The Petersburg Campaign

Vol II: The Western Front Battles,
September 1864 – April 1865

Edwin C. Bearss

with Bryce Suderow

SB

Savas Beatie

California

Library of Congress Cataloging-in-Publication Data
Bearss, Edwin C.
The Petersburg Campaign / Edwin C. Bearss, with Bryce Suderow.
p. cm.
Includes bibliographical references and index.
"The Attack on Petersburg, June 9, 1864 — The Second Assault on Petersburg, June 15-18, 1864 — The Battle of the Jerusalem Plank Road, June 21-24, 1864 — The Crater, July 30, 1864 — The Battle of the Weldon Railroad, August 18-21, 1864 —The Second Battle of Ream's Station, August 25, 1864"—Vol. 1, table of contents.
ISBN: 978-1-61121-104-7
1. Virginia—History—Civil War, 1861-1865—Campaigns. 2. Petersburg (Va.)—History—Siege, 1864-1865. I. Suderow, Bryce A. II. Title.
E476.59.B43 2012
975.5'03—dc23
2012028512

SB

Published by
Savas Beatie LLC
989 Governor Drive, Suite 102
El Dorado Hills, CA 95762

Phone: 916-941-6896
(E-mail) customerservice@savasbeatie.com

05 04 03 02 01   5 4 3 2 1
First edition, first printing

Unless otherwise indicated, all photographs are from the Library of Congress.

Savas Beatie titles are available at special discounts for bulk purchases in the United States by corporations, institutions, and other organizations. For more details, please contact Special Sales, P.O. Box 4527, El Dorado Hills, CA 95762, or you may e-mail us at sales@savasbeatie.com, or visit our website at www.savasbeatie.com for additional information.

Proudly published, printed, and warehoused in the United States of America.

To Mary Virginia Bearss

Inside Fort Stedman, Petersburg, Virginia, April 2, 1865

Library of Congress

Contents

Contents (continued)

List of Maps

List of Maps (continued)

List of Maps (continued)

Photos and illustrations have been placed throughout the book
for the convenience of the reader.

Introduction by Edwin C. Bearss

At the request of Theodore P. Savas of Savas Beatie publishers, I have prepared an Introduction for Volume 2 of *The Petersburg Campaign: The Western Front Battles, September 1864-April 1865.* The first volume of this publication, as readers recall, was subtitled *The Eastern Front Battles, June – August, 1864* (2012).

To avoid being too repetitive, I have revisited the subtitle to reflect a step back to provide insights into the history of how the U.S. Government and the National Park Service came to be involved in the management, preservation, and interpretation of many of the nation's Civil War battlefields.

On August 17, 1890, Congress authorized the Chickamauga and Chattanooga National Military Park, America's first. Three more national military parks followed by the end of the nineteenth century: Shiloh in 1894, Gettysburg in 1895, and Vicksburg in 1899. The War Department purchased and managed their lands while participating states, military units, and associations positioned monuments at appropriate locations. At Antietam on August 30, 1890, Congress provided for acquisition of token lands where monuments and markers could be placed. It and other places where this less expensive policy was adopted were later designated national battlefield sites. In subsequent years Antietam and most of the latter sites bearing this designation would be enlarged and re-designated national battlefields.

Congress, in 1907 authorized Chalmette National Monument and Grounds commemorating the War of 1812's Battle of New Orleans, departing from its recent focus on the Civil War. This was followed on March 2, 1917, with our first Revolutionary War site with the authorization of Guilford Courthouse National Military Park. Four weeks before in early February, Congress had authorized another Civil War site at Kennesaw Mountain, Georgia.

In 1926, Congress called upon the War Department to survey all the national's historic battlefields and provide recommendations for their preservation or commemoration. This led Congress to add more areas to the battle sites before the August 11, 1933, reorganization that transferred the management of the nation's military history sites to the National Park Service, a bureau in the Department of the Interior, which was then headed by the power-hungry and formidable Harold Ickes.

Civil War sites not heretofore listed (and their date of authorization) are as follows: Petersburg NMP, July 3, 1926; Fredericksburg and Spotsylvania County Battlefields NMP, February 14, 1927; Stones River NMP, March 3,

1927; Fort Donelson NMP, March 26, 1928; Brices Cross Roads NBS and Tupelo NBS, February 21, 1929; and Appomattox Court House NBS, June 18, 1930. Some six years later Congress authorized the Richmond NBP.

Although Petersburg National Battlefield and Richmond National Battlefield Park are separate units within the National Park system, each has its own staff and the degree of cooperation is dependent upon the personalities of the respective incumbents. The focus of the staff of Richmond NBP is on the interpretation of Richmond as capital of the Confederacy, the Seven Days' Battles and Drewry's Bluff; the 1864 Overland Campaign from the Union crossing of the Pamunkey River through Grant's crossing of the James River; and, sites such as Battery Parker's and Fort Stevens associated with much of Bermuda Hundred. The staff of Petersburg NMP is given priority interpreting and protecting Grant's City Point headquarters; the Petersburg home front; the Five Forks battlefield; and the Western Front Visitor Contact Station and the Eastern Front Visitor Center.

*   *   *

Lt. Gen. Ulysses S. Grant, in the days following his June 3 bloody repulse at Cold Harbor, determined to give Gen. Robert E. Lee the slip, cross south over the James River, and attack Petersburg from the east. This would enable Maj. Gen. George G. Meade to cooperate with Maj. Gen. Benjamin F. Butler's Army of the James that had occupied Bermuda Hundred and either capture Petersburg by *coup de main* or, if that failed, sever the railroads connecting the Cockade City with Richmond and the Deep South. Although Grant stole a march on Lee, the heavily outnumbered Confederates under Gen. P. G. T. Beauregard, in the four days comprising June 15-18, stood tall until Lee and the Army of Northern Virginia arrived about noon on the 18th. Their arrival and Union failure to take the city as hoped led to a long and bloody investment of Petersburg and Richmond that would not end until the night of April 2, 1865. Taking advantage of Maj. Gen. Philip Sheridan's Five Forks victory on April 1, the Union Sixth Corps scored a breakthrough at dawn on April 2 of the Rebel breastworks located on land preserved and interpreted in Pamplin Historical Park. This compelled the Confederates to evacuate their extensive lines and thus both cities that night. Lee's and Grant's date with destiny at Appomattox Court House was one week in the future.

Because the boundary between Richmond NBP and Petersburg NBP was determined by legislation and not military history, sites associated with the investment of Petersburg north of the James are included in the Richmond

NBP. Among these are First Deep Bottom (July 27-29), coupled with the Crater (July 30); Second Deep Bottom (August 13-23), coupled with the Weldon Railroad (August 18-21); Chaffin's Farm—Fort Harrison (September 29-30), coupled with Peebles' Farm (September 30-October 2); Boydton Plank Road (October 27-28) coupled with Fair Oaks and Darbytown Road (October 27-28).

Readers familiar with the Introduction to the first volume of *The Petersburg Campaign* know that the reports I was tasked to prepare to document the Draft Troop Movement Map overlays were only undertaken for sites embraced within the Petersburg park. Consequently, documented narratives were not prepared for those sites north of the James River. Readers interested in the Union September 29-30, 1864, attacks aimed at the capture of Fort Harrison—New Market Heights—Chaffin's Farm and their association with the fighting south of the James River at Peebles' Farm are referred to Dr. Richard Sommers' tour de force *Richmond Redeemed: The Story of Petersburg.* This monumental study, originally published more than three decades ago by Doubleday, will be widely available once again later this year (2014) when Savas Beatie offers it in a revised Sesquicentennial edition.

Stepping back to Volume I, I want to commend my publisher Ted Savas and his staff of Savas Beatie for the selection of the subtitle and other past favors. After checking with my longtime friend and associate Chris Calkins, I learned that in 2004 the park in a key planning document had divided sites for interpretation and enriching their driving tours of Petersburg National Battlefield into Eastern and Western fronts. To me, this was an inspired decision and one I wished I had thought of at the time of the Civil War Centennial.

The subtitle "Western Front Battles" takes me back to Hardin, Montana, when I was in the third grade. In that year, 1931, I saw the movie "All Quiet on the Western Front." It was judged the top motion picture in the previous year. In the years since I have seen it a number of times, both while in the U.S. Marine Corps and as a civilian. Not until the outbreak of World War II in Europe on September 1, 1939, did I realize the movie was an anti-war blockbuster based on the novel of the same name published in Germany in 1929 by Erich Maria Remarque, followed by *The Road Back* two years later. Both books were banned and burned in Germany just months after Adolf Hitler came to power in 1933. Fortunately for Remarque and his family, they had fled to Switzerland the previous year.

Even today, I vividly recall certain scenes in that movie: Schoolmaster Kantorek, as he urges his students to enlist and they rush off to fight for the glory of the Fatherland. The main character Paul Baumer, played by actor Lew Ayres, who returns home wounded and suffers a breakdown and weeps when Kantorek encourages him to speak to a younger class about his heroism on the field of battle; the moving scene of Paul sharing a shell crater with a French soldier he has mortally wounded; and of course, the final sequence when Paul is killed on a quiet day by a nameless French sharpshooter.

Ayers was so affected by his role as Paul that he was classified as a conscientious objector in World War II. He then showed his character by entering the service as a medic. Slim Summerville as Tjaden (one of Paul's pre-war friends) and Louis Wolheim as old soldier Stanislaus "Kat" Katczinsky, remind me of comrades with whom I served in World War II. (Dr. Glenn Clay, a doctor from Davis, California, and a frequent companion on many battlefield tours, gave me a T-shirt sporting a photograph highlighting schoolmaster Kantorek.) Looking to the future, "All Quiet on the Western Front" had a similar effect on life and my career as did the Jeb Stuart biography by John Thomason, read to me by my father during the harsh Montana winter of 1935-36.

*   *   *

This set of essays in this second volume of *The Petersburg Campaign* brings to a close my work of so many decades ago on this fascinating campaign. Petersburg in all its rich complexity has been overlooked for much too long. It is my hope that the publication of this set, together with some of the other outstanding recently published studies, elevates Petersburg to its rightful place in the pantheon of Civil War campaigns.

And now, it is "On to the Western Front battles!"

Edwin C. Bearss
Historian Emeritus
National Park Service

Introduction by Bryce A. Suderow

Lieutenant General Ulysses S. Grant's operations of June through August of 1864 began with an assault on the city of Petersburg on June 15. For the next four days, Grant and the commander of the Army of the Potomac, Maj. Gen. George G. Meade, dribbled troops into action in an effort to capture the important logistical center. Sufficient troops to pierce a vulnerable part of the Rebel line, however, were never committed. The attacks were called off on the afternoon of June 18, ending what would later be styled as "Grant's First Offensive."

Despite the fact that the Army of the Potomac's morale was very low, Grant did not cease or even pause his military operations against Petersburg. Three days later on June 21, he sent Maj. Gen. Winfield Hancock's II Corps and Maj. Gen. Horatio Wright's VI Corps southwest in an effort to seize the Weldon Railroad before turning north to sever the South Side Railroad ("Grant's Second Offensive"). In effect, Petersburg would be surrounded by troops on the east, south, and eventually the west. The fragile state of the Federal army was revealed on the afternoon of June 22 when a Confederate division under William Mahone struck a gap between the two Federal corps, routing much of Hancock's command with a devastating flank attack. The next day, June 23, VI Corps commander Wright did not act with sufficient vigor and indeed seemed paralyzed while two Southern brigades routed a Vermont brigade busy tearing up the Weldon Railroad. This operation was but the first of many attempts by Grant to extend his line west to outflank Gen. Robert E. Lee's Confederate line and steal a march north to cut the South Side railroad. Although the Rebels maintained control of the Weldon line, Lee's lines were stretched farther west.

Grant spent most of the month of July without engaging in any major active operation. Although the army spent this time resting and refitting, this was not Grant's reason for delaying operations. Instead, he was awaiting the return of Wright's VI Corps from Washington D.C., for William Smith's XVIII Corps to join his army, and for his cavalry to replace losses in men and horses suffered during the Trevilian Station and Wilson-Kautz raid, both of which were aimed at tearing up railroads supplying Lee's men. As the month began its last week, Grant realized he wasn't going to be reinforced by either the VI Corps or XVIII Corps anytime soon, and by this time his cavalry had sufficiently recovered to resume operations. Consequently, he tried a new strategy. Grant would send II Corps and Sheridan's cavalry north to threaten Richmond, which he hoped would compel Lee to strip his front before Petersburg. Once this occurred, Grant intended to set off a mine beneath the Confederate lines at Pegram's Salient opposite Ambrose E. Burnside's IX Corps. This "Third Offensive" (July 26-30, 1864) was at least a partial success because Lee did as Grant hoped and shifted large troop formations north of the James River away from Petersburg. Unfortunately for Northern arms, the large mine assault ("The Battle of the Crater") failed because although the mine exploded, the Confederate defenders stood their ground and prevented a breakthrough into Petersburg. A counterattack by Mahone's brigades drove the Federals back to their original lines. The battles during these final days of July were known as the First Battle of Deep Bottom (July 27-29) and the Battle of the Crater (July 30). Union losses that July were 6,367, and Confederate losses totaled at least 3,000.

The direct attacks against the Rebel lines during the First and Third Offensives were the exception rather than the rule. Grant would eventually launch eight offensives, but only three of them involved assaults against the main Confederate lines: the June 15-18 attacks, the July 30 Crater attack, and the April 2, 1865, attack that fractured the lines and ended the long siege. The other five offensives were aimed at seizing roads and railroads. It is important to realize that the so-called "Siege of Petersburg" wasn't really a siege at all. Lee managed to keep supplies flowing into the city to the very end. After June 23, 1864, Grant never attempted to directly besiege Petersburg. Instead, his operations involved stabs southwest and west to stretch or break Lee's line in an effort to reach and cut the South Side Railroad. Most of these movements gained ground that the Federals promptly fortified, extending the Union and Confederate lines ever westward.

Grant's Fourth Offensive was launched to force Lee to recall troops en route for the Shenandoah Valley. The operation was similar to the one in July. The Federals threatened Richmond and Lee weakened the Petersburg front. This allowed Warren to seize the Weldon Railroad in the vicinity of Globe Tavern. Grant decided to send the II Corps south along the railroad to destroy it as far south as Ream's Station. On August 25, Lee attacked the isolated corps and routed it. The offensive lasted from August 14-25, 1864 and consisted of the Second Battle of Deep Bottom, the Battle of Globe Tavern, and the Battle of Ream's Station. Federal losses for August were 10,996 and for the Confederates, 5,500.

It should be pointed out that Grant's original plan did not include extending the Federal line as far west as Globe Tavern. He planned to order Warren back to the main Federal line after the Globe Tavern combat. Warren presented Grant with a *fait accompli* by fortifying Globe Tavern and building entrenchments in cooperation with Meade that connected his isolated position to the main Union line east of the Jerusalem Plank Road. To Grant's credit, he saw the wisdom of extending the Union line westward and allowed Warren to maintain his new position. More importantly, in his future offensives Grant often held the ground seized and fortified it. The Fourth Offensive was a turning point in the siege because by extending the lines west, Grant forced Lee to lengthen his own lines. This spread out his men and weakened his lines.

We should also note that Grant never had a master plan to seize Petersburg. Contrary to popular history, he did not decide to extend the Union lines in order to outflank Lee and capture Petersburg. He usually made up his plans on the spur of the moment and, as often as not, they were embarrassingly bad ideas. His offensives did have the goal of extending the lines westward. Instead, they were aimed at cutting Lee's supply lines. If Grant felt like holding the ground he gained during an offensive, he held it. If he felt like abandoning it, he abandoned it.

One of his worst plans shifted Sheridan's cavalry corps from Deep Bottom on July 29 and sent it on a raid (without a chance to rest) against the Weldon Railroad on July 30 in coordination with the Crater attack. The long ride so exhausted the Union horsemen that they were forced to stop when they reached the Union left flank. They never reached the Weldon Railroad.

The Fourth Offensive was also a turning point for the Confederates. Hitherto, Lee had relied on the Dimmock Line that ringed the city on three sides to defend Petersburg. In the battles along the Jerusalem Plank Road on June 22-23, he had dispatched troops from the line when Hancock's and Wright's Federals tried to move westward toward the South Side Railroad. This advance successfully assaulted the two corps and forced Grant to pull them back into the Union lines. During the Fourth Offensive, however, Lee's tactic did not work because the Confederate assaults on Warren were repulsed and the Federals seized Globe Tavern.

After the Fourth Offensive, the Confederates began building two new lines of defensive works jutting out from the Dimmock Line in a southwesterly direction. By working on two lines simultaneously, they insured that neither line was complete by the time Grant launched his Fifth Offensive on September 29, 1864. The first was a forward line to protect the Squirrel Level Road. This two-mile line consisted of four forts and earthworks. Unfortunately, the earthworks along the line at Fort Archer were only three feet high, with no slashing or chevaux de fries to slow down attackers. The second line was farther north, parallel to and south of the Boydton Plank Road. This line was intended to protect the Boydton Plank Road and the South Side Railroad. It was three miles long and very weak, consisting of only logs with earth thrown over them.

At the end of three months of operations Grant had succeeded in seizing ground as far west as the Weldon Railroad, but the railroad was still being used by Lee, who supplied Petersburg by sending wagons to haul supplies into the city via the Boydton Plank Road from a point south of the Federal lodgment on the railroad at Globe Tavern.

*   *   *

This second volume of The Petersburg Campaign chronicles the last six months of the campaign. It begins the Union's Fifth Offensive at Peebles' Farm on September 30, 1864, and ends with the final offensive that broke through the Confederate lines on April 2, 1865 and forced the evacuation of both Petersburg and Richmond.

During these six months Grant launched five offensives. Two of them—Peebles' Farm and Burgess Mill—were attempts to seize the South Side Railroad. One, the fighting at Hatcher's Run, was an attempt to capture the supply wagons traversing the Boydton Plank road and delivering supplies from the broken Weldon Railroad north to Petersburg. The other two offensives consisted of Federal assaults against entrenched Confederates. The Eighth Offensive also included a Federal assault, but was in reality a mixed bag of four separate battles that should collectively be known as the Five Forks Campaign.

Grant ordered Sheridan to Five Forks, an important road junction a short distance below the South Side Railroad, with the hope that threatening the railroad would induce the Confederates to come out of their entrenchments so he could defeat them in the open. General Robert E. Lee assembled a force under George Pickett and Fitzhugh Lee to defeat Sheridan and end the threat to the railroad. Sheridan was still at Dinwiddie Court House when the Confederates struck him. They came close to defeating him on March 31 at Dinwiddie Court House, after which Pickett fell back to Five Forks when Warren's V Corps moved to reinforce Sheridan. The next day, April 1, Sheridan and Warren attacked and defeated Pickett at Five Forks. In the other two battles on March 29 and 31, Lee attacked Warren at the Lewis Farm and White Oak Road, respectively, when the Federals threatened R. H. Anderson's line along the White Oak Road.

After the fall of Richmond and Petersburg on April 2, the Confederates withdrew westward in an effort to get around and south of Grant's pursuing Federals with an eye toward joining Gen. Joseph E. Johnston's command in North Carolina. The effort was unsuccessful for a number of reasons, and on April 9, 1865, Lee surrendered his Army of Northern Virginia at Appomattox Court House.

Acknowledgments

As always, there are many people who have helped make the second volume of this project a reality. If I miss someone, you know who you are, and please know I appreciate all you have done.

As before, I would like to thank Theodore P. Savas of Savas Beatie for his eagerness to publish this book and for all his help along the way. Because Ed did not produce a chapter on Fort Stedman, Ted arranged with author William Wyrick, through the good graces and courtesy of *Blue & Gray* magazine publisher Dave Roth, to utilize a lengthy General's Tour article as the foundation for an updated and expanded study on the subject. The lengthy chapters covering the Five Forks "Campaign" as it should be known, were reviewed by Five Forks expert Mike McCarthy, who made a number of observations large and small based upon sources discovered after Ed prepared his original study. Although it was beyond the focus of this study, we believed a brief Postscript covering the retreat to Appomattox was in order. Ted called upon the leading expert on that subject, Chris Calkins, to produce it, which he did most ably. All of these chapters, as with the first volume, were enhanced with George Skoch's master cartography. Many of these actions have never been properly mapped before. As always, George did a magnificent job.

Many others from Savas Beatie also helped on a variety of fronts, as they always do: Production Manager Lee Merideth worked overtime with all the issues that crept into play, and fielded my emails and (most of) my calls during and after hours; Marketing Director Sarah Keeney reviewed some of the formatted book and has been laying the groundwork on the promotional front; and Veronica Kane proofed the final incarnation. Thank you one and all.

Lamar Williams ensured the text adhered to the house style sheet and proofed an early version of the transcribed original Bearss manuscript. David Van Dusen worked with the Savas Beatie team to create an outstanding book trailer, which really captured the thrust and intent of this volume and can be found on the Savas Beatie home page, and on YouTube.

Many others typed computer files from the original manuscripts, proofed them, or made certain there was uniformity in the chapters: Alice J. Gayley, Shelley Lewis, Debbie McMahon, Donald R. Parker, Keith and Terri Saunders, and Becky Waid.

Bryce A. Suderow
Washington, DC

Chapter 1

The Battle of Peebles' Farm

September 30-October 2, 1864

Editor's Introduction

The stalemate in the Shenandoah Valley frustrated Lt. Gen. U. S. Grant. He urged Maj. Gen. Phil Sheridan, the commander of the Union Army of the Shenandoah, to attack and defeat Confederate Lt. Gen. Jubal Early and the Confederate forces sent to operate there by Gen. Robert E. Lee. After weeks of maneuvering and a series of sharp skirmishes, Sheridan finally caught Early at Winchester and soundly defeated him there on September 19, 1864. Three days later he routed the depleted Southern Army of the Valley again at Fisher's Hill. Both were serious defeats for the Confederacy. Assuming Early was finished as a threat, Sheridan set out south, burning farms and seizing crops and livestock for Federal use. Lee, however, was not done in the Valley and dispatched additional reinforcements in the form of Joseph Kershaw's infantry division and Tom Rosser's cavalry brigade. Both would play key roles in October at Cedar Creek.

Grant launched his Fifth Offensive at the end of September to cut General Lee's lines of communication southwest of Petersburg and to prevent Lee from further reinforcing Early in the Shenandoah. He decided on a similar strategy he had used before: make another attack on the Richmond lines with his right flank, followed by a heavy movement with his left below Petersburg. His decision to follow this course of action was strongly influenced by intelligence gathered by Army of the James commander Maj. Gen. Benjamin F. Butler that indicated Richmond's garrison had been gravely weakened that August when Lee husbanded his forces below the James River to drive the Federals away from the vital Weldon Railroad.

Grant's plan called for Butler to attack Richmond's defenses on September 29, followed by a march on the South Side Railroad by parts of Maj. Gen. Gouverneur K. Warren's V Corps and Maj. Gen. John G. Parke's IX Corps on August 14.

Lieutenant General Ulysses S. Grant
Library of Congress

Part I

Grant Prepares to Push for the South Side Railroad

To cover and exploit the surprise attack Maj. Gen. Benjamin F. Butler's Army of the James was scheduled to make September 29, 1864, on the Confederate defenses north of the James River, Lt. Gen. Ulysses S. Grant called on the commander of the Army of the Potomac, Maj. Gen. George G. Meade, to cooperate. Meade would see that his troops were "under arms at 4:00 a.m. on the 29th ready to move in any direction." Officers were to see that their men had three or four days' rations in their haversacks and 60 rounds of ammunition on their persons.

Originally, Grant had intended to give Meade "specific instructions for the concentration" of all his reserves and for a demonstration as if the Federals planned to extend their investment line westward from the Weldon Railroad. But on studying the subject, Grant determined to leave the details of the projected undertaking to Meade. Grant, however, wanted Meade to exert himself to convince the Rebels that the South Side Railroad and Petersburg were primary objectives.

Should the Confederates rush heavy reinforcements north of the James to contain Butler's thrust toward Richmond, Grant wanted Meade to be ready to take advantage of the situation. If Meade's troops gained the South Side Railroad or a position from where their artillery could command the right of way, Meade was to hold the ground seized at all hazards. To do so, Meade was authorized to reduce the number of men assigned to hold the Petersburg investment line, provided he didn't strip the garrisons posted in the enclosed works.

All teams assigned to the trains should be harnessed and hitched. Stockpiling of supplies at the depots along the Military Railroad was to be stopped. So far as practicable, all supplies on hand should be loaded onto wagons.[1]

Before retiring on the night of September 27, Grant forwarded additional instructions to Meade. If Meade could move some troops in the morning the Confederates might believe that the Army of the Potomac was massing for a drive against the South Side Railroad, Grant felt it would be helpful. In addition, Grant

---

1 *The War of the Rebellion: A Compilation of the Official Records of the Union and Confederate Armies*, 128 vols. (Washington, D.C. 1880-1901), Series 1, vol. 42, pt. 2, 1046-1047. Hereafter references are to Series 1 unless noted.

General Robert E. Lee
Library of Congress

thought it would be advisable for Meade to send scouts "some distance to the southeast to discover" if Confederate cavalry was feeling its way toward the James.[2]

Meade was perplexed by Grant's orders. At 10:30 p.m. he wired Grant, "Do you refer to movements within or without our lines?"

After discussing the situation with his staff, Meade was satisfied that in the morning he could send two divisions of Maj. Gen. John G. Parke's IX Corps "beyond our left and beyond where Warren was the other day." If assailed, Parke's troops could be reinforced by two divisions from Maj. Gen. Gouverneur K. Warren's V Corps.[3]

"What I meant," Grant replied, "was for you to move troops within our lines: not openly." Grant wanted the Rebels to glimpse soldiers and believe that the Army of the Potomac was massing for a blow toward the South Side Railroad. The X Corps, then *en-route* to Bermuda Hundred, Grant reasoned, would be missed by the Southerners in the morning, and it would be to the Federals' advantage if the foe could be deceived into believing the Army of the James was being shifted to the left.[4]

Before bed, General Meade had Chief of Staff Maj. Gen. Andrew A. Humphreys telegraph his cavalry commander, Brig. Gen. David McMurtrie Gregg. Gregg was to have the officer at Prince George Court House order out a strong patrol. This force was to ride out in the morning in a southeasterly direction to see if the Confederates were moving any cavalry toward the James.[5]

On September 28, General Meade worked out a plan to implement Grant's orders. The Army of the Potomac was to be under arms and ready to march as Grant had designated. All supply trains would be loaded with six days' rations for the troops. Surplus stores were to be removed at once from the depots to City Point.

---

2 *Ibid.*, 1047.

3 *Ibid.*, 1047. A forced reconnaissance out onto Vaughan Road by the 2nd brigade of Crawford's division had been made on September 15. Encountering the Confederates near Poplar Spring Church, the Federals, after driving in their pickets, returned to their camp near Globe Tavern.

4 OR 42, pt. 2, 1048.

5 *Ibid.*, 1057. On the morning of the 27th, Brig. Gen. Henry E. Davies' brigade had ridden to Prince George Court House and relieved Brig. Gen. August V. Kautz's division. Davies' troopers assumed responsibility for watching the approaches to the rear of the Army of the Potomac from the James River to the Norfolk Railroad. Gregg's 2nd brigade led by Col. Charles H. Smith patrolled the countryside from the Norfolk Railroad to the left of the picket line manned by the V Corps. Davies' headquarters were at Prince George Court House; Smith's reserves were on the Jerusalem Plank Road at McCann's.

General Warren was to march "with not less than two divisions of his corps." His remaining troops would be left to garrison Forts Wadsworth, Dushane, and Davison; the enclosed batteries; and the line of rifle pits connecting Forts Wadsworth and Howard. General Parke was to be ready to leave the defense of the investment line between Forts Davis and Howard to his Third Division and the garrisons of Forts Alexander Hays and Howard. He would mass Brig. Gen. Orlando B. Willcox's and Robert B. Potter's divisions and the reserve artillery near Gurley's house ready for movement.

All corps commanders were to be prepared in case the forthcoming battle developed favorable to pull their soldiers out of the rifle pits linking the enclosed works, leaving the line from the Appomattox to Fort Davison to be held by the troops garrisoning the redoubts and the enclosed batteries.

General Gregg was to recall his patrols and concentrate his cavalry division near Robertson's on the Weldon Railroad. Upon doing so, Gregg was to make suitable dispositions to cover the Jerusalem Plank Road and the Ream's Station sector.

When they took the field, the troops were to take along their entrenching tools. Since rapid marches would be called for, each brigade was to reduce its train. Only one-half the stipulated number of ambulances, small-arms ammunition wagons, and "reserve ammunition wagons" for the 12-pounder guns would be taken along. One medicine and one hospital wagon would be allowed for each brigade. The spring wagons and pack-mules allowed by regulations for headquarters could accompany the troops, but no supply trains, forage wagons, baggage wagons, or sutlers' wagons were to be permitted.[6]

Three days before, on September 25, two divisions of the IX Corps (Willcox's and Potter's) had been withdrawn from the front line. On the left, they were relieved by a detachment from the V corps and on the right by Brig. Gen. Edward Ferrero's black division. Ferrero's troops on moving into the rifle pits extended to the right as far as Fort Davis on Jerusalem Plank Road, relieving several units from the II Corps. General Willcox's First Division, after being pulled out of the trenches, had been posted in reserve behind the sector of the investment line held by the blacks, while General Potter's division camped east of the Plank Road in close supporting distance of the II Corps.[7]

At 1:00 a.m. on the 28th, Chief of Staff Humphreys contacted General Parke. In compliance with Grant's instructions, Meade wanted Parke to march Potter's

---

6   *Ibid.*, 1069.

7   OR 42, pt. 1, 545.

division as soon as it was light from its camp near Avery's house to the neighborhood of the Gurley house. In carrying out this movement, Potter was to go out of his way to attract the Confederates' attention.

Upon receipt of these instructions, Potter issued orders for his brigade commanders to have their units ready to move at daybreak. Reveille was to be beaten with as much fanfare as possible.[8]

A diarist in the 7th Rhode Island, one of Potter's regiments, recorded:

> At 3 a.m. we were aroused and ordered to be in readiness to move at daylight. Earliest rays of the rising sun found us in line with arms stacked. Thirty minutes later we started for our old camp near the Weldon Railroad, arriving there at nine. At one, orders were issued to occupy it, but the hint was also given not to fix it up much, as we would probably tarry but a few hours. At sunset tents were erected for the night.[9]

Because he hadn't received his copy of Meade's circular, Parke was mystified by Potter's movements. Consequently, at 9:30 a.m. he telegraphed Humphreys, "If compatible with public interest, I would like to know whether the movement of the Second Division to the vicinity of the Gurley House is permanent or merely temporary . . ."[10]

Humphreys replied that before the day was over, Parke would see the logic behind Potter's movement.[11]

Two deserters from the 8th Georgia Cavalry on the morning of the 28th were brought before General Warren. The Georgians told Warren that their regiment was stationed at Poplar Spring Church. At the time they had deserted, they reported, Confederate fatigue parties were extending the entrenchments southwest from Petersburg. Works were being thrown up on Peebles' farm. When Warren asked, "How far to the southwest do the new rifle pits extend?"

The deserters shook their heads. They informed the Union officers that Rebel infantry was "pretty thick" around their camp.[12]

Warren was so impressed with what he heard that he promptly transferred the deserters to Meade's headquarters. Chief of Staff Humphreys was no more

---

8   OR 42, pt. 2, 1076.

9   William P. Hopkins, *The Seventh Regiment Rhode Island Volunteers in the Civil War, 1862-1865* (Providence, 1903), 214-215.

10   OR 42, pt. 2, 1076-1077.

11   *Ibid.*, 1077.

12   *Ibid.*, 1074.

Major General Andrew A. Humphreys (seated, second from right).
Library of Congress

successful than Warren in obtaining information from the two Georgians as to how far beyond Peebles' farm the new fortifications extended. They told Humphreys that they were building a large redoubt with embrasures for 16 guns near the tobacco warehouse in Peebles' field. This redoubt, they said was about 1,000 yards from the forks of the Squirrel Level and Church Roads, which its guns would command. The taller of the two stated that the Confederates had rifle pits paralleling the Boydton Plank Road for a distance of five to six miles from Petersburg.[13]

The staff officer with Meade's plan of operations for the 20th reached General Warren's Globe Tavern headquarters a little before 7:30 p.m. Acknowledging the dispatch, Warren pointed out that he had directed his pickets to remain where they were, as they could be withdrawn, "as fast as needed in the morning." Warren was taken aback when he saw that he was to have his men ready to march at 4:00 a.m.

13 *Ibid.*, 1065. When Meade relayed this information to Grant, he informed his superior that Peebles' farm was just north of Poplar Spring Church. *Ibid.*, 1064.

He informed Meade that it would be 5:00 a.m. before it was light enough to move out.[14]

Soon thereafter, Warren was handed a telegram signed by Humphreys. Warren now learned that Gregg's cavalry was "to make a demonstration upon the enemy's left." As early as practicable in the morning, Gregg was to concentrate his division at Robertson's. Should Gregg need infantry support, he was to notify Warren.[15]

Orders were drafted by Warren's staff alerting Brig. Gen. Charles Griffin of the First Division, Brig. Gen. Romeyn B. Ayres of the Second Division, and Col. J. William Hofmann of the 3rd Brigade, Third Division, to have their troops formed, inspected, and ready to march at 4:00 a.m. Colonel Charles S. Wainwright was to designate the batteries which were to accompany this force. At the same time, Brig. Gen. Samuel W. Crawford of the Third Division was notified that he would hold the line westward from Fort Howard with Brig. Gen. Edward S. Bragg's brigade.[16]

Meanwhile, General Gregg had moved to carry out Meade's instructions. Brigadier General Henry E. Davies was to recall his patrols, concentrate his brigade, and move it to McCann's on the Jerusalem Plank Road. The brigade commissary and quartermaster people were to see that each man in the command was issued three days' rations and two days' forage. Only one wagon, belonging to brigade headquarters, was to accompany the column on its march to Robertson's. The rest of the wagons were to be packed and sent to park with the division train.[17]

At the same time, Gregg issued orders for Col. Charles H. Smith to withdraw all his pickets and patrols from the area east of the Weldon Railroad. The brigade would be massed at McCann's and be prepared to ride at 4:00 a.m. One regiment, the 16th Pennsylvania, would be detached and left to watch the Jerusalem Plank Road and the countryside toward Ream's Station when the division moved out. Like Davies, Smith was to see that his men carried only the designated amount of rations, forage, and ammunition. Except for artillery and headquarters wagons, the only wheeled vehicles that were to accompany Gregg would be the hospital train, consisting of one medicine wagon and ten ambulances.[18]

---

14 *Ibid.*, 1075.

15 *Ibid.*, 1074.

16 *Ibid.*, 1075.

17 *Ibid.*, 1078.

18 *Ibid.*, 1078-1079; OR 42, pt. 1, 619. While in the field, Battery H, 1st U.S. Light Artillery would report to Colonel Smith and Battery A, 2nd U.S. Light Artillery to General Davies. OR 42, pt. 2, 1078.

It had been deemed advisable by General Grant for General Meade to put his infantry in motion toward the South Side Railroad on September 29. The reason was that Grant didn't feel the Confederate high command had pulled enough troops out of the Petersburg defenses to justify such a movement.[19]

*   *   *

Long before 4:00 a.m. on the 29th, reveille sounded in the camps of General Gregg's cavalry division. By the designated hour, Gregg had given the command to mount and the troopers moved out, taking the road to Globe Tavern. At Globe Tavern, Gregg turned his column onto the Halifax Road. The horsemen rode down the Halifax Road to its intersection with the Wyatt Road. Here Gregg called a brief halt; Davies' brigade was detached and ordered to hold the junction.

Gregg, hoping to find a byway leading to Vaughan Road and a bridge across Rowanty Creek, led Smith's brigade down the Wyatt Road. At the same time, the general sent a combat patrol to make a dash on Ream's Station.

At 7:00 a.m., Gregg reined up his horse and wrote a brief note for delivery to Chief of Staff Humphreys. Besides reporting what had occurred since breaking camp, Gregg observed that if he was unable to locate a road to the Rowanty, he would "demonstrate toward Poplar Spring Church or wherever I find the enemy."[20]

By 9:30 a.m., when he made his next report, Gregg's troopers had encountered mounted Confederates from Maj. Gen. Wade Hampton's Confederate Cavalry Corps. The troopers sent to Ream's Station had thundered into the village, routed the Rebel pickets, and driven them a mile down the Halifax Road. At that point the Federals had encountered the Johnnies in force. The leader of the Union patrol recalled his people and rejoined the main column on the Wyatt Road.

Meanwhile, Gregg, accompanied by Smith's brigade, had pushed on. Confederate vedettes were encountered by Smith's vanguard. A running fight ensued. The butternuts fell back and the bluecoats reached Vaughan Road. Questioning the citizens encountered, Gregg learned from a talkative one that General Hampton planned to review part of his corps during the day on a field three miles west of Ream's Station.[21]

19 Andrew A. Humphreys, *The Virginia Campaign of '64 and '65* (New York, 1883), 290-291.

20 *OR* 42, pt. 1, 619; pt. 2, 1106.

21 *OR* 42, pt. 2, 1106-1107.

After reaching Wilkenson's on Vaughan Road, Gregg sent a strong patrol to reconnoiter a wood road, which local people said gave access to the Boydton Plank Road. The Federals, as they advanced toward Rocky Branch, were compelled to smash several roadblocks defended by detachments from Brig. Gen. Mathew C. Butler's division of Hampton's cavalry. Several Confederates were captured. When Gregg questioned them, he was unable to obtain much information as to the geography of the area, as the prisoners were also strangers to this section of Dinwiddie County. At the same time, the region into which the blue clads had pushed was covered with a dense growth of pines. Besides favoring the defenders, the pines and undergrowth seemed to wall in the Yanks.[22]

The Confederate vedettes on retiring fell back toward Hatcher's Run.[23] At the point where Vaughan Road crossed the run, there was a camp for dismounted casuals from Hampton's Corps commanded by Maj. Richard S. Farley.[24]

The patrol sent toward the Boydton Plank Road by Gregg reached Armstrong's Mill. Before rejoining the brigade, the troopers cut the telegraph line linking Petersburg with Stony Creek Depot. According to Mr. Armstrong, personnel from the Confederate Signal Corps had completed this line three or four days before. Besides taking down and rolling up a section of wire, the Federals chopped down a number of poles. A strong force of Rebel horsemen followed the bluecoats as they retired. Meanwhile, an attack on Maj. Farley's camp by a strong combat patrol from Smith's brigade had been repulsed.[25]

About noon, a courier reached Gregg's command post with a message from Chief of Staff Humphreys. This dispatch was in reply to Gregg's 7:00 a.m. communication. Humphreys cautioned the cavalryman that he would probably be unable to reconnoiter the Poplar Spring Road beyond Squirrel Level Road, because the Confederates had thrown up rifle pits across Peebles' field.[26]

When he acknowledged this dispatch at 12:12 p.m., Gregg advised headquarters of his probe toward Armstrong's Mill and the clash with Farley's dismounted troopers. Having failed to reach the Boydton Plank Road, Gregg

---

22 *Ibid.*, 1107.

23 There are three variations on the spelling of this stream: Hatcher's Run, Hatchers Run and Hatchers' Run.

24 *Ibid.*, 1106-1107.

25 *Ibid.*, 619, 947; OR 42, pt. 2, 1107.

26 OR 42, pt. 2, 1106.

planned to withdraw Smith's brigade to Wyatt's and "try the enemy toward Poplar Spring Meeting House."[27]

Gregg's forced reconnaissance was already having repercussions. Since the activities of the Union troopers appeared "serious," General Hampton got in touch with one of his division commanders, Maj. Gen. W. H. F. "Rooney" Lee. Rooney Lee's division had been camped at Chappell's farm until two days before. On that day, the 27th, Brig. Gen. Thomas Rosser's Laurel Brigade had been detached and ordered to the Shenandoah Valley. The rest of the division, during the day, had crossed Hatcher's Run and established its camps closer to Petersburg.

Rooney Lee's division, under orders from Gen. Robert E. Lee, had started for the north side of the James on the 29th, to reinforce the troops struggling to contain General Butler's onslaught. Hampton suspended this movement. Instead, Rooney Lee was to rush one of his two brigades down Vaughan Road, while the other was to halt and take position near Petersburg, covering the Boydton Plank Road.[28]

Before falling back to Wyatt's, Gregg sent a patrol up Vaughan Road toward Poplar Spring Church. The troopers reached Miss Pegram's without encountering any resistance beyond a few scattered shots from Rebel pickets, who beat a hurried retreat. At Miss Pegram's the leader of the patrol learned there was a strong force of Rebel infantry at Peebles', one-half mile farther up the road.

Gregg would have liked to check out this story, but the presence of Farley's dismounted troopers at the crossing of Hatcher's Run prevented a sufficient force from being detached to push the reconnaissance beyond Miss Pegram's. Recalling his patrols, Gregg marched Smith's brigade to Wyatt's. Gregg investigated the possibility of sending a column northward from Wyatt's to Poplar Spring Church, but was told that the road was heavily barricaded and picketed.[29]

Upon establishing his headquarters at Wyatt's, Gregg posted a strong outpost at McDowell's farm. Rooney Lee, late in the afternoon, reached McDowell's with Brig. Gen. Rufus Barringer's hard-riding North Carolina Brigade. As soon as the gunners of McGregor's Virginia Battery had unlimbered their pieces and opened fire, the greyclads moved to the attack. The Federals manning the line of outposts at McDowell's farm were hurled back. As they retired toward Wyatt's, a number of their comrades were overtaken and grounded their arms.

27 *Ibid.*, 1107.

28 OR 42, pt. 1, 947; R. L. T. Beale, *History of the Ninth Virginia Cavalry, in the War Between the States* (Richmond, 1899), 146; Edward L. Wells, *Hampton and his Cavalry in '64* (Richmond, 1899), 313.

29 OR 42, pt. 2, 1107.

Alerted by the firing on the picket line, Gregg called for Colonel Smith to form his brigade for battle. The cannoneers of Batteries H and I, 1st U.S. Light Artillery, threw their four Napoleons into battery. Within a few minutes, the regulars were engaged in a sharp duel with the gunners of McGregor's battery. The butternuts drew first blood; one of their projectiles blew up a limber and disabled one of the Federals' guns. Barringer now threw his men forward, but they were repulsed by the Yankees' well-aimed volleys.[30]

Early in the afternoon, General Warren had issued instructions for General Crawford to have one of his brigades, Brig. Gen. Henry Baxter's, make a reconnaissance toward Poplar Spring Church. Baxter's column, covered by a strong force of skirmishers, moved out at 3:00 p.m. Passing through the line near Fort Dushane, Baxter's foot soldiers took the country road leading to Poplar Spring Church. Before they had proceeded far, the Yanks encountered Rebel pickets. The Federals forged ahead, driving the Confederates before them. As Baxter's skirmish line approached the church, it was shelled by Southern artillery. While Baxter was examining the area to satisfy himself that Rebel guns commanded the road leading westward by the church, his scouts reported a strong force of grey clads maneuvering to turn his right. Not wishing to chance an engagement so far in front of friendly lines, Baxter recalled his scouts and withdrew his brigade. The Federals re-entered their works, and Baxter reported that he had encountered the foe in force.[31]

General Gregg called for help when he was attacked by the dismounted Rebel cavalry. In response to Gregg's call, General Warren issued marching orders to one of General Griffin's brigades. The brigade was to hasten to the cavalry's assistance.

Guided by one of Gregg's aides, the brigade moved out of the works on the double. The infantry, however, didn't arrive in time to participate in the fighting at Wyatt's.

Just before dark, Rooney Lee had hurled Barringer's cheering North Carolinians forward. Although they drove ahead with their characteristic abandon, the Johnnies were unable to dislodge the Union cavalrymen.

Recalling Barringer's men, Rooney Lee had them remount. He led the column northwestward and rendezvoused with Col. J. Lucius Davis' brigade on the

---

30 *Ibid.*, 1108; *OR* 42, pt. 1, 619, 647.

31 *OR* 42, pt. 1, 65-66; *OR* 42, pt. 2, 1094, 1104. Baxter's command consisted of the 11th, 88th, and 90th Pennsylvania; the 39th Massachusetts, and the 104th New York. No casualties were suffered by Baxter's brigade during the forced reconnaissance to Poplar Spring Church. *OR* 42, pt. 1, 65-66.

Boydton Plank Road. General Butler took advantage of the Federals' withdrawal at Wyatt's to re-establish his picket line.[32]

Soon after the repulse of Barringer's attack, General Griffin recalled his infantry brigade. Before retiring for the night, Gregg redeployed his command. Davies' brigade was called up from reserve and given the task of manning the picket line extending from Wyatt's to Ream's Station. Smith's brigade was sent to the rear and camped at Perkins' house, where there was a good supply of water. As Smith's troopers hadn't watered their horses since the previous day, the animals were badly gaited.[33]

*   *   *

At 1:30 p.m., General Grant telegraphed Meade from Deep Bottom. Up until that hour, Butler's troops north of the James had scored several important successes—Fort Harrison had been captured and the Confederates abandoned their position centering on Four Mile Creek and commanding the River Road (today's Virginia 5) retired into Fort Gilmer. Grant wrote that reinforcements from Petersburg were beginning to reach the Southerners fighting to check the Union surge toward Richmond. Grant, as yet, didn't feel the Rebels had pulled sufficient troops out of their Petersburg defenses to insure that a thrust by the Army of the Potomac toward the South Side Railroad would be a success. He would defer to Meade's judgment, whether it would be advisable for the Army of the Potomac to undertake any offensive operations this evening.

Before handing this dispatch to the telegrapher, Grant received reports from the signal corps people that large numbers of Rebel troops had been spotted "moving from Petersburg toward Richmond." Should these movements continue, Grant notified Meade, "it may be well for you to attack this evening."[34]

At 3:30 p.m., Meade informed Grant that Gregg had encountered Rebels in force in the country west of the Weldon Railroad. A reconnaissance by soldiers from General Ferrero's division had disclosed that the Confederates hadn't pulled any troops out of their works in the sector between Forts Mahone and Walker. Officers manning the signal stations were unanimous in reporting "no movement

---

32 *OR* 42, pt. 1, 947; pt. 2, 1108.

33 *OR* 42, pt. 2, 1108-1109. At the beginning of the engagement at Wyatt's, Gregg's Chief Surgeon had established the division hospital at Perkins' house. The tent-flies were put up and the injured were received, fed, and had their wounds examined. *OR* 42, pt. 1, 619-620.

34 *OR* 42, pt. 2, 1092.

or change in the enemy in our front." Consequently, Meade was satisfied that the foot soldiers seen going to Richmond belonged to Maj. Gen. Robert F. Hoke's division, which had been in reserve on the Confederates' left. In view of these developments, Meade had determined not to "make a movement to the left today, as it would hardly amount to anything, it being now so late."

Grant was advised that Baxter's brigade had been ordered to make a reconnaissance to Poplar Spring Church, and that the Army of the Potomac would be "prepared to advance at daylight tomorrow." Meade observed, "We are all delighted to hear of the brilliant success of the movements today."[35]

At 10:30 p.m., Meade sent Grant another telegram. After summarizing the afternoon's actions (the engagement at Wyatt's and Baxter's reconnaissance to Poplar Spring Church), Meade reported that, according to Maj. Gen. Winfield S. Hancock, large numbers of Confederate soldiers had been observed marching along the road from Petersburg to Port Walthall. Meade interpreted this movement to be a threat to his right on the Appomattox.

According to Meade's signal officer, approximately 7,000 Rebel infantry had left Petersburg during the day for Richmond, while another 5,000 had marched to bolster the Confederate right. When he studied these reports, Meade became discouraged. He didn't believe he could assemble a sufficient force for maneuver to justify an attempt to reach the South Side Railroad. Checking with Warren and Parke, Meade learned that the four divisions they had ready for field service mustered only 16,000 strong, whereas when he had broken the Weldon Railroad, he had employed six divisions of the V and IX Corps.

What he planned to do, however, was to throw out a force to Poplar Spring Church to engage the foe. The value of such an undertaking, Meade noted, was open to question, because it would extend the Federal lines without "a commensurate object."

Grant returned to City Point for the night. Telegraphing Meade at 11:30 p.m., Grant observed, "You need not move out at daylight in the morning, but be prepared to start at, say, 8:00 a.m., if you find the enemy still further reduced." Grant planned to return to Deep Bottom at 5:00 a.m. When he did, he might be able to secure definite information as to how many troops the rebels had shifted from the Petersburg area to contain Butler's attack north of the James.

When Meade's striking force did take the field, Grant thought it would be wise if it were maneuvered "to get a good position from which to attack." Should the Confederates be routed, Grant wanted them followed into Petersburg. At the same

---

35 *Ibid.*, 1093.

time, Grant opposed the extension of the investment line to the South Side Railroad, unless a large part of Lee's Army of Northern Virginia was drawn across the James to oppose Butler's advance.[36]

Upon receipt of Grant's 11:30 p.m. dispatch, Chief of Staff Humphreys notified Warren, Parke, and Gregg that they were to have their troops formed and ready to march at 8:00 a.m.[37]

Earlier in the day, Warren and Parke had alerted the divisions of their commands that were to move out and engage the Confederates to be ready to take the field "precisely at 5:30 a.m.," on September 30.

General Warren had prepared orders for the guidance of his division commanders. Griffin was to recall all his pickets south of the road leading to Poplar Spring Church. All his other outposts, along with those detailed from Ayres' and Crawford's divisions, were to remain in position. When the corps moved out, Griffin was to have the advance. He was to be followed by Ayres' division, reinforced by Hofmann's brigade. One battery was to accompany Griffin's division; two batteries were to march with Ayres. No guards would be left in the camps and all wagons were to be parked between corps headquarters and the Gurley house. The corps pioneers were to be at Warren's headquarters at 5:30 a.m. When the column marched, General Crawford would assume charge of all troops left behind.[38]

Griffin found the order for him to withdraw part of his picket line vague, for he didn't know the location of Poplar Spring Church. He wished corps headquarters to clarify this point for him.[39]

Lieutenant Colonel Frederick Locke replied for Warren, informing the First Division commander that he was to recall all pickets posted south of a line running due west from Fort Dushane.[40]

Upon receipt of General Orders 43, Griffin, Ayres, and Hofmann notified their subordinates that the troops were to be awakened at 4:30 a.m. and have

---

36 *Ibid.*, 1094.

37 *Ibid.*, 1130, 1139.

38 *Ibid.*, 1103-1104.

39 *Ibid.*, 1104. At this time, Griffin observed, the right flank of his picket line connected with Aryes' outposts at Flowers' house.

40 *Ibid.*, 1105.

breakfast. The brigade commanders were to have their units formed, mustered, inspected, and ready to take the field at 5:20 a.m.[41]

Part II

The Confederates Assail the IX Corps

In compliance with General Meade's directive, Generals Gregg, Parke, and Warren had their commands ready to take the field early on September 30. Warren, having heard nothing from army headquarters since midnight, soon became apprehensive. Deciding to check with Chief of Staff Humphreys, Warren inquired at 7:35 a.m., "Am I to move at 8 o'clock without further orders?"

Before replying, Humphreys checked with General Meade. The army commander remarked that it might be wise to wait until he heard something definite from General Grant. Humphreys accordingly telegraphed Warren, "You are not to move without further orders."[42]

Grant, following a flying visit to Deep Bottom, was back at City Point by 8:15 a.m. Upon his return, Grant wired Meade that for the time being Butler's army would remain north of the James, ready to resume its drive on Richmond, should it be found practicable. Grant wanted Meade to move out now and see if an advantage could be gained. All that he had heard or seen during the past 48 hours convinced Grant that the Confederates "must be weak enough at one or the other place to let us in."[43]

Meade promptly ordered Warren's, Parke's and Gregg's commands into action. Warren was to march his striking force "out past Poplar Spring Church and endeavor to secure the intersection of the Squirrel Level Road, so as to enable us to gain a position on the right of the enemy."[44] General Parke was to march Potter's and Willcox's divisions out after Warren "and cooperate with him in endeavoring to secure a position on the right" of the Confederates' works. Soldiers from the IX

---

41 *Ibid.*, 1105. Hofmann's brigade was to move out as follows: the 2nd and 6th Wisconsin, 7th Wisconsin, 19th Indiana, 24th Michigan, 149th Pennsylvania, 150th Pennsylvania, and 143rd Pennsylvania.

42 *OR* 42, pt. 2, 1130.

43 *Ibid.*, 1118.

44 *Ibid.*, 1131.

Corps would also try to open a route across Arthur Swamp to the vicinity of Miss Pegram's, south of Poplar Spring Church, and take post on Warren's left.[45] General Gregg's mounted division was to return to Wilkinson's.[46]

A message was forwarded to Grant at 8:30 a.m. by Meade, advising him of his operational plan. If all went well, the Federals would turn the Rebels' right.

A contraband, who had escaped from Petersburg and had passed through the Union lines that morning, had been questioned by Meade's officers. He told Col. George H. Sharpe that on the morning of the 29th, the Confederate high command sent troops out on the Lynchburg Road, and that Maj. Gen. Henry Heth's division had been rushed northward to reinforce the troops opposing Butler's drive. The only other news which Meade had for Grant at this time concerning the foe's movements was that the men in one of the signal stations had spotted an ambulance train rolling toward the Union left.[47]

It was after 9:00 a.m. when Warren put his column into motion. In accordance with the corps commander's instructions, General Griffin's First Division took the lead, as the troops passed through the lines. Griffin had assigned the advance to his 3rd Brigade commanded by Col. James Gwyn.

After leaving the frowning parapets at Fort Dushane behind, the Federals crossed a large open field and entered the woods, which consisted for the most part of scrubby pines. The column cautiously felt its way ahead. After having marched about two and one-half miles, a halt was called, and General Griffin, who was riding at the head of his division, told Gwyn to throw out skirmishers. Colonel Gwyn gave the officer in charge of the 118th Pennsylvania, Capt. James B. Wilson, the responsibility for seeing that this task was carried out. One officer—Lt. John Conahay—and 20 men were deployed and sent forward. The skirmishers hadn't advanced very far before they encountered Rebel pickets behind light fieldworks thrown up alongside the road in front of Poplar Spring Church. Shots were exchanged and the grey clads retired. Lieutenant Conahay was killed in this fighting and General Griffin was standing next to him when he fell.[48]

---

45 *Ibid.*, 1137.

46 *Ibid.*, 1139-1140.

47 *Ibid.*, 1118.

48 Survivors' Association, *History of the Corn Exchange Regiment 118th Pennsylvania Volunteers, From Their First Engagement at Antietam to Appomattox* (Philadelphia, 1888), 513-514; William H. Powell, *The Fifth Army Corps (Army of the Potomac), A Record of Operations During the Civil War in the United States of America, 1861-1865* (New York, 1896), 730.

General Warren and his staff reached Poplar Spring Church hard on the heels of Griffin's vanguard. The officers watched as Gwyn deployed his brigade into line of battle. When formed, the brigade's line was at an angle to the large redoubt and rifle pits into which the Confederate outposts had retired. Gwyn's soldiers were partially screened from the fire of the guns emplaced in the redoubt by the crest of a small hillock and the thick forest.[49]

Before pushing on, Warren (at 11:00 a.m.) dashed off a note to Chief of Staff Humphreys. Warren informed headquarters that Griffin's troops were being shelled by Rebel artillery, but that the pines screened the grey clads from his view. The pioneers had been turned to widening the road to facilitate the advance of Ayres' division and the IX Corps. As the situation now stood, Warren continued, he would have Ayres halt his troops; Parke and his two divisions would then pass behind the V Corps and try to outflank the Southerners. Unless Meade should decide differently, Warren proposed to "operate" against the Confederates in the Peebles' farm sector.[50]

Considerable time was wasted as Gwyn completed his dispositions. Before resuming the advance, the brigade effected a change of front. As the bluecoats of the 118th Pennsylvania changed "front forward on the right company," the regiment came in "full view of a four-gun battery and a long line of infantry parapets."

When Gwyn gave the word, the troops moved out of the pines and into the field fronting the Rebel redoubt, 600 yards away. Here, they were raked by fierce discharges of canister and scattered small-arms fire. The 118th Pennsylvania and the regiment on its right, the 16th Michigan, raced forward. After passing over about 500 yards of cleared ground, the two regiments encountered an abatis.[51] A team of husky pioneers leaped forward and with axes speedily cut a path through the obstructions, wide enough for eight men to pass. Through this breach, the 16th Michigan went by fours by the left flank, and the 118th Pennsylvania by the right flank. Captain A. Wilson led his regiment; Col. Norval E. Welch headed the 16th Michigan.[52]

---

49 Survivors' Association, *History of the Corn Exchange Regiment*, 514; Powell, *The Fifth Army Corps*, 730.

50 *OR* 42, pt. 2, 1131.

51 Survivors' Association, *History of the Corn Exchange Regiment*, 514. The abatis were "built of rails firmly planted and connected by string pieces."

52 *Ibid.*; Powell, *The Fifth Army Corps*, 730.

Pressing on, the assaulting Union columns crossed the ditch and started to ascend the parapet of Fort Archer, which was defended by dismounted troopers of the 7th Virginia Cavalry from Brig. Gen. James Dearing's brigade. One Rebel aimed his carbine at Colonel Welch, squeezed off a round, and killed the colonel. Color-Corporal William H. Wild at the same moment was cut down and mortally wounded, as he planted the colors of his regiment, the 118th Pennsylvania, on the superior slope of Fort Archer. As the Federals stormed over the works, the grey clads took to their heels. Soldiers from the 20th Maine entered the redoubt hard on the heels of the 118th Pennsylvania and the 16th Michigan.

Just before the bluecoats came pouring over the works, Confederate cannoneers of the Petersburg Virginia Artillery brought up their teams. The horses were hitched to the guns, and three of them were driven from the redoubt before the Federals could intervene. The remaining gun would likewise have been saved by the Rebels had it not been for Lt. A. E. Fernald of the 20th Maine. Fernald had raced ahead, and, sizing up the situation, dashed through the gorge, and called upon the cannoneers to halt. They hesitated for a moment. Whipping out his revolver, Fernald pointed it at the head of one of the drivers. Several Rebel troopers opened fire on the daring lieutenant, but they missed their mark. William Kilpatrick of Company D, 118th Pennsylvania rushed to Fernald's assistance, mounting "a wheel-horse while the struggle for the piece was taking place," whereupon, the Confederates surrendered the gun.

Colonel Gwyn sought to ride his horse up the steep exterior slope of Fort Archer. As he did, the animal slipped and fell on him, badly injuring his leg and breaking open the scar tissue covering an old wound. Unable to continue in command, Gwyn was assisted to the rear by several of his aides. With Gwyn out of action, Maj. Ellis Spear of the 20th Maine, as senior officer present, assumed charge of the 3rd Brigade.[53]

After storming Fort Archer, Major Spear quickly reformed the brigade. As soon as the units had been mustered, Spear, in accordance with instructions from General Griffin, posted his troops about 200 yards in front of Fort Archer.

After the firing ceased, Col. Horatio G. Sickel's brigade of Griffin's division advanced and took position west of the captured redoubt. Within a few minutes, the officers had put their men to work throwing up breastworks. The line occupied

---

[53] Survivors' Association, *History of the Corn Exchange Regiment*, 514, 516; Powell, *The Fifth Army Corps*, 730-731. Since General Dearing was ill, Col. Joel R. Griffin of the 8th Georgia commanded the brigade on September 30. *OR* 42, pt. 1, 947; Theodore Gerrish, *Army Life, A Private's Reminiscences of the Civil War* (Portland, 1882), 215-216; Eugene A. Nash, *A History of the Forty-Fourth Regiment New York Volunteer Infantry in the Civil War, 1861-1865* (Chicago, 1911), 209-211.

by Sickel's soldiers "extended across a large open field, at the ends of which were thick woods. . . ."[54]

At 1:30 p.m., following the capture of Fort Archer, General Warren addressed a terse note to Chief of Staff Humphreys. Griffin's troops, Warren boasted, had "just carried the entrenchments on Peebles' farm in splendid style." The Union "loss was not very great" and the bluecoats had taken a number of prisoners. Subsequently, Warren learned from the Provost-Marshal that the prisoners totaled about 70.[55]

Before another 15 minutes had passed, Warren received an interesting note from General Humphreys. The chief of staff wanted Warren to know that Ferrero had been directed to extend the front held by his black troops from Fort Howard to Fort Wadsworth. Such action on Ferrero's part would enable his division to relieve one of Crawford's brigades, which would be held in reserve for "exigencies." Humphreys wanted to know if there was "a road or route direct from Fort Wadsworth to Poplar Spring Church" that could be opened to facilitate communications.[56]

Acknowledging Humphreys' dispatch, Warren pointed out that a feasible route could be opened westward across the fields from Fort Wadsworth to Vaughan Road.[57]

Soldiers of Potter's and Willcox's divisions of the IX Corps "arose early, formed line, stacked arms, ate breakfast and laid down to rest." General Parke's striking force took up the march at 10:30 a.m., Potter's troops moving from their camp near Aiken's house and Willcox's from their bivouac at Gurley's. Potter's division took the lead as the IX Corps crossed the Weldon Railroad and headed westward over the road pioneered by Warren's bluecoats. Soon the troops were in a countryside untouched by the ravages of war.

Approaching Vaughan Road, the men of the IX Corps spotted Ayres' soldiers posted in the fields and woods north of their line of march. The head of Potter's column overtook Griffin's division at Poplar Spring Church. At this time, the Rebel

---

54 Survivors' Association, *History of the Corn Exchange Regiment*, 517; Survivors' Association, *History of the 121st Regiment Pennsylvania Volunteers* (Philadelphia, 1893), 85.

55 *OR* 42, pt. 2, 1131; *OR* 42, pt. 1, 55.

56 *OR* 42, pt 2, 1131. The brigade commanded by General Bragg would constitute Crawford's reserve.

57 *Ibid.*, 1131.

artillery was growling while Griffin was preparing him men to attack Fort MacRae.[58]

As one of the regiments was crossing a valley east of the church, a soldier in the 35th Massachusetts of Potter's division recalled, the Confederate cannoneers fired "a solid shot which raked the whole length of the regiment, passing just over the men, and causing a laughable bobbing of heads."[59]

Parke halted the head of his column and rode on to Warren's command post. After discussing the situation with Generals Warren and Griffin, and while waiting for his troops to close up, Parke made a hurried reconnaissance.

Returning, Parke told Potter to deploy part of his division at the church in support of Griffin. Potter accordingly approached the commander of his lead brigade, Col. John I. Curtin, and gave him his instructions.

The brigade was promptly formed at right angles to the Poplar Spring Church Road. Curtin's two left flank regiments (the 21st Massachusetts and the 48th Pennsylvania) took position at Smith's house. The 7th Rhode Island, in accordance with Parke's instructions, was sent to open a road through Arthur Swamp from Smith's to Miss Pegram's.

Before the Rhode Islanders had gone very far, they were fired on by Rebel sharpshooters. Dropping their tools, the rugged infantrymen deployed alongside the 48th Pennsylvania and the 21st Massachusetts. The three regiments pressed forward compelling the grey clads to take to their heels. Parke hoped to use the route cut by the Rhode Islanders to wheel his corps into position on Griffin's left.[60]

A diarist in the 7th Rhode Island described these events:

> From our tool wagon each man was supplied with a spade, axe, or a pick. This looked like work. Three-quarters of an hour later we were instructed to leave our tools upon the ground, take our muskets and fall in. Presently we were taken into the woods and in front of the brigade to the skirmish line. After advancing through the woods nearly three-quarters of a mile we reached a field bordering on the Squirrel Level Road. . . . Here to our surprise we were ordered to return to our tool wagon where we belonged, and to remain with it until otherwise directed. We promptly obeyed and were soon

58 OR 42, pt. 1, 545-546, 578, 581, 586; Hopkins, *The Seventh Regiment Rhode Island*, 215; Committee of the Regiment, *History of the Thirty-Fifth Regiment Massachusetts Volunteers, 1862-1865* (Boston, 1884), 296.

59 Committee, *History of the Thirty-Fifth Regiment Massachusetts Volunteers*, 296.

60 OR 42, pt. 1, 545, 546, 578, 581, 586.

back whence we started. We promptly stacked and dinner was prepared, it now being 4 p.m. and the day very warm.[61]

Fast moving developments on another part of the field caused Parke to cancel his orders for the opening of the road. Parke ordered Potter's division to deploy to the left of the V Corps.

"We were at once ordered forward at the double-quick," recalled the historians of the 36th Massachusetts, "and, coming out into fields and fronting, followed the other lines of battle across the open and up to the captured works, which were quite strong, especially the redoubt, which had a deep ditch."[62]

As they moved forward, the IX Corps troops passed the men of the V Corps, "who were quietly resting with stacked arms . . . ."[63]

Curtin's brigade of Potter's division advanced to the right of the captured works. Passing beyond Peebles' house, Curtin's battle line, covered by a strong force of skirmishers, beat its way through the pines until its right flank unit gained an open field adjoining the Squirrel Level Road. The ground occupied was "considerable in advance" of Fort MacRae.[64]

Here a halt was called. To Curtin's soldiers, this delay was inexplicable, because it was evident that the advantage of surprise was being thrown away by their leaders. Surely, they reasoned, the Confederate generals must have already been alerted to their presence by the men driven from the redoubt by Warren's bluecoats.[65]

Meanwhile, Potter's 2nd Brigade, led by Brig. Gen. Simon G. Griffin, advanced over the ground to the west of Fort MacRae. As soon as his battle line drew abreast of the V Corps soldiers on its right, Griffin called a halt.[66]

As soon as Willcox's division reached Poplar Spring Church, Parke drafted a plan to exploit the success gained by Warren's troops. The IX Corps would pursue the foe and drive for the Boydton Plank Road. As the first step in this undertaking, Parke had Potter get in touch with Gen. Simon Griffin. Griffin was to advance his brigade beyond Oscar Pegram's house.

---

61 Hopkins, *The Seventh Regiment Rhode Island,* 215.

62 Committee, *History of the Thirty-Fifth Massachusetts Volunteers,* 296-297.

63 Committee of the Regiment, *History of the Thirty-Sixth Regiment Massachusetts Volunteers, 1862-1865* (Boston, 1884), 259.

64 *OR* 42, pt. 1, 546, 578, 581.

65 Committee, *History of the Thirty-Sixth Massachusetts Volunteers,* 259.

66 *OR* 42, pt. 1, 578, 587.

When Griffin gave the word, the 2nd Brigade pushed forward in column of attack—the 11th New Hampshire to the right and the 6th New Hampshire to the left. After leaving the captured works, the column marched to the northwest, passed through a narrow belt of timber, and entered a large clearing, near the eastern end where Widow Pegram's house stood.

Passing the V Corps' pickets near Widow Pegram's, Griffin's skirmishers encountered Rebel outposts in the pines beyond. Potter, who was riding with Griffin, told his brigade commander to strengthen his skirmish line, and the 2nd New York Mounted Rifles moved out on the double. A cautious advance toward B. H. Jones' house was resumed.[67]

About 400 yards beyond Widow Pegram's house, the Federals came to a Old Town Creek. The skirmishers reported Confederates in considerable strength on the opposite side of the hollow. A Rebel battery started shelling the road where Griffin's column marched. At this, Griffin formed his brigade into double line of battle.

As soon as Colonel Curtin's IX Corps troops had been relieved by units from Ayres' division, General Potter sent an aide with instructions for Curtin to move to the left out of the woods and follow the route taken by Griffin's column. Before recalling his skirmishers and forming his brigade into column, Curtin sent a runner racing to recall the 7th Rhode Island from its road-cutting duties.

Marching northwestward across Church Road, the brigade reached Widow Pegram's. As they pressed ahead, Curtin's troops were hailed by scouts, who gave them the grim news that the Rebels had taken advantage of the delay to reinforce the works against which they were advancing. Except for a few solid bolts and shells that whizzed overhead or struck in the pines to their right, all was quiet. News that Griffin's troops were in contact with Confederate skirmishers, resulted in orders from Potter for Curtin to deploy his troops in double line of battle on the left of the 2nd Brigade. The troops formed along the ridge passing through Pegram's cornfield, with their right flank anchored on the road from Pegram's that intersected Church Road to the left of Boisseau's house.[68]

---

67 *Ibid.*, 587. The 2nd New York Mounted Rifles had been dismounted.

68 *Ibid.*, 578-579. From left to right the first line was composed of the 9th, 11th and 6th New Hampshire, and the 2nd Maryland. Griffin's second line consisted of the 17th Vermont, the 31st and 32nd Maine, the 56th Massachusetts, and the 179th New York. *Ibid.*, 579, 581, 583, 586; Committee, *History of the Thirty-Fifth Massachusetts Volunteers*, 260; Committee, *History of the Thirty-Sixth Massachusetts Volunteers*, 297. Prior to drawing abreast of Griffin's brigade, Curtin's left had rested at the Peebles' house, and his right occupied the road along the edge of the woods in front of Oscar Pegram's house. *OR* 42, pt.1, 581.

When General Potter instructed Curtin to form to the left to cover the Church Road, he had been led to believe that a brigade from Willcox's division would look after Griffin's right. Up to this moment, all reports reaching Potter from his scouts indicated that the butternuts were pulling back toward the Boydton Plank Road. In their hurry to push ahead, the soldiers of Potter's division had forged at least one-quarter mile in advance of the picket line manned by the V Corps. There were no Union troops on Potter's left, but this caused no apprehension, because the leader of the Second Division had been told by General Parke that there were no Rebels in that direction. Orders now arrived for Potter "to push on with . . . [his] whole force as rapidly as practicable, without reference to anyone else."[69]

Potter relayed these instructions to his brigade commanders. Covered by a strong skirmish line, Griffin's brigade moved out. Crossing Old Town Creek, the bluecoats forged ahead; skirmishers from the 2nd New York Rifles swept away the grey clads before them. The New Yorkers dashed up a hill and reached the open ground near R. Jones' house, which they seized and held after a brisk clash. Griffin's first assault wave rolled forward and occupied the crest at the edge of the pines fronting Jones' house.[70]

Cognizant of meeting Confederate resistance, Griffin halted his advance to wait for friendly troops to come up and "make connections" on his right and left. General Potter in the meantime had told Curtin to post his brigade on Griffin's left. As his right flank drew abreast of Griffin's first line of battle, Curtin called a halt.[71]

Curtin made a hurried reconnaissance and saw that there was an open field to his front. To capitalize on this situation, Curtin had his men take cover behind a "thickly-grown hedge and fence." At this time, the 35th Massachusetts, 45th Pennsylvania, 58th Massachusetts, and 51st New York constituted Curtin's first line; the 48th Pennsylvania, and the 21st and 36th Massachusetts were on the left of the brigade:

> Soldiers of the 36th Massachusetts on the left of the brigade halted for a few moments near the Boisseau house, at a fence with the skirmishers of the regiment, covered the front and left of the regiment, the line extending from the woods to the Boisseau house. The firing on our right now increased and the Second Brigade became hotly engaged, and our line was ordered over the fence, which was hastily crossed, and an advance of a few yards made into an open field, which extended a long distance to the

69 OR 42, pt. 1, 579.

70 *Ibid.*, 579, 587.

71 *Ibid.*, 579, 581, 583, 586.

right, exposing to view a large part of the brigade line of battle, while the enemy was concealed in the woods beyond. Here the regiment first met the whizzing Rebel bullets, which became so troublesome as to cause the men to lie down; and, although the prostrate attitude was eminently adapted to the situation, the recumbent warriors may have been shamed, and were certainly encouraged, by the example of General Curtin, who at this junction reached the front, and followed by a single orderly, rode along the line of his brigade, as coolly as if on review. His horse was soon after shot from under, and a valuable saddle, sent as a present from his friends in Pennsylvania, fell into the hands of the enemy.[72]

When they crossed the rail fence, the men of the 35th Massachusetts reached the edge of a grove of trees overlooking the fields near Jones' house. This "movement was effected slowly in good order, and the men lay down in line pending further action, a few bullets from a line of the enemy in front clicking in the tree tops."[73]

The 7th Rhode Island, still carrying their entrenching tools, had overtaken the brigade. In accordance with Curtin's instructions, the Rhode Islanders halted in the cornfield in front of Oscar Pegram's house. The 4th Rhode Island, its term of service having expired, established and manned the straggler line.[74]

While Curtin's troops were forming on Griffin's left, one of Willcox's staff officers rode up and told Griffin that he wanted to pinpoint his right flank. This information, he observed, was necessary as one of Willcox's brigades was to take position there.[75]

General Willcox's First Division had followed Curtin's brigade as far as Oscar Pegram's. Here, Willcox received orders from his corps commander to post one brigade to the left of Potter's division with its left sharply refused. Willcox entrusted the dependable 2nd Brigade led by Brig. Gen. John F. Hartranft with this mission. Hartranft promptly formed his brigade into line of battle, facing northwest, his right connecting with Potter's left near Boisseau's.[76]

---

72 Committee, *History of the Thirty-Sixth Massachusetts Volunteers*, 260-261.

73 Committee, *History of the Thirty-Fifth Massachusetts Volunteers*, 297.

74 Hopkins, *The Seventh Regiment Rhode Island*, 316; *OR* 42, pt. 1, 579, 581, 583, 586. At this stage of the conflict, Boisseau's house was unoccupied.

75 *OR* 42, pt. 1, 577.

76 *Ibid.*, 546, 552, 565. From right to left, Hartranft's brigade was comprised of the 1st Michigan Sharpshooters, 2nd Michigan, 50th Pennsylvania, 24th New York Cavalry (dismounted), 46th New York, 60th Ohio, and 20th Michigan. *Ibid.*, 565.

The brigade advanced in support of Potter's thrust. As it did, Hartranft proposed to establish a line from the left of Potter's division to the Clements' house. Having entered the pines, Hartranft sent Lt. Col. Byron M. Cutcheon with two regiments, the 2nd and 20th Michigan, to guard the road running westward to Armstrong's Mill. After establishing and manning a roadblock, Colonel Cutcheon sent several scouts up the road. Within a short time, the scouts returned and reported they had sighted no Confederates.[77]

Soon after Cutcheon's troops had set up the roadblock, Hartranft received instructions from General Parke to recall his command and shift to the right. Hartranft, as soon as the units had assembled, moved his soldiers up the road beyond Oscar Pegram's. There he called a halt and formed his brigade into line of battle, facing west and at a right angle to Potter's division. Hartranft's right was anchored near Boisseau's. In front of Hartranft's left was a morass. A patrol from the 20th Michigan penetrated the swamp and reported that it could be passed, "but with difficulty." Between the right of his line and the bog was a cleared field about 200 yards in width. About 1,000 yards west of Hartranft's front could be seen Confederate rifle pits, presumably occupied by cavalry.

Hartranft's skirmishers waded the swamp and took post on the low crest beyond. When Potter's division advanced, Hartranft moved his "brigade by the right flank, preserving the formation." After Potter's troops entered the pines north of W. J. Pegram's cornfield, Curtin's brigade extended to the left, thus throwing its flank into the field beyond Boisseau's and about 300 yards in advance of Hartranft's right. Hartranft then changed front, forming his line parallel to, and, en echelon to the right of Curtin's bluecoats;[78] his right was about 150 yards in advance of Boisseau's; the left rested on the swamp.

Willcox's two other brigades, in compliance with Parke's instructions, were held in reserve. Colonel Samuel Harriman's 1st Brigade was posted to the left of Oscar Pegram's. One of Harriman's regiments, the 109th New York, was given the mission of picketing the wood road leading to the southwest. Harriman was admonished to have his troops ready to reinforce Potter's division or Hartranft's brigade as circumstances demanded.[79] Willcox's 3rd Brigade, Col. Napoleon B. McLaughlen commanding, was massed in the woods east of Oscar Pegram's.

---

77 *Ibid.*, 552, 565, 570.

78 *Ibid.*, 565, 570, 572, 573. When he formed his brigade en echelon to Curtin's, Hartranft's right was about 150 yards beyond Boisseau's, while his left rested on the swamp.

79 *Ibid.*, 553, 558. When the IX Corps halted near Poplar Spring Church, Harriman's brigade had been formed into line of battle in the woods near the road and to the left of the Peebles'

As soon as he heard the crack of small-arms to his front, Willcox knew that Potter had found the foe. Orders were issued for Harriman to extend his flank to the right to the Pegram House Road and to be ready to march to Potter's support.

Moments later, an orderly on a sweat-streaked horse galloped up to Willcox's command post. The aide told Willcox that Parke wanted him to advance the reserve to the "crest" in Pegram's cornfield. Willcox issued the necessary instructions to Harriman and McLaughlen.

Harriman's battle line swept forward and occupied the crest; McLaughlen's troops beat their way through the woods east of the field. To guard against surprise, McLaughlen deployed and threw forward the 100th Pennsylvania as skirmishers. The Pennsylvanians were to plug the gap between Griffin's right and the the V Corps' left. McLaughlen's battle line followed the skirmishers. Before McLaughlen's line drew abreast of Griffin's troops, one of Willcox's staff officers thundered up. The aide told McLaughlen to countermarch his troops and take position in Pegram's field. Without pausing to recall the 100th Pennsylvania, McLaughlen led his command westward. As the head of the brigade debouched into the cornfield, McLaughlen was directed to post his troops to the east of Mr. Pegram's. By the time the panting troops had filed into position, the shooting to the north had increased in intensity until it was a continuous roar.[80]

Meanwhile, sharp firing from the direction of Boisseau's reached Colonel Curtin's ears. Instructions now arrived for Curtin to rush one of his regiments to reinforce Griffin's brigade. Marching orders were issued to the 35th Massachusetts. When the Massachusetts regiment reported to him, General Griffin told the unit commander, Maj. John W. Hudson, to post his troops in the pines in rear of his brigade.[81]

These shifts of position were beyond the comprehension of the men of the 35th Massachusetts. One of the soldiers recalled that the regimental adjutant had asked the staff officers "what there was upon our immediate right."

---

house. Harriman's task was to protect the left flank of the army. A patrol was advanced beyond the forks of the road, but the scouts were unable to spot any signs of hostile activity. Soon thereafter, Harriman advanced his battle line across a nearby ravine and took position across the road. A lieutenant and 20 men, accompanied by a staff officer, marched westward. After advancing about a mile and one-half, the patrol crossed a line of rifle-pits. An inspection revealed that the late occupants had made a hurried evacuation. Contact was established with pickets from Gregg's cavalry brigade. It was nearly 3:00 p.m. when Harriman reassembled his brigade and marched to the northeast and reported to General Willcox near Oscar Pegram's. *Ibid.*, 558, 562, 563.

80 *Ibid.*, 553, 574.

81 *Ibid.*, 582, 583.

The aide replied, "Nothing but a few pickets."

Since the soldiers knew there was "nothing but skirmishers upon" their left, "it seemed a queer position to be in, thus cast loose at night-fall upon the extreme left of the army."[82]

The withdrawal of the 35th Massachusetts had left a gap between Curtin's right and Griffin's left. Curtin therefore shifted his battle line to the right until the opening was closed.[83]

Observing that his brigade commanders were re-adjusting their lines, General Potter prepared to push on. As soon as it was reported that Curtin's troops were in position on Griffin's left, Potter waved his division forward. On doing so, he glanced at his watch. It was 5:00 p.m.

Griffin was troubled. When the order to resume the advance arrived, the only troops on his right were skirmishers from the 100th Pennsylvania.

With a deafening cheer, Griffin's battle line surged ahead. By the time Griffin reached Jones' house, he spotted a strong force of Confederates low to the ground sweeping out of the woods to his front and right. The Rebel battle line extended well beyond Griffin's right.[84]

Curtin's bluecoats, on entering Jones' field, saw only a few Confederates, and these were in front of the sector against which Griffin's lines were pressing. The advance continued until the first line of battle drew abreast of Jones' house. Here, Curtin halted his troops and rode to the left, but he was unable to pinpoint any Rebels in that direction. Curtin retraced his route. Heavy firing had broken out by this time along Griffin's front, while Curtin's right flank units were briskly engaged.[85]

General Potter, on seeing that the Rebels were in force and overlapped his right, feared that the butternuts would brush the skirmishers of the 100th Pennsylvania aside and reach Church Road, over which his division had marched northward from Peebles' farm. If this occurred, his division would be isolated. Potter rushed several aides to tell Curtin and Griffin to change front to the right.[86]

Meanwhile, General Griffin had moved to cope with the danger. Trusting to Curtin's brigade to protect his left, Griffin threw the 17th Vermont forward,

---

82 Committee, *History of the Thirty-Fifth Massachusetts Volunteers,* 298.

83 *OR* 42, pt. 1, 582, 583.

84 *Ibid.,* 579, 587.

85 *Ibid.,* 582.

86 *Ibid.,* 579.

Major General Cadmus Wilcox
Library of Congress

wheeling its front to the right. At the same time, the brigade commander called up the rest of his reserve, less the 179th New York, to bolster his front line.[87]

* * *

Early on September 30 the camps occupied by Confederate Maj. Gen. Cadmus M. Wilcox's division were astir. Soon after the troops had eaten their breakfasts, orders arrived for Brig. Gen. Samuel McGowan and James H. Lane to march their brigades to the north side of the James River. By 9:00 a.m., the troops had packed their gear. When Lane and McGowan gave the word, the regimental commanders formed their units and the column moved off. Passing through the outskirts of Petersburg, the North and South Carolinians crossed the Appomattox, and started up the turnpike toward Richmond.

About two or three miles north of Petersburg, a staff officer overtook the column and directed the officers in charge to have their troops retrace their steps. The brigades marched to a marshaling area near Battery No. 45. Here, Lane and McGowan halted their soldiers and allowed them to take a welcomed break.[88]

Following the loss of Fort MacRae, General Hampton had contacted Maj. Gen. Henry Heth. (Lt. Gen. Ambrose P. Hill, who was in charge at Petersburg while Lee was directing operations north of the James, had placed Heth in charge of

87 *Ibid.*, 587-588.

88 James H. Lane, "History of Lane's North Carolina Brigade," in *Southern Historical Society Papers*, vol. 9, 254, 356; J. F. J. Caldwell, *The History of a Brigade of South Carolinians, Known First as "Gregg's," and Subsequently as "McGowan's Brigade,"* (Philadelphia, 1866), 182; W. S. Dunlop, *Lee's Sharpshooters; or, The Forefront of Battle* (Little Rock, 1899), 209-210.

the infantry being assembled to oppose the Union thrust northward from Poplar Spring Church toward the Boydton Plank Road.) Heth and Hampton, after discussing the situation, decided to launch a counter-offensive. Heth, with his infantry, was to hit the Yanks in front, while Hampton's troopers assailed their left.

Before carrying out his assignment, Hampton moved Rooney Lee's division from its camp down the Boydton Plank Road. Dismounting the troopers, Hampton and Lee placed them behind some works to the right of where Heth was massing his infantry. Hampton would now wait for Heth's troops to begin the attack.[89]

Simultaneously, Heth put Lane's and McGowan's brigades of Wilcox's division, and MacRae's brigade of his division into motion. When the troops marched, they took the Boydton Plank Road. Upon reaching the Church Road crossing, Heth called a halt, and the troops were formed into line of battle behind some half-finished rifle pits. Reports reached the grey clads that the Federals were sweeping toward them. At first, the Johnnies believed that they would stand on the defensive and receive the Yanks' attack. They soon found that they were mistaken. The brigade commanders passed the word to move out.

McGowan's South Carolinians marched by the flank across a ravine northeast of Jones' house. Calling a stop just beyond the hollow, McGowan formed his brigade into line of battle. General Lane's North Carolina Brigade was posted on McGowan's right. The Church Road separated the brigades. The brigade led by Brig. Gen. William MacRae was formed in support.[90]

Through the pines, McGowan's and Lane's grey clads could see the Jones' house and bluecoated skirmishers of the 2nd New York Mounted Rifles. To cover the deployment of their brigades, McGowan and Lane advanced their sharpshooters. The Rebel marksmen and Union skirmishers peppered away. General Heth, sensing that the time was ripe, told Wilcox to put his men into action.

Letting go a terrible "Rebel Yell," the Confederate battle lines charged out of the woods. McGowan's sharpshooters, led by Capt. W. S. Dunlop, reached the Jones' house well ahead of the battle line. A short but desperate contest ensued,

89 Humphreys, *Virginia Campaign of '64 and '65*, 292; OR 42, pt. 1, 947; Beale, *History of the Ninth Virginia Cavalry*, 146; Wells, *Hampton and His Cavalry*, 319.

90 Caldwell, *History of a Brigade of South Carolinians*, 182-183; Dunlop, *Lee's Sharpshooters*, 210; W. J. Martin, "History of the 11th North Carolina Regiment," in *Southern Historical Society Papers*, 52 vols (Richmond, 1876), vol. 23, 53.

before the South Carolinians routed the 2nd New York Mounted Rifles from the house and outbuildings, capturing 32 prisoners.[91]

Captain Dunlop of the sharpshooters recalled:

The sharpshooters were deployed and advanced under a stringing fire into a basin shaped depression in the face of the hill this side of the Jones' house, where we were protected from the enemy's fire by the rising ground in front. Here our line was adjusted to the work in hand, and orders extended to prepare for action.

When everything was ready, with arms at a trail and bodies well stooped, the beautiful line slipped across and up the sloping side of the inclining basin, until our movements could no longer be concealed, when at the command, "up, guards, and at 'em! Fire and charge!" the entire line rose and fired; then with a rousing cheer stormed up the hill, broke and routed their entire line, and sent them flying across the field to cover of the woods beyond, save and except those occupying the Jones' house, who fought savagely for their position for a little while. The sharpshooters closed upon the house and poured into the doors and windows of the brick basement a murderous cross fire, which soon moderated their zeal and caused them to cry out for quarter.[92] "My line was formed:" General Lane reminisced: just beyond a stream of water, and the ground in front, particularly on the right, was rising, and served, somewhat, to shelter my men. I put the Thirty-third [North Carolina] on the right, as I feared a flank movement in that direction, and I had unbounded confidence in the bravery, coolness, and judgment of its Colonel, R. V. Cowan. I made known my fears to Cowan and instructed him, should such a movement be attempted, to maneuver his regiment at once to meet it and not await orders from me.

Not long after leaving him, and a short time before the general advance, there was heard a volley and a shout on the right. A large body of the enemy had formed perpendicular to Major [Thomas] Wooten's line of sharpshooters, under the impression . . . that it was my line of battle, and were advancing rapidly. But Cowan was on the alert, his men were brought to attention, and when the Yankee line was nearly opposite his colors, he moved his command to the top of the hill, and with a well directed, converging, flank fire, broke the whole line . . . .[93]

---

91 Caldwell, *History of a Brigade of South Carolinians*, 183; OR 42, pt. 1, 582, 588.

92 Dunlop, *Lee's Sharpshooters*, 210-211.

93 Lane, "History of Lane's North Carolina Brigade," 355.

Griffin's battle line prepared to counterattack. But before they could dislodge the South Carolina sharpshooters, Lane's and McGowan's brigades came up on the double. The bluecoats brought their rifle-muskets to the ready, got off one ragged volley, and took to their heels "in the wildest disorder." Halting, the grey clads sent several well-aimed volleys crashing into the demoralized fleeing mass.[94]

"While we were thus situated and quietly watching a line of battle approaching in front," the historians of the 36th Massachusetts reported:

upon whom we expected immediate orders to charge or open fire, a battalion, said to be bounty jumpers, came up behind us, appearing to be forming, when suddenly they left for the rear with a haste truly amazing—what could it mean? In a moment the mystery was explained, a column of Confederates charged upon our right-rear from the direction of the Church Road, coming upon us through the underbrush before we discovered their approach.

It would have been impossible to devise a worse plight for our regiment as then constituted. For a change of direction there was no time. Defense was out of the question; we should have shot our own men. In front was the line we had been watching on our right and rear where the new enemies, already seizing men from our right companies as they broke towards [sic] the left. The only thing to do was to collar our recruits, shout "Git!" in the best German at our command . . ., and then take ourselves off over the fence to the left into a field of sorghum, many of the men, however, getting in a shot before crossing the fence, which hindered the enemy a little, their foremost men also stopping to gather in those of our regiment who still clung to earth too much surprised to rise.

Crossing the fence, the [Battalion, 21st Massachusetts], under Captain [Orange S.] Sampson, deployed as skirmishers, covered our flight of a few rods to the ridge in [Mr. Pegram's cornfield].[95]

As they retreated in confusion, Griffin's troops crowded in on Curtin's second line. Such was the pressure upon the flank of this line that it was compelled to fall back and take position at the right angles to the first line. As soon as the Yanks had disappeared into the pines, the Southerners resumed their advance. The grey clads as they approached the south side of Jones' field were raked by the fire of Curtin's

---

94 Caldwell, *History of a Brigade of South Carolinians*, 183; OR 42, pt. 1, 582, 588.

95 Committee, *History of the Thirty-Fifth Massachusetts Volunteers*, 298-299.

second line—the 36th Massachusetts, the 48th Pennsylvania, and the 21st Massachusetts.[96]

Curtin's three regiments blazed away at McGowan's and Lane's onrushing battle lines. For a few moments, the Federals held their own. But in the end, the numbers told the story: overpowered, the Yanks were compelled to withdraw.[97]

"As the whole force covering our right vanished," a soldier in the 36th Massachusetts related:

> The regiment was subjected to a galling fire from that direction as well as the front. [Lieutenant] Colonel [William] Draper then ordered a change of front, but seeing that the enemy's movements threatened to cut us off from our forces in the rear he changed the order to a movement by the left flank in the same direction.

> The sorghum . . . gave us a slight shelter, and we hurriedly made our way through it, the vicious "zip" of the rebel bullets giving us an incentive to haste. Reaching the ravine between the Boisseau house and the sorghum field we found remnants of several regiments of the First Division [Willcox's], which had fallen into disorder, still gallantly holding their ground, gathered in little groups around their colors.[98]

General Potter was distressed to see Griffin's troops "falling back in considerable confusion." The general and his staff sought to rally the men, but the Rebels "were in so much force and so close that it could not be done." An aide was sent racing with orders to deploy the 7th Rhode Island, the division reserve, and to organize a new line of resistance near W. J. Pegram's. Soldiers of the 2nd Rhode Island, manning the straggler line, were to halt all men coming to the rear and compel them to rejoin their units. A second staff officer was dispatched with instructions for Colonel Curtin to have his troops pull back and reform along the new line. The aide, however, found the woods full of Confederates and turned back without contacting Colonel Curtin.[99]

The staff officer sent to look after the 7th Rhode Island found that regiment halted in the cornfield near Mr. Pegram's. Assisted by the aide, Lt. Col. Percy Daniels formed his regiment into line of battle among the stalks.[100]

---

96 Caldwell, *History of a Brigade of South Carolinians*, 183; *OR* 42, pt. 1, 582, 588.

97 *OR* 42, pt. 1, 582; Caldwell, *History of a Brigade of South Carolinians*, 183.

98 Committee, *History of the Thirty-Sixth Massachusetts Volunteers*, 261-262.

99 *OR* 42, pt. 1, 579.

100 *Ibid.*, 586; Hopkins, *The Seventh Regiment Rhode Island*, 216.

As he passed through the Jones' garden, General Lane spotted a number of his brigade who had stopped to plunder, when "a real soldier" from the 7th North Carolina arose from one of the walks to his left and told the general that "he was neither a plunderer nor skulker, but was there with his brother who had just been wounded."

Lane went to him. The general saw that the brother, who had been shot through the head, was unconscious and would soon be dead. Turning to the soldier, Lane remarked, "you know the orders—the ambulance corps is detailed to take care of all such cases—but as I know what it is to lose a brother under similar circumstances I cannot order you forward."

The general then passed on. As he was about to enter the woods beyond the garden, the soldier overtook him, and said, "Here I am, General, I have thought over what you said and I am going to the front."[101]

The appearance of Curtin's regiments on their right had been disconcerting to MacRae's North Carolinians. Since they didn't know that Rooney Lee's cavalry was about to intervene, the commanders of the 11th and 52nd North Carolina feared that they had been outflanked. On their own initiative, they wheeled their units to the right and assailed Curtin's blue clads.[102]

General Wade Hampton and the dismounted troopers of Rooney Lee's Division had been listening, when the rattle of small-arms and the shouts indicated that Heth had launched his assault and was rolling the Yankees back. Hampton called for Rooney Lee. Through the woods, the Rebel leaders could see the left flank of Curtin's brigade as it maneuvered frantically to cope with the sledgehammer-like blow delivered by the Confederate infantry. Hampton told Lee to attack. Placing himself at the head of the 9th and 10th Virginia, Rooney Lee rode off. The dismounted troopers advanced out of the earthworks covering the Boydton Plank Road and through the pines in line of battle, holding their fire until the last moment. Striking the left flank and rear of Curtin's first line, the troopers quickly effected a junction with MacRae's right flank units—the 11th and 52nd North Carolina. Three of Curtin's regiments (the 45th Pennsylvania, 58th Massachusetts, and 51st New York) found themselves encircled. Unable to fight their way out of the trap, the men grounded their arms.[103]

When the 35th and 36th Massachusetts fell back, they had passed through the sector occupied by Hartranft's brigade. Hartranft and several of his aides rallied the

---

101 Lane, "History of Lane's North Carolina Brigade," 355-356.

102 Martin, "History of the 11th North Carolina Regiment," 53-54.

103 *OR* 42, pt. 1, 579, 582, 584, 585, 948; Beale, *History of the Ninth Virginia Cavalry*, 146.

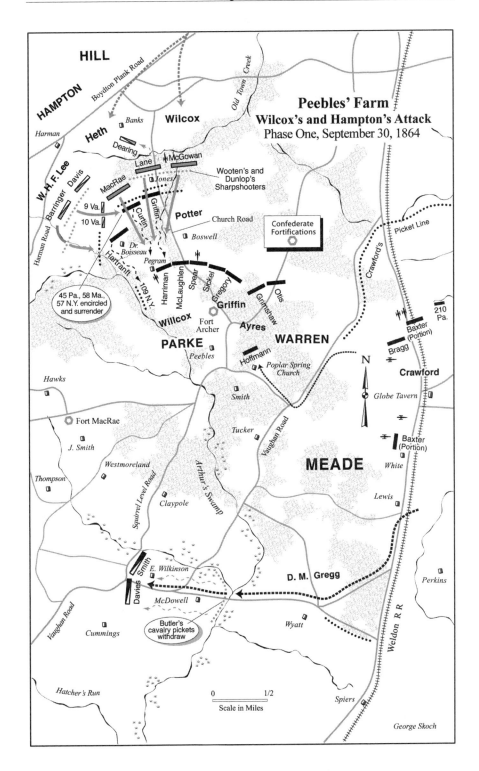

HILL

HAMPTON

Boydton Plank Road

Old Town Creek

Peebles' Farm
Wilcox's and Hampton's Attack
Phase One, September 30, 1864

Harman

Banks

Wilcox

Heth

Dearing

Lane

McGowan

Wooten's and
Dunlop's
Sharpshooters

W.H.F. Lee

Davis

MacRae

Jones

Barringer

9 Va.

Curtin

Griffin

Potter

Church Road

Confederate
Fortifications

Crawford's

Picket Line

Harman Road

10 Va.

Dr.
Boisseau

Boswell

Hartranft

Pegram

Harriman

McLaughlen

Spear

Sickel

Gregory

Otis

Grimshaw

210
Pa.

Baxter
(Portion)

45 Pa., 58 Ma.,
57 N.Y. encircled
and surrender

109 N.Y.

Willcox

Fort
Archer

Griffin

Ayres

WARREN

Bragg

Crawford

PARKE

Peebles

Hoffmann

Poplar Spring
Church

N

Hawks

Smith

Globe Tavern

Fort MacRae

Tucker

Baxter
(Portion)

J. Smith

Westmoreland

MEADE

White

Thompson

Claypole

Arthur's Swamp

Squirrel Level Road

Vaughan Road

Lewis

Smith

E. Wilkinson

D. M. Gregg

Perkins

Davies

McDowell

Vaughan Road

Cummings

Butler's
cavalry pickets
withdraw

Wyatt

Weldon R R

Hatcher's Run

0   1/2

Scale in Miles

Spiers

George Skoch

two Massachusetts regiments and placed them on the right of their line. At this time, there was little action, except for sporadic firing along the skirmish line, and in this area.

To help restore a semblance of order to the 35th Massachusetts, Sgt. Thomas Castle took position with the colors, and "the men began to rally in good position for defense, except that it was open to the left."

Our recruits, one of the veterans recalled, "were full of fight, and some of them began firing recklessly from behind the ridge through our forming line, one shot killing First Sergeant Young, of Company E . . . This back fire discouraged the formation, and now, to our surprise . . . on looking to the right we saw the whole of our Brigade coming rapidly to the rear . . ."[104]

A staff officer galloped up to Hartranft's command post with an urgent message from Chief of Staff Humphreys. Hartranft was to withdraw his troops. Because of the dense growth of sorghum in which his right rested, Hartranft had been unable to see that Potter's division was in wild retreat, consequently, he didn't see that there was any need to retire. Orders were orders, however. The brigade pulled back about 100 yards and redeployed along a road, a short distance in front of Boisseau's house. Here, Hartranft discovered by cocking his ear toward the roar of battle that Potter's division "had been well driven back."

Shortly thereafter, Rooney Lee's dismounted troopers attacked and forced the skirmishers that Hartranft had sent to the opposite side of the swamp to call for help. In view of the Confederate successes to his right and left, which if exploited could result in his command being surrounded, Hartranft determined on a farther withdrawal. This retirement would be carried out from left to right.

As the first step, Hartranft sent an orderly to tell Colonel Cutcheon to recall the 2nd and 20th Michigan. The Michiganders encountered no difficulty until they reached the swamp, separating them from the rest of the brigade. As they waded the morass, they were attacked by Lee's troopers, who charged their left and blazed away as the bluecoats worked their way through the vines and brambles. A number of men were cut down. After extricating themselves from the swamp, the Michiganders reformed in the woods west of Oscar Pegram's. The other regiments followed. Under General Willcox's supervision, Hartranft reformed his line, the right resting west of Pegram's and the left "very much refused." Skirmishers were advanced about 100 yards.[105]

---

104 Committee, *History of the Thirty-Fifth Massachusetts Volunteers*, 299.

105 *OR* 42, pt. 1, 553, 565-566, 571-573. On the left, Hartranft's skirmishers connected with the *line* of outposts manned by the 109th New York.

Willcox's two reserve brigades (Harriman's and McLaughlen's) were marching toward the "crest" in the field fronting W. J. Pegram's, when the Confederates routed Potter's division. As they flooded back from the front, frightened rabble passed, before the onrushing grey clads were sighted. At this time, Harriman's battle line was in the open field in front of and east of W. J. Pegram's.

The 7th Rhode Island was posted in the cornfield on Harriman's left. Covered by the Rhode Islanders, the cannoneers of the 34th New York Battery drove their teams forward. Unlimbering their four 3-inch rifles under a galling fire, the artillerists pointed their guns on a left oblique to the front, and opened on the Rebels with shot and shell. One of Lt. Col. William Pegram's batteries, which had been assigned to support Heth's attack, answered the New Yorkers' rifles. Projectiles from the Rebels' guns struck around Oscar Pegram's house "and even through it," killing and wounding a number of Federals.[106]

McLaughlen's brigade, at the time the Confederates were sighted, was advancing across the field southeast of Mr. Pegram's. Suddenly, the Confederate artillery roared forth. McLaughlen's troops were subjected to a fearful hammering. To protect his command, McLaughlen directed the soldiers toward a small hillock that lay between his line of march and the Rebel guns. As soon as his brigade reached the defiladed area, McLaughlen redeployed his regiments "into column of battalions closed in mass."[107]

*   *   *

General Heth's infantry sought to capitalize on the rout of Potter's division. Southeast of Jones' house there was a fork in the road, which heretofore had separated McGowan's right from Lane's left. The Church Road veered to the left, the other went to the right and on to Mr. Pegram's. Between these roads there was an all but impassable "swampy marsh." Lane's North Carolinians and the larger part of McGowan's brigade advanced to the west of the thicket. Large numbers of Johnnies crowded into the road leading through the pines toward Oscar Pegram's. As the Confederates forged rapidly ahead, the units became scrambled. McGowan and Lane deemed it best not to dampen the ardor of their victorious troops by stopping to reform.

As the butternuts debouched from the woods, they were hammered with shell and canister by the 34th New York Battery. Seemingly undaunted, the grim foot

---

106 *Ibid.*, 553, 586, 603; Hopkins, *The Seventh Regiment Rhode Island*, 216.

107 *OR* 42, pt. 1, 553, 574.

soldiers charged the guns and the supporting infantry—Harriman's brigade reinforced by the 7th Rhode Island.[108]

"Ere long," a diarist in the 7th Rhode Island recorded:

> the brigade [Curtin's] on our front became hard pressed, broke in places, and came back in confusion. At first we thought they were all wounded men, but soon discovered such was not the case. Leaving our wagon of tools Colonel Daniel then quickly formed a rear guard with the regiment, deploying the four right companies under Captain [George A.] Wilbur, and partially succeeded in stopping the stampede. They came so thick and fast, however, we could not hold them all in check, though a considerable number rallied on our right and left. We held our position believing there was a line of battle held in front of us. So there was, but not of the complexion we supposed. A little rise of ground in our front prevented us from knowing exactly what was occurring beyond. Suddenly a line of gray appeared over the crest.[109]

McGowan's, Lane's, and McRae's foot soldiers assailed the Yanks' reorganized main line of resistance. Harriman's bluecoats held their ground for about 15 minutes in the face of a slashing attack by the Johnnies. One of the Rhode Islanders heard the general call, "For God's sake move up and help that little Seventh Rhode Island!" General Griffin likewise was conspicuous as he sought to reform his men.

Harriman's troops now began to give way—the right wing (the 37th Wisconsin, and the 8th and 27th Michigan) retired in good order to a rail fence to the east of W. J. Pegram's. Here, the regiments halted, faced about, and threw down the fence. Within seconds, the soldiers had thrown up fence rail barricades, behind which they crouched and blazed away at their pursuers. The 13th Ohio Cavalry (dismounted) on the right of Harriman's battle line panicked. Taking to their heels, the Ohioans "fled ingloriously from the field." As they did, many of the dismounted troopers overran the 38th Wisconsin, throwing the Wisconsin regiment into disorder. The officers of the 38th Wisconsin rallied their regiment in the woods.[110]

---

108 Caldwell, *History of a Brigade of South Carolinians*, 183-184; Dunlop, *Lee's Sharpshooters*, 212-213.

109 Hopkins, *The Seventh Regiment Rhode Island*, 216.

110 OR 42, pt. 1, 553, 558, 562-563. Upon being reformed, the 38th Wisconsin took position on Hartranft's battle line. Capts. Richard H. Wheeler and Joshua Gore were able to collect a number of men from the 13th Ohio Cavalry (dismounted) and lead them back to the front.

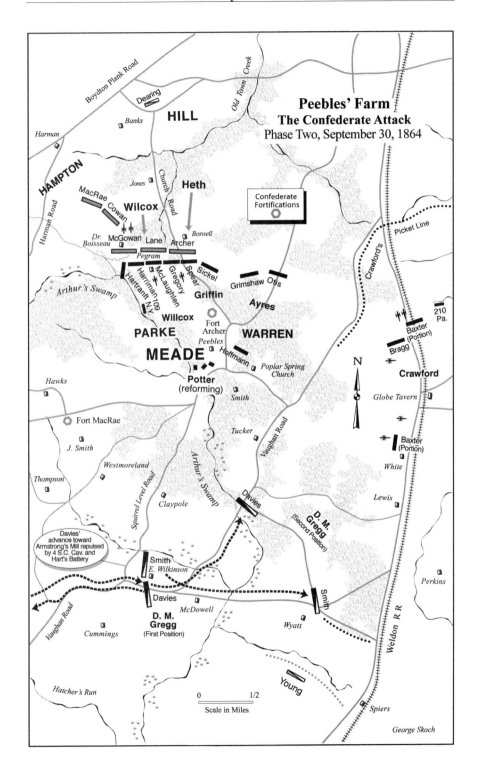

Peebles' Farm
The Confederate Attack
Phase Two, September 30, 1864

Soldiers of the 7th Rhode Island, after covering the withdrawal of the 34th New York Battery, fell back about ten rods and posted themselves behind the fence enclosing Mr. Pegram's.[111]

McLaughlen's brigade held the knoll southeast of W. J. Pegram's until Harriman's left flank units bolted. Whereupon, McLaughlen deployed his brigade into line of battle on the double. McLaughlen shouted for his men to stop the stragglers. Orders were now received from General Willcox for the brigade to form into line of battle on the double and to advance to Harriman's assistance. Urged on by Colonel McLaughlen, the 3rd Brigade took position at W. J. Pegram's, its left connecting with Harriman's command and its right with Griffin's division of the V Corps.[112]

When the 34th New York Battery retired, the hard-charging Confederates almost captured one of the pieces which had careened against a gate post.[113]

The Southerners were distressed to see that the Federals were rapidly forming a new line of resistance in rear of Oscar Pegram's and along the elevation upon which the house stood. General McGowan reported:

> We had now driven them [the bluecoats] near a mile, in confusion and rout, and there was considerable disorder in our ranks. The impulse of the first charge had spent itself; we had no supports; both flanks were uncovered; night was approaching; and, therefore, it was impossible to make a fresh charge and carry the position of the Pegram house, which was a strong one, defended, I believe, by overwhelming numbers of fresh troops.

Seeing that cannoneers of the 34th New York Battery had put their four 3-inch rifles back in battery, General McGowan sent word for "Willie" Pegram to rush one of his batteries to the South Carolinians assistance. Within a few minutes, McGowan sighted a battery thundering up the road toward him. Just then, the Yanks got off several well-aimed volleys which discouraged the cannoneers. Turning their teams around, the artillerists drew back without having put their guns into action.[114]

---

111 *Ibid.*, 586; Hopkins, *The Seventh Regiment Rhode Island*, 217.

112 *OR* 42, pt. 1, 553, 574.

113 Caldwell, *History of a Brigade of South Carolinians*, 183-184.

114 *Ibid.*, 184.

*   *   *

There had been considerable misgivings in the V Corps, when it was learned that the IX Corps was driving for the Boydton Plank Road. Lieutenant Isaac H. Seesholtz of the 118th Pennsylvania was heard to wager that Griffin's division "would soon be summoned to the fore." He was continuing "to better and better his stakes, with no takers" when heavy firing and fierce shouts were heard off to the left and front.[115]

The afternoon of Sept. 30 was almost spent before Griffin was ordered to support the IX Corps. So urgent was the need for reinforcements that the regiments of Griffin's division marched to the sound of the guns by the flank and at the double quick. Soldiers from Potter's IX Corps division were encountered retreating on the run. The forward movement soon changed to one by the left flank. Before they had proceeded very far in this new direction, the units were quickly faced about and ordered to march by the right flank. Word spread that the Confederates were pressing their advantage.

Griffin's troops occupied a crest, facing a dense woods through which led a roadway down which the Rebels surged. As the soldiers recalled, this prompt action on the part of Griffin and his officers alone kept them from suffering a fate similar to that suffered by Potter's division. The line of battle was established just in time to hold the grey clads, who were becoming somewhat disorganized by their pursuit of Potter in the timber.[116]

Immediately after filing into position, troops of Spear's brigade sighted a number of men clad "partly in blue" to their front. Fears were voiced that these might be stragglers from the IX Corps. In spite of being "fired upon with telling severity," the officers shouted for their men to hold fire. But the soldiers knew better, and, notwithstanding the command, they blazed away in time to avert disaster.[117]

For 30 minutes, Spear's brigade on the left of Griffin's main line of resistance stood in the open, receiving the fire of Confederates posted in the edge of the pines, scarcely 100 yards away. A shell from one of the Rebel cannon burst over the right of the 20th Maine. A dozen men were cut down. The crest held by Spear's bluecoats was so sharp that the artillerists to the rear, to avoid hitting their comrades, put an

---

115 Survivors' Association, *History of the Corn Exchange Regiment*, 518.

116 *Ibid.*, 519; Powell, *The Fifth Army Corps*, 732.

117 Survivors' Association, *History of the Corn Exchange Regiment*, 518-519. The 20th Maine was posted on the left and the 16th Michigan on the right of the 118th Pennsylvania.

extra turn on the elevating screws, and the projectiles overshot friend and foe. No reinforcements were in sight. When they exhausted their supply of ammunition, the soldiers rifled the cartridge-boxes of the dead and wounded.

Officers shouted encouragement to their men. The color-bearer of the 118th Pennsylvania fell; Lieutenant Seeholtz seized the colors and bore them forward a pace or two, until a minie ball struck him in the wrist, disabling him. Captain Wilson snatched up the colors and handed them to Thomas Crealy of Company C.[118]

There was some wavering, but General Griffin rode "along, with his resolute, heroic bearing and gave assuring words," whereupon the lines stiffened. Griffin ordered up Capt. Charles E. Mink and his battery—Battery H, 1st New York Light Artillery. Mink, "the one-armed artilleryman of intrepid valor," was directed to push his Napoleons "right up to the front."

"It's as bad as putting artillery on the skirmish line," cried Mink.

Turning to Captain Wilson of the 118th Pennsylvania, Mink said, "throw back your three or four left companies, sir, and let me get a section in there and I will clear the woods for you."

Back went the companies, while the gunners manhandled the pieces forward. "Double shot with canister and fire by section," Mink commanded. The gun captains pulled the lanyards, sending a storm of canister belching into the woods to their front. At such close range, the "stoutest soldiers" could not stand the punishment. The woods to the brigade's front were soon cleared of Confederates. It was now starting to get dark and the fighting waned.[119]

Captain Wilbur and his four companies of the 7th Rhode Island had become separated from the rest of the regiment. A diarist wrote of what ensued:

---

118 *Ibid.*, 519; Powell, *History of the Fifth Corps*, 732.

119 Survivors' Association, *History of the Corn Exchange Regiment*, 519-520; Powell, *The Fifth Army Corps*, 732; Gerrish, *Reminiscences of the Civil War*, 216-217; Nash, *History of the Forty-Fourth New York*, 210-211. At the close of fighting, Captain Wilson of the 118th Pennsylvania moved out to establish a line of outposts in the woods fronting his position. As he did, the Captain approached a giant oak about 60 feet in front of his line. As the Captain threw his arm around the tree, he felt another human. Peeking around the forest giant, Wilson saw "A tall, gaunt North Carolinian, so great in statue that he towered giant-like above him." In the advance, the North Carolinian had gone too far forward, and when the artillery opened, he felt that his only safety lay in hugging the tree. Wilson escorted the frightened North Carolinian back to the Union lines. Apparently, the Confederate felt that the term "Yankee" was one of reproach and its use would insure him harsh treatment. He addressed his captors as "you Northerners," and was particular to explain that he had never spoken of the Union soldiers by any other name. Survivors' Association, *History of the Corn Exchange Regiment*, 520.

When the rebs came over the hill those on our front of course commenced firing at us, but as we were well scattered we did not make much of a target. Then came the order to lie down, which was promptly obeyed. The hostile line continued to advance, however, until just in the nick of time a brigade of the Fifth Corps [Spear's] came out of the woods on the side of the hill, directly behind us and delivered a terrible volley. This checked its progress, and diverted attention from us. For quite a while we lay there between two heavy fires not daring to raise our heads. Finally, the captain [Wilbur] instructed us to fall back if we could without getting killed. It was somewhat dark when we did start, and good time was made getting out of that hot hole.

As we arose, the Johnnies dropped their bullets among us like hailstones, shouting, "Stop you Yankee sons of _____! Stop! Throw down your arms and stop!" Their demand was unheeded.[120]

West of the position held by Griffin's V Corps division, the soldiers of the IX Corps were glad to see the Confederates retire into the woods north of W. J. Pegram's fields. A detachment from the 1st and 14th South Carolina of McGowan's brigade, which had penetrated to the gate within 50 yards of Pegram's house, grumbled at the order to pull back. Rebel officers reformed their units behind the rail fence fronting the fields. Here, although partially sheltered by the "crest" in the middle of the cornfield, the grey clads were harassed by a desultory fire from small-arms and artillery. About 9:00 p.m., orders were received from General Heth for the infantry brigades to return to the Jones' farm. After checking the rolls and detailing men to man the picket line, the unit commanders formed their men into line of battle and told them to rest on their arms.[121]

As soon as the fighting had ebbed, the Confederates, to their delight, harvested from the battlefield hundreds of "oil cloths, blankets, knapsacks and the like." A number of knapsacks, judging from the appearance of the straps, had been "cut from the shoulders of their owners in their hasty retreat under a murderous fire accompanied with that well-known rebel yell."[122]

Rooney Lee and the men of the 9th and 10th Virginia Cavalry, along with McGregor's battery, reported back to General Hampton with 900 prisoners and 10 stands of colors, captured in the late afternoon's fighting. Hampton, expecting that the Confederates in the morning would attempt to recover the works at Peebles'

120 Hopkins, *The Seventh Regiment Rhode Island*, 217.

121 Caldwell, *History of a Brigade of South Carolinians*, 184-185.

122 James H. Lane, "Twenty-eighth North Carolina Infantry," in *Southern Historical Society Papers*, vol. 24, 337.

farm captured by the V Corps, saw that Lee's division and Dearing's brigade were posted in the rifle pits northeast of Fort MacRae.[123]

The soldiers of the IX Corps were glad to see the Confederates go. As darkness settled over the area, there was sniping on the right of Willcox's division, but mostly by the Federals.[124]

General Meade (who had visited Warren's command post late in the afternoon) decided that it might be wise to have the troops fall back into prepared positions. In making this decision, Meade was guided by two factors—the approach of darkness and the fluid condition of the lines. Orders were accordingly issued by Chief of Staff Humphreys instructing Warren's left was to be posted in Fort MacRae, while his right connected with the investment line at Fort Wadsworth. The V Corps officers were to see that their men entrenched.[125]

To carry out his mission, Warren saw that Ayres' 2nd Brigade occupied the redoubt near the Chappell house.[126] The remainder of Ayres' division, reinforced by Hofmann's troops, was posted and began entrenching along a line from Fort MacRae to the Chappell house.[127] Griffin's troops on being recalled, occupied the ground on the left of Ayres' division.[128]

At 7:45 p.m., Chief of Staff Humphreys in compliance with Meade's instructions, instructed General Parke to withdraw his troops from Oscar Pegram's. The IX Corps was to retire and occupy the entrenchments captured earlier in the day from the Rebels. Parke was to anchor his right on Fort MacRae and his left on Arthur Swamp; his troops were to dig in across "the road running past Peebles' toward J. Hawks' or J. Smith's."[129]

Parke promptly relayed this order to his division commanders. After detailing a strong force of pickets to hold his line, Willcox put his troops in motion for

123 OR 42, pt. 1, 948; Beale, *History of the Ninth Virginia Cavalry*, 146. While the fighting was in progress, McGregor's artillerists had moved forward and joined the 9th and 10th Virginia.

124 OR 42, pt. 1, 553.

125 OR 42, pt. 2, 1132-1133.

126 OR 42, pt. 1, 477-478. The brigade commander, Lt. Col. Elwell S. Otis, saw that the 12th and 14th U.S. Infantry dug in on the right of the redoubt; the 5th and 146th New York were posted in the redoubt; the 11th U.S. Infantry and the 15th New York Heavy Artillery threw up breastworks on the left of the strongpoint. As soon as it was dark, the 10th and 12th U.S. Infantry were thrown forward as pickets. *Ibid.*, 478.

127 OR 42, pt. 2, 1135.

128 Survivors' Association, *History of the Corn Exchange Regiment*, 520-522; Powell, *The Fifth Army Corps*, 63.

129 OR 42, pt. 2, 1137.

Peebles' house. There was considerable confusion as Willcox sought to redeploy his troops in the dark.

Colonel Harriman's brigade had taken the lead as Willcox's division tramped southward. At a point indicated by his guide, Harriman halted and deployed his troops on either side of the road, facing northwest. As soon as the men had shucked their gear, they began erecting fortifications.[130]

It was almost midnight before Hartranft's skirmishers were relieved by the 24th New York Cavalry (dismounted). Guided by several staff officers, Hartranft's troops occupied the ground on the right of Harriman's brigade and began digging in on the ridge near Clements' house.[131]

Colonel McLaughlen had been told to post his brigade on the right of Potter's division. The brigade took position on Hartranft's left, but McLaughlen was unable to find Potter's troops. When orders were received to throw up earthworks, McLaughlen was unable to tell the direction the line was to run. He therefore advanced his brigade and occupied a strong defensive position on the crest of a hill. Outposts were established and the men allowed to bivouac.[132]

Potter and his brigade commanders spent most of the night collecting and reforming their shattered units. Typical was the condition of the 35th Massachusetts. The regimental historians admitted that when the 35th was withdrawn from Oscar Pegram's "great confusion resulted." Part of the regiment under Lt. Samuel Patch:

> succeeded in getting in with the left flank of the brigade, and did some service there. Another part was with Captain [Albert A.] Pope and the regimental colors. The major, adjutant and several other officers and another part of the regiment got lost in the darkness and strange locality, and went wandering to the westward, where they came upon a Confederate line of entrenchments newly dug. The Major sprang over them, revolver in hand, but they were entirely vacant, their men having been drawn to their left, where our cavalry was posted, and reached Poplar Spring Church, from whence they rejoined the other men in the morning.[133]

---

130 OR 42, pt. 1, 558, 562, 563.

131 *Ibid.*, 566, 571-573.

132 *Ibid.*, 575.

133 Committee, *History of the Thirty-Fifth Massachusetts Volunteers*, 299-300.

After mustering and reorganizing their commands, Potter and his officers posted their men in the line of works taken from the Confederates north of Peebles' house, Curtin's brigade on the left and Griffin's on the right.[134]

Upon checking the rolls, the officers of the IX Corps found that in the day's fighting their units had suffered 1,994 casualties: 67 killed, 418 wounded, and 1,509 missing. Over seventy-five percent of the casualties had been inflicted on Potter's division.[135] When he filed his after- action report on October 30, Potter observed:

> The majority of the troops behaved well, but the recruits (mostly substitutes, and many unable to speak English) behaved badly, and the greatest inconvenience and serious trouble resulted from the scarcity of officers, large numbers of both field and line officers having been recently mustered out of service. By this serious want I found my efforts to rally the troops nearly paralyzed. The conduct of the few officers remaining, as far as came to my knowledge or observation, was good.[136]

General Gregg's Union cavalry division left Perkin's during the morning and again rode westward to Wilkinson's on Vaughan Road. The few pickets encountered by the bluecoats, after exchanging a few shots with Gregg's vanguard, retired across the Rowanty. Although he questioned a number of citizens, Gregg by mid-afternoon was unable to pinpoint Hampton's cavalry. When he relayed this news to Chief of Staff Humphreys, Gregg complained that the necessity of picketing the roads leading from his left toward Ream's Station seriously embarrassed his command.[137]

Generals Meade and Humphreys had reached Warren's command post shortly after 2:00 p.m. After discussing the situation at the front with Warren, Meade telegraphed Grant the latest news—the capture of Fort MacRae by Griffin's division, and the disappearance of the Confederate cavalry from Gregg's front.

Grant replied promptly, "If the enemy can be broken and started, follow him up closely. I can't help believing that the enemy are prepared to leave Petersburg." If the Rebel cavalry had vanished from Gregg's front, Grant telegraphed, the Union

---

134 *OR* 42, pt. 1, 579, 582, 588.

135 *Ibid.*, 546.

136 *Ibid.*, 579-580.

137 *OR* 42, pt. 2, 1139-1140.

cavalry ought to be pushed ahead, and if no obstacles were encountered turn the Confederate infantry's right.[138]

At 4:15 p.m., General Humphreys notified Gregg that Meade wanted him to send a brigade up the road reconnoitered by his troopers on the 29th to establish contact with General Parke. The column sent to carry out this task was to guard the IX Corps' left and endeavor to reach the Boydton Plank Road. For Gregg's information, the IX Corps was striking northwest from Peebles' and planned to reach the Plank Road near Boisseau's.[139]

Upon receipt of Humphreys' dispatch, Gregg gave General Davies' brigade the task of guarding Parke's left. Davies and his troopers encountered the 4th South Carolina Cavalry, supported by Hart's Battery, on the Telegraph Road, near Armstrong's Mill. A sharp engagement ensued, but the Federals were unable to dislodge the Rebel horsemen.[140]

The near disaster suffered by the IX Corps caused Meade to get in touch with Gregg. Meade wanted Gregg to recall Davies' troopers. When he fell back, Davies was to have one of his regiments report to General Parke. The people at army headquarters also wanted all the information Gregg had regarding the whereabouts of the Confederate cavalry.[141]

It was after dark when General Davies detached the 1st New Jersey Cavalry with orders to communicate with Parke's IX Corps at Oscar Pegram's. As the troopers moved out, Davies decided to accompany them. When he wheeled his horse about, Davies directed his second in command, Col. William Stedman, to recall the brigade and return to Davis', where Gregg had established his command post.

The night was very dark and the road along which the 1st New Jersey rode was a strange one. Since the Confederates were known to be on their left and to their front, the column proceeded cautiously. As the advance slowly rode up the little hill fronting Armstrong's house, the troopers could hear talking and the clattering of sabers.[142]

Confederate Brig. Gen. John Dunovant, about dark, put his brigade of South Carolinians in the saddle. Dunovant, according to the orders he had recently

138 *Ibid.*, 1119.

139 *Ibid.*, 1140.

140 *Ibid.*, 1140-1141; OR 42, pt. 3, 27; U. R. Brooks, *Butler and His Cavalry in the War of Secession, 1861-1865* (Columbia, 1909), 325.

141 OR 42, pt. 2, 1141.

142 OR 42, pt. 1, 635; OR 42, pt. 3, 27.

received from his immediate superior, General Butler, was to reinforce Brig. Gen. Pierce M. B. Young's brigade then picketing the crossings of the Rowanty. Charles Montague of the 6th South Carolina was assigned to the advance guard. As Montague recalled:

> We were soon overtaken by General Dunovant and his staff, who requested us to move to one side of the road so that they could pass. Captain Sullivan answered that we were the advance guard, and the general replied, "Oh, there is no danger on this road; I will be the advance guard myself tonight."
>
> So we moved to one side, and as we did so, a limb knocked my hat off, and it fell under the horses' feet as they rode by. It was a very dark night, misting rain, and it was useless to attempt to get it, so I tied a handkerchief over my head, and after the General and his staff had passed, we fell in behind. . . . After riding about a mile or a mile and a half, while going through what was apparently a field, we were suddenly halted by a voice not more than 25 or 30 steps in advance of us, yelling out, "Halt, halt, or we fire!"[143]

"Who goes there?" another voice snapped.

"Butler's South Carolina Brigade," came this starling reply.

"Who are you?"

"First New Jersey Cavalry." "Charge" commanded the leader of the vanguard.

With "a Jersey yell," the Federals thundered through the "thick darkness upon an invisible foe." A sharp volley was given, the rapid and continued rattle of hoofs on the gravel road in front gave "notice" that the Federals had scattered the Confederates advance guard. Several grey clads, including Lt. O. N. Butler, a brother of the general, were captured.

When they searched Butler, the Yanks found several reports indicating that Hampton's cavalry had participated in the attack on the V and IX Corps. Ascertaining that the grey clads were closing in on the column from all sides, General Davies concluded that it would be unwise to continue along the road. The regiment retraced its steps and rejoined the brigade after midnight at Davis' house.[144]

---

143 Brooks, *Butler and His Cavalry*, 325-326.

144 *Ibid.*, 326-327; OR 42, pt. 1, 625.

Just before dark, the blue clad troopers of Smith's brigade occupying the picket line covering the approaches from Ream's Station and on the road running south from Wyatt's were attacked by General Young's Confederate horsemen. Although hard-pressed, the Yanks succeeded in beating off the butternuts.[145]

*   *   *

At 9:00 p.m. on the last day of September, General Meade telegraphed Grant, reporting that Parke's Corps, as it was driving toward Boydton Plank Road, had been "vigorously" assailed by two divisions of Hill's Corps. The IX Corps in severe fighting had been pushed back; orders had been issued for Warren and Parke to dig in. Meade was of the opinion that it would be injudicious for the Army of the Potomac "to make another advance tomorrow unless reinforced or some evidence can be obtained of the weakening of the enemy."

After studying Meade's communication, Grant replied at 9:40 p.m., "You need not advance tomorrow," he wrote, "unless in your judgment an advantage can be gained." Meade would hold on to what his troops had gained, and be ready to advance if the opportunity presented itself. Grant advised his general, "We must be greatly superior to the enemy in numbers on one flank or the other, and by working around at each end, we will find where the enemy's weak point is." During the day, Grant continued, Butler's troops north of the James had been assailed three times, but they had held firm.[146]

Shortly thereafter, Grant sent a dispatch notifying Meade that two new regiments and a part of another had been sent as reinforcements to the Army of the Potomac. Grant accordingly inquired, "Can they not be put in the line so as to spare some old troops to reinforce the left?"

Before going to bed, Meade wired that the fresh regiments on their arrival were to be placed in the rifle pits on either side of the Weldon Railroad. Already one of the regiments, the 210th Pennsylvania, had filed into the earthworks, east of Fort Wadsworth. This, with an extension of the frontage occupied by Ferrero's division, had enabled Crawford to relieve Bragg's brigade. In addition, Meade had ordered Hancock to hold his lines with two divisions and to hold the third (Mott's) "in reserve ready for contingencies."

According to the best available information at his headquarters, Meade observed, Field's and Hoke's divisions, which had constituted the Confederate

145 *OR* 42, pt. 2, 1141.

146 *Ibid.*, 1121.

strategic reserve, had been rushed from Petersburg to the north side of the James. This had left four divisions south of the Appomattox. Units from two of these, Wilcox's and Heth's, had been identified as being in the force which had assailed the IX Corps at Jones' farm, while the other two—Mahone's and Johnson's—were holding the Petersburg lines.[147]

Meade at the same time issued instructions to guide the early morning activities of Warren, Parke, and Gregg. The corps commanders were to send out strong reconnaissance patrols at daylight "to ascertain the position of the enemy." The picket lines were to be advanced simultaneously.[148]

General Gregg with his cavalry division was to advance at daylight up the road which passed Boisseau's and feel the position of the foe. The cavalry leader was to keep in touch with and to cooperate with General Parke.[149]

Meanwhile, General Warren had contacted Crawford. At early dawn, Crawford was to march Bragg's brigade out to the Flowers' house. Captain Emmor Cope, with two batteries, would be sent to assist Bragg in forming his line. Before throwing up any breastworks, Bragg was "to carefully push a skirmish line a little north of west, to connect with General Ayres at the Chappell house. Crawford was to retain and deploy the new units sent from City Point by Grant to bolster the V Corps.[150]

Part III

Hampton's Rebel Horsemen Fail to Drive Gregg's Cavalry from Davis' Plantation

Chief of Staff Humphreys at 12:15 a.m. on October 1, 1864, sent identical messages to Generals Parke and Warren. The corps commanders were informed that according to the latest news from Grant's headquarters, General Butler's troops on the north side of the James were confronted by Maj. Gen. Charles W. Field's and Robert F. Hoke's divisions, and part of George E. Pickett's. Should the

---

147 *Ibid.*, 1122.

148 *Ibid.*, 1133, 1138.

149 *Ibid.*, 1141-1142.

150 *Ibid.*, 1135.

forced reconnaissance they were to undertake at dawn show the Rebels were rushing additional troops to oppose Butler's thrust, they were to drive for the Boydton Plank Road.[151]

It was 5:15 a.m. before Humphreys' 11:50 p.m. and 12:15 a.m. dispatches reached Parke's command post. Replying immediately, Parke notified headquarters that he feared his losses on the previous afternoon would be "much heavier" than preliminary reports had indicated. Before his troops pulled back to their present position, scouts had reported that the Rebs were posted in the "woods just north" of Oscar Pegram's. Before ordering out any reconnaissance patrols, Parke would prefer to have his troops make their present position secure, which would be impossible until after daylight.[152]

As day broke along the front, it started to rain. Parke, on examining his front and discussing the situation with his chief subordinates, learned that in the darkness some of his units had failed to occupy good defensive positions. Several hours were lost as units were shifted to ground that met with the engineers' approval. Hartranft's brigade was moved to the right, and posted with its right resting near Peebles' house and its left extending across the flats toward Clements'. The troops of McLaughlen's brigade were deployed on Hartranft's left, their left anchored on Harriman's unit. As soon as he had re-adjusted his line, General Willcox had his brigade commanders put their rain-drenched, miserable men to work entrenching and slashing timber.[153]

Potter's division, to Willcox's right, spent the morning strengthening the breastworks in front of Peebles' house. Besides felling an abatis, the troops threw up several redoubts.[154]

A soldier in the 7th Rhode Island of Potter's division wrote of the day's activities:

> called at 4 a.m., formed line and stacked arms behind the breastworks thrown up last night. At 8 a.m. rain began to fall. At 10 a.m. we took axes and went out to cut away some pine woods that obstructed the view. They were situated quite near the enemy's pickets who ere long opened fire and drove us back to our lines. Thomas Quinlan was shot through both thighs, while John Moore and William Weldon were injured by a falling tree. Work was then commenced on an earthwork to shelter a battery. . . .

151 OR 42, pt. 2, 17, 25.

152 *Ibid.*, 25.

153 OR 42, pt. 1, 558, 566, 571-573, 575.

154 *Ibid.*, 582, 586.

Meanwhile a section of Durell's [Pennsylvania] Battery came up and vigorously shelled the rebel picket compelling it to fall back. Thereupon our line advanced farther out and constructed sheltering pits to hold the additional ground. After dinner we returned to the pine grove, and, at 4 p.m., finished leveling the trees without molestation. At night we pitched our tents in the mud close behind the breastworks. . . .[155]

Warren, as directed, sent several patrols to feel for the Confederates. After passing beyond the picket line, the scouts encountered large numbers of Rebels beyond W. J. Pegram's house, and on the right of General Ayres' position near the Chappell house. Shortly after the blue clads had returned with this news, the Rebel artillery roared into action, pounding the area held by the V Corps. When he relayed this information to General Meade at 8:00 a.m., Warren cautioned, "I expect a hard time."[156]

Prior to the receipt of the dispatch from Warren, Meade had telegraphed Grant. Copies of his 5:15 a.m. message from Parke, as well as the latest messages from Hancock and the Signal Corps people were forwarded to Grant by Meade. Personnel manning the Plank Road signal station at 6:45 a.m. had spotted a column of Rebel infantry as it debouched from the pines near Battery No. 40 and turned into the Halifax Road. It had taken the Southerners 15 minutes to pass a given point.[157]

Hancock, at 7:00 a.m., had notified Meade that a deserter from the 16th Alabama, Brig. Gen. Archibald Gracie's brigade, had been brought in by his outposts. When questioned, the Alabamian said that there was "nothing new," the Petersburg lines were being held by two divisions: Johnson's and Mahone's.[158]

These reports, Meade pointed out to Grant, indicated that the Rebels were still in force to Parke's front and were bringing up fresh formations. The statement made by the deserter reinforced Meade in his belief that only two divisions were holding the Petersburg lines, while two others (Wilcox's and Heth's) had been rushed to meet his thrust on the left. Parke and Warren had been ordered to advance if they deemed it practicable. If they attacked, Meade promised to

155 Hopkins, *The Seventh Regiment Rhode Island*, 217-218.

156 *OR* 42, pt. 3, 18.

157 *Ibid.*, 9.

158 *Ibid.*, 11. Gracie commanded a brigade in General Johnson's division.

reinforce them with one of Hancock's divisions, "and put in all the troops" he could lay his hands on.[159]

Meade sent a second telegram with two attachments at 9:20 a.m. to Grant. In addition to Warren's 8:00 a.m. communication telling of the Confederate concentrations near Pegram's and Chappell's, there was an enclosure from Provost Marshal John C. Babcock.

Colonel Babcock had just finished questioning the deserter from the 16th Alabama. Besides the information previously gleaned by Hancock's staff, Babcock got the man to say that Hoke's and Field's divisions had left Petersburg, either to reinforce Lt. Gen. Jubal A. Early in the Valley or the troops struggling to contain Butler's drive toward Richmond. So far, the only prisoners captured in the fighting west of the Weldon Railroad interrogated by the provost marshal had belonged to Dearing's cavalry brigade.[160]

Due to the apparent continued build up by the Confederates in the sector southeast of the Boydton Plank Road, Meade issued orders for General Hancock to send him Brig. Gen. Greshom Mott's division. As soon as Mott's troops arrived at Poplar Spring Church, Meade assured Grant, he would resume the offensive. The departure of Mott's troops would leave less than 15,000 soldiers to hold the investment line from the Appomattox to the Weldon Railroad.[161]

*   *   *

The Confederate brigade commanders, in accordance with instructions from General Heth, saw that their men were formed and supplied with ammunition early on October 1. It was about 7:00 a.m. when the wet, muddy columns were put into motion. On the right, Lane's North Carolina brigade tramped down the road leading to Oscar Pegram's, while McGowan's South Carolinians took the Church Road. As the Southerners approached the edge of the woods, they were halted and deployed—the North Carolinians to the right and the South Carolinians to the left. Sharpshooters were deployed and sent to relieve the men who had spent an uncomfortable night on the picket line.

According to the plan worked out by General Hill, Wilcox was to assail the IX Corps, while Heth's column moved out on Squirrel Level Road and assailed the V Corps. Soon after Lane and McGowan had completed their dispositions, the

159 Ibid., 4.

160 Ibid., 8-9.

161 Ibid., 4.

gunners of the Letcher Virginia Artillery emplaced their guns on Lane's right, where they could enfilade the Federals' works.[162]

General Heth, accompanied by Brig. Gen. James J. Archer's and Joseph R. Davis' brigades, had moved out. Breaking camp at 3:00 a.m., Heth's column had taken up the march for the right. Halting near Battery No. 42, the soldiers anxiously waited for dawn. As soon as it was light enough to see, Archer and Davis led their troops down the Squirrel Level Road to its intersection with the Confederate earthworks. Passing through the rifle pits, the grey clads entered an open field, where their officers formed them into line of battle, preparatory to assailing the fortifications defended by General Ayres' bluecoats.

While the infantry officers were marshaling their units into line of battle, Colonel Pegram's cannoneers unlimbered their guns. When Pegram gave a pre-arranged signal, the guns of the Letcher and the Purcell Virginia Batteries roared into action. Hofmann's brigade which was massed in reserve near Poplar Spring Church found itself caught in a deadly crossfire. Observing this, General Warren had Hofmann withdraw his troops and march them eastward to bolster Ayres' right flank, which was being threatened by Rebel infantry.[163]

General Heth, satisfied that Pegram's guns had softened up the Union defenses, passed the word to attack. Covered by a strong skirmish line, Archer's and Davis' foot soldiers swept forward.

Shortly before the beginning of the bombardment, Colonel Otis sent the 17th U.S. and the 140th New York to relieve the 10th and 12th U.S. on the picket line. Suddenly, the Confederate artillery fell silent. Moments later, Rebel skirmishers were sighted. Close behind through the dripping pines came Archer's and Davis' battle lines.

The 10th U.S. Infantry, which hadn't yet taken position in the works, countermarched, and led by Lt. Theodore Schwan, hastened to the pickets' assistance. The Johnnies, who advanced in double line of battle, proved too much for the Federals. Despite the presence of the 10th U.S., the Union skirmishers were compelled to retreat. As they retired on their fortified line, they exchanged volleys with the onrushing butternuts. Re-entering the works, the pickets filed into position alongside their comrades. Without bothering to halt and regroup, the Rebs attempted to storm the rifle pits, but they were repulsed with heavy losses. Among the bluecoats cut down in this fighting was the commander of Ayres' 1st Brigade,

---

162 Caldwell, *History of a Brigade of South Carolinians*, 185; Dunlop, *Lee's Sharpshooters*, 213; Lane, "History of Lane's North Carolina Brigade," 356.

163 *OR* 42, pt. 3, 18; *OR* 42 pt. 1, 859, 949.

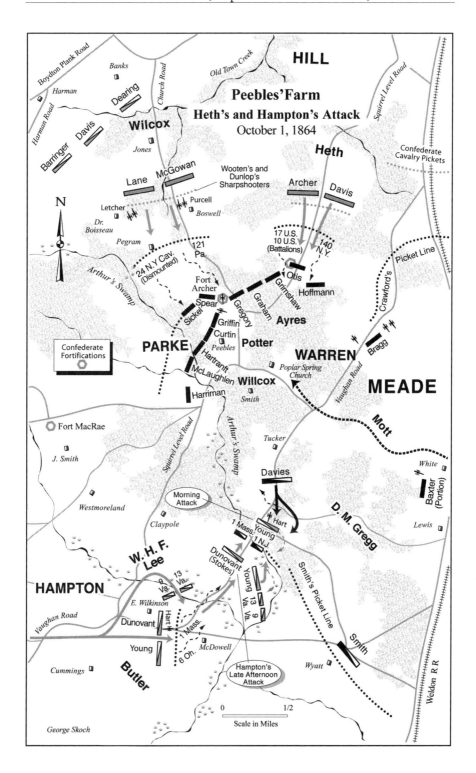

Peebles' Farm

Heth's and Hampton's Attack

October 1, 1864

Colonel Otis, who was carried to the rear badly wounded. With Otis out of action, Maj. James Grindlay of the 146th New York, as senior officer present, took charge of the brigade. Upon the repulse of the Johnnies, Major Grindlay had the soldiers of the 17th U.S. and the 140th New York reoccupy the picket line from which they had been dislodged.[164]

The sharpshooter battalions from McGowan's and Lane's brigades were advanced, while the brigades stood to arms in line of battle. As soon as the Confederate artillery fell silent, the sharpshooters left the protection of the woods and entered the fields beyond. Union skirmishers from the 24th New York Cavalry (dismounted) were encountered "in strong rifle pits" near Oscar Pegram's house. Without halting to get off a volley, the grey clads charged and put the New Yorkers to flight. Captain Dunlop of McGowan's sharpshooters recalled that we "pursued them up a sloping ridge, yelling and firing at every jump."[165]

Soldiers from Sickel's brigade held the works east of the picket line manned by the New Yorkers. Word had been sent along the line that the brigade should fall back "as soon as hotly pressed by the enemy." This order never reached the commander of the 121st Pennsylvania, Lt. Col. James S. Warner. The Pennsylvanians were therefore surprised to see the soldiers to "their right relinquishing their ground without, so far as they could see, any plausible reason for doing so. "Most of the regiment—fortunately for themselves—instinctively followed, leaving Colonel Warner, the adjutant, 7 other commissioned officers, and 43 enlisted men behind."

Along with a number of men from other units who had failed to get the word, the Pennsylvanians snatched up their small-arms when a strong force of Confederates appeared to their front. Letting go three "rousing cheers" for the Union, these soldiers "settled down to defend their position to the last." But unfortunately for them, Lane's and McGowan's sharpshooters swept out of the woods to their left and rear, and "scooped in the whole party, making prisoners of them all."[166]

The rattle of small-arms and the shouts of the Johnnies caused the soldiers of the IX Corps who were throwing up breastworks and slashing timber to redouble

---

164 OR 42, pt. 1, 478, 942; OR 42 pt. 3, 18.

165 Dunlop, *Lee's Sharpshooters*, 213-214.

166 Survivors' Association, *History of the 121st Pennsylvania Volunteers*, 85-86.

their efforts. After driving in the IX Corps picket line, the sharpshooters were recalled, bringing with them 240 prisoners and many stand of arms.[167]

When the sharpshooters returned with twice as many prisoners as they had men, the Rebel cannoneers were taken aback. Thinking that the foe was advancing, the Letcher Virginia Artillery turned its cannons on the sharpshooters and their prisoners. Several rounds were fired before they discovered their mistake. A number of bluecoats were killed and wounded, while General Wilcox had a narrow escape as one of the projectiles burst "almost at his feet."[168]

Following Ayres' repulse of the Confederate attack, at 11:30 a.m., Warren wrote Chief of Staff Humphreys, reporting that his men were busy strengthening the earthworks and opening roads. The inactivity of the Rebels since their mid-morning attack indicated to Warren that they were either entrenching or massing for a new thrust. "We," Warren complained, "are not strong enough to act offensively, in view of the uncertainties of the enemy's positions, numbers, and movements, but we keep feeling them." A mistake on the Federals' part, Warren warned, might enable the Confederates to recover the ground "we have taken." Warren wanted to know if his policy of watchful waiting met with Meade's approval.[169]

While waiting for headquarters to reply, Warren and his staff visited the line held by Spear's brigade of Griffin's division. Evidently, the work was not being prosecuted with as much vigor as the general had hoped. He vented the opinion, "I never saw a lazier set of men in my life; they are good for nothing but fight. I could take my staff and cut down more trees than the whole brigade." Some of the troops interpreted the general's remarks as "an indirect compliment for the valorous deeds of the day before." The reference to "fight" was an incentive to activity and, for a time at least, the men worked harder.[170]

It was after 2:00 p.m. when Warren received an answer to his 11:30 a.m. communication. Chief of Staff Humphreys observed that Meade had sanctioned Warren's passive attitude pending the arrival of Mott's division. As soon as Mott showed up, Warren was to make dispositions to attack.[171]

---

167 Caldwell, *History of a Brigade of South Carolinians*, 185; OR 42, pt. 1, 554, 566. Although they had been driven back, the dismounted troopers of the 24th New York were kept on picket duty throughout the remainder of the day.

168 Lane, "History of Lane's North Carolina Brigade," 356.

169 OR 42, pt. 3, 18-19.

170 Survivors' Association, *History of the Corn Exchange Regiment*, 523.

171 OR 42, pt. 3, 19.

Meanwhile, Meade had forwarded several messages he had received during the late morning to General Grant, who had left City Point and was visiting General Butler's Deep Bottom headquarters.[172]

The first of these dispatches had been received from General Crawford. Crawford had closely questioned 13 prisoners captured by his patrols following the repulse of the attack on Ayres' division. Three of the prisoners said they belonged to Walker's brigade, several to Archer's brigade, three to Dearing's cavalry brigade, while one claimed to be an aide to General Dunovant. On checking with his staff, Crawford learned that Walker's and Archer's brigades were assigned to Heth's Division. A deserter from the 26th Mississippi had also been brought to Crawford's Globe Tavern headquarters. This man proved to be verbose, telling the Federal officers that his regiment belonged to Davis' brigade, Heth's division. Moreover, he continued, Heth's entire division was massed to Warren's front, while Wilcox was operating farther to the west.[173]

The other message originated with Colonel Babcock. Provost Marshal Babcock announced that a lieutenant and 27 enlisted men, who had been captured "last evening and this morning," had been received from the V Corps. These men had been examined and had been found to represent nearly every regiment in Heth's division. Four or five of them belonged to the cavalry—Young's and Dearing's brigades. One infantryman identified his unit as the 10th Georgia [battalion], Wright's brigade, Mahone's division. Beyond their name, rank, and unit, the Rebels refused to give any information.[174]

Meade in his covering memorandum wrote that this intelligence left no doubt that "Wilcox and Heth" were in front of "Warren and Parke, and that part, if not all, of Mahone's [Division], will be there today." As soon as Mott arrived, Meade promised "to try" the Confederates again.[175]

The 185th New York, which had marched from City Point the previous afternoon, reported to General Crawford during the morning. When he checked with the colonel prior to sending his unit into the trenches, Crawford discovered that the New Yorkers had left their tents, rations, and ammunition at the landing.

---

172 *Ibid.*, 4-5.

173 *Ibid.*, 22. At this stage of the conflict, Archer's and Walker's brigades had been consolidated. *OR* 42, pt. 2, 1309.

174 *OR* 42, pt. 3, 9.

175 *Ibid.*, 5.

The hardboiled Crawford telegraphed the chief quartermaster at the big City Point depot to forward the regiment's gear and supplies to Globe Tavern immediately.[176]

As the morning progressed, personnel occupying the V Corps' signal station kept a close watch on the countryside toward Petersburg. Fog and rain, however, hindered their vision. When the officer in charge filed his report at 11:25 a.m., he observed that the Confederate works about W. Davis' house were full of men. He theorized that they were probably the troops repulsed earlier in the day by Ayres' division. Soldiers could also be seen moving westward along the Boydton Plank Road, but the fog was so dense that the observers were unable to determine their character or number.[177]

At 12:15 p.m., the people in the signal station warned General Crawford that a Rebel skirmish line was moving against the sector held by his men east of the Weldon Railroad.[178] Alerted, the Union outposts were readied for the Southerners. There was a crackle of musketry as skirmishers in grey and pickets in blue clashed in the mist-shrouded woods, where the Confederates had scored their breakthrough on August 19. Finding that the Yanks were waiting for them, the Johnnies retired into their rifle pits.[179]

*   *   *

General Mott's troops, in accordance with a directive from Meade, had been relieved early on October 1 from duty in the forts and rifle pits along the section of the investment line from Fort Morton to Fort Alexander Hays. Soldiers from the First and Second Divisions of the II Corps assumed the responsibility for defending the works formerly held by Mott's bluecoats.[180] Upon being replaced in the rifle pits, Mott's brigade commanders massed their troops in the woods. Part of the soldiers were collected behind Avery's house; the rest on the Jerusalem Plank Road in rear of the Chieves' house.[181]

---

176 *Ibid.*, 22.

177 *Ibid.*, 21. The signalmen had watched as the Rebels swept forward and engaged Ayres' skirmishers along Squirrel Level Road.

178 *Ibid.*, 21.

179 *Ibid.*, 22-23.

180 *Ibid.*, 13-14; OR 42, pt. 1, 344. General Miles' division held the earthworks between the Appomattox and Fort Meikel, while Gibbon's troops occupied those from Fort Meikel to Fort Davis.

181 OR 42, pt. 3, 11.

At 9:10 a.m., Hancock notified Meade that all of Mott's division, except the pickets had been replaced.[182] Replying for Meade, Chief of Staff Humphreys directed Hancock to have Mott's division report to General Parke at the Peebles' house. No artillery was to accompany the division on its move to the west. The troops were to be transported as far as the Weldon Railroad on the recently completed United States Military Railroad. Near Globe Tavern, Mott would be met by a guide who was to show him the road to Peebles'.

To expedite the movement, the troops concentrated near Avery's were to be marched to Hancock's Station, while those on the Plank Road were to be moved to the trestle bridge. Sixty cars, all that there were on the railroad, were to be employed to shuttle the division to Globe Tavern.[183]

Mott's units would take their ammunition train, along with their ambulances and the headquarters spring wagons, with them. One hospital and one medicine wagon per brigade would be allowed. The division supply train was to be sent to the Weldon Railroad by road, so that the troops could fill their haversacks.[184]

At 10:30 a.m., General Hancock advised Mott of what was expected of his command.[185]

Some two and one half hours later, Mott was notified by the chief quartermaster that the cars were ready. Orders to move out were given. The brigade commanders began entraining their men at the designated sites. There were three trains, and each was required to make three round trips before the last of Mott's bluecoats detrained at Globe Tavern.

The first troops to arrive at Globe Tavern belonged to Brig. Gen. Byron R. Pierce's brigade. As soon as he had met the guide and formed his troops, Pierce started for Peebles' house. The rain, which had been beating down throughout the day, had turned the road into a ribbon of mud. After a hard two and one-half mile march, Pierce reported to General Parke, who directed him to mass his command and await the arrival of the rest of the division.

Mott and his staff remained behind to supervise the entraining, consequently, it was 3:30 p.m. before the train with the general aboard chugged up to Globe Tavern. Before starting for Parke's headquarters, Mott spoke briefly with General Crawford. He told Crawford that 3,000 men had preceded him, and that 1,500 soldiers were aboard the three trains now arriving.

---

182 *Ibid.*, 12.

183 *Ibid.*, 12; OR 42, pt. 1, 344.

184 OR 42, pt. 3, 13.

185 *Ibid.*, 16.

The troops accompanying Mott found the road leading westward from Globe Tavern across the fields and through the pines cut to pieces by the two columns that had gone before. Reaching Peebles' at 5:00 p.m., General Mott called on General Parke. The IX Corps commander had Mott mass the new arrivals alongside their comrades in rear of Peebles' house. As soon as the division had been marshaled, Mott told his brigade commanders to have their men camp.[186]

*   *   *

Meade's 11:50 p.m. order for Gen. Gregg to move out at daybreak on the road running by Boisseau's didn't reach the cavalry leader till after 5:00 a.m. Gregg was hard pressed to get his troopers in the saddle by the time stipulated. It was after 6:00 a.m. when the column marched. Gregg rode with Davies' vanguard, as the bluecoats in a drizzling rain moved out of their encampment at the Davis' house.

Gregg and his troopers encountered no difficulty beyond a muddy road in reaching Peebles' house. There, Gregg reported to General Parke, who told him that the object of the intended reconnaissance had been accomplished—the Confederates had been found. General Warren now showed up. Upon discussing the situation, the three generals decided that Gregg should deploy his horsemen to guard the approaches to Parke's left and rear.

When he notified Chief of Staff Humphreys of this decision at 8:30 a.m., Gregg pointed out that the best area for him to post his command to discharge this mission was on Vaughan Road at Davis' house. According to the latest information brought in by his scouts, Dunovant's South Carolina cavalry brigade was near Armstrong's.[187]

Just as the last of Gregg's troopers were leaving Davis', they had been assailed by a strong detachment from General Young's cavalry brigade. Bringing up Hart's South Carolina Battery, the butternuts drove the Federals from Davis'. Gregg at the time of his meeting with Parke and Warren didn't know about this development. When notified by his rear guard of what had occurred, Gregg wheeled his command about.

Spearheaded by Davies' troopers, the Union horsemen drove back down Church Road. There was sharp skirmishing as the Yanks drove Young's

---

186 OR 42, pt. 1, 344, 366, 393. Pierce's brigade had entrained at Hancock's Station and McAllister's at the trestle bridge. Of the 1,500 troops which rode aboard the three trains that reached Globe Tavern at 3:30 p.m., 600 belonged to de Trobriand's brigade, 700 to Pierce's, and 125 to McAllister's. OR 42, pt. 3, 23.

187 OR 42, pt. 1, 620, 635; OR 42 pt. 3, 27-28.

outnumbered Confederate horsemen from Davis'. While most of the Rebels fought from their horses, some were dismounted. To dislodge the butternuts, Gregg was compelled to dismount his troopers. Gregg and his men continued to force the fighting until they had pushed Young's troopers back to Wilkinson's. There, the Confederates unlimbered a section of Hart's guns and braced for another stand.[188]

General Dunovant's South Carolina cavalry brigade had marched from Armstrong's to Young's assistance. The reinforcing column reached Wilkinson's soon after Young's troopers had fallen back. One of Dunovant's troopers recalled that as his regiment, the 6th South Carolina, rode up:

> We saw our division commander, Maj. Gen. M. C. Butler, and General Young, sitting on their horses upon a brink of a ridge overlooking an open valley or field on the right, in which some of the brave Georgians were deployed and fighting with the enemy, who were slowly advancing from out of a wood on the other side of this open field. Young was cursing and storming in that stentorian voice of his, which could be heard for half a mile. "Hold your ground down there, you damned scoundrels," was one of his mildest expressions. The men were fighting gallantly against heavy odds, as we could plainly see, and I remember well how indignant I was at General Young, much as I admired him, for cursing them so outrageously.[189]

Dunovant promptly deployed his brigade to the left and right of Vaughan Road. Covered by the South Carolinians, General Young recalled and regrouped his brigade, preparatory to resuming offensive operations. Dunovant's troopers, after repulsing a feeble Federal attack, encountered no difficulty in holding their ground.[190]

After sending a courier at 12:45 p.m. with a report to Chief of Staff Humphreys describing what had happened, Gregg formed his command to discharge his day's task—to guard the approaches to the IX Corps' left and rear. Davies' brigade was to occupy the position at Davis' farm. To accomplish this, General Davies deployed and advanced the 6th Ohio and the 1st Massachusetts Cavalry regiments toward Wilkinson's, while holding the 1st New Jersey in reserve. Colonel Smith's 2nd

---

188   OR 42, pt. 1, 635; OR 42, pt. 2, 28; Brooks, *Butler and His Cavalry*, 327.

189   *Ibid.*

190   *Ibid.*, 327-329.

Brigade was posted on Davies' left, its left flank extending in the direction of Halifax Road.[191]

General Humphreys read Gregg's 12:45 p.m. dispatch with interest. At 2:00 p.m., he wrote Gregg telling him to attack the Confederate force at Wilkinson's and develop its strength. If at all possible, Gregg was to drive the Rebel cavalry back across the Rowanty. It was important, Humphreys admonished that "our whole force should engage the enemy in this quarter—that is, outside of the entrenchments."

Humphreys let Gregg know that Mott's advance brigade had just reached Globe Tavern and was en route to join Parke. As soon as Mott's other two brigades were up, an attack would be launched against the Confederates in the Peebles' house sector. The chances for success of this thrust would be enhanced, if Gregg could keep a force equal to or greater than his pinned down.[192]

Meanwhile, word had reached General Hampton that Butler's division had engaged Union cavalry on Vaughan Road. Placing himself at the head of two of Rooney Lee's regiments, the 9th and 13th Virginia, Hampton headed for the Boydton Plank Road. A circuitous march brought Hampton out on the Squirrel Level Road east of Armstrong's Mill.[193]

The Confederates beat the Yanks to the punch. Seeing that it had almost ceased raining, at 3:30 p.m., General Butler ordered Dunovant and Young to assail the Federals to their front. General Hampton, at the same time, was to fall upon the Federals' right with the 9th and 13th Virginia Cavalry.

As couriers passed along Dunovant's and Young's lines relaying the orders to attack to the regimental commanders, many of the men who had participated in the "Cattle Raid" were "bellowing like bulls, and shouting over to the Yankees, 'Good, fat beef over here; come over and get some," and then a fellow would jump up and bellow, and by the time he dropped, bullets would be whistling over our heads and rattling on the rail piles."[194]

Young's and Dunovant's butternuts assailed the skirmish line at Wilkinson's held by dismounted troopers of the 6th Ohio and 1st Massachusetts. Within a few minutes, the Southerners had gained the upper hand. Notwithstanding the determined resistance offered by the bluecoats from Massachusetts on the right, the Federals were rolled back. At first, the retreat was orderly, but a charge by one

191 OR 42, pt. 1, 620, 635.

192 OR 42, pt. 3, 28.

193 OR 42, pt. 1, 948; Beale, *History of the Ninth Virginia Cavalry*, 146.

194 Brooks, *Butler and His Cavalry*, 330.

of the Confederate regiments broke the 6th Ohio. Leaving a number of prisoners in the Rebels' hands, the Ohioans skedaddled. At this moment, Hampton led the 9th and 13th Virginia cavalry regiments in a slashing attack on the right flank of the 1st Massachusetts. Giving way, the Massachusetts bluecoats followed the Ohioans up Vaughan Road. It was only after the troopers passed through the lines of the 1st New Jersey that the officers rallied and reformed their regiments.[195]

Dunovant's South Carolinians were compelled to curtail their pursuit of the Yankees, when they became entangled with the Virginians. General Butler, who was leading the South Carolinians on the left, had leveled his revolver at one of the Virginia officers and was ready to squeeze off a round, when he recognized him.[196]

As Dunovant was regrouping his brigade, General Butler rode up. Calling to Dunovant, Butler asked if he was familiar with the ground.

"No!" Dunovant replied.

Butler, turning to a dismounted officer, said, "Major Farley, had you not been over the ground before?"

"Yes," Farley answered, "I reconnoitered it two or three days ago."

"Does this creek not make a bend here, and if I move down the creek, can I not get enfilade fire upon the enemy's position on the other side?" Butler inquired.

Farley answered, "Yes."

Whereupon, Butler turned to Dunovant and said, "General, move the brigade by the right flank down this creek until you get that position, then attack."

Throughout this conversation, Dunovant gave the impression of being very impatient, and when Butler finished speaking, he replied, "Oh, General, let me charge'em. We've got'em going and let us keep'em going."

Butler replied, "General, I am afraid I will lose too many men."

"Oh, no we won't," Dunovant retorted, "my men are perfectly enthusiastic and ready to charge, and we've got the Yankees demoralized, one more charge will finish'em. Let me charge them."

Butler's expression changed, his eyes grew darker, and in a voice short, sharp and stern, he called to Dunovant, "Charge them, sir, if you wish."

At this, Dunovant wheeled his horse about, and called to his brigade, "Forward, charge!"

After their frightened comrades had passed, the men of the 1st New Jersey dressed their ranks. An ominous silence gripped the area. Suddenly all hell seemed to break loose, as the dense woods to the bluecoats' "front became alive with rebels,

---

195 *OR* 42, pt. 1, 620, 637, 948; *OR* 42, pt. 3, 29.

196 Brooks, *Butler and His Cavalry*, 330-331.

who came on at a double-quick, shouting and yelling like so many fiends, firing as they advanced."[197] The commander of the 1st New Jersey Cavalry, Maj. Myron H. Beaumont, reported:

> The Jersey boys stood cool and calm though exposed to a fire from the whole rebel line, as well as six guns, which had been run up to within 300 yards of our lines. The spiteful buzz of bullets, the shriek of solid shot and shell, and the fierce tearing whirr of canister, were enough to terrify brave hearts and older heads, but with our colors planted in the center of the line my gallant men stood without firing a shot until, with the enemy twenty-four paces in front, I gave the order to commence firing. Old soldiers and veterans of the bloodiest fights of the war join in saying that our rapidity of firing was wonderful and unsurpassed.[198]

General Dunovant was shot from his horse by Sgt. James T. Clancy of Company C, 1st New Jersey. Dr. John B. Fontaine, Hampton's Medical Director, was mortally wounded as he rushed to the stricken general's assistance. Two of the grey clads picked up their general. As they did, General Butler called, "Who is that shot?"

Charles Montague of Company B, 6th South Carolina replied, "General Dunovant."

"Is he killed?" Butler inquired.

"Yes, I think so."

Butler then told the men who had gone to their general's aid, "Carry him back, and don't let the men know it." Turning to Lt. Col. William Stokes, the senior officer present, Butler said, "Colonel, take command of the brigade."[199]

Three frontal assaults were made on the 1st New Jersey and the 1st Massachusetts, which on being reformed had been deployed on the Jersey men's right. After the repulse of the South Carolinians rushes, the Confederates fell back and disappeared into the woods "apparently whipped."

A counterattack was ordered by Major Beaumont. To Sgt. Gilbert L. Johnson of Company G, 1st New Jersey, fell the honor of being the first man to scramble over the works. The color guard followed, and the 1st New Jersey, with a wild shout, dashed into the woods. By the time the bluecoats had advanced 200 yards,

---

197 *Ibid.*, 331.

198 *OR* 42, pt. 1, 635-636.

199 Brooks, *Butler and His Cavalry*, 331-332.

they were recalled. The reason: Young's Georgia brigade had launched a sharp assault on the left of Gregg's position at Davis'.

At this time, Company C, 1st New Jersey was picketing the area in front of the Union left. The officer in charge, Lt. William Hughes, seeing that his company was surrounded, called for his men to cut their way out. The lieutenant and most of his troopers succeeded in reaching Davis' house and warning their comrades to watch out for the flank attack. Among the men isolated by the advance of the Georgians was Sgt. Charles Watts. The sergeant spotted a group of men dressed like Yanks. He rode up to one who proved to be General Young and asked, "How in thunder are we going to get out of this?"

The general seemed to be as puzzled as Watts; he had mistaken the charge by Company C for the advance of a mounted force of Federals, thus delaying his attack long enough to allow the 1st New Jersey to regain their works. One of the men with Sergeant Watts, Pvt. Miles Downey, realized that the newcomers were Confederates and pulled a gun on Young's adjutant general, Capt. John M. Jones. Bluffing the Rebs, Watts and Downey returned to their lines with their embarrassed prisoner.

Subsequently, Major Beaumont learned from Captain Jones that the charge by Company C on the rear of Young's brigade, probably saved the day for the Yanks. It seems that General Young had been so badly shaken by this development that he sent a runner to General Hampton with news that he had been surrounded and would probably be captured.[200]

General Hampton in the meantime had sent a courier with orders for Rooney Lee to send him two additional regiments. Before the reinforcements could be deployed, a galloper reached Hampton with news that the Federals had gained the rear of Young's brigade. This compelled Hampton to post three fresh units to meet this "new threat." By the time it was ascertained that Young had been hoodwinked, it was too late in the day to mount another attack. Recalling his corps at dusk, Hampton pulled back, taking with him the 30 to 40 prisoners captured in the afternoon's fighting.[201]

It was 6:30 p.m. before General Gregg caught his second wind and notified headquarters of the fighting at Davis'. After tersely describing what had transpired, Gregg observed cautiously, "the enemy are withdrawing their dismounted forces and establishing pickets." During the action, the Rebels had broken through "the chain of vedettes in front of Vaughan Road on the right of Davis', "but they were

---

200 *OR* 42, pt. 1, 636.

201 *Ibid.*, 948; Brooks, *Butler and His Cavalry*, 332-333.

now being re-established. This position, Gregg complained, was difficult to hold, as the dense woods concealed the movements of the butternuts, whenever they abandoned their horses to fight afoot.[202]

After questioning the Confederate prisoners taken at Davis', Gregg was shocked by what he heard. One of the grey clads claimed to belong to Brig. Gen. Joseph R. Davis' infantry brigade, while Captain Jones said that four brigades of Hampton's cavalry corps were on the field. Since the necessity of picketing the approaches to the left and rear of the Army of the Potomac occupied a considerable part of his strength, Gregg advised headquarters that if the Rebels resumed the fight in the morning, he would only be able to deploy six regiments and one battery against this overwhelming force.[203]

The receipt of this startling information had immediate repercussions at headquarters. At 10:00 p.m., General Meade issued orders for Gregg to call on the IX Corps for a brigade of infantry, if he deemed it necessary.[204]

*   *   *

At 2:30 p.m., General Meade forwarded to Grant's headquarters a summary of the day's happenings up to that hour. Meade had received bad news from a Confederate prisoner captured in the morning's attack on Ayres' division. This man told Meade that he had seen a 700-man column of prisoners from the IX Crops marching into Petersburg. Meade warned Grant that from what General Potter had reported, the Rebel's story was probably true.

Mott's division, he continued, was now arriving at Globe Tavern by rail and going forward. Within the next several hours, Meade planned to see Parke and Warren; he would then determine his next move. He hoped to attack, provided such an undertaking wasn't considered injudicious by his corps commanders. At the moment, it was raining hard at Globe Tavern, and the roads east of the Weldon Railroad were said to be in "bad" shape.[205]

Upon his return to City Point from Deep Bottom, Grant studied the reports from the Union left. Grant, when he read of the advance of the Confederate skirmishers against the sector of Crawford's line east of the Weldon Railroad, concluded that the foe had made a forced reconnaissance "to see if they could strip

202   OR 42, pt. 3, 29.

203   *Ibid.*, 29.

204   *Ibid.*, 27, 29.

205   *Ibid.*, 5.

that part of their line." Satisfied the Rebels had found that they could, Grant warned Meade that they were probably pulling troops out of that sector to bolster their right. Consequently, Grant believed that Crawford in the morning should launch a powerful attack "directly down the railroad . . . and either make the enemy hold that part of his line strongly or go through."[206]

Meanwhile, Meade had taken up the situation with Parke and Warren. Parke told Meade that if his troops undertook an offensive before dark, about all that could be expected was the reoccupation of the area about W. J. Pegram's. Although his scouts reported the Southerners had artillery at that point, they had been unable to determine if it were supported by a "heavy force" of infantry. To make matters worse, the ground in the IX Corps' sector was getting very soft. As soon as all of Mott's units were up, Parke proposed to advance Willcox's and Potter's lines of battle on Mr. Pegram's, while employing Mott's division to support and extend his left.[207]

Meade returned to Globe Tavern before maturing his plans. It was 6:45 p.m. when he telegraphed Parke that he was to hold his command ready to "move forward as soon after daylight tomorrow as practicable and attack the enemy." When putting his troops in motion, Parke was to throw his left forward and endeavor to turn the Confederates' right. His object would be to effect a lodgment upon the Boydton Plank Road, within easy reach of the South Side Railroad. Or if the Army of the Potomac proved strong enough, Parke was to be prepared "to follow the enemy closer to Petersburg."[208] Warren's corps, except for Crawford's command, was to advance in conjunction with Parke's bluecoats.[209]

General Parke would employ Gregg's cavalry "in such manner as will most effectually aid" his command. As Meade and his staff saw it, there were two ways that the cavalry could assist Parke: It could force its way up the Squirrel Level Road past Hawks' and come in on the left of the IX Corps, or it could assail the Rebels in front of Davis'.[210]

At 7:00 p.m., Meade notified Grant that the last of Mott's troops didn't reach the Peebles' farm marshaling area until almost 6:00 p.m. The late arrival of Mott's people, in conjunction with the weather, had prevented the Army of the Potomac

206   *Ibid.*, 6.

207   *Ibid.*, 26.

208   *Ibid.*, 26-27.

209   *Ibid.*, 19, 27.

210   *Ibid.*, 27, 29-30.

from undertaking any offensive operations during the day. Grant was assured that orders had been issued for Parke and Warren to advance at daybreak and "endeavor to effect a lodgment on the Boydton Plank Road."[211]

Two hours before he received his orders to be prepared to attack at daybreak, General Warren had contacted Crawford. Warren wanted Crawford to see that Ayres' pickets were relieved during the evening.[212]

At 5:55 p.m., Crawford acknowledged the dispatch, and observed that he would see that Ayres' outposts were relieved by soldiers from General Baxter's brigade, as he couldn't spare any more men from General Bragg's command. At this time, Crawford explained, Bragg's people were picketing in front of Ferrero's division at Fort Howard. Ferrero had reported the Confederates were feeling his line east of Fort Howard, but they hadn't shown any force. After being fired on by Ferrero's blacks, the Rebel skirmishers had pulled back. At the moment, the fog was very heavy, and the personnel in the signal station were unable to see the Southerners' lines.[213]

At dark, the soldiers in the Peebles' farm sector pitched their tents in the mud behind the breastworks and made themselves as comfortable as the rain allowed.[214]

Tragedy struck during the night in the 35th Massachusetts. Sergeant Robert McCulloch of Company C, Chief of Pioneers, was killed by a falling tree, which struck him while he was sitting upon a log. A grave was dug upon the ground the regiment occupied, and McCulloch's remains laid to rest, a group of sorrowing comrades assisting in the interment.[215]

---

211 *Ibid.*, 6-7.

212 *Ibid.*, 24. Since these men were only supposed to keep watch and not fight, Warren believed that 200 would be sufficient.

213 *Ibid.*, 24. Crawford notified Warren that the two regiments which had reported to him, were in the works from Fort Wadsworth to the right.

214 Hopkins, *The Seventh Regiment Rhode Island*, 218.

215 Committee, *History of the Thirty-Fifth Massachusetts Volunteers*, 302.

Part IV

Meade's Troops Dig In to Protect Their Gains

Long before daybreak on October 2, 1864, General Parke notified his division commanders (Willcox, Potter, and Mott) to see that their troops were up and under arms by dawn.[216] Reveille sounded early. As soon as the soldiers had eaten a hurried breakfast, the units were formed and mustered.

The division commanders assembled at Parke's command post at 6:00 a.m. Parke tersely told the officers that they were to make a forced reconnaissance and develop "the force of the enemy and position of his works." To accomplish this, Potter's division was to advance and take position on a line with W. J. Pegram's house. Willcox's division was to press ahead on the left of Potter's battle line, pivoting on the Second Division so as to form a line facing northward. General Mott's II Corps division was to march out the Squirrel Level Road and deploy on the left of Willcox's troops. Mott would then advance in conjunction with Willcox's battle line, "keeping up the connection on . . . [his] right, and to keep a good lookout for . . . [his] left flank." The officers had no questions, so Parke told them to rejoin their units.[217]

It was almost 8:00 a.m. before Mott had maneuvered his division into position. The brigade commanded by General Pierce was deployed in line of battle on the left of the rifle pits occupied by Willcox's bluecoats. Pierce threw forward three regiments (the 1st U.S. Sharpshooters, and the 84th and 141st Pennsylvania) as skirmishers.[218] Colonel McAllister massed his brigade close behind Pierce's; his orders were "to deploy as soon as the movement commenced and the nature of the ground would admit."[219] The 1st Brigade, Brig. Gen. P. Regis de Trobriand commanding, was to constitute the division reserve. General de Trobriand would

---

216 *OR 42*, pt. 1, 344; *OR 42*, pt. 3, 46.

217 *OR 42*, pt. 1, 344, 546.

218 *Ibid.*, 344, 366. From right to left the skirmishers were deployed: 1st U.S. Sharpshooters, and the 84th and 141st Pennsylvania. Pierce's battle line from right to left consisted of the 1st Massachusetts Heavy Artillery, 57th Pennsylvania, 93rd New York, and 105th Pennsylvania.

219 *Ibid.*, 344, 392.

send out flankers and leave a regiment to guard the point where the roads forked near Clements' house.[220]

General Parke, realizing that Meade was probably becoming impatient, telegraphed headquarters that Mott was taking position. After Mott had completed his dispositions, Parke promised to "advance the whole line."[221] Meade forwarded this communication to Grant. In a covering memorandum, Meade observed that incomplete returns indicated that in the past two days' fighting on the left, the Army of the Potomac had suffered at least 2,500 casualties. Mott had been accompanied by 4,500 men, thus the reinforcements totaled about 2,000.[222]

Upon being notified that Mott was ready, Parke sent a staff officer galloping to tell Potter to put his division in motion. Covered by a strong skirmish line, Potter's infantry (Griffin's brigade on the left and Curtin's on the right) climbed out of the rifle pits and started forward. The morning was bright and clear; the sun seemed to smile as Potter's men beat their way through the woods. Potter's division encountered no difficulty in gaining the ridge passing through W. J. Pegram's cornfield. Here, Potter halted his battle line, while his skirmishers advanced to the edge of the woods beyond.[223]

Willcox's division (Hartranft's brigade on the right, McLaughlen's in the center, and Harriman's on the left) advanced on Potter's left. The division pushed beyond W. J. Pegram's, Hartranft's skirmishers occupying the area about Boisseau's house.[224]

As the troops crossed the field beyond W. J. Pegram's, they were shelled by several 6-pounders, but the Confederate artillerists put too much elevation on their pieces and overshot their targets.[225]

Willcox's left flank brigade, Harriman's, encountered no Rebels as it worked its way through the woods. Debouching from the pines, Harriman's skirmishers (the 27th Michigan) exchanged shots with Rebel sharpshooters, who retired as soon as

220 *Ibid.*, 344.

221 OR 42, pt. 3, 44.

222 *Ibid.*, 36.

223 OR 42, pt. 1, 580, 582-583; Committee, *History of the Thirty-Sixth Massachusetts Volunteers*, 266; Committee, *History of the Thirty-Fifth Massachusetts Volunteers*, 302.

224 OR 42, pt. 1, 554, 566. Hartranft's brigade advanced in double line of battle, with skirmishers in front. The skirmish line consisted of the 60th Ohio; the first line of the 20th Michigan and 46th New York; the second line of the 24th New York Cavalry (dismounted), 1st Michigan Sharpshooters, 2nd Michigan, and 50th Pennsylvania.

225 *Ibid.*, 571.

they spotted Willcox's battle line. When Harriman halted his soldiers, he saw that they were posted in the field 50 paces to the left and rear of McLaughlen's unit.[226]

General Pierce's brigade of Mott's division, after advancing about three-quarters of a mile through the woods, came upon a line of rifle pits defended by Confederates.

As Pierce's troops forged ahead, McAllister's brigade had marched up the Squirrel Level Road. Pierce's battle line had swung slowly to the right. McAllister took advantage of this situation to deploy and throw forward several of his regiments as skirmishers. Pierce's bluecoats, supported on the left by three of McAllister's regiments (the 120th New York, and the 5th and 7th New Jersey), surged through a belt of felled timber and dislodged the small force of Rebels, apparently dismounted cavalry, posted behind these breastworks.[227]

Mott's troops paused for about 30 minutes before pushing on. As the advance continued, bluecoated skirmishers drove Confederate pickets before them. The Federals, after advancing about a mile, entered an open field and found themselves confronted by another line of works, which appeared to be stronger than those already carried. Scouts came back with the news that these rifle pits were manned by artillery and infantry. While awaiting instructions from Parke, Mott had Pierce and McAllister feel the Southerners' defenses with their skirmishers. The Union skirmishers, as they worked their way ahead, were sniped at by Confederate sharpshooters and shelled by artillery.[228]

Pierce promptly organized a storming party from the 1st Massachusetts Heavy Artillery, and the 84th, 105th and 141st Pennsylvania. The 1st U.S. Sharpshooters were to advance to the right of the storming party. Lieutenant Colonel George Zinn of the 84th Pennsylvania was placed in charge of this force. Zinn formed his men in a ravine about 200 yards from the Rebels' works and to the right of a canister-belching, four-gun battery—Ellett's Virginia Battery.[229]

Pierce asked McAllister to shift one of his regiments to the left and into position opposite Ellett's guns. When Zinn's storming party advanced, this

---

226 *Ibid.*, 558-559. Five hundred men of the 38th Wisconsin, which had joined the division on the previous day, were left to hold the works.

227 *Ibid.*, 344, 366, 377, 385, 393, 403. McAllister's left at this time extended beyond the white house (Smith's).

228 *Ibid.*, 344, 366, 393. When the advance was resumed, McAllister saw that all of his brigade, except two regiments, was deployed as skirmishers.

229 *Ibid.*, 344, 366, 377, 382, 385. From left to right the storming party was formed by the 1st Massachusetts Heavy Artillery, 141st Pennsylvania, and 84th Pennsylvania. The 105th Pennsylvania was posted 50 paces in rear of the 1st Massachusetts Heavy Artillery.

regiment was to open a "severe fire" upon the battery to draw its attention and to pin down the cannoneers.[230] McAllister assigned this task to the 11th Massachusetts Infantry, Maj. Charles C. Rivers commanding.[231]

At 3:00 p.m. Mott, feeling that his subordinates had completed their dispositions, told Pierce to send his men in. When Pierce gave him the word to advance, Colonel Zinn charged at the head of the storming party. The cheering Federals, although subjected to the well-aimed volleys of Rebel foot soldiers and deadly charges of canister, closed to within a few rods of the works. Seeing that the Confederates' fire was beginning to take a heavy toll, Zinn called for his men to fall back. The bluecoats retired in good order, having lost 5 killed, 49 wounded, and 14 missing in the futile rush. Among the wounded was Colonel Zinn.[232]

The 11th Massachusetts was not in position when Zinn's column started, consequently, the regiment was unable to carry out its mission of silencing Ellett's Battery. When the Confederates opened fire, the soldiers from the 11th Massachusetts dropped. Though exposed to the galling fire, they grimly held their ground, even after the storming party had been repelled.[233]

At 1:00 p.m., Willcox's left flank brigade, Harriman's (moved up into line with McLaughlen's troops on their right. Here, the brigade was massed in double line of battle.[234] Instructions were received by Harriman from Willcox "to keep a sharp lookout on the left." In case Pierce's brigade advanced, Harriman was to see that contact was maintained. When Colonel Zinn organized his storming party, three regiments were pulled out of the line adjoining Harriman's left. Harriman promptly relayed this information to General Willcox, and at the same time he shifted his brigade so that the gap which had opened was quickly plugged.[235]

Meanwhile, along the sector of the front west of the Weldon Railroad held by the V Corps, General Griffin's division kept pace with the IX Corps. General Ayres on Griffin's right had given the Maryland brigade the task of making a forced reconnaissance up Vaughan Road toward W. Davis' house. When the Maryland

---

230 *Ibid.*, 366.

231 *Ibid.*, 393. When the word to move to the left arrived, the 11th Massachusetts took cover in a ravine, to escape the fire of the Rebel artillery. *Ibid.*, 401.

232 *Ibid.*, 366-367, 377, 382, 385.

233 *Ibid.*, 393-394, 401.

234 *Ibid.*, 554, 559. The 109th New York and 37th Wisconsin were posted in Harriman's first line, the 38th Wisconsin and 13th Ohio Cavalry (dismounted) in support.

235 *Ibid.*, 554, 559, 563-564, 566, 571.

brigade moved out of the rifle pits, it was supported by two of Grindlay's regiments, the 5th and 140th New York.[236]

Prior to the advance of the Federals, the Confederates had recalled all their artillery and most of their foot soldiers from the area about W. Davis' house. As the Marylanders and New Yorkers closed in on W. Davis', a thin line of grey clad skirmishers retired into the rifle pits about the house. Little time or effort was required by the Yanks in dislodging the Johnnies from these light entrenchments. The retreating men were intercepted and reformed by their officers about the barn north of Davis' house.[237]

At 11:00 a.m., the personnel manning the signal station of the Weldon Railroad spotted a four-gun Confederate battery and 25 wagons moving eastward along the Boydton Plank Road. The skirmishers contesting the advance of the Maryland brigade at the same time took position in the field northeast of Davis'.[238]

Warren, upon being notified the Maryland brigade had reached the vicinity of Davis', dashed off a message to General Ayres. If Ayres thought his troops could take the redoubt at Davis', he was to "give it a trial, and if captured hold it." Such an attack, Warren believed, would compel the Confederates to commit themselves.[239]

The Maryland brigade occupied the redoubt and rifle pits about W. Davis' without difficulty. Learning that the Rebels occupied in force a line of works northeast of Davis', Warren rushed word for Ayres to recall his troops. Before doing so, a demolition team from the 14th U.S. Infantry advanced and set fire to the buildings. As the Federals pulled back from Davis', the Southerners pushed forward and reoccupied the area.[240]

*   *   *

By 11:00 a.m., Meade had learned enough from the reports sent in by Parke and Warren to conclude that the Confederates had pulled back "from some of the positions occupied" on October 1. His signal officers at the same time reported the Rebels' "main line of works as far as seen heavily manned." In view of this intelligence, Meade felt the foe would not await attack outside his fortifications.

---

236 *Ibid.*, 478.

237 OR 42, pt. 3, 41-42.

238 *Ibid.*, 42.

239 *Ibid.*, 43.

240 *Ibid.*, 42; OR 42, pt. 1, 478.

Relaying this information to Grant, Meade observed that without orders from higher authority, he wouldn't assail the entrenchments. Upon being satisfied the Confederates had pulled back into their works, he would take up the best position he could, "connecting with the Weldon Railroad and extending as far to the left as practicable, having in view the protection of . . . [his] left flank, and then entrench."[241]

Grant, who was at Deep Bottom, replied at 11:10 a.m., "Carry out what you propose . . . that is, entrench and hold what you can, but make no attack against defended fortifications."[242]

Following receipt of Grant's message, Chief of Staff Humphreys addressed identical telegrams to Generals Parke and Warren. As soon as it was ascertained that the foe had pulled back into his main line of works, they were "to take up the best line for connecting with the Weldon railroad," make their left secure, and dig in. All orders providing for the effecting of a lodgment on the Boydton Plank Road and an attack on the Petersburg perimeter were cancelled.[243]

General Parke, upon receipt of Meade's directive, put the men of his right flank division, Potter's, to work entrenching. A strong redoubt, subsequently designated Fort Fisher, was started on the right of the 35th Massachusetts, which rested on Church Road. Fort Welch was commenced on the ground where W. J. Pegram's house had stood.[244]

During the forenoon, one of Potter's regiments, the 36th Massachusetts, was greatly annoyed by a sharpshooter and by the raking fire of artillery. The regimental historians reported that the fire of this unseen battery:

occasionally caused a lively scattering by sending a shell whizzing diagonally across our lines. One of these burst in the ranks of Company K, wounding three men and killing two. . . . The fire from the battery slackened in the afternoon, but the "reb" sharpshooter kept at his work so persistently that it seemed extremely desirable to put a stop to his fun. Accordingly Colonel Draper detailed James Knowlton, of Company E, and Corporal Frank Bell, of Company F, two good shots, to relieve us from this annoyance if possible.

---

241 OR 42, pt. 3, 36.

242 *Ibid.*, 36.

243 *Ibid.*, 41.

244 Committee, *History of the Thirty-Fifth Massachusetts Volunteers*, 302-303.

They crept out some distance beyond the picket line, found cover, and waited for indications. They had not long to wait, for soon the crack of a rifle was heard, and from a tree in the edge of the woods back of the enemy's picket line rose a telltale puff of smoke. Both took careful aim, fired, and to their delight saw a gray-clad Johnny come tumbling heels over head out of the tree. After this successful shot the work in the trenches was pursued with more safety and peace of mind, and by nightfall a strong rifle-pit stood between us and the enemy.[245]

General Meade, "accompanied by a brilliant staff," visited the sector of the line held by Potter's troops during the morning. The general and his party, some of the soldiers recalled, probably furnished "an additional inducement to the rebel gunners to serve their pieces well."[246]

Pickets led by first Lt. William N. Meserve of the 35th Massachusetts occupied most of the ground where Potter's division had been overwhelmed on the 30th. The pickets "recovered most of the dead, whose bodies had been stripped; the needs of the Confederates requiring the clothing, but not requiring the mangling and ill usage which some of the bodies had received, as if stabbed or bayoneted in mere wantonness or hatred."[247]

Confederate outposts called for the Federals to send over to them the rest of the 58th Massachusetts, "as they had most of that regiment, they would like to have the specimen complete." Referring to the 35th Massachusetts, the Rebs called, "We have caught some real live Yankees this time, they can't speak a word of English!"[248]

To Potter's left, Willcox's troops held the ground gained in the forced reconnaissance till sunset, when they were recalled. The division's position faced west, its right resting in rear of Pegram's, and its left flank connected with the rifle pits occupied by Mott's troops near the Clements' house. As soon as the men were posted along the line laid out by the engineers, a picket line was established and the soldiers turned to throwing up earthworks.[249]

Soon after the failure of Pierce's thrust, General Mott received a message from General Parke. The IX Corps commander wrote that he had just seen Meade, who had remarked that he didn't want Mott's division "to run any great risk, but to take

245 Committee, *History of the Thirty-Sixth Massachusetts Volunteers*, 266-267.

246 *Ibid.*, 267.

247 Committee, *History of the Thirty-Fifth Massachusetts Volunteers*, 303.

248 *Ibid.*, 303.

249 *OR* 42, pt. 1, 554, 559, 563-564, 566, 571.

up a line and entrench." Staff officers were sent by Mott, with instructions for the brigade commanders to get their men under cover.[250]

At 5:15 p.m., a courier reached Mott's command post with orders from Parke to withdraw the II Corps division into the line of works near the Clements' house. The rifle pits would be occupied, while a strong force was detailed to picket well to the front.[251] Before this information could be relayed to the brigade commanders, a strong party of Confederates left the protection of their earthworks and assailed the 11th Massachusetts. A sharp fire-fight ensued.

Late in the afternoon, the commander of the 99th Pennsylvania Infantry of Gen. de Trobriand's brigade, which was posted to the left of McAllister's skirmishers, had sent word that he was withdrawing his regiment and McAllister must look out for his left flank. According to the scheme worked out by Mott, de Trobriand's brigade was to take the lead as the division marched to the rear. A few minutes later, McAllister was notified by Mott that he was to recall his brigade. Before doing anything else, McAllister disengaged the 11th Massachusetts from its critical position. The brigade then pulled back and was posted in the rifle pits east of Squirrel Level Road.[252]

General Pierce, before evacuating the ground in front of the Confederate works, called for the officer in charge of the 93rd New York. The New Yorkers were deployed as skirmishers and left to cover the withdrawal of the brigade. As soon as the column was well under way, the division officer of the day recalled the 93rd New York. It was after dark when Pierce's troops re-entered the fortifications near Peebles' house and camped in a field near Poplar Spring Church.[253]

On Parke's right, General Griffin's V Corps division had re-adjusted its line to conform to the re-occupation of the area about Pegram's by the IX Crops. As soon as the engineers had selected a line, the V Corps soldiers were turned to entrenching and slashing timber.[254]

Gregg's cavalry division remained encamped at Davis' and Wyatt's throughout the day. Patrols were advanced some distance to the southwest on Vaughan and

250 *Ibid.*, 344-345.

251 *Ibid.*, 345.

252 *Ibid.*, 394, 401, 403, 404.

253 *Ibid.*, 367, 371, 377, 382.

254 OR 42, pt. 3, 41; Survivors' Association, *History of the Corn Exchange Regiment*, 523-525.

Squirrel Level Roads. The 8th Pennsylvania Cavalry, as it rode down Vaughan Road, clashed with a Confederate outpost.[255]

The next morning, October 3, General Meade forwarded a report to Grant, tersely describing the previous day's operations. Nightfall on the 2nd, Meade wrote, found his troops securely in possession of the area about Mr. Pegram's, with their "left refused and the cavalry to the rear on the Vaughan and . . . [Duncan] Roads." The line occupied represented a two and one-half mile extension of the Union left from its former position at Fort Wadsworth on the Weldon Railroad. At the moment, the Army of the Potomac's left was "a little over a mile from the Boydton Plank Road," and only a slightly greater distance from the South Side Railroad. Generals Parke and Warren, Meade reported, were "busily occupied entrenching in this position and rendering it such that, should the enemy turn the left, they will have an available force to meet the movement."[256]

Editor's Conclusion

The preparations for the fifth offensive and the offensive itself led to major changes in the troops positions both north and south of the James. To concentrate against Richmond, Butler needed Maj. Gen. David B. Birney's X Corps, which was ordered withdrawn from the Petersburg trenches, as was the cavalry division of Maj. Gen. August Kautz. Lee reacted to Butler's September 29 attack by withdrawing Maj. Gen. Robert Hoke's division from the position it had held on the extreme left since June 15. Lee also recalled to Richmond from Petersburg Charles Field's division for use above the James.

In the operation north of the James, Butler attacked both New Market Heights and Chaffin's Bluff. The entire Confederate line—which had confined the Federals to Deep Bottom and Curle's Neck with a minimum of Rebel manpower—collapsed but the attack ultimately failed and did not take the Southern capital. The Federal attackers remained north of the James throughout the rest of the Petersburg Campaign. Lee restored his front only with vigorous effort and cost. He was forced to improvise a long line of works extending from New Market Road all the way to the Nine Mile Road, a distance of eight miles. Both Hoke's and Field's divisions arrived from the

---

255 *OR* 42, pt. 1, 82, 85, 89, 92, 636. Davies' brigade camped at Davis', while Smith's bivouacked at Wyatt's.

256 *OR* 42, pt. 3, 50-51.

Petersburg front to file into this new position and man the new line, which remained woefully weak in many places.

Outside Petersburg, meanwhile, Maj. Gens. Wade Hampton, Cadmus Wilcox and Henry Heth attacked and routed the IX Corps at Peebles' Farm but were fought to a standstill by Warren's V Corps. The Federals held the captured ground and fortified it. The tactical stalemate that was the Fifth Offensive added another five miles of manned trenches below Petersburg. Union losses totaled 2,889, while the Confederates lost about 1,300.[257]

---

257 John Horn, *The Petersburg Campaign: June 1864-April 1865* (Combined, 1999), 33. Horn is a fine historian and writer, and this title includes some of Bryce Suderow's original research into numbers and losses regarding various aspects of the Petersburg Campaign fighting.

Chapter 2

The Battle of
Burgess Mill

October 27, 1864

Editor's Introduction

In early October 1864, Secretary of War Edwin M. Stanton visited Petersburg. General Grant gave him a tour of the siege lines before meeting with him to discuss the course of the war. Almost certainly the upcoming presidential election was one of the topics on the table, and it is likely Stanton advised Grant not to risk another battle before the November election. After seeing Stanton off Grant ignored his advice and decided a successful attack against General Lee would aid Lincoln's reelection, and thus began exploring where he should next strike the Confederates. He directed his chief engineer, John G. Barnard, to examine the chances of success of a movement west and then north to seize the South Side Railroad, or an attack on Bermuda Hundred. Barnard's report, which he issued on October 15, ruled out a Bermuda Hundred operation and informed Grant that a thrust at the railroad was possible, but would require a column of 40,000 men in order to succeed.

Combined with other troops, Horatio Wright's VI Corps, which was then serving with Phil Sheridan in the Shenandoah Valley, would provide Grant the men he needed. Sheridan had defeated Jubal Early at Third Winchester and Fisher's Hill on September 19 and 22, respectively, and had yet to undertake any further significant military operations. Grant told Sheridan to either resume operations or send the VI Corps to Petersburg. Sheridan decided to return Wright's corps, but Early launched a devastating surprise attack on October 19. Although Sheridan's troops eventually defeated the Confederates and routed them from the field, the offensive delayed the dispatch of the corps at a time when Grant was in a hurry to press his own operations. On October 21, Grant and Meade surveyed the western end of the Union line southwest of Petersburg, and Grant was ready to move.

In his previous four offensives Grant had used a two-front strategy that threatened one sector (Richmond) to compel Lee to weaken his lines along the Petersburg front, before striking west below Petersburg against supply lines feeding and arming the Confederates. (Grant's First Offensive was a direct assault against Petersburg in mid-June.) Each effort included the ultimate goal, not yet realized, of reaching and cutting the South Side Railroad. This time, however, Grant decided to launch simultaneous attacks against Petersburg and Richmond.

Inquiries to three corps commanders determined how many troops would be required to hold the Federal lines, and thus how many would be available for the operation. Reports back on October 21 and 22 indicated that Winfield S. Hancock's II Corps could hold its line with one division, John G. Parke's IX Corps with about 1,500 men, and Gouverneur K. Warren's V Corps with just one brigade. Deducting these men from the army's strength left Meade with 36,000 infantry and 5,000 cavalry to drive west, skirt or break through Confederate fortifications, and strike north a few miles to seize the railroad. With Barnard's recommendation of 40,000 men having been met, Grant discussed plans for the two-pronged offensive with Meade and Ben Butler on October 23 and the next day issued orders for the offensive.

Grant's plan called for Hancock to move via the Vaughan Road, turn onto the Boydton Plank Road, and from there travel west on the White Oak Road to reach the railroad via Claiborne's Road. Meanwhile, Parke and the IX Corps would seize the Confederate works at Hatcher's Run, which Union intelligence suggested were incomplete. If Parke succeeded, Warren and the V Corps would support him. If he did not, Warren would move to join Hancock.

Part I

General Meade Plans an Offensive

The leader of the Army of the Potomac, Major General George G. Meade visited Lieutanant General Ulysses S. Grant's City Point, Virginia, headquarters on October 23, 1864. While there, Meade proposed that he employ three of his four corps to turn the Army of Northern Virginia right beyond Hatcher's Run and drive for the South Side Railroad. Grant told Meade that he would have to give additional thought to the subject. Meade then returned to his headquarters.

On October 24, Meade was handed a telegram from Grant marked confidential. Unfolding the message, Meade found that he was to:

> Make your preparations to march out at an early hour on the 27th to gain possession of the South Side Railroad, and to hold it and fortify back to your present left. In commencing your advance, move in three columns . . . with the same force you proposed to take. [Major General John G.] Parke, who starts out nearest to the enemy, should be instructed that if he finds the enemy entrenched and their works well manned, he is not to attack but confront him, and be prepared to advance promptly when he finds that by the movement of the other two columns to the right and rear of them they begin to give way.

When the columns marched, each soldier was to carry three days' rations in his haversack and 60 rounds of ammunition on his person. Wagons and ambulances were to be parked a considerable distance in front of the Rebel picket line. Another 20 rounds of small arms ammunition per man, along with a reserve supply of artillery projectiles, were to be loaded into wagons by the ordnance people and held ready to roll when called for. Depots along the Military Railroad were to be cleared of stores, and all wagons, ambulances, and artillery horses not accompanying the corps were to be sent to City Point on the night of the 26th.[1]

According to information obtained by Meade's officers from Rebel deserters, the Petersburg earthworks were being extended by Confederate fatigue details and black work gangs to Hatcher's Run. These rifle pits were to terminate at redoubts previously thrown up by Rebel horse soldiers on the south bank of Hatcher's Run,

---

1   OR 42, pt. 3, 317-318.

about one mile above Armstrong's Mill, and were said not to cross or extend up the run. At Burgess Mill, where Boydton Plank Road crossed Hatcher's Run, there were artillery emplacements and some infantry parapets, but no entrenchment lines.

The Petersburg lines from the Appomattox below the city to Battery No. 31 were reportedly defended by Major General Bushrod R. Johnson's combat-ready division. Lieutenant General Ambrose P. Hill's III Corps held the remainder of the line from Battery No. 31 to Arthur Swamp with Major General Henry Heth's division on the left; Major General Cadmus M. Wilcox's on the right; and Major General William Mahone's in reserve. Major General Wade Hampton's two cavalry divisions (Lee's and Butler's) and Brigadier General James Dearing's mounted brigade were on the right of the Confederate infantry.[2]

Meade and Chief of Staff Major General Andrew A. Humphreys prepared to alert their corps and cavalry commanders to get ready for another big offensive. Several changes were made by Meade as to the amount of rations and ammunition to be taken along by his army. The soldiers were to carry three full days' rations in their haversacks, and "three days' bread and small rations in knapsack." Sixty rounds of ammunition were to be taken on the person; with another 40 rounds per man in the ordnance wagons. The artillery was to bring along 250 projectiles per gun, using the caissons of the field pieces emplaced in the redoubts instead of additional wagons. Half of the ambulances were to go with the troops, while each brigade was to be allotted one medicine and one hospital wagon. No baggage or headquarters wagons were allowed to accompany the columns, but pack mules could be used to bring up the officers' rations and tents. Clerks, orderlies, and others on detached or special assignment (unless their services were deemed essential) were to be armed and instructed to report back to their units. Each corps was to designate an officer to take charge of the horses and caissons belonging to the batteries posted in the redoubts, with orders to see that they were "parked with the train of the Artillery Reserve."[3]

How to organize a striking force of 30,000 to 35,000 infantry and still have sufficient manpower to hold the investment line plagued Meade. The withdrawal of large numbers of troops from the earthworks would have to be done with finesse to keep Gen. Robert E. Lee and his generals from ascertaining that the Army of the Potomac was about to strike a mighty blow. Major General Winfield S. Hancock (his II Corps held the fortifications from Battery No. 24 on the left to the redoubts

2 *Ibid.*, 318-319; Humphreys, *The Virginia Campaign of '64 and '65*, 294.

3 *OR* 42, pt. 3, 322-323, 325-326, 328, 330.

at Spring Hill) was to see that Brigadier General Nelson Miles' First Division relieved the Second and Third Divisions on the line. On being relieved by Miles' bluecoats, Brigadier General Gershom Mott was to mass his Third Division on the cleared ground near Southall's house. Brigadier General Thomas W. Egan was to concentrate his Second Division near Fort Bross. These movements were to begin as soon as it was dark, and Mott's and Egan's soldiers "must be massed beyond the view of the enemy by daylight" on October 25.[4]

Major General Gouverneur K. Warren was notified to have his V Corps ready to march by Wednesday night, the 26th. Meanwhile, Warren and his staff were to see that the troops left behind "to hold the redoubts and enclosed batteries" from Battery No. 24 to Fort Conahey were posted. According to an estimate prepared by Warren's staff, 2,200 infantry and 32 guns would be sufficient to discharge this mission. Warren was to form the rest of his foot soldiers and guns out of the Confederates' sight.[5]

Like Warren, General Parke of the IX Corps was ordered to have his men ready to move on the night of the 26th. Fifteen hundred foot soldiers and 24 guns were to be stationed in the redoubts and enclosed works from Fort Fisher on the right to Fort Cummings on the left. All other IX Corps combat personnel were to be concentrated "at convenient points for movement, out of view of the enemy."[6]

Brigadier General David McM. Gregg of the cavalry was to alert his division to be ready to ride on Wednesday night. Preparatory to taking the field, Gregg was to recall his pickets.[7]

Evidently, Meade and his staff were not too well versed in the ways of horse soldiers. General Gregg soon notified Chief of Staff Humphreys that "it will scarcely be possible for the cavalry to carry on their persons three days' bread and small rations in addition to three days' rations in the haversacks." Since every trooper would have to take 20 pounds of forage in his haversack, there would be no room for extra rations. Gregg would therefore have his men cram four days' rations into their knapsacks, and caution them that the rations would have to last five days.[8]

---

4   *Ibid.*, 323-324.

5   *Ibid.*, 325. Brigadier General Charles Griffin was on leave, but Warren valued the services of the leader of his First Division so highly that he sent him a telegram, urging him to rejoin the army. Griffin, never one to miss a fight, rejoined his division in time to lead it into battle.

6   *Ibid.*, 328. Troops left to hold the redoubts were to be provided with 200 rounds of ammunition per person and to be supplied with rations to see them through six days. *Ibid.*, 329.

7   *Ibid.*, 330.

8   *Ibid.*, 331.

As soon as it was dark on October 24, Miles' division marched from its camps, and the troops moved into the trenches, relieving Egan's and Mott's soldiers.

After being replaced in the rifle pits at 2:20 a.m., Egan's brigade commanders put their units in motion for Fort Bross. A temporary camp was established a short distance behind the redoubt. A large fatigue detail from Egan's 2nd Brigade (Colonel James M. Willett's) had remained behind until 4:00 a.m., strengthening the earthworks. When these men were secured, the project engineer told the officer in charge to proceed to Avery's house. The troops were kept standing in ranks at Avery's until well after daybreak, awaiting additional instructions from Colonel Willett. Orders finally came to march to Fort Bross, but nothing was said about concealing their movements from Rebel lookouts, consequently, General Hancock was distressed to learn that when the column moved south, its line of march was in view of the Confederates.[9]

At 10:00 p.m., the troops from Mott's division garrisoning Forts Sedgwick, Davis, and Alexander Hays had been relieved by units from Miles' division, and falling in behind their guides, they hiked to the rendezvous at Southall's. Men of the Third Division posted in Forts Blaisdell, Bross, and Stevenson were scheduled to rejoin their units on the morning of the 26th.[10]

At 9:00 a.m. on October 25, General Hancock notified Meade's headquarters that Egan's and Mott's troops had been relieved. A 900-man fatigue detail had spent the night working on fortifications near the Dunn and Avery houses. At the same time, the Confederates had been building bomb-proofs and covered ways behind their rifle pits opposite Fort McGilvery.

Miles notified Hancock that 1,900 men would be required to man the picket line, but he only had 6,200 riflemen, which was insufficient. If the regiment currently guarding the depot at Cedar Level was ordered to report to him, Miles was of the opinion that he would have enough men to discharge his mission.[11]

Chief of Staff Humphreys, on learning of Miles' problems, issued orders for the regiment at Cedar Level to report to the First Division, when the depot was abandoned.[12]

9 OR 42, pt. 1, 295, 325; OR 42, pt. 3, 347-348.

10 OR 42, pt. 1, 345, 394; OR 42, pt. 3, 348. Miles' brigades were posted: the 1st Brigade from the Appomattox to Fort Morton; the Consolidated Brigade from Fort Morton to Battery No. 21; the 4th Brigade from Battery No. 21 to Battery No. 24, including Forts Sedgwick, Davis, and Alexander Hays. Ibid., 45, 48.

11 OR 42, pt. 3, 344-345.

12 Ibid., 345.

On October 25, Hancock notified Egan and Mott that tents would be struck at noon tomorrow. Forage, rations, and ammunition "required from the trains must be drawn and issued by" that time. Several changes were made in the amount of rations to be taken along on the expedition. Each man was to carry four days' rations on his person instead of six, "to count from the morning of the 27th." One day's supply of salt meat was to be taken in haversacks and three days' beef on the hoof. All public and personal property in excess of what the officers and men could carry on their persons or horses were to be turned over to the corps' chief quartermaster for safekeeping. The troops were to be prepared to march at 2:00 p.m. To hide their destination from the Rebels, it was announced that the order to march would not be issued until the morning of the 26th.[13]

Major John G. Hazard, who commanded the II Corps' artillery, had a tough assignment getting his batteries ready to roll. On the night of the 24th, a section of the 4th Battery, Maine Light Artillery, which had been withdrawn from Fort Haskell, relieved the section of Battery F, 1st Pennsylvania posted in Battery No. 10. The other section of Battery F was recalled from Fort Stedman, rejoining its parent unit near Baxter Road in the rear of the deserted house. Battery H, 1st Ohio Light Artillery was moved from Fort Sedgwick, one section being ordered into Battery No. 13 and the other into Battery No. 14, relieving the 10th Battery, Massachusetts Light Artillery. The Massachusetts cannoneers marched from the earthworks to the Fort Bross rendezvous, where they found Battery K, 4th U.S. Light Artillery. Corps reserve troops—Batteries C and I, 5th U.S. Light Artillery, and the 1st Battery, New Hampshire Light Artillery— reported to General Mott at Southall's.[14]

A staff meeting was held on the 25th in General Parke's command post at the Peebles' house. Assisted by his staff, Parke designated the units that would be left to hold the IX Corps' line. Fort Fisher was to be garrisoned by the 31st Maine and the 45th Pennsylvania; Fort Welch by the 51st New York, the 59th Massachusetts, and the 17th Vermont; Fort Gregg by the 8th Michigan and recruits from the 51st Pennsylvania; Fort Sampson by the 3rd Maryland; Fort Cummings by the 46th New York. Each unit was to camp in the "immediate vicinity" of the fort garrisoned, and was to picket their entire front. Lieutenant Colonel Ralph Ely of the 8th Michigan,

---

13 *Ibid.*, 345-346.

14 *Ibid.*, 346. The 14th Massachusetts Battery withdrew one section from Fort Bross and one from the rear of Fort Sedgwick; the 3rd Battery, Vermont Light Artillery, was pulled out of Battery No. 16; while the 3rd Battery, Maine Light Artillery, was relieved in Fort Rice by a section of Battery A, 1st New Jersey Light Artillery. These three batteries proceeded to City Point, where the officers in charge reported to Brigadier General Henry W. Benham.

as senior officer, was to be in charge of the fortified line when the IX Corps marched out.[15]

By this time, General Meade and his headquarters people had finished studying their maps. The routes that the various units were to take were plotted. Orders were drafted and distributed. On the afternoon of the 26th, Hancock was to move Egan's and Mott's divisions "to the Vaughan Road just outside the line of rear entrenchments." To reach this area, the troops who wore the clover-leaf were to take a route well to the rear, so as to be out of sight of Confederate observation posts. At 2:00 a.m. on the 27th, Hancock was to march his corps via Vaughan Road, cross Hatcher's Run, "pass by Dabney's Mill and Wilson and Arnold's steam saw-mill on Boydton Plank Road; cross the open country to Claiborne's Road near its intersection" with White Oak Road, and re-cross Hatcher's Run. His column would then march to the South Side Railroad, striking it at a point about three miles east of Sutherland Station.

General Gregg was to assemble his cavalry division (about 3,000 strong) on the afternoon of the 26th near Hatcher's Run. When his troopers rode out on the 27th, they were to cross the stream by the first crossing below the one used by Hancock's corps. Upon reaching the west bank of the creek, Gregg, who was to look to Hancock for his orders, was to advance his horse soldiers on the left of the infantry, probably following Quaker Road as far as Boydton Plank Road. Gregg's movements would be governed by Hancock's.

Parke's IX Corps was to march "at such hour" on the 27th as to enable it to surprise at daybreak the small Confederate force posted in the recently opened earthworks between Hatcher's Run and Hawks'. If successful, Parke was to pursue the Confederates, wheeling his columns to the right as they forged ahead. Should Parke fail to break through, he was to remain in position, keeping the butternuts pinned down, while the II and V Corps turned their right.

The V Corps was to march simultaneously with the IX Corps proceeding to the crossing of Hatcher's Run, below Boydton Plank Road Bridge, from where Warren was to support Parke. If the IX Corps broke through, Warren's was to push ahead, taking position on the left of Parke's battle line. Should Parke's assault fail, Warren was to cross Hatcher's Run and endeavor to turn the Rebels right by re-crossing the run above Burgess Mill, holding a position on Hancock's right.[16]

Wagons and extra caissons that were to accompany the expedition would not move on the morning of the 27th, but would be "left parked at the most secure

15 *Ibid.*, 350-351.

16 *Ibid.*, 340-341; Humphreys, *The Virginia Campaign of '64 and '65*, 294-295.

point near" the bivouacs, to be ordered to the front when convenient. Ambulances, however, would go with the troops.

Army headquarters on the 26th would be transferred to the neighborhood of Poplar Spring Church. Meade, during the early phases of the offensive, would be with the right wing. Headquarters personnel and the engineers were to be held in reserve at Meade's Station, along with a "full supply" of entrenching tools.[17]

Meade was delighted to learn that a deserter from the 27th North Carolina had turned himself in to the IX Corps' pickets. When questioned, he reported that fatigue parties from his division (Heth's) had been detailed to throw up fortifications to the right of Brigadier General Samuel McGowan's South Carolina brigade. While engaged in this work, the man remarked, he and his late comrades had been nearly two miles to the right of their brigade, Brigadier General John R. Cooke's, which was posted on McGowan's left. The newly dug rifle pits to McGowan's right (which were held by dismounted cavalry) were not extensive, the North Carolinian told his interrogators, but they were fronted by an abatis.[18]

It was 2:30 p.m. on October 26 before Grant completed his review of Meade's plan of operations. He liked everything he read, except for one point. Grant suggested that if Parke, on advancing, found the Confederate "fortifications in defensible condition and manned," he should not attack but "confront them until the movement of the other two corps had its effect."

Meade modified his master plan to partially meet his superior's objection. But, Meade added, as Parke was scheduled to be in front of the Rebel fortifications at dawn, he would have to make a forced reconnaissance "to ascertain the exact condition of affairs unless he waits until after daylight."[19]

Early on October 26, Hancock, as he had promised, laid out the route that Egan's and Mott's divisions were to follow in gaining the area near Vaughan Road, where they were to spend the night. The two divisions were to move out at 2:00 p.m. with Mott's in advance. Mott's line of march would be from Southall's, through the pines by the Widow Smith's, Williams', and Dr. Gurley's houses, and the frowning parapets of Fort Dushane. A halt for the night would be called "just outside the line and near" Vaughan's house. Three batteries were to accompany the corps, one assigned to Egan's division by Major Hazard and the others to Mott's. Ambulances and wagons were to follow the division to which they belonged. When the soldiers went into bivouac, they were to be confined to their camps. No drum

---

17 OR 42, pt. 3, 341-342; Lieutenant Colonel Ira Spaulding commanded the engineers.

18 *Ibid.*, 338.

19 *Ibid.*, 355.

Major General Winfield S. Hancock
Library of Congress

or bugle calls were to be sounded. The officers were to caution their men to hold down the size of their campfires.[20]

By the designated hour, the brigade commanders had formed, mustered, and inspected their units. Mott's division took the lead as the II Corps took the field. No difficulties were encountered until the vanguard, with which Hancock and his staff rode, reached the Weldon Railroad. It was understood by Hancock that Meade expected the corps to bivouac on Vaughan Road near Davis'. A personal reconnaissance satisfied the corps commander that it would take his pioneers hours to make the road from Fort Dushane to Davis' passable for his columns. Discussing the geography of the area with his scouts, Hancock learned that he could turn his troops into the Halifax Road. A short distance down the Halifax Road was a fork, and the road branching to the right led to Colonel Wyatt's on Church Road. The road passing in front of Colonel Wyatt's was said to connect with Vaughan at Mrs. Davis'.

Observing that the sun was about to set, Hancock determined to halt his corps and have his troops bivouac in the fields south of Fort Dushane. Hancock then dashed off a note to Meade at 6:30 p.m., reporting that Egan's rear brigade was just coming in. He had stopped, because there was considerable confusion whether Fort Dushane or Fort Cummings anchored the left flank of the Federals' fortified

---

20 *Ibid.*, 359; *OR* 42, pt. 1, 410-411. Batteries C and I, 5th U.S. (armed with six Napoleons) reported to General Egan, while the 10th Massachusetts Battery (six 10-pounder Parrotts), and Battery K, 4th U.S. (four Napoleons) was attached to Mott's command.

line. If Meade still wanted his corps to march via Vaughan's house, the hour that the troops were to move out in the morning could be pushed ahead.[21]

Chief of Staff Humphreys acknowledged Hancock's communication. It would be unnecessary, he wrote, for the II Corps to go by way of Vaughan's headquarters. He had no objection however to taking the route via Colonel Wyatt's as long as it was the shortest.[22]

General Gregg during the afternoon had called in his outposts and had concentrated his cavalry at Perkins'. When he rode over to Lewis' house to report to General Hancock, Gregg had bad news for the corps commander. Gregg had talked with several Confederate deserters. They told him that Vaughan Road, particularly near the Hatcher's Run crossing, was obstructed with felled timber. This information troubled Hancock, because he didn't relish marching his columns through obstructions in the dark. Since it would not be light until 5:30 a.m., Hancock inquired of Humphreys, "Why not let the soldiers start at a later hour?"[23]

Meanwhile, Hancock had made his plans for the morning. At 2:00 a.m., the corps, with Egan's division in the lead, was to move out. The line of march was to be Church Road to Vaughan Road, then across Hatcher's Run by way of Dabney's Mill to Boydton Plank Road. Egan was to cover his column with a strong advance guard, pushed a considerable distance to the front. Great care would be taken to keep the soldiers closed up, and the cadence would be held down till daybreak.

Gregg, after detaching a squadron to reconnoiter in advance of the infantry, was to march his division via Rowanty Post Office to Vaughan Road. Whenever the opportunity presented itself, Gregg was to communicate with Hancock. When riding down Halifax Road, to avoid confusion, the cavalry was to keep to the left and the infantry to the right.

A guide, thoroughly familiar with this section of Dinwiddie County, reported to General Egan. All wagons, except the ambulances, were to be parked between the camp and Dr. Gurley's.[24]

---

21 *OR 42*, pt. 3, 358; *OR 42*, pt. 1, 230, 295, 303, 319, 325, 346, 351, 394. Fort Dushane had been erected in late August and early September, following the battle of the Weldon Railroad, and anchored the defense line covering the railroad from the west. Fort Cummings had been thrown up in early October, after the battle of Peebles' Farm, and anchored the Union line laid out to secure the ground gained at that time.

22 *OR 42*, pt. 3, 358.

23 *OR 42*, pt. 1, 608.

24 *OR 42*, pt. 3, 359-360.

Meade, upon receipt of Hancock's message regarding a need to reschedule the hour the march was to commence, was agreeable. The II Corps could start at 3:30 a.m., which would bring Hancock into the vicinity of Hatcher's Run at dawn.[25]

General Warren was thrown into a quandary by Meade's instructions for him to "move simultaneously with the IX Corps, and proceed to the crossing of" Hatcher's Run, below Boydton Plank Road Bridge, because he knew of no road that would bring the V Corps into position between the II and IX Corps. Major Washington A. Roebling was detailed to explore the road network between the fortifications held by the IX Corps and Hatcher's Run, but he was unable to venture beyond the Union pickets, a short distance in front of the earthworks.

General Parke's pioneers, however, came to Warren's assistance. A road was opened by them through the abatis and pines to the left of Fort Cummings, via an open field, to a cart road. When Chief of Staff Humphreys relayed this information to Warren, he pointed out that this cart road would enable the V Corps to reach Duncan Road, which led by Westmoreland's house. The people at army headquarters were unable to see why the V Corps could not move simultaneously with the IX Corps as far as Duncan Road. From there, it was believed that Warren's scouts should be able to locate a route to Hatcher's Run.[26]

After acknowledging Humphreys' telegram, Warren issued orders for his division commanders to have their troops at Parke's house, ready to take the field at 5:30 a.m. on the 27th. Heavy battle losses and the discharge of men whose enlistments had expired had reduced the once proud and formidable V Corps to little more than a skeleton. When the corps marched, Brigadier General Charles Griffin's First Division was to have the advance, to be followed by Brigadier General Romeyn B. Ayres', with Brigadier General Samuel W. Crawford's bringing up the rear. The corps was to keep closed up, Griffin's vanguard following hard on the heels of Parke's rear division. Of his 11,000 effectives, Warren complained, 3,913 had never fired a shot in anger, while 1,649 were "ignorant of the manual." Five batteries, 3 armed with light 12-pounders (14 guns) and 2 with 3-inch ordnance rifles (10 guns), were to accompany the expedition. The earthworks from Battery No. 24 to Fort Fisher, formerly held by the entire corps, would be entrusted to Brigadier General Henry Baxter's brigade, about 2,500 strong and 8 batteries of 34 guns. Surplus transportation and baggage had been sent to City Point.[27]

---

25 *Ibid.*, 359.

26 *Ibid.*, 361; OR 42, pt. 1, 434.

27 OR 42, pt. 1, 434; OR 42, pt. 3, 362-363. General Baxter commanded Crawford's 2nd Brigade. The V Corps batteries left to hold the works were posted: Battery No. 24, two 3-inch

Meade, when he reviewed Warren's orders, disapproved of the starting time—5:30 a.m.—it was not early enough. General Parke, having alerted his division commanders to have their troops on the road by 3:00 a.m., prompted Meade to telegraph Warren to put his corps in motion at 4:00 a.m.[28]

The troops of the IX Corps spent October 26 getting ready to take the offensive. Rations and ammunition in the stipulated quantities were drawn, while the units earmarked to hold the forts took position. Besides cutting a passage through the parapets and abatis to the left of Fort Cummings for the V Corps, Parke's pioneers opened a route through the fortifications to the right of that stronghold for the IX Corps.

General Parke, before retiring, notified Brigadier General Orlando Willcox, whose First Division was to have the advance, that he was to move his "command promptly at 3:30 in the morning, keeping . . . [his] brigades well closed, and taking the road cut through the parapet to the right of Fort Cummings . . ."[29] The Third Division led by Brigadier General Edward Ferrero and Brigadier General Robert Potter's Second Division, as named, were to follow Willcox through the gap opened in the earthworks.[30]

Tattoo was beaten as usual in the IX Corps' camps that evening. After tattoo, the officer of the day made his rounds to see that the men had retired and that no unnecessary campfires were burning. At 2:30 a.m., the officers awakened their men, being careful to hold down the noise. The units were formed, mustered, and ready to march at 3:00 a.m.[31]

---

rifles; Battery No. 25, two 12-pounder Napoleons; Fort Howard, two 12-pounder Napoleons and two 3-inch rifles; Battery No. 26, two 12-pounder Napoleons and two 3-inch rifles; Fort Wadsworth, four 3-inch rifles and four 12-pounder Napoleons; Fort Keene, two 3-inch rifles and two 12-pounder Napoleons; Fort Urmston, four 12-pounder Napoleons and two 3-inch rifles; Fort Conahey, two 3-inch rifles and two 12-pounder Napoleons. *OR* 42, pt 3, 363-364; Humphreys, *The Virginia Campaign of '64 and '65*, 295-296; Powell, *The Fifth Army Corps*, 738-739.

28 *OR* 42, pt. 1, 361.

29 *OR* 42, pt. 3, 364-365; *OR* 42, pt. 1, 548-549.

30 *OR* 42, pt. 1, 548, 580, 592.

31 *OR* 42, pt. 3, 365.

Part II

Hampton Establishes a Roadblock

At 3:30 a.m. on October 27, 1864, General Hancock learned that his divisions were formed and passed the word to move out. In accordance with Hancock's orders, Egan's division took the lead. As soon as Egan's rear regiment had moved from its camp and turned into Halifax Road, Mott's lead brigade marched from its bivouac. Egan's 3rd Brigade commanded by Brigadier General Thomas A. Smyth had the advance, followed by Colonel James M. Willett's 2nd Brigade, while Lieutenant Colonel Horace P. Rugg's 1st Brigade brought up the rear. A squadron from the 6th Ohio Cavalry preceded Smyth's lead regiment. Rumbling along between Willett's and Rugg's brigades were the six Napoleons manned by Batteries C and I, 5th U.S. Light Artillery.[32]

For the first one-half mile of the march, the infantry had little "elbow room." Although they held to the right as directed, Halifax Road was hardly wide enough for both the foot soldiers and Gregg's cavalry. Tempers flared. Insults were exchanged as infantrymen and cavalrymen got in each other's way. The situation improved after the head of the columns reached the junction, and the II Corps took the road on the right, while Gregg's cavalry continued down Halifax Road.

General Egan and his guide rode with the troopers of the 6th Ohio. At Colonel Wyatt's, the column turned into Church Road and pushed on across Arthur Swamp. Day was breaking as the vanguard entered Vaughan Road. There were several sharp reports, as Confederate pickets posted at a house about 200 yards north of the road blazed away at the Ohio horse soldiers. Egan called a brief halt, to enable General Smyth to organize a force to dislodge the Rebels. Within a few moments, Lieutenant Colonel Frank J. Spalter had reported to Egan with his 4th Ohio Infantry Battalion. Close behind came the 7th West Virginia. Egan had Spalter deploy his Ohioans as skirmishers to the right and left of Vaughan Road. The West Virginians were told to load their rifle muskets and advance as a support to the Ohioans. By the time Spalter's battalion had taken position, the Confederates had secured their mounts and had disappeared down the road.[33]

---

32 *OR* 42, pt. 1, 231, 295, 427.

33 *Ibid.*, 295, 325, 338-339.

Brigadier General Thomas W. Egan
Miller's Photographic History of the Civil War

The march was resumed. It was apparent to the veterans that their officers anticipated trouble, as they asked one another, "Why else has Egan called in the cavalry and deployed infantry to screen the advance?" There was no more delay at this time, and the column tramped rapidly along until Spalter and his Ohioans approached Hatcher's Run. Spalter and his foot soldiers sensed trouble. Here the road had been obstructed: trees had been toppled and brush thrown into the stream, so as to disorganize a force attempting to assail the rifle pits dug on the opposite side to cover the crossing.

Without waiting for the 7th West Virginia, Colonel Spalter barked the command "Double-quick!" The Ohioans crossed an open field and dashed down the slope. There was a crashing volley. Spalter and several of his men were knocked off their feet. Unable to cross Hatcher's Run, the Ohioans took cover and returned the Rebels' fire. By this time the 7th West Virginia had deployed as skirmishers and moved to the attack. The West Virginians stormed into the abatis, but like the Ohioans, they were repulsed.

With Spalter dead, Captain John Fordyce of the West Virginia unit was senior officer present. After posting his men behind trees, he dashed to the rear and hailed Generals Egan and Smyth. The generals listened as Fordyce explained the situation. Egan turned to Smyth and told him to form his brigade across the road. Staff officers galloped to the rear with instructions for Willett and Rugg to hurry to the front with their brigades and form a second line behind Smyth's. Willett was to post his bluecoats on the right, while Rugg massed his on the left of Vaughan Road.[34]

---

34 *Ibid.*, 295, 303, 319, 325, 338-339.

Major Henry S. Farley of South Carolina led the small detachment of dismounted troopers from Brigadier General Pierce M. B. Young's brigade charged with guarding the Vaughan Road crossing of Hatcher's Run. The Confederates, their fighting blood up, let go a terrible "Rebel Yell" as the Yankee skirmishers scrambled for cover. The sight of Egan's battle lines had a sobering influence.

Egan, having completed his dispositions, told Smyth to charge. Supported by Willett's and Rugg's brigades, Smyth's battle line swept forward. Men dropped, but on the Federals came. Tearing gaps in the abatis, the Yanks, holding their cartridge boxes and rifle muskets above their heads, plunged into the run. The water was waist deep. By the time they had scrambled up the slippery west bank, the Rebels had abandoned their rifle pits and were fleeing down the road. A number of grey clads, not as fleet as their comrades, were captured.

Smyth's soldiers continued the pursuit to Young's Store, where the general called a halt to reform his brigade. While waiting for the rest of the division, Smyth had the 1st Delaware relieve the 4th Ohio Battalion and the 7th West Virginia on the skirmish line. The men from Delaware pushed out about three-quarters of a mile, driving the Confederates before them.[35]

General Hancock, while waiting impatiently for his pioneers to remove the obstructions from the ford so his artillery could pass, dashed off a note to Chief of Staff Humphreys. He reported his column had forced its way across Hatcher's Run. It was now around 7:30 a.m., and firing could be heard off to the south where Gregg's cavalry was operating, but there were no sounds of battle from the IX Corps off to the northeast. This caused Hancock to feel "some uneasiness," because he realized that his "small column could affect nothing if the enemy were permitted to concentrate against it, and that he could not even attempt to reach the South Side Railroad unless the enemy were kept occupied meeting the attacks" launched by Parke and Warren.[36]

As soon as the rest of Egan's brigades and Mott's division had forded Hatcher's Run, Hancock told Egan to march "by the nearest road to Dabney's Mill." Mott's column was to move out along Vaughan Road a mile or so, and then strike for the mill by way of a cart road, shown on the Federals' maps of eastern Dinwiddie County.[37]

---

35 *Ibid.*, 338-339.

36 *Ibid.*, 231; *OR* 42, pt. 3, 379; Francis A. Walker, "The Expedition to the Boydton Plank Road, October, 1864," in *Papers of the Military Historical Society of Massachusetts*, 15 vols, (Boston, 1906), vol. 5, 325.

37 *OR* 42, pt. 1, 231.

Major General Gershom Mott
Library of Congress

Egan, after reforming his division, called for Rugg to take the advance. Smyth's brigade was to bring up the rear. Rugg's lead regiment—the 19th Massachusetts —turned off Vaughan Road and into Telegraph Road. At the point where Telegraph Road struck Hatcher's Run, Egan had Rugg form his brigade into battle line across the road, while skirmishers of the 19th Massachusetts waded into the stream. Not encountering any Confederates, they withdrew. The march resumed along a cart road when Rugg reassembled his troops. The head of the column reached Dabney's Mill at 9:15 a.m., where the vanguard (two companies of the 19th Maine) captured Major Andrew R. Venable, Hampton's adjutant general. While Egan's soldiers were halted, waiting for Mott to arrive, Venable was questioned by Egan and his staff, but refused to tell the Federals anything except his name and rank.[38]

Mott's division, with Brigadier General P. Regis de Trobriand's brigade leading the way, had waded Hatcher's Run at 8:00 a.m. Preparatory to moving out Vaughan Road, Mott had de Trobriand advance the 2nd U.S. Sharpshooters and the 73rd New York as skirmishers. De Trobriand's advance guard, as it approached a cornfield near where the road to Dabney's Mill branched off from Vaughan Road, spotted Confederates digging rifle pits. The Yanks surged forward, and the Confederates dropped their entrenching tools, swung into their saddles, and pounded off in swift retreat. Nothing further out of the ordinary occurred to slow the march to Dabney's Mill. Since Egan's troops had reached the mill well ahead of

---

38 *Ibid.*, 295-296, 303, 306, 309, 312, 314, 319, 325.

them, Mott's soldiers were subjected to considerable good-natured guying as they tramped up.[39]

All the while, the sound of Gregg's guns was getting nearer. Hancock knew that with Gregg advancing, he would have to strike rapidly for Boydton Plank Road, if he were to intercept the Confederates that the Union cavalry were driving in. Orders were given for Egan to push on toward Plank Road.[40]

Egan soon had his division in motion along a wood road, which his guide assured him led into Boydton Plank Road at Bevill's. At 10:30 a.m., Rugg's advance debouched from the pines into a field and reached their goal. Looking up Plank Road toward Hatcher's Run, the Yanks could see the canvas tops of Confederate military wagons as they rolled northeastward.

Hancock, who was riding with Egan, was disappointed because he believed that a small force of cavalry, if one were available, might have captured part of the train before it crossed the run at Burgess Mill. As soon as the last of his foot soldiers had emerged from the woods, Egan had Rugg form his brigade into line of battle across Boydton Plank Road. The 19th and 20th Massachusetts were sent to report to Capt. A. Henry Embler of Hancock's staff. Embler deployed the Massachusetts infantrymen as skirmishers to the right of the road and advanced to feel the foe. At the same time, Hancock called for Rugg to move his brigade across Boydton Plank Road, anchoring its right on the road.[41]

As soon as Willett's 2nd Brigade entered the clearing, Egan had the colonel form his troops with their left on Plank Road. The position taken by Willett's troops was parallel with the road and faced the commanding ground, known to the soldiers as Burgess farm. Willett was told by Egan to advance "to the support of Captain Embler's skirmishers, until his left connected" with Rugg's right.[42]

While Willett was preparing to do as directed and before the head of Smyth's column came out of the pines, a Confederate battery roared into action, hammering Rugg's skirmishers and battle line with case-shot. Two Rebel guns were quickly pinpointed on the south side of Hatcher's Run, near Burgess Tavern, while a second section had unlimbered its piece off to the west near White Oak Road.[43]

39 *Ibid.*, 346, 359, 367, 394.

40 *Ibid.*, 231.

41 *Ibid.*, 296, 303, 309-310, 314; Walker, "The Expedition to the Boydton Plank Road," 325.

42 *OR* 42, pt. 1, 296, 319.

43 *Ibid.*, 231, 297; Walker, "The Expedition to the Boydton Plank Road," 325.

The cannoneers of Batteries C and I, 5th U.S. Light Artillery heard the boom of the Southerners' cannon. Lieutenant W. Butler Beck put his "battery into a trot." Driving their teams out into the field, the regulars put their Napoleons into action, concentrating their fire on the Confederate guns on the ridge near Burgess. The range was only 800 yards, and the Federal cannoneers quickly registered on their mark. Within a few minutes, the grey clads had had enough, and limbering up their guns they withdrew north of the run.[44]

General Hancock did not deem it prudent to continue his march for the White Oak Road, while any Confederates remained south of Hatcher's Run. Orders were now issued for Egan to push for the bridge at Burgess and to drive everything across. General Gregg at this time rode up and reported to Hancock.

*   *   *

When Gregg's horse soldiers took the field before daybreak on October 27, Colonel Charles H. Smith's brigade was assigned the advance, to be followed by Colonel Michael Kerwin's, with Brigadier General Henry E. Davies' brigade covering the rear. The cavalrymen were delighted when Hancock's II Corps left them in possession of Halifax Road. A mile north of Ream's Station, the long column turned into the Dinwiddie Court House Road, which would bring it to the Monk's Neck Bridge crossing of Rowanty Creek.

Colonel Smith, before saddling up, assigned the advance to the dependable 6th Ohio Cavalry. A Confederate outpost was encountered by the Ohioans at J. Hargrave's, about one mile northeast of Monk's Neck Bridge. A few shots were exchanged and the Rebel vedettes fled. The bluecoats followed, close on the Johnnies' heels.[45]

As they approached the bridge, the Ohioans pulled up their horses because on the opposite side, about 200 yards to their front, they could see a line of breastworks behind which Rebel cavalrymen assigned to watch the crossing were waiting. Colonel Smith galloped up and made a hurried estimate of the situation. The 6th Ohio and a battalion of the 1st Maine were dismounted. After the troopers had counted off, every fifth man was detailed as a horse holder. Next, the men were deployed on the run as skirmishers. Several well aimed volleys kept the butternuts pinned in their rifle pits, and then the bluecoats charged, wading into the Rowanty

---

44 OR 42, pt. 1, 427. 2nd Lieutenant Thomas Barnes of the regular battery was mortally wounded at this time. A Confederate sharpshooter cut him down with a minie in the abdomen.

45 Walker, "The Expedition to the Boydton Plank Road," 325.

above and below the bridge. Pressing on, the Yanks stormed the works, capturing several prisoners.

A bridgehead established, Gregg had his pioneers cut away the barricades placed on the approaches to the bridge. The division then crossed Rowanty Creek, as the horse holders brought up the mounts, and the advance was resumed. Smith's brigade, preceded by troopers of the 6th Ohio, continued to lead. As the column forged deeper into Dinwiddie County, the Ohioans were in constant contact with Rebel horsemen, routing them from the roadblock. Much powder was burned, but with both sides moving rapidly, there were few casualties.

Two and one-half miles west of Monk's Neck Bridge, the Federals turned into Vaughan Road and crossed Little Cattail Run. Upon reaching the intersection of Vaughan and Quaker Roads, Gregg's vanguard wheeled into Quaker Road. As the 6th Ohio started down the slope leading to Gravelly Run, Major George W. Dickinson threw up his right arm as a signal to halt. Most of the leaves having withered and fallen, the advance guard could see a number of Rebels posted on the north side of the stream, prepared to resist their crossing.[46]

Several couriers had been bagged by the Yanks during their lightning-like ride from the Rowanty to Gravelly Run. Gregg closely questioned these men and learned that two Confederate cavalry divisions were based in eastern Dinwiddie County. Major General W. H. F. "Rooney" Lee's division was camped on Stony Creek, to Gregg's left and about three miles distant, while Brigadier General Matthew C. Butler's division was camped on Quaker Road to his front.[47]

Major General Wade Hampton's cavalry corps was charged with guarding the southwest extension of the Petersburg fortifications. On October 24, the cavalry chieftain had notified General Lee that his horse soldiers had been employed "in assisting the infantry in completing a new line of works, which extends" to Hatcher's Run. Hampton posted his corps when this task was completed. Seven hundred dismounted cavalrymen had been sent into the newly completed earthworks, their right resting on Hatcher's Run, about one and one-half miles above Armstrong's Mill. Troopers from Butler's division picketed the countryside from the rifle pits to Monk's Neck Bridge, while Rooney Lee's horse soldiers watched the ground between Monk's Neck Bridge and the point where Halifax Road spanned Stony Creek. Brigadier General James Dearing's brigade was

---

46 OR 42, pt. 1, 609, 621, 648.

47 *Ibid.*, 608.

encamped at Burgess Mill with orders—on receipt of news of a Union advance—to take position at once in the trenches on the right of the infantry.[48]

Lt. Gen. Ambrose P. Hill, on the 24th, joined Hampton for a ride along the recently finished earthworks. As they jogged along, Hampton suggested to Hill that if the infantry could hold the line to Hatcher's Run, he could pull his dismounted troopers out of the rifle pits north of the stream and place them in the works guarding the south bank. The cavalry corps would then be concentrated within supporting distance of the fortified zone, and if the Federals attacked, Hampton could throw a force of "400 to 4,000 men" on their flank by crossing at one of the five dams, reserving at the same time a sufficient mounted force to cope with their cavalry. Before Hill could act on this suggestion, however, the Army of the Potomac lashed out toward them.[49]

Shortly after daybreak on October 27, excited couriers began reaching Hampton's command post with reports that a number of Union columns were advancing and driving in Butler's pickets from Squirrel Level Road on the left to Dinwiddie Court House Road on the right. Next came evil-tidings that Union infantry and artillery had forced crossings of Hatcher's Run at Armstrong's Mill and Vaughan Road, while Yankee cavalry had stormed the Monk's Neck Bridge. Orders were given for Butler to reinforce his outposts. The brigade commanders ordered their regiments "to get into the saddle" without allowing their cavalrymen to attend to the "niceties of the toilette, or to breakfast. . . ." Some dismounted men, "who were in camp, always as wretched as fish out of water, were forced, much against their will, to move in undignified haste, swearing like orthodox troopers, amid much pleasant chaff from their more fortunate comrades on horseback." Butler, accompanied by a combat patrol, rode out to engage the Union column (Hancock's corps) that was advancing via Vaughan Road.

Learning from his scouts that Gregg's cavalry was driving up Quaker Road, Hampton headed south with a strong detachment from Butler's division. Hampton soon encountered the pickets as they retreated before Gregg's vanguard. Reacting to this emergency with his characteristic vigor, Hampton dismounted and formed his men on a ridge overlooking Gravelly Run. Butler now rode up and reported that he had been unable to locate Hancock's column. Meanwhile, the cannoneers of the

---

48 OR 42, pt. 3, 1161-1162. To strengthen their line behind Hatcher's Run, the Confederates had erected five dams, covering them with works on the south bank.

49 *Ibid.*, 1162.

Washington South Carolina Artillery emplaced two of their 3-inch rifles on a commanding knoll.[50]

Before riding out of Butler's camp, Hampton had dispatched an aide with instructions for Rooney Lee to take the field with all his division, except those men on picket duty. Lee was to ride from his Stony Creek camp, up the military road, so as to strike Gregg's cavalry in the rear as it advanced up Quaker Road.

Hampton, as a good soldier, knew that the gap which had opened between Butler's left and Hatcher's Run would have to be covered. If not, Hancock's column would make an unopposed march to Burgess Mill. He therefore gave Major Venable the task of telling Dearing to pull his troopers out of the rifle pits north of Hatcher's Run, and to post them on Boydton Plank Road near Bevill's house. Dearing, upon reaching Bevill's, would have a twofold mission: watching Butler's flank and rear and guarding the roads leading from Armstrong's and Dabney's Mill to Plank Road.

Major General Henry Heth, placed in charge of the forces opposing Hancock by Hill, quashed the order for Dearing to proceed to Bevill's because he did not feel that the brigade could be spared from the works. Dearing and his troopers would continue to be responsible for the defense of the Burgess Mill crossing of Hatcher's Run. It was while hastening to tell Hampton of Hill's refusal to release Dearing that Venable was captured by Hancock's vanguard. Hampton therefore, did not know that the approach to his rear was unguarded.

Upon the departure of Hampton's column for Gravelly Run, the men remaining in camp quickly packed the wagons and started for Burgess Mill. These were the vehicles seen by Hancock as he rode out onto Boydton Plank Road.[51]

General Gregg had joined Colonel Smith and Major Dickinson on the ridge south of the Quaker Road crossing of Gravelly Run. While the officers were discussing the tactical situation, the cannoneers of the Washington South Carolina Artillery opened fire. Gregg, studying the opposite slope through his glasses, pinpointed a strong skirmish line. Smith prepared to attack. The 6th Ohio and the 1st Maine were dismounted and deployed as skirmishers. Wading the run, the bluecoats carved out a narrow bridgehead. Butler's Confederates, however, held their ground along the brow of the ridge and prepared to counterattack. Smith determined to commit another regiment. The 21st Pennsylvania was called up and rode across the stream, forming on the flanks of the skirmish line. As soon as the Pennsylvanians were in position, Smith's brigade began to fight its way up the

50 *OR* 42, pt. 1, 608, 648, 949; Wells, *Hampton and His Cavalry*, 329.

51 *OR* 42, pt. 1, 949; Wells, *Hampton and His Cavalry*, 329-330.

slope. Suddenly, the butternuts broke off the engagement, secured their horses, and retired up the valley of Gravelly Run.[52]

It was not long before Gregg and Smith's bluecoats discovered the reason for the Confederates' precipitant withdrawal. Hampton had first learned that Dearing had not taken position at Bevill's, when several ashen-faced men rode up and reported a powerful Union column (Hancock's) was astride Boydton Plank Road. If Butler's butternuts held their ground, they would be trapped between the Yank cavalry to their front and Hancock's infantry to their rear. It was mandatory for Hampton to change his front, so as to meet the Federals on the Boydton Plank and White Oak roads. After dispatching a combat patrol with one gun up Quaker Road to harass Hancock, Hampton ordered Butler to disengage his division, move to the left, and take post near J. Wilson's on Plank Road. Covered by a strong rear guard, Butler broke contact with Gregg's horse soldiers and headed for Wilson's.[53]

While Smith's brigade battled Butler's division along Gravelly Run, Rooney Lee's division came thundering up the military road from Stony Creek. General Davies' brigade, reinforced by the 2nd Pennsylvania of Kerwin's brigade, was posted at the junction of the Quaker and Military roads. Lee's grey clads made a spirited attack, but they were repulsed.

As soon as Butler's division had abandoned the ridge overlooking Gravelly Run, Gregg resumed his march up Quaker Road. Davies' rear guard—the 1st Pennsylvania Cavalry—was cautioned to keep a strong lookout. Rooney Lee's butternuts harassed the Yanks as far as Gravelly Run.[54]

Rooney Lee was hailed by one of Hampton's aides. The staff officer told Lee that he was to find a wood road, south of Gravelly Run, and take his division over to Boydton Plank Road. He would then cross the stream, advance up the Plank Road, and assail the Federals. Lee moved to carry out Hampton's instructions.[55]

Upon reaching Wilson's, Hampton had Butler detail a small force and post it there to draw Hancock's attention toward the southwest. Accompanied by Butler and the remainder of the division, Hampton took the wood road leading by Holliday's and connecting with White Oak Road at Butler's house. Although the Confederates drove their mounts hard, they reached White Oak Road with only

---

52 *OR* 42, pt. 1, 608-609, 621, 649.

53 *Ibid.*, 949; Wells, *Hampton and His Cavalry*, 332-333; Brooks, *Butler and His Cavalry*, 357.

54 *OR* 42, pt. 1, 609, 629, 641; Beale, *History of the Ninth Virginia Cavalry*, 147.

55 *OR* 42, pt. 1, 949.

minutes to spare. A short distance to the east, and sweeping rapidly toward them, was a Union skirmish line.[56]

Butler's troopers dismounted and deployed on the double. Young's brigade took position on the left, its flank resting on Burgess Mill Pond, with an open field to its front. Colonel Hugh Aiken's South Carolina brigade was on the right, picketing the ground to a considerable distance south of White Oak Road. Butler was told by Hampton that he was to advance as soon as he heard Rooney Lee's guns. While waiting for Lee to get into position on Boydton Plank Road, Butler sent the horse holders to the rear, and his cavalrymen threw up temporary barricades of "fence rails, logs and such material as . . . [they] could get." Captain James F. Hart had the gunners of his Washington South Carolina Artillery unlimber their six guns along the division's line, commanding the field in front.[57]

Hancock, with the Confederates having established a roadblock on White Oak Road, was especially glad to see Gregg. He told the cavalryman to form his division on the left of the II Corps—Kerwin's brigade "close upon the infantry and west of the Plank Road," Davies' on the Plank Road, and Smith's on the Quaker Road. Davies' and Smith's horse soldiers were to watch for Confederate thrusts up these roads and guard the II Corps' rear.[58]

With Gregg's division on the field, Hancock prepared to turn his command into White Oak Road. Orders were given for Egan to advance his battle line down Boydton Plank Road, driving the Rebels posted on the high ground at Burgess across Hatcher's Run. Meanwhile, Mott's column had come up. Before leaving Dabney's Mill, a lieutenant and 150 cavalrymen had reported to Mott. The general told the lieutenant "to look well after the rear and to throw vedettes well out on all by-roads; also to drive up all the stragglers." At a word from Mott, the march was resumed with flankers thrown out. Mott's lead brigade reached Plank Road at 12:30 p.m.

In accordance with orders from Hancock, Mott told de Trobriand to cover the left flank by "a curved line of battle facing to the left and rear (west and south, across Boydton Plank Road)." The 73rd, 86th, and 124th New York were deployed and advanced as skirmishers in front of de Trobriand's position. This skirmish line connected on the right with Rugg's Second Division brigade and on the left with Gregg's vedettes. The 2nd U.S. Sharpshooters soon reinforced the three New York

---

56 *Ibid.*, Wells, *Hampton and His Cavalry*, 333-334.

57 Brooks, *Butler and His Cavalry*, 357. Butler's 3rd Brigade, Rosser's, had been detached and sent to join Lt. Gen. Jubal Early in the Valley.

58 *OR* 42, pt. 1, 609, 621, 629, 641, 648.

regiments on the skirmish line. De Trobriand's battle line—the 99th and 110th Pennsylvania; the 20th Indiana; the 40th New York; the 1st Maine Heavy Artillery; and the 17th Maine Infantry—extended across the fields on both sides of a wood road, leading to the northwest, and was covered on its flanks by a dense growth of pines.[59]

Brigadier General Byron R. Pierce's 2nd Brigade was massed in a field, near the junction of Dabney's Mill and Boydton Plank roads.[60] Colonel Robert McAllister's 3rd Brigade was emerging from the pine as a cavalcade of horsemen rode up. One of the officers, whom McAllister recognized as General Meade, told the brigade commander to halt his column.[61]

At noon, a courier rode up and handed Hancock a note from Chief of Staff Humphreys, drafted at 10:40 a.m. Humphreys wanted Hancock to know that the V Corps had found the Rebels "entrenched on a line running near to Armstrong's Mill pond." No V Corps troops had yet forded Hatcher's Run, but Warren was to cross a division at once and follow with the rest of his corps. Meanwhile, Hancock was to look out for his right and to confirm there was no enemy between his corps and Hatcher's Run.[62]

Replying, Hancock observed that he was at the Burgess house, and that General Gregg and his cavalry had "just come up." The foe having been driven across Hatcher's Run, the II Corps was about to move out on White Oak Road. By the route that he proposed to follow, it was six miles to the South Side Railroad.[63]

One of Hancock's officers now told Mott to put his division in motion for White Oak Road. Before Mott could do as directed, Hancock received an order from General Meade requiring him to halt where he was. While awaiting additional instructions, Hancock watched as de Trobriand's brigade formed.

Generals Grant and Meade rode up to Hancock's command post. Calling Hancock aside, Meade told him that Crawford's V Corps division was working its way up Hatcher's Run. Meade wanted Hancock to extend his line to the right and link up with Crawford's troops.[64]

---

59 *Ibid.*, 346, 359.

60 *Ibid.*, 346, 367.

61 *Ibid.*, 346, 395.

62 OR 42, pt. 3, 379.

63 *Ibid.*, 380.

64 Walker, "The Expedition to the Boydton Plank Road," 325-326; OR 42, pt. 1, 231.

Part III

General Heth Strikes

General Parke's IX Corps was formed and ready to march at 3:00 a.m. on October 27. Parke, like other people at Meade's headquarters, was of the opinion that the Confederates' fortifications had not yet been extended to Hatcher's Run, or if such a line had been marked out by General Lee's skilled engineers, the earthworks had not been completed.

Brigadier General Orlando B. Willcox's lead brigade, Colonel Bryon M. Cutcheon's, marched at 3:30 a.m., passing by Parke's Peebles' house command post, en route to Fort Cummings. Moving through the gap cut in the earthworks and abatis to the right of Fort Cummings, the head of the column was halted by Willcox at the picket line. Here Cutcheon's bluecoats waited in the darkness, while the next brigade in line, Colonel Napoleon B. McLaughlen's, marched up.

Filing to the right, McLaughlen's troops passed in front of the earthworks from which the Rebels had been driven the previous month. McLaughlen's mission was to surprise the Confederate outpost known to be stationed at the redoubt. At what he considered a secure distance from the redoubt, McLaughlen halted his troops. Major James Doherty with 40 volunteers from the 57th Massachusetts crept forward—their task was to take the pickets from the rear. One of Doherty's party was trigger-happy. There was a loud bang. One of the four Confederate sentries was knocked to the ground by a minie, and his companions leaped to their feet and in the confusion eluded Doherty's patrol. Reaching their lines, the grey clads sounded the alarm.[65]

McLaughlen, on hearing the shot, led his brigade forward and joined Doherty at the redoubt. Here he halted his column to allow Brigadier General John F. Hartranft and his 1st Brigade to pass. Willcox rode up and told McLaughlen to have his column follow Hartranft's.[66]

Cutcheon, by this time, had deployed the 2nd Michigan as skirmishers along the edge of the woods east of C. Smith's house. The 20th Michigan was posted in support and the rest of the brigade was held ready to file by the left flank. Upon hearing that McLaughlen's troops had botched their assignment, Cutcheon

---

65 *OR* 42, pt. 1, 548, 556, 568, 576.

66 *Ibid.*, 576.

advanced his brigade toward Smith's house. At Smith's, Cutcheon swung his left forward, and the brigade drove westward. Contact with McLaughlen's troops to the right was soon lost, so Cutcheon directed his "skirmishers to gain ground in that direction as they advanced, until they should cover the road running westward from the Hawks house." The right of the skirmish line had a difficult time wading the branch of Arthur Swamp in front of Hawks' thus causing the left of the skirmish line to swing ahead until it was nearly perpendicular with Duncan Road. Cutcheon discovered what had occurred, but 20 minutes of valuable time was lost while the alignment was corrected. When the advance was resumed, Cutcheon told Lieutenant Colonel Edwin March of the 2nd Michigan "to push forward vigorously and attack promptly any force of the enemy he might encounter."

The Union skirmishers forged ahead. Confederate pickets from Heth's division were encountered in the pines east of Watkins'. Shots were exchanged, and the butternuts fell back. General Willcox heard the musketry and had Cutcheon hold his ground, while he called up Hartranft's people. Hartranft's brigade came up on Cutcheon's left. As soon as Hartranft's skirmishers were in position on the left of the 2nd Michigan, Willcox told his brigade commanders to push on. Hartranft's and Cutcheon's brigades closely supported the skirmishers as they drove in Heth's outposts.

It had been daylight for several hours, when the skirmishers emerged from the pine thickets west of the Clements house, and found themselves confronted by a line of rifle pits "well filled with men and protected by an almost impervious slashing." March advanced his bluecoats close up to the abatis, the left of his line entering the felled timber. Seeing that the Confederate position was too strong to be assailed, he sent a runner racing to the rear to tell Cutcheon what he had discovered. Cutcheon reinforced March with the 20th Michigan and the 51st Pennsylvania. Hartranft at the same time strengthened his skirmish line. Taking position in front of the abatis, the Federals dug in.[67]

Under Willcox's eye, Hartranft and Cutcheon formed their brigades for attack. Colonel McLaughlen's brigade was called up, so it could be a ready reserve. All the while patrols from the two advance brigades probed for soft spots in the fortified line held by Heth's veterans.[68]

Brigadier General Edward Ferrero's black division had followed the route pioneered by Willcox's troops through the breastworks and abatis and across the

67 *Ibid.*, 556, 568-569; OR 42, pt. 3, 389; Augustus Woodbury, *Major General Ambrose E. Burnside and the Ninth Army Corps* (Providence, 1867), 469-470.

68 OR 42, pt. 1, 556, 576.

countryside beyond. When Willcox's advance came to a halt before the Rebel earthworks west of Clements' field, Ferrero jockeyed his brigades into position on Willcox's right, swinging his right flank back to link up with Brigadier General Robert R. Potter's Second Division near the Hawks house.[69]

Screened by a strong line of skirmishers, Ferrero pushed his battle line through the pines and dense undergrowth. Ferrero's men, like Willcox's, were compelled to halt when they came upon a line of recently dug earthworks. Obstructions (slashed timber and abatis) warned Ferrero and his officers that an attack against the sector to their front would be attended with frightful casualties. Ferrero, after notifying Parke of the situation, received permission to fortify his position.[70]

There was a glow in the eastern sky, as Potter's advance brigade—Brigadier General Simon G. Griffin's—passed Fort Cummings. Rapidly marching ahead, Griffin's troops relieved McLaughlen's at the abandoned Rebel redoubt. To cover the advance of Willcox's and Ferrero's divisions, Griffin sent a strong force of skirmishers toward the northwest. After all the soldiers had passed the redoubt, Potter brought up his 1st Brigade, Colonel John I. Curtin commanding. Potter now deployed his division, "the center on the road to the right of the Hawks house and in line with that house," his right in the abandoned Confederate rifle pits about one-eighth mile from the slashings in front of the Union main line of resistance, and his left in contact with Ferrero's right. A picket line was established well to the front, connecting on the right with the pickets in front of Fort Welch.[71]

Potter had his men entrench their position during the afternoon. The 19th Battery, New York Light Artillery had reported to him, so Potter had the cannoneers emplace four guns near the Hawks house and the remaining section on his right.[72]

At 9:45 a.m., General Parke notified Chief of Staff Humphreys that "Willcox is up with the enemy's line, and is now engaged, skirmishing." Willcox was now extending to the left to connect with Warren, and, if he found a soft spot, he was to attempt a breakthrough. Potter at this hour was across the road north of the Hawks' house redoubt, while Ferrero occupied the interval between Willcox and Potter.[73]

---

69 OR 42, pt. 3, 388; OR 42, pt. 1, 592. Colonel Ozora P. Stearns' 1st Brigade was on the left, while Colonel Henry G. Thomas' 2nd Brigade was on the right.

70 OR 42, pt. 1, 592.

71 *Ibid.*, 580; Committee, *History of the Thirty-Fifth Regiment Massachusetts Volunteers,* 306; Committee, *History of the Thirty-Sixth Regiment Massachusetts Volunteers,* 271.

72 OR 42, pt. 1, 592.

73 OR 42, pt. 3, 388.

Warren's V Corps, as directed, had marched at 4:00 a.m. It started to sprinkle at 4:45 a.m., and because of the overcast, it was unusually dark. Owing to the gloom, parts of the long column became scrambled. Brigades lost contact with the preceding unit. It was light enough for the soldiers to see the road at 5:30 a.m., and Warren, having passed to the left of Fort Cummings, turned the head of his column into the woods. Warren was disgusted to discover that the IX Corps' people had not cleared all the obstructions from the road, so he called on General Griffin for pioneers. Keeping to the left of the IX Corps' flankers, the column moved in a southwesterly direction to R. Thompson's house.

Ascertaining that he was getting too far south and that all roads encountered ran north and south, Warren had his pioneers cut a road through the pines in a westerly direction for one-half mile. This led the corps' vanguard into Duncan Road, southeast of the Clements house. Here Warren found a cart road leading west. A short tramp down the cart road brought Warren's advance guard up against Heth's picket line.[74]

General Griffin, in response to instructions from Warren, told Colonel Edgar M. Gregory, the commander of his lead brigade, to form his men in the pines to the left of the road. Gregory deployed his unit in double line—the 188th New York Battalion and the 91st Pennsylvania in front, and the 187th New York Battalion and the 159th Pennsylvania in support. Skirmishers from the 91st Pennsylvania were advanced, while the 155th Pennsylvania, in the same formation, took position to cover the 2nd Brigade's left. As soon as Gregory reported that he was prepared, Griffin sent him forward. The men who wore the red maltese cross, although subjected to a "lively fire," advanced through the pines, driving Heth's outposts back into their fortifications. Upon penetrating to within 100 to 200 yards of the Rebels' main line of resistance, Gregory's skirmishers encountered felled timber and came under a scathing fire from riflemen sheltered behind recently erected breastworks. A hasty reconnaissance convinced Griffin that the slashings and abatis would make an assault on the rifle pits costly. Orders were given for Gregory's troops, who had already seen 100 of their comrades shot down, to take position and start fortifying. Contact was established at this time with Hartranft's IX Corps troops on the right.[75]

It was now 9:30 a.m. Warren had already received word from General Meade that Parke's people had met the Confederates, but they would probably be unable

74 OR 42, pt. 1, 437; Powell, *The Fifth Army Corps*, 739.

75 OR 42, pt. 1, 437, 459.

to crack the Rebels' fortified line. Meade therefore wanted Warren to send part of his corps across Hatcher's Run and communicate with General Hancock.[76]

Replying to Meade's communication, Warren told of his advance and of Gregory's repulse. Warren was satisfied with all that he had seen and because of the strength of the Rebels' works to his front; it would be impractical for his corps to force a crossing of Hatcher's Run above Armstrong's Mill.

Hancock, at the same time, was notified that the V Corps was "about one mile north of Armstrong's Mill, on the Duncan Road."[77]

After ordering Generals Ayres and Crawford to mass their divisions close behind Griffin's, Warren called for two of his staff—Major Washington A. Roebling and Capt. William T. Gentry. Roebling was to take the general's escort (a detachment from the 4th Pennsylvania Cavalry) and feel to the left, and see if he could locate where the Rebel right anchored on Hatcher's Run. Captain Gentry was entrusted with the 9:30 a.m. message to Hancock. Pending the return of his aides, Warren would reconnoiter to his front and ascertain the practicability of forcing Heth's position.[78]

Major Roebling rode toward Armstrong's Mill. On the opposite side of Hatcher's Run at the mill, he could see a regiment of troops wearing the III Corps clover-leaf badge. As Roebling and the horse soldiers watched, the II Corps foot soldiers moved out of what looked like rifle pits. The major assumed that these were abandoned Confederate earthworks; that they were continuous along the right bank of the stream; and that they re-crossed Hatcher's Run somewhere opposite Griffin's left, connecting with the fortifications before which Gregory's advance had stalled. As it rode up the creek, Roebling's party was fired on by a grey clad picket, who took to his heels. Roebling reported back to Warren at 10:15 a.m. and told his general that besides being fortified, the south bank of the run was heavily timbered.[79]

Generals Grant and Meade, accompanied by a large number of horsemen, rode up to Warren's command post at 10:30 a.m. After Warren had briefed his important visitors as to his dispositions and the formidable character of the Rebels' works, Major Roebling explained to the generals that Griffin's skirmish line extended a considerable distance down Hatcher's Run. Captain Gentry now showed up.

76 OR 42, pt. 3, 384.

77 Ibid., 385.

78 OR 42, pt. 1, 437.

79 Ibid., 440; Powell, The Fifth Army Corps, 740.

Questioned by Warren, he reported that the rear of General Hancock's column had passed Dabney's Mill en route to the Plank Road.[80]

Grant, after reflecting on the situation and checking his maps, told Warren "to send a division across Hatcher's Run, place its right flank on the run, and then move up, supporting General Hancock, and upon arriving at the enemy's right of the line in front of General Griffin to attack it in flank, and endeavor to cause him to abandon the line, and thus open the way for the rest of . . ." the V and IX Corps.[81]

Checking with his staff, Warren learned that Crawford's division was conveniently situated to undertake this special assignment. Lieutenant Charles Ricketts was sent to tell Crawford to bring up his division. When Ricketts trotted up, he found the Third Division halted in Thompson's field. After listening to Ricketts, Crawford turned the head of his column into Duncan Road. Before he had gone far, Crawford encountered Major Roebling. The major, who was to conduct the division to its position, told Crawford that he was to cross Hatcher's Run at Armstrong's Mill, advance up the right bank, resting his right on the stream, and link up with Griffin's left. From Roebling, Crawford learned that the II Corps was on his left and had advanced a considerable distance. While questioning the staff officer about the topography of the area into which he was to take his troops, the general was told that if he advanced as he planned with a two-brigade front, he would "overlap" the II Corps.[82]

Meanwhile, Warren increased the force with which Crawford would cross Hatcher's Run. Orders were issued for General Ayres to reinforce Crawford with a brigade. Ayres detached the Maryland Brigade, Colonel Andrew W. Denison commanding. Warren would travel with Crawford's column since it was a mission fraught with danger. Griffin was expected to employ his own division and two brigades of Ayres' to keep Heth's attention focused on his front, while Crawford maneuvered for position on the Rebels' flank or rear.[83]

As Warren trotted off, Griffin called up two regiments from his 3rd Brigade—Brigadier General Joseph J. Bartlett's—sending them to the left. There they took position, their right resting on Gregory's left and their left on Hatcher's Run. The rest of Bartlett's brigade was formed in line north of the road opened that

80 *OR* 42, pt. 1, 437, 440.

81 *Ibid.*, 437.

82 *Ibid.*, 440, 495-496.

83 *Ibid.*, 437.

morning by the division pioneers. General Ayres massed his 1st and 3rd Brigades as a strategic reserve in the pines behind Bartlett's battle line.[84]

Crawford's vanguard reached the run opposite Armstrong's Mill by 11:45 a.m. and started to cross. Because of the heavy growth of timber and underbrush on the opposite side of the stream, Crawford was compelled to leave his battery, the 9th Battery, Massachusetts Light Artillery, at the mill. Warren joined Crawford by the time his rear brigade—Colonel J. William Hofmann's—had scrambled up the south bank. Colonel Denison and the Maryland Brigade overtook the division at this time. While Crawford's bluecoats were deploying, Warren reviewed for Crawford's benefit what was expected. Using a map, the corps commander indicated to his subordinate the point where the earthworks confronting Griffin's people were believed to anchor on the run. Warren wanted Crawford to turn these fortifications.[85]

In forming his command, Crawford placed Brigadier General Edward S. Bragg's brigade in advance. Bragg was told "to throw out a strong line of skirmishers, to double them, and to advance them half a mile in his front, their right resting upon the creek." Colonel Hofmann's brigade was formed in rear of Bragg's, its right anchored on Hatcher's Run. In accordance with instructions from Crawford, Hofmann threw out the 147th New York as flankers to guard his left. As the dense undergrowth made it impossible to advance along the creek, two regiments of the Maryland Brigade were ordered "to advance in rear, and supporting the right flank, and two others on the left flank," and Colonel Denison was instructed to hold his Marylanders ready to reinforce any portion of the line that might be necessary.

After checking with the brigade commanders and learning that they were ready, Crawford "broke the command by the right of companies to the front, and advanced into the forest. Forward progress was attended with great difficulty. So thick were the trees and so tangled the undergrowth that the troops became confused as to directions. Officers were compelled to rely on their compasses. To help Crawford and his top subordinates guide their movements, Warren dispatched an aide with instructions for Griffin to have his skirmish line open on the foe to its front. Much difficulty was experienced by the brigade and regimental commanders in maintaining a semblance of an alignment. Hatcher's Run made a horseshoe bend to the west, and Crawford, to avoid having his right wing wade the stream twice, filed his brigades by the flank a considerable distance to the southwest.

84 *Ibid.*, 437, 459; Survivors' Association, *History of the Corn Exchange Regiment*, 528.

85 *OR* 42, pt. 1, 437, 496.

Reconnoitering in front of his left, Crawford rode into the clearing at Dabney's Mill, where he spotted a cavalry detachment. Told by the horse soldiers that the II Corps was a considerable distance to his front, Crawford urged his men on. The pace of the advance was snail-like. After what seemed like hours, Crawford reached Crow's farm—"a wide open space under cultivation." To the east, about 200 yards away, Hatcher's Run made a sharp meander. Here the timber had been felled, so as to make any movement up the bank of the stream impracticable.

Crawford now lost valuable time as he mistook the branch which discharges into Hatcher's Run at this point for the main stream. After the general had oriented himself, he sent Hofmann's brigade forward by the flank, while Bragg's battle line crossed Crow's field. Hofmann's soldiers, covered by a line of skirmishers, moved so rapidly that without realizing it, they passed Bragg's battle line. Hofmann sent out scouts when he discovered that Bragg's troops were no longer to his front. Within a few minutes, they returned and reported that because of the jungle-like conditions, they had been unable to locate Bragg's troops.

Hofmann halted his column. Before resuming his advance, he formed his brigade into line of battle, covering it with a strong force of skirmishers. A 200-yard advance brought the Federals up against a "heavy line" of Confederate sharpshooters. The Rebels banged away at Hofmann's bluecoats. An eyewitness reported, "The troops were a little scared, and many stragglers began running to the rear; but few bullets seemed to come from the enemy. Our line then commenced to cheer, and advance rapidly, firing all the while. The firing from the enemy was very feeble." The engagement which ensued was short but decisive; the grey clads being driven across Hatcher's Run.[86]

Another group of Confederates at the same time had assailed Bragg's skirmish line, as it entered the woods north of Crow's farm. The bluecoats held their ground, and, reinforced by the 150th Pennsylvania, they drove back the butternuts, capturing one of Brigadier General John R. Cooke's North Carolinians.[87]

The shooting served as a guide, and enabled Bragg and Hofmann to re-establish contact. One of Bragg's aides galloped up and told Hofmann to retire. In answer to Hofmann's inquiry, the staff officer pinpointed Bragg's brigade as 500 yards to his left and rear. Before the order could be executed, it was

---

86　*Ibid.*, 438, 441, 496, 507, 525. Hofmann's brigade included: the 56th Pennsylvania, 200 strong; the 121st Pennsylvania, 58 officers and men; the 142nd Pennsylvania, 150 strong; the 76th New York, 133 rank and file; the 95th New York, 213 strong; the 147th New York, 179 strong; the headquarters guard and pioneers, 43 officers and men; total, 1,013. *Ibid.*, 525.

87　*Ibid.*, 496.

countermanded. Subsequently, the order was repeated, and the brigade moved back and fell in on Bragg's left.[88]

General Crawford, on making a reconnaissance, found that Bragg's skirmishers had advanced 150 yards beyond the point where Griffin's left anchored on the north bank of Hatcher's Run. This was the reason for Hofmann's recall. After Hofmann's bluecoats had taken position on Bragg's left, Crawford "detached a regiment to examine the right bank of the creek near my present position, and to feel the enemy's works." The regiment took position and blazed away, enfilading one of Heth's units posted in the rifle pits north of the run. This fire disconcerted the grey clads, but being veterans they did not panic. After redeploying to meet this threat to their flank and rear, the Confederates returned the Federals' fire.[89]

By 1:00 p.m., Heth was confronted by his first crisis of the day. He was paying Brigadier General Joseph R. Davis (the President's nephew) a visit when everyone heard firing to the right. A few minutes later Lieutenant G.W. Cornelius of the 2nd Mississippi reported to General Davis from the right. "General, they have broken our line and my command has been forced to retreat." Crawford had sent one of his regiments across Hatcher's Run and it had begun firing into the rear and flank of Davis' Brigade, which was already under fire from Griffin's troops in its front.[90] General Davis summoned Colonel John M. Stone who commanded the 2nd Mississippi and placed him in charge of the three, right-flank regiments of the brigade and ordered him to drive back the Federals. Stone pulled his men out of the line and faced the Federals. Believing the Federals had more men than he did, he informed his officers, "We are going to advance and I expect will be cut to pieces." Fortunately for the Confederates, Crawford only sent one regiment and not a brigade to threaten the Confederate flank. Stone and his regiments charged them and drove them across Hatcher's Run.

At 1:00 p.m., General Warren rode up to Crawford's command post. A hasty inspection demonstrated to the corps commander that Crawford's troops were just where he wanted them—"on the right flank of the enemy's position fronting Griffin." He could see that the steep banks and slashed timber at this point would make it difficult for Crawford's troops to force a crossing of Hatcher's Run. Moreover, as Crawford explained to Warren, the march through the "jungle" had

88 *Ibid.*, 525.

89 *Ibid.*, 496.

90 Lieutenant Charles R. Jones, "Historical Sketch of Fifty-Fifth North Carolina Infantry" in Our Living and Our Dead, May 13, 1874, 1; Charles M. Cooke, "Fifty Fifth Regiment" in Clark's *Histories of the Several Regiments and Battalions from North Carolina in the Great War 1861-1865, vol. 3,* 311.

caused whole regiments to lose their way. Warren told Crawford to hold his ground and press the foe with his skirmishers, while he rode to discuss the situation with Meade, who was reportedly at Hancock's headquarters. As Warren galloped off, Crawford checked the time: it was 4:00 p.m.[91]

Major Roebling in the meantime had been riding along Bragg's skirmish line, and he found its right was on the creek, directly in front of the Rebel rifle pits on the left bank. The breastworks near Hatcher's Run had been evacuated. At this moment, a 20-man Confederate squad appeared atop a knoll north of the run and fired at the major's party, killing an orderly. As he retired downstream, Roebling saw that Griffin's skirmish line connected with Bragg's battle line. A dozen of Griffin's men were on Crawford's side of the stream, having crossed on a log. There was no officer with them. Roebling told them to find their officer and tell him that the Rebels had pulled out of their breastworks, and "to go up and occupy them." Roebling contacted Crawford next and inquired, "Why have you halted when victory is in your grasp?"

"I have positive orders from Warren not to advance another step," was the reply.

Captain Dennis Dailey of Warren's staff now rode up and begged to be allowed to ford the stream, which was waist-deep, with 50 volunteers to mop-up the line of rifle pits.

"Permission refused," Crawford snapped.

Whereupon, Roebling thundered off up a cart road to see if he could find Warren and explain to him the situation.[92]

*   *   *

At this time, Gen. Robert E. Lee was at Chaffin's Bluff, north of the James, Lieutenant General Ambrose P. Hill having been left to look after the units charged with holding the Petersburg lines. On October 25-26 there were signs of stepped-up Union activities on the north side of the James, and on the morning of the 27th elements from Major General Benjamin F. Butler's Army of the James attacked vigorously along the entire front from the New Market to the Charles City Roads.[93] Simultaneously, Lee received reports that the bluecoats had crossed Hatcher's Run and were driving for Boydton Plank Road. Colonel Walter H. Taylor

---

91 *Ibid.*, 438.

92 *Ibid.*, 441-442.

93 *Ibid.*, 871.

of Lee's staff remarked, "It looks like a sure enough advance,"[94] while Colonel Charles Marshall, in more formal phrase, notified Secretary of War James A. Seddon, "There . . . appears to be a simultaneous movement on both flanks." The government was profoundly alarmed and called the last available reserves, the munitions workers and the cadets, to its defense.[95]

Counter-operations on the South Side had to be left to the judgment of Generals Hill and Hampton. North of the James, Lee left the dispositions to Lieutenant General James Longstreet, who had returned to duty eight days before. Never did Lee have better reason to trust the military judgment of Longstreet. The front opposite Fort Burnham had been carefully planted with subterra shells or "land mines," after its capture by the Federals on September 29, so Longstreet had nothing to fear along that sector, which the Chaffin's Bluff garrison manned. He massed two divisions—Hoke's and Field's—on the front of attack, and soon became convinced that the bluecoats might be preparing to turn the upper end of the outer line, which was undefended. Boldly shifting his infantry as far northward as Williamsburg Road, Longstreet sent Brigadier General Martin W. Gary's cavalry to occupy the fortifications on Nine Mile Road. In the course of a few hours, he repulsed the foe, capturing 600 prisoners and 11 battle flags. No drive north of the James, during the entire investment of Richmond, had been broken up so readily.[96]

On the South Side, the Federals' numbers were large and their advance rapid. If he determined to march to meet the Federals, General Hill would be compelled to leave thousands of soldiers to hold the extensive Petersburg earthworks. Hill liked to fight, however, so it was not difficult for a man of his temperament to make this decision. Major General Henry Heth was responsible for the sector of the Confederate line closest to the attacking Federals.

On the morning of October 27, Heth commanded his own division; Lane's and McGowan's brigades from Wilcox's division; Dearing's cavalry brigade; and 600-800 dismounted cavalry occupying the Confederate army's extreme right.[97]

Hill put Heth in charge of stopping Hancock's drive toward the South Side Railroad. Word reached Heth that Federal troops were moving down his lines to

94 Douglas S. Freeman, *R. E. Lee: A Biography*, 4 vols. (New York, 1934-1935), vol. 3, 513.

95 *OR* 42, pt. 3, 1178.

96 Freeman, *R. E. Lee*, vol. 3, 513. On May 6, 1864, Longstreet had been seriously wounded in the battle of the Wilderness.

97 Heth's report, Janet Hewitt, *Supplement to the Official Records of the Union and Confederate Armies*. 100 vols. Wilmington, NC: Broadfoot 1997, vol. 7, 480. Hereafter referred to as Supplement to the *OR*.

turn his right. He dispatched Brigadier General Joseph R. Davis' Mississippi brigade to reinforce the dismounted cavalry on his right flank. About this time, Brigadier General James Dearing sent Heth word that Hampton had ordered him to leave his section of the line and report to him with the mounted portion of his command. Heth informed Dearing that this would not be possible until he replaced his force with a brigade of infantry. Heth ordered Gen. John R. Cooke to take Dearing's place.[98]

Generals Hill, Heth, and Hampton, on the afternoon of October 27, soon to be joined by Major General William Mahone, proved to be an unbeatable combination as they took advantage of Union errors to more than hold their own.

Through the use of couriers Heth and Hampton worked out a plan of attack.

Heth would be in field command as General Mahone capitalized on blunders by General Meade and his corps commanders. With this force, Heth was to cross Hatcher's Run, advance into the wilderness beyond, and see if he could interpose between the II and V Corps. If he could, Heth was to assail Hancock's right, while Hampton's dismounted troopers struck the II Corps' left and rear. Dearing's dismounted troopers would strike the II Corps' left and rear and hold the rifle pits to Hancock's front, covering the bridge at Burgess Mill, while Heth was feeling his way into position.[99]

When Heth took the field, Brigadier General Bushrod Johnson with his division (reinforced by Brigadier General Joseph Finegan's and Colonel William Gibson's brigades of Mahone's division, and Archer's 3rd Battalion, Virginia Reserves) occupied the fortifications from the Appomattox to Battery No. 45.[100] Three brigades of Major General Cadmus Wilcox's Light Division held the works from a point opposite Fort Welch to Battery No. 45. Wilcox's other brigade—Brigadier General Edward L. Thomas—was north of the Appomattox and had been stationed there since July 4. It was on the night of October 2 that Wilcox's butternuts had taken position in this area, and the next morning they had commenced erecting breastworks. This was the beginning of the line of fortifications extending from Battery No. 45 to Hatcher's Run. Heth's division threw up and occupied the rifle pits on Wilcox's right. From right to left Wilcox's brigades were posted: Brigadier General Samuel McGowan's, "Little Jim" Lane's, and Alfred M. Scales'.

---

98 Clark, *North Carolina Regiments*, vol. 2, 449.

99 Walker, "The Expedition to the Boydton Plank Road," 335-336.

100 *OR* 42, pt. 3, 1180.

Major General Henry Heth
Library of Congress

General Heth's division was responsible for the defense of the newly erected rifle pits from Hatcher's Run on the right to Wilcox's left. General Cooke's North Carolina brigade was on the right; Colonel Robert M. Mayo's Consolidated brigade on the right center; Brigadier General Joseph R. Davis' Mississippi brigade on the left center; and Brigadier General William MacRae's North Carolina brigade anchored the left. MacRae's command post was at Hart's house.

General Hill's ready reserve consisted of three of General Mahone's brigades—Brig. Gen's. Nathaniel Harris', David A. Weisiger's, and Colonel J. Horace King's—which were camped between the Weldon Railroad and Battery No. 45. There was an air of expectancy on October 24, as Sgt. John F. Sale of the 12th Virginia, Weisiger's brigade, wrote in his diary:

> Nothing of interest has transpired for some time. Considerable artillery firing & picket firing has been going on for some time, but no movements of any importance has taken place. Large numbers of conscripts are daily being sent forward to recruit our army, and with but a few days drilling and the example of the old soldiers they will be as good as any, and our army will be as large as before the campaign. Where on earth the new men come from I cannot see, but they do come from somewhere is a visible certainty, our regiment alone having received about 100. Deserters are coming out of the enemy's lines to join us, some 35 or 40 persons having come to my knowledge.[101]

---

101 Caldwell, *The History of the Brigade of South Carolinians*, 187. Sergeant John F. Sale, Diary, n.d., Virginia State Library.

As soon as the outposts raised the alarm on the 27th, Generals Heth and Wilcox's brigade commanders saw that the "'long roll" was beaten. The troops were turned out on the double and the lines manned. By 9:00 a.m., the pickets had been driven in, and the bluecoats of the V and IX Corps had appeared before the felled timber fronting the works held by Cooke's, Mayo's, and Davis' brigades.

General Hill, upon being alerted that the Yankees were attempting to turn his right, called for General Mahone to bring up the portion of his division that could be spared from the line. Even before the order to fall out was heard in the trenches occupied by Weisiger's and King's troops, the sound of heavy firing off to the southwest told the soldiers that the much dreaded thrust toward the Army of Northern Virginia's right was under way. Mahone also ordered General Harris to withdraw his Mississippi brigade from its position in the trenches as soon as he was relieved and to follow the division on Boydton Plank Road in the direction of Burgess Mill. It was not until noon that Harris was relieved from trench duty.[102]

At 9:00 a.m. Mahone told his brigade commanders to form their units. Within a short time, the troops had turned out under arms and in light marching order. When Mahone passed the order to move out, Weisiger's Virginia brigade took the lead. There was a 30-minute halt at Battery No. 45, while Mahone checked with General Hill. Instructions having been received to report to General Heth, Mahone turned his two brigades into Boydton Plank Road. Accompanying Mahone were portions of two batteries from Lieutenant Colonel William J. Pegram's Artillery Battalion: Ellet's under Lieutenant Edward G. Hollis and Gregg's. At Gill's plantation, the infantry abandoned the Plank Road in favor of the Military Road to Stony Creek. Here General Mahone was met by a guide sent by General Heth. The artillery continued its march to join Dearing at the bridge over Hatcher's Run.[103]

The guide, familiar with the area, led the way as Weisiger's Virginians and King's Alabamians tramped along seldom frequented byroads. Off to the east and southwest, the soldiers heard the rattle of musketry and the roar of cannon. The head of the column soon reached the dam Confederate pioneers had built across Hatcher's Run, to back up water toward the bridge at Burgess Mill.

Not long before Mahone's vanguard arrived at the dam, General Heth learned that Crawford's division, having crossed Hatcher's Run at Armstrong's Mill, was pressing up the south bank of that stream in a drive to establish contact with Hancock's corps at Burgess Mill. To gain time, Heth called on General Cooke for 75 picked marksmen. Crossing the run on the double, the North Carolina

---

102 Supplement to *OR*, vol. 7, 471.

103 *OR* vol. 42, pt. 1, 860.

sharpshooters moved off into the dense pines. Taking advantage of the terrain, the North Carolinians stalled Crawford's division in the jungle north of Crow's clearing.

Satisfied that the V and IX Corps did not intend to make a serious assault on the Rebel works northeast of Hatcher's Run, Heth called in his left flank brigade—MacRae's—to take the North Carolinians' place behind the breastworks. McGowan's brigade extended to the right. MacRae's butternuts reported to Heth at the dam.

Generals Heth and Mahone now listened intently as several of Cooke's scouts, who had just re-crossed the run, reported that there was a gap between Hancock's right and Crawford's troops. Heth decided to capitalize on this Union blunder. Before putting his infantry in motion, Heth contacted General Hampton. Between them, the two generals perfected their plans. As soon as the foot soldiers had crossed Hatcher's Run, Heth was to notify Hampton. When the roar of battle indicating that Mahone had attacked reached his command post, Hampton would send Butler's dismounted cavalrymen sweeping down White Oak Road against Hancock's left.

Heth and Mahone now crossed the dam with two of Mahone's brigades—Weisiger's and King's and MacRae's North Carolinians—and, piloted part of the way by Heth, followed "an old blind wood road" through the wilderness toward Boydton Plank Road. While they were on the march Heth explained that Hampton would attack from the west and south as soon as he heard Mahone's guns and that Dearing would attack with his brigade and Harris' Mississippi brigade and possibly Scales' North Carolina brigade if the latter came up in time.[104]

At this point Heth received word from General Dearing that Hancock had driven him from the bridge over Hatcher's Run, that he had fallen back, and that all the roads leading into Heth's rear were open to the Federals, so Heth left Mahone to join Dearing.[105]

Because of the dense woods, Heth had left his artillery north of Hatcher's Run. Slipping his column through the gap separating Hancock's right and Crawford's front, Mahone soon learned from his scouts that he had gained an excellent position from which to launch an attack on Hancock's right and rear.

A halt was called to allow the brigade commanders to form their units into line of battle. Weisiger's Virginia brigade was posted on the left, MacRae's North Carolina brigade on the right, and King's Alabamians in support. The 12th Virginia

---

104 Supplement to *OR* vol. 7, 481-482.

105 Supplement to *OR* vol. 7, 482.

was on the extreme left, so General Weisiger called for the company to which Sergeant Sale was assigned to deploy as flankers. While his butternuts were filing into position, General MacRae reconnoitered to his front, and observed that the Federals had blundered in positioning their artillery too near the woods. As soon as skirmishers had been advanced, Mahone passed the word for the assault to begin. Forty-five hundred combat-harden veterans forged through the woods toward the fields occupied by Hancock's right flank unit, Pierce's brigade.[106]

Late in the afternoon, it started to rain and Heth called for reinforcements, and King's Alabamians crossed Hatcher's Run.[107]

*　　*　　*

For a better understanding of the tactical situation in which the Federals found themselves at the time that the Confederates were deploying for a counterstroke, we must recall that in accordance with the latest orders from army headquarters, Parke, having entered a fortified zone, was to confront the foe in his works, "until the operations on the left (should) draw off the Confederates." In which case, he was to attack without regard to the strength of the Rebels' position to his front.

Meade's alternate plan was now ready to execute, though it was not a course of action upon which he was "disposed to insist." As we shall see, Meade, with Grant's concurrence, gave the order to cancel it, although no disaster or check, except from the nature of the geography of eastern Dinwiddie County, had been experienced.

What was this "plan?" It was to employ Parke's IX Corps to keep the Rebels pinned in their defenses east of Hatcher's Run and throw Warren's V Corps across that stream. Warren's men would then be left to hold Boydton Plank Road, while Hancock struck for the South Side Railroad by way of White Oak Road.

It is apparent that the revised master plan was much less sweeping in its scope. With less manpower being committed, there was less chance of success. First, the "active force" had been reduced from three corps to two. Second, considerable time had been squandered in "defining" the Confederates' position and in reaching the conclusion that an attack on the Rebel fortifications by Parke would be unprofitable. Hours, every minute of which was precious, had elapsed, during

---

106　*Ibid.*, Walker, "The Expedition to the Boydton Plank Road," 335-336, 348-349; Caldwell, *The History of a Brigade of South Carolinians*, 187; Dunbar Rowland, *The Official and Statistical Register of the State of Mississippi, 1908* (Nashville, 1908), 436, 450, 466, 493, 507, 511, 514; Charles Stedman, "The Forty-Fourth North Carolina Infantry," in *Southern Historical Society Papers*, (Richmond, 1876), vol. 25, 343.

107　OR 42, pt. 1, 457.

which a vigilant and resourceful foe was making preparations to counter the impending blow.

Reduced in size and possible importance, as was Meade's modified plan, it was soon emasculated by action by Union brass. Instead of pushing Warren as far as possible across Hatcher's Run with his entire corps, thus throwing upon Parke the responsibility of holding the Confederates in their breastworks northeast of the stream, Meade had informed Hancock that only one division of the V Corps—Crawford's—was to ford Hatcher's Run.

What Meade hoped to gain by these new dispositions was that Crawford, by advancing rapidly up the south bank of the run, would compel the Confederates defending the rifle pits fronting the V and IX Corps to abandon their positions. With the Rebels gone, Warren and Parke could then cross Hatcher's Run and in conjunction with Hancock, slash deeply into the rear of the Petersburg defenses. Whether it was Meade's intention to push on out White Oak Road, or to wheel his column to the right and roll up the Confederate line, we do not know.

There was always another possibility—that General Hill, feeling the heavy hand of the foe upon Boydton Plank Road, would seize the initiative and advance to strike the intruding force a fearful blow. This possibility, which was made a strong probability by the often and bitterly experienced audacity of the Confederates, made it imperative that Crawford waste no time in establishing contact with Hancock. Delay on Crawford's part could result in losing a chance for victory, or worse, it could invite defeat and disaster.[108]

Promptly on being notified by Meade of the changed plan, Hancock moved to open communications with Crawford. Unknown to the Federal leaders, the Confederates were already moving to capitalize on their errors.

---

108 Walker, "The Expedition to the Boydton Plank Road," 327-328. People who like to "Monday morning quarterback" speculate that Meade should have pushed Warren's entire corps across Hatcher's Run, throwing on Parke the responsibility for keeping the Rebels pinned in their earthworks northeast of Armstrong's Mill. With the entire V Corps across Hatcher's Run, Warren could have assumed responsibility of holding the area embraced within the angle of the stream, including the bridge at Burgess Mill. Hancock would have thus been free to strike for the South Side Railroad with his two infantry divisions, reinforced by Gregg's cavalry.

Part IV

The II Corps Gamely Holds On in the Face of Heth's Onslaught

General Hancock, immediately after General Gregg and his horse soldiers had reported, ordered General Egan's II Corps division to drive the Rebels posted on the high ground at Burgess Mill across Hatcher's Run. While Rugg's and Willett's battle lines, covered by a strong force of skirmishers, moved forward, Lieutenant Beck's cannoneers of Batteries C and I, 5th U.S. Light Artillery engaged the Rebel battery emplaced at Burgess Tavern. General Smyth's brigade emerged from the pines flanking the road to Dabney's Mill at this time.

Hancock hailed Egan and told him to deploy Smyth's troops to cover the division's left and rear. To do this, Smyth formed his men into battle line on the left of the Dabney's Mill Road, and advanced skirmishers. As soon as Mott's lead brigade tramped into view, Egan recalled Smyth's bluecoats. Egan directed Smyth to redeploy his soldiers on the right of Rugg's brigade and in support of Willett's. As Smyth's men fell in on their colors, preparatory to carrying out their new assignment, Mott's 1st Brigade (de Trobriand's) came up and assumed responsibility for guarding the II Corps' left and rear. Crossing a plantation road, Smyth promptly formed his men in an "open field on the right of and on the prolongation of Colonel Rugg's line."[109]

General Egan, as soon as he saw Smyth's column marching up Plank Road, ordered Willett (whose brigade had heretofore been posted on Rugg's left) "to advance and carry the enemy's position on the hill crest near the Burgess house." Captain Embler and the skirmishers of the 19th and 20th Massachusetts, reinforced by the 69th Pennsylvania, charged on the double, followed closely by Willett's brigade. As he would be advancing across open ground, Willett, to reduce casualties, had deployed his brigade as skirmishers. With Captain Embler riding in advance, the bluecoats stormed ahead. General Dearing's dismounted troopers were driven through a belt of timber and across a "swampy ravine." Valuable time

---

109 OR 42, pt. 1, 296, 326, 330, 331, 333, 335, 336, 411. The regulars had emplaced their Napoleons at the junction of the Dabney's Mill and Boydton Plank roads. A Confederate battery (possibly the Washington South Carolina Artillery) had taken position near Mrs. Rainey's and had fired several rounds, taking the II Corps' battle lines in reverse. The approach of Gregg's column compelled the Rebels to retire these guns.

Major General William Mahone
Library of Congress

was lost as Embler's and Willett's skirmish lines worked their way down and up the other side of the underbrush-choked hollow.

As they scrambled up the north slope, Embler and Willett called a halt to reform their lines. Dearing's pickets by this time had joined their comrades on the high ground at Burgess barn, east of the Plank Road. Resuming their advance, the Yanks dislodged Dearing's butter-nuts and smashed the roadblock. The Confederates had barricaded Boydton Plank Road at a tollgate, but as General Egan wrote in his after-action report, his men failed to observe Virginia highway regulations and no toll was paid.[110]

Embler and his skirmishers sought to cut off the Rebels as they "retreated to the right and across [a] wide sheet of water, where their horses waited them." North of the pond, the cannoneers of the Petersburg Virginia Artillery had unlimbered a gun, which opened on the bluecoats.

Colonel Willett, after his foot soldiers had mopped-up the area, redeployed his brigade into line of battle on the commanding ground from which they had driven Dearing's dismounted troopers. The brigade, except for the left wing which was refused at nearly a right angle, held the military crest of the ridge overlooking Hatcher's Run. To strengthen their position, the men turned to throwing up breastworks.[111]

---

110 *Ibid.*, 296, 309-310, 319.

111 *Ibid.*, 296, 309-310, 319, 337. Willett's left flank was anchored on the left side of the Plank Road.

As soon as General Egan saw Willett's battleflags reach Burgess barn, he ordered Colonel Rugg's battle line forward. Rugg's brigade moved up Plank Road and formed on Willett's left. Rugg, after examining the terrain, anchored his left on a ravine. The 1st Minnesota Battalion and the 7th Michigan were thrown out as skirmishers and given the task of protecting the brigade's left. The 19th and 20th Massachusetts reported back to Rugg and were assigned positions behind the barricades being erected by soldiers of the 1st Brigade.[112]

General Smyth's 3rd Brigade was now advanced and formed in an open field on Willett's right. As they hiked up Plank Road, Smyth's column was shelled by the Petersburg Artillery posted north of Hatcher's Run. To protect his right, Smyth saw that the 10th New York and the 12th New Jersey were positioned in echelon on that flank.[113]

Having advanced his division 800 yards, Egan called upon Lieutenant Beck to post two of his Napoleons on the ridge from which Willett's brigade had dislodged the Rebels. The right section, 2nd Lieutenant Richard Metcalf commanding, was advanced and unlimbered its guns in a cornfield on the right of Plank Road. Beck's left section was to be emplaced on the crest near the Burgess house. As the cannoneers of the left section drove their teams up Plank Road, they came under a well-aimed fire from rifled guns of the Washington South Carolina Artillery, posted some distance up White Oak Road. Beck had his regulars in action practically as soon as the trails struck the ground. While the left section fought the South Carolinians' guns, Metcalf's hammered away at Butler's dismounted troopers as they filed into position in the woods, one-half mile to the west.

Within a short time, a second rifled Confederate battery (the Petersburg Artillery) added the weight of its metal to the duel. The gun crew threw their pieces into battery near the dam. At a range of 800 yards, they enfiladed Beck's left section. Beck, after telling the section leader to concentrate on the rifles to his left, rode to the rear and brought up at a gallop his center section. The artillerists threw these Napoleons into battery at right angles to the left section, and blazed away at the Rebel rifles at the dam. Ellett's Virginia Battery now reached the field and put two 3-inch rifles into action at a point east of the dam. Beck sent word for Metcalf to take care of this threat.

The Confederate gunners did their best to drive the regulars from the commanding ground at Burgess Mill. But for the "bad practice of their gunners,"

112 *Ibid.*, 296, 303, 306, 308, 310, 312, 314.

113 *Ibid.*, 296, 326, 330, 333-335, 337.

Beck reported, he feared "there would have been but little left of my battery." As it was, most of the Confederates' projectiles either passed overhead or fell short.[114]

At 1:10 p.m. on October 27, General Hancock dispatched Major Henry H. Bingham to ascertain the whereabouts of General Crawford's V Corps troops while the field pieces bellowed. Accompanied by ten cavalrymen, the major took a road leading to the southeast. Bingham, after a mile ride, encountered General Crawford at Crow's house. He informed the V Corps general that at the moment his people were within three-quarters of a mile of Hancock's right. On Crawford's map, Bingham pointed out the Burgess house, "designating it as a point held by the line of the Second Corps and part of its front." At the time that he had ridden off on his mission, the major continued, the Confederates still held the bridge carrying Boydton Plank Road across Hatcher's Run, but Hancock and his officers had been discussing the "propriety of its capture."

Crawford, in turn, indicated on the map a point which he expected to reach whereupon, he planned to throw "around his left" and connect "with the right of the Second Corps."[115]

While Bingham was absent, Generals Grant and Meade and their entourage had visited the II Corps' front. As soon as Major Bingham returned and reported Crawford's position, Generals Grant and Meade took leave of Hancock's command post. On doing so, they gave Hancock verbal orders to hold his position until the following morning, when he was to retire by the road over which he had advanced.[116]

It seems to this observer that the responsibility of making the connection rested on Crawford. Hancock, engaged with the foe at Burgess Mill and holding a key position, could hardly be expected to shift to the right to contact Crawford. Crawford was to advance from the southeast and place his division on Hancock's right. To facilitate a link-up between their commands, Hancock had ordered Smyth's brigade into position on Willett's right, and called for skirmishers to be pushed farther toward the southeast.[117]

While these dispositions were being effected, the dismounted Rebel cavalry pressed Hancock's left and front. Dearing's troopers undertook a determined

---

114 *Ibid.*, 296, 411, 427. Metcalf's Napoleons were unlimbered "on the crest in rear of the ravine near the tavern," while the left section was posted west of the ravine and about one-fourth mile to the left of Metcalf's section.

115 *Ibid.*, 238-239.

116 *Ibid.*, 232.

117 Walker, "The Expedition to the Boydton Plank Road," 329.

sortie. Re-crossing Hatcher's Run, they drove in Willett's skirmishers and surged up the slope toward Burgess Mill where the center and left sections of Batteries C and I were emplaced. Beck waited anxiously until the grey clads had closed to within 200 yards, before he shouted for his cannoneers to shift targets. Pointing their four Napoleons at the onrushing Johnnies, the regulars blasted "them with canister, and with such good effect that they halted" and took cover. Fearing that Dearing might renew the attack as soon as he had regrouped, Beck shifted his left section, bringing it up on line with the center section.[118]

General Hancock now sent word for Egan to throw forward Smyth's brigade—his right wing. At a word from Smyth, skirmishers of the 1st Delaware and the 108th New York advanced across the field east of the Plank Road. Close behind came Smyth's battle line. Dearing's dismounted horse soldiers were dislodged from the toehold they had secured in front of Beck's Napoleons. Continuing their push, the bluecoats compelled the Southerners to abandon their rifle pits south of the run. Some of Smyth's soldiers followed the retreating butternuts across Hatcher's Run, penetrated the swamp beyond, and started to ascend the ridge. On their left, the 164th New York of Willett's brigade had moved out. Near the bridge, the New Yorkers captured a 12-pounder gun, limber, and caisson abandoned by the Petersburg Artillery. While the Yanks brought off the caisson, they were unable to locate enough rope to drag off gun and limber, which were left behind when they were recalled.[119]

As soon as General Egan saw that Smyth's bluecoats had driven the Confederates across the run, he sent an aide to recall the men who had forded the stream and another to order Colonel Willett to report to Smyth. In its advance, Smyth's battle line had inclined to the left and was now between Willett's brigade and Hatcher's Run. When Willett reported to him, Smyth placed the 170th and 182nd New York in the rifle pits west of the Plank Road, while the 164th New York and 8th New York Heavy Artillery were posted on the right of the Third Brigade.[120]

---

118 OR 42, pt. 1, 427.

119 *Ibid.*, 297, 326, 331, 334-335, 337. Captain T. J. Burke of the 164th New York reported, after Willett's brigade had occupied the hill on Burgess' farm, and Smyth's brigade "had united on the right, he saw the line advancing, and believing it to be the whole line he also moved forward upon the left . . . of [Smyth's] brigade, and entering the woods soon found himself, with ten men of his company, in rear of the enemy's works, who were hastily evacuating the same, and captured one 12-pounder gun and 1 small caisson, which, being unable to remove, they broke off the axles of the gun carriage, and threw the gun into the stream . . . ; that they drew off the caisson. . . ." *Ibid.*, 320.

120 *Ibid.*, 297, 326. General Smyth led the 3rd Brigade, Second Division, II Army Corps.

Egan, having been notified that Crawford's division was somewhere off to his right, told Smyth to see if he could establish contact with the V Corps. Smyth called for the 10th New York, and Lieutenant Colonel George F. Hopper was told to take his regiment and go into position on the right of the 8th New York Heavy Artillery. Although he deployed his infantrymen at 10-pace intervals, Hopper was unable to establish contact with Crawford. Shots could be heard off to the southeast, so a six-man patrol was ordered out by Hopper "to ascertain what troops were engaged in that direction."[121]

The enfilading fire of the Washington South Carolina Artillery rifled guns emplaced out on White Oak Road so annoyed Hancock that he called for General Gregg to capture or drive them away. Gregg delegated to Colonel Kerwin the task of dealing with the battery. Three regiments—the 8th, 13th, and 16th Pennsylvania Cavalry—moved out. Before proceeding very far, Gregg told the men to halt, while he and his escort reconnoitered the Rebels' position. Gregg mistook Butler's dismounted cavalry for infantry. Seeing that the Confederates were posted behind hurriedly erected barricades, Gregg decided that it would be foolish to attack; he told Kerwin to hold his ground.[122]

At 3:00 p.m., Hancock decided to launch a frontal assault across Hatcher's Run and establish a bridgehead. Egan, whose division held the high ground at Burgess Tavern, would be in charge of the attacking force, but needed to be reinforced first. Colonel Robert McAllister's brigade of Mott's division was ordered to Egan's support.

McAllister's brigade hiked up the Plank Road, turning to the right along the crest of the ridge overlooking the dam. McAllister reported to Egan here, and in accordance with Egan's instructions, McAllister formed his brigade in double line of battle in rear of the 10th New York.[123]

By this time, Lieutenant Beck had been warned by the chiefs of his left center sections that they were running short of ammunition. If Egan's attacking infantry were to be assured of proper artillery support, a fresh battery should be called up. Chief of Artillery John C. Hazard arrived on the field with the 10th Battery, Massachusetts Light Artillery and Battery K of the 4th U.S. Light Artillery. These guns were parked near the junction of the Dabney Mill and Plank Roads. Seeing

---

121 *Ibid.*, 326, 334.

122 *Ibid.*, 232, 641; Walker, "The Expedition to the Boydton Plank Road," 330-331.

123 OR 42, pt. 1, 297, 395. Within 15 minutes of the time he had formed his brigade in double line of battle, McAllister redeployed his troops in single line extending his left to the Plank Road. *Ibid.*, 395.

that Beck needed assistance, Hazard told Lieutenant Henry H. Granger of the Massachusetts battery to take his six 10-pounder Parrotts and place them in position alongside Beck's Napoleons.

The battery historian recalled:

> Twas but a moment, however, for we are wanted at the front, and leaving caissons behind, out upon the Plank Road dash the pieces at a lively trot. We have a half-mile run before us ere getting into position, and no sooner are we fairly on the road than we become the object of warm attention from the enemy's guns, whose shells crash through the trees and fence by the roadside as we go. But on we press, galloping up the rise in the road just south of where it meets the White Oak Road, and wheel to the right into a field, unlimbering near a barn. We are opposite the entrance of the White Oak Road . . . on the corner of it and the Plank Road stands . . . an unpretentious wood-colored hostelry, known as Burgess Tavern or house. We at once join battle with the enemy's batteries posted across the Run near Burgess Mill.

As they unlimbered their Parrotts, the Massachusetts cannoneers observed that the fire of the Confederate guns, which had caught Beck's regulars in a crossfire, had slowed. Egan ordered Beck to the rear with his center and left sections. When his men parked their four Napoleons next to Battery K, Beck reported to Hazard that "he had expended all of his ammunition except canister."[124]

The Confederates at this time brought up Gregg's South Carolina battery. Gregg's cannoneers quickly threw their four Napoleons into battery and dueled with the 10th Massachusetts' Parrotts.

Rugg's brigade of Mott's division continued to guard Hancock's left. While his skirmishers sniped at Butler's dismounted troopers, Rugg's battle line was shelled by the guns of the Washington South Carolina Artillery, but the configuration of the terrain was such that casualties were slight.[125]

General Mott had stayed with his 2nd Brigade, General Pierce's. Early in the afternoon, Mott had received instructions from Hancock to detail two regiments to support Lieutenant Metcalf's section. Pierce accordingly ordered out the 5th Michigan and the 93rd New York. These two regiments were posted in the woods east of the cornfield in which Metcalf's regulars manned their two brass Napoleons.

---

124 *Ibid.*, 411-412, 427; John D. Billings, *The History of the Tenth Massachusetts Battery of Light Artillery in the War of the Rebellion* (Boston, 1909), 356-357. So far, Beck's battery had lost 3 killed and 7 wounded.

125 *OR* 42, pt. 1, 232, 359.

Colonel John Pulford, as senior officer, formed the two regiments at right angles to the battery, with skirmishers well forward. Mott, within a short time, told Pierce to advance the rest of the brigade and position it on the left of Metcalf's guns. Here the brigade remained for one hour and were subjected to a severe shelling.[126]

By 4:00 p.m., Egan had completed his dispositions and was prepared to wave his men forward. After approving Egan's battle plan, Hancock dispatched Lieutenant May H. Stacey to alert General Crawford that the II Corps was "about to assail the bridge, for which preparations were complete."[127]

About the same time, General Smyth, over on the right of Egan's battle line, had organized a patrol to ascertain Crawford's whereabouts. Lieutenant Charles W. Cowtan and six enlisted men started from the right of the 10th New York in a southeasterly direction. Before going very far, Cowtan and his men spotted a column of Rebel infantry. This force, which proved to be Heth's command, was moving by the flank toward the II Corps' rear. Retracing their steps, the New Yorkers told Smyth what they had seen. Smyth lost no time in relaying this news to Egan.

A fighting Irishman, Egan was determined to beat the foe to the punch. He told Smyth to force a crossing of Hatcher's Run at the mill dam.[128]

When the blue clads moved out, they were accompanied by Lieutenant Asa Smith's center section of the 10th Massachusetts Battery. Little difficulty was encountered by the Federal infantry in reaching Hatcher's Run. The 14th Connecticut crossed the run downstream from the bridge, while Smith and his artillerists unlimbered their Parrotts near the approach to the bridge, and hammered the Confederates posted on the ridge beyond with shot and shell. Smyth had alerted the 164th New York to be prepared to charge across the bridge, when a crashing volley of musketry off to the right and rear caused him to hesitate.[129]

Shortly before Egan told Smyth to attack, General Grant had ridden up to Burgess Mill to get a better view of the Confederate positions north of the run. He was trailed by his own and Meade's staff. The mounted cavalcade made a conspicuous target for the Rebel batteries, and the group was shelled. Several men were hit by flying fragments of iron; one was killed.

Several Grant aides rode out to reconnoiter. Their reports, however, were conflicting. It seemed as if no eyes but his own could determine exactly what Grant

126 *Ibid.*, 346, 367.

127 *Ibid.*, 232.

128 *Ibid.*, 326-334.

129 *Ibid.*, 297, 236, 330, 411; Billings, *History of the Tenth Massachusetts Battery*, 357-358.

wanted to know. Calling to Lieutenant Colonel Orville E. Babcock of his staff, Grant galloped down the Plank Road to within a few yards of the bridge, "exposed not only to the enemy's sharpshooters, but to the cross-fire of two Rebel batteries." The telegraph had been cut, and the feet of Grant's horse became entangled. Babcock was obliged to dismount and free them, while the officers on the ridge looked on in "suspense and thought how many campaigns depended on the life that now was endangered." But the general and his aide rode on until Grant could "clearly discern the Rebel line, the condition of the country, the course of the stream, and the nature of the banks."

Grant saw that Dearing's dismounted cavalry was in force north of Hatcher's Run, with strong defenses protecting their front. The Rebels entrenched line extended far beyond the area, where it had been presumed to veer to the north. When the Army of the Potomac had marched westward, units of Lee's Army of Northern Virginia had shifted to the right to counter this movement. Grant now concluded that the Confederates' redeployment made Meade's revised plan "impracticable." While the Southerners' fortified line north of Hatcher's Run might be stormed, it could only be done so at great risk. The advantage gained, in Grant's opinion, "would not compensate, while in the event of repulse, disaster might be grave," stretched out as the army was, with its flanks six miles apart, and Hatcher's Run dividing Warren's corps.

Any serious rebuff to Union arms was to be avoided with the presidential election only ten days away, and the Democrats certain to exaggerate every mishap. Politics for the moment were all important. It would therefore be unwise to take any risks.

When Grant returned from the bridge, he called to General Meade. After a brief conference, Meade gave verbal orders for Hancock to hold his position until morning, when he was to retire by the same road over which his column had advanced. The two ranking generals and their staffs then started for Armstrong's Mill.[130]

The volley that caused Smyth to pause had originated in the pines in front of Pierce's brigade. General Mott, a short time before, heard the shouts and shots in the woods east of the cornfield. A staff officer was told to investigate. He soon returned with news from General Pierce that the skirmishers were shooting at stragglers falling back before Crawford's advance.

---

130 Adam Badeau, *Military History of U. S. Grant*, 3 vols. (New York, 1868-1881), vol. 3, 120-121; *OR* 42, pt. 1, 232.

The firing got louder, so Mott instructed Pierce to reinforce his picket line. Pierce ordered out the 1st U.S. Sharpshooters. When the regulars reported to him in the pines, Colonel Pulford used them to prolong the right of his skirmish line. Hardly had the sharpshooters filed into position, before the fighting flared to a point where Pierce sent forward another regiment, the 105th Pennsylvania, with instructions to bolster the 5th Michigan.[131]

Heth's Confederate scouts, as they beat their way through the woods, ran afoul of Pierce's skirmish line. While runners raced to tell Heth what they had seen, the Confederate and Union skirmishers banged away. Mahone, whom Heth had placed in tactical command, ordered his three brigades to attack.

Meanwhile, Pierce shouted to his regiments lying in line in the cornfield, "Change front and face the woods!" Before this could be done, the grey clad battle line charged Pierce's skirmishers with vigor. A crashing volley, delivered by the blue clads, caused the Confederates to slow their front a few steps. Mahone's battle line, however, overlapped the right of Pierce's picket line for a considerable distance and MacRae's North Carolinians quickly enveloped the 93rd New York.

At the same time, a hard hitting Confederate detachment from Weisiger's brigade struck the right angle, where the 5th Michigan and the 1st U.S. Sharpshooters connected. Breaking through, the Virginians fanned out to the left and right. Sergeant Alonzo Woodruff and Cpl. John M. Howard of the 1st U.S. Sharpshooters were posted to the left of where the butternuts had ripped a gaping hole in Pierce's skirmish line. As the Virginians pressed forward, the two Yanks discharged their pieces. Unable to reload, Howard threw down his piece and tackled a big Rebel, "who seemed to be leading that part of their line." Overpowered by the Virginian, Howard fell wounded in both legs. Sergeant Woodruff rushed to his comrade's aid. Clubbing his rifle musket, Woodruff, in a desperate hand-to-hand encounter fended off the Confederates long enough to enable Howard and him to escape.

Following the Confederate breakthrough to their left, the men of the 1st U.S. Sharpshooters pulled back and reformed. Unable to hold their ground, the regiment then retreated to the edge of the woods, where it took cover behind a rail fence.[132]

General Pierce, seeing that the Rebels had rolled back the 1st U.S. Sharpshooters, bellowed for the 141st Pennsylvania "to charge the left of the enemy's line." As the 141st crossed the cornfield and approached the pines, the 1st

131 OR 42, pt. 1, 347, 368, 388.

132 Ibid., 347, 368, 388-389.

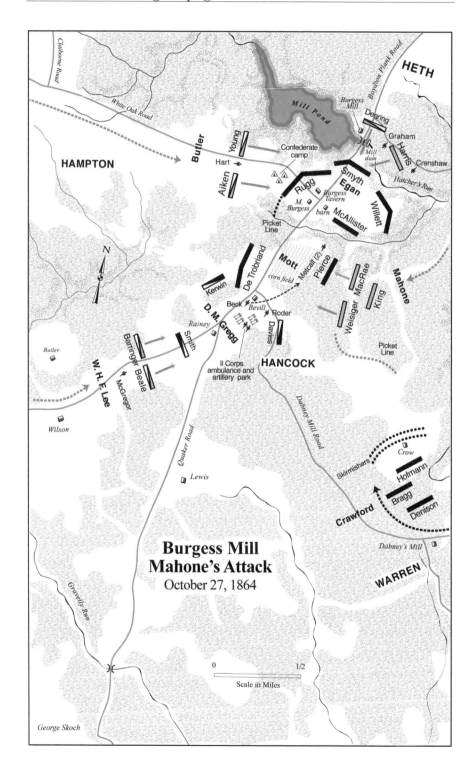

**Burgess Mill
Mahone's Attack**
October 27, 1864

George Skoch

U.S. Sharpshooters could be seen falling back in confusion hounded by "great masses" of Confederates. Lieutenant Colonel Casper W. Tyler ordered his Pennsylvanians to fire. The regiment was excited and difficult to control. Most of the men panicked. Tyler succeeded in holding the two or three companies nearest him at the point of the woods. Although exposed to a murderous fire, the Pennsylvanians "exchanged fifteen or twenty rounds with the enemy," before they were compelled to give way. Tyler and his men retreated and took cover behind the rail fence, where the officers of the 1st U.S. Sharpshooters rallied and reformed their men.[133]

The battle-hardened Confederates by now had all but encircled the troops, holding the left and center of Pierce's skirmish line. With Rebels to their front, right, and left, it became "root hog or die." Facing their foot soldiers to the rear, the officers in charge of the 5th Michigan, the 13th New York, and the 105th Pennsylvania sought to fight their way out of the woods, before the jaws of the trap snapped. Already, large numbers of Johnnies had infiltrated the ground over which they had to pass. On the left, the 93rd New York lost heavily, 41 men being captured by MacRae's North Carolinians. Of these, 12 subsequently escaped, after having been stripped of their arms, accoutrements, knapsacks, and pocketbooks. The 105th Pennsylvania saw its two ranking officers slain, and the colors and many enlisted men captured. Colonel Pulford's 5th Michigan was decimated before it emerged from the woods. Retreating across the cornfield, the three regiments were finally halted along the Plank Road.[134]

The three regiments (the 1st Massachusetts Heavy Artillery, and the 7th and 87th Pennsylvania) which, along with the 141st Pennsylvania, had constituted Pierce's reserve, were wheeling to the right as the Confederate battle lines surged out of the pines. Unnerved by the sight of their fleeing comrades, these three regiments were in no condition to withstand an assault by MacRae's and Weisiger's veterans. Very little powder was burned before the former heavy artillerists and the Pennsylvanians took to their heels. The troops retired in disorder to the Plank Road, where they were rallied on their colors.[135]

Lieutenant Metcalf's brass Napoleons, upon the rout of Pierce's brigade, were left to face the Confederates' onset. Metcalf and his gunners of Batteries C and I, 5th U.S. Artillery had time to fire only a half-dozen rounds of canister from their two pieces, before MacRae's grim North Carolinians were upon them. As they

133 *Ibid.*, 368, 386.

134 *Ibid.*, 368, 374-375, 383-384.

135 *Ibid.*, 347 372, 378, 380.

drove forward, Confederate sharpshooters of Company A, 44th North Carolina blazed away at the teams, killing or wounding all the horses. Metcalf was cut down—badly wounded and captured—along with his Napoleons. Flushed with success, the butternuts rushed on toward the Plank Road. As soon as they had crossed the road, Mahone wheeled MacRae's brigade to the left. The sight that met the Rebels' gaze was a pleasant one, for it promised a rich harvest.[136]

The clearing formed by the angle between the Plank and Dabney's Mill roads was jammed with the shattered remnants of Pierce's brigade, ambulances, led horses, and artillery. Moreover, if the Confederates could hold their grip on the Plank Road, it would be the end for the II Corps' Second and Third Divisions, caught as they were between Heth's and Hampton's converging columns.

General Hancock kept his head. He and his generals moved promptly to establish a new line of resistance, designed to keep the Confederates from gaining additional ground in the direction of Plank Road, while a column was organized to assail Heth's right and rear. While helping Pierce reform his shattered brigade, General Mott suddenly realized that if unchecked, the Confederates would establish a roadblock on the road to Dabney's Mill. Major John William of Mott's staff galloped off with orders for de Trobriand to redeploy his brigade. De Trobriand effected a change of front to the rear by countermarching six of his regiments. In accordance with instructions from Mott, he posted these six regiments facing north along Dabney Mill's Road. The 1st Maine Heavy Artillery was stationed along Plank Road. De Trobriand cautioned his men that they must hold their ground at all hazards.[137]

Upon the collapse of Pierce's command, Lieutenant John W. Roder of Battery K, 4th U.S. Light Artillery was directed to put his four 12-pounder Napoleons into battery on the right of Plank Road, near Bevill's house. Extricating itself from the mass of ambulances, wagons, and led horses, Roder's regulars put their brass guns into battery and opened with shot and shell on Mahone's battle lines at a range of 500 yards. Lieutenant Beck, having secured ammunition from Roder, placed his four Napoleons in position on the left of the Plank Road, and "opened fire upon the point of woods, where the enemy broke through and captured" Metcalf's guns.

The assault on Hancock's right caused General Gregg to dismount all available regiments of Kerwin's and Smith's brigades. Two of Smith's regiments (the 1st Maine and the 6th Ohio) moved up smartly to take position on de Trobriand's

---

136 *Ibid.*, 412, 427; Walker, "The Expedition to the Boydton Plank Road," 336; Stedman, "The Forty-Fourth North Carolina Infantry," 343. Lieutenant R. W. Stedman led Company A, 44th North Carolina.

137 *OR* 42, pt. 1, 347, 359.

right, while Kerwin's came handsomely into position on the 1st brigade's other flank.[138]

Just as Weisiger's brigade had started forward, Sergeant Sale and his fellow flankers of the 12th Virginia spotted a Union officer riding toward them. The newcomer, who proved to be Lieutenant Colonel George Harney of the 147th New York, in the dense undergrowth had mistaken the Rebels for his own men. When called on to surrender, Colonel Harney had only one course open to him, as a dozen rifle muskets were pointed toward him. That night, after the fight, Sergeant Sale wrote in his diary:

> He [Colonel Harney] was hurrying up his regiment to deploy them as skirmishers, when he was captured. I got a very fine haversack, sword belt, & revolver from him. He had on a fine hat & gold watch but I could not muster meanness sufficient to rob him of these. I knew that if I were captured everything I had would have been taken from me, but I have not yet become mean enough to take private property from them.[139]

Hancock, as was his custom, rushed to the point of danger. As soon as de Trobriand's infantry and Gregg's dismounted troopers were ready, Hancock planned to lead a counterattack. Just as de Trobriand and Gregg were reporting their units formed, confusion gripped the Confederates. Some of the butternuts faced about and began shooting toward their rear.

At the first sound of the Confederate onslaught against Pierce, Hancock had dispatched his senior aide-de-camp, Major William G. Mitchell, to General Egan with instructions for him to abandon the attack aimed at securing the heights beyond Hatcher's Run. Egan was to face about and assail, with his entire line, the Rebel column that was driving Pierce.[140]

Egan had surmised that the Rebels were up to no good, when his right and rear were fired on. Orders were issued for General Smyth to halt his battle line and to recall the 14th Connecticut, which had already crossed the run. Colonel McAllister was instructed to countermarch his brigade and attack the Confederates that were rolling over Pierce's bluecoats. When he galloped up, Major Mitchell thus found that Egan had anticipated his superior.

---

138 *Ibid.*, 234, 412, 425, 428, 609, 641, 648; Walker, "The Expedition to the Boydton Plank Road," 336-337.

139 Sale, Diary, n.d.

140 *OR* 42, pt. 1, 234.

At Egan's position near the Burgess dwelling, Mitchell asked Rugg to charge with his brigade at the Rebels that had gained Plank Road to Egan's rear. Rugg refused on three points:

1) He had recently received orders from Egan to hold his position at all hazards.
2) Butler's dismounted cavalry was threatening his left and front.
3) The enemy on the road was not in force, but [only] a disorganized body.

Rugg, believing that a good-sized regiment charging down the road in line would be as effective as the whole brigade, told Mitchell to take the 36th Wisconsin. The major therefore placed himself at the head of the Wisconsin unit and moved out.

MacRae's North Carolinians occupied a ridge and were preoccupied with preparations for storming Mott's reorganized main line of resistance, covering the Dabney's Mill Road. Consequently, they were oblivious to the approach of McAllister's bluecoats and the 36th Wisconsin until it was too late. Egan's legions burst upon MacRae's right and rear like a bolt out of the blue.[141]

Since there were a large number of recruits in his brigade and time was precious, McAllister deemed it best to have his battle line "about-face and move on the enemy with my rear rank in front." Two regiments (the 5th and 7th New Jersey) would remain where they were as a support to Smyth's battle line, when the brigade advanced to dislodge the Confederates.

McAllister's battle line advanced to the "slope of the hill and halted a few moments." To their front, McAllister and his men saw MacRae's North Carolinians pressing back Pierce's shattered command. McAllister shouted to Colonel John Schoonover, whose 11th New Jersey was on the right, to move against the butternuts that had blocked Plank Road. With the rest of his brigade (the 120th New York, the 8th New Jersey, the 11th Massachusetts, and a battalion of the 11th New Jersey), McAllister marched down the slope. The cheering bluecoats surged across gulleys, breaking down the thick "hazel-brush" which bounded them. Reaching the high ground beyond, McAllister called a halt and reformed his command.

---

141 *Ibid.*, 234, 297, 303, 326, 379. Charges were subsequently brought against Colonel Rugg by General Hancock for "neglect of duty and disobedience of orders." Tried and convicted by court-martial, Rugg was dismissed from the service. On January 26, 1865, his disability, consequent upon dismissal, was removed. He did not, however, re-enter the service. Walker, "The Expedition to the Boydton Plank Road," 326, 338.

MacRae and several of his ranking officers by this time had sighted McAllister's battle line. The historian of the 44th North Carolina recalled:

The Federal commander [Hancock], seeing that MacRae was not supported, closed in upon his flanks and attacked with great vigor. Undismayed by the large force which surrounded him, and unwilling to surrender the prize of victory already within his grasp, MacRae formed a portion of his brigade obliquely to his main line of battle, driving back the foe at every point, whilst the deafening shouts and obstinate fighting of his brigade showed their entire confidence in their commander, although every man of them knew their situation to be critical, and their loss had already been great. Awaiting reinforcements, which long since ought to have been with him, he held his vantage gained at all hazards, and against enormous odds. No help came whilst his men toiled, bled, and died.

Wheeling part of his brigade to the right, MacRae prepared to cope with McAllister's threat to his flank and rear. McAllister's bluecoats sent several well-aimed volleys crashing into the oncoming North Carolinians. Men were cut down in large numbers, and MacRae's butternuts to McAllister's front retired into the pines.

McAllister bellowed, "Forward!" As the bluecoats charged, it appeared that the North Carolinians were attempting to get a battery into position. (Actually, the Southerners were seeking to limber up Metcalf's two Napoleons.) The 120th New York on McAllister's left tried to reach the guns, but it was beaten back by the 44th North Carolina. Heth now committed his reserve brigade, and Harris and his Mississippians advanced out of the woods and rushed to MacRae's assistance. For a brief period, McAllister's brigade was all but engulfed with Rebels on all sides. "Had our line broken while in this critical situation all would have been lost," Colonel McAllister recalled.[142]

As the situation began to turn bleak for McAllister, Major Mitchell, at the head of the 36th Wisconsin, charged down the Plank Road. Striking Harris' Mississippian's flank, the soldiers from Wisconsin swept to a spectacular success, and smashed the Rebel roadblock; 100 grey clads surrendered; and a stand of colors was captured.[143]

The charge by the 36th Wisconsin took the pressure off McAllister. Most of the North Carolinians and Mississippians, having retired into the pines east of the

---

142 OR 42, pt. 1, 395-396; Stedman, "The Forty-Fourth North Carolina Infantry," 343; Rowland, *Mississippi Official and Statistical Register*, 450, 493, 511.

143 OR 42, pt. 1, 297, 303, 316. This stand of colors was subsequently recovered by the Rebels.

Plank Road, General Egan sent word for McAllister to change his front to the left and re-establish contact with Mott. As McAllister redeployed his battle line, it came under a galling small-arms fire.[144]

When Egan redeployed his command to cope with Heth's assault, one of his staff officers notified Lieutenant Smith to withdraw his two 10-pounder Parrotts, retire to Burgess' Tavern, and rejoin his battery—the 10th Massachusetts. Being without ammunition, Smith's guns stood by the barn unserviceable. Scarcely had Smith reported to his superior, Lieutenant Granger, before he was knocked from his horse, shot through the bowels, and mortally wounded. Lieutenant Granger now had his gunners point the pieces of his left and right sections to the southeast and hammer the woods into which the Rebel infantry had retired. Not having brought up the battery's caissons, the supply of ammunition in the limbers was soon exhausted. After the charge of the 36th Wisconsin, communications were reopened along the Plank Road, and the 10th Massachusetts battery retired down the road and massed near Bevill's.[145]

Witnessing the charge of the 36th Wisconsin, General Hancock called for Mott to counterattack. De Trobriand placed himself at the head of the 40th New York, the 20th Indiana, the 99th, and part of the 110th Pennsylvania, positioned facing north along Dabney's Mill Road, and prepared to carry out this assignment. Cheering "lustily," de Trobriand and his men went forward, driving the Confederates before them. Within a short time, they had mopped up the field to their front.

Major Mitchell, after leading the 36th Wisconsin into battle, contacted the officers commanding the 1st Maine Heavy Artillery and a battalion of the 110th Pennsylvania. Mitchell told them to follow him. Rushing out into the cornfield, the two regiments rolled back the Confederates, who were already reeling, because of McAllister's and de Trobriand's slashing assaults. Within a few minutes, Metcalf's Napoleons had been retaken. Not less than 150 Rebels, along with the colors of the 26th North Carolina of MacRae's brigade, fell into the onrushing Federals' hands. Fifty of the grey clads were disarmed by the 1st Maine in and around Burgess barn, while the rest were surrounded by the 110th Pennsylvania in a cluster of pines.

Soldiers from the 5th Michigan, the 1st Massachusetts Heavy Artillery, and the 57th Pennsylvania had accompanied the 1st Maine Heavy Artillery and the 110th

---

144 *Ibid.*, 396.

145 *Ibid.*, 412; Billings, *History of the Tenth Massachusetts Battery*, 357-364.

Pennsylvania. After the guns had been recaptured, volunteers secured ropes and drew off the two Napoleons.[146]

The two regiments led into battle by Major Mitchell now took position on the left of McAllister and on the right of the regiments that had followed de Trobriand.

The advance of de Trobriand's troops having checked the Confederates; the fire of Roder's and Beck's eight guns emplaced near Bevill's house, reinforced by the infantry's musketry, compelled the butternuts to retire into the pines. Union skirmishers followed the Johnnies into the edge of the woods. Because the infantry battle line was posted only a few yards in front of the guns, the use of canister was precluded. Following the repulse of Heth's infantry, Lieutenant Beck advanced his four Napoleons and placed them in battery at the junction of Dabney's Mill and Plank Road. In accordance with Major Hazard's instructions, Beck unlimbered his guns and shelled the point of the woods 800 yards to his right and front. The battery held this position until 8:00 p.m.[147]

Meanwhile, Dearing's dismounted Rebel troopers and Harris's Mississippi brigade had taken advantage of the recall of McAllister's brigade to threaten Smyth's front. Leaping over the breastworks, they came down off the ridge toward Hatcher's Run, only to be checked by well-aimed volleys fired by the 8th New York Heavy Artillery and 164th New York. Recalling the 10th New York, which was deployed as skirmishers to his front, Smyth had Colonel Hopper post his men in line of battle near the edge of the pines, so they could watch the brigade's right and rear.[148]

The left of Rugg's skirmish line began near Boydton Plank Road and straddled White Oak Road and the right of the mill pond. On the left was the 1st Battalion, 106th Pennsylvania Infantry; in the center was the 69th Pennsylvania; and on the right was part of the 1st Minnesota. Rugg's brigade was in the timber 100 yards to the rear.[149]

The Confederate leaders (Mahone and Hampton) had failed to coordinate their movements. Heth's infantry column, which had opened the attack, lost the

---

146 OR 42, pt. 1, 347, 359-360, 370, 374, 378, 379; United States Department of the Army, *The Medal of Honor of the United States Army* (Washington, 1948), 179. General de Trobriand charged that the battleflag of the 26th North Carolina, "in one way or other, passed afterwards in the hands of the Seventh Michigan." Sergeant Alonzo Smith of the Michigan regiment was awarded the Medal of Honor for capturing the colors of the 26th North Carolina.

147 OR 42, pt. 1, 412, 428.

148 *Ibid.*, 297, 326, 334.

149 Testimony of Capt. A.S. White, Company B, 19th Maine, Horace Rugg Court Martial Transcript, Record Group 153 (LL-649), NARA.

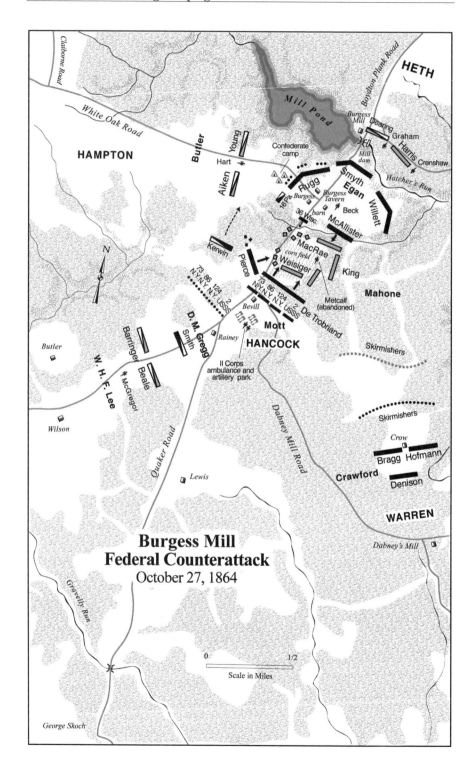

Burgess Mill
Federal Counterattack
October 27, 1864

George Skoch

0   1/2
Scale in Miles

initiative before Hampton's dismounted cavalry assailed the Union left. Butler's battle line, deployed to the right and left of White Oak Road, now drove in from the west, while Rooney Lee's division advanced up Plank Road from the southwest.[150]

When Hampton gave the word, General Butler sent orders for his battle line to take up the advance. Supported by the fire of the Washington Artillery's guns, Young's brigade on the left and Aiken's on the right bounded over their barricades and drove against the picket line defended by four of Rugg's regiments. The bluecoats were posted at the "edge of a dense pine wood," an open field to their front. As Butler's dismounted troopers debouched from the pines on the opposite side of the field, the Yankees banged away.

Captain Charles McAnnally of the 69th Pennsylvania noted the rebels "came on in a mob" and that the Federals had "six men deep at the point they charged." The firing was so intense that the 69th Pennsylvania ran out of ammunition. They kept their fire going by rifling the pockets and ammunition pouches of the dead and wounded and by ammunition passed forward by the 19th and other regiments sending forward two cartridges per man. At one point, the Rebels pushed the 69th back, but the regiment rallied and helped repel the attack. A second Rebel attack was also repulsed.[151]

Rebel losses were high as they sought to smash pockets of Union resistance and reach the Plank Road. Lieutenant Colonel Robert J. Jeffords was killed at the head of his regiment, the 5th South Carolina Cavalry.

The 16th Pennsylvania Cavalry was posted south of the White Oak Road on the left of de Trobriand's jittery regiments opposite Aiken's brigade. The Keystoners either lay on the ground or crouched five or six feet apart behind a worm fence on the edge of the woods. As the sun set they could hear Butler's division assembling in the woods on the far side of the field. Colonel John K. Robison passed the word "Hold the line at all hazards, old 16th." Adjutant Samuel Cormany walked along the line telling the company officers not to open fire until the colonel gave the word and then to fire deliberately and aim to kill. Each man could lose 13 rounds without reloading, 7 from their Spencer carbines and 6 from their revolvers. The orders were to use the Spencers for the start of the attack and the revolvers for close quarter fighting.

As Cormany returned to the colonel, rebel bullets began buzzing around his head. Looking over his shoulder he saw the first Confederates coming towards him

---

150 *Ibid.*, 949, 953; Stedman, "The Forty-Fourth North Carolina Infantry," 343-344.

151 Testimony of Capt. A.S. White, Horace Rugg Court Martial Transcript, Record Group 153 (LL-649), NARA, 54.

out of the woods. "All orders given to the whole line," he informed his commander. Robison replied, "Bully, adjutant and they are coming." Out of the dark came a long line of dismounted rebel cavalry. At Robison's command "Fire" the Spencers let loose the first volley. Despite a pounding, some of the Confederates got within 40 or 50 yards of the fence. The air was full of noise: the Federals yelling like hyenas and shooting at will; and the rebel-wounded crying out. The rebel survivors fled.

The Confederates attacked a second time; and although some nearly crossed the open field, they were too few to accomplish anything and fell back. That was the end of the battle.[152]

As Aiken's brigade swept forward to connect its right with Rooney Lee's left, General Butler missed two of his aides (Major T. G. Barker and Capt. Nat Butler), and glancing to his right, he spotted them and Lieutenant William Preston Hampton "riding in the midst of the line of advancing men, waving their hats and cheering them on. They were perhaps a hundred yards to his right and the heavy firing prevented their hearing him." General Butler finally succeeded in getting their attention. Nat Butler wheeled his horse about, while Preston Hampton prepared to return to his father's command post.

As young Hampton galloped off in one direction and Nat in the other, he called, "Hurrah, Nat," and moments later a minie ball struck him in the groin, inflicting a mortal wound. Within a few minutes, Preston Hampton was dead.

When General Hampton saw his dying son lying on the ground he dismounted and kissed the brave boy, wiped a tear from his eyes, remounted and went on giving orders as though nothing had happened.

General Butler now trotted up and asked General Hampton "Who has been wounded?"

"Poor Preston," the father replied, "has been mortally wounded."

General Butler called for a one-horse wagon, so that the remains might be removed. Meantime, the Federals, observing the crowd, concentrated a galling fire on the group. One shot struck Preston's brother, Wade, in the spine, badly injuring him."[153]

Between White Oak Road and Hatcher's Run, General Young's dismounted cavalry fought Rugg's skirmishers, reinforced by the 69th Pennsylvania. Dearing, to assist his comrades to the right and left, again urged his brigade forward. Infiltrating

---

152 Cormany Diaries, 487.

153 OR 42, pt. 1, 347, 360, 949; Wells, *Hampton and His Cavalry*, 334-335; Brooks, *Butler and His Cavalry*, 358-359.

Major General Wade Hampton
Library of Congress

the underbrush north of Hatcher's Run, Dearing's men again opened on Smyth's battle line, posted on the ridge south of the stream. A half-hearted thrust was made at this time by Harris' Mississippians and MacRae's North Carolinians against the sector defended by McAllister's troops. Egan's division during this phase of the engagement formed a crude square—Rugg's skirmishers, reinforced by the 69th Pennsylvania, in the pines west of Burgess Tavern; Smyth's battle line on the ridge south of Hatcher's Run and in the woods east of Plank Road; and Rugg's line of battle on Smyth's right, partially extended behind McAllister, whose right crossed Boydton Plank Road.[154]

Egan's soldiers held firm on all fronts, and at 5:30 p.m., Egan's division withstood another assault. Since this attack was feeble, Egan and his officers believed that the Rebels were almost ready to call it a day. Mopping up in front of their position, Rugg's skirmishers disarmed a Confederate major, several line officers, and 40 enlisted men. Sergeant Daniel Murphy of the 19th Massachusetts got himself a real prize—the colors of the 47th North Carolina, MacRae's brigade, were captured.[155]

* * *

154 *Ibid.*, 297-298.

155 *OR* 42, pt. 1, 297, 303, 316. This stand of colors was subsequently recovered by the Rebels.

Major General Rooney Lee's division was up and mounted by 7:00 a.m. when a courier brought news that the Federals were on the move. Lee sent Barringer's North Carolinians to the junction of the Vaughan and Quaker Roads. Meanwhile he reached the Quaker Road further up with Beale's Virginians and pressed the Federals toward the intersection of the roads, intending to trap them between his two brigades. After receiving orders to attack, Barringer dismounted parts of the 1st and 2nd regiments and sent them forward, but they found the Federals already retiring. Only a few shots were fired by each party.

At 10:00 a.m., Lee received orders from Hampton to march up Quaker Road toward Burgess Mill and strike the Federals. However, before Lee could make contact, Hampton was flanked out of his camp. Hampton ordered Butler to ride to White Oak Road and Lee to move to Boydton Plank Road.

Lee was riding at the head of his division with his old regiment, the 9th Virginia Cavalry, when he spied a Federal cavalry regiment approaching. Thinking there was time to dismount the regiment and greet the Federals with carbine fire, he gave the order. Then realizing the Yankees were coming so quickly that there wasn't enough time for his men to obey, he countermanded the order. The 9th Virginia regiment was in disarray with some men mounted and others dismounted when the 21st Pennsylvania struck them and charged into their midst, slashing at the Virginians with their sabers and firing into them with their pistols. Stout wooden fences on either side of the narrow road made it impossible for Lieutenant Colonel Thomas C. Waller and his officers to reform their regiment's ranks. Under this pressure the regiment was routed. Some troopers tried to force their horses to leap over the fence. Lieutenant Colonel Samuel A. Swann who was in the rear when the Yankees struck the head of the regiment, prevented panic from spreading by drawing his pistol and threatening to shoot the more timid and calling upon other troopers to help rally the men. His actions made this part of the regiment stand firm.[156]

Fearing the 9th Virginia would flee to the rear and run through his regiment, Lieutenant Colonel Robert A. Caskie, commanding the 10th Virginia Cavalry, in column behind the beleaguered 9th, ordered his men to draw their sabers. Caskie became impatient and rode over to Swann and told him, "your regiment is stampeded" and asked him to cease trying to rally his men and instead clear the road so the 10th could charge the Yankees. Swann replied with an indignant denial.

At that crucial moment Captain Luther of Company B jumped from his horse, leaped onto the fence and shouted, carbine in hand, "Rally 9th and we will drive them back!" In a moment all the dismounted men near him rallied around him.

156 Byrd C. Willis diary.

These men, numbering 50 or more, pushed to the head of the column and poured a terrible fire into the Yankees. The federals recoiled and retreated.

It was getting dark when Lee's division advanced towards the woods. During their march they heard the roar of rifles coming from the infantry battle to the north. After advancing half a mile the Confederates struck the Federals. Ordered to attack by Lee, Barringer dismounted the 1st and 2nd North Carolina Cavalry regiments and positioned them on the left side of Boydton Plank Road, forming a line of battle with the 9th and 13th Virginia Cavalry on the right of the road, still actively engaged with the Federal cavalry. Ordered to advance their lines, Colonel William H. Cheek and Major McNeil soon outdistanced the Virginia regiments. The two North Carolina regiments overlapped the right flank of the de Trobriand's infantry and drove them back. Then they opened fire on the main line of the Federals who were concealed in the woods.

Shortly afterwards, Lee received word from Hampton that he should attack. The signal to go in would be the sounds of Mahone's gunfire. The 3rd and 4th North Carolina cavalry regiments were in the rear supporting McGregor's battery. Barringer fed them into his line. Placing the 1st and 5th regiments on either side of the road with the Virginia cavalry to their right, Barringer moved McGregor's battery forward and placed it in the road among the cavalrymen of the 5th North Carolina regiment. The tarheels of the 2nd North Carolina were moved back to support the battery.[157]

Rooney Lee's division now struck. General Gregg heard the clash of arms as the 21st Pennsylvania fought a stout delaying action against Beale's Virginians east of Boydton Plank Road. Wheeling his horse about, Gregg galloped down Plank Road. Gregg, upon reaching the point of danger, found the Pennsylvanians resisting Lee's onset. The 6th Ohio Cavalry at this time filed into position alongside the 21st Pennsylvania. Even so, Gregg could see that his men were outnumbered. Aides raced off with word for the brigade commanders to rush to Gregg all their available manpower.

The 1st Maine came down the road on the run. Colonel Smith formed the Maine men on the right of the 21st, the Pennsylvanians having closed to the left, while the 6th Ohio was posted on the right of the 1st Maine. With the arrival of these units, General Beale's Virginians was slowed. Nevertheless, the butternuts continued to gain ground, foot by foot. A section of guns manned by Battery I, 1st U.S. Light Artillery was called up.

---

157 "Barringer's NC Brigade of Cavalry," *Raleigh Daily Confederate*, February 23, 1865.

Barringer's North Carolina Cavalry brigade drove against the picket line defended by four of de Trobriand's regiments—the 73rd, 86th, 124th New York; and the 2nd U.S. Sharpshooters. The bluecoats were posted at the "edge of a dense pine wood," an open field to their front. As the dismounted tarheel state troopers debouched from the pines on the opposite side of the field, the Yankees banged away. The Confederates came on with great determination. Dismayed by their failure to check Barringer's horse soldiers, whom they mistook for infantry, some of the bluecoats fled. Much of the picket line was thrown into confusion, and only "the exertions of officers and steadiness" of the veterans kept it from entirely disintegrating.

Fortunately for the II Corps, Rooney Lee's attack came after Heth's foot soldiers had spent their strength. Mott, observing that the firing to his left had increased and was getting louder, instructed de Trobriand to recall the regiments of the 1st Brigade that had just beaten back the Rebel infantry. Detaching a line of skirmishers to hold the ground gained, de Trobriand marched his troops back to the position along Plank Road previously held.[158]

With the redeployment of de Trobriand's brigade along Boydton Plank Road, much of the steam went out of Barringer's attack on the units manning de Trobriand's picket line. This enabled officers of the 73rd, 86th, and 124th New York and the 2nd U.S. Sharpshooters to rally their men.[159]

Gregg dispatched a staffer with an urgent request that Hancock support him with all mounted regiments he could spare. Hancock sent the 2nd, 4th, and 13th Pennsylvania. These units came up "successively as fast as their legs could carry them," and entered the fight. Hancock would have liked to have reinforced Gregg with infantry, but this he could not do, because he expected the Rebel infantry at any minute to renew its attacks.[160]

At the time of Rooney Lee's attack on Gregg's cavalry, Major Hazard, as a precautionary measure, told Lieutenant Granger to throw his 10-pounder Parrotts into battery west of the Plank Road, and facing the point of danger. Here Granger was cut down by a fragment from an exploding shell. The battery had lost all its officers in the day's fighting, so Major Hazard told Lieutenant E. S. Smith of

---

158 OR 42, pt. 1, 347, 360.

159 OR 42, pt. 1, 360, 950; Wells, *Hampton and His Cavalry* 335-341; Brooks, *Butler and His Cavalry*, 359-360.

160 OR 42, pt. 1, 234-235, 609, 621, 641, 644, 648; Beale, *History of the Ninth Virginia Cavalry*, 147.

Battery K, 4th U.S. Light Artillery to take charge of the 10th Massachusetts Battery.[161]

The situation at this time was fluid. Although the assaults by Heth's infantry and Butler's and Dearing's dismounted cavalry on the II Corps' front, right, and center had been repulsed, Rebel artillery emplaced north of Hatcher's Run and on White Oak Road still hammered the men who wore the clover-leaf. At the same time, rifled projectiles from McGregor's battery passed over Gregg's line and burst among the II Corps infantry. Renewed efforts were made at this hour to establish contact with Crawford's troops, but they were unsuccessful.

At 4:50 p.m., General Hancock told Major Bingham to communicate with Generals Warren and Crawford. He was to inform the V Corps leaders that the Rebels had assailed the II Corps' right; that the attack had been repulsed; that Hancock was in need of reinforcements; that the V Corps should advance and connect its left with Hancock's right.

Bingham sought to reach Crawford's command post at Crow's house by following the cart road he had traveled earlier in the day. Before going far, however, the major ran into a Confederate roadblock. Wheeling his horse about, Bingham, "as expeditiously as possible struck the road leading to Dabney's Mill." Upon reaching the mill, the major was directed by one of the cavalrymen posted there into the road leading to the left. The trooper told Bingham that Crawford's division had tramped out that road.

After riding what he believed to be several miles, Bingham encountered Confederates, who, bringing their rifle muskets to their shoulders, called on him to surrender. Bingham, seeing that flight was hopeless, handed over his side-arms to the North Carolina colonel. In addition to Bingham, the North Carolinians captured three ambulances, a score of horses, and 20 soldiers of the II Corps.[162]

Because of the dense woods and a strong wind blowing from southeast to northwest, the roar of battle along Boydton Plank Road was not audible at Warren's headquarters.

Hancock received a message around 5:20 p.m. drafted by Chief of Staff Humphreys 65 minutes earlier. Unfolding the paper, Hancock learned that Union signal officers had observed Confederate troops en route down the Plank Road. Though it was feared by the people at army headquarters that the foe was massing

---

161 OR 42, pt. 1, 412; Billings, *History of the Tenth Massachusetts Battery*, 363-365. The battery had exchanged its empty limbers for full ones from the caissons.

162 OR 42, pt 1, 239. The night of the 27th being very dark, Bingham succeeded in giving his captors the slip. He then made his way to Hancock's command post, where he reported that he had failed in his mission.

against Hancock, the orders for the II Corps to withdraw on the following morning remained unchanged. Crawford's division was to be recalled at the same time. As the road linking Hancock's and Meade's command posts was "infested by small parties" of Rebel cavalry, Hancock was to see that it was "heavily patrolled."[163]

Meade was seemingly unaware of what had transpired on the Plank Road since he had left the field, and Hancock explained to Capt. Addison G. Mason (the staff officer who had carried Humphreys' dispatch) the situation confronting the II Corps. It was starting to get dark by the time Mason started on his return ride to army headquarters.

Soon after the captain's departure, Hancock received a discouraging report from Chief of Artillery Hazard. When the corps had taken the field that morning, the wagons with the reserve ammunition, in compliance with orders, had been left at Perkins'. Of the three batteries that had accompanied the column, only one, the 10th Massachusetts, had any projectiles left. At the same time, the Massachusetts battery had lost all its officers, and Lieutenant Smith reported that he had but three men left per gun.

The corps had been marching and fighting throughout the day and as "a consequence was in considerable disorder." A heavy rain was falling, and the narrow cart road to Dabney's Mill (the only direct link with the rest of the Army of the Potomac) was not only threatened by the foe, but was being turned into a ribbon of mud by the precipitation.

Hancock questioned whether the reserve ammunition (which was 13 miles in the rear) could be brought up and issued in time for a fight in the morning.[164]

Two staff officers were sent by Hancock to convey this information to Meade.

About 6:30 p.m., a courier reached Hancock's command post with two messages signed by General Humphreys. Studying these documents, which had been drafted 75 minutes before, Hancock learned that General Ayres' V Corps division had been ordered to his support. But because of the hour, it would be impossible for the reinforcing column to get beyond Armstrong's Mill before dark. If Hancock could attack successfully in the morning with the addition of Ayres' and Crawford's divisions, it was Meade's desire that he do so. If not, Hancock was authorized to withdraw his troops under the cover of darkness.[165]

These instructions added to Hancock's embarrassment, because they made him reluctant to abandon his position. On his shoulders had been thrown the

163 *Ibid.*, 235; *OR* 42, pt. 3, 380.

164 *OR* 42, pt. 1, 235; Walker, "The Expedition to the Boydton Plank Road," 341.

165 *OR* 42, pt. 1, 235; pt. 3, 381.

responsibility for determining whether reinforcements could be gathered, and the needed ammunition for his corps brought up and issued in time for battle at daylight. Yet these were subjects which were in no way under his control. Certainly, if no greater energy were shown in getting up ammunition and reinforcements during the night, than had been displayed in pushing Crawford forward during the day, Hancock had reason to shake his head.

General Gregg, having checked Rooney Lee's advance up the Plank Road, joined Hancock at this time. It was now dark, and Gregg had further evil tidings for his superior. His cavalry, Gregg reported, "a considerable proportion being armed with repeating rifles, had almost wholly exhausted their ammunition." Owing to the commingling of his regiments in the woods, together with the rain and extreme darkness, "Gregg did not think it practicable to get ammunition up and issued to the men during the night."[166]

Reluctant as he was to abandon the field, his conversation with "an officer so reliable and trustworthy as General Gregg," determined Hancock "to order a withdrawal rather than risk disaster by awaiting an attack in the morning only partly prepared."[167]

Part V

Meade Cuts His Commitments and Pulls Back

Not long after he had arrived at his decision to pull back, at 8:35 p.m. on October 27, Hancock received another communication from General Humphreys. The staff officers detailed by Hancock to explain the situation to Meade and his people reached army headquarters around 6:15 p.m. Meade, after listening to what they had to say, dictated a message to Hancock, couched in a similar vein to Chief of Staff Humphreys' 5:15 p.m. dispatches. If he should retire during the night, Hancock was to "leave some force at Dabney's Mill to aid in withdrawing Crawford."[168]

---

166 OR 42, pt. 1, 235; pt. 3, 383.

167 OR 42, pt. 1, 236.

168 OR 42, pt. 3, 381-382.

At 9:00 p.m., Hancock notified Humphreys that orders had been issued for his corps "to return to the vicinity of the Gurley house." Egan with his division was to hold Dabney's Mill and to communicate with General Crawford.

At 10:30 p.m., Humphreys replied, notifying Hancock that Meade wished the II Corps to halt as soon as it had re-crossed Hatcher's Run and had replenished its ammunition. Additional orders would be awaiting Hancock at that point. General Warren was to "attend to drawing in General Crawford, and will see that General Egan is notified when he can withdraw."[169]

Hancock scheduled the retreat to commence at 10:00 p.m., to provide sufficient time to permit the staff officers sent to army headquarters to rejoin the corps. To insure an orderly withdrawal, all available ambulances were loaded with the wounded—155 being removed. Because Dabney's Mill Road was passable in only one direction at a time, the medical officers reported it would be impossible to bring up additional ambulances and move troops to the rear at the same time. Therefore, Hancock was forced to leave behind approximately 250 wounded soldiers. So far as practicable, these men were collected and placed in the Rainey's house and barns. Three competent surgeons and a number of hospital stewards were detailed to stay with them.[170]

Prior to the receipt of orders that the field was to be abandoned, General Mott, believing that the fight would be resumed at daybreak, redeployed his division. General Pierce had reformed his brigade along the Dabney's Mill Road to the left of de Trobriand, with pickets (two regiments) advanced at a considerable distance. The 1st Maine Heavy Artillery was stationed along the Plank Road on de Trobriand's right with orders to maintain contact with Egan's division. Four of de Trobriand's regiments (the 73rd, 86th, and 124th New York, and the 2nd U.S. Sharpshooters) continued to picket the countryside west of the Plank Road. Slight breastworks were erected.[171]

About 8:00 p.m., Mott received orders from Hancock "to start the ambulances, pack mules, and the two batteries" that had exhausted their ammunition for Globe Tavern. This column would be escorted by the 17th Maine. The division was to follow at 10:00 p.m. While waiting to put his column in motion, Mott was to recall McAllister's brigade.[172]

169 *Ibid.*, 382.

170 OR 42, pt. 1, 194, 236.

171 *Ibid.*, 348, 360, 368.

172 *Ibid.*, 348.

The ambulance train, accompanied by the 10th Massachusetts and Beck's batteries, rolled as scheduled. Beck's regulars, because of the loss of 14 horses, had to abandon one caisson, which the lieutenant had his men cut to pieces, so as to be of no service to the foe. One of the battery's limbers was also missing, having fallen into the Confederates' hands. Except for hard pulling caused by the muddy roads, the train escorted by the 17th Maine encountered little difficulty in reaching Globe Tavern. The sun was just breaking through the overcast, as the troops crossed the railroad.[173]

McAllister, whose brigade had been posted in support of Rugg's, reported to Mott at 8:30 p.m. While Mott was checking with his brigade commanders to insure that there would be no errors, he learned from de Trobriand that shortly after dark someone had blundered. At that hour, two of the regiments deployed as skirmishers west of the Plank Road had "misunderstood an order to keep a close connection on their right, and reformed in line in that direction." De Trobriand, taking into consideration the extreme darkness, decided it would be not only difficult but hazardous to re-establish the picket line in the woods. As general field officer of the day, de Trobriand relocated his line of outposts much closer to the II Corps' main line of resistance, so it would facilitate their recall.[174]

Mott put his division, except the men on picket, in motion as scheduled. He had sent his provost guards ahead to clear the road of stragglers. Near Dabney's Mill, Mott was overtaken by one of Meade's aides with orders from army headquarters for the Third Division to halt after it had re-crossed Hatcher's Run.

By 1:00 a.m. on October 28, Mott's division had crossed the stream. On doing so, the troops were massed near Widow Smith's.[175]

General Egan's division (accompanied by Battery K, 4th U.S. Light Artillery) trailed Mott's division down the cart road. As directed, Egan halted his soldiers at Dabney's Mill. To expedite contact with Crawford's division, Hancock's escort had reported to Egan before he left the Plank Road. While en route to the mill, the escort disappeared. Since he was unfamiliar with the area, Egan, upon reaching the mill, halted his division. He would allow his men to rest and await the dawn, before attempting to connect with Crawford.[176]

---

173 *Ibid.*, 412, 428; Billings, *History of the Tenth Massachusetts Battery*, 366. In the battle, Batteries C and I, 5th U.S. Light Artillery, expended 237 rounds of solid shot, 147 shells, 248 rounds of spherical case, and 34 rounds of canister.

174 *OR* 42, pt. 1, 348, 360.

175 *Ibid.*, 348, 368, 395.

176 *Ibid.*, 298, 303, 320, 327.

Gregg's horse soldiers left the field by way of the Quaker Road at 10:30 p.m. Davies' brigade, which during the day (even when Gregg was hardest pressed) had been held in reserve at the junction of the Quaker and Boydton Plank Roads, became the rear guard as the cavalry rode southward. Because of the destruction of the Gravelly Run Bridge earlier in the day, Gregg's column was slowed. Only the lead brigade, Colonel Kerwin's, had succeeded in re-crossing the Rowanty by daybreak. The division reached Perkins' house about 7:30 a.m., on the 28th, without having seen any signs of the foe on its return march.[177]

With the withdrawal of the cavalry, the only Federals remaining on the field were the wounded, who had been left behind, and the infantrymen manning the picket line. In obedience to Hancock's instructions, at 1:00 a.m., General de Trobriand recalled his outposts. All Third Division pickets, with the exception of three officers and 26 enlisted men of the 73rd New York, got the word and reported to the general on the Plank Road. When de Trobriand had reorganized his picket line earlier in the evening, contact had been lost with the 70-man detachment from the 7th Michigan and the 1st Minnesota. These men, who were on outpost in the pines north of White Oak Road, were left behind, when de Trobriand called in the Second Division pickets. De Trobriand, as soon as the pickets had fallen in, moved out after the main column. Upon reporting to Hancock, de Trobriand was told to rejoin his division, which he did.[178]

*   *   *

At 4:30 p.m., General Warren had left Crawford's command post to consult with General Meade, whom he presumed to be with Hancock on the Plank Road. As Warren neared the Plank Road, he encountered Major William Riddle of Meade's staff, who told him that the army commander had returned to Dabney's Mill. Warren accordingly hastened to that point, and he had been at Meade's command post for only a few minutes, when word arrived that the Rebels had penetrated the gap between Hancock and Crawford and were assailing the II Corps

---

177 *Ibid.*, 609, 622, 641, 648. Before moving out, Gregg's hospital stewards had collected all the division's wounded. As all the injured could not be placed in ambulances, Doctor Elias J. Marsh used the wagons captured in the morning, along with two infantry ammunition wagons. In this fashion, he was able to carry about 100 wounded horse soldiers off the field. A field hospital was established after reaching the Perkins' house, and the wounded were removed from the ambulances. By dark all the wounds had been dressed, the necessary operations performed, and the patients placed on cars that could carry them to the big base hospital at City Point. *Ibid.*, 622.

178 *Ibid.*, 236, 298, 304, 360.

"with great violence." Meade told Warren to rush Crawford to Hancock's support. Warren, however, countered with the suggestion that Ayres' division "could more readily be got there," because there was no direct road leading from Crawford's front to Hancock. Meade was agreeable. Orders were drafted for Ayres to march at once.[179]

Major Bingham had been at Crawford's command post about an hour ahead of Warren. Not long after Warren had ridden off, another one of Hancock's people arrived and told Crawford that the II Corps was to storm the bridge at Burgess Mill and advance beyond it. This would explain the heavy firing that could be heard off to the northwest.[180]

About an hour before dark, as Crawford's soldiers were throwing up a "light" line of works, Confederate stragglers, who had become bewildered and had lost their way in the wilderness, began running afoul of Crawford's picket line. These Rebels, many of whom had been engaged with the II Corps, were ignorant of Crawford's position. One group of grey clads had with them (when disarmed by Crawford's skirmishers) three ambulances they had captured. Six of them had taken Capt. Emmor B. Cope of Warren's staff prisoner, but finding themselves behind the Union lines, they surrendered to him, and he brought them in. All told, Crawford's troops disarmed 238 Confederate enlisted men and three officers.[181]

When questioned by Crawford's staff, the Confederates, most of whom identified themselves as belonging to Weisiger's and Harris' brigades, remarked that they had flanked and broken the II Corps. This was the first intimation Crawford had had that matters had gone badly with Hancock.

As he was returning to the Crow house, Major Roebling heard someone shout out in the pines, "Stop that man on horseback." As he reined up his horse, Roebling saw that the newcomers were eight Rebels in charge of two Yanks. All had lost their way in the wilderness. The Federals had been the Confederates' prisoners, but not one in the group knew the way, so they had agreed to follow the first man who knew where he was going.[182]

---

179 *Ibid.*, 438.

180 *Ibid.*, 496-497.

181 *Ibid.*, 438, 497, 507.

182 *Ibid.*, 442. At 4:00 p.m., Major Roebling visited Meade's headquarters. While there he had explained the situation, and received an order for Crawford to take possession of the breastworks in front of Griffin, provided he could cross the run. At the time that Roebling rejoined Crawford, he was astonished to see Rebel stragglers coming in from the left and rear. They reported King's Alabama brigade in the woods, a short distance to the southeast.

Crawford now ordered scouts out on his left. One, an intelligence officer, returned at 6:45 p.m. to report that he had spotted a strong column of Rebel infantry (probably King's Alabama brigade) passing to Crawford's left along a cart road which crossed Hatcher's Run, one-half mile above the V Corps' position. Relaying this information to Warren, Crawford warned that unless the interval between his left and the II Corps was closed, he anticipated a fierce fight in the morning. Within the past few minutes, a North Carolinian belonging to MacRae's brigade had been questioned. In addition, large numbers of Confederates from Weisiger's brigade of Mahone's division had been made prisoner, when they blundered into the Third Division's line.[183]

In the event his division was unable to hold its own in face of the expected Confederate onslaught, Crawford had his pioneers at dark bridge Hatcher's Run, in rear of Griffin's skirmish line.[184]

Warren, on learning that Hancock would withdraw his corps under the cover of darkness, contacted Crawford. It would be best, Warren wrote, for Crawford to begin withdrawing his troops as soon as it was light, "taking care to bring in all your pickets, and drive in the stragglers." Not knowing that Crawford's pioneers had already bridged the run, Warren granted his division commander permission to do so. Or if he wished, Crawford could retire via the way he had come. Whichever route he took, Crawford was to make certain that the division (Egan's) that Hancock was to leave at Dabney's Mill was kept posted. If he re-crossed Hatcher's Run above Armstrong's Mill, Crawford was to deploy his troops into double line of battle on Griffin's left.[185]

Upon receipt of this message from his immediate superior, it didn't take Crawford long to make up his mind as to the route his division would take. He, as well as his officers and men, had had enough of the wilderness through which they had marched. When the division moved, it would be across the bridge.

As a precautionary measure, Crawford reinforced his line of outposts. At 3:00 a.m., he commenced pulling his troops out of the bridgehead. By daylight, the three brigades had reached the north bank of Hatcher's Run. Before destroying the

---

Crawford, to cope with this situation, had Hofmann change his front. In view of this situation, Crawford decided against sending his division across Hatcher's Run.

183 OR 42, pt. 3, 387.

184 OR 42, pt.1, 497.

185 OR 42, pt. 3, 387.

bridge, Crawford called in his pickets. The division was formed as directed on Griffin's left and facing the stream.[186]

Upon being notified that Crawford had retired across the run, Warren dispatched Major Roebling to convey this information to General Egan. At the same time, Egan was directed to report to Warren. On doing so, he massed his division near Armstrong's Mill.[187]

Meanwhile, Crawford had discovered, on discussing the situation with his brigade commanders, that some of their pickets had not come in. The bridge was quickly repaired, and the 7th Wisconsin sent back across Hatcher's Run. Major Hollon Richardson formed his men into line, and they beat their way slowly forward.

After leaving General Egan's command post, Major Roebling had ridden over to Crow's field, where he spotted three abandoned V Corps ambulances. Here Roebling encountered an officer and two men sent out to recall the 7th Wisconsin. As they rode through the woods beyond Crow's, Roebling and his companions rounded up 20 Union stragglers. They then encountered the 7th Wisconsin, bringing in 82 prisoners. The officer in charge explained that they had lost their way, and Major Richardson had ridden off in search of assistance. Within a short time Richardson returned, accompanied by Major Dailey. With Dailey as their guide, the regiment found its way back to the bridge. The last of Crawford's people passed the bridge at 9:00 a.m., and the pioneers for the second time wrecked the structure.

At 7:30 a.m., Warren was advised that Meade wanted him to send Ayres with two of his brigades to occupy the "vacant space" between the IX Corps' left and Clements' house. Appropriate orders were issued.

Stragglers from the II Corps continued to wander into the V Corps' lines, so Warren sent ten men from his escort to Dabney's Mill. Major James H. Walsh with his battalion of the 3rd Pennsylvania Cavalry would continue to picket the road from Dabney's Mill to the Vaughan Road crossing of Hatcher's Run. Walsh notified Warren at 10:00 a.m. that the road was nearly clear of wagons and stragglers.[188]

---

186 *Ibid.*, 413; *OR* 42, pt. 1, 497, 507, 525. Bragg's brigade was posted on the left, Hofmann's to the right, and Denison's in reserve.

187 *OR* 42, pt. 1, 298, 442.

188 *Ibid.*, 439, 442-443, 497; *OR* 42, pt. 3, 414. The pickets brought with them between 30 and 40 Confederates.

Warren now issued orders authorizing Egan and Crawford to withdraw. Screened by Walsh's horse soldiers, Egan's II Corps division moved down the right bank of Hatcher's Run to Vaughan Road. Hancock, upon learning that Egan's division was in motion, instructed Mott to hold his division ready to take up the march. The decision having been made to abandon for the time being offensive operations designed to turn the right flank of the Petersburg defenses, Hancock directed Mott and Egan to return their divisions to their old camps near the Norfolk & Petersburg Railroad.

While waiting at Widow Smith's for Egan's column to appear, Mott sent Pierce's brigade to Colonel Wyatt's. It was starting to get dark by the time Egan's troops were back in the camp in the rear of Fort Bross, out of which they had marched 52 hours earlier. Mott's division returned to Southall's at 5:00 p.m., where the general massed Pierce's and McAllister's brigades, while de Trobriand's brigade camped near Chieves' house.[189]

Crawford's division was the first V Corps unit to retire from Hatcher's Run; taking the road back to Fort Cummings. By 10:30 p.m., Egan's and Crawford's troops were out of sight, so Warren notified Parke that he was ready to recall Griffin's division.[190]

At 6:45 a.m., Chief of Staff Humphreys notified Parke that he was to be prepared to withdraw during the morning into the entrenchments from which his IX Corps had marched on the 27th. Either Meade's headquarters or Warren would notify Parke when to retire, as he was to pull back simultaneously with the V Corps. Should Parke not require his artillery to cover his retrograde, it could precede him.

Acknowledging Humphreys' communication, Parke announced that two batteries had accompanied his columns; one was with Potter at Hawks' and the other in Ferrero's rear at Watkins'. Orders had been given for all wheeled vehicles to start for the rear.[191]

Parke's people had spent the afternoon and evening of the 27th erecting breastworks. Willcox's division on the left had dug in within 250 yards of the fortifications held by Heth's division. Some of the bluecoated skirmishers had advanced into the slashed timber fronting the Rebels' works. On Willcox's left, Hartranft's battle line was in contact with Sickel's brigade of Griffin's division. While Hartranft's troops were digging in, the 51st Pennsylvania held the picket line. Hartranft at dusk had recalled the Pennsylvanians, and each regiment was made

189 *OR* 42, pt. 1, 236, 298, 348; pt. 3, 413.

190 *OR* 42, pt. 1, 439.

191 *OR* 42, pt. 3, 415.

responsible for manning the line of outposts to its front. Colonel Cutcheon, whose brigade was in position on Hartranft's right, learned from Colonel March at 2:00 p.m. that the 2nd Michigan was nearly out of cartridges. The 60th Ohio was advanced and relieved the 2nd Michigan on the skirmish line. On the extreme left, soldiers of the 2nd Michigan had penetrated so deeply into the felled timber that it was impossible for them to retire by daylight. Along toward dark, Confederates from Davis' Mississippi brigade made a sortie and captured these people. Willcox's 3rd brigade, McLaughlen's, had been held in reserve until 5:00 p.m. McLaughlen at that hour shifted one wing to Wilkins' to cover the 34th New York Battery, and the other to the right to constitute a reserve to Ferrero's black division.[192]

Their troops were a greater distance from the Confederates than Willcox's, so there was little activity along Ferrero's and Potter's picket lines. Large fatigue parties were kept employed throughout the afternoon and well into the night slashing timber and opening roads.[193]

At 11:00 a.m. on October 28, Griffin and Willcox, whose divisions were separated from the Confederate fortifications by several hundred yards of timber strewn ground, prepared to retire. Breaking contact with an aggressive foe, such as the Army of Northern Virginia, can be a difficult task. To conceal their intentions, Griffin and Willcox had their brigade commanders push skirmishers up against the slashings. The Confederates, at daybreak, had rushed the outposts held by Griffin's left flank brigade (Gregory's), but they had been repulsed. Griffin on the left encountered no difficulty in withdrawing Gregory's and Sickel's units.

A dark and stormy night had compelled General Hampton to suspend his attack, shortly after Butler's division on the left and Rooney Lee's on the right had established contact. Hampton told Lee and Butler to picket their fronts and be prepared to resume the fight with the II Corps at daybreak.

Hampton and Heth met in the rain to perfect their plans for the next day. A plan for joint action having been agreed to, Hampton returned to his command post. One of Heth's aides rode up at 3:30 a.m., and told the cavalry leader that his general had been unable to get the reinforcements he had anticipated. Consequently, Heth would not be able to cooperate with the cavalry.

Daybreak revealed to Hampton and his troopers that the II Corps had given them the slip. Several hours passed before Hampton organized a pursuit. When the Confederate horse soldiers moved out, Dearing's brigade took the lead. A short

192 OR 42, pt. 1, 556, 561, 569, 576; pt. 3, 389.

193 OR 42, pt. 1, 580.

distance beyond Dabney's Mill on the road to Armstrong's, Dearing's vanguard clashed with Walsh's troopers. The bluecoats were chased across Hatcher's Run.

General Griffin sent his reserve brigade, Bartlett's, to cope with this threat. Bartlett deployed his foot soldiers to the left and right of Duncan Road, advanced the 1st Michigan and the 118th Pennsylvania as skirmishers, and waited for the butternuts. Dearing's troopers crossed Hatcher's Run at Armstrong's. But on sighting Bartlett's waiting battle line, Dearing called a halt. After some harmless skirmishing at extreme ranges, the Confederates melted back into the pines out of which they had advanced.[194]

The V Corps, upon Dearing's retirement, returned to its camps by way of Duncan and Squirrel Level roads, without further adventure.

Willcox's division was assigned the task of covering the IX Corps' retirement. Cutcheon's brigade extended to the right and relieved Ferrero's outposts. As soon as his skirmishers reported to their units, Ferrero put his division in motion for Fort Cummings. Covered by a strong skirmish line posted behind the barricades, Willcox's brigade commanders retired their units a short distance and reformed them into line of battle. The pickets then pulled back. Over on the left, while Hartranft's battle line was in Watkins' field and his skirmishers in Clements' field, Davis' Mississippians charged over the abandoned breastworks with wild "Rebel Yells." They, however, chose not to press their advantage.

Continuing the retrograde, Willcox next drew up his troops near the abandoned Rebel Redoubt and waited until the V Corps' rear guard, Walsh's cavalry, had filed up Squirrel Level Road. Meanwhile, General Potter had pulled his troops out of the newly erected works, posting Colonel John I. Curtin's brigade, supported by a section of the 19th New York Battery, a short distance west of Fort Cummings. As soon as the V Corps was out of the way, Willcox's troops withdrew into the fortified zone out of which they had advanced the previous day. Curtin's infantrymen, as soon as Willcox's skirmishers had passed, followed. By 6:00 p.m. on October 28, Parke had all of his troops in their old positions and his picket line re-established.[195]

The last bluecoats (not counting wounded and stragglers) to leave the area about Burgess Mill were 70 men of the 1st Minnesota and the 7th Michigan. They had manned the picket line in the woods between the White Oak and Plank roads. At daybreak it was discovered that all their comrades had gone. Captain James C.

---

194 *Ibid.*, 439, 459, 950; Wells, *Hampton and His Cavalry*, 339-341; Brooks, *Butler and His Cavalry*, 359-360; Survivors' Association, *History of the Corn Exchange Regiment*, 529-530.

195 OR 42, pt. 1, 549, 556, 561, 569, 576, 580; Committee, *History of the Thirty-Fifth Regiment Massachusetts*, 306.

Farwell of the 1st Minnesota, as senior officer present, took charge. He and his men remained undercover until after Hampton's horse soldiers had moved out in pursuit of the II Corps. Crossing the field north of Mrs. Rainey's on the double, the Yanks made for the pines between Quaker and Dabney's Mill roads. Avoiding roads wherever possible, Farwell and his men headed southeast, and succeeded in regaining the Union lines by way of Ream's Station. In making their getaway, the foot soldiers twice clashed with roving mounted Confederate patrols.[196]

*   *   *

Brigadier General Nelson Miles on the evening of October 27 ordered out two combat patrols. These groups were to probe the Confederate defenses to their front to ascertain if the Rebel generals were withdrawing men to oppose the Army of the Potomac's drive toward the South Side Railroad. Captain Jeremiah Z. Brown of the 148th Pennsylvania with 100 men moved out of the Union rifle pits in front of Fort Morton. About the same time, 130 bluecoats led by Lieutenant Colonel Denis F. Burke of the 88th New York braced themselves to charge the Rebel picket line at the Chimneys, opposite Fort Sedgwick.[197]

General Bushrod Johnson, whose division held the earthworks to Miles' front, had made several changes in his deployment. Brigadier General William H. Wallace's South Carolina brigade had been shifted to the right to relieve King's and Harris' brigades of Mahone's division in the trenches. Colonel John T. Goode's Virginia brigade was called up from the reserve to occupy the rifle pits vacated by the South Carolinians. These changes left Johnson holding the sector from the Appomattox to Battery No. 30.[198]

Unwittingly, Miles had selected points to be probed that were held by troops unfamiliar with their surroundings. Brown and his Pennsylvanians had only 40 yards to cover, after they left the protection afforded by their trenches, to reach their goal—Davidson's Battery. It was the hour for posting and relieving sentries, so the division officer of the day mistook the Yanks for pickets returning to the line. He passed the word for his men to hold their fire. Troops posted in the rifle pits in rear of the Crater had the impression that Brown and his Pennsylvanians were deserters coming over to their side. A light fire, however, was opened by the butternuts stationed in the rifle pits to the right and left of Davidson's Battery.

196 OR 42, pt. 1, 236.

197 Ibid., 254.

198 Ibid., 906.

Major General Nelson A. Miles
Library of Congress

With their axes, the Federals in the meantime had opened a passage through the chevaux-de-frise. Pressing quickly on, they entered the battery, capturing 4 officers and 13 enlisted men of the 37th and 47th Virginia. The Confederates now realized that they had been mistaken. A savage counterattack was launched by one of Goode's regiments from the southwest. Before Miles had a chance to take advantage of the success scored by Brown's patrol, the butternuts had recovered Davidson's Battery, taking 15 prisoners.[199]

It was 10:00 p.m. when Burke's patrol charged the Confederate line of outposts west of the Rives Salient. The "intense darkness and rain" covered the bluecoats' advance, and they carried about 200 yards of picket line held by the Holcombe South Carolina Legion, capturing eight Southerners. Next, the Confederate artillery opened along the entire front and the Union cannoneers replied. A furious cannonade ensued, lasting for about 30 minutes. Covered by this bombardment, General Wallace organized a 200-man detachment from the Legion and the 18th South Carolina. Headed by Captain A. V. Brown of the Legion, the volunteers advanced to recover the line of outposts. The South Carolinians cautiously approached to within 20 or 30 yards of the picket line and then charged, recovering the works and "capturing 14 prisoners, with their arms and accouterments, and a small lot of entrenching tools."[200]

---

199 *Ibid.*, 254, 906.

200 *Ibid.*, 254-256, 906, 933. On these two raids, General Miles reported that he lost 4 officers and 63 men, killed, wounded, and missing.

Miles' twin thrusts against Johnson's division had immediate and important repercussions. General Hill, who had been willing to increase the strength of Heth's striking force, now had a change of heart. No reinforcements would be forthcoming, and Hampton and Heth would have to forego the joint infantry-cavalry attack on the II Corps scheduled for daybreak on the 28th. Indeed, Hill was so alarmed for the safety of the sector held by Johnson's division that orders were issued recalling Mahone and the three brigades with which he had marched to meet the Federals.[201]

Under the cover of darkness, Heth had recalled the four infantry brigades that had crossed Hatcher's Run to carry the fight to the Army of the Potomac. MacRae's and Weisiger's brigades retired in considerable disorder. When Major J. R. Lewellen mustered the 12th Virginia, he found that he had lost 3 killed, 13 wounded, and 76 missing and presumed to be prisoners.[202] One of MacRae's veterans recalled, "The affair at Burgess Mill was marred by the misunderstanding of his orders by an officer in high rank, by which he failed to reinforce as instructed" our brigade, thereby causing us to suffer a heavy loss.[203]

News that the II Corps had stolen a march on Hampton and Heth caused Hill to fret. He feared that unless Mahone marched rapidly, the Federals would effect such a concentration in front of Johnson's sector that they would be able to score a breakthrough. Sergeant Sale reported that his brigade, along with Harris' and King's, hurried back to our "old positions." It was discovered "on getting to our old place that the enemy had attacked in addition to our right, our extreme left, and also on the Baxter Road, but were defeated in all their attempts. So ends, another 'On to Richmond.'"[204]

The Army of the Potomac listed its casualties in the battle of Burgess Mill as 166 killed, 1,028 wounded, and 564 missing. Of these, the II Corps had lost the lion's share—99 killed, 539 wounded, and 420 missing. Confederate casualties were never completely reported. The Union provost-marshal reported that 530 Confederate prisoners from Weisiger's, Cooke's, and MacRae's brigades were sent in by the II Corps, while 148 soldiers (all from Weisiger's brigade, except for a few

201 *Ibid.*, 906.

202 Sale, Diary, n.d.

203 Stedman, "The Forty-Fourth North Carolina Infantry," 343-344.

204 Sale, Diary, n.d.

stragglers from Cooke's brigade) had been turned over to his people by the V Corps. Twenty Rebel cavalrymen had also been counted.[205]

Thus ended the most ambitious Union attempts in the autumn of 1864 to outflank the Richmond-Petersburg line. It closed with a Confederate victory. Many soldiers hoped that this would be the last great battle in this sector for the year, because of the weather, which had been mild and open in October, but became uncertain with the opening of November.

It should have been apparent by now to Grant and Meade that by sending columns out to threaten the flanks of the Richmond-Petersburg line that they were playing into General Lee's hands. Each time that it was tried, the Confederates used their entrenchments to hold the Federals to their front in check with a comparatively small force, while they concentrated, against the flanking column a sufficient force to repel it back, or at least cripple its advance.

Editor's Conclusion

This Sixth Offensive failed because the Confederate line at Hatcher's Run was not unfinished, Parke moved much too slow and without sufficient aggression when he met the enemy, and the Confederates shuffled troops to prevent the breakthrough that should have taken place. When Parke's failure became clear, Warren was dispatched to link up with Hancock. Unfortunately, deep woods and swamps delayed Warren and the Confederates attacked Hancock before a junction could be formed. In effect, the Union plan failed because two-thirds of the Federals were tied down in front of the Confederate lines doing nothing. They did not even prevent the Confederates from assembling a large force to strike Hancock. Union losses were 1,758, while Confederate casualties totaled about 1,300.[206]

---

205   *OR* 42, pt. 1, 160; pt. 3, 406.

206   Horn, *The Petersburg Campaign* p. 33

Chapter 3

The Battle of Hatcher's Run

February 5-7, 1865

Editor's Introduction

There were changes in the high command of both armies between October and December of 1864. Confederate First Corps commander Lieutenant General James Longstreet returned from his convalescence in October after his nearly fatal wound in the Wilderness the previous May to resume command of his corps. His return left Lieutenant General Richard H. Anderson, who had been leading Longstreet's men since Old Pete's fall, without a command. Anderson, who had displayed generally reliable if unspectacular command abilities, was put in charge of two infantry divisions—Robert Hoke's and Bushrod Johnson's—that had served under General P. G. T. Beauregard. This decision formed what was in essence (but not officially) a fourth corps within Lee's army. On the Union side, Ben Butler was finally relieved of command of the Army of the James after his failure to take Fort Fisher off Wilmington, North Carolina, on Christmas day. With his re-election President Lincoln no longer needed the political general. Butler was replaced by Major General Edward O. C. Ord.

There were also important changes in the composition of the opposing armies during the last two months of 1864 and January 1865. Between December 4 and 16, after its extended sojourn in the Shenandoah Valley, the VI Corps rejoined the Army of the Potomac at Petersburg. Major General Horatio Wright's corps took position on the Union left southwest of the city.

Major General Joseph Kershaw's Confederate division, part of Longstreet's corps, also returned from the Valley in late November and joined the rest of Longstreet in the trenches north of the James River defending Richmond. The much-reduced Confederate II Corps under Major General John Gordon left the Shenandoah Valley between December 8 and 14 and rejoined the Army of Northern Virginia, taking position on the right of Lieutenant General A. P. Hill's III Corps.

In another gamble to slow down Union advances elsewhere, General Lee weakened his army in December of 1864 and January of 1865 by detaching Hoke's infantry division and Brigadier General Matthew Butler's cavalry division to oppose Major General William T. Sherman's thrust through the Carolinas. Cavalryman Wade Hampton returned to his native South Carolina to help raise troops and assist in stopping Union successes there. Also that January, Grant dispatched men from the Army of the James under Major General Alfred Terry to capture Fort Fisher at Wilmington.

The lull in the fighting before Petersburg and Richmond between the end of October 1864 and early February of 1865 allowed Meade's exhausted and demoralized Army of the Potomac a much-needed opportunity to rest, drill, and regain faith in itself and in its leaders. During this same period across the lines, however, many Confederates reached the unmistakable conclusion that the South would almost certainly lose the war. Morale sank lower during this prolonged lull, and men deserted in large numbers.

In December 1864, Major General Gouverneur Warren marched his V Corps 40 miles down the Weldon Railroad as far south as Hicksford, tearing up large portions of the line between that point and Stony Creek. Lee, however, continued to supply his army by using wagons to haul war material from below Hicksford to Petersburg via the Boydton Plank Road. In February 1865, Grant dispatched Brigadier General David M. Gregg's cavalry to sever the Boydton Plank Road and seize these Rebel supply wagons to stop this method of supply. The II Corps, now under the command of Major General Andrew Humphreys, together with Warren's V Corps, supported the cavalry operation.

Part I

Meade and His Generals Prepare to Strike

Reports reached Lieutenant General Ulysses S. Grant's City Point, Virginia, headquarters at the beginning of February 1865, that the Confederates were employing huge wagon trains to haul supplies into Petersburg for consumption by the Army of Northern Virginia. Rations stockpiled at depots in North Carolina, it was said, were being shipped as far as Hicksford, 40 miles south of Petersburg, over the Petersburg & Weldon Railroad. At Hicksford, the commissary supplies were removed from the cars and loaded onto wagons. Upon leaving the temporary railhead, the wagon trains rolled up the Meherrin River valley to the Boydton Plank Road, and then along that road through Dinwiddie Court House and on to Petersburg.[1]

General Grant, hoping to intercept these trains and break up this supply route, addressed a memorandum to the commander of his Army of the Potomac, Major General George G. Meade on February 4. To take advantage of the dry, spring-like weather of the past few days which had dried the area's roads, Grant wanted "to destroy or capture as much as possibly" of the quartermaster trains being used to "partially supply" Gen. Robert E. Lee's troops in and about Petersburg. To accomplish this, Meade was to prepare his cavalry to take the field as soon as possible, and in no case later than the 6th. When the troopers rode out, they were to travel light, taking "no wagons and but few ambulances."

The II Corps was to march at the same time, but independent of the cavalry, "as far south as Stony Creek Station." The foot soldiers were to stay there till the cavalry had done the foe all the harm it could and had returned to its base. When it took the field, the infantry was to take along four days' rations in haversacks and one and one-half days' forage for the cavalry in wagons. A limited amount of artillery was to accompany the II Corps.

The V Corps was to be held ready to assist the II Corps should the Confederates march out of the Petersburg perimeter to attack. It might be wise, Grant observed, for Meade to send out the V Corps at the same time as the II, marching "it by a road west of the one taken by the latter, and to go but about half way to Stony Creek, unless required to do so to meet movements of the enemy."

---

1 Humphreys, *The Virginia Campaign of '64 and '65*, 312.

Grant entrusted his letter, which was marked confidential, to a trusted staff officer for delivery to General Meade. After studying the memorandum, Meade concluded that chances for the operation's success would be enhanced if several changes were made.

As one of the II Corps' divisions was in the rifle pits, valuable time would be squandered and there would a risk of attracting the Confederates' attention should this unit be withdrawn. Meade accordingly thought it would be better if he sent the V Corps to Stony Creek and the two divisions of the II Corps to Ream's Station. There, the II Corps would be in position to support the V Corps, "or return to our left flank if threatened."

Meade telegraphed Grant at 1:45 p.m. for permission to make these changes to his master plan.[2]

Grant approved Meade's suggestions. Upon doing so, he pointed out that he had mentioned the II Corps for the longer march simply because the V Corps had undertaken the last expedition.[3]

While awaiting Grant's reply, Meade discussed the situation with his staff. One of the officers revealed that the Confederate trains moving along the Boydton Plank Road had been crossing the Nottoway at Birchett's Bridge. If Grant would give him the go-ahead, Meade would send the V Corps to the crossing of Stony Creek via Vaughan Road, while the II Corps followed the same road as far as Rowanty Creek. Thus, the infantry would be advanced to within supporting distance of Dinwiddie Court House, where the cavalry was to strike the Boydton Plank Road. Meade believed that his horse soldiers had as good a chance of intercepting the trains near Dinwiddie as at Belfield, while his infantry columns would simultaneously not have so far to march. Should the Rebels choose to come out and fight, the II and V Corps would be "in good position to invite them."

While he forwarded this information to Grant, Meade inquired, "Are the objects to be attained commensurate with the disappointment which the public are sure to entertain if you make any movement and return without some striking result?"[4]

---

2   OR 46, pt. 2, 367.

3   *Ibid.* The V Corps, reinforced by the Third Division of the II Corps and Brigadier General David McM. Gregg's cavalry, in December had destroyed the Weldon Railroad, as far as the Meherrin River. Humphreys, *The Virginia Campaign of '64 and '65*, 310.

4   OR 46, pt. 2, 367-368.

Replying at 6:45 p.m., Grant assured Meade, "Your arrangements are satisfactory," and that the "objects to be attained are of importance."[5] Grant had inquired as to when the troops would march, so Meade (at 7:45 p.m.) wired, "the cavalry will move out at 3:00 a.m. and the infantry at 7:00 a.m." Since his last telegram, several "contrabands" had entered the Union lines. When questioned, they reported that Major General Matthew C. Butler's Confederate cavalry division had left the Petersburg area the previous week for North Carolina. With Butler gone, Lee would only have one mounted division, Major General W. H. F. "Rooney" Lee's, to oppose the Federal horse soldiers.[6] News of the probable departure of Butler's Division caused Grant to again contact Meade. If the Union cavalry could possibly go to Belfield, it was to do so, because there was said to be a large quantity of stores stockpiled there.[7]

Meade and his staff in the meantime had prepared a "circular" for the guidance of the corps commanders and Brigadier General David McM. Gregg, the leader of the Army of the Potomac's cavalry. Gregg was to have his division on the road at 3:00 a.m. the following day, to proceed via Ream's Station to the Boydton Plank Road for the purpose of intercepting and capturing Rebel wagon trains carrying supplies from Belfield. Should an opportunity occur to inflict "injury on the enemy," Gregg was to take advantage of the situation. The cavalryman was to leave with the V Corps one of his cavalry regiments and a supply train, loaded with "one and a half day's forage" and his reserve ammunition. The troopers were to be rationed for "four days from tomorrow morning." Gregg was to keep the leader of the V Corps posted, and in the event of an engagement, he was to look to him for orders.[8]

Major General Gouverneur K. Warren was to march his V Corps at 7:00 a.m. to J. Hargrave's house, on the road leading from Rowanty Post office to Dinwiddie Court House. There, he was to take post in support of Gregg's cavalry. When it took the field, the V Corps was to be accompanied by "two batteries, one rifled and one smooth-bore, and the usual amount of ammunition in limbers and caissons." Like troopers, the foot soldiers were to carry along four days' rations. Ninety

---

5 *Ibid.*, 368. In early January, the Confederate leaders decided to send General Butler and two (Rutledge's and Young's) of his three brigades to South Carolina to check the advance of Major General William T. Sherman's powerful "Army Group." On January 19, an order to this effect was issued. Around the same time, Major General Wade Hampton was directed to proceed to South Carolina. Wells, *Hampton and His Cavalry*, 389.

6 *OR* 46, pt. 2, 368, 370.

7 *Ibid.*, 368.

8 *Ibid.*, 370, 380-381.

rounds of ammunition would be allocated by the corps' ordinance officer for each man taken along on the expedition, 50 rounds in cartridge boxes and the rest in reserve. "One-half the usual allowance of ambulances, with one hospital and one medicine wagon to each brigade, together with one-half the entrenching tools, besides the pioneer tools," would be taken by the corps. Should Warren need reinforcements, he was to look to the II Corps.[9]

Major General Andrew A. Humphreys was to move out at 7:00 a.m. with his two divisions "on the line to the crossing of the Vaughn Road over Hatcher's Run and the Armstrong's Mills." He would "hold these two points and the communications with General Warren" to his front and the VI Corps in his rear. The II Corps was to march with two batteries, while the allowance as to rations, ammunition, tools, and medical would be identical to that of Warren's people.[10]

As a situation could develop where the entire Army of the Potomac might be called on to take the field, Major General John G. Parke of the IX Corps and Brigadier General George W. Getty of the VI Corps, along with the leader of Humphreys' First Division (Brigadier General Nelson A. Miles), were alerted to hold their commands ready to march on short notice. They were to be prepared to withdraw "all the troops except the minimum number necessary to maintain the picket-line and the garrisons of the works." Meade's staff was put on call to be ready to accompany their general when he took the field at 8:00 p.m.[11]

By 8:50 p.m. on February 4, General Gregg had prepared and distributed final instructions to his brigade commanders. When the division took the field at 3:00 a.m., the march order would be: "First, Second Brigade; second, Third Brigade; third, one-half the ambulances of the division; fourth, First Brigade." After leaving camp, the horse soldiers were to proceed down the Jerusalem Plank Road to Gary's Church, and then to Ream's Station, where the commander of the advance brigade, Col. J. Irwin Gregg, was to receive additional instructions. No batteries would be taken along on the expedition, while the leader of the 3rd Brigade was to designate one of his regiments to report to General Warren.[12]

---

9   *Ibid.*, 370, 377-378. A telegraph line was to be run from army headquarters to the II Corps' command post on Hatcher's Run.

10   *Ibid.*, 370, 372. General Miles' division, which was posted in the earthworks, was to report during the corps absence to army headquarters.

11   *Ibid.*, 370-371.

12   *Ibid.*, 382. Colonel Gregg of the 2nd Brigade was to recall two-thirds of the force that he had on picket at dusk. The troopers remaining on picket were to maintain their present line, with such modifications as Colonel Gregg might direct. *Ibid.*

Meanwhile, General Warren had announced the order in which his V Corps was to move out. Realizing that there would be delays, Warren wanted his division commanders to have their people formed and ready to march by 6:30 a.m. Brigadier General Romeyn B. Ayres' Second Division was to take the lead, followed by Brigadier General Charles Griffin's First Division, the artillery, Brigadier General Samuel W. Crawford's Third Division, the ambulances, and finally the reserve ordnance wagons. The usual number of spring wagons would be allowed to accompany the "several headquarters." At 6:30 a.m., all the corps' pioneers were to assemble at Dr. Gurley's house. A three days' supply of beef cattle on the hoof were to be driven along on the expedition. Guards were to be detailed to protect the camps during the corps' absence.

V Corps troops currently on the picket line were to be left when the long blue columns moved out. Rations to subsist the 1,400 pickets were to be issued by the corps' chief of commissary.[13]

General Humphreys, having served for months as Meade's Chief of Staff, was more conscious of security concerns than Warren and Gregg. Like General Grant, he marked the circular prepared for the guidance of his division commanders as "confidential." Brigadier General Thomas Smyth was to march his Second Division down Vaughan Road at 7:00 a.m., past Cummings' house, and via a crossroad to the vicinity of Armstrong's Mill. There, he was to post his troops and hold the Hatcher's Run crossing. Other units of Smyth's command were to guard the crossroad over which the Second Division had marched from Vaughan Road and "look up the Duncan Road toward the Watkins house." Smyth's column was to be preceded by 350 horse soldiers, who were to drive the Rebel vedettes beyond Hatcher's Run. The troopers were then to cross the stream, pushing on to Dabney's Mill.

The Third Division, under the command of Brigadier General Gershom Mott, was to follow Smyth. One brigade was to cross Hatcher's Run, and hold the roads beyond leading to Armstrong's and Dabney's Mills. A second brigade was to be posted at the crossing of Hatcher's Run, while a third was to be positioned at the point where the crossroad to Armstrong's Mill left Vaughan Road.

During the advance, Smyth's people were to look out for their right and front, and, in conjunction with Mott's division, "establish a line connecting with the corps picket-line near the Tucker house. . ."[14]

---

13 *Ibid.*, 378-379.

14 *Ibid.*, 373-374. General Miles was to hold his division, "including the garrison of the rear works, ready to move, excepting the force heretofore specified for garrisons, pickets, as the

To insure that Smyth and Mott took the field with as many effectives as possible, Humphreys ordered that the 355 men from Smyth's division currently on picket were to be relieved by soldiers from General Miles' First Division during the night. Mott's pickets would not be relieved, but would be withdrawn when the division moved out, "excepting a sufficient force to protect the camps in their rear against guerrillas." Miles was to send garrisons to Forts Emory and Siebert at 8:00 a.m. on February 5.[15]

Part II

The Confederates Come Out

Reveille sounded at 2:00 a.m. on February 5, 1865, in the encampments occupied by General Gregg's fast-moving cavalry division. Before an hour had passed, the troopers had wolfed down a hurried breakfast, squared away their gear, and saddled their horses. The three brigades had been formed, mustered, and inspected by 3:00 a.m. General Gregg now gave the word, and the division moved out. The 2nd Brigade, Col. J. Irwin Gregg commanding, took the lead as the long column rode through the darkness down the Jerusalem Plank Road.[16]

As the leading regiment, the 13th Pennsylvania turned off the Plank Road at Gary's Church and into a road leading westward. The early risers were getting up, as the column passed Wood's Shop. Daylight found the horse soldiers at Ream's Station, where General Gregg directed the advance into the Halifax Road. Veterans pointed out to replacements the sites associated with previous Rebel encounters in and about Ream's Station. At Malone's Crossing, the cavalry entered the Malone's Bridge Road.

About a mile from Malone's Bridge, men of the 13th Pennsylvania spotted Rebel pickets. Captain Nathaniel S. Sneyd ordered the gait quickened as he observed the Confederates swinging into their saddles and retiring rapidly down the road. Troopers of the 13th Pennsylvania pounded along close on their heels.

---

picket-line south of the road running west from Fort Cummings will require to be changed quickly by orders from the commanding general."

15 *Ibid.*, 374-375. Heretofore, Smyth's division had garrisoned Forts Emory and Siebert.

16 OR 46, pt. 1, 113, 365-367, 371. The 6th Ohio Cavalry, in accordance with instructions, was detached and ordered to report to General Warren. The 1st Brigade was camped at Westbrook's house, one mile west of McCann's Station, on the Petersburg & Norfolk Railroad.

Crossing Rowanty Creek, the grey clads sounded the alarm and took cover in a line of rifle pits. Alerted by shouts and shots, the reserve had already filed into the earthworks. As soon as the last of the pickets had crossed and moments before the Federals came into view, the Confederates removed a number of planks which they had previously loosened from the bridge.

General Gregg, who rode with the vanguard, saw the fortifications and called for the commander of the 13th Pennsylvania to form his troopers for battle. As soon as the cavalrymen had dismounted and the horse-holders had been detailed, the Pennsylvanians deployed as skirmishers to the left and right of the road, "with orders to advance and drive the enemy from his position. . . ."

The troopers fought their way, "Indian-fashion," toward the edge of the stream. Within a few minutes, the bluecoats had gained the upper hand and were able to keep the Rebels pinned down. Covered by the fire of these sharpshooters, volunteers dashed forward and repaired the bridge. Colonel Gregg now called up the 2nd Pennsylvania. Putting the spurs to their horses, the 2nd Pennsylvania Cavalry clattered across the bridge, scattering the Confederates—who had abandoned their position and were racings for their mounts—in all directions. An officer and 15 men, less fleet than their comrades, were overtaken by the Federals.[17]

When the march was renewed, the 8th Pennsylvania Cavalry of Gregg's brigade took the lead, as the division pounded westward toward Dinwiddie Court House by way of the Military and Vaughan roads. No further opposition was encountered as the Yankee horse soldiers pounded ahead. The Confederates, who they had bested in the engagement at Malone's Bridge, had retired toward Stony Creek. Galloping into Dinwiddie Court House at noon, troopers of the 8th Pennsylvania surprised and captured a small train of nine wagons.

While the division rested, Colonel Gregg organized and sent out three combat patrols. The 8th Pennsylvania Cavalry rode down the Boydton Plank Road toward Belfield, while the 16th Pennsylvania Cavalry headed up the Plank Road in the direction of Petersburg. A detachment from the 2nd Pennsylvania Cavalry headed out on the Flat Foot Road.

Lieutenant Colonel William A. Corrie and his horse soldiers of the 8th Pennsylvania drove down the Plank Road to a point beyond the crossing of Butterwood Creek, without intercepting any more wagons. Spearheaded by Captain McDowell's squadron (Companies A and B), the 16th Pennsylvania rode up the Plank Road about 5 miles, overtaking 12 wagons and an ambulance, and capturing 3 officers and 12 enlisted Confederates. The 16th Pennsylvania, not

17 *Ibid.*, 115, 366-368, 370. In this clash, the 2nd Pennsylvania lost 1 killed, 2 wounded, and 1 missing.

having fired a shot, then returned its steps. Of the three patrols ordered out, only the 2nd Pennsylvania exchanged shots with the Rebels. As they advanced down Flat Foot Road, the horse soldiers of the 2nd Pennsylvania clashed with a small mounted detachment.[18]

General Gregg, after questioning the prisoners and the residents of the village, concluded that information indicating the Rebels were moving large quantities of supplies into Petersburg by way of the Boydton Plank Road was false. During the past ten days, he wrote Chief of Staff Alexander S. Webb that there had been very little wagon traffic along that road. Although he had driven his men hard, only 18 wagons had been captured.

Important information regarding Confederate troop movements, however, had been secured. One of Gen. Robert E. Lee's infantry divisions had camped on the night of the 4th, four miles northeast of Dinwiddie Court House. This force had broken camp at dawn and had marched up the Boydton Plank Road, rejoining the Army of Northern Virginia inside the Petersburg perimeter.

According to the prisoners, Col. B. Huger Rutledge's South Carolina cavalry brigade had gone south. The remainder of Lee's cavalry, currently operating on the Southside, was said to be "about Belfield and north toward Jarratt's." Because of the destruction of the railroad bridge across the Meherrin River, there was reportedly only a small quantity of supplies at Belfield; consequently, Gregg decided that leading his division to that point wasn't worth the risk.[19]

Satisfied that he had inflicted all the damage he could to the Confederate military in the Dinwiddie Court House area, Gregg started his division back for the Rowanty. As his vanguard was turning into the military road at Kidd's, General Gregg sent a patrol down Vaughan Road to relay to General Warren the information that the horse soldiers had collected regarding Rebel activities in the area. The cavalry division was back at Malone's Bridge at 10:00 p.m. On the return march, a half dozen mounted butternuts harassed Gregg's rear guard, Captain Oliphant's squadron (Companies G and H), 16th Pennsylvania Cavalry.[20]

* * *

18 *Ibid.*, 115, 117, 368-370. In addition to the wagons, the 8th Pennsylvania captured 50 mules and 10 men.

19 *OR* 46, pt. 2, 396.

20 *OR* 46, pt. 1, 116, 366, 368, 370-371.

General Humphreys and his staff were up and about long before daybreak on February 5. Checking his order of battle at 5:25 a.m., Humphreys was disturbed to learn that the cavalry officer (who was to have reported with his detachment at 1:00 a.m.) had not shown up. Upon investigating, Humphreys discovered that there had been a miscommunication: the cavalry was to report at 6:00 a.m. At the designated hour, Maj. Frank W. Hess, with 200 officers and men of the 3rd Pennsylvania Cavalry, showed up at Humphreys' headquarters.[21]

Communicating with General Smyth, Humphreys was delighted to learn that the Second Division's picket line had been relieved by troops from Miles' command.[22] Smyth assured his corps commander that at this hour his troops were massed at McDougall's house and were ready and eager to take the field.[23]

Preceded by Major Hess and his troopers, Smyth's division took up the march at 7:00 a.m. Immediately behind the cavalry, as the Second Division turned into Vaughan Road, came Col. William A. Olmsted's 1st Brigade, followed by Col. Mathew Murphy's 2nd Brigade, the 10th Massachusetts Battery, and Lieutenant Colonel Francis E. Pierce's 3rd Brigade. Before the column had hiked very far down Vaughan Road, Colonel Olmsted, in compliance with instructions from General Smyth, sent the 19th Massachusetts forward to support Hess' cavalry.[24]

General Mott had turned his division out at daybreak. Forty minutes before the Third Division was slated to move out, Lt. John W. Roder reported to Mott with his unit—Battery K, 4th U.S. Light Artillery. Mott put his division in motion at 7:00 a.m. The Third Division, with Brigadier General Regis de Trobriand's 1st Brigade in the lead, followed Smyth's column down Vaughan Road. Near McDowell's house, one of Humphreys' staff officers hailed General Mott. Humphreys wanted Mott to send forward the brigade that was to force a crossing of Hatcher's Run. Mott told de Trobriand to accompany the aide and he halted Smyth's division.

The 1st Brigade and one section of Battery K followed de Trobriand, as he rode through the picket line. De Trobriand's mission was twofold. Besides forcing a crossing of Hatcher's Run at Vaughan Road, he was also to "make disposition to

---

21 *Ibid.*, 191; *OR* 46, pt. 2, 396.

22 *OR* 46, pt. 1, 195. At 8:00 a.m., the 39th New York was placed in a garrison at Fort Emory, while the 125th New York occupied Fort Siebert.

23 *Ibid.*, 212.

24 *Ibid.*, 212, 214-215. At this stage of the conflict, Smyth's division numbered 4,607 effective. *Ibid.*, 191.

hold the roads leading to Armstrong's and Dabney's Mills." Screened by Hess and his horse soldiers, de Trobriand's bluecoats sped rapidly along.[25]

Shots were exchanged near Cummings' house, as Hess' cavalrymen charged and drove Confederate vedettes down the road toward the ford. Approaching Hatcher's Run, Major Hess and his scouts saw that there was a small detachment of Rebels posted in rifle pits on the opposite bank to guard the Vaughan Road crossing. A hurried reconnaissance satisfied Hess that his troopers would be unable to force a "passage" as planned, because the crossing had been obstructed with felled timber.

Upon receiving this news from Hess, de Trobriand prepared to employ his infantry to establish the bridgehead. Soldiers of the 2nd U.S. Sharpshooters were called up and deployed as skirmishers to the front and right of the Rebels' breastworks. While the sharpshooters engaged the Johnnies, the 99th and 110th Pennsylvania worked their way through the woods south of Vaughan Road. Col. Edwin R. Biles of the 99th was to take advantage of the diversion effected by the regulars to force a passage of Hatcher's Run at the broken dam, 200 yards south of the crossing.

After waiting about 15 minutes and hearing nothing further from Colonel. Biles, General de Trobriand rode to the left to ascertain the cause of the delay. As his horse trotted into the woods, de Trobriand was shaken to see the two Pennsylvania regiments lying down among the trees. Infuriated, he confronted Biles and demanded an explanation. Biles answered, "The cavalrymen told me the run was impassable for foot soldiers," while "he supposed that he was to regulate his movements" on the sharpshooters.

"You are mistaken!" de Trobriand exclaimed, and he repeated his orders.

The misunderstanding resolved, the 99th Pennsylvania, supported by the 110th, moved out of the woods and charged across a small, open field to the bank of the run. Without waiting for the bluecoats to attempt a crossing, the butternuts abandoned their earthworks and disappeared into the timber beyond. Even with no opposition the Yanks experienced considerable difficulty in reaching the right bank of Hatcher's Run. The water was deep and cold, and the men had to jump, one after the other, from log to log. General de Trobriand was compelled to dismount and pass the stream in similar fashion.[26]

---

25 *Ibid.*, 191, 224. The cavalry had a twofold mission: to drive in the Rebel pickets and to secure the crossing, "so as to conceal temporarily the fact from the enemy that the movement was made by an infantry force."

26 *Ibid.*, 164, 224, 226-227; Francis A. Walker, *History of the Second Army Corps in the Army of the Potomac* (New York, 1886), 647.

Having gained the west bank of the run by 9:30 a.m., General de Trobriand had the mission of posting his men to cover the bridgehead and watch the roads leading to Armstrong's and Dabney's Mills. An arc-shaped line was laid out across the two roads, the right resting on the run and the left on a swamp. The units filed into position as the regiments of the 1st Brigade slowly worked their way across Hatcher's Run. Outposts were pushed out, connecting on the left with the captured rifle pits in which de Trobriand posted two companies. The brigade's numerically strongest regiment, the 1st Maine Heavy Artillery, was held in reserve, ready to move on the double to any point on the perimeter where its services were required. Observing that Rebel skirmishers occupied the woods to their center and right, the Yanks dug in.[27]

Meanwhile, the division pioneers had been called up and put to work bridging the run. One bridge was thrown across the stream at the Vaughan Road crossing and a second at the broken dam. The latter bridge was completed first. As soon as the bridge was declared ready for traffic, Major Hess and his horse soldiers crossed and reported to de Trobriand.

As soon as de Trobriand's rear guard had passed, General Smyth told Colonel Olmsted to resume the march. The leader of the II Corps, General Humphreys, wanted Smyth to secure a crossing of Hatcher's Run at Armstrong's Mill. After covering the bridgehead, Smyth was to extend to the right beyond R. Armstrong's house, anchoring his right on Rocking Branch. Preceded by a company of the 3rd Pennsylvania Cavalry, the Second Division followed de Trobriand's column to within one-half mile of the Vaughan Road crossing of Hatcher's Run. Here it turned into a cart road leading westward through the woods to Armstrong's Mill. As the horse soldiers approached Rocky Branch, they were fired on by Confederate outposts. Supported by the 19th Massachusetts Infantry, the Pennsylvania charged, driving the Rebels across the stream. A short distance beyond, the butternuts rallied and checked the Union cavalry. Three companies of the 19th Massachusetts, deployed as skirmishers, now took the lead. Smashing the Confederate roadblock, the infantry chased the Johnnies across Hatcher's Run. Here their advance was stopped by the fire of sharpshooters posted in rifle pits on the opposite bank. The officer in charge of the skirmishers shouted, "Take cover!"[28]

General Smyth, hearing shots in the woods of to his left, called on Colonel Olmsted for another regiment. The brigade commander sent the 19th Maine. The general told Lieutenant Colonel Joseph B. Spaulding of the Maine regiment to

27 *OR* 46, pt. 1, 227.

28 *Ibid.*, 164, 224, 227.

move his people "in line of battle off to the left." Covered by two companies, deployed as skirmishers, the 19th Maine worked its way through woods and dense undergrowth. The Maine men reached Hatcher's Run and saw Rebel infantry picketing the opposite bank. Several shots sent the grey clads diving into their rifle pits, which paralleled the bank at a distance of about ten rods.

Capitalizing on the failure of the foe to clear fields of fire, Spaulding's skirmishers crossed the run, one at a time on a fallen tree, and took cover in a defiladed area between the water and top of the bank. Although it was slow going, the rest of the regiment followed, using the route pioneered by the skirmishers. All his men across, Spaulding advanced his skirmishers. As soon as they showed themselves, there was a sharp outburst of firing. Within 15 minutes, the soldiers of the 19th Maine had gained the upper hand, and the Rebels took to their heels. Spaudling's skirmishers lost no time taking possession of the abandoned breastworks. Reinforced by two additional companies, the skirmishers extended to the right. Visual contact was soon established with the picket line of the 19th Massachusetts on the north side of Hatcher's Run.[29]

While the 19th Maine was carving out a bridgehead, General Smyth began deploying his division, keeping in mind General Humphreys' instructions to extend to his right. The troops were marched up the road leading to Armstrong's house and placed in line of battle. Colonel Olmsted's brigade was posted with its left flank—the 19th Massachusetts—resting on Hatcher's Run, but keeping in contact with the 19th Maine on the south bank. The 1st Brigade was in a field, facing the woods and occupied by much of the ground. Skirmishers advanced into the pines, while the rest of the troops were put to work erecting breastworks. As the 7th Michigan and the 1st Minnesota advanced into the timber to the left and front, they drove in Confederate pickets, capturing two.[30]

Colonel Mathew Murphy's 2nd Brigade was posted on the right of Olmsted's, its right resting on Rocky Branch. The line along which Murphy's troops entrenched "was in advance of the Armstrong house and in the rear of the Armstrong, Jr. house." One regiment, the 164th New York, was advanced as pickets.

Shortly before noon, a unit from the 3rd Brigade, the 1st Delaware, reported to Colonel Murphy. The Delaware people were posted on the right, "refusing their

---

29 *Ibid.*, 212, 214-215.

30 *Ibid.*, 212, 214, 216-219. From left to right the units posted along Olmsted's main line of resistance were: the 184th Pennsylvania, the 36th Wisconsin, and the 152nd New York. The left flank of the skirmish line held by the 1st Minnesota rested on Hatcher's Run, where it connected with the right flank of the 19th Massachusetts.

right wing, with their two right companies thrown perpendicularly to the rear." About 100 yards in front of his right, across the intervening cleared ground, Murphy saw the profile of a Rebel redoubt, with "connecting curtains." While the soldiers were digging in, a gun emplaced in this work sent an occasional round screaming overhead, shaking up the recruits , but doing no damage.[31]

The 3rd Brigade was Smyth's ready reserve, consequently, it was massed "under cover of a slight ridge," near Armstrong's. By noon, Colonel Pierce had been called upon for four units besides the 1st Delaware. At 11:00 a.m., the 7th West Virginia Battalion was ordered to report to Colonel Olmsted. Led by a staff officer, the West Virginians crossed Hatcher's Run on a dam, under a galling small arms fire, and took position alongside the 19th Maine. The 14th Connecticut was rushed up from the reserve to be posted in support of two sections of the 10th Massachusetts Battery. The left section, Lt. Milbrey Green commanding, had emplaced its 10-pounder Parrotts near young Armstrong's house, commanding Duncan Road and covering the front and right of the Second Division; the center section had unlimbered its rifled Parrotts to command the ford across Hatcher's Run and Smyth's left flank.

Lieutenant Colonel George F. Hopper advanced with his battalion of the 10th New York to reinforce Olmsted's skirmish line, while at 2:00 p.m., the 12th New Jersey was organized into fatigue parties and detailed to construct a corduroy road.[32]

General Mott's 2nd and 3rd Brigade had trailed Smyth's division down Vaughan Road to Cummings' house. Here Mott called a brief halt. In accordance with Meade's master plan, Mott sent Col. Robert McAllister's 3rd Brigade down a wood road toward Tucker's. McAllister was to place his organization in "line of battle near the Tucker house, across the road leading past it, and to throw out pickets on . . . [the] left; also, to guard well . . . [his] right." Col. George S. West's 2nd Brigade was to push on down Vaughan Road to Hatcher's Run.[33]

Within a short time, McAllister's infantry had filed into position in the woods at Tucker's. A line of outposts was established and manned by the 120th New York and the 11th New Jersey, and a connection made with Murphy's Second Division pickets along a cart road. McAllister spent most of the afternoon exploring the

---

31 *Ibid.*, 192, 212, 220, 222.

32 *Ibid.*, 212, 222, 249-250, Billings, *History of the Tenth Massachusetts Battery*, 382.

33 OR 46, pt. 1, 224, 238.

woods in front of the sector occupied by his brigade, familiarizing himself with the topography.[34]

At 12:30 p.m., orders were received from General Humphreys to build breastworks. McAllister's people went to work with a will. McAllister feared that a Rebel column might infiltrate the ground between his right and a branch of Arthur Swamp, so he had his soldiers extend their rifle pits in that direction.[35]

General Humphreys had been studying his maps. On doing so, he concluded that, if past experiences were a guide, the Confederates would soon leave the protection of their fortifications, and launch a vigorous counterattack. Humphreys felt that the Rebels would aim their initial blow at the area between Hatcher's Run and the headwaters of Arthur Swamp, where Smyth's and McAllister's men were entrenching. Consequently, he rode to his right to examine Smyth's and McAllister's positions. The corps commander saw that McAllister's brigade, although it was stretched to the breaking point, was unable to cover the wide expanse of front between Rocky Branch and Arthur Swamp.

After checking with General Meade, Humphreys telegraphed General Miles at 2:00 p.m. to dispatch "a strong brigade to relieve . . . McAllister in the position now occupied by him near the Tucker house."[36]

An able and vigorous officer, Miles did not quibble. Contacting the leader of his 4th Brigade, Colonel John Ramsey, the general told him to move out with all of his "disposable force." As soon as the soldiers could be turned out under arms Colonel Ramsey put his column in motion down Vaughan Road.[37]

Miles, after he saw Ramsey's troops hit the road, wired Humphreys that they were en route to Tucker's. If all went according to schedule, the brigade should be there by 3:45 p.m.[38]

Ramsey's people marched more rapidly than anticipated. At 3:30 p.m., a member of Ramsey's staff rode up to McAllister's command post, and handed the leader of the 3rd Brigade a copy of General Humphreys' 2:00 p.m. telegram. By this hour, McAllister's bluecoats had nearly completed the line of works on which they

---

34 *Ibid.*, 238, 242-246. The 11th New Jersey held the picket line to the left, while the 120th New York was deployed to the right.

35 *Ibid.*, 238.

36 *Ibid.*, 192; *OR* 46, pt. 2, 398.

37 *OR* 46, pt. 1, 207, 208, 211. The disposable force of Ramsey's brigade included: the 8th New York Heavy Artillery, the 64th New York, and the 53rd, 116th, and 144th Pennsylvania.

38 *OR* 46, pt. 2, 398.

had been working, but before McAllister could recover from the effect of this bombshell, Colonel Ramsey rode up at the head of his brigade.

Inside of 30 minutes, Ramsey's soldiers had replaced McAllister's in the rifle pits and along the picket line. After being relieved, McAllister massed his regiments in a field 200 yards behind the fortifications, while he sent his adjutant-general, Capt. John P. Finkelmeier, to division headquarters for fresh instructions. Needless to say, McAllister's soldiers did a lot of complaining about having the fruits of their labor enjoyed by troops from another division. At 4:00 p.m., orders were received for McAllister to redeploy his brigade on Ramsey's left.

After posting their units, Ramsey's regimental commanders deployed and advanced some of their men as pickets. The rest of the soldiers stacked arms and were turned to strengthening the barricades.[39]

Meanwhile, accompanied by General Mott, West's brigade had reached Hatcher's Run to find de Trobriand's bluecoats in possession of the opposite bank and the pioneers bridging the stream. Mott told West to form his brigade into battle line across Vaughan Road.

While West's infantry was taking position, Generals Humphreys and Mott crossed Hatcher's Run to inspect the bridgehead. Before returning to the east bank, Humphreys outlined to General de Trobriand and Major Hess what their next moves should be. De Trobriand was to push out along Vaughan Road, "so as to take possession of the Dabney's Mill Road at F. B. Keys' house." Hess and his horse soldiers were to open communications with the 19th Maine at Armstrong's Ford. A 30-man outpost was to be established by the major at Dabney's Mill.[40]

Hess moved first since he had the smaller command. On the road to Armstrong's Ford, one-fourth mile beyond the perimeter held by de Trobriand's infantry, Hess' cavalry encountered Rebel pickets. The grey clads were formed along the edge of a wood and posted behind a rail fence. Company A, Capt. Louis R. Stille commanding, was dismounted and ordered to drive in the Rebels, but they were too strong. Major Hess called for Company E to charge, mounted, on Company A's left, while Company M advanced on Stille's right. Sweeping forward, the Yanks routed the butternuts from behind the fence, capturing five. As they felt their way through the pines beyond, the Pennsylvania cavalrymen encountered the Confederates in "considerable force." Hess was satisfied that he could not dislodge these rugged foot soldiers, unless he was reinforced.

39 OR 46, pt. 1, 207, 208, 211, 238, 242-243, 245-247. From left to right, Ramsey's brigade was posted: the 64th New York, the 53rd and 116th Pennsylvania, the 8th New York Heavy Artillery, and the 144th Pennsylvania.

40 *Ibid.*, 164, 227, 235.

When notified of this, General Humphreys directed Hess to return to Vaughan Road, and open communications with the V Corps at J. Hargraves'. After a two-mile ride toward Hargraves', Hess' vanguard was fired on by snipers posted in the pines east of Vaughan Road.[41]

At 2:00 p.m., Colonel West crossed Hatcher's Run with his brigade. On doing so, he had formed a line of battle with his right resting on Vaughan Road and his left, which was refused, anchored on the run. De Trobriand was now free to take possession of the Dabney's Mill Road. Three regiments, two from his brigade (the 30th New York and the 110th Pennsylvania) and one from West's (the 105th Pennsylvania) were entrusted with this mission. As they pressed forward, the Yankee foot soldiers swept back the Rebel pickets, and soon gained their goal.

Hess' cavalry battalion was fired on, as it felt its way along Vaughan Road, so the 105th Pennsylvania was ordered to the horse soldiers' assistance. Supported by infantry, the troopers charged and smashed the Rebel roadblock. The advance along Vaughan Road was continued until contact was established with the V Corps. After reporting to General Warren, the column retraced its steps, and Major Hess notified General Humphreys that the road was open.[42]

From atop the signal tower behind Fort Fisher, signal corps personnel kept the Rebel lines to their front under observation, and at 3:15 p.m., warned Miles that the Rebels were "moving a very heavy column to their right." Miles telegraphed this important information to his superior, General Humphreys. Orders were issued, alerting the division commanders to be on guard against a counterattack.[43]

*   *   *

Past experiences, many of them bitter, enabled veteran officers and men of the Army of the Potomac to predict what Gen. Robert E. Lee's response to their surge toward the Boydton Plank Road would be. Indeed, they were able to calculate the length of time it would take Lee and his generals to ready a powerful counterblow.

Lee was attending church in Petersburg, when an aide entered, and, in a hushed voice told his general that Union infantry had forced a passage of Hatcher's Run at the Vaughan Road crossing. Lee waited quietly until communion; then, contrary to

---

41 *Ibid.*, 164. Hess failed to open direct communications between the two bridgeheads, so the only direct contact between the troops at the Vaughan Road crossing and Armstrong's Ford was along the picket lines posted on the left bank of Hatcher's Run.

42 *Ibid.*, 164, 192, 227, 235.

43 *OR* 46, pt. 2, 398.

his custom, went with the first group to the chancel. He received the communion and, taking up his hat and gloves from the pew, left immediately.[44]

Before riding for the point of danger, Lee stopped in at his headquarters for a few minutes. A telegram was dispatched at 2:45 p.m. to the War Department relaying news of the Union advance, and announcing that the general was preparing to meet the foe. At the same time, Chief of Artillery William N. Pendleton was notified, "The enemy are advancing on the Vaughan Road, cavalry and infantry crossing at Hatcher's Run. This may be a strong movement. Have the artillery on the whole line on the alert and in readiness for any emergency."

In the past, the Federals had always made a thrust north of the James toward Richmond, in conjunction with attempts to extend their left, so Lt. Gen. James Longstreet was contacted. Longstreet in turn alerted his subordinates charged with guarding the approaches to Richmond that General Lee "anticipates a simultaneous move on our left."[45]

To cope with this new Union offensive, General Lee had available a ready reserve of four infantry divisions and one division of cavalry. Major General John B. Gordon had reached Petersburg from the Valley with two badly battered divisions of the old II Corps (Pegram's and Evans') on December 8, 1864. A month later, Grimes' division of the II Corps had detrained at Dunlop's Station and had gone into camp on Swift Creek, three and one-half miles north of Petersburg.[46]

General Gordon in the meantime had camped the division commanded by Brigadier General Clement A. Evans on the Boydton Plank Road, about one mile northeast of Burgess Mill. Brigadier General John Pegram's division established winter quarters on White Oak Road, one mile west of Burgess Mill. These two divisions took turns furnishing the 800 men detailed to picket Hatcher's Run, from where the fortifications held by Major General Henry Heth's right flank brigade anchored on the stream to a point beyond Vaughan Road. Horse soldiers from Gen. Rooney Lee's cavalry division were charged with covering the crossings of the Rowanty. On February 5, soldiers from Pegram's division were manning the picket line.[47]

44 *Ibid.*, 1204; Freeman, *R. E. Lee*, vol. 3, 535-536.

45 *OR* 46, pt. 2, 1204.

46 *Ibid.*, 477.

47 *Ibid.*, 134-135; Randolph Barton, "The Battle of Hatcher's Run," in *Confederate Veteran*, vol. 17 (1909), 119.

Up until now Gordon's Corps had not seen any action since returning from the Valley, where they had suffered disasters of which the veterans didn't like to talk. Major Randolph Barton, a staff officer in the Stonewall Brigade, preferred to recall:

> The superb picture of Mrs. Pegram, formerly the lovely Hetty Cary, of Baltimore, and a bride of about two weeks, handsomely mounted, and General Lee, on foot, with his hand resting on her horse's neck, engaged in conversation while awaiting the coming of the division to be reviewed by General Lee. You can imagine the splendor of the group: a beautiful woman, a noble man in appearance in every other respect, and handsome horse.[48]

In addition to Evans' and Pegram's infantry divisions, Major General William Mahone's, which was camped one and one-half mile west of Battery No. 45, would be available for the counterattack Lee was planning.[49]

Rooney Lee's cavalry division, except for squadrons out on picket, was in "comfortable winter quarters" near Belfield. This was almost 40 miles away, a long day's march for men riding horses and mules that had been on short forage for months.[50]

As they had since early October, units from Major General Henry Heth's and Cadmus M. Wilcox's divisions occupied the line of earthworks extending from Battery No. 45 on the left to Hatcher's Run on the right. Heth's division was on the right and Wilcox's on the left. The prong of Arthur Swamp heading several hundred yards northwest of Boisseau's house (Tudor Hall) separated Heth's left from Wilcox's right. From right to left Heth's brigades were posted: Brigadier General John R. Cooke's; Colonel William McComb's; Brigadier General Joseph R. Davis'; and Brigadier General William R. MacRae's. Three of Wilcox's four brigades were in the works—McGowan's on the right, Lane's in the center, and Scales' on the left. Wilcox's other brigade, Thomas', was north of the Appomattox and had been stationed there since July 4.[51]

48 Barton, "The Battle of Hatcher's Run," 119; Henry Kyd Douglas, *I Rode With Stonewall: Being Chiefly the War Experiences of the Youngest Member of Jackson's Staff from the John Brown Raid to the Hanging of Mrs. Surratt* Chapel Hill, (1940), 335-336.

49 OR 46, pt. 1, 134-135. Mahone's Division was in the habit of providing about 200 men every day to picket in front of Lane's and Scales' brigades of Wilcox's division.

50 *Ibid.*, 1210; Beale, *History of the Ninth Virginia Cavalry*, 147.

51 OR 46, pt. 1, 134-135; Caldwell, *The History of a Brigade of South Carolinians*, 199.

Brigadier General Joseph Finegan
Library of Congress

Accompanied by his staff, at 3:00 p.m., General Lee rode out of Petersburg, taking the Boydton Plank Road. Already a number of Lee's generals, in accordance with his instructions, had put their columns in motion.

General Mahone was sick, so Brigadier General Joseph Finegan, as senior officer present, turned out the division. As soon as the brigade commanders had formed, mustered, and inspected their men, the units marched from their camps. Time being all important, Finegan permitted each brigade to start for Hatcher's Run, as soon as the officer in charge reported that it was ready. In marching to the southwest, several of Finegan's brigades took Cox Road, while others followed the Boydton Plank Road. Union signal personnel stationed in the tower behind Fort Fisher kept sections of these roads under observation. It was 3:00 p.m. before the men in the tower caught their first glimpse of one of Finegan's brigades, "going at quick time to our left on the Cox Road."[52]

An hour earlier, General Wilcox had contacted Brigadier General Samuel McGowan. The leader of the South Carolina brigade was told by his superior to prepare his men to take the field. The order to move out came within the hour. Upon leaving his camp at Boisseau's, McGowan had his lead regiment, the 1st South Carolina, fall in behind MacRae's North Carolinians. The South Carolina brigade followed MacRae's troops down the works toward Hatcher's Run. Near the center of Heth's camps, McGowan called a halt. Taking position behind the breastworks, the South Carolinians nervously fingered their rifle muskets, as they listened to the rattle of musketry and the roar of cannon in the woods to their front.

52 OR 46, pt. 2, 393-394.

Questioning several soldiers who were guarding the huts, the South Carolinians learned that the troops formerly holding this sector, Davis' Mississippians had been ordered out to attack Union troops feeling their way up Duncan Road.[53]

General Gordon, learning of the Union advance, had ordered out Evans' and Pegram's divisions. North of Hatcher's Run, Evans marched his three brigades from their camps to Burgess Mill, then down the north bank of the run to the line of works fronting General Cooke's winter quarters. The division then moved to the left along the works, about one mile. After a brief halt, at 4:00 p.m., Evans' grey clads crossed the fortifications. Before entering the woods and underbrush skirting Rocky Branch, Evans formed his division into battle line: Brigadier General William Terry's Virginia brigade on the left, Colonel William R. Peck's Louisiana brigade in the center, and Colonel John H. Lowe's Georgia brigade on the right. After the brigade commanders reported that they had completed their dispositions, General Evans told them they were to guide on Terry. He then waved his battle line forward. The division advanced to where the artillerists had unlimbered their guns and halted. Skirmishers were pushed out, as the batteries shelled the woods to the front.

Heth had massed his division on the left of Evans' troops. When he advanced, Heth would do so on a two-brigade front. Cooke's and McComb's brigades, supported by Davis' and MacRae's would spearhead the counterattack. General Lee reached the field about the time that Heth and Evans were completing their preparations. Since the hour was late, Lee decided to send Heth's troops forward, although Finegan's division was not yet up.[54]

South of Hatcher's Run, General Pegram prepared to resist the Union column that had established a bridgehead on the west side of Hatcher's Run.

About 3:00 p.m., Heth's Confederates began probing the sector held by Smyth's left flank brigade, Olmsted's. A thrust against the picket line on the left of Armstrong's house was repulsed. Shortly thereafter, Pegram's grey clads advanced toward the bridgehead held by the 19th Maine and 7th West Virginia Battalion. Colonel Spaulding reinforced the men posted in the rifle pits with two fresh companies, and the Rebels pulled back. It appeared to General Smyth that these were feints to cover an all-out assault on his left, so he had Colonel Olmsted deploy the 20th Massachusetts as skirmishers to plug a gap that had opened between Murphy's right and McAllister's left.[55]

---

53 Caldwell, *The History of a Brigade of South Carolinians*, 200.

54 *OR* 46, pt. 1, 391; *OR* pt. 2, 423, 438, 499.

55 *OR* 46, pt. 1, 212, 214, 217-218.

At 4:00 p.m., two Rebel batteries began shelling Murphy's breastworks. While one battery hammered the brigades left, the guns emplaced in redoubt pounded his front. Satisfied the Confederates were endeavoring to soften up his position before attacking; Murphy asked the cannoneers of the 10th Massachusetts Battery to hold their fire, while sending word for his pickets to keep their eyes open.[56]

McAllister in the meantime moved to carry out his instructions to post his brigade on Ramsey's left. His right regiments were just filing into position, when Heth struck. Advancing in double line of battle, covered by a strong skirmish line, Heth's division pressed forward on the left and right of Rocky Branch. Yankee pickets fired a few scattered shots and fled. Colonel McAllister bellowed, "Double-Quick!" and his troops quickly completed their deployment.

Lieutenant Colonel John William of Humphreys' staff galloped up at this moment, shouting that a gap had opened on the right, where Ramsey's brigade had closed to the right. To cope with this situation, the rear regiment (the 11th New Jersey) was diverted from the left. As men of the 11th New Jersey scrambled into position behind the breastworks, frightened pickets, many of them belonging to the Second Division, ran toward them. A Rebel battery emplaced to the left and rear of Thompson's house, shelled the bluecoats, hurrying them along. Moments after the 11th New Jersey had occupied the works, Heth's skirmishers sheltered in the pines and ravine to the left opened fire.

On the left of McAllister's line, the barricades faded out, and the left battalion of the 8th New Jersey found itself with no protection, except trees and underbrush. Following hard on the heels of the retreating pickets, Heth's battle lines appeared in front of the sector defended by the 8th New Jersey, which greeted the butternuts with a terrific volley, causing them to fall back in confusion. Again, they advanced in strong force, seemingly unmindful of the Yanks' fire, and took cover behind stumps and felled timber east of Rocky Branch. Now sheltered, the Johnnies punished the exposed wing of the 8th New Jersey.

From left to right, the 120th New York, the 7th New Jersey, and the 11th Massachusetts held the brigade front to the left of the 8th New Jersey. Heth's battle lines came on "with a yell known to . . . all." Volley after volley ripped into the oncoming Confederates, and compelling them to recoil.[57]

West of Rocky Branch, Evans' skirmishers assailed the right of Murphy's picket line defended by the 182nd New York. The New Yorkers and butternuts engaged in a spirited fire-fight. After about 15 minutes, the Johnnies pulled back.

56 *Ibid.*, 220.

57 *Ibid.*, 238-239, 242-246, 248.

The Rebel artillery now resumed its bombardment of Murphy's main line of resistance. While the Yanks were exchanging mutual congratulations at having beaten off the Southerners, Evans' grey clads came on a second time, but again they were repulsed by Murphy's skirmishers. Colonel Murphy at this time was disabled, a minie ball striking him in the knee. After turning command of the brigade over to the senior regimental commander, Colonel James P. McIvor of the 170th New York, Murphy was carried to a field hospital.[58]

General Smyth, learning that his pickets east of Rocky Branch were retreating before Heth's Confederates, called up the 108th New York and a battalion of the 4th Ohio from his reserve brigade.

Simultaneously, orders were given for the 14th Connecticut to change front to the right and take position covering Rocky Branch. Although they had to cross an area swept by artillery, the Connecticut regiment "changed front forward on first company, bringing . . . [its] line at a right angle with the line attacked." The 12th New Jersey had returned from its road building assignment just as Smyth was preparing to move out with the 4th Ohio and 108th New York. A change in plans was made. Since he believed that two regiments would be sufficient for the mission, Smyth crossed the branch at the head of the 4th Ohio and 12th New Jersey to discover McAllister's men "filing in to occupy that ground that . . . [he], intended to occupy. . . ." Smyth accordingly ordered the Ohio battalion to report back to Colonel Pierce, while the 12th New Jersey was posted in support of McAllister's brigade. The 108th New York in the meantime had been employed to bolster Olmsted's picket line.[59]

Two sections of the 10th Massachusetts Battery were emplaced west of Rocky Branch at the hour of Heth's advance. General Smyth, seeing that the butternuts were driving toward the 300-yard gap separating his right from McAllister's left, sent word for Lieutenant J. Webb Adams to wheel his guns about. Since being unlimbered, Adams' and Green's sections had only been slightly engaged, having fired an occasional round at the cannons to their front which were harassing Murphy's infantry. Green, whose section was in battery near young Armstrong's, found that on reversing his 10-pounder Parrotts he was able to enfilade the advancing Rebel lines, 300 yards to his front. Adams' pieces from near the ford delivered "an oblique fire on the center and left" of Heth's battle lines. "Never did shells do more effective work," bragged the batteries historian:

58 *Ibid.,* 220-221.

59 *Ibid.,* 212, 222-223.

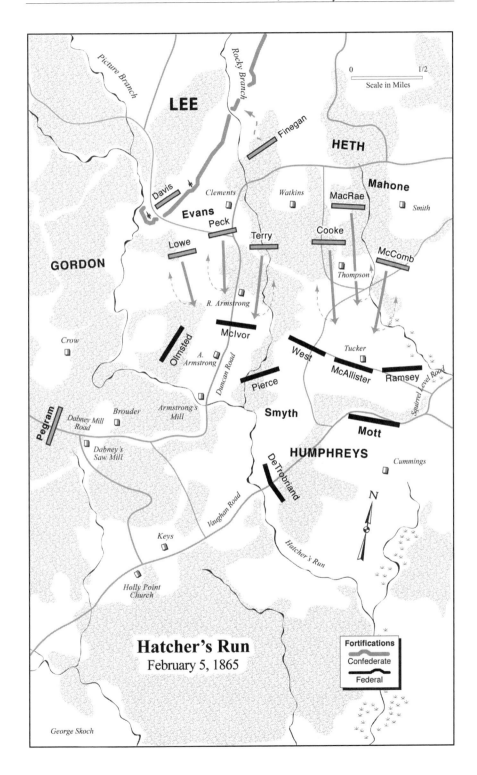

Hatcher's Run
February 5, 1865

George Skoch

Than did those fired by these two sections. Their opportunity was a rare one, and most rarely did they improve it. The Rebel advance first appeared in view in a somewhat scattered tract of woods, mainly pines and oaks, and amid these the havoc was greatest. Five men were afterwards found lying dead near a tree, killed by a shell which, singularly enough first passed completely through the trunk of the tree, exploding on the further side.[60]

As soon as Heth's attack began, General Mott, who was at the Vaughan Road crossing, sent an aide to see how Colonel McAllister was doing. The staff officer returned with news that McAllister "was most gallantly encouraging his command," and that he had sent "word that he was fighting with and without breastworks; also, that he could whip the rebels away." Although Mott liked McAllister's spirit, he determined to rush him some assistance. At 5:00 p.m., orders were issued for Colonel West to pull two regiments out the bridgehead and march them to the point of danger.

In accordance with these instructions, West directed the 141st Pennsylvania and the 1st Massachusetts Heavy Artillery to re-cross Hatcher's Run and to report to Colonel McAllister near Tucker's. Shortly after these two units had moved out, West was instructed by Mott to hasten to McAllister's assistance with his entire brigade, except the 105th Pennsylvania which was on patrol.[61]

All told, General Heth launched three attacks against the sector defended by McAllister's reinforced brigade. Colonel McAllister recalled that not long after the initial repulse:

the well-known Rebel yell rolled out on the evening breeze, and on rushed their massed columns. My line now opened a most destructive fire . . . again the enemy were repulsed. The fire slackening some, I rode along the lines encouraging the men to stand firm and the day would be ours. They all struck up the song "Rally around the Flag, Boys." The Rebels replied, "We will rally around your flag, boys!" The heavy firing had now ceased for the time being, but the pause was of short duration. The Rebel [Heth] with his famous fighting division made a rush for the gap in our lines . . . but our boys were ready for them, and as the darkness of the night had closed in upon us, the discharge of musketry and burning, flashing powder, illuminating the battle-scene . . .

60 Billings, *History of the Tenth Massachusetts Battery*, 384-387; OR 46, pt. 1, 24-25.

61 OR 46, pt. 1, 225, 235.

and the loud thundering of the artillery, made the scene one of more than ordinary grandeur. We then rolled back the Rebel columns for the last time."[62]

Before Heth's third attack, the 141st Pennsylvania and the 1st Massachusetts Heavy Artillery reinforced McAllister. The Pennsylvanians took the lead as the two regiments filed into position in a field in support of McAllister's battle line. Here the newcomers were exposed to a severe small-arms fire.

Colonel West arrived with the head of his column at a most opportune moment for the Army of the Potomac. A strong force of Heth's grey clads, advancing down the east bank of Rocky Branch, was threatening to turn McAllister's left. West's lead regiment, the 57th Pennsylvania, deployed into the battle line on the double. Charging into the bottom, the Pennsylvanians checked the Confederates' surge. Following close on the heels of the 57th, soldiers of the 5th Michigan formed on the Pennsylvanians' left. In pressing forward, the Michiganders passed a number of Second Division soldiers, who had been routed from the picket line, huddled behind trees. Not long after West and his men had taken position, night closed in, and the fighting ceased.[63]

Along the front held by Ramsey's brigade, there was action on the picket line in front of the two left flank regiments—the 64th New York and the 53rd Pennsylvania. To assist McAllister's hard-pressed troops on their left, the colonels of these two regiments had their men "fire to the left and front . . . thus subjecting the enemy to a cross-fire."[64]

During the night, patrols were thrown out to reoccupy the picket line from which the Second Division had been dislodged. A score or more Confederates were encountered wandering about the woods, and, after being disarmed, they were forwarded to the provost marshal for interrogation. Large numbers of men were turned to by their officers to erect breastworks by felling timber on either side of Rocky Branch. Troops not assigned to fatigue parties and outpost duty were permitted to rest on their arms.[65]

---

62 Billings, *History of the Tenth Massachusetts Battery*, 385. In front of the sector held by the 8th New Jersey, the Rebels were able to close within 80 yards of the Federals' main line of resistance.

63 *OR* 46, pt. 1, 235-236, 239, 242-245, 247-248.

64 *Ibid.*, 207-208, 210. While the fighting to their left was at its height, Rebel artillery hurled a few shells into the works held by Ramsey's troops.

65 *Ibid.*, 236, 239.

Checking with his division commanders, General Humphreys learned that the men who wore the "Clover Leaf" had suffered 125 casualties in the engagement, while Rebel losses were "comparatively severe and must have been six or seven times greater than ours."[66]

At 5:30 p.m., while Heth's attack was at its height, General Miles was directed by his corps commander to have a second brigade report to Colonel Ramsey. Miles designated the brigade led by Colonel George von Schack, who marched to Tucker's house with four of his regiments: the 7th, 52nd, 39th, and 111th New York. When Von Schack reported, Ramsey had him form his troops on the right of his brigade. The firing to the left had nearly ceased when the newcomers arrived. After remaining in line about three hours, during which time his troops were engaged in throwing up earthworks, Ramsey told Von Schack that the crisis having passed, he was to return to his camp.[67]

General Finegan had reached the scene of the fighting with his division about the time that Heth was mounting his third assault. Recognizing how late it was and that the Federals were already entrenched, General Lee did not pursue the action, and issued orders for Heth to recall his troops. Covered by Evans' skirmishers, Heth pulled back. Despite the darkness and the woods, there was little confusion as the Confederates broke contact with the Federals and withdrew into their fortifications.

In accordance with instructions, Evans' troops marched back to their quarters, while Finegan's division bivouacked for the night in rear of Heth's camps. McGowan's South Carolinians were alerted when Davis' Mississippians returned from the fight. The next morning, McGowan's brigade returned to its sector.[68]

*   *   *

General Warren's V Corps had marched from its camps at 7:00 a.m. on February 5, turning into Halifax Road at Globe Tavern. Three squadrons of the 6th Ohio Cavalry, which had reported to Warren, had the lead, followed by Ayers' Second Division, Griffin's First Division, and Crawford's Third Division. Behind

---

66 *Ibid.*, 193.

67 *Ibid.*, 195, 202.

68 *Ibid.*, 381, 391; Caldwell, *The History of a Brigade of South Carolinians*, 200, OR 46, pt. 1, 389, 397, 423.

Griffin's bluecoats and in front of Crawford's were 12 field guns, with eight horses hitched to each piece and caisson. The trains brought up the rear.[69]

At Rowanty Post Office, the column left Halifax Road, taking the "right-hand road to Rowanty Creek." Captain Emmor B. Cope of Warren's staff rode with the cavalry and hoped that the horse soldiers might seize Monk's Neck Bridge via a vigorous dash before the Confederates could destroy the structure. The area between Halifax Road and Rowanty Creek was "fairly open for that region. What timber there was . . . skirted one side of the road at a time." Even so, the Rebels had obstructed the road, so the cavalry's march was slowed.

It was 10:00 a.m. before the 6th Ohio Cavalry reached the Rowanty, where the troopers found the bridge destroyed, and the stream deep and unfordable. As if this weren't bad enough, there were rifle pits on the opposite side. Behind these breastworks, a small but determined band of Rebels had taken cover, prepared to dispute the crossing. Captain John Saxon of the 6th Ohio dismounted one of his squadrons, deploying the troopers as skirmishers. Posted behind recently erected barricades, the Johnnies more than held their own against the Yankee cavalry.

Generals Warren and Ayers now rode up, accompanied by Ayers' lead brigade, Colonel James Gwyn's. After conversing hurriedly with Captain Cope, Warren told Ayers to have Gwyn and his infantry establish a bridgehead.

Gwyn moved promptly. The 190th and 191st Pennsylvania were advanced as skirmishers, supported by the 4th Delaware. While soldiers of the 4th Delaware kept the Rebels pinned down by pouring volley after volley into the breastworks, the Pennsylvanians worked their way down to the water's edge. The stream was 60 feet wide at this point, and where there was slack water, there was ice. Overcoming these difficulties, the foot soldiers managed a crossing by swimming and wading across the creek—a few on the ice. Gaining the west bank, the Pennsylvanians routed the Rebels from their rifle pits, capturing 23.[70]

Trees were felled by the pioneers helping the remainder of Gwyn's brigade to cross. The brigade then pushed out about one-half mile, halted, and took position covering the bridgehead.

General Warren took personal command of the pioneers and the fatigue parties given the task of bridging the Rowanty. A bridge for the cavalry to cross had

69 Powell, *The Fifth Army Corps*, 755; OR 46, pt. 1, 253. The V Corps' camps were located between the Jerusalem Plank and Halifax roads. Besides the ambulances, the corps' train included: 50 ordnance wagons and 56 wagons heavily loaded with forage and ammunition for the cavalry.

70 OR 46, pt. 1, 253, 258-259, 259-260, 283-284; Powell, *The Fifth Army Corps*, 756.

been completed by 1:00 p.m., but it was 3:45 p.m. before "a bridge practicable for the artillery and the trains" was declared open for traffic.[71]

At 11:30 a.m., Warren forwarded a message to Meade's headquarters, reporting that his troops had forced their way across the Rowanty. He had yet to hear anything from Gregg and the cavalry.

Chief of Staff Webb, at the same hour, wrote Warren that Humphreys' troops had forced a crossing of Hatcher's Run. The telegraph had been extended to the Vaughan Road crossing, where for the time being General Meade had established his command post.[72]

The corps, as rapidly as it crossed the Rowanty, moved out Monk's Neck Road to where it intersected with Vaughan Road. Captain Cope took the 6th Ohio Cavalry and pushed ahead, proceeding down Vaughan Road to Little Cattail Creek. Here Cope met Major Henry E. Tremain of General Gregg's staff, who tersely explained that the cavalry division, having been at Dinwiddie Court House several hours before, was currently en route back to Malone's Bridge, where it was to bivouac for the night. Contact was also made at this time with the patrol (Major Hess) sent down Vaughan Road by General Humphreys.[73]

Immediately after Cope's and Tremain's conversation, a mounted Rebel patrol led by Rooney Lee came pounding up Vaughan Road from Dinwiddie Court House. According to General Warren, "the meeting was quite unexpected to them from the way they scampered off, and to me, as I had supposed General Gregg would send information to me as soon as he had uncovered the road leading to my position. The enemy's cavalry thus picked up one or two stragglers and caught sight of our infantry. . ."[74]

His troops having reached J. Hargrave's, Warren ordered his divisions to take their assigned positions. General Ayers' troops covered the Quaker and other roads leading north; General Griffin's were posted on Oliver Chappell's farm, watching Vaughan Road and the roads to the west; Crawford's people were positioned in a field east of Vaughan Road, the artillery and trains parked nearby.[75]

71 *OR* 46, pt. 1, 253, 258, 260, 284.

72 *OR* 46, pt. 2, 400.

73 *OR* 46, pt. 1, 253, 258, 260; *OR* 46, pt. 2, 401.

74 *OR* 46, pt. 1, 253; John Esten Cooke, *Wearing of the Gray: Being Personal Portraits, Scenes, and Adventures of the War* (Bloomington, 1959), 540-541.

75 *OR* 46, pt. 1, 256, 260. Corps headquarters were established at the crossing of the Quaker and Vaughan roads. Gwyn's brigade of Ayres' division was on the left, Bowerman's in the center, and Winthrop's on the right. Griffin's brigades were posted from left to right: Pearson,

While the men who wore the Maltese cross on their caps were gathered around campfires brewing coffee and discussing the day's events, they were startled to hear heavy firing off to the northeast. "The Johnnies have found the II Corps," they told one another.[76]

At 5:00 p.m., while the fighting along McAllister's front was raging, General Meade issued orders for Gregg to immediately report to Warren with his cavalry division. A cover letter was addressed to Warren, apprising him of this development. When Gregg showed up, Meade wanted Warren to place the cavalrymen on the left of his infantry. Army headquarters also wished Warren to know that the Rebels had assailed Humphreys' right, but they had been repulsed. It might become necessary, however, to march the V Corps up Vaughan Road to support Humphreys.[77]

Heth's attack on the II Corps' right made it vital that the Army of the Potomac maintain its grip on the section of Vaughan Road between de Trobriand's bridgehead and Warren's corps. Instructions were issued for Warren to hold with his command at "a point in the vicinity of Mr. Hargrave's and Mrs. Davis' instead of the point designated as J. Hargrave's" in his instructions.[78]

The courier with this order reached Warren's command post at 6:45 p.m. From him, Warren learned that it had become necessary to recall part of Mott's division (West's brigade) to assist the soldiers struggling to contain the Confederate counterattack east of Hatcher's Run. Checking his field maps on which he had plotted his troop positions, Warren saw that to comply with Meade's latest instructions (for the V Corps to be in force at the junction of the Monk's Neck and Vaughan roads) he would have to recall Crawford's division. When this was done, Griffin would have to "make arrangements to hold the road to Dinwiddie Court House. . ."[79]

Crawford's troops were collecting wood and building fires, "the night being very cold and the men weary after the long march of the day," when orders were

---

Sickel, and Burr. Burr's right rested on Ayres' left, while Pearson's pickets connected on the left with Crawford. *Ibid.*, 269-270, 277, 284.

76 *Ibid.*, 260.

77 *OR* 46, pt. 2, 401, 409.

78 *Ibid.*, 402.

79 *Ibid.*, 404.

barked to fall in. The division then returned to the junction of the Monk's Neck and Vaughan roads.[80]

Meanwhile, intelligence officers of Col. George H. Sharpe's at Meade's headquarters had been questioning deserters, who told them Lieutenant General Ambrose P. Hill's entire corps, reinforced by other divisions, was massing to assail the II Corps. Consequently, it might become necessary to recall the V Corps to bolster Humphreys. If this occurred, Warren was to move his troops along Vaughan Road, bringing with him only his "reserve ammunition, sending everything else, artillery, ambulances, and wagons, back with General Gregg." This dispatch was in Warren's hands at 8:00 p.m.[81]

By 9:00 p.m., Meade had made his decision. Warren was to march his corps via Vaughan Road to Hatcher's Run, and cross one division to the east side. The other two were to hold a line from Armstrong's Mill to de Trobriand's bridgehead, whose troops the V Corps was to relieve. Warren was to bring with him all of Gregg's cavalry, except those horse soldiers detailed to escort the trains.[82]

It took the staff officer, entrusted with this communication, 30 minutes to ride from army headquarters to Warren's command post. Warren could move rapidly when he wanted. Griffin, whose division was to take the lead, was to march as soon as he could recall his pickets. On reaching Hatcher's Run, unless instructed differently by General Meade, Griffin was to relieve de Trobriand. The wagon train was to follow Griffin, and the commander of the First Division was to see that it was parked as near the crossing as feasible.[83]

So much time was lost relieving the pickets that it was nearly midnight before Griffin's bluecoats were "fairly on the road."[84] The trains followed Griffin, then Ayers' division, and the artillery.[85] Crawford's division brought up the rear.[86]

It was 11:00 p.m. before Gregg learned that he was to join General Warren. Gregg let his men and horses get another hour of rest before he had his brigade commanders arouse their units. At 1:00 a.m. on February 6, the cavalry division broke camp. Marching via the Stage and Monk's Neck roads, near the Vaughan

---

80 *OR* 46, pt. 1, 287, 292-293.

81 *OR* 46, pt. 2, 402.

82 *Ibid.*, 402-403.

83 *Ibid.*, 404.

84 *OR* 46, pt. 1, 254, 258, 266, 269-270.

85 *Ibid.*, 254, 277, 282, 284.

86 *Ibid.*, 254, 287, 293.

Road crossing of Gravelly Run, at 4:00 a.m., Gregg reported to General Warren. Warren gave Gregg his first mission: he and his troopers were to cover the corps movement to Hatcher's Run.

While waiting for Crawford's foot soldiers to cross Gravelly Run, Gregg posted Brigadier General Henry E. Davies' 1st Brigade to cover approaches to the stream. Troopers of the 2nd and 3rd Brigades took advantage of this respite to dismount, build fires, and prepare coffee. Both the infantry and cavalry had had but little rest. The night was very cold and the roads were frozen hard before morning.[87]

By 6:00 a.m., the V Corps had reached the left bank of Gravelly Run.

*   *   *

General Lee's lightning-like response to the Union thrusts across Hatcher's Run and the Rowanty caused Federal leaders to commit additional troops and then change their plans. At 2:30 p.m., General Meade notified General Grant's City Point headquarters that bridgeheads had been established by the II and V Corps. By forcing a crossing of Hatcher's Run, the II Corps captured nine prisoners, all from General Pegram's infantry division. So far, nothing had been heard of Gregg and his cavalry. Information gathered from the prisoners led Meade and his staff to believe that General Lee might "attempt to interpose between Warren and Humphreys." To cope with this possibility, it was decided to call up General Parke's reserve division.[88]

At the time this decision was made, Parke's IX Corps held the front from the Appomattox to Battery No. 24 with its First and Second Divisions. Brigadier General John F. Hartranft's Third Division was in reserve. In accordance with Meade's "circular," Parke alerted Hartranft to hold his troops ready to march from their camps at a moment's notice. The message for Parke to "send General Hartranft['s] division, without artillery, promptly and rapidly down the Vaughan Road, to report to" General Humphreys at Hatcher's Run was received at 1:45 p.m.[89]

Should the Rebels take advantage of the withdrawal of Hartranft's people to launch an attack on the IX Corps' sector, orders were issued by Meade for the Engineer Brigade to march from City Point to the Meade's station area to augment

87 *Ibid.*, 254, 366, 368, 371; Powell, *The Fifth Army Corps*, 758.

88 *OR* 46, pt. 2, 389.

89 *Ibid.*, 407-409; *OR* 46, pt. 1, 315, 344.

the IX Corps. There the leader of the brigade, Col. Wesley Brainerd, was to report to Parke.[90]

Hartranft's troops moved out of their camps in light marching order. By 4:00 p.m., the division, which had been massed near Fort Blaisdell, had pushed on, taking the road that led westward and crossed the Weldon Railroad at Globe Tavern. Four hours later, at a point on Vaughan Road two miles beyond Fort Siebert, Hartranft reported to General Humphreys. The II Corps leader was delighted to see that the reinforcing column was well closed up. Few, if any, men had straggled.

Humphreys positioned Hartranft on Ramsey's right, with orders to have his men entrenched immediately. After his troops had been posted, Hartranft found that his left rested "on a wide, impenetrable swamp," and his right a few rods in front of Claypool's house. The general direction of his line was north and south. By daylight, the division "had a good line of works 1,000 yards in length. . . ."[91]

Heth's assault on Humphreys' right had caused Meade a few anxious moments. At 5:30 p.m., Brigadier General George W. Getty of the VI Corps was telegraphed to "withdraw from your line that portion of one division not on picket and in the works, and hold it in readiness to move at a moment's notice." The division recalled was to be concentrated on "Vaughan Road just outside the works."[92]

Getty, to comply with Meade's orders, would have to redeploy his troops. He decided to hold the First Division, Brigadier General Frank Wheaton commanding, ready to march to Humphreys' assistance. But to do so, Getty would have to "distribute" two of his divisions to hold with them what had formerly been occupied by three. Troops of the Third Division were directed to extend on the right and take position on the line between Fort Wadsworth and Battery No. 24, currently defended by Wheaton's bluecoats. These changes took time.[93]

At 6:30 p.m., Chief of Staff Webb telegraphed Getty that as soon as Hartranft's column passed, he was to put Wheaton's division into motion. When the Rebels

---

90 *OR* 46, pt. 1, 315; *OR* 46, pt. 2, 395, 407-408. The Engineer Brigade reported to Parke on the evening of the 5th, and was posted as a reserve near Avery's house.

91 *OR* 46, pt. 1, 344.

92 *OR* 46, pt. 2, 405. Getty, as senior officer present, had been in charge of the VI Corps since January 17; Major General Horatio G. Wright having received a leave of absence.

93 *Ibid.*, 405-406.

hurled a third attack against Humphreys' line, Webb wired, "Should your division be ready to move before General Hartranft arrives let it move at once. . . ."[94]

Seeing that Hartranft's column was passing, Getty ordered Wheaton to follow as soon as the road was clear.[95]

General Wheaton checked his watch when his division moved out: it was 8:00 p.m. Near Fort Siebert, one of Humphreys' staff officers hailed Wheaton, telling him that he was "to form on and covering the Squirrel Level Road," to the right of Hartranft's IX Corps division. Soon after Wheaton's lead brigade marched up, the right of the IX Corps was established, and Wheaton formed his line: the 3rd Brigade on the left; the 1st Brigade on the right; and the 2nd Brigade in reserve, in the rear of the left of the line which rested near Claypool's house. The right of Lieutenant Colonel Edward L. Campbell's 1st Brigade nearly reached the abatis fronting Fort Cummings. All of Wheaton's troops were in position by 11:30 p.m., and within two hours "an excellent rifle pit had been constructed all along our front and slashings made across the two swamps through which our line ran."[96]

At 6:45 p.m., Meade telegraphed Grant that Humphreys' troops, up to that hour, had repulsed all Confederate attacks. Even so, orders had been issued calling up a VI Corps division. At this time, Meade continued, the V Corps was in position at Hargrave's, about three and one-half miles southwest of the Vaughan Road crossing of Hatcher's Run. Gregg had been to Dinwiddie Court House, but as there was little military traffic on the Boydton Plank Road, he had returned to Malone's Bridge. Orders had gone out for Gregg to join Warren.

Evaluating the Confederates' actions, Meade opined that General Lee planned "to turn Humphreys' right and cut our communications with our line of works." Besides Pegram's and Evans' divisions from Gordon's corps, deserters had reported the presence of units from Heth's and Mahone's commands. Unless there were new developments, Meade informed Grant, he proposed to "leave Humphreys and Warren in their present positions, with directions to support each other."[97]

Grant, a believer in the power of the offensive, saw the situation in a different light than did the conservative Meade. Replying to his army commander's telegram at 7:15 p.m., Grant directed Meade to recall Warren and the cavalry. Upon their

94 *Ibid.*, 405.

95 *Ibid.*, 406.

96 *OR* 46, pt. 1, 297-298.

97 *OR* 46, pt. 2, 389.

arrival the Vaughan Road crossing, Meade was to recover the initiative, follow up the Confederate repulse, and push for the South Side Railroad.

At 8:22 p.m., Meade notified Grant that orders had been issued withdrawing Warren and the cavalry. Humphreys at the same time had been directed "to await developments, and to attack, if advantageous, and drive the enemy into their works." Patrols had reported that the foe had a strong line of works passing through the Clements house. Unless his soldiers could crack this line, Meade felt they could "hardly reach the Boydton Plank Road or South Side Railroad without a flank movement considerably to the left."[98]

Meade, before retiring, forwarded to Grant a summary of the day's activities. If, in the morning, he found the Rebels that had assailed Humphreys' right still outside the works, he would "attack and drive him into them, taking advantage of anything disclosed by the operation."[99]

Part III

General Gordon and His Confederates Win the Second Round

By 8:00 a.m. on February 6, 1865, General Warren's three V Corps divisions were massed near Hatcher's Run. In accordance with instructions from Warren, General Griffin saw that the soldiers of his First Division relieved de Trobriand's II Corps bluecoats in the rifle pits covering the approaches to the bridges.[100] Ayres' Second Division was massed behind the rifle pits held by Griffin's troops, while Crawford's Third Division crossed the run and bivouacked.

Twelve hours before, General Mott had been alerted by his corps commander, General Humphreys, that Warren was to relieve his people holding the bridgehead. As soon as it had been replaced, de Trobriand's brigade was to re-cross Hatcher's Run and take position behind McAllister's and Ramsey's brigades. Mott was to take

---

98 *Ibid.*, 390.

99 *Ibid.*, 391-392.

100 OR 46, pt. 1, 260, 266, 269-271, 287, 293. Pearson's 3rd Brigade was posted in the works on the right, its right resting at Armstrong's Mill and its left extending to within 50 yards of Vaughan Road. Pearson, after advancing a strong picket line, put his troops to work strengthening the rifle pits. Crawford's division was to constitute a strategic reserve, ready to march at a moment's notice to either Warren or Humphreys' support.

charge of Ramsey's First Division troops in addition to his own. Hess' cavalry battalion was recalled at the same time.[101]

As soon as he had assembled his brigade on the morning of the 6th, de Trobriand marched the troops, reinforced by the 105th Pennsylvania, across Hatcher's Run and up Vaughan Road. In accordance with Mott's instructions, de Trobriand massed his troops near Tucker's house.[102]

Rooney Lee's Confederate cavalry followed Gregg's horse soldiers, as they screened the rear of the V Corps as it marched up Vaughan Road. General Davies' brigade easily parried Lee's initial thrusts. General Gregg, however, was of the opinion that the butternuts might be disposed to press the attack, so he posted Brigadier General Henry E. Davies' 1st Brigade and Col. Oliver B. Knowles' 3rd Brigade across Vaughan Road and in a large field, near the Keys house. The troopers were dismounted, horse holders detailed, and skirmishers advanced. After the troopers fed and watered their horses, Colonel Gregg's 2nd Brigade remounted and took position in support of their comrades.[103]

On the evening of the 5th, General Meade made a serious error. At 9:00 p.m., Humphreys had been informed that Warren and Gregg had been directed to report to him. With these troops, and Wheaton's and Hartranft's divisions, Humphreys was to hold his "present position, extending as far as possible toward our line of works." Should the Confederates attack again and be repulsed, Humphreys was to launch a counterattack and drive them into their fortifications. Meade's mistake was in assuming that Humphreys was the senior corps commander on the field, which he was not.[104] Warren's commission as major general of volunteers predated Humphreys' by two months.

At 7:50 a.m. the next morning, Chief of Staff Webb sent identical telegrams to Humphreys and Warren. They were to feel the enemy in their "front and determine whether or not they are outside their line of works." In case the Rebels were, the corps commanders were to attack at once and drive them within their fortifications.

---

101 OR 46, pt. 2, 399-400.

102 OR 46, pt. 1, 225-227. The 105th Pennsylvania of West's brigade had reported to de Trobriand on its return from the reconnaissance down Vaughan Road. Major Hess and his troopers of the 3rd Pennsylvania, having patrolled Vaughan Road during the night, took position at Cummings' house after re-crossing the run.

103 *Ibid.*, 254, 258, 260, 366, 368, 371. The 6th Ohio rejoined Knowles' brigade at this time.

104 OR 46, pt. 2, 396. Meade spent the night of the 5th at Aiken's house.

If, however, the Southerners were posted behind their lines, there was to be no assault.[105]

At 8:00 a.m., Warren received his copy of Webb's message. Since he outranked Humphreys, Warren considered the area where the fighting had occurred the previous evening as part of his front.

While endeavoring to ascertain what Meade intended, Warren received a note from General Humphreys that the II Corps "was about to attack the enemy if outside his works." Warren, accordingly, deemed it best to await the results of Humphreys' operations, holding the V Corps and Gregg's cavalry in hand to cooperate if needed.[106]

While awaiting additional news from Humphreys, Warren, learning that Rooney Lee's horse soldiers were growing bolder, determined to reinforce Gregg with one of his V Corps infantry brigades. Col. Frederick Winthrop's brigade of Ayres' division was ordered forward. Marching out Vaughan Road, Winthrop posted his troops on the right of the road, near Key's house.[107]

In accordance with Meade's orders, Humphreys had told Mott and Hartranft to organize and send out strong reconnaissance patrols. At the same time, instructions were issued by Humphreys for all division commanders reporting to him, including General Miles, to hold their units "ready to attack the enemy should he be found outside his works."[108]

Mott assigned the task of undertaking the forced reconnaissance to his reserve brigade, de Trobriand's. De Trobriand took with him four regiments.

The 2nd U.S. Sharpshooters, deployed as skirmishers to the left and right of the road running north from Tucker's, had the advance. On the left of Thompson's house, de Trobriand found a cart road through the woods. Two companies of the 20th Indiana were detached to hold this position. No Confederates were encountered as the Yanks beat their way through the woods, so the general concluded that they had called in their outposts. Reaching a clearing, the Federals spotted a "light work" held by a small number of grey clads. Several shots sent the butternuts scampering toward the northwest. Beyond Watkins' house, de Trobriand and his sharpshooters were able to make out "a continuous line of works occupied by the enemy." Moving in that direction, the regulars, as they approached the house, flushed several Confederate pickets.

---

105 *Ibid.*, 423.

106 *Ibid. OR* 46, pt. 1, 254.

107 *OR* 46, pt. 1, 254, 258, 280.

108 *OR* 46, pt. 2, 423; pt. 1, 193.

It was becoming apparent to de Trobriand by this time that he was in front of the Rebels' works. To develop their strategy, he pushed his skirmishers closer. As he did, he saw a Confederate column dash toward the cart road, where he had left the two Indiana companies. Suspecting that the grey clads intended to cut his line of retreat, de Trobriand sent back all his command, except the skirmishers. The regulars were then turned into the road running west of Thompson's house, paralleling the route taken by the Johnnies. The butternuts showed no disposition to attack, so de Trobriand pushed two companies, deployed as skirmishers, through the woods and into a morass.

Advancing across the swamp, the sharpshooters found themselves in front of a line of breastworks, with a redoubt, armed with two guns, commanding the road. The Federals banged away at "the rebels visible above the parapet." Taking position in the rifle pits fronting their main lines of resistance, the Southerners returned the Yanks' fire. De Trobriand, by this time (11:00 a.m.), had accomplished his mission. Orders were now received to return to the Union lines.[109]

It was 10:00 a.m. when General Hartranft sent the 200th Pennsylvania to "move by way of the Smith and Hawks houses, and ascertain, if possible, the position and force of the enemy outside of their main works. . . ." The regiment advanced beyond the abandoned Rebel redoubt and found Confederate pickets occupying the same line, as they had at the time of the battle of the Boydton Plank Road in October. Satisfied that the butternuts were not in force outside their main defensive works, the Pennsylvanians retraced their steps and told Hartranft what they had seen.[110]

At 11:00 a.m., General Humphreys informed Warren that the Confederates to the II Corps' front had retired into their entrenchments. Seventy five minutes later, Warren received a sharp note signed by Chief of Staff Webb, notifying him that he had misinterpreted Meade's dispatch of 7:40 a.m. Meade had wanted both the II and V Corps, not just Humphreys', to reconnoiter to determine whether the foe was to their front.

---

109 OR 46, pt. 1, 225; pt. 2, 424. De Trobriand was accompanied on his forced reconnaissance by the 2nd U.S. Sharpshooters, the 20th Indiana, the 17th Maine, and the 1st Maine Heavy Artillery. The redoubt was on rising ground, near a barn in front of Armstrong's house.

110 OR 46, pt. 1, 344; OR 46, pt. 2, 424.

Meade now visited Warren's command post. While there, he made it clear that the V Corps was "to make a reconnaissance south and west of Hatcher's Run, to ascertain the whereabouts of the enemy's line in that direction."[111]

Warren made his plans accordingly. Crawford's division was to cross Hatcher's Run and "move out on the Vaughan Road to where it turns off to Dabney's Mill, and then follow up that road toward the mill, driving back the enemy and ascertaining the position of the enemy's entrenched line. . . ." Ayres was to support Crawford. Part of Gregg's cavalry was to push down Vaughan Road, driving the Rebel horse soldiers across Gravelly Run, while a second detachment was to screen Crawford and Ayres' left. Finally, Gregg was to dispatch a small mounted force to watch the road leading down the east side of Hatcher's Run and Rowanty Creek to Monk's Neck Bridge.[112]

Warren believed Gregg would encounter no difficulty in carrying out this assignment, because only an inconsequential Rebel force had been reported lurking to the V Corps' left. Griffin's division would continue to hold the earthworks covering the bridgehead and be prepared in an emergency to support either the infantry or the cavalry.[113]

Should he encounter the Confederates in strength, Warren could look to Humphreys for reinforcements. Humphreys had told Warren that Wheaton's division, 4,500 strong, was en route to Cummings' house, adjacent to the Vaughan Road Crossing of Hatcher's Run, while de Trobriand's brigade was available and could be ordered to the V Corps' support.[114]

At 2:30 p.m., General Wheaton was directed by Humphreys to pull his VI Corps troops out of the breastworks covering Squirrel Level Road and march them "to the vicinity of the Cummings house on the Vaughan Road. . . ." The rear brigade had reached Cummings', when one of Humphreys' staff officers hailed Wheaton, telling him to push on down Vaughan Road. An aide at the same time was to be sent to see whether Warren wanted him to mass his VI Corps on the east or west side of Hatcher's Run.[115]

Soldiers from General Hartranft's division replaced Wheaton's in the earthworks to their right. By placing his reserve regiments on the line, Hartranft

---

111 *OR 46*, pt. 1, 254; *OR 46*, pt. 2, 431-432. Confederate deserters had stated that their works extended south to Gravelly Run, about a mile southwest of Dabney's Mill.

112 *OR 46*, pt. 2, 434.

113 *OR 46*, pt. 1, 254-255.

114 *Ibid.*, 255.

115 *Ibid.*, 298.

"still had a reasonably strong one." Large details were turned to slashing timber to further strengthen the position held by the IX Corps division.[116]

*   *   *

Crawford's division, with Brigadier General Edward S. Bragg's brigade in the lead, crossed Hatcher's Run at 2:00 p.m.; Colonel Henry A. Morrow's 3rd Brigade followed Bragg's; and Brigadier General Henry Baxter's brought up the rear. As they passed through the breastworks, Crawford's people bantered with Griffin's soldiers. One-third of a mile beyond the bridge, the head of the column turned into the road to Dabney's Mill. Crawford glanced at his map and saw that he was within a mile of his goal.

A brief halt was called in a cleared field to allow General Bragg to form his brigade into battle line and to cover his front with skirmishers. The ground across which Crawford would be called on to advance was "rolling and principally covered with a heavy growth of wood, part of it thick underbrush, a swamp, and several old fields."[117]

Bragg's brigade, as it entered the timber, encountered an entrenched picket line defended by troops from Col. John S. Hoffman's Confederate brigade. While Bragg's skirmishers and the butternuts banged away, Crawford formed Morrow's brigade into battle line 300 yards to the rear to extend beyond Bragg's left. Baxter's 2nd Brigade was hustled into line on Morrow's left. As soon as Morrow had refused his right, Crawford shouted, "Forward!" The bluecoats swept through the woods, routing the outnumbered butternuts from their breastworks, and pursuing them to Dabney's Mill.[118]

Like General Meade, General Lee wanted to know what the foe was doing. General Rooney Lee, who had followed Gregg's horse soldiers across Gravelly Run, reported that the Yankees were pulling back to the east bank of Hatcher's Run. As yet, not all of Rooney Lee's cavalry had arrived from the camp near Belfield, and until all his men were up, young Lee hesitated to assail Gregg's roadblock.

Since the cavalry was unable to secure the desired information in regard to Meade's movements, General Lee told his corps commander General Gordon, to

---

116 *Ibid.*, 344.

117 *Ibid.*, 287, 293; OR Vol. II, pt. I, 286.

118 OR 46, pt. 1, 287, 293, 296, 390; OR Vol. II, pt. I, 286, 288, 290.

have his infantry make a forced reconnaissance toward the Vaughan Road Crossing.[119]

General John Pegram's division, which was encamped south of Hatcher's Run, was given this mission by Gordon. Pegram, to carry out his task, divided his command into two columns. Colonel John S. Hoffman, with his five-regiment Virginia brigade, was to reconnoiter the road leading past Dabney's Mill, while Pegram's other two brigades (Brigadier General Robert D. Johnston's and William G. Lewis') were to march down Quaker Road to its junction with Vaughan Road, then up Vaughan Road. It was almost noon before the two columns moved out in search of the enemy. General Pegram accompanied Hoffman's brigade.

At Dabney's Mill, Pegram told Hoffman to halt and post his brigade. Scattered shots could be heard off to the south, where Rooney Lee's horse soldiers skirmished with Gregg's troopers. Pegram, believing that there was only cavalry to his front, called for Major Henry K. Douglas. The young major was to take two of Hoffman's regiments and feel for the Federals' position. As he approached the bridgehead, Douglas sighted Crawford's oncoming column. After deploying a small holding force behind the rifle pits, erected during previous fighting in this area, Douglas galloped back to Dabney's Mill to warn his general that a powerful Union force had advanced out of the bridgehead.[120]

While Hoffman's Virginians took position covering the ruins of the mill, Pegram dispatched a messenger to ask Gordon for help. Gordon issued marching orders to General Evans' division, and then sent an aide to notify General Lee that the situation had drastically changed. If the Union advance was being made in the force Pegram reported, Gordon would have to be reinforced.

Earlier in the day, the "long roll" had been beaten in Evans' camps. The troops had been turned out under arms and marched rapidly down the Boydton Plank Road to Burgess Mill. Evans' three infantry brigades remained here until about 11:00 a.m., when Generals Lee and Gordon, satisfied by the reports forwarded by Rooney Lee that the Federal infantry had re-crossed Hatcher's Run, ordered them back to their encampments. When the division retraced its steps, a small detachment from Colonel Peck's Louisiana brigade was left to guard the bridge.

Not long after the regimental commanders had dismissed their units, the "long roll" sounded. Once again, the men fell out on the double. Many of the men were heard to complain that this was probably another false alarm. As soon as the brigades had formed, the division moved out and hiked down the Boydton Plank

119 *OR* 46, pt. 1, 381.

120 *Ibid.*, 381, 390; Douglas, *I Rode With Stonewall*, 326.

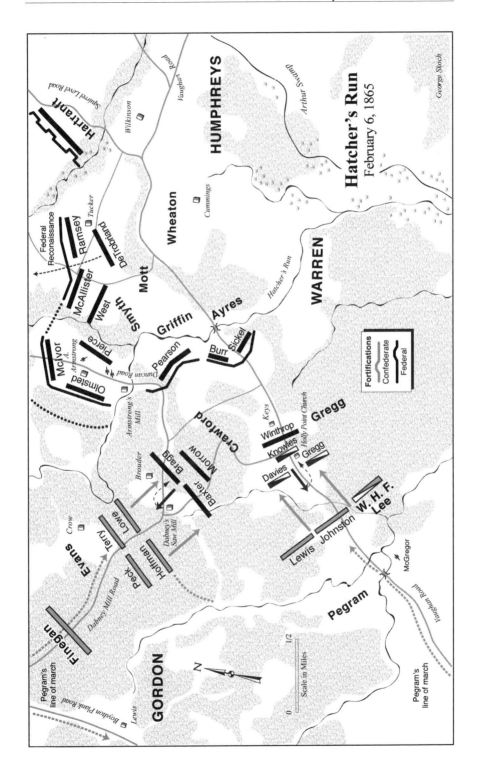

Hatcher's Run
February 6, 1865

Road. Crossing Hatcher's Run and passing Burgess Tavern, the head of the column turned into a wood road, leading to the southeast. Hearing the firing in the woods to their front, Evans' men knew this time there would be a fight. As Peck's brigade crossed the bridge, it was rejoined by the men who had been on picket.[121]

Evans' vanguard reached Dabney's Mill at a critical moment for the Confederates. As Hoffman's brigade retired beyond the mill site, Evans had his commanders file their troops into line of battle in the woods on the Virginians' left.[122]

From left to right, Evans' brigades were posted: Col. John H. Lowe's; Brigadier General William Terry's; and Col. William R. Peck's. Peck's right flank companies were in contact with Hoffman's left. When he drafted his after-action report, Colonel Peck wrote, "My command was much reduced by this time by the heavy picket detail still on duty, and I was forced, with the mere handful left, to conform my movements entirely to those of the larger commands on my right and left."[123]

As soon as the brigade commanders reported their lines formed, General Gordon passed the word to counterattack. The shrill "Rebel Yell" burst forth, as the lean, combat-hardened veterans stormed forward. Within a matter of moments, the butternuts had stopped Crawford's division in its tracks.

Morrow's supporting brigade closed up on Bragg's bluecoats, who were battling the Confederates for possession of the clearing where the mill had stood. Bragg's left began to give ground. General Baxter, on the left, was told by Crawford to advance his lines and take position on Bragg's left, which was hard pressed.

The 39th Massachusetts and the 16th Maine, supported by the 97th New York, came up with a cheer; the Maine regiment was anchoring the left on Bragg's right. Baxter posted his other regiments to the left and rear. Although they took heavy losses, the 39th Massachusetts, the 16th Maine, and the 97th New York forged ahead and drove Hoffman's Virginians and Peck's Louisianans from the mill site. Bragg's regiments on their right, however, continued to be hammered back by Lowe's Georgians and Terry's Virginians. (Terry's brigade included units that had won fame as the "Stonewall Brigade.") Bragg's men broke and took to their heels. As they retreated, they rushed through Morrow's lines. Morrow and his officers experienced considerable difficulty holding their soldiers in ranks. As soon as Bragg's bluecoats were out of the way, Morrow's line sent volley after volley crashing into the "advancing columns of the enemy." The Rebel surge was checked

---

121 OR 46, pt. 1, 290-292; Barton, "The Battle of Hatcher's Run," 119.

122 OR 46, pt. 1, 390.

123 *Ibid.*, 390, 392; Barton, "The Battle of Hatcher's Run," 119.

and Evans' brigades halted on the opposite side of the clearing. With a cheer, Morrow's brigade dashed across the field, chasing the Confederates into the pines beyond.

Baxter's three regiments, on the left of Bragg's line, were unable to hold their position when the troops to their right fled. Although reinforced by the rest of the brigade, they were pressed back about 200 yards by Hoffman and Peck's grey clads before they held. Baxter's soldiers took advantage of the success scored by Morrow's battle line to regain the pile of sawdust marking the mill site.[124]

Having entrusted the conduct of operations on Vaughan Road to General Gregg, Warren accompanied Crawford's infantry as it drove toward Dabney's Mill. Before he had ridden very far, the sound of heavy firing came rolling in from the southwest. An excited aide soon rode up with word that Colonel Winthrop's brigade had been assailed by the foe in force and could not rejoin Ayres' division as it marched to Crawford's support. Indeed, he continued, Gregg and Winthrop had all they could do to hold their ground, and they needed assistance. Warren sent word via Captain Cope for General Griffin to reinforce Winthrop with a brigade and to take personal charge of operations on Vaughan Road. Griffin, at the same time, was to order Pearson's brigade, "his largest and best," to accompany Ayres in place of Winthrop's.

Within a few minutes, Warren had received a second call from Gregg for reinforcements, as the Rebels were turning to his left. Not having any more V Corps to commit, Warren called on Humphreys for help.[125]

Unknown to the Federals, two of General Pegram's brigades (Johnston's and Lewis') had reached Vaughan Road to Gregg's front and had taken position on the left of Rooney Lee's cavalrymen, who were fighting dismounted. At the time that Winthrop's brigade reported to Gregg at Keys', the cavalry was heavily skirmishing with Pegram's soldiers some distance down Vaughan Road. In compliance with Gregg's request, Winthrop had relieved the cavalry pickets with the 146th New York. Winthrop then deployed the 5th and 140th New York to the right of the road in a large open field. These dispositions had hardly been completed before Gregg's troopers started forward.[126]

---

124 OR 46, pt. 1, 287, 293, 392; OR 51, pt. 1, 286, 288, 291, 293, 295. Colonel Charles W. Tilden, of the 16th Maine, reported that in this advance, Color Sergeant Luther Bradford "was wounded in the left arm (causing amputation of same) while gallantly bearing the colors in advance of the line, urging the men on to their work. This is the third time he has been wounded. . . ." OR 51, pt. 1, 288.

125 OR 46, pt. 1, 255, 260; OR 46, pt. 2, 432.

126 OR 46, pt. 1, 280; Beale, History of the Ninth Virginia Cavalry, 147.

When the cavalry moved out, Davies' brigade was to the right of the road, Gregg's to the left, and Knowles' in support. Colonel Gregg's brigade, which went into action mounted, established contact with the Rebels first. The 4th Pennsylvania, followed by the 8th Pennsylvania, charged down the road in sections of eights. As the horsemen approached the ground where Johnston's brigade was posted, a deadly volley crashed into the head of the column, causing the horse soldiers to recoil. Among the casualties was Colonel Gregg, who was shot in the leg. Before leaving the field, Gregg turned over command of the 2nd Brigade to Col. Michael Kerwin of the 13th Pennsylvania. Colonel Samuel B. N. Young, of the 4th Pennsylvania, quickly reformed his regiment. A second charge was made across an open field, with the same result. A third charge was undertaken, but failed. Young and his men finally realized they were fighting Confederate infantry, who were not about to be dislodged by horsemen.[127]

On the right of the 4th Pennsylvania, the 16th Pennsylvania went into action on foot. While their comrades of the 2nd Brigade were being battered, the troopers of the 16th had dislodged a strong Rebel detachment holed up on Myers' farm, capturing 30 of Johnston's North Carolinians. A grey clad standard bearer was shot down, but a horse soldier in the 13th Pennsylvania, which came up mounted, reached the colors first. No time was given for the Yanks to argue over the colors because a Confederate counterattack rolled them back.[128]

North of Vaughan Road, Davies' cavalrymen had been mauled by the butternuts. Davies, along with the colonels of the 1st New Jersey and the 10th New York, was shot from his horse. As Gregg's bluecoats fell back in confusion, they were closely followed by Rebel infantry.[129]

When he saw that the horse soldiers had been repulsed, Colonel Winthrop ordered up the 5th and 140th New York, and the 15th New York Heavy Artillery. After opening their ranks to allow the retreating troopers to pass, the foot soldiers moved forward on the double and delivered several well-aimed volleys which checked the Confederates' advance. Recoiling, Johnston's and Lewis' North Carolinians retired into the woods out of which they had chased Gregg's cavalry. As soon as they had reformed their lines, Johnston and Lewis led their cheering troops out of the timber and into the field beyond, only to be repulsed a second time. A

127 OR 46, pt. 1, 366, 368-370.

128 *Ibid.*, 368, 370.

129 *Ibid.*, 280, 366. Colonel H. A. Janeway, of the 1st New Jersey, recovered, while Lieutenant Colonel F. L. Tremain, of the 10th New York, died.

third, but very half-hearted, attempt by the grey clads to close with Winthrop's brigade was easily repelled.[130]

At 5:00 p.m., Winthrop was warned by his subordinates that ammunition was running short. Meanwhile, General Griffin pulled his 1st Brigade—Sickel's—out of the earthworks covering the bridgehead, and ordered it to report to General Gregg out on Vaughan Road. Reaching Keys', Colonel Sickel found Winthrop's troops closely engaged with Rebel battle lines in the open ground west of the road.

General Gregg told Sickel to support Winthrop, "whose line at the time was being pressed by a vigorous assault of superior numbers of the enemy." Forming his brigade into line of battle, facing southwest, Sickel put his bluecoats into motion. As Sickel came by, Winthrop's troops, most of whom had emptied their cartridge-boxes, retired.

Sickel now called for a charge. At the first volley from the fresh brigade, Johnston's and Lewis' North Carolina brigades, abandoned "the field in great disorder, leaving their killed and wounded" in Union hands, together with several prisoners. The blue clad infantry followed the Rebel infantry for "some distance," only halting when confronted by an ammunition shortage. Sickel reported his difficulties to General Griffin who, in turn, told Sickel to hold the ground gained and to advance a strong skirmish line, which was done.

By now, it was starting to get dark, and as the firing off to the north increased in intensity, Griffin shouted for Sickel to change front to the northwest. As the Union infantry was being reformed, Colonel Knowles' brigade of dismounted cavalry was posted on the left, facing west. Winthrop's soldiers, having visited the ordnance wagons, were deployed on Sickel's right, their right anchored on Vaughan Road.[131]

Having broken the back of the Confederate thrust up Vaughan Road, General Gregg called for Davies' and Knowles' brigades to harass the retreating butternuts. Advancing to the left and right of Vaughan Road, the cavalry drove for the Gravelly Run crossing. Johnston's and Lewis' infantry brigades retired toward the northwest, to join General Gordon at Dabney's Mill; and Rooney Lee's cavalry retreated down Vaughan Road, followed at a respectful distance by the Yankee horse soldiers. The 4th Pennsylvania, having remounted, took the lead. As the Federals neared the Gravelly Run crossing, they were shelled by two guns of McGregor's Virginia Battery, unlimbered on the opposite side. This checked their

130 *Ibid.*, 280-281; H. C. Wall, "The Twenty-Third North Carolina Infantry," in *Southern Historical Society Papers*, vol. 25, 175.

131 OR 46, pt. 1, 266, 280-281. After being relieved by Sickel's troops, Winthrop reported, his men retired "75 to 100 yards in rear of my position and replenished my boxes with the ammunition which I had just then succeeded in procuring."

pursuit and, because it was almost dark, the brigade commanders recalled their troops and returned to Key's farm.[132]

*   *   *

Earlier in the day, General Ayres rapidly pushed forward to support the left of Crawford's division at Dabney's Mill, which he understood was hard-pressed. Because of the thick undergrowth, Ayres marched his troops in two lines by the flank. As the foot soldiers were ascending a ridge, a mounted detachment of Gregg's cavalry, riding rapidly, overran the left of Col. James Gwyn's brigade, throwing that unit into confusion. Without halting to reform, Ayres pushed on with Col. Richard N. Bowerman's Maryland brigade and soon engaged the foe. The Marylanders took position on Crawford's left at the mill site. Gwyn, on rallying his troops, moved up and occupied ground on Bowerman's left.[133]

In the meantime, Colonel Pearson's First Division—guided by one of Warren's staff—filed out of the works covering the bridgehead. As the troops were passing through a "strip of woods," they were shelled by 3-inch rifles mounted in the fortifications off to their right. Several men were struck down. General Warren now hailed Colonel Pearson and told him to form his brigade in line of battle. When he deployed his unit, its right rested behind the center of one of Crawford's brigades and extended to the left behind Ayres' battle formation. Pearson's troops had scarcely formed before the Rebel artillery opened fire. Shells shrieked overhead, tearing limbs and boughs from the tall pines. The area where the brigade had formed was marshy and the underbrush close and heavy. Even if there had not been opposition, a march across such terrain would have been fraught with difficulty.[134]

At 4:30 p.m., Pearson's brigade of Griffin's division advanced in line to a position in close support. All the while, the shooting to their front constantly continued and was severe. The line halted in an open field in which there were a few scattered trees and came under a fierce artillery fire.[135]

132 *Ibid.*, 366, 368, 370.

133 *Ibid.*, 277-278, 282, 284.

134 *Ibid.*, 281; Survivors, *History of the Corn Exchange Regiment*, 551. The brigade was posted from right to left by the following units: the 32nd Massachusetts, the 155th Pennsylvania, the 16th Michigan, the 118th Pennsylvania, the 20th Maine, the 83rd Pennsylvania, and the 1st Michigan.

135 *OR* 46, pt. 1, 271, 277-278.

Lieutenant Colonel William J. Pegram (Gen. John Pegram's younger brother), in accordance with instructions from General Heth, had sent several of his batteries down the Boydton Plank Road. After crossing Hatcher's Run, the cannoneers of Ellett's Virginia Battery drove the teams hitched to their four 3-inch rifles down the road to Dabney's Mill. Reaching an open field, the gunners unlimbered their pieces and began hammering the Federals to their front.[136]

Orders were received from General Warren, who rode up on a "splendid white horse," for Pearson to reinforce Ayres with part of his brigade. Accompanied by the 155th Pennsylvania and the 32nd Massachusetts, Pearson hastened forward and deployed these units on Bowerman's left, "where they immediately became fiercely engaged with the enemy." In accordance with instructions from Ayres, Pearson retraced his steps and brought up another regiment, the 16th Michigan, which was posted on Bowerman's right. Before returning to his brigade, Pearson told Lieutenant Colonel Benjamin F. Partridge of the Michigan unit that he was to hold this ground for as long as feasible.[137]

General Gordon and his division commanders, Pegram and Evans, had regrouped their brigades in the woods northwest of Dabney's Mill. While the arrival of Ayres' division and Pearson's brigade had tipped the scales momentarily in favor of the Yankees, the Rebels were far from ready to abandon the field. As soon as the brigade commanders reported that they were ready and the battery commanders had unlimbered their guns and found the range, Gordon ordered, "Attack!" Pegram's and Evans' divisions advanced with their characteristic ardor. Hoffman's brigade of Pegram's division changed the Union left, while Evans' battle lines assailed Warren's center and right.[138]

As soon as Pearson's troops had taken post on Bowerman's left and right, Ayres passed the word for the troops to roll up log barricades. While the Marylanders were doing this, the 32nd Massachusetts and 155th Pennsylvania suddenly moved—without orders—300 yards farther to the front, where they formed a line at an angle with Bowerman's. The sawdust pile that marked the mill site was at this line's apex. To the right of the clearing was a thick grove of small pines, covering Crawford's left—Baxter's regiments.

Gordon's battle lines, covered by skirmishers, beat their way through the pines and underbrush. Over on the Union right, Terry's Virginians and Lowe's Georgians

136 J. C. Goolsby, "Crenshaw Battery, Pegram's Battalion, C S Artillery," in *Southern Historical Society Papers*, vol. 28, 368-369.

137 *OR* 46, pt. 1, 271, 277-278.

138 *Ibid.*, 390.

Brigadier General John Pegram
Library of Congress

forced Morrow's brigade to give ground. With Morrow's troops falling back, Evans maneuvered his men so as to enfilade Baxter's advance regiments (the 16th Maine, 39th Massachusetts, and the 97th New York). Baxter's bluecoats, up to this point, had been blazing away at the Rebels (Peck's Louisianans) who threatened their front. These volleys ripped through the pines, whistling across the ground defended by the 32nd Massachusetts and the 155th Pennsylvania. These two regiments (against whose lines Hoffman's Virginians were advancing) broke. The retreat of the 32nd Massachusetts and the 155th Pennsylvania enabled Hoffman to roll back the Maryland brigade. Baxter's three regiments, with the units to their right and left retreating, found their position untenable. "The men of the different regiments, mingling together, fell back in some confusion, but soon rallied around their colors. . . ."[139]

Encouraged by their gains, the Rebel leaders urged their men on. As General Pegram shouted encouragement to his Virginians, he was shot through the body near the heart. Major Douglas, who was riding with the general, leaped from his horse and caught him as he fell. Assisted by several others, Douglas took Pegram from his horse. He died in the major's arms, almost as soon as he touched the ground. Colonel Hoffman was also severely wounded. Deprived of two of their

139 OR 51, pt. 1, 286, 288, 290-291; OR 46, pt. 1, 279, 282, 293.

leaders, Hoffman's brigade was thrown into confusion. Valuable time was lost while General Gordon reorganized the brigade and placed the senior regimental commander, Col. John G. Kasey, in command. To make matters worse, Hoffman's and Evans' troops had diverged to the left and right, and a large gap had opened in Gordon's battle line, near the mill site.[140]

Union leaders took advantage of the Confederates' discomfort to regroup. General Baxter, in the center, had his troops erect barricades about 200 yards southeast of Dabney's Mill. To Baxter's right, Morrow called for a counterattack. As the troops of Crawford's 3rd Brigade started through Dabney's orchard, Colonel Morrow was seriously wounded. His senior regimental commander, Col. Thomas F. McCoy of the 107th Pennsylvania, was nearby when Morrow fell. As he turned over command, Morrow placed the brigade flag which he had been carrying in McCoy's hands. McCoy, seeing that the brigade had come up into line with Baxter's troops to the left, called a halt, and shouted for his men to entrench.[141] Colonel Pearson and his officers, "after much hard labor and exertion," reformed the 3rd Brigade on Baxter's left.[142] Bowerman's Marylanders, on Pearson's left, braced themselves for a stand at the sawdust pile. Checking with his regimental commanders, Bowerman was dismayed to learn the ammunition was running short.[143]

Meanwhile, Confederate reinforcements had reached the field. General Finegan marched up at the head of his division. In accordance with orders from General Gordon, Finegan formed his troops to fill the gap that had opened between Evans' right and Kasey's left. Many of his men had been killed or wounded, and with many of his men having fired their last round, Colonel Peck, on the arrival of Finegan's division, withdrew the Louisiana brigade a short distance to

---

140 OR 46, pt. 1, 390, 392; Douglas, *I Rode With Stonewall*, 326-327. After the fighting for the day was over, Major Douglas recalled, the question was asked, "Who will tell Mrs. Pegram?" "You must do it, Douglas," snapped General Gordon. "Heavens! General—I'll lead a forlorn hope—do anything that is war—but not that.Send New. He's married and knows women; I don't." "Major New went on his unenviable duty and I took the general's body back to my room at headquarters. An hour after, as the general lay dead on my bed, I heard the ambulance pass just outside the window, taking Mrs. Pegram back to their quarters. New had not seen her yet and she did not know; but her mother was with her. A fiancée of three years, a bride of three weeks, now a widow!" Douglas, *I Rode With Stonewall*, 327.

141 OR 46, pt. 1, 287, 289, 293; OR 51, pt. 1, 286, 288, 291.

142 OR 46, pt. 1, 271-272, 276; OR 51, pt. 1, 293, 295-296.

143 OR 46, pt. 1, 282.

where the ordnance wagons were parked. Within a few minutes, the aggressive Gordon had completed his dispositions and the entire line advanced.[144]

From left to right, the Union line, assailed by the hard-driving Confederates, was defended by Bowerman's, Pearson's, Baxter's, and McCoy's brigades. An anxiously expected ordnance train failed to reach the front in time. The cry, "We need cartridges!" was raised by a number of the bluecoats fighting to check Gordon's steamroller.

A volley from the rear threw Pearson's brigade into a panic and a stampede ensued. The brigade on Pearson's right (Baxter's) was the next to collapse. Having caved in Warren's center, the grey clads swung to the left and right, intent on rolling up Bowerman's and McCoy's units. McCoy, seeing that his brigade was in danger of being encircled, called for a retreat. With empty cartridge-boxes and their flanks exposed, Bowerman's Marylanders pulled back. Unless the Confederates could be checked, it would spell the end of the war for the V Corps.[145]

General Ayres remembered that there were several ridges, with marshy terrain intervening, between Dabney's Mill and the field fronting the bridgehead. Assisted by his staff, Ayres tried to rally the troops for a holding action along these ridges. So shaken were the soldiers who wore the Maltese cross on their caps that on only one occasion was Ayres able to bring a semblance of order out of chaos. But, when the troops that had been positioned saw an armed mob pass to their left, they took to their heels.[146]

Fortunately for the V Corps, reinforcements were at hand. As he rode down Vaughan Road to confer with General Warren, General Wheaton heard firing off to the southwest. Wheaton, satisfied that the V Corps had engaged the foe, ordered his division to push on, while he galloped ahead to Warren's command post. Warren had gone to the front, so Wheaton was directed by Meade "to move over Hatcher's Run, and be in position to support the Fifth Corps on the Vaughan Road or elsewhere."

As he rode out Vaughan Road, Wheaton met Generals Griffin and Gregg, who told him that they could cope with the Rebels to their front; consequently, they had no immediate use for any VI Corps troops. While the three generals conversed, one of Warren's staff raced up on a sweat-flaked horse. He reported that he had just

---

144 *Ibid.*, 390, 392; G. Moxley Sorrel, *Recollections of a Confederate Staff Officer* (Jackson, Tenn., 1958), 272-273.

145 *OR* 46, pt. 1, 271-272, 277, 279, 282, 289; *OR* 51, pt. 1, 286.

146 *OR* 46, pt. 1, 279.

come from the right, where Crawford and Ayres were engaged and that reinforcements were needed.

Wheaton's lead brigade, by this time, had crossed Hatcher's Run. Guided by one of Warren's aides, Col. James Hubbard's 2nd Brigade was conducted through the entrenchments and out the road to Dabney's Mill. Overtaking the brigade, Wheaton learned from the staff officer that Warren had told them to bring up only one brigade. Before riding on for the point of danger, Wheaton ordered his other two brigades to form behind the entrenchments and await further instructions.

Three-quarters of a mile beyond the run, Wheaton began to encounter stragglers. A glance at their badges told the general that these fugitives belonged to Crawford's division. Within a few moments, the number of troops fleeing toward the perimeter so flooded the road that Wheaton knew that some grave misfortune had befallen the V Corps troops at Dabney's Mill. To be on the safe side, he called for Colonel Hubbard to halt and deploy his brigade into line of battle. Before Hubbard could complete his dispositions, "the mass of troops in front came rushing through the dense woods and quite over us, and it was with the greatest difficulty that the line could be formed, so obstructed was it by the fugitives, who were deaf to every entreaty . . . and refused to rally on the flanks or in support of the brigade there forming. Squads, companies, and regiments went rapidly to the rear despite our greatest efforts to halt them."

While the confusion was at its height, Wheaton was joined by General Warren, who remarked that "the line in front had broken irreparably." Up until this moment, there had been only sniping in the woods to Hubbard's front. While Hubbard was preparing to throw out skirmishers, his men received several volleys from a line of troops clad in blue uniforms to their left. Fortunately for the VI Corps, these volleys were fired too high to inflict many casualties.

These crashing volleys were discharged by Burr's brigade of Griffin's division. Burr's troops had followed Sickel's down Vaughan Road. Before he reached Key's, his orders were countermanded and he was directed to follow Hubbard's brigade to the scene of action at Dabney's Mill. When the VI Corps disappeared into the pines; Burr halted and formed his troops into line of battle in a field. Without doing much checking, Burr bellowed, "Fire!"

To avoid having his troops slaughtered by the V Corps, Wheaton told Hubbard to withdraw from the pines. Falling back about 300 yards, Hubbard redeployed his brigade in a field. As the VI Corps retired, they were followed by Confederate sharpshooters, who infiltrated the woods to their front.

The gathering darkness and "general confusion" made it difficult for Hubbard to effect his disposition. Pearson's brigade, having been reformed, filed into position on Hubbard's left. Three regiments (the 1st Michigan and the 118th

Pennsylvania of Pearson's brigade, and the 121st New York of Hubbard's) were deployed and advanced as skirmishers.[147]

Burr's brigade, in the meantime, had disintegrated, retreating in great disorder, "their officers having no control of them whatever." Losing all sense of direction, many of Burr's bluecoats became so frightened that they continued to fire into the backs of units to their front. Others discharged their weapons into the air. Colonel Burr finally rallied a small force, which he posted on Hubbard's right.[148]

When Ayres advanced to Dabney's Mill, he presumed that Gwyn's brigade, having been disorganized by the horse soldiers breaking through its ranks, would rejoin him as soon as the man had been reformed. But, in going forward, Gwyn became confused as to directions and had wandered to the left. He encountered a Rebel picket line, which he engaged. Isolated and unsupported, the brigade soon collapsed.[149]

Lieutenant Colonel Frederick T. Locke was en route to the front line from Meade's Cummings' house command post, when he saw stragglers coming toward him. He quickly deployed the corps' provost guard and Warren's escort across the open field, with instructions to round up the refugees. Sighting "a mass of troops with colors retiring through the woods to the left" of the field, Locke rode over to learn who they were. Most of them were found to belong to Gwyn's brigade.

Locke shouted for them to halt and form on their colors. Gwyn galloped up shortly thereafter and explained that "his brigade had broken after receiving but a slight fire from the enemy." "Reform your brigade, advance to the woods, and deploy so as to stop the retreat," Locke snapped, as he pointed toward his front.

A number of Bowerman's Marylanders were now encountered wandering about the field. Locke rallied a number, telling "Gwyn to take charge of them along with his own command."[150]

Night had closed in, so the fighting soon ceased. Taking advantage of a full moon, Warren reorganized his corps. The five brigades (Burr's, Bowerman's, Gwyn's, Bragg's, and Baxter's) that had disintegrated were reformed and mustered inside the breastworks defended by Wheaton's 1st and 3rd Brigades.

Colonel Winthrop's brigade, of Ayres' division, was recalled from Keys' farm. Marching to the right, Winthrop's bluecoats relieved Pearson's, and assumed responsibility for picketing the pines to the left and right of the Dabney's Mill Road.

---

147 *Ibid.*, 261, 269, 272-273, 298-299.

148 *Ibid.*, 259, 269.

149 *Ibid.*, 279, 284.

150 *Ibid.*, 258-259.

Pearson, as soon as he had recalled his regiments, moved back into the rifle pits out of which he had led his troops several hours before.[151]

Upon the withdrawal of Winthrop's brigade, Colonel Sickel discovered that his people were the only ones remaining in Keys' field. He accordingly redeployed his troops along "a new and more eligible line for defensive operations and remained under arms all night." Sickel's pickets on the right were in contact with Winthrop's, while on the left, they connected with Gregg's cavalry.[152]

Hubbard's outposts were relieved by Winthrop's soldiers at 8:00 p.m. Orders were now received for Wheaton to withdraw his division east of Hatcher's Run and "mass in some convenient place." As Hubbard's troops tramped through the earthworks, the 1st and 3rd Brigades fell in behind. Crossing the stream, Wheaton's division went into bivouac near Cummings' house.[153]

The Confederates pursued the Federals through the forest. Darkness was at hand by the time Gordon's battle lines gained the fields fronting the breastworks, guarding the approaches to the Vaughan Road crossing. Gordon's units had been disorganized by the rapid advance and it would take time to regroup for an assault on the barricades to his front. Gordon accordingly decided to recall his troops and return to Dabney's Mill.

Before beginning the return march, Gordon saw that a strong line of outposts was established, while fatigue parties were organized to police the battlefield and collect arms and accoutrements abandoned by the V Corps people in their wild flight. Men also had to be detailed to escort into Petersburg the numerous prisoners bagged in the fighting.

There was little rest in the Southern camps, as Gordon and his generals, certain that the battle would be renewed, saw that their men entrenched their position at Dabney's Mill.[154] While the surgeons and hospital stewards dressed the wounds of the injured, burial details went about their grim task.

*   *   *

At 3:00 p.m., General Mott sent Colonel McAllister with a patrol to reconnoiter the ground explored during the morning by de Trobriand. A one and one-half mile advance brought the bluecoats out in front of the Rebel's

---

151 *Ibid.*, 266, 272, 280.

152 *Ibid.*, 266.

153 *Ibid.*, 299; OR 46, pt. 2, 437.

154 OR 46, pt. 1, 381, 390-392; Sorrel, *Recollections of a Confederate Staff Officer*, 272-273.

breastworks, but the butternuts were so engrossed in the fighting beyond Hatcher's Run that they ignored the patrol.[155]

News that the Confederates were sweeping back the V Corps caused Meade a few unpleasant moments. At 5:45 p.m., Chief of Staff Webb telegraphed II Corps commander Humphreys to hold all the troops he could "spare in readiness to move to Warren promptly and rapidly." Humphreys' command post barely clicked out this information, before a wire was received to rush troops to the Vaughan Road crossing of Hatcher's Run.[156]

Humphreys told Mott to put de Trobriand's 1st Brigade in motion. While de Trobriand's troops—2,500 strong—were falling out, orders reached Mott from II Corps headquarters to withdraw West's brigade from the line and to follow de Trobriand. Mott called on Ramsey and McAllister to each bring up a regiment to strengthen the column marching to Warren's assistance.[157] De Trobriand's brigade took the lead as the relief column started down Vaughan Road. Near the bridge, General Meade halted de Trobriand and told him that Warren's troops had checked the Confederate onset and that he was to return to his former position.[158] West's brigade was likewise stopped and countermarched. While the regiments from McAllister's and Ramsey's brigades were returned to the breastworks, de Trobriand's and West's brigades were massed in the woods.[159]

At the time that de Trobriand and West were instructed to reinforce Warren, Humphreys telegraphed General Miles to rush a brigade down Vaughan Road. At 7:00 p.m., Miles (replied that his 2nd Brigade, Col. Richard C. Duryea commanding, had been ordered out. Duryea's troops had gone only a short distance when Miles was notified that the emergency had passed, so he was to recall his 2nd Brigade.[160]

Two sections of the II Corps artillery (one from Battery K, 4th U.S., and the other belonging to the 10th Massachusetts) employed their guns to support the V Corps. As the men who wore the Maltese cross retreated, the four guns emplaced near Armstrong's shelled the woods across the run.[161]

---

155   *OR* 46, pt. 1, 225, 239; *OR* pt. 2, 425.

156   *OR* 46, pt. 2, 425.

157   *Ibid.*, 425; *OR* 46, pt. 1, 225.

158   *OR* 46, pt. 1, 228; *OR* 46, pt. 2, 426-427.

159   *OR* 46, pt. 1, 225, 236. West's brigade was positioned in the woods on the right of Smyth's main line of resistance.

160   *Ibid.*, 195; *OR* 46, pt. 2, 428-429.

161   *OR* 46, pt. 1, 212, 222, 250; Billings, *History of the Tenth Massachusetts Battery*, 391.

At the time the V Corps broke, two units of Colonel Pierce's brigade—the 69th Pennsylvania and 4th Ohio Battalion—were called up from the reserve and took position covering the dam and a bridge that had been thrown across Hatcher's Run, near Armstrong's Mill. As they double-timed into position, they were fired on by Rebel sharpshooters posted in the timber and underbrush on the south bank.

Meade, realizing that the VI Corps had been materially weakened by the need to employ Wheaton to strengthen his field force, issued orders for General Parke to rush the Engineer Brigade to Aiken's house.[162] After reporting to Getty, the brigade occupied the line between Battery Nos. 24 and 26, its right resting on Battery No. 24. A 287-man detail from the Engineer Brigade relieved the men Wheaton had left on the picket line.[163]

After the results of the forced reconnaissance undertaken that morning by the II Corps had been studied, Meade telegraphed General Grant at 2:00 p.m. that if Warren's troops, who were then preparing to move out, encountered the Confederates behind fortifications, he would require fresh instructions. Because, he added, he would have "accomplished all originally designed or now practicable." The condition of the roads, which was very bad and the lack of trains and supplies precluded any extended movement to the west. As far as Meade could see, he only had two options: to entrench where he was or withdraw. Meade decided that if further operations were contemplated, the Army of the Potomac should extend its entrenched line to Hatcher's Run.

Grant opposed making an attack on a fortified line, but went along with Meade's suggestion that "it will be well to hold out to Hatcher's Run."[164]

Part IV

The Federals Fortify a Line from Fort Sampson to Hatcher's Run

It had clouded up and a cold rain was falling at daybreak on February 7, 1865. As his first order of business, General Warren began shifting his brigades, "so as to bring all of each division together." At 8:15 a.m., Warren telegraphed Chief of Staff

162 OR 46, pt. 2, 435.

163 OR 46, pt. 1, 72.

164 OR 46, pt. 2, 417.

Webb that since the fighting had ceased; all had been quiet along the V Corps' front. Out on the picket line, Winthrop's men could see Confederate troops moving about in their picket posts. Warren speculated that the foe was either relieving their outposts or reinforcing them.[165]

Webb, in replying, observed that General Meade wanted a report on the V Corps' condition and an estimate of the casualties suffered in yesterday's battle. Warren was to push out skirmishers to ascertain if the Rebels were still in force to his front. If they were, he was to exercise his judgment as to the wisdom of attacking.[166]

Rooney Lee's cavalry meanwhile, trailed by an infantry skirmish line, was spotted advancing across the fields south of Vaughan Road. Colonel Sickel's outposts and the grey clads soon opened fire, and for the next 45 minutes the two skirmish lines banged away.

As soon as he spotted the butternuts, Colonel Sickel contacted Generals Griffin and Gregg. The cavalry leader promptly called up one of his regiments, which he positioned on the left of Sickel's infantry. The cannoneers of Battery D, 1st New York Light Artillery were also ordered up. Because of the dense woods in the fight of the 6th, the artillerists were unable to employ their guns, so they were glad to see, as the battery drove down Vaughan Road, that the country hereabouts was open. The rain soon changed to sleet by the time the gunners reached the front. The Confederates, who had been sent to gather arms abandoned in the previous afternoon's fight, now pulled back into the woods.[167]

At 9:20 a.m., Warren received another note signed by General Webb. The chief of staff wanted the V Corps leader to give due consideration in drafting his plans to meet Meade's desire that Gregg's cavalry be withdrawn at the earliest opportunity.

Twenty minutes later, Warren advised headquarters of the "slight demonstration" made by the Confederates on Vaughan Road. So far, all that he had seen and heard satisfied him that the Rebels would not make a stand this side of Dabney's Mill. He was convinced that the V Corps could drive the Rebels "that far, if at all, without the aid of more than one of Gregg's brigades." If Meade so wished, the other two cavalry brigades could be recalled at once.[168]

At 10:40 a.m., Meade issued instructions for Warren to "order General Gregg to take two of his brigades to Rowanty Post Office, with their horses, etc." There

165 OR 46, pt. 1, 256; OR 46, pt. 2, 454.

166 OR 46, pt. 2, 454.

167 *Ibid.*, 454; OR 46, pt. 1, 267, 297, 368.

168 OR 46, pt. 2, 454.

Gregg would see that his troopers were provisioned and kept well in hand, so they would be ready to march against the foe's cavalry or to the support of the II Corps. This message was delivered to Warren at 12:30 p.m., who forwarded a copy to Gregg with a notation "to carry out the instructions contained therein."[169]

Gregg moved promptly. By 1:00 p.m., the two brigades—Davies' and Knowles'—that were to accompany the cavalry leader across Hatcher's Run were ready to ride. Just as he was putting his horse soldiers into motion, a courier rode up with additional instructions from army headquarters. Gregg now learned that he could post his command in the most suitable place to watch the Halifax and Perkins roads. Should he find it difficult to supply his division at that point, he was authorized to move back to Fort Dushane.[170]

Gregg posted his two brigades by dusk at the junction of the Halifax and Wyatt roads. One regiment—the 21st Pennsylvania Cavalry—was advanced to the Rowanty Post Office, with pickets thrown out on the Perkins and Ream's Station roads. Another regiment was sent to reconnoiter the country between Ream's Station and Stony Creek. Troopers from the 21st Pennsylvania, occupying an outpost near Monk's Neck Bridge, had watched as a brigade of Rebel infantry marched down the road on the opposite side of the Rowanty. Union and Confederate pickets in this sector confronted each other with the stream between.[171]

Several hours before he left the west side of Hatcher's Run, Gregg had the troopers from Kerwin's brigade remain behind to relieve Sickel's infantrymen, so they could rejoin their parent unit—Griffin's division. By 11:00 a.m., Kerwin's horse soldiers had moved into position across Vaughan Road, and Sickel's brigade marched up the road.[172]

Not long after Gregg had departed, Colonel Kerwin received orders from Warren's headquarters to send a combat patrol down Vaughan Road. This force was to try and push the Rebels to their front across Gravelly Run. If the Confederates were encountered in force, the patrol was to retire on the brigade.[173]

The 4th Pennsylvania—Colonel Young commanding—was selected to make the sweep toward Gravelly Run. No Confederates were encountered by the

Pennsylvanians as they rode down Vaughan Road, until they had penetrated to within one-half mile of their goal. Striking the Rebel picket line at this point, Colonel Young shouted for his bugler to sound "Charge!" The butternuts were forced back to the stream, where they braced for a stand. A lightning-like movement by Young's dismounted 1st Battalion drove the grey clads across Gravelly Run and into rifle pits on the other side.

Cannoneers now opened on the Yanks with their two 3-inch Whitworths. Recalling his troopers, Colonel Young headed back up Vaughan Road, as the hexagonal bolts knocked branches and boughs from the trees to the troopers' right and left. A squadron of Rooney Lee's dismounted Confederates followed the bluecoats as far as the point where the pickets had been assailed. Young now wheeled his column about and the rebels finally rejoined their comrades beyond the stream.

On his return, Colonel Young explained to Colonel Kerwin that the Confederates appeared "to have one brigade of cavalry" in the trenches south of Gravelly Run.[174]

General Ayres had spent a good part of the morning on the picket line. What he saw and heard from Colonel Winthrop convinced the general that this rugged duty had taken its toll, because the infantrymen of the 1st Brigade appeared to be exhausted. Returning to his command post, Ayres, recalling that Warren had expressed an intention to retrieve Winthrop's bluecoats "as soon as some other troops could be fitted out to take" their place, wrote Colonel Locke. Ayres, after explaining the situation, urged that Winthrop's brigade be replaced.[175]

Warren consented to Ayres' request. As soon as Sickel's troops reentered the perimeter, they replaced Burr's brigade behind the earthworks on Pearson's left. Burr's people then moved out and relieved Winthrop's on the picket line. Troops of his unit not assigned to outpost duty were formed into line of battle by Burr, and turned to erecting breastworks. At periodic intervals during the cold, wet afternoon, the woods occupied by Burr's brigade were shelled by Rebel artillery.[176]

---

174 *Ibid.*, 465-466; OR 46, pt. 1, 368-369.

175 OR 46, pt. 2, 460. While Ayres was visiting Winthrop, he heard the chopping of axes and the crash of timber in the woods to his front, a certain indication to the veterans that the Rebels were felling timber and throwing up breastworks.

176 *Ibid.*, 459; OR 46, pt. 1, 269. The left of Burr's picket line anchored on Vaughan Road, while the right joined Ayres' line of outposts.

Forming and mustering his troops as soon as they were relieved, Winthrop led them back into the bridgehead, where they camped behind the units manning the barricades.[177]

On the morning of February 7, Warren dispatched Captain Cope to examine the ground to the right and locate a battery position, where the Federals could emplace guns to reply to the Rebels' cannons at Dabney's Mill. Near Armstrong's Mill, the captain found ground having the necessary prerequisites. He also observed that the II Corps' batteries at Armstrong's house could be helpful in neutralizing the troublesome Confederate guns.

Fording Hatcher's Run where Pearson's right anchored, Cope crossed the open ground in front of the works and visited the II Corps pickets. Seeing no signs of the Johnnies, the captain concluded that they must have pulled in their line of outposts. Rejoining Warren, Cope told what he had seen.[178]

Warren, after listening to what Cope had to say, determined to see if he could dislodge the Rebels from their advance rifle pits. At 10:00 a.m., he reduced his plan to writing. General Crawford was to move out from the right of the bridgehead and assail the foe; Wheaton's VI Corps division would be held ready to reinforce Crawford.[179]

When Captain Cope delivered his copy of the circular to Crawford, he explained that the Third Division was to "push out as far as possible toward Dabney's Mill, bury his dead of the day before, and see what was going on."[180]

By the time that Cope reached Crawford's command post, the troops had refilled their cartridge-boxes. When Crawford passed the word to prepare to move out, the brigade commanders called for their units to fall in on their color lines.

Baxter's brigade took the lead as the column marched up the west side of Hatcher's Run, the breastworks behind which Pearson's troops crouched to their left. Opposite Armstrong's Mill, the column turned to the left and passed through the works. A short distance beyond the rifle pits, Crawford called for General Baxter to halt and deploy his troops into line of battle. Covered by a double line of skirmishers—the 39th Massachusetts in advance and the 11th Pennsylvania in support—the brigade resumed the advance. Crawford's other brigades followed Baxter's battle line—Bragg's on the left and McCoy's on the right.

---

177 OR 46, pt. 2, 459.

178 OR 46, pt. 1, 261.

179 OR 46, pt. 2, 458-459.

180 OR 46, pt. 1, 261.

Baxter's skirmishers were fired on by Rebel pickets who were posted behind light earthworks. These grey clads belonged to Brigadier General G. Moxley Sorrel's Georgia brigade of Finegan's division. The 11th Pennsylvania advanced to assist the 39th Massachusetts, and the Georgians were quickly dislodged. Closely followed by the battle line, Baxter's skirmishers forged ahead through the sodden forest, driving the grey clads before them. General Sorrel was among the casualties in this phase of the fighting. A Union rifleman put a minie ball through his chest, piercing the general's "right lung, smashing the ribs front and rear." Sorrel was carried to the rear by his aides. Although he recovered, the war was over for Sorrel. A three-quarter mile advance brought Baxter's people to a clearing. Out in the field in front of the skirmishers was a formidable line of works held in force by Confederate infantry. A short distance to their right was a parapet with embrasures, through which protruded the ugly muzzles of several cannon.[181]

The Confederates had spent a miserable morning strengthening the line of works, marked out the previous evening, covering their position at Dabney's Mill. Guns manned by Ellett's and several other batteries of Col. William J. Pegram's Artillery Battalion were manhandled along muddy trails and into position at strategic points behind the parapets. A brigade from General Finegan's division led by General Sorrel had been sent forward at dawn to hold the picket line.

As soon as he was notified by Sorrel that the Federals were advancing in force, General Gordon had the "long roll" beaten. In forming his troops to meet the renewed Union advance, Gordon posted Pegram's division (now commanded by General Johnston) on the right, while Finegan's division filed into position on Johnston's left. General Evans' division was held in reserve, ready to move forward at a moment's notice.[182]

After Baxter's troops had chased Sorrel's Georgians out of their advance rifle pits, these fortifications were occupied by Colonel McCoy's brigade. In accordance with instructions from Crawford, McCoy had his men start strengthening and refacing the trenches and slashing timber. While engaged in this work, the soldiers were shelled by artillery emplaced north of the run, and fired on by Tar Heel sharpshooters of Cooke's brigade posted in the underbrush north of Hatcher's Run. Apprehensive lest the grey clads slip a column across the stream to turn his position, McCoy dispatched skirmishers to cope with this threat. When General

---

181 *Ibid.*, 290; OR 51, pt. 1, 286-287, 289-292; Sorrel, *Recollections of a Confederate Staff Officer*, 272-273.

182 *Ibid.*, 273; OR 46, pt. 1, 392. Another casualty of the day's troop movements was "Sally," the promiscuous bitch dog mascot of the 11th Pennsylvania. She is a popular figure on the unit's Gettysburg monument.

Crawford learned of this situation, he personally positioned several of Bragg's regiments between McCoy's right and Hatcher's Run.[183]

To hold his position fronting the Rebels' main line of resistance, Baxter called up and deployed his three remaining regiments—the 16th Maine, 97th New York, and 88th Pennsylvania—as skirmishers to the right and left. McCoy's 56th Pennsylvania was brought up and posted as a reserve to Baxter's skirmish line.[184]

Shortly after Crawford had passed through the barricades, Meade telegraphed Warren at 11:45 a.m. that in view of the inclement weather and General Grant's strong feelings against attacking a fortified line, an assault at this time would be inadvisable, unless great advantages could be gained. Plans at army headquarters were being prepared to withdraw the V Corps "tonight or tomorrow" to the east bank of Hatcher's Run.[185]

His fighting blood aroused, Warren determined to ignore his superiors and push matters. At 3:45 p.m., Crawford was directed to "drive the enemy just as far as you can in the daylight that is left you, and use all your supports I have sent you."[186]

Writing Chief of Staff Webb at 4:30 p.m., Warren placed himself on record that if it were necessary to fall back across Hatcher's Run, he would prefer to do so in the morning. In an effort to get Grant and Meade to change their minds, he reported, "We have regained most of the ground we held yesterday, and drawn the artillery fire from the enemy's works, and we could hold the south side of Hatcher's Run toward Dabney's Mill so long as may be required."[187]

The supports referred to by Warren in his 3:45 p.m. communication to Crawford belonged to Wheaton's division. At the time of the Rebels' morning demonstration on Vaughan Road, General Warren had called for Wheaton to rush one of his brigades to V Corps headquarters. With this threat evaporating, Col. Joseph E. Hamblin's brigade was massed in a field east of the run. At 12:00 p.m., Hamblin's men were ordered across the stream to support General Crawford. Colonel Hubbard's 2nd Brigade was then concentrated in the field vacated by

---

183 OR 46, pt. 1, 290, 295-296; OR 51, pt. 1, 294-296.

184 OR 51, pt. 1, 287, 295; OR 46, pt. 1, 290.

185 OR 46, pt. 2, 455.

186 *Ibid.*, 461.

187 *Ibid.*, 456.

Hamblin. Within the hour, Hubbard's bluecoats crossed the run and formed near the bridge, prepared to march to Hamblin's assistance on Crawford's call.[188]

Before assailing the earthworks covering Dabney's Mill, Crawford had the remainder of Bragg's troops take position between McCoy's and Hatcher's Run. To afford sufficient space for Bragg's men behind the captured works, McCoy's battle line filed to the left several hundred yards, resting its left on a morass. As soon as this movement was completed, orders were received from Crawford for McCoy to advance and take position on the left of Baxter's skirmishers. Hamblin's VI Corps brigade marched up and occupied the works just before McCoy's men started forward. As his troops drew abreast of Baxter's, McCoy refused his left wing.[189]

When Crawford passed word that all was ready, Baxter's and McCoy's troops advanced against the manned barricades to their front. Sleet was falling and a thin crust of ice had formed on many of the soldiers' arms and accoutrements. Baxter's skirmishers on the right drove to within 100 yards of the newly erected breastworks, before their thrust was blunted by the well-aimed volleys of Finegan's foot soldiers.[190]

McCoy's battle line came forward through the pines on the run. When "Willie" Pegram's artillery to their front swept the woods with canister, part of McCoy's line "gave way and retired to the works in their rear before they could be rallied." Other individuals, such as Maj. H. J. Sheafer and the color guard of the 107th Pennsylvania only retired about 100 yards and reformed.[191]

Gordon's Confederates made no effort to follow up this success. On the Union right, Baxter's bluecoats retired to the ground held prior to the attack. The troops on McCoy's left, who hadn't bolted, threw up breastworks within 300 yards of the Confederates' entrenchments. Here they were joined, as soon as it was dark, by the rest of the brigade.[192]

At 6:20 p.m., Crawford wrote Warren that he had advanced his lines, driving the rebels into their "new lines of works." Prisoners bagged by the Yanks reported that the V Corps was opposed by the same units it had fought yesterday. His division was extended as far as the exhausted condition of the men would allow, so

188 *Ibid.*, 462; OR 46, pt. 1, 299. Wheaton's 1st Brigade at 3:00 p.m. was assembled in the field east of the run, recently vacated by Hubbard's bluecoats.

189 OR 46, pt. 1, 290, 292, 295; OR 51, pt. 1, 294-296.

190 OR 51, pt. 1, 287, 289-291, 295.

191 OR 46, pt. 1, 290, 292; OR 51, pt. 1, 294, 296.

192 OR 51, pt. 1, 287, 289; OR 46, pt. 1, 291, 295.

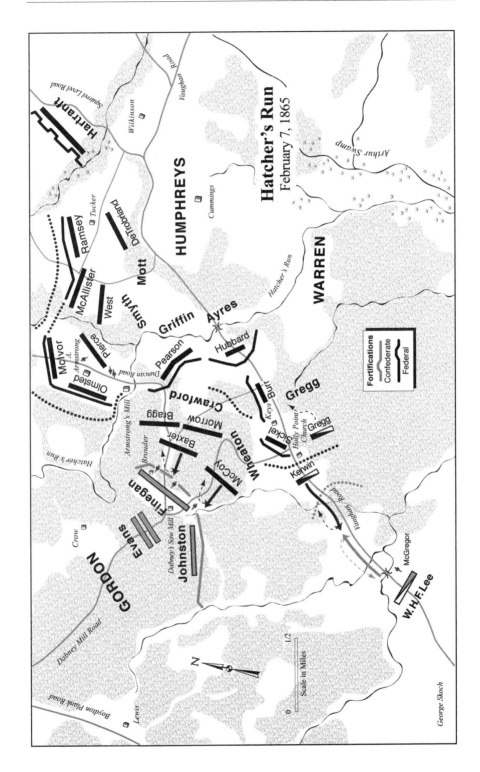

Hatcher's Run
February 7, 1865

George Skoch

orders had been issued for one of Wheaton's brigades to take position on McCoy's left.[193]

Baxter's skirmishers, at 9:00 p.m., were relieved by picked men from Hamblin's and McCoy's brigades. Retiring about 100 yards, Baxter's soldiers formed line and began erecting works within one-quarter mile of the Rebel rifle pits, connecting on the right with McCoy's brigade and on the left with Hamblin's.[194] Bragg's brigade by this time had been advanced and occupied the ground between McCoy's right and Hatcher's Run.[195] There in the pines, the soldiers, chilled to their bones by the sleet, grimly held their ground. Needless to say, the ranks had been thinned, as the sunshine patriots and summer soldiers slipped to the rear.[196]

General Crawford at the time notified Warren that his advance line had dug in. He had just returned to his command post from inspecting the picket line. From the road which he was on, the Rebel fortifications ran northeast and southwest. His troops, he observed, badly needed rest, not having had an opportunity to build fires and make coffee for over ten hours.[197]

Because of the shoddy condition of many of the units' uniforms, the Confederates undoubtedly suffered greater discomfort from the hostile elements than the Federals. General Lee, after visiting the front, wrote Secretary of War James A. Seddon on the 8th:

> All the disposable force of the right wing of the army has been operating against the enemy beyond Hatcher's Run since Sunday. Yesterday, the most inclement day of the winter, they had to be retained in line of battle, having been in the same condition the two previous days and nights. I regret to be obliged to state that under these circumstances, heightened assaults, and fire of the enemy, some of the men had been without meat for three days, and all were suffering from reduced rations and scant clothing, exposed to battle, cold, hail and sleet.[198]

General Humphreys' II Corps held its ground on February 7. At the time of Warren's decision to undertake a forced reconnaissance, Humphreys was directed

---

193 *OR* 46, pt. 2, 461.

194 *OR* 51, pt. 1, 287, 289, 291-292.

195 *OR* 46, pt. 1, 291; *OR* 51, pt. 1, 294-295.

196 *OR* 46, pt. 1, 291.

197 *OR* 46, pt. 2, 461.

198 *OR* 46, pt. 1, 381-382.

by Meade to support the men who wore the "Maltese cross" with all his available force, if called upon. Contacting Warren at 12:35 p.m., Humphreys reported that he had two brigades in ready reserve—de Trobriand's and West's.

Replying for his boss, Colonel Locke inquired into the possibility of the II Corps batteries, emplaced near Armstrong's, giving Crawford's frontal fire support, "more for the moral effect it will produce on our troops than anything else."[199] Warren, at this time, did not believe he would require any II Corps troops.[200]

But, in accordance with this request, cannoneers of Smith's section, Battery K, 4th United States Artillery shelled the woods in front of Crawford's advancing line. The regulars continued to fire until the men of the V Corps had pushed deep into the woods and closed up against the Rebel position at Dabney's Mill. Along toward dark, a section of the 10th Massachusetts Battery opened on a Rebel battery near Dabney's Mill, at a range of one mile. After the redlegs had expended 25 rounds, the butternuts ceased fire.[201]

*   *   *

At 10:15 a.m., Meade telegraphed Grant that foul weather, "and the ignorance I am under of the exact moral condition of Warren's corps, and his losses from stragglers, has restrained me from giving him positive orders to attack." Even so, Warren had been instructed to undertake a forced reconnaissance.

In regard to the plan of holding to Hatcher's Run broached late on the 6th, Meade explained, his "idea was to hold it permanently by a strong line, which a small force could hold, if we moved farther to the left." Humphreys' and Warren's men had already thrown up a line of light works, but if Meade's suggestions were adopted, a permanent line with redoubts, could be quickly established.[202]

Grant replied that as Meade was on the ground, he should know "better than the people at City Point what line the troops should occupy." In Grant's opinion, "we should hold from our present left to Armstrong's Mill. The cavalry could then picket down Hatcher's Run and cover our rear easier than at present." The weather

---

199 OR 46, pt. 2, 451.

200 *Ibid.*, 452.

201 OR 46, pt. 1, 213, 250, 252, 261; OR 51, pt. 1, 285; Billings, *History of the Tenth Massachusetts Battery*, 392.

202 OR 46, pt. 2, 447.

having turned bad, Grant thought it would be wise to get the soldiers "back to the position you intend them to occupy."[203]

At 1:30 p.m., Grant wired Meade that he had been called to Washington to testify before the Committee on the Conduct of the War. He hoped to leave via boat for the capital in the morning, but he would defer his departure until Meade notified him the "troops now out are in the new position they are to occupy."

Meade answered that he would advise Grant as soon as the troops were in position. He doubted however, if they would be by tomorrow, because "some works" had to be constructed before he could "unmass the forces on the left."[204]

Meeting with his staff and Chief Engineer J. C. Duane, Meade drafted a circular, sketching the fortified position the troops were to take up. Major Duane was "to lay out and construct an entrenched line from Fort Sampson to Armstrong's Mill placing works at the latter point and the crossing of the Vaughan Road, so as to hold and command both these crossings." Suitable artillery emplacements were to be selected and connected by rifle pits, timber was to be slashed, dams built on Hatcher's Run, and the stream obstructed.

As soon as these works had been surveyed, the Petersburg investment line would be held: the IX Corps from the Appomattox to Fort Howard; the VI Corps from Fort Howard to Fort Gregg, inclusive; and the II Corps from Fort Gregg to Armstrong's Mill. Warren's V Corps was to occupy fortifications covering the Vaughan Road crossing, picketing Hatcher's Run above and below, "and will be posted on a line from the crossing of the Vaughan Road via Cummins' and Wyatt's houses, and so held as to meet any attack from the rear, or to support" the II or VI Corps, if they were attacked. Warren's men were to also hold a line of outposts from Hatcher's Run to the intersection of Church and Halifax Roads. Gregg's cavalry was to take position on Jerusalem Plank Road, and picket from the left of the V Corps to the James River.[205]

Chief of Staff Webb wrote Warren at 5:15 p.m. to prepare him for this bombshell. Meade, Webb observed, was pleased to learn of the success registered by Crawford's command. Nevertheless, his troops were to be withdrawn, but not at night. When Warren redeployed his corps, the soldiers were not to return to the camps from which they had marched on the road.[206]

203 *Ibid.*, 447-448.

204 *Ibid.*, 448.

205 *Ibid.*, 450.

206 *Ibid.*, 456-457.

After studying Meade's circular and Webb's communication, Warren replied, we will forsake our old quarters cheerfully, because "when any extension of our line is to be made, we have the privilege of doing it."[207]

Shortly after dark, General Meade called on Warren for information as to when he would have no further need for Wheaton's infantry and Kerwin's cavalry.

Warren replied that it would be possible to withdraw Wheaton's division at any time, while he would see that Kerwin's horse soldiers were relieved in the morning.[208]

Upon being informed that Wheaton would be recalled, Crawford advised Warren that he would then be unable to maintain his position if the Confederates attacked in force. Warren thereupon directed Crawford to recall his division simultaneously.

While Crawford was strengthening his picket line, Wheaton sent for Hamblin's and Hubbard's brigades. Re-crossing Hatcher's Run, the two VI Corps brigades fell in behind Campbell's. Wheaton then put his column in motion up Vaughan Road. Daybreak on February 8 saw Wheaton's VI Corps division back in the camps from which the troops had marched 56 hours earlier.[209]

Screened by a formidable rear guard, Crawford's division followed Wheaton's through the breastworks and across the run. At 3:00 a.m., near Cummings' house, a halt was called, and the exhausted troops allowed to bivouac in the surrounding fields. Having left their shelter-halves behind when they took the field, Crawford's bluecoats were unable to rest comfortably because of the frightful weather.[210]

Colonel Kerwin's troopers were holding the roadblock at Keys' farm, and were relieved by a detachment from Ayres' division by 7:45 a.m. on February 8. Riding

---

207 *Ibid.*, 457.

208 *Ibid.*, 457-458.

209 OR 46, pt. 1, 299; pt. 2, 485, 491. General Getty, upon the return of Wheaton's command, posted his divisions as follows: Wheaton's division occupied the line from Fort Howard to Fort Keene (not including the latter), besides garrisoning Forts Davison and McMahon on the rear line; Mackenzie's division would hold the line from Fort Keene to Fort Fisher (not including the latter), while garrisoning Fort Dushane; Seymour's division was to defend the line from Fort Fisher to Fort Gregg. The Engineer Brigade was to occupy the works extending from Battery No. 24 to Fort Howard, not including the latter. OR 46, pt. 2, 491-492.

210 OR 46, pt. 2, 485, 487-488, 490; OR pt. 1, 256, 291, 295. In fighting on the 7th, Crawford's division had lost 23 killed, 152 wounded, and 158 missing. Losses in the division on February 6 and 7 totaled 1,168.

up Vaughan Road, the horse soldiers marched eastward to Globe Tavern, where Kerwin reported to General Gregg.[211]

In accordance with Meade's circular of the previous afternoon, General Gregg, on the arrival of Kerwin's unit, ordered two of his brigades to return to their camps east of Jerusalem Plank Road, while a third (Kerwin's) would watch Halifax Road.

During the day, Gregg was notified that his resignation from the army had been accepted. One of the cavalry leader's last official acts was to inform Chief of Staff Webb that at dark, soldiers from Crawford's division had assumed responsibility for picketing the countryside from Halifax Road to Hatcher's Run. Meanwhile, his troopers had taken station to enable them to picket the area from Halifax Road to the James River. With Crawford's foot soldiers on duty, Gregg wished to relieve Kerwin's brigade so the horses could be foraged.[212]

Two of Warren's divisions—Griffin's and Ayres'—continued to be responsible for the defense of the bridgehead. Warren, as an officer who had belonged to the Corps of Engineers, was understandably interested in the extension of the fortified zone from Fort Sampson to Hatcher's Run. On February 8 at 12:35 p.m., he telegraphed Meade's headquarters that unless the Federals constructed a work on the south bank of Hatcher's Run at Armstrong's Mill, the line held by Humphreys' left division (Smyth's) could be untenable. A reconnaissance had disclosed that the foe, if this redoubt were not erected, would possess "commanding ground that will overlook and take the line in rear in front of Armstrong's house." It appeared to Warren that the best line the Army of the Potomac could take would be from Fort Cummings via Westmoreland's and Tucker's houses to C. W. Cummings'. "No matter where we put the line on the left bank," Warren cautioned, "if the enemy establishes one on the other side along the high ridge from Armstrong's Mill to the Vaughan Road a small force would be able to prevent us from crossing the stream."[213]

Meade was impressed with Warren's comments, so Chief Engineer Duane's instructions to him were amended to read, "proceed to lay out and construct an entrenched line from Fort Sampson to the crossing of the Vaughan Road, placing a work at the latter point to hold and command that crossing."[214]

On the afternoon of the 8th, Crawford sent his 3rd Brigade, McCoy's, to relieve Kerwin's horse soldiers on the picket line extending eastward from Monk's

---

211 *OR* 46, pt. 2, 485; *OR* 46, pt. 1, 116, 118.

212 *OR* 46, pt. 2, 494.

213 *Ibid.*, 488.

214 *Ibid.*, 480.

Neck Bridge to Halifax Road. Soldiers from Ayres' division held the line of outposts from the left of the earthworks guarding the approach to the bridgehead to the point where McCoy's picket line anchored on the east bank of the Rowanty.[215]

General Humphreys' II Corps held its ground on the 8th, while the engineers surveyed the new line the men wearing the "Clover leaf" were to take up. After studying the area between Fort Gregg and Armstrong's Mill, and discussing the situation with his generals, Humphreys issued a directive. At 8:00 a.m. on the morning of February 9, General Miles was to be relieved along the sector of the entrenched line between Forts Fisher and Gregg by Brigadier General Truman Seymour's VI Corps division. One hour later, Miles was to march his troops and "take position in the new line, from Fort Sampson to the chimneys of the Westmoreland house."

Mott at the same hour was to shift that part of his division slated "to occupy the new line on the right of the battery to be erected on McAllister's front, and take position on the new line," his right resting at the chimneys of the Westmoreland house. Both division commanders were to see that their men slashed the woods to a distance of 700 yards to their fronts, and threw up a substantial parapet, with a ditch on the side facing the foe. Details from the 4th New York Heavy Artillery were to be given the task of supervising the construction of the five batteries that were to be erected along the new line.[216]

In accordance with instructions from Meade's headquarters, Humphreys, on the morning of February 9, saw that his First and Third Divisions took up the positions assigned them along the new line. Ramsey's brigade at this time reported back to Miles, having completed its assignment with Mott's Third Division.[217]

There was no hostile activity in front of the bridgehead held by the V Corps during the 36 hours beginning at daybreak on the 8th and ending at nightfall on February 9. Ayres' troops were kept employed erecting a strong work "on the Vaughan Road, below the run," while Griffin's held the breastworks covering the crossing of Hatcher's Run. A line of outposts was established by Griffin,

215 *Ibid.*, 490; OR 46, pt. 1, 291.

216 OR 46, pt. 2, 483-484, 500. Miles' division for the time being would continue to be responsible for the defense of the line between Forts Gregg and Sampson, as well as for garrisoning Fort Cummings. Mott announced that de Trobriand was to move up from the reserve and post his troops on Miles' left.

217 OR 46, pt. 1, 81, 193. Miles' brigades were posted from right to left: Ramsey's, Macy's, and Von Schack's, with Duryea's in reserve, about 500 yards in rear of Von Schack's brigade. Mott established his command post at Claypole's house.

connecting with Smyth's II Corps division on the right. East of the run, Crawford's troops continued to man the picket line, "starting from a point near the burnt sawmill, thence running easterly, passing through Rowanty Post Office, and connecting with the cavalry pickets at the intersection of the Church and Halifax Roads."[218]

Before retiring on the evening of the 9th, General Warren prepared a set of instructions that were to govern his corps' activities on the following day. Crawford was to have a large working party at Cummings' at 7:00 a.m. This force would be assigned the task of corduroying Vaughan Road. General Griffin would begin relieving Ayres' pickets at 6:00 a.m. Ayres with his division was to report to corps headquarters at 7:00 a.m., prepared "to construct a new line of entrenchments." Griffin's pioneers were to spend the day felling "all the timber between the line of breastworks on the right bank of Hatcher's Run and the edge of the stream."[219]

On February 10 at 10:00 a.m., Warren wrote Chief of Staff Webb that by nightfall, Ayres' fatigue parties would have completed the breastworks to the battery on Hatcher's Run. He therefore wished to know, "How much of this line will be the responsibility of the II Corps?"

Since his last communication, Warren had had a survey made of Hatcher's Run below the Vaughan Road crossing. On doing so, he found that the stream ran "south 40 degrees east for one mile and three-fourths. . . ." His pickets at this time extended a mile below the crossing on the left bank, then due east along a road to J. W. Spiers' on Halifax Road.

Replying, Webb informed Warren that the V Corps was to hold the works at the Vaughan Road crossing, while Humphreys' men held to that point. The right of Warren's picket line west of Hatcher's Run was to connect with the left of Humphreys' northeast of the stream.[220]

The task of corduroying Vaughan Road was completed by late afternoon, so General Crawford was authorized to return with his division to the camps they had left on the 5th. There the troops were to collect from their old quarters all their gear, and be ready to head west at 6:00 a.m. On reaching the area near Colonel Wyatt's, Crawford would mass his troops and await further orders.[221]

General Bragg's brigade would be detached at this time from the Third Division and marched to Warren Station. At noon on the 11th, Bragg's troops were

218 *OR* 46, pt. 2, 500-501.

219 *Ibid.*, 501-502.

220 *Ibid.*, 518-519.

221 *Ibid.*, 520.

to board the cars that were to carry them to City Point, where they were to embark on transports. After casting off, the ships were to proceed down the James and up Chesapeake Bay to Baltimore. As soon as he had disembarked at Baltimore, General Bragg was to report by telegraph to Major General Henry W. Halleck.[222]

Upon being notified that the earthworks between McAllister's left and the Vaughan Road crossing had been completed, General Humphreys notified General Smyth that at daylight on the 11th, he was to withdraw his division from its position at Armstrong's and occupy these works. When he did, Smyth was to post two brigades in the rifle pits, while holding one in reserve. The artillery was to be retired at midnight, under the direction of Major Hazard. Before recalling his troops, Smyth was to see that they destroyed "such rifle pits . . . as might be useful to the enemy."[223]

General Mott, prior to Smyth's recall, was to withdraw West's brigade and mass it in rear of McAllister's. During the morning, de Trobriand was to relieve troops of General Miles' division on his right as far as the first redoubt (Battery C) to the right of the ruins of Westmoreland's house. To accomplish this, de Trobriand was to deploy one or both of his reserve regiments.[224]

General Hartranft, whose IX Corps division had been opening and building roads since the 8th, was notified on February 10 at 7:00 p.m. that his troops had been relieved of duty with the II Corps. It took Hartranft's men less than one hour to pack their gear before moving out. As soon as the two brigades had been formed and mustered, Hartranft passed the word to move out. Marching by way of Globe Tavern, Hartranft's bluecoats were back in their camps by midnight.[225]

As directed, shortly before daybreak on the 11th, General Smyth withdrew his division from its position, covering the Armstrong's Mill crossing of Hatcher's Run. The troops marched back and moved into the newly constructed earthworks, their right anchored on McAllister's left and their left resting on Vaughan Road. Cannoneers of the 10th Massachusetts and Battery K, 4th U.S. Light Artillery had previously limbered up their guns and driven them to the rear.[226]

---

222 *Ibid.*, 519-520.

223 *Ibid.*, 516-517.

224 *Ibid.*, 517-518.

225 *Ibid.*, 521-522; OR 46, pt. 1, 344. As soon as Hartranft's troops returned to their camps, Brigadier General Robert Potter of the 2nd Division extended his line to the left, relieving the Engineer Brigade. Upon being replaced in the rifle pits, the Engineer Brigade returned to City Point on the 11th.

226 OR 46, pt. 1, 193, 212, 252; OR 51, pt. 1, 285; OR 46, pt. 2, 526.

At the same time, General Griffin's V Corps division evacuated the bridgehead and went into camp east of Hatcher's Run.[227]

General Lee was informed on the morning of February 8 that the Federals had pulled back into the breastworks covering the Vaughan Road crossing, and concluded that Generals Grant and Meade, for the time being, had abandoned their efforts to cut the Army of Northern Virginia's supply lines. In view of the bad weather, which compounded the hardships of the underfed and inadequately clothed Confederates, Lee ordered the units massed to cope with Meade's latest thrust to return to their camps. By nightfall, Finegan's and Evans' infantry divisions and Rooney Lee's horse soldiers were back in their comfortable winter quarters out of which they had marched on Sunday, the 5th. Johnston's division drew the unpleasant task of manning the earthworks covering Dabney's Mill.[228]

*   *   *

Union casualty lists for the operation were forwarded by the corps commanders to General Meade's headquarters for tabulation. Checking the figures, Meade determined that the units involved in the battle of Hatcher's Run of February 5–7, had suffered 1,539 battle casualties—171 killed, 1,181 wounded, and 187 missing. As expected, Warren's V Corps had been hardest hit, losing 131 killed, 970 wounded, and 159 missing. Despite the stampede of a number of V Corps units on the 6th, the number of Union missing was surprisingly small. This undoubtedly resulted from two factors: the comparatively short distance that separated the commands that broke from a haven of refuge behind the breastworks covering the Vaughan Road crossing; and a failure on the Confederates' part to pursue.[229]

Although few of the war-weary soldiers in blue realized it, the battle of Hatcher's Run was a pre-cursor to the early collapse of the Army of Northern Virginia. On February 5, although several divisions of his ready reserve were close at hand, it was late in the day before General Lee could mount a counterattack. And, when the counterthrust was delivered, the Confederates failed to drive ahead with their former abandon. There were reports that orders to charge were

227   *OR* 46, pt. 1, 88-90.

228   *OR* 46, pt. 2, 499.

229   *OR* 46, pt. 1, 69; Powell, *The Fifth Army Corps*, 763-766.

repeatedly ignored by certain units. General Lee was said to have "wept like a child" when he witnessed this breakdown of discipline in his army.[230]

On the 6th, General Gordon and his men failed to capitalize on the V Corps' stampede. A powerful blow, delivered at the proper moment, could have doomed Warren's command, as frightened bluecoats came pounding out of the woods and over the breastworks guarding the approach to the bridges.

The breakdown of the Confederate cavalry was evident. To forage their mounts, the mounted units had to be posted a considerable distance from the Petersburg lines. Consequently, the Federals had been out of their works for over 24 hours, before Rooney Lee's cavalry division reached the field. When the Rebel horse soldiers did arrive, they and their mounts were already fatigued by the long march up from Belfield, and they failed to demonstrate any of the dash that had characterized their operations, even as late as the battle of the Boydton Plank Road on October 27–28, 1864.

As for tangible gains, Meade and his generals succeeded in extending their fortified line from Fort Sampson to the Vaughan Road crossing of Hatcher's Run. To cope with this extension, General Lee had to spread his troops even thinner than heretofore. Where he had been able to hold three divisions as a strategic reserve, he was soon compelled to reduce his ready reserve to one infantry division.

No report was made by Confederate leaders of their losses in the battle of Hatcher's Run.

Editor's Conclusion

Hatcher's Run is one of the most fascinating battles of the Petersburg Campaign because there are several important aspects about it we are unable to fully grasp and understand. There are fewer accounts for this battle than for any other major battles in the Petersburg Campaign.

In broad strokes, we know that David McM. Gregg's cavalry raid turned into a pitched battle when General Lee committed his troops. At the close of three days, Grant fortified the new Union positions rather than order the men to retreat. The Federals lost 1,539 men to all causes and the Confederates about 1,000.[231]

But significant questions of lasting interest remain. For example, how well did John Gordon's II Corps fight in the first significant action of 1865?

---

230 OR 46, pt. 2, 499.

231 Horn, *The Petersburg Campaign*, p. 33.

Some scholars of Lee's army believe that by this time, Gordon's II Corps had recovered most or all of its morale after the terrible defeats it had suffered at Third Winchester, Fisher's Hill and Cedar Creek the previous September and October in the Shenandoah Valley. Other historians, however, point to accounts by Gordon's men that indicate some of the II Corps's regiments did not perform well. Unfortunately, there is not enough data to reach a firm conclusion.

Another important unresolved question centers on the Army of the Potomac's morale, and whether it had recovered after the massive bloodletting and string of defeats it had suffered during 1864. According to conventional wisdom, by early 1865 the Union army had once again found its elan and fought well at Hatcher's Run. On the other hand, some of Gouverneur Warren's V Corps brigades broke and ran, seemingly without sufficient cause. Perhaps this was so because large numbers of untrained recruits had recently joined, but again we can't be sure because there is not sufficient data upon which to base a conclusion.

We know less about the role played by David McM. Gregg's division of cavalry at Hatcher's Run than for cavalry in any other battle of the campaign. We do know the horsemen faced heavy opposition, and two brigade commanders fell wounded. Exactly what the cavalry accomplished there, however, remains impossible to determine.

A firm understanding of what took place at Hatcher's Run will remain beyond our grasp until more information surfaces about the fascinating and still rather mysterious Feb 5-7, 1865, fighting.

Chapter 4

The Confederate Attack and Union Defense of Fort Stedman

March 25, 1865

by William Wyrick

Editor's Introduction

By March of 1865, Lee's Army of Northern Virginia was outnumbered more than two to one outside Richmond and Petersburg, with the entire Confederate command tied to tens of miles of trenches and forts. Desertions were increasing, morale was falling, disease coursed through his troops, and supplies were dwindling. Union armies elsewhere were reducing what was left of the Confederacy, collapsing Southern-controlled terrain inexorably toward Virginia. With nothing of substance left to do in the Shenandoah Valley, it was likely Phil Sheridan's 9,000 men would move east. The initiative remained firmly in the hands of Lee's opponents. Once the rainy season passed, he knew Generals Grant and Meade would resume active operations. The odds of stopping them increased with each passing day.

On the night of March 4, 1865, Major General William Mahone's Rebel infantry division left its position on the far left of Lee's line, which it had occupied since June of 1864, and replaced Major General George Pickett's division on Bermuda Hundred. Pickett moved his men north and joined the rest of James Longstreet's I Corps above the James River. After much discussion, Lee informed Major General John Gordon that "there seemed to be but one thing that we could do—fight. To stand still was death. It could

Major General George G. Meade
Library of Congress

only be death if we fought and failed." After more than two weeks of planning, Gordon suggested that Lee strike the Union right at Fort Stedman. The lines were close there, and important Union supply bases were behind Stedman, including City Point. A breakthrough might capture these areas. In addition to disrupting Union operations and logistics, a successful attack would help protect the South Side Railroad from further Union attacks by forcing Grant to weaken his own left to confront the victorious Confederates.

The passing of the 1864-1865 winter, one of "unusual severity," brought no relief to Robert E. Lee's embattled Army of Northern Virginia. Double-shotted salutes from 100 Federal guns had announced to the Southern capital that the cities of Savannah, Charleston, Wilmington, and Columbia had fallen in rapid succession. With the Confederacy collapsing on Richmond and Petersburg, General Lee knew he had to pursue a new strategy to avoid a final checkmate.[1]

In early March 1865, Lee met with President Jefferson Davis to warn that the evacuations of Richmond and its transportation hub of Petersburg were but a question of time. Any retreat, he cautioned, "should be in a southwesterly direction toward the country from which we were drawing supplies, and from which a large portion of our forces had been derived." Lee, recently promoted to general in chief of the Confederate armed forces, proposed withdrawing his Army of Northern Virginia toward Danville, Virginia, to achieve a junction with the troops of Gen. Joe E. Johnston, which were being driven northward across North Carolina by Major General William T. Sherman's Federals. If that could be completed, "the combined force would then be hurled upon Sherman with the hope of defeating him before Grant could come to his aid . . . and Grant, drawn far from his base of supplies in the midst of a hostile population . . . might yet be defeated, and Virginia delivered from the invader."

Such an escape from the trenches of Petersburg and Richmond, however, required that Lee strike such a blow against Ulysses S. Grant as to throw Union forces into disarray, thus allowing him to withdraw his army before Grant's troops could recover from their "consternation." Lee bypassed his senior leadership in favor of counsel from 33-year-old Major General John B. Gordon of Georgia, one of the few young commanders proven in the cauldron of the 1864 battlefields and upon whom Lee still relied. Gordon was aggressive and creative, just what Lee needed for realizing this "tremendous possibility." Even though he was the youngest of Lee's corps commanders, Gordon had already established a reputation for being "crammed with courage and brimming with enterprise." He had sustained five wounds leading his brigade at Antietam in September 1862, and served with distinction within the past year from the Wilderness to Petersburg, and then

---

1   This chapter is a revised and expanded version of Mr. Wyrick's narrative on Fort Stedman that originally appeared in *Blue & Gray Magazine*, Volume XXV, Issue 1. Dave Roth was kind enough to allow its use in this book because Ed Bearss did not originally prepare a separate essay on this topic.

Major General John B. Gordon
Library of Congress

capably under Jubal Early in the Shenandoah Valley. Now he led the Second Corps— Stonewall Jackson's legendary former "foot cavalry."[2]

According to Gordon, he was called out into a miserable night at 2:00 a.m. When he arrived at Lee's headquarters on the outskirts of Petersburg, Lee greeted Gordon with a face reflecting "painful depression." The overwrought Lee launched into a discussion of field reports indicating the dire nature of their predicament. On paper, Lee's Army of Northern Virginia numbered only 57,000; the effective count was much less. The addition of Joe Johnston's army in the Carolinas, disintegrating before Sherman's relentless advance, would raise the total available to Lee to no more than 80,000. In contrast, Lee estimated the strength of Grant's forces already fronting Richmond and Petersburg—the Armies of the Potomac and the James—to be well above 100,000 troops. Lee knew the imminent arrival of Phil Sheridan's divisions from the Shenandoah Valley would make it impossible for him to hold his lines. The armies of Gens. Sherman and John M. Schofield in North Carolina and Thomas in Tennessee raised the number of troops "within Grant's reach" to about 280,000—making the odds that much more impossible.[3]

According to Gordon, Lee shared reports indicating that, in addition to being vastly outmanned, Lee's troops were in a terrible state. "I was not prepared for the picture of extreme destitution—of the lack of shoes, of hats, and of blankets, as well as food," admitted Gordon. The Southern commander said the number of his

---

2 Humphreys, *The Virginia Campaign, 1864 and 1865*, 311-312; William H. Hodgkins, *Battle of Fort Stedman (Petersburg, Virginia), March 25, 1865* (Boston, 1889), 16; Jeffersosn Davis, *The Rise and Fall of the Confederate Government*, 2 vols. (New York, 1881), vol. 2, 550-551; John Brown Gordon, *Reminiscences of the Civil War* (Baton Rouge, 1993), 385, also Introduction's by Ralph Lowell Eckert, 88-91 (Antietam), 309-313 (Monocacy), and 332 (Cedar Creek).

3 Gordon, *Reminiscences*, 385, 388. Gordon's recollection of Lee's estimate of the Federal troops available to Grant includes Union armies in Tennessee and North Carolina. This far exceeds the numbers provided by Humphreys, *The Virginia Campaign*, 323. The latter includes only those troops already on the Richmond-Petersburg front.

starving horses had dwindled to half that needed to move his artillery and supply trains. Sheridan had plundered the Shenandoah of food and fodder. At the same time, the Army of the Potomac was being supplied daily by the U.S. Military Railroad that provided a direct link between the bustling port at City Point and the Petersburg front.

Lee asked Gordon for his reading of the options left to them. Gordon outlined three courses of action in order of preference: (1) Negotiate a peace with the Federals; (2) Abandon Richmond and Petersburg and unite Lee's Army of Northern Virginia with Joe Johnston's in North Carolina; or (3) Attack the Federals "without delay."

The Georgian related that when Lee seemed to challenge this assessment, he strongly reaffirmed his position and pressed the general in chief for his own views. Lee relented, agreeing with Gordon "fully." In the ensuing discussion Lee raised the difficulties posed by each course of action. Pursuing the favored alternative, Gordon urged Lee to convince Jefferson Davis to sue for peace on the best terms available. It was almost dawn before the "intensely absorbing, and in many respects harrowing" interview ended with Lee pledging to present the "tremendous issue" and proposed path of action to President Davis. Lee took the train to Richmond that same morning.[4]

Lee summoned Gordon days later to inform him of the outcome of the Richmond meeting. The "most pertinacious" President Davis had rejected the preferred course of negotiations, remaining adamant that there could be no peace without guarantees of Southern independence. Abraham Lincoln had rejected such assurances a month earlier at the Hampton Roads peace conference. Regarding the issue of evacuating Richmond and Petersburg, Lee recognized that the Confederate leadership seemed to be in a state of denial of the situation and was thus not prepared to relinquish the capital. Given the Richmond mindset, Lee concluded: "There was but one thing that we could do—fight. To stand still was death. . . ."[5]

In mid-March, Lee moved Gordon's infantry corps into the trenches extending southward from the Appomattox River with directions that Gordon "study General Grant's works at all points, consider carefully all plans and possibilities, and then tell me what you can do to help us in our dilemma."[6]

The long blue line encircling the Confederate capital extended 37 miles from White Oak Swamp (east of Richmond) to Hatcher's Run (southwest of

---

4 *Ibid.*, 393.

5 *Ibid.*, 394.

6 *Ibid.*, 397.

Petersburg). It was divided by natural boundaries into three distinctly separate segments: Richmond, Bermuda Hundred, and Petersburg. Toward the north end, the James River formed the boundary between the Richmond and Bermuda Hundred fronts. The Petersburg front lay to the south, below the confluence of the James and Appomattox rivers. The trenches began on the Appomattox River only two miles from the center of the city and ran generally south from the river about three miles before curving south and west across the Jerusalem Plank Road for another eight miles. Near the Appomattox River, the no-man's-land corridor separating the opposing forces was only a few hundred yards wide. To the west, the two lines splayed out from one another as much as two miles as they meandered beyond the Weldon Railroad to Hatcher's Run.

The armies on both sides were well entrenched, protected by layers of obstructions: tangled abatis—man-made thickets constructed of felled trees and brush; moveable cheveaux de frise—"horse rakes" made of sharpened rails bristling from central axles and chained together; and spiked fraise—barricades mounted with sharpened logs anchored in the ground and wired together so as to point outward at shoulder height.

Forts dotted the entire siege line. Spaced at intervals of one-fourth to one-half mile, and with batteries interspersed between them, these strongpoints were positioned to sweep the ground in front with artillery fire. Lines of skirmishers, or pickets, were posted in rifle pits well in front of the works to observe the enemy and warn of attack. Both sides had strung telegraph lines to provide instant communication along the length of the front. Behind the Union entrenchments was a line of secondary works and the Military Railroad that carried supplies from the teeming wharves of City Point to the front lines several times a day.[7]

Given his limited resources, Lee had not attempted a major offensive of his own since the protracted conflict at Petersburg had begun about nine months earlier. Now it was Gordon's task to coordinate such an endeavor. The Georgian considered every detail and contingency that might affect the outcome—any vulnerability in the enemy's defenses, the time required to breach them, the distances between lines, the terrain, the hour of attack, weather, and the available resources.

Then, as now, reliable intelligence was of the utmost importance. "My efficient staff—Majors Moore, Hunter, Dabney, and Pace, and Captains Markoe, Wilmer, and Jones—were constantly engaged gathering information from every possible source." The reports of his own units were augmented with interviews of enemy

---

7   Chris Calkins, National Park Service Lecture, June 1, 2004.

prisoners, deserters, and spies. Regarding the penetration by spies, Gordon recalled how Grant had chided Lee, through an emissary: "I keep in such close touch with him [Lee] that I know what he eats for breakfast every morning." The indomitable Southern commander responded through the Union officer that, for his part, he knew "perhaps as much about his [Grant's] dinners as he knew about my breakfasts."[8]

While surveying the front near the Appomattox River, Gordon consulted with Brigadier General James A. Walker, the commander of Early's division. Walker recalled that Gordon took note of the short distance between the Confederate positions at Colquitt's Salient and the Federal works on Hare's Hill called Fort Stedman. Gordon inquired of Walker whether he was vulnerable to attack from Fort Stedman. Walker replied, "I did not think I could hold my position against an assault because the enemy's lines were so close that they could clash over our works any night before we were aware of their coming." But, added Walker, it was also true: "I can take their front line any morning before breakfast." Gordon replied, "Don't forget what you have said; I may call on you to make your words good."[9]

Gordon reckoned that after a week of "laborious examination and intense thought," his plan of attack was "fully developed in his own mind." On March 22, Lee called a meeting with Gordon to determine whether he had found a weakness in the Federal defenses, and, if so, how he would exploit it. According to Gordon, he told Lee, "I can take Fort Stedman, sir."[10]

Part I

Scene of The Fight

Fort Stedman stood on Hare's Hill, two miles east of the center of Petersburg and one mile south of the Appomattox River. The men of the 17th South Carolina claimed they built the original structure when Union Major General George B. McClellan marched up the Virginia peninsula to threaten Richmond in 1862. The fort lay on the second line of Confederate defenses overrun by Northern divisions

8   Gordon, *Reminiscences*, 391-392, 398.

9   James A. Walker, "Gordon's Assault on Fort Stedman, March 25, 1865: A Brilliant Achievement," *Southern Historical Society Papers*, 52 vols. (Wilmington, 1991), vol. 31, 23.

10 Gordon, *Reminiscences*, 401.

during their attacks of June 15-18, 1864. Turned to Federal use, the bastion was named for Brigadier General Griffin A. Stedman of the 11th Connecticut Volunteers (Martindale's brigade), who was mortally wounded on August 5, 1864, following a failed Confederate attempt to explode a mine there.[11]

Fort Stedman faced west toward Spring Hill, where the Confederates manned the heavily fortified Colquitt's Salient. Located only 200 yards from Fort Stedman, Colquitt's Salient provided a strong base for staging an attack. Union Capt. William Hodgkins, who studied the fortifications of both sides and later wrote a book about the battle, recalled: "The batteries in and around this position mounted twenty guns of various calibers. A formidable triple row of cheveaux-de-frise protected it from assault. In rear was a road twenty feet wide, in a broad deep ravine. In great numbers troops could be massed; and the road was continued as a completely covered way as far as Blandford, a suburb of Petersburg." To the rear, formidable Confederate artillery batteries occupied the high ground on both sides of the Appomattox River.[12]

Though formidable in appearance, Fort Stedman was among the weakest links in the Federal line of defenses. The artillery officer of the IX Corps, Bvt. Brigadier General John C. Tidball, said that it "was no fort in the engineering sense of the term, but a struggling work of no regular shape." "It was a comparatively small work without bastions," wrote Captain Hodgkins, "covering about three-quarters of an acre of ground. In the fort and around it, in rear, was a grove of large shade-trees. . . . Its nearness to the enemy prevented even the slightest repairs." Its close proximity to the enemy also rendered it vulnerable to a surprise rush from the Southern lines.[13]

North of Fort Stedman was Fort McGilvery, located near the Appomattox River. A line of breastworks extended southward from McGilvery through Union Batteries No. 8 and 9. The quarter- mile space between Fort Stedman and Battery No. 9 was the most vulnerable point on the line. The ground sloped down to an

---

11 Robert J. Stevens, *Captain Bill: The Records and Writings of Captain William Henry Edwards (and Others) Company A, 17th Regiment, South Carolina Volunteers, Confederate States of America. A History and Genealogy of Chester County, S. C.*, 5 vols. (Richburg, SC., 1985) Book One, 22. The author claimed "Fort Steadman" was named for the colonel of the 6th South Carolina Volunteers, and that the 6th Regiment had built the works some two years prior to this date: "When we rearranged our lines around Petersburg, in the summer of 1864, our engineers left this fort in the Yankee lines." Calkins, Lecture, June 1, 2004.

12 Hodgkins, *Battle of Fort Stedman*, 11-12; "The Battle Before Petersburg: Diagram of the Ground," *Philadelphia Inquirer*, March 28, 1865, 1.

13 Eugene C. Tidball, *"No Disgrace to My Country": The Life of John C. Tidball* (Kent, 2002), 358; Hodgkins, *Battle of Fort Stedman*, 10.

Brigadier General John F. Hartranft
Library of Congress

open plain, low-lying and often wet. The men of the 1st Maine Heavy Artillery had suffered the worst single-action loss of any Civil War regiment in their ill-fated charge across this field on June 18, 1864. Constant picket fire from the enemy prevented completion of the Union works on this exposed site.[14]

According to Gen. John C. Tidball, Fort Stedman, with Batteries No. 10, 11, and 12, were "to all intents and purposes, one work." Shielding Fort Stedman on the right, Battery No. 10 was "an open work" mounting two cannon and mortars. On the ridge to the left, Battery No. 11 was a small, V-shaped "ravelin for two guns." A curtain extended beyond Battery No. 11 to Battery No. 12, "a nearly square redoubt mounting four Coehorn mortars." In front of Batteries No. 11 and 12, the ground fell down into shallow, creek-lined and brush clogged ravines. Situated on high ground one-half mile to the south of Fort Stedman was Fort Haskell, "a strong fortification mounting six guns, besides mortars."

"The crest upon which Stedman stood," continued Captain Hodgkins, "was commanded in the immediate rear by two hills of nearly equal height—the Dunn House hill, seven-eighths of a mile distant, on which stood the Dunn House Battery and Fort Friend; and the Friend House hill, one mile and one-quarter distant, a little east of north. Both hills were partly fortified, and artillery covered the rear and flanks." Tidball added that these works and others formed "an interior line for

---

14 Noah Andre Trudeau, *The Last Citadel: Petersburg, Virginia, June 1864–April 1865* (Baton Rouge, 1993), 54.

Major General John G. Parke
Library of Congress

some distance in rear of the
Stedman front, and then turning to
the left, near the Jerusalem Plank
Road, made a return line facing to
the rear."[15]

John F. Hartranft, then a
Union brigadier general, observed
that Fort Stedman was strategically
located: "Fort Stedman, with Batteries No. 9 and 10 on its right and Batteries No.
11 and 12 and Fort Haskell on its left, covered Meade's Station on the United States
Military Railroad, the supply route of the Army of the Potomac." Meade's Station,
only 2,200 yards to the rear, was the supply depot of the IX Corps. Seizure of the
high ground between Fort Stedman and Meade's Station would cut Grant's long
blue line in two, isolating the Union left and exposing it to a flanking attack.[16]

Gordon also made a detailed analysis of the enemy occupying the defenses
opposite his Second Corps. The first seven miles of the Union front located south
of the Appomattox River were manned by the IX Corps under Major General John
G. Parke. Parke's First Division, led by Bvt. Major General Orlando B. Willcox,
occupied the four-mile segment extending south from the river past Fort Stedman
to Fort Morton. Brig. Gen. Napoleon Bonaparte McLaughlen, commanding the
3rd Brigade, was responsible for most of the line on either side of Fort Stedman.

A paper provided by Union Col. Thomas W. Clarke of the 3rd Maryland
Infantry suggested that fewer than 2,000 soldiers of the Third Brigade manned the
trenches between the gaps at Battery No. 9 and Fort Haskell. The infantry on the
front line included the 57th Massachusetts (175 men north of Stedman), 29th

15 Hodgkins, *Battle of Fort Stedman*, 9.

16 John Hartranft, "The Recapture of Fort Stedman," in Johnson and Buell, eds., *Battles and
Leaders of the Civil War*, 4 vols. (New York, 1884-1887), vol. 4, 584.

Massachusetts (125 at Battery No. 11), and the 3rd Maryland (200 left of Fort Haskell). About 500 men of the 14th New York Heavy Artillery occupied Stedman and Haskell. Additional artillerymen under Tidball were assigned to field pieces in the forts. Another 500 men of the 100th Pennsylvania occupied a position immediately behind and to the left of Stedman. The 59th Massachusetts was positioned in an old line of works near Battery No. 13 to the south. A veteran artillery officer, Tidball was responsible for the operation of all the IX Corps batteries. The Third Division, consisting largely of new recruits and commanded by General Hartranft, was held in reserve and strung out along the secondary line that extended southward from the Dunn house behind Fort Stedman to a point near Fort Howard, a distance of about three miles.[17]

Finally, the officers of Willcox's division were concerned that in Grant's mounting efforts to turn Lee's flank to the west, he had left the segment of the Federal line below the Appomattox River undermanned. Capt. Joseph Carter, who was entrenched with the 3rd Maryland between Battery No. 12 and Fort Haskell, agreed: "Again it may be stated that there was an interval or vacant space of 300 yards or more to the right of Fort Steadman [sic] . . . and there was another 500 yards between Fort Haskell and Fort Morton that would have taken several regiments to fill. This weakness in the lines and the insufficiency of the troops at other points was well-known at Corps Headquarters."[18]

Rather than fill the gaps in the line, Gen. Parke positioned the brigades of Hartranft's Third Division in the rear so that they could move up quickly to reinforce either Willcox on the Appomattox or Major General Robert B. Potter's Second Division opposite the site of the July 30, 1864, battle of the Crater. IX Corps's disastrous role in that action had been much maligned by the rest of the army. Troops from the IX Corps had charged Confederate entrenchments opposite Fort Morton, located only a mile south of Fort Stedman, after detonating 8,000 pounds of gunpowder placed in an underground tunnel beneath the Southern works. Commanded at that time by Major General Ambrose E. Burnside, the IX Corps troops were poorly led and failed to deeply penetrate the works. In the melee that followed, Confederates rallied to slaughter the disorganized Federals. A court of inquiry censured Union leadership: Parke replaced Burnside, and two division commanders were relieved. The court also cited General Willcox, the

17 John Anderson, *The Fifty-Seventh Regiment of Massachusetts Volunteers* (Boston, 1896), 266-267; Hartranft, "The Recapture of Fort Stedman," 584.

18 Anderson, *Fifty-Seventh Regiment of Massachusetts Volunteers*, 277; Joseph Carter, "History of the Third Brigade, First Division, Ninth Corps" [n.p., n.d.], quoted in "The Battle of Fort Stedman," Pennsylvania Historical Society Collections, 6.

division commander now defending the line around Fort Stedman, for "lack of energy" in advancing his men through the confused scene at the Crater.[19]

If an attack on Federal entrenchments had to be made, the works about Fort Stedman offered some of the necessary elements for success: close proximity to the enemy, flawed defenses, undermanned works, and a disrespected opponent. However, a creative plan of attack was needed for the Confederates to take full advantage of these perceived weaknesses.

Part II

Gordon's Plan

It was well known among the combatants that the proximity of the lines between Fort Stedman and Colquitt's Salient rendered the works on both sides of the corridor vulnerable to attack. Still, General Grant, recognizing the risks of mounting a frontal attack on fortified positions, had shelved proposals by Generals Potter and McLaughlen for a strike that could be launched from the left of Fort Stedman. General Lee, however, was compelled by circumstance to seriously consider the results of Gordon's investigations and act accordingly.[20]

While writing his memoir *The Rise and Fall of the Confederate Government*, Jefferson Davis asked Gordon to supply him with a summary of this pivotal action. Gordon responded with this brief statement of his plan of attack:

> The general plan of assault and battle was this: To take the fort by a rush across the narrow space that lay between it and Colquitt's Salient, and then surprise and capture, by a stratagem, the commanding forts in the rear, thus opening a way for our troops to pass to the rear, and upon the flank of the left wing of Grant's Army, which was to be broken to pieces by a concentration of all the forces at my command upon that flank.[21]

Gordon's objective went far beyond the mere capture of a portion of Grant's front. Lee, he reported in his postwar account, listened intently as he described his plan. "The prisoners and guns we might thus capture would not justify the peril of

---

19 Hartranft, "The Recapture of Fort Stedman," 587-588; Humphreys, *The Virginia Campaign of '64 and '65*, Appendix K, "Opinion, Finding V," 430-431.

20 *OR* 46, part 2, 805-806.

21 Davis, *The Rise and Fall of the Confederate Government*, vol. 2, 551-552.

the undertaking," Gordon claims he explained to Lee. "The tremendous possibility was the disintegration of the whole left wing of the Federal army, or at least the dealing of such a staggering blow upon it as would disable it temporarily, enabling us to withdraw from Petersburg in safety and join Johnston . . ."[22]

PHASE 1: The attack would begin in the "hour before dawn," the well known favorite time with officers of both sides for attempting a surprise:[23] By 4:00 a.m. "a few, select men" would work through the night to remove the rows of cheveaux de frise in front of the Confederate works, thus opening a passageway for an assault by a large force. These moveable but cumbersome barricades could be pulled aside only when the chains linking them were removed.

To ensure that the attack was a surprise, Confederate pickets would move out from their forward positions and neutralize their Federal peers quietly before they could sound the alarm. To make this happen, Gordon would take advantage of Grant's own initiative to accelerate Rebel desertions—the well-advertised promise that turncoats would receive payment for their guns and the guarantee of safe passage northward.[24] Advance troops would approach Federal lines in the manner of deserters "coming in," and they would quietly seize or slay the Federal pickets. At the given signal, 50 "brave and especially robust and active men," armed only with axes, would move in the darkness to cut paths through the Northern fraise. These men would be drawn from the squads of pioneers in each regiment who felled trees and honed logs for everything from firewood to fortifications.

To further ensure surprise of the enemy, the first wave of 300 Confederate infantrymen, with unloaded weapons, would advance silently on the heels of the axmen. They would use their bayonets and the butts of their muskets to subdue the garrison at Fort Stedman.

Gordon realized that the occupation of Fort Stedman would complete only the first phase of this major offensive: "It was simply the opening of a road through the wilderness of hostile works nearest to us in order that my corps and the additional

---

22 Gordon, *Reminiscences*, 403.

23 Lieutenant Thomas Sturgis, by companion, "Prisoners of War," *Personal Recollections of the War of the Rebellion: Addresses Delivered Before the Commandery of the State of New York, Military Order of the Loyal Legion of the United States*, Fourth Series, edited by A. Noel Blakeman (New York and London, 1912). Quote is from a typed paper in the files at Petersburg National Battlefield (February 1, 1911), 3.

24 Joseph Warren Kiefer, *Slavery and Four Years of War: A Political History of Slavery in the United States*, 2 vols. (New York, 1900), vol. 2, 187.

forces to be sent me could pass toward the rear of Grant's lines and then turn upon his flanks."[25]

PHASE 2: To effect a sustainable breakthrough of the Union lines Gordon knew that he would have to gain possession of the commanding ridge in the rear, where a second line of fortifications was visible on the crest. Both Lee and Gordon had determined that the "three forts" in the rear, protected by abatis, were nearly invulnerable to a frontal attack. Thus, the redoubts must be taken by a stratagem: As soon as Fort Stedman was carried, three Confederate officers would each lead 100 men in a rush on one of the forts on the ridge. When challenged by Union soldiers, the Confederate officers would identify themselves as Union commanders, shouting, "The Rebels have carried Fort Stedman and our front lines!" Pretending to lead Federal troops in retreat, each Confederate officer would move with his 100 men to seize a designated fort on the commanding ridge. Securing the forts and the high ground on which they stood would give the Confederates a strong position from which to push on with the third phase.

PHASE 3: Once the fortifications on the ridge were secured, the attack would be fully developed. A division of infantry would cross, and be prepared to move down, Grant's lines to the left, pushing the Federals out of their trenches and forcing them "to form at right angles to his line of works." Cavalry would ride through the breach to the rear so as to cut Federal communications with City Point, interrupt the military railroad, destroy pontoons, and otherwise prevent reinforcements from crossing the Appomattox River. Finally, Lee's whole force would move up, change front, and push back the Union defenders to widen the gap between Grant's left and the Appomattox River.

Having often reconnoitered the front lines over the past nine months, Lee knew the ground well. Recognizing the risks inherent in this complicated plan, Gordon claimed Lee subjected him to an intense grilling on the feasibility of the enterprise. Gordon parried Lee's every thrust. In the end they agreed that the taking of the second line of forts was the key to their success. Failing this, the Confederates would be forced to leave the commanding ridge to the Federals and "to rush with all troops available toward Grant's left, meeting emergencies as best we can."[26]

---

25 Gordon, *Reminiscences*, 403.

26 *Ibid.*, 404.

Lee reacted favorably to the presentation and directed Gordon to assign men to the varied tasks required to complete the mission. He was not to notify those selected until Lee had reviewed the plan again and found the guides needed for the thrust beyond Fort Stedman. Within 24 hours Gordon was again conferring with Lee to finalize orders. Gordon's reconstructed account captures the gravity of that fateful meeting:

> With the exception of the last council of war on the night before the surrender, I believe this conference on the night of March 23rd was the most serious and impressive of my experience. General Lee had thought of all the chances: he had found three men, whom he did not know in person, but who were recommended for the three guides; he had selected different troops to send from other corps, making with mine, nearly one half of his army; and had decided that we should make one supreme effort to break the cordon tightening around us. . . . With full recognition by both the commander and myself of the hopelessness of our cause if we waited longer on Grant's advance, and also the great hazard of moving against him, the tremendous undertaking was ordered.[27]

Gordon's several accounts of the evolution and Lee's ultimate approval of his plan contain an important omission. Lee approved the enterprise, but he did so with the caveat that the operation must be undertaken without "great sacrifice."[28]

Part III

The Preparations

On March 23, 1865, the time had arrived for Lee to actively implement his offensive. Having destroyed the last element of Southern resistance in the Shenandoah Valley, Phil Sheridan would soon arrive at City Point with his cavalry. At the same time Lee was placed under additional pressure by an urgent plea from Joe Johnston, whose army was disintegrating before the northward thrust of Sherman's juggernaut. Now that Sherman was being resupplied at Goldsboro, North Carolina, Johnston had to alert Lee: "Sherman's course cannot be hindered

---

27 *Ibid.*, 406.

28 *OR* 46, pt. 1, 382.

by the small force I have. I can do no more than annoy him. I respectfully suggest that it is no longer a question of whether you leave your present position. You have only to decide where to meet Sherman."[29]

Lee agreed the assault on Fort Stedman would be built around Gordon's Second Corps, which consisted of the three divisions under Major General Bryan Grimes and Brig. Gens. James A. Walker and Clement A. Evans. Gordon's corps would be augmented with infantry brigades from the Richmond front, including those in the division of George E. Pickett. If those troops were not available, other men from the corps of Lt. Gens. Ambrose P. Hill and Richard H. Anderson could be drawn from the Western front. Cavalry was also promised for the purpose of destroying communications and transportation links with Grant's forces north of the Appomattox River. If Lee's staff was correct in their estimate that 40,000 troops remained to him, their commander's commitment of a force of 18,000 represented nearly half of the Army of Northern Virginia.[30]

The massive undertaking was fraught with risk. One of the most daunting issues was timing. Lee's decision was not revealed until Thursday night, March 23. The assault would begin before dawn on Saturday morning, the 25th. Eighteen thousand men must be assembled and readied for action within the next 30 hours. General Walker described some of what had to be done:

> The preparations for the movement were simple, but required some little time. In the first place, rations for three days had to be issued, cooked, brought up, and distributed. The cartridge boxes had to be examined and filled up with cartridges; muskets had to be inspected; the sick and disabled sent to hospitals; the storming party selected, and instructed what was required of them.[31]

Once that was complete, the many units had to be massed at the point of attack. The main force (Gordon's corps) had manned the trenches at Colquitt's Salient since March 15, but still had to be formed for battle. To preserve the crucial element of surprise, the Confederates would not begin moving to the front until nightfall. Operating in darkness, Gordon's divisions would be pulled out of the trenches between the Appomattox River and the Crater, aligned in three columns

29 Douglas Southall Freeman, ed., *Lee's Dispatches: Unpublished Letters of General Robert E. Lee to Jefferson Davis and the War Department of the Confederate States of America, 1862-65* (New York, 1915), No. 192, 339.

30 James Longstreet, *From Manassas to Appomattox: Memoirs of the Civil War in America* (Philadelphia, 1896), 509-510.

31 Walker, "Gordon's Assault on Fort Stedman," 23.

before Blandford Church to the rear, and moved back up to the front line at Colquitt's Salient. The men in gray would also have to wrench openings in their own barricades for the rush against Fort Stedman.

Gordon had been promised additional troops to support the attack, but they would have to come from a long way off. Pickett's division, now back with Major General James Longstreet's First Corps, was entrenched more than 15 miles to the north in the Richmond defenses. Given the distance and only 24 hours' notice, these troops would have to be moved by rail. However, the trains had not been marshaled in advance, and they would be slow in coming.[32]

Early on March 24, Longstreet requested railroad transportation for 8,000 men, most of them from Pickett's command. That afternoon Lee received word that rolling stock sufficient for only 1,200 men would be available for departure at 9:00 p.m., and for another 2,000 at 2:00 a.m. No other troops from Pickett's force could entrain until after the attack had begun. At 4:30 p.m. Lee transmitted this message to Gordon: "Genl: I have received yours of 2:30 P.M. and telegraphed for Pickett's division, but I do not think it will reach here in time. But we will try. If you need more troops one or both of Heth's brigades can be called to Colquitt's Salient and Wilcox's to the Baxter Road."[33]

A. P. Hill's Corps comprised the divisions of Maj. Gens. William Mahone, Henry Heth, and Cadmus Wilcox. With Mahone's division now defending Richmond, Hill's two remaining divisions were strung out along the works extending from Hatcher's Run to Lieutenant Run, more than seven miles southwest of Colquitt's Salient. Gordon would have to call up all the substitute troops pledged by Lee, and more. Heth's division comprised a brigade of North Carolinians led by Brigadier General John R. Cooke and of Tennesseans commanded by Brigadier General William McComb. These troops would support Gordon's right. The brigades of Brigadier General James H. Lane (Tarheels) and Brigadier General Edward L. Thomas (Georgians) were drawn from Cadmus Wilcox's division. With Wilcox now ill, General Lane assumed command of the division and would lead the two brigades to a reserve position along Lieutenant Run.[34]

32 OR 46, pt. 3. 1341-1346.

33 R. E. Lee dispatch to Major General J. B. Gordon, 4:30 p.m., March 24, 1865, quoted in Gordon, *Reminiscences*, 407.

34 Lane, "History of Lane's North Carolina Brigade," in *Southern Historical Society Papers*, vol. 9, 494; Samuel Walkup, typed transcript of unpublished diary, University of North Carolina Manuscript Department (UNCMS), 77; Cadmus Marcellus Wilcox, Papers, 1846-1887 (Library of Congress Manuscripts), Folder 1023, 29.

Gordon would also draw on Major General Bushrod R. Johnson's division, now assigned to Lt. Gen. Richard H. Anderson's corps, held in reserve at Burgess Mill west of Hatcher's Run. Brigadier General Matthew Ransom assumed overall command of two of Johnson's brigades for the attack on Stedman. The first was his own contingent from North Carolina, to be led by Col. Henry M. Rutledge. Ransom's charges would assume the positions they had occupied opposite Stedman before being relieved by Gordon's troops in mid-March. The second of Johnson's brigades were South Carolinians serving under Brigadier General William H. Wallace. These soldiers would assume a position near the Appomattox River to the left of Ransom.[35]

All of these additional troops began their long trek to the jump-off point after dark on the 24th to preserve secrecy. Colonel Samuel Walkup of the 48th North Carolina wrote about the trek in his diary: "We . . . left after 10 p.m. . . . We were all night dragging in weary impatience to between Petersburg & the trenches where we bivouaced on the old ground behind a bluff. The city had a gloomy, desolate, haunted appearance like some plague had depopulated it. And spread its deadly still over its remains. . ."[36]

Ironically, some of Gordon's own units were scattered too far afield to get back to Petersburg in time. Regimental historians Capt. V. E. Turner and Sgt. H. C. Wall wrote that when Robert D. Johnston's brigade was recalled on March 23, a number of companies had been detached to round up truant soldiers: "The return from North Carolina was so sudden that the troops, far up the river near Clarksville, did not reach their railroad in time, and with the detached companies, in other parts of the State, joined us in Petersburg some days later."[37]

Back at the Petersburg front, Gordon and his officers labored through the night to organize the strike force into three columns. To lead the storming party from his division, General Walker chose Captain Joseph Anderson of the 49th Virginia and Lieutenant Hugh P. Powell of Co. A, 13th Virginia—"the bravest of the brave."[38]

35 Robert D. Graham, "Fifty-Sixth Regiment," in Walter Clark, ed., *Histories of the Several Regiments and Battalions from North Carolina in the Great War 1861-'65*, 5 vols. (Wilmington, 1996), vol. 3, 390, hereafter Clark, *North Carolina Regiments*; Stevens, *Captain Bill*, 22.

36 Walkup, Unpublished Diary, UNCMS, 76-77.

37 V. E. Turner and H. C. Wall, "Twenty-Third Regiment," in Clark, *North Carolina Regiments*, vol. 2, 263.

38 Walker, "Gordon's Assault on Fort Stedman," 24.

Brigadier General Clement A. Evans
Library of Congress

Colonel Hamilton Jones of the 57th North Carolina, also of Walker's division, had returned from a Federal prisoner of war camp so recently that some of his men did not know he was back. Still, at 3:00 a.m., Jones was summoned to a meeting of general officers and told he would lead a column into Fort Stedman. When asked to select two regiments for the task, he chose his own 57th and "the gallant Sixth [North Carolina]" commanded by Lieutenant Colonel Samuel McDowell Tate.[39]

General Clement Evans chose York's combined Louisiana Brigade commanded by Lieutenant Colonel Eugene Waggaman to represent his division. Evans told Waggaman, "On account of the valor of your troops, you will be allowed the honor of leading off the attack. This you will make with unloaded muskets."[40]

Gordon worked throughout the night to coordinate the movements of the troops massing behind Colquitt's Salient. The enterprising Georgian said that preparations even extended to his own residence in Petersburg, where his wife and others prepared cloth strips to be worn by advance troops for identification purposes. Gordon's host, J. Pinkney Williamson, also assisted the preparations. "The General requested Mr. W. to procure some white cloth to tie around his

39 Colonel Hamilton C. Jones, "Fifty-Seventh Regiment," in Clark, *North Carolina Regiments*, vol. 3, 422-423.

40 Napier Bartlett, *Military Record of Louisiana, Including Biographical and Historical Papers Relating to the Military Organizations of the State* (Baton Rouge, 1992), 40.

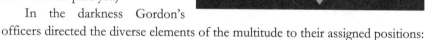

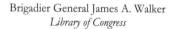

Brigadier General James A. Walker
Library of Congress

sharpshooters' arms so they might recognize each other in the dark," he recalled. "It was torn into four-inch strips by Mr. and Mrs. W. and the General sent it to the camp about 12 o'clock at night.... (Note: This cloth cost Mr. W. $300 and he has not been paid yet.)"[41]

In the darkness Gordon's officers directed the diverse elements of the multitude to their assigned positions:

From each division hardy pioneers, armed with "keen-edged axes," who would clear openings in Union obstructions, plus a storming party comprising sharpshooters and volunteers.

Three detachments of 100 men, identified by white strips of cloth tied about their bodies or arms, commanded by officers bearing the alternate names of their Union counterparts, accompanied by local guides who would lead them to the second line of Union forts to the rear.

A company of artillerists, led by Lieutenant Colonel Robert B. Stribling of the Fauquier Battery, who would turn the guns of the captured fortifications against the Federal entrenchments.

The main assault force, formed into three columns.

Formidable batteries about Colquitt's Salient, readied under the personal supervision of Colonel Hilary P. Jones, the artillery officer for Gordon's Second Corps.

41 J. Pinkney Williamson, *History of the Crater and Ten Months Siege of Petersburg* (n.p., n.d.), 6.

Cavalry assigned to disrupt Federal communications in the rear were to report for duty at the intersection of Halifax Road and the Norfolk Railroad. "Marse" Robert's own son, Major General William Henry Fitzhugh "Rooney" Lee, was tasked to bring his cavalry up to the vicinity of Monk's Corner Road at 6:00 a.m.[42]

According to General Walker, the myriad tasks required for the massive undertaking were "done quietly and with the least possible noise. No commands were given, but the words were passed in low tones from man to man. About an hour before daylight my storming party pressed cautiously and silently one by one over the breastworks, and crept up close to one of our solitary pickets in his pit and lay down on the ground."[43]

Part IV

The Attack Begins

General Gordon planned to strike the Federals at 4:00 a.m. so that his storming parties could take advantage of the darkness in moving on Fort Stedman and the second line of forts beyond. However, some witnesses recalled seeing the first light of dawn before they received the signal to advance. While his two regiments still lay poised for attack behind their axmen, Col. Hamilton Jones saw that, "Away in the east there was a band of white light in the sky which marked the approach of day."[44]

In his reminiscences, Gordon tells the tale of how at 4:00 a.m. he mounted his breastworks with no one other than a private to signal the advance. However, he found that his men were still moving the three rows of cheveaux-de-frise in front of Colquitt's Salient to create an opening for his columns. Gordon claimed a Federal

---

42 Regarding the plan of attack, General Bryan Grimes's courier, H. A. London, wrote that the "storming party" consisted "of about 500 sharpshooters [and a] number of pioneers" who rushed into Battery No. 10 and Fort Stedman before the garrison was aroused. The main body of troops then advanced. See H. A. London, editor, "Battle of Fort Stedman," *The Chatham Record*, Wednesday, March 27, 1912 (page not indicated). General Walker recalled that 50 pioneers would lead each of Gordon's three divisions. See Walker, "Gordon's Assault on Fort Stedman," 24. Regarding the artillerists, see OR 46, pt. 1, 391. Regarding the use of additional troops and cavalry, see Gordon, *Reminiscences*, 407.

43 Walker, "Gordon's Assault on Fort Stedman," 24.

44 Jones, "Fifty-Seventh Regiment," 422-423.

Major General Bryan Grimes
Library of Congress

picket called out through the darkness to the Confederate private, "What are you doing over there, Johnny? What is that noise? Answer quick or I'll shoot."

Passing long nights in close proximity to one another, the rival pickets often shared their plight by conversing and trading. Gordon feared this Union soldier might sound the alarm, but the Confederate private tasked with firing the shot signaling the attack responded, "Never mind, Yank. Lie down and go to sleep. We are just gathering a little corn. You know rations are mighty short over here." The Union picket relaxed. "All right, Johnny: go ahead and get your corn. I'll not shoot at you while you are drawing your rations."

When the last of the barricades was pulled aside, Gordon wrote that he ordered the private to fire the shot that would set the attacking force in motion. The soldier balked at crossing his fellow sentry in blue. Gordon said that when he repeated the order in a threatening manner, the private called out, "Hello, Yank! Wake up; we are going to shell the woods. Look out; we are coming." Having repaid his enemy's favor, the young man fired his gun, sounding the call to battle.[45]

General Walker, leading Early's division toward the left of the Confederate attacking force, offered another version of the beginning of the assault. The usual suspense was mounting, he explained, when, "General Gordon came down the line to where the head of my column rested, and, finding my command ready to move, stepped to one side and fired three pistol shots in rapid succession." Walker

---

45 Gordon, *Reminiscences*, 408-409.

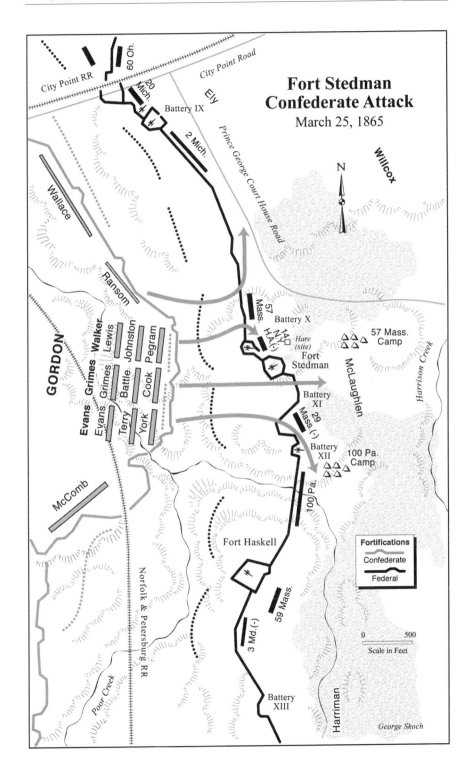

Fort Stedman
Confederate Attack
March 25, 1865

George Skoch

recalled that Capt. Joseph Anderson commanded the division storming party to advance silently at the double-quick, trailing their unloaded muskets. Walker continued: "I have read many accounts, both in history and fiction, of such attacks, and my blood has been stirred in reading them; but I never read an account of one so dashing, so orderly, and so quiet as this. The cool, frosty morning made every sound distinct and clear, and the only sound heard was the Tramp! Tramp! of the men as they kept step as regularly as if on drill."[46]

Near the Confederate center, Captain Joseph P. Carson, of the 4th Georgia Regiment (Cooke's Brigade), claimed that he led 100 sharpshooters, each armed with "the celebrated Whitworth rifle." Carson recalled that Gen. Gordon appeared about 3:00 a.m. He supplied them with white strips of cloth to be drawn over the shoulder and wrapped about the waist so that friend could be distinguished from foe in the darkness. According to Carson, Gordon spoke to the waiting troops: "It was a stirring and impressive speech as we heard it, standing there in the night, with the awful task and eternity staring us in the face. The assault," continued Carson, "was to be made at a given signal and at last it came. In an instant we were over our works and heading for the fort with all the speed we could command."[47]

The first Confederate objective was to neutralize the Yankee pickets. Hamilton Jones's storming party, chosen from William Lewis's brigade of Walker's division, was led by two youthful lieutenants—the infantry by Jim Edmondson of the 57th North Carolina, and the pioneers by W. W. Flemming of the 6th North Carolina. Edmondson's squadron appeared to be just another party of deserters advancing through the darkness toward the Union lines as he called out, "Oh, boys, come back! Don't go!" When the graycoats called out, "Don't shoot Yank, we are coming in," Federal sentinels were heard to reply, "It's okay, Johnnie, come on in. We won't shoot." Most of the Federal pickets were thus subdued with bayonets or clubbed muskets before they could react to the ruse. Lieutenant Flemming's pioneers sprang into action. According to one witness, "as soon as Lieutenant Edmondson's success was apparent, a gallant corps of pioneers dashed upon the enemy's obstructions and with their axes chopped and battered them down to make way for the two regiments to enter and take the enemy's line of defense."[48]

---

46 Walker, "Gordon's Assault on Fort Stedman," 25.

47 According to Captain Joseph P. Carson, this "graphic account . . . was given by him to a reporter of the press several years after the close of the war," quoted in Henry W. Thomas, *History of Doles-Cook Brigade: Army of Northern Virginia, 1861-1865* (Atlanta, 1903), 35.

48 J. D. Barrier, "Breaking Grant's Line," in *Confederate Veteran*, 43 vols. (Wilmington, 1986-1988), vol. 33, 417; *Richmond Times Dispatch*, March 28, 1865, 1.

Union General Willcox, commanding the First Division of the IX Corps, reported that the Rebels struck in three columns: one swept across the low ground toward Fort Stedman and Battery No. 10 in its front, one moved directly on Fort Stedman, and the third advanced toward a point between Fort Stedman and Battery No. 11 to the south. Battery No. 10 was but a small enclosure that connected with the front of Fort Stedman, and the Southern storming party quickly swept over it. Because no alarm had been given, Lieutenant Ephraim B. Nye of the 14th Massachusetts Light Artillery was killed before his men could fire more than a single round from two three-inch rifles. Captain John M. Twiss of the 1st Connecticut Heavy Artillery, in charge of three coehorn and four eight-inch mortars, was wounded. Those few Federals who were not killed, wounded, or captured fled toward the Reserve Camp at Meade's Station more than a mile to the rear.[49]

"The capture of Battery No. 10 gave the enemy a wide opening on the right and rear, and great advantage over Stedman," recalled Union Captain Hodgkins, "the ground just in rear being on a level with the parapet of the Fort, and they entered the sally-port almost undiscovered." As Confederates poured into the fort, Captain Edwin W. Rogers of the 19th New York Light Battery rallied his cannoneers long enough to discharge a dozen rounds from his four 12-pounders. But the surprised Federals, some of whom were accused of engaging in a drunken card game, were overcome in hand-to-hand combat. Continued Hodgkins: "It was so dark that foe could not be distinguished from friend, and at one time the enemy were firing a part of the guns and our men the others. The firing revealed the position of our men, and the cannoneers were immediately seized and thrown over the works into the ditch."[50]

The two trailing North Carolina regiments of Lewis's brigade advanced sluggishly at first, the young color-bearer of the 57th urging them into line:

His flag could not be seen the length of a company, however much he might wave it, so he kept his voice going loud enough to be heard all along the line of the regiment

---

49 OR 46, pt. 1, 322-325.

50 Hodgkins, *Battle of Fort Stedman*, 24; OR 46, pt. 1, 341; George L. Kilmer, "Assault and Repulse at Fort Stedman," *Century Magazine* (September, 1887), vol. 34, No. 5, 783-791. A virtually identical version of Kilmer's account is found in Johnson and Buell, *Battles and Leaders of the Civil War*, vol. 4, 579. Colonel Thomas W. Clarke, adjutant-general of the Third Brigade, vehemently denied the accusation that the men in Fort Stedman had been drinking or gambling. Clarke also stated that, "Standing orders required the troops to be under arms half an hour before daybreak." Anderson, *The Fifty-Seventh Regiment of Massachusetts Volunteers*, 268; Hodgkins, *Battle of Fort Stedman*, 24.

saying: Here's your flag; come on men, keep in line. . . . The men could not be urged to a double-quick, and it seemed a long time getting across that open field. The enemy, however, had been struck with such consternation at the boldness of the well-nigh exhausted gray lines that they fled in dismay after a feeble effort at resistance and left the attacking force in complete possession of Fort Stedman. The two regiments entered the Federal line, and no enemy appeared near.[51]

During the night, Ransom's brigade, part of Bushrod Johnson's division, had moved back into the positions opposite Stedman its members had vacated only ten days previously. The Tar Heels formed opposite the fort and the unfinished works that stretched northward toward the Appomattox River. "The left of the Fifty-sixth, the regiment to-day again under Major [John] Graham," recorded one member, "is near the City Point road, and to its right is the Forty-ninth and then the Twenty-fifth." Lieutenant Thomas Roulhac of the 49th North Carolina took his sharpshooters out behind Flemming and Edmondson. Also in the forefront was Lieutenant Hawkins of the 25th, who was ordered "Not to attack Fort Stedman, but to take it." Ransom's line of battle followed "on their heels."[52]

According to Captain Robert Graham of the 56th North Carolina, "Gordon's people, who had replaced us here on the 15th instant, have just been moved up to the line and are to advance in line abreast with us." Captain Joseph Anderson of the 49th Virginia and Lieutenant Hugh P. Powell of the 13th Virginia led the sharpshooters of John Pegram's brigade (now led by Lieutenant Colonel John G. Kasey) directly toward Fort Stedman. Before the pioneers could clear a path through the Federal fraise, Anderson and Powell were cut down by enemy fire, both mortally wounded. Captain Robert Daniel Funkhouser of the 49th Virginia recalled that he and his comrades "charged through the gap in two ranks with fixed bayonets, filed to the right, fronted into line of battle, and rushed into the fort without a moment's hesitation."[53]

The flash of cannon fire immediately illuminated Captain Joseph Carson's sharpshooters when they emerged from their entrenchments. Carson said that when his men mounted the rise in front of Fort Stedman, "The wind from the cannon and the flying balls was so strong we could not keep our hats on, while the frightful roar of the guns drowned every other sound." Carson recalled that after

---

51 Barrier, "Breaking Grant's Line," 417.

52 Thomas R. Roulhac, "Forty-Ninth Regiment," in Clark, *North Carolina Regiments*, vol. 3, 144, and Graham, "Fifty-Sixth Regiment," 390.

53 Laura Virginia Hale and Stanley S. Phillips, *History of the Forty-Ninth Virginia Regiment: "Extra Billy Smith's Boys"* (Lanham, 1981), 203.

his men breached the perimeter of sharpened rails, they came upon the moat directly in front of the fort. He recalled the Union defenders firing straight down on them until the attackers found a low place to the right and scrambled to get inside the fort. "Forming my line we struck the enemy at right angles, and they in a few minutes surrendered," he continued. "As soon as they laid down their arms I ordered them to form into line and double-quick to our works, which they did in a hurry."[54]

Colonel Eugene Waggaman's combined Louisiana brigade had slow going across the boggy ground south of Fort Stedman. Waggaman himself had to be "extricated from the mud of a ditch" before leading his men out of the darkness and into the fort through an embrasure. The scene within was bedlam as the several Confederate storming parties piled into the crowded enclosure, and "such was the excitement and desperate energy of the struggle, that the combatants fought as was afterwards said, 'as if they had drank two quarts of brandy.' The fort was finally carried, though it was rough and tumble fighting, the opposing soldiers being locked together like serpents."[55]

Amid the confusion, the commanding officer of the Federal Third Brigade, General McLaughlen, appeared in Fort Stedman and began issuing orders to the men around him. Private I. G. Bradwell of the 31st Georgia related how McLaughlen "happened to face with Lieutenant Guinn, who was advancing, pistol in hand, with the foremost men. He asked: 'Are you a Rebel?' To this Guinn replied, 'I am,' and commanded him to surrender. When asked if he was an officer, Guinn replied that it did not matter and told the general to surrender immediately or he would blow his head off." McLaughlen complied, but was allowed to keep his sword until General Gordon arrived to assume command of the fort for the Confederacy. Private Bradwell escorted McLaughlen to the rear for safekeeping, leaving him "mad enough to die for his bad luck." Ironically, only the day before McLaughlen had explained to visitors his own proposal for a Union attack against Confederate lines from the left of Fort Stedman.[56]

Captain Carson recalled that another Union officer—evidence suggests it was Captain Henry Swords of Willcox's staff, division officer of the day—rode into the line forming behind Fort Stedman. "He was magnificently mounted and reined up almost against me," Carson recalled, "with the words, 'Hello, boys, how are things going?'" Carson replied, "They are going pretty well," before inviting him to

---

54 Thomas, *Doles-Cook Brigade*, 40.

55 Bartlett, *Military Record of Louisiana*, 40.

56 I. G. Bradwell, "Holding the Line at Petersburg," *Confederate Veteran*, vol. 28, 457.

dismount. When two of Carson's men leveled their rifles at him, the Union officer dismounted and gave up his horse, "with the injunction to take good care of him." After waiting "some little time" for the arrival of General Gordon, Carson deployed his sharpshooters as skirmishers behind Fort Stedman. Cook's brigade would soon come up behind them as the sharpshooters moved toward the second line of forts farther to the east.[57]

Meanwhile, Colonel Stribling had led two detachments from the Fauquier Artillery and two men each from other batteries of his artillery battalion into Fort Stedman. Stribling's detachment turned at least two of the captured cannon and began firing the guns into Federal troops manning the works up and down the line.[58]

The Confederates on the left—with Ransom's and Lewis's Carolinians in the lead—swung northward from the captured fort toward the Appomattox River. They swept the line of the 57th Massachusetts from the flank and the rear, forcing them to abandon their camp. Ransom's brigade moved swiftly toward Battery No. 9 to the north, the 56th North Carolina forming the extreme left of the Confederate forces. The regiments of Lewis's brigade, led by Hamilton Jones of the 57th North Carolina, pushed northeast toward Fort Friend (formerly Confederate Battery 8) located 1,200 yards in the rear.[59]

Below Fort Stedman, Colonel Waggaman emerged on the right of the fort with only about half of his Louisiana Tigers contingent intact. They moved slowly to the south. They may have been among the troops seen plundering the baggage of the Federals who had abandoned the area. For a time, the 100th Pennsylvania under Lieutenant Colonel Joseph H. Pentecost stoutly resisted Confederate skirmishers advancing on the works to the south and toward Meade's Station in the rear. The 29th and 59th Massachusetts Veteran Volunteers rallied briefly to retake Battery No. 11.[60]

The Confederates kept coming. After their advance to the south was initially blunted by Federal defenders, the men in gray pushed south and east past Batteries No. 11 and 12. According to division commander Clement Evans, fighting on the right of the Confederate assaulting line, Brigadier General William Terry's consolidated brigade of Virginians "formed and advanced along the breastworks

---

57 Thomas, *Doles-Cook Brigade*, 41.

58 Michael J. Andrus, *The Brooke, Fauquier, Loudoun, and Alexandria Artillery* (Lynchburg, 1990), 85.

59 Jones, "Fifty-Seventh Regiment," 424.

60 Bartlett, *Military Record of Louisiana*, 40; *OR* 46, pt. 1, 331.

on rear of [the Federals], driving the enemy for a space of about six or seven hundred yards. . . . Evans' brigade commanded by Col. [John H.] Baker [13th Georgia] cooperated with Brigadier General Terry as soon as the Brigade was crossed from our breastworks to those of the enemy." Terry's men pushed on toward Fort Haskell. Evans claimed the capture of "the south half of Fort Stedman and about six or seven hundred yards of the breastworks in which were very many mortars and other pieces of artillery and at least four hundred of the prisoners captured."[61]

Thus far the assault had unfolded better than anyone could have reasonably expected, and Gordon sent word of his initial success to General Lee, who was observing the attack from "a commanding position near the old Blandford Church." Up to this point, recalled Gordon:

> the success had exceeded my most sanguine expectations. We had taken Fort Stedman and a long line of breastworks on either side. We had captured nine heavy cannon, eleven mortars, nearly 1,000 prisoners, including General McLaughlen, with the loss of less than half a dozen men. . . . I was in the fort myself, and relieved General McLaughlen by assuming command of Fort Stedman.

Gordon had indeed breached the Federals' front line. Now he awaited word from the three detachments advancing on the second line of Federal forts.[62]

The *Philadelphia Inquirer* later reported that all the forces on the field now came into play: "At five o'clock the rebels opened from their works—Spring Hill Battery, opposite Steadman, the 8-inch mortar on its right, the Gooseneck, Clifton and Chesterfield on the north side of the river. . . . Our artillerists still supposing it nothing more than a challenge to one of the old duels so common between them, sprang to their guns. . . . 'The rocket's red glare, bombs bursting in air,' were literal facts, and no mere phantasies of a poetic frenzy."[63]

61 Robert Grier Stephens, ed., *Intrepid Warrior, Clement Anselm Evans: Confederate General from Georgia; Life, Letters, and Diaries of the War Years* (Dayton, 1992), 535.

62 Gordon, *Reminiscences*, 411. London, ed., "Battle of Fort Stedman," *The Chatham Record*, March 27, 1912 (page not indicated).

63 "Mr. Edward Crapsey's Letter," *Philadelphia Inquirer*, March 28, 1865, 1.

Part V

The Federal Response

Gordon's assault had taken McLaughlen's Third Brigade by surprise, but they were not unprepared for battle. As early as February 22, General Grant had warned his officers that Lee might stage an attack and attempt to withdraw to the west before the Federals could recover. In response to this warning, Northern officers adopted various measures to bolster their defenses. For example, all of Parke's artillerists kept their cannons primed and ready to fire on a moment's notice. On the night of March 24, General McLaughlen ordered his men to hold their fire at nightfall—except in the case of an attack. The muskets of the Confederate pickets also fell silent as they ceased harassing the enemy and discouraging deserters. Without the "monotonous concert" of fitful musketry at Fort Stedman, the eve of battle had been "unusually quiet."[64]

The Federal brigade picket officer, Captain John Burch of the 3rd Maryland, claimed he visited the picket line in front of Battery No. 11 and Fort Stedman about 4:00 a.m. Once he confirmed his men were on the alert, he returned to his post. A short time later he "got word from a lookout that the enemy were approaching." When the sound of gunfire reached him, he fell back to the Federal entrenchments. At the same time, the captain of the picket, Lieutenant Henry C. Joslyn of the 29th Massachusetts, sent word to brigade headquarters that "an unusual number of deserters were coming over with arms." Matters were confusing indeed; Joslyn requested instructions as to how to proceed.[65]

The officer of the day for the Third Brigade, Captain Henry C. Ward of the 57th Massachusetts, later claimed that he began reconnoitering the mile and a half stretch of picket line at 3:00 a.m. When he crawled out to investigate an "unusual noise," Ward saw that "a corps of pioneers were removing the obstructions in front of the works of the enemy, and that troops were forming for an attack, some of the men having a white band on the arm to distinguish them in the dark." After crawling back to his lines, Ward reported that he "directed the firing of the pickets on the entire line and sent messengers to the commanding officer of the troops in

---

64 Horace Porter, "Campaigning with Grant", in *Century Magazine*, August, 1897, 596; OR 46, pt. 1, 345; I. G. Bradwell, "Gordon's Brigade after the Valley Campaign," *Confederate Veteran*, vol. 18, 418-419; Anderson, *The Fifty-Seventh Regiment of Massachusetts Volunteers*, 278.

65 OR 46, pt. 1, 331, 337.

Fort Stedman in my rear that an attack was being made. All at once a thin line of battle made its appearance in our front, joined by pickets of the enemy." Ward was clubbed to the ground by a Confederate soldier and taken prisoner.[66]

General McLaughlen was encamped 800 yards behind Fort Haskell that early morning. He was shaken awake and flooded with messages. The general sent word to Lieutenant Joslyn to detain the deserters, called out the 59th Massachusetts to receive the turncoats at Fort Stedman, and ordered all his regiments to get "under arms." With the sound of battle spattering down the line from Fort Stedman, McLaughlen dispatched staff officers along his front and went to Fort Haskell to see the situation for himself. In the fort he found that the battalion of the 14th New York Heavy Artillery was "alert and ready to resist an attack," and as he passed along the works toward Fort Stedman found "everything right" with the 100th Pennsylvania Infantry.

McLaughlen next encountered Maj. Charles C. Richardson, who offered the shocking news that Fort Stedman had been overrun and that his 29th Massachusetts had been driven from Battery No. 11. Acting decisively, McLaughlen ordered the men in Battery No. 12 to turn their mortars on the captured redoubt. When the 59th Massachusetts came up from its reserve position, McLaughlen recorded that he "put them into work with fixed bayonets and recaptured it [Battery No. 11] at once. Supposing that I had restored the only break in the line, I crossed the parapet into Fort Stedman on the right." Perhaps the general did not believe the major's report that the fort had been captured. Once inside, McLaughlen failed to realize that the troops he was directing were Confederates until he was captured by Lieutenant Guinn of the 31st Georgia.[67]

Back at Third Brigade headquarters, meanwhile, Acting Assistant Adjutant Colonel Thomas W. Clarke reported that "word was sent to Colonel [Samuel] Harriman on our left that he had better get under arms, and, if he could, get a regiment loose from his lines to support us. A messenger was also sent to General Hartranft, commanding the reserve division of Pennsylvania troops beyond the railroad to ask him to get under arms and move to our support, as we dreaded an attack."[68]

By 5:15 a.m., word of the attack had been passed to Gen. Willcox and IX Corps commander John Parke, both of whom had their headquarters a short distance to the rear, Willcox's at the Friend house and Parke's along the Baxter Road. Parke

---

66 Anderson, *The Fifty-Seventh Regiment of Massachusetts Volunteers*, 278.

67 OR 46, pt. 1, 331.

68 Anderson, *The Fifty-Seventh Regiment of Massachusetts Volunteers*, 268-269.

requested that Major General George G. Meade, commanding the Army of the Potomac, reinforce him with the IX Corps's Provisional Brigade. Parke sent several messages to army headquarters before receiving this unexpected response at 5:55 a.m.: "General Meade is not here, and the command devolves on you." On the day before, President Lincoln had journeyed aboard a chartered steamer, the *River Queen*, up the James River to City Point for a visit with General Grant. Unbeknownst to Parke, Grant had invited Meade, his wife, and his adjutant to spend the evening with them at City Point. While Gordon was launching his attack against Fort Stedman, General and Mrs. Meade were still aboard the *Thomas Collyer* anchored in the James River. While Parke focused on directing the IX Corps's response along his front, Major General Henry Hunt of Meade's staff coordinated the supporting movements of Meade's entire army.[69]

Because Gordon's men had cut the telegraph line to City Point, Hunt sent a courier to inform Meade of the offensive: "Enemy are reported as having broken through our lines near Fort Stedman, and also that he is making a heavy attack on Willcox's right. I have notified corps commanders and am sending down Wainwright's artillery. The troops around us are getting under arms." Within thirty minutes VI Corps commander Horatio G. Wright ordered out Frank Wheaton's division from the trenches west of the Weldon Railroad. By 7:00 a.m., all the "available force" of Gouverneur K. Warren's V Corps, held in reserve southwest of Petersburg, was in motion toward Fort Stedman.[70]

These supporting troops, however, would have to march at least four or more miles to reach the unfolding battle. Reinforcement of the IX Corps would take time, and time was now of the essence. Parke's IX Corps would have to fend for itself along the contested front that extended southward from Battery No. 9, through Fort Stedman to Batteries No. 11 and 12, and to Fort Haskell to the south.

---

69 OR 46, pt. 3, 146, 147; Porter, "Campaigning with Grant," 596; Allan Nevins, ed., *A Diary of Battle: The Personal Journals of Colonel Charles S. Wainwright, 1861-1865* (New York, 1962), 504.

70 OR 46, pt. 3, 113, 148.

Part VI

Battery No. 9 and Fort McGilvery

General Matthew Ransom's Confederate brigade rushed into combat on the heels of Flemming and Roulhac's storming parties on the north side of Fort Stedman. The men struck the fort and turned northward, taking the breastworks of the 57th Massachusetts from the flank and rear. Given all they had experienced during this long war, the morning of March 25 was easy work. The defenses were unfinished, and the wet ground in the swale north of Stedman had prompted most of the Northern defenders to pass the night in their camp 100 yards northeast of the fort. It was the clamor of the Rebel charge that roused the New Englanders from their tents that dawn.

Sergeant-Major Charles H. Pinkham was making his escape from the camp of the 57th Massachusetts when he was accosted by his temporary commander, Maj. James Doherty. Spouting colorful language, Doherty demanded to know the location of the regimental flag. When Pinkham replied that the colors had been left in his tent, Doherty ordered him back to retrieve the banner. The 57th had lost its flag in the battle of the Crater, and Doherty was not about to have his regiment dishonored like that again. According to Pinkham, for a short time he approached the level of professional sprinter, successfully running the gauntlet of fire to camp and back again without injury, "save being half frightened to death by the bullets whizzing around my ears."[71]

Though embarrassed by the Carolinians, the Bay Staters of the 57th Massachusetts rallied to do some hard fighting. They reformed several times during their retreat to send fusillades into their yelling pursuers. Fighting desperately to slow down the enemy advance, recorded the regimental historian, "They made a final stand behind an old abandoned rebel fort known as Dunn House Battery, near the Prince George Court House Road." The fighting cut up the 57th regiment. The hard-nosed Major Doherty fell during the fighting and would die the next day. By bravely "standing up to the work," the men of Massachusetts slowed the Confederate rush toward Meade's Station and the Military Railroad.[72]

---

71 Anderson, *The Fifty-Seventh Regiment of Massachusetts Volunteers*, 275.

72 *Ibid.*, 255.

Battery No. 9 and Fort McGilvery stood between Ransom's brigade and the Appomattox River farther north. Confederate skirmishers advanced in that direction until their path was blocked by the 2nd Michigan. The Carolinians tried to bluff their way into Battery No. 9, calling out to the Federal defenders, "It's of no use now; it's all over, you might as well throw down your guns." The Rebels set about to take prisoners when Captain John C. Boughton called their bluff and ordered his regiment to open fire and take cover in front of the battery. The violent reply gave the Carolinians pause. "Our movement has been covered by the darkness, and we now look for troops to come up on our left," recalled Capt. Graham of the 56th North Carolina. "We understood that Pickett was to come from Butler's front at Drewry's Bluff, and the line from our left to the river." The Tar Heels had not received word that the trains carrying Pickett's division would not arrive from Richmond in time for the assault. When he finally realized that support would not be forthcoming, Graham pushed his men on toward Battery No. 9 and Fort McGilvery.[73]

Inside Battery No. 9, meanwhile, Lieutenant Val Stone of the 5th U.S. Artillery reported: "I could just see in the gray of dawn (it was then about 5.15 a.m.) a line of battle drawn up, moving toward me, their right being inside of our works, this line extended along the ravine between Battery No. 9 and Fort Stedman, their left resting near the rebel lines. I immediately ordered my section to open on them with spherical case; they were in easy range, about 400 yards." Stone and his gunner would not cease firing for hours.[74]

The left of the 2nd Michigan fell back into Battery No. 9, but Captain Boughton threw the remainder of his men across the wagon road and "checked the enemy in a splendid manner." Captain Albert Day of the 20th Michigan, which manned Battery No. 9, also targeted Confederates still within the cover of their works. The bluecoats were quickly reinforced by elements of the 1st Michigan Sharpshooters and the 50th Pennsylvania, brought up by Col. Ralph Ely commanding the Second Brigade. The 60th Ohio supplied flank fire from the rear.[75]

Farther north in Fort McGilvery, Major Jacob Roemer of the 34th Battery, New York Light Artillery, had been aroused sometime after 4:00 a.m. by the commotion around Fort Stedman. The artillery officer had already alerted Colonel Ely to the attack when he commenced firing to the south. Roemer wrote that

73 OR 46, pt. 1, 327; Graham, "Fifty-Sixth Regiment," Clark, *North Carolina Regiments*, 390-391.

74 OR 46, pt. 1, 190.

75 OR 46, pt. 1, 325-327.

"things were becoming very lively on our left, when I noticed a column of the enemy advancing on the rear and left of the fort along the Norfolk Road where there was a deep cut through a hill . . . placing our infantry at the enemy's mercy. . . . The situation was very critical." With no gun portals on the backside of the fort, Roemer had one of his cannons pushed along the rear traverse and hoisted onto the parapet. Taking personal charge of the gun, he fired low through the cut and watched his shells explode just in front of the column. The fire brought the enemy advance to an abrupt halt.[76]

Part VII

Behind Fort Stedman

General Gordon knew the breakthrough at Fort Stedman was but the first stage of the Confederate assault, and likely the easiest of his objectives. The ultimate goal was the "tremendous possibility" of cutting Grant's forces in two, if only for the time needed for General Lee to escape with his army westward into the heart of Virginia. To complete the task, Gordon's storming parties had to seize the "three forts" deep in the rear before the Federals could rally to their defense.

Orlando Willcox, defending the Federal line with his First Division, reported that when he arrived on the plain behind Fort Stedman, "The enemy's skirmishers now came down the hill directly to the rear of Stedman, and moved toward my head-quarters at the Friend House, the Dunn House Battery, and in the direction of Meade's Station, and this, for a time, rendered my communication with the Third Brigade long and circuitous."[77]

Confederate Col. Hamilton Jones led his 57th North Carolina regiment to the left and rear toward Fort Friend. When they reached the ravine that held Harrison Creek they were met by blasts of gunfire from Captain Edward Jones's 11th Massachusetts Battery. Alerted to the danger by prisoners captured overnight, Jones "took his guns out of Fort Friend, placed them on the edge of the ravine, and depressed them at such an angle as would permit him to hurl canister into the advancing column of the enemy." Colonel Hamilton Jones fell wounded during the thrust, and the Federal guns repulsed the attack. The flag bearer of the 57th North

---

76 *OR* 46, pt. 1, 363-364.

77 *OR* 46, pt. 1, 322-325.

Carolina was standing in line in full view of the fort "when a shell, evidently aimed at the colors, burst so near that he seemed in the very midst of the shock. Both the color guards fell."[78]

"Meantime," reported General Willcox, "I had ordered out the Seventeenth Michigan [Acting] Engineer Regiment, at my headquarters, and sent word to the commanding officers of the 200th and 209th Pennsylvania—encamped between Meade's Station and the Dunn House Battery—to move, respectively, one to the Friend House, the other in front of the Dunn House Battery. These regiments promptly appeared."[79]

General Hartranft, the Third Division's new commander, arrived while most of his troops were still en route from their respective camps in the rear. After conferring with Willcox near the Friend house, Hartranft "promptly and gallantly" led his 200th Pennsylvania and remnants of the 57th Massachusetts in an attack on the camp of the displaced New Englanders. Advancing back down the Prince George Court House Road, they doggedly cleared out the skirmishers in their front, pushed through the camp of the 57th Massachusetts and engaged Ransom's North Carolinians, strung out between Fort Stedman and Battery No. 9.[80]

As Captain Graham of the 56th North Carolina recalled it, "A solid column of blue appears upon the rising ground to our front and right. Their alignment is perfect, and down they dash only to be repulsed by the steady volleys from our line. Over again they come, and again they are driven back. The third time they meet with no better success." General Hartranft and his charges were thus "obliged to retire through the camp of the Fifty-Seventh Massachusetts, and take shelter in an old line of works about forty yards in its rear and to the right." Even though they had repulsed Hartranft's counterattack, Ransom's Carolinians were no longer on the attack. Instead, they were now using their bayonets to dig in where they were—stalled between Battery No. 9 on the north and Fort Stedman on the south. The attack was beginning to bog down.[81]

Hartranft later claimed that, during their advance down the road extending from Meade's Station to Fort Stedman, the 200th Pennsylvania had done the best fighting of the day, paving the way for the recapture of Fort Stedman. He lauded the troops who were never "before in action who not only rallied . . . but resolutely

---

78 Hodgkins, *Battle of Fort Stedman*, 35; Barrier, "Breaking Grant's Line," 417; Jones, "Fifty-Seventh Regiment," 424.

79 *OR* 46, pt. 1, 322-325.

80 Hartranft, "The Recapture of Fort Stedman," 587-588.

81 Graham, "Fifty-Sixth Regiment," Clark, *North Carolina Regiments*, 391.

recharged . . . and again re-rallied on the first available ground. No veterans could have done better." Meantime, "The 209th had been able to push its way to a good position, its left resting on the old works to which the 200th had fallen back. . . ." Willcox's Provost Guard, the 17th Michigan [Acting] Engineers, moved up on their right. Colonel Ely's skirmishers of the Second Brigade came next. Anchoring the far right side of the battlefield for the Federals were the 2nd and 20th Michigan regiments, still in firm possession of Battery No. 9. When Captain J. C. Bracket of Willcox's staff brought word to Hartranft that a "solid line was thus formed against the advance of the enemy" to the Federal right, Hartranft relinquished command of the 200th Pennsylvania and circled back to the Federal left, where he would personally assess the situation at General McLaughlen's head-quarters and Fort Haskell.[82]

The advance of Hartranft's Pennsylvanians toward the Federal right had uncovered the Prince George Court House Road leading from Fort Stedman back to the Dunn House Battery and Meade's Station. To block the enemy's advance in this direction, Parke ordered General Tidball, commanding the IX Corps artillery, to provide support from the crest of the hill behind Stedman. Tidball brought up two sections of 12-pounders of the 1st New York Light Artillery and the 19th New York Battery from the artillery park near Meade's Station to a position 1,200 yards behind Stedman and to the left of Jones's guns at Fort Friend.

Tidball's artillery took position "on the crest of the hill in front of the station [and] opened fire on the enemy's skirmish line, which by this time had advanced to the ravine between this hill and Fort Stedman." Tidball's guns rendered an immediate impact by forcing the Southern skirmishers to retrace their advance on Meade's Station to a line of old works 200 yards from Stedman. The "straggling fire" from two captured cannons, which the Confederates had wrestled to the back of the fort, stopped.[83] Tidball later claimed that his artillery was joined by a strange collection of personages who appeared to the enemy to be reinforcements. As Tidball put it, a small town had cropped up around Meade's Station:

Near the station were the 9th Corps Hospital, some camps of reserve artillery, and a large collection of Sutler and Christian Commission establishments. At first alarm the people of all these places turned out in force to see what was going on. In the haziness of dawn these sightseers appeared to those at Stedman a compact line of troops

82 Hartranft, "The Recapture of Fort Stedman," 587.

83 *OR* 46, pt. 1, 355-358.

stretching along the hill, and some of the pieces of the reserve batteries being brought forward and opening fire gave reality to the delusion.[84]

Part VIII

Fort Haskell

Fort Haskell was strategically located atop a ridge one-half mile south of Fort Stedman. Ideally sited for artillery, Fort Haskell afforded a commanding view of the Union defenses extending northward to Fort Stedman and of the plain behind it. Eyewitness George L. Kilmer of Co. I, 14th New York Heavy Artillery, asserted: "If Stedman and all the works north of it to the river were cut away by the enemy, so long as Haskell remained intact it projected our line into the vast open space which must necessarily become the main field of action." It was thus imperative that the Confederates capture this source of enfilading fire on their right flank and turn it to their advantage.

Both Stedman and Haskell were garrisoned by the 14th New York Heavy Artillery (armed with muskets), the 3rd New Jersey Battery (rifled cannon), and the 1st Connecticut Heavy Artillery (with Coehorn mortars). Unlike their comrades in Fort Stedman, all the men in Fort Haskell were fully alert when Private Hough, an enterprising picket reconnoitering the area, sounded the alarm. The defenders were already at the parapets because their battalion commander, Charles H. Houghton, had a premonition of an attack and wanted his men ready for battle at 4:00 a.m. A nervous sergeant had misread the directive and ordered the garrison out three-quarters of an hour before the appointed time, so when Confederate infantry from Evans's division was heard advancing through the darkness, the Northern gunners were ready and waiting. They held their fire and listened as a Southern officer advised his line of battle, "Steady! We'll have their works. Steady, my men." When the enemy approached into point-blank range the Federal gunners opened fire. "Not a word was spoken but in perfect concert the cannon belched forth grape and our muskets were discharged upon the hapless band," recorded one eyewitness. "It was an awful surprise for the surprisers, and fifty mangled bodies lay

---

84 Tidball, *"No Disgrace to My Country,"* 361.

there in the abatis. . . . Then they split into squads and moved on the flanks, keeping up the by-play until there were none left."[85]

Dawn was breaking when Terry and Evans's brigades of Evans's division finally overran Batteries No. 11 and 12. Evans's brigade deflected toward the rear, but Terry's men pushed down the Union entrenchments toward Fort Haskell. Lieutenant Colonel Joseph H. Pentecost, commanding the 100th Pennsylvania, fought bravely but was killed in the onslaught. Elements of the 59th Massachusetts, 100th Pennsylvania, and 3rd Maryland regiments sought refuge in Fort Haskell or fell back to the cookhouses in the rear. Survivors from the 1st Connecticut Heavy Artillery escaped with two of their mortars, mounted the parapet of Haskell, and resumed firing. Joining the gunners in Haskell was Lieutenant Joslyn of the 29th Massachusetts, who had first sounded the alarm on the picket line in front of Battery No. 11. Joslyn had slipped through a line of advancing Confederates to reach the safety of the fort. Major Jacob Woerner, the veteran German commander of the 3rd New Jersey Artillery, arrived to send the advancing graycoats reeling with the one gun he could fire from the right-rear angle of Haskell. The situation grew more desperate as Confederate sharpshooters showered the fort with minie balls and the enemy batteries at Colquitt's Salient intensified their fire. Three wounds disabled garrison commander Major Houghton in three minutes. Crammed into an area the size of a steamer's deck, the several hundred cannoneers and survivors fought valiantly, "the wounded and sick men loading the muskets, while those with sound arms stood to the parapets and blazed away."[86]

With Fort Haskell now isolated and a quarter-mile from the nearest Union troops, a Federal battery far to the rear started shelling the stronghold on the presumption that it had fallen into enemy hands. About this time, the commanding officer of the 14th New York Heavy Artillery, Major George M. Randall, who had been captured in the initial assault on Stedman, appeared at Haskell. He had escaped his Rebel captors with his unit's colors wrapped around his body. To halt the Federal shelling of Haskell, Randall pulled together a color guard—Haskell's flag-bearer Kiley and eight other men—and marched them bravely out the rear of the fort to brandish their flag "conspicuously in view of the Federal batteries behind them. Four of the guard were hit, one mortally." Fortunately the tactic worked and the "friendly fire" on Fort Haskell stopped. A third charge by scattered squads of Terry's brigade ended on the slopes of Fort Haskell with blasts of grape shot from Woerner's guns. "With this the aggressive spirit of that famous

85 Kilmer, "Assault and Repulse at Fort Stedman," 783-791.

86 OR 46, pt. 1, 338; Kilmer, "Assault and Repulse at Fort Stedman," 787.

movement melted away forever," 14th New York Heavy Artillerist George Kilmer recalled. "The sortie was a failure, and daylight found the invaders stalled in the breach." But the Southerners were not yet finished. "The Confederate problem of the day was reduced to the silencing of Haskell, and it was the target of more guns than had been concentrated upon one point during the siege. Here for once," Kilmer waxed poetically, "after all the prosy months of stupid carnage, was the realization of the grand and the terrible in the war."[87]

Part IX

Gordon's Plan Unravels

In his reminiscences, General Gordon recorded that the success of the first stage of the assault "had exceeded my most sanguine expectations. We had taken Fort Stedman and a long line of breastworks on either side." Gordon sent word to Lee at Blandford Church that he was in the fort itself. Further, 300 picked men led by three officers representing themselves as retreating Federals were on their way to seize the three forts in the second line of Union works. It was then that the good news devolved into disappointment. "Soon I received a message from one of these three officers, I believe General Lewis of North Carolina, that he had passed the line of Federal infantry without trouble by representing himself as Colonel —— of the Hundredth Pennsylvania, but that he could not find his fort, as the guide had been lost in the rush upon Stedman," recalled Gordon. "I soon received a similar message from the other two. . . ." The failure of the guides meant that the second line of forts on the commanding hills would not be taken by surprise in the darkness. Both Gordon and Lee knew that after seizing Stedman, the "three forts" had to be taken with their planned ruse in order for the effort to have a real chance of success. Assaulting these fortified works using conventional tactics in daylight would be too costly. The advance was frozen in place.[88]

As General Walker later recorded, "General Gordon seemed loath to give up his cherished plans, and waited to communicate with General Lee, and for an hour or two longer we held our captured fort and breastworks." By the time Gordon and his officers urged their men on, the attack had lost all its momentum in the

---

87 *OR* 46, pt. 1, 341; Kilmer, "Assault and Repulse at Fort Stedman," 789.

88 Gordon, *Reminiscences*, 410-411.

confused scene around Fort Stedman. During the delay, the logistics of moving long columns of troops through the breach into the Federal works proved more difficult than anticipated, and the breach had not been widened because of the enfilading fire from Battery No. 9 to the north, the commanding hills in the rear, and Fort Haskell to the south. Delays in the advance eliminated the advantage of surprise, and the rising sun dissipated the cover of darkness.[89]

"It took more than an hour for the entire division to come up and form into line, and it was sunrise before we were ready to advance," confirmed Walker. "The attacks made by the other columns were either not made, or, if made, were unsuccessful, and these troops came to my aid in Fort Stedman." General Evans agreed, adding, "Day was breaking" before Terry's brigade was formed to move on Batteries No. 11 and 12 and Fort Haskell.[90]

A variety of causes contributed to the delays. In addition to those listed above, the sheer numbers of combatants overwhelmed the site. The structure, which normally garrisoned perhaps 300 men, encompassed less than an acre of ground but was overrun by elements of at least two Confederate divisions pushing forward past a conglomeration of huts and bomb-proofs. Six hundred Federal prisoners and several captured cannon were being taken to the rear. General Grimes and other officers could not get their horses through the battlements, so they rode captured mounts on the line behind Stedman. Soldiers engaging in the time-honored practice of looting further snarled the heavy traffic. Private H. A. London, a courier with the 32nd North Carolina, told his family that the plundering was "no worse than usual, even though there was plenty of everything to tempt them." London himself stopped long enough to pilfer a bluecoat's personal letters for a souvenir.[91]

Some soldiers balked at moving forward because by this time they viewed the battle as a "forlorn hope." General Walker claimed at one point, "The leading files were lying down behind the breastworks at the point where those before them had crossed." The general alleged that when he ordered the men forward, their company captain tried to block the advance because he did not want to see his men slaughtered. After a dramatic confrontation that included an attempt by Walker to shoot the mutinous officer, the captain finally led his men into battle, where he disappeared into history. Walker suspected the dissident was part of the "Red

89 Walker, "Gordon's Assault on Fort Stedman," 28.

90 *Ibid.*, 28; Stephens, *Intrepid Warrior*, 535.

91 Pulaski Cowper, compiler, and Gary W. Gallagher, ed., *Extracts of Letters of Major-General Bryan Grimes, to his Wife . . . Together with Some Personal Recollections of the War* (Wilmington, 1986), 98; *Washington Daily Times*, March 26th, 1865, 1; H. A. London Papers, UNCMS.

Strings," soldiers who attached red strings to their uniforms to signify their intent to surrender when confronted by the enemy.[92]

Other Confederate troops willing to join the fight didn't come up at all because they weren't called up. The courier sent to find the 4th North Carolina of Cox's brigade, as an example, was alleged to have lost his way in the darkness and, consequently, failed to summon these men to battle. Indeed, of all the soldiers in Cox's brigade, only the sharpshooters of his 1st and 3rd regiments sallied forth from Colquitt's Salient. Some units were set in motion toward the battlefield but never arrived at Fort Stedman. Foremost among these was Pickett's division, which was to have come from Richmond to support Ransom's brigade in its thrust toward the Appomattox River. However, on the previous day when it became evident to General Longstreet that the troop trains from Richmond could not be marshaled in sufficient number, Lee selected other troops from the divisions of Cadmus Wilcox, Henry Heth, and Bushrod Johnson, then deployed west of Petersburg.[93]

In order to reach the battlefield, the troops from Cadmus Wilcox's division—Lane and Thomas's brigades—had to march from their entrenchments on the far side of Petersburg. Even though they were not pulled out of their line until after dark, they still completed their trek through the city by 2:00 a.m. General Wilcox, although not present at the battle due to illness, had visited his assigned location "about 150 yards in rear of our occupied line in an old pit." He reported that his men were subsequently "moved back near a mile" by Gordon's staff. Regarding his troops' alleged failure to support the attack, Wilcox claimed that his two brigades were never ordered to join the assault, even though Gordon's adjutant knew of their changed position.[94]

The men of Henry Heth's division would later be accused of delaying the start of the entire enterprise. The *New York Times* reported that the supporting troops from Cooke's North Carolina and McComb's Tennessee brigades were late coming up. As a result, with "daylight making its appearance the enemy became desperate" and the charge was made without them. However, Lieutenant T. H. Tolson of the

---

92 Walker, "Gordon's Assault on Fort Stedman," 26.

93 E. A. Osborne, "Fourth Regiment," in Clark, *North Carolina Regiments*, vol. 1, 264; Brigadier General William R. Cox, "The Anderson-Ramseur-Cox Brigade," in Clark, *North Carolina Regiments*, vol. 4, 450. Cox's 1st and 3rd North Carolina regiments were among the storming parties that first struck Fort Stedman, and the rest of the brigade was not brought up until Cox himself sought out General Lee, and then only to be deployed along the main Confederate line; OR 46, pt. 1, 188. Some of Pickett's men were seen arriving in Richmond that morning, but they were not sent to the fighting east of Petersburg.

94 Cadmus M. Wilcox, Petersburg Campaign Report, Lee Headquarters Collection, Virginia Historical Society and Papers 1846-1887, Library of Congress, Folder 1023, 29.

2nd Maryland Confederate Battalion (assigned to McComb's Tennessee Brigade) claimed the Marylanders were not summoned to battle until dawn, and even then they were not directed to Fort Stedman. Tolson claimed he was "[a]wakened at daylight by the gentle voice of a 100-pound Federal Parrott shell passing over my head. . . . We go into the trenches and halt in the works, our right resting near the Crater. . . . We were to support them some say, but by somebody's mistake, did not participate at all." Colonel Samuel Walkup's men of the 48th North Carolina and Cooke's brigade were also not roused until sunup. They were diverted to the right of the Crater for the apparent purpose of securing the Confederate line between Fort Stedman and the Crater to the south, which had been stripped of troops for the assault. An 18-year-old named Hampden Osbourne claimed he had been left in charge of a detail of no more than 50 men to demonstrate along the line in front of the Crater during the attack.[95]

The supporting troops on Gordon's left were led by General Matt Ransom, who took his own brigade and that of Brigadier General William H. Wallace on the long march from Bushrod Johnson's camp at Burgess Mill. Before dawn, Col. Henry M. Rutledge promptly led Ransom's brigade on the thrust toward the Appomattox River. Wallace's brigade, however, didn't make it onto the battlefield until some Confederates soldiers were seen falling back from Fort Stedman. General Johnson yelled, "General Wallace, don't you see those men leaving the fort? Have your men take it and hold it." By the time Wallace's troops belatedly crossed over to Fort Stedman, they were blanketed by "the most terrible rain of shot and shell that we ever experienced." They hunkered down inside the fort. "The idea of formally forming the regiment was abandoned and the men were allowed to fire from every available point."[96]

The columns in front of Wallace had broken up as their movements became "disjointed." Union General Tidball explained that "Fort Stedman, with Battery No. 10 on its right, and Nos. 11 and 12, on the left, were, to all intents and purposes, one work . . . and had become a labyrinth of bomb-proofs, traverses, gopher holes, huts, and all in all every imaginable manner of irregularity." The combination of darkness and confused surroundings proved to be more challenging than expected.

95 *New York Times*, March 28, 1865, 1; S. Z. Ammen, *Maryland Troops in the Confederate Army from Original Sources: Material Gathered in 1879 from the Men Who Led and Fought*, Thomas Clemens Collection, American Military History Education Center (Carlisle, PA), 171; Walkup, Unpublished Diary, UNCMS, 76; Hampden Osbourne, "The Struggle for Fort Mahone," *Confederate Veteran*, vol. 25, 227.

96 DeWitt Boyd Stone, Jr., ed., *Wandering to Glory: Confederate Veterans Remember Evans' Brigade* (Columbia, 2002), 216.

Captain John Anderson of the 57th Massachusetts observed that "to accomplish anything through the intricate entanglements of our works was impossible. What [the Confederates] needed was daylight and a pocket guide for each man."[97]

The coming of daylight, however, only worsened the plight of the Southern soldiers. The *Petersburg Express* reported what happened when the sun rose: "The enemy now opened every gun that could be brought to bear on our troops, and subjected them to a rain of iron, before which the experiences of Malvern Hill and Gettysburg are said by veterans to pale almost into insignificance. It was painfully distinct in this city, where our very dwellings were shaken to their foundations." Given these circumstances, concluded Confederate General Evans, "Many of the troops behaved well, but in this as in former actions, I could but observe how sadly we need organization and discipline. It is almost impossible at times to maneuver the troops at all."[98]

General Tidball concluded that it was the combination of confusing landscape and enfilading artillery fire that frustrated Gordon's plan: "Getting over and into this labyrinth broke entirely the enemy's formation, and before they could reform for a forward movement, such a pelting fire of artillery was brought to bear upon them as to cause them to seek shelter in the bomb-proofs, behind traverses or wherever else they could find cover."[99]

Before publishing his memoirs in 1903, Gordon was quoted as saying that the failure to take Fort Haskell was the cue for withdrawal. Regarding the failed attacks at Haskell, division commander Clement Evans wrote that he had "communicated my situation to the Major General commanding [Gordon] with the statement that to advance further I must charge a strong line of the enemy aided by their artillery." Gordon's objective was "To roll up the Union line . . . beginning with Fort Haskell, and as soon as he saw that Haskell could not be silenced he determined to withdraw. He did not do this immediately because it required Lee's sanction."[100] General Lee's commitment to the assault included the caveat that the objectives be achieved without "great sacrifice." When he learned the second line of Union forts could not be taken by the agreed-upon stratagem, and upon seeing the failure to

---

97 Tidball, *"No Disgrace to My Country,"* 360-361; Anderson, *The Fifty-Seventh Regiment Massachusetts Volunteers*, 264.

98 Unidentified Correspondent, *Petersburg Express*, quoted in *Richmond Dispatch*, March 28, 1865, 1; Stephens, *Intrepid Warrior*, 535.

99 Robert Garth Scott, *Forgotten Valor: The Memoirs, Journals, & Civil War Letters of Orlando B. Willcox* (Kent, 1999), 634.

100 Stephens, *Intrepid Warrior*, 535; Kilmer, "Assault and Repulse at Fort Stedman," 791.

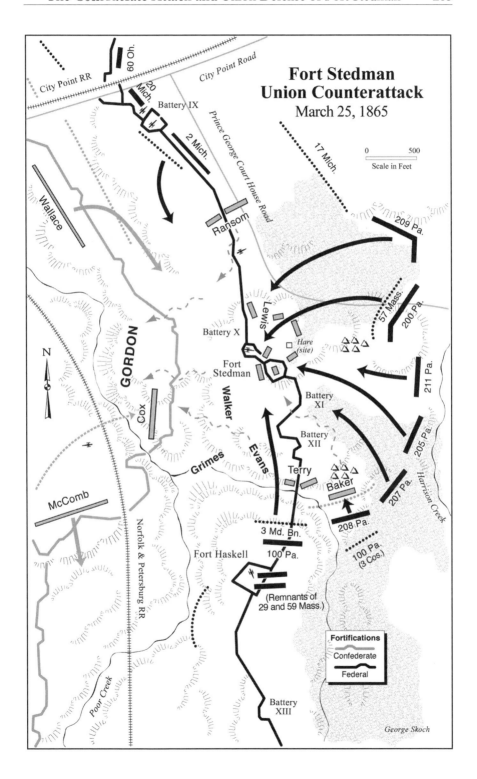

Fort Stedman
Union Counterattack
March 25, 1865

60 Oh.

City Point RR

City Point Road

20 Mich.

Battery IX

Prince George Court House Road

2 Mich.

17 Mich.

0   500
Scale in Feet

209 Pa.

Wallace

Ransom

Lewis

57 Mass.

200 Pa.

Battery X

Hare
(site)

N

GORDON

Fort
Stedman

211 Pa.

Cox

Walker

Battery
XI

205 Pa.

Grimes

Evans

Battery
XII

Terry

Baker

207 Pa.

Harrison Creek

McComb

3 Md. Bn.

208 Pa.

Fort Haskell

100 Pa.

100 Pa.
(3 Cos.)

Norfolk & Petersburg RR

(Remnants of
29 and 59 Mass.)

Fortifications

Confederate

Federal

Poor Creek

Battery
XIII

George Skoch

widen the breach, Lee ordered Gordon's troops and all supporting units to abandon the attack and return to their works.[101]

Part X

The Federal Countercharge

The Federal defenders were now aligned with deadly symmetry. Fort Stedman lay at the center of the arc proscribed by the old Confederate Batteries No. 4 and 5 on the north (part of the old Dimmock Line), Fort McGilvery, Battery No. 9, Fort Friend, the ridge in front of Meade's Station, Fort Haskell on the south, and Fort Morton beyond. "As soon as the haze of the morning cleared away sufficiently to enable the artillery to direct their fire with accuracy," artillery commander Tidball reported, "all the pieces . . . that could be brought to bear upon Fort Stedman, opened, and concentrating a fire of about thirty pieces upon and around the fort, soon made the place untenable."[102]

As Gordon looked out over the field of fire surrounding Fort Stedman, he saw his well-planned attack bogged down and his troops taking heavy casualties. Despite his personal appearance on the field behind Stedman, the troops, pinned down by murderous fire, could be driven eastward no farther. On Gordon's left, the several brigades of Carolinians were absorbing heavy casualties along the Federal works extending toward Battery No. 9 and Fort McGilvery. Generals Ransom and Wallace were well on the way to losing more than 1,200 soldiers in their two brigades. Major Graham of the 56th North Carolina was cut down when a single bullet passed through both knees. By the end of the fighting General Lewis would lose all of his brigade's field officers, including Colonel Jones of the 57th Regiment, who had led the advance on Fort Friend. Brigadier General Robert D. Johnston left the field with a severe ankle injury.[103]

---

101 Gordon, *Reminiscences*, 411.

102 *OR* 46, pt. 1, 355-358.

103 R. H. Anderson, *Narrative of Services Oct '64—April '65*, Lee Headquarters Collection, Virginia Historical Society, 2; Graham, "Fifty-Sixth Regiment," vol. 3, 392; William Gaston Lewis, Personal Papers, 1865-1911, Letter to Wife, March 27, 1865, UNCMS Collection (Chapel Hill, NC); Turner and Wall, "Twenty-Third Regiment," Clark, *North Carolina Regiments*, 264.

Behind Fort Stedman, division commander Bryan Grimes had sent Phil Cook's brigade to an eminence 300 yards out when they were faced down by Tidball's batteries firing from Fort Friend, the Dunn House Battery, and from the commanding hills. The unsupported Georgians fell back to a line of former Confederate works and Brigadier General Philip Cook was escorted from the field with a badly broken arm. Grimes's division would sustain 478 casualties that morning.[104]

At Fort Stedman, Wallace's South Carolina brigade and elements of others crowded in and around the redoubt. The brigadier shed his coat to personally man one of the captured guns. Many more men from the attacking force huddled on the slope leading up to Stedman from the Confederate works, where they took enfilading fire from Federal guns firing on both flanks. On Gordon's right, the repeated assaults against Fort Haskell had failed. Colonel Baker of Evans's brigade and General Terry both fell with wounds.[105]

Even though Lee's decision to abandon the attack and fall back was necessary and proper, the memory of both the order and the manner in which it was executed would always be painful for Gordon. Withdrawing, recalled the commander many years later, "was not easily accomplished. Foiled by the failure of the guides, deprived of the great bodies of infantry which Lee had ordered to my support, I had necessarily stretched out my corps to occupy the entrenchments which we had captured." Just getting the retreat order to commanders strung out along the half-mile front was a wretched task requiring messages to be hand-carried through a "consuming fire." "I happened to be near General Gordon when he issued orders to retreat to our own works and made up my mind not to wait for the regular channel of communication," Major Phil Alexander recalled, "through staff officers, but 'called on feet to save the body,' and they responded quite lively, you may rest assured."[106]

Union General Hartranft had ridden to McLaughlen's abandoned headquarters 800 yards behind Fort Haskell to deploy his Second Brigade under Colonel J. A. Mathews. He saw the United States flag still flying over Haskell, its guns gamely manned by the 14th New York Heavy Artillery, 3rd New Jersey Battery, and 1st Connecticut Light Artillery. Infantry inside the fort included the

---

104 Thomas, *Doles-Cook Brigade*, 36; Cowper and Gallagher, *Extracts of Letters of Major-General Bryan Grimes*, 98.

105 Stone Jr., ed., *Wandering to Glory*, 219; Stephens, *Intrepid Warrior*, 535.

106 Gordon, *Reminiscences*, 411; Anderson, *The Fifty-Seventh Regiment Massachusetts Volunteers*, 282.

3rd Maryland and displaced elements of the 100th Pennsylvania and 29th and 59th Massachusetts regiments. The garrison of survivors had just repelled what would prove to be the last Confederate charge—this one by about 300 infantry, apparently led by General Terry himself.[107]

When he arrived at McLaughlen's headquarters about 7:00 a.m., Hartranft found that his 208th Pennsylvania had moved up to a "good position . . . its left connected with Fort Haskell by about 200 men mostly from the 100th Pennsylvania, and some few of the 3rd Maryland, who had been driven from Batteries No. 11 and 12."[108] It was Hartranft who had earlier sent his staff officer of the day, Captain Prosper Dalien, to deploy the 208th Pennsylvania there. Riding ahead, Major George Shorkley had rallied the survivors of the first Confederate assault and McLaughlen's non-combatants with orders to stand their ground until help arrived: "Sergeant Randolph," announced the captain, "the head of Gordon's division is coming up that road. Deploy your pioneers as skirmishers and whip it."

Stunned, Randolph asked, "I am to whip a division with pioneers, sir?"

"Certainly," Shorkley replied. "You shall be relieved with a line of battle in ten minutes. Make lots of racket."

The audacious charge by the 208th Pennsylvania and disparate units, led by Lieutenant Colonel M. T. Heintzelman, met with success even though the Federals were badly handled during the brief but sharp fighting. The blue line was not turned back until it had pushed the graycoats into the ravine behind Battery No. 12.[109]

Hartranft worked tirelessly to complete a semicircle of blue around Fort Stedman by sending the newly arrived men of his second brigade—the 205th and 207th Pennsylvania regiments—to the right toward the road stretching from Stedman to Meade's Station. Hartranft's 211th Pennsylvania, which had just completed its march from the Avery house, covered the road to Meade's Station in the Federal center. Colonel Samuel Harriman, commanding the First Brigade of Willcox's division, had also come up behind Fort Haskell with the 37th Wisconsin and 109th New York regiments.[110]

From his vantage point atop the crest in the rear, General Tidball could clearly see that by 7:30 a.m., the momentum of the battle had shifted in favor of the Union. The enemy, he reported, "were seen breaking away in small detachments from Stedman back to their own lines. This was quickly perceived by our troops on all

107 Kilmer, "Assault and Repulse at Fort Stedman," 783-791.

108 Hartranft, "The Recapture of Fort Stedman," 587-588.

109 Anderson, *The Fifty-Seventh Regiment Massachusetts Volunteers*, 271.

110 Hartranft, "The Recapture of Fort Stedman," 587-588.

sides." Mounting the high ground behind Fort Haskell, Hartranft was greeted by an extraordinary view: "Riding along the other flank, the whole scene of operations on the opposite slope was spread out before me. On a semicircle of a mile and a half, five regiments and detachments, nearly 4,000 men, were ready to charge."[111]

As Third Brigade Adjutant Thomas W. Clarke reported, "a little before eight, an aide from General Hartranft came with his compliments to say to the commanding officer of the Third Brigade, that he would charge in five minutes, and would be pleased to have the Third Brigade co-operate. [Brevet Colonel Gilbert P. Robinson, now in command of McLaughlen's brigade] . . . at once replied: 'Give my compliments to General Hartranft, and say I am charging now, immediately giving the order to rise up and charge."[112]

Both Hartranft and Robinson were encouraged by the sight of Union soldiers already streaming along the works from Fort Haskell toward Fort Stedman. Captain Joseph Carter asserted these men comprised the greater part of the 3rd Maryland, with most of the 100th Pennsylvania close behind, who initiated the charge on Fort Stedman. Carter claimed he assumed leadership of the 3rd Maryland soon after the Confederate assault on Fort Haskell began. Colonel Robinson had withdrawn to the rear, unaware that McLaughlen's capture had thrust him into command of the third brigade.

Captain Carter reported that he led his contingent of the 3rd Maryland along the works from Fort Haskell through Fort Stedman, with the 100th Pennsylvania close behind, a full half-hour before Hartranft arrived. (Captain Hodgkins of Hartranft's staff conceded that Batteries No. 11 and 12 were already back in Union hands by 7:30 a.m.) Carter affirmed that Color-Sergeant Charles Oliver of the 100th Pennsylvania, who had wrenched the regimental colors from a desperate Confederate flag-bearer, was the first to plant a Federal battle flag inside Fort Stedman. Carter's Marylanders would claim the capture of two battle flags. The 100th Pennsylvania, now under Major N. J. Maxwell, would boast of the capture of five stands of colors.[113]

Colonel Robinson's attacking force consisted of the survivors from the same units that had fled Batteries No. 11 and 12, except these men had rallied behind Hartranft's 208th Pennsylvania to roll back the initial Confederate thrust behind Fort Haskell. Like Carter, Robinson claimed his contingent regained the Federal lines just ahead of Hartranft's Pennsylvanians, "carrying the trenches and batteries

---

111 OR 46, pt. 1, 355-358; Hartranft, "The Recapture of Fort Stedman," 588.

112 OR 46, pt. 1, 345.

113 Hodgkins, *Battle of Fort Stedman*, 41; OR 46, pt. 1, 336.

as far as Fort Stedman, into which, almost immediately, from a direction about perpendicular to the line of our charge, came a portion of the Third Division."[114]

Adjutant Clarke wrote that Hartranft's two brigades charged with "the right aiming at Fort Stedman, the left to sweep up the line, and the center directed on Battery No. 11 . . . the 57th Massachusetts swept up to their own works, and every gap of escape was promptly closed, except on the right of Battery No. 10 to a point about halfway to Battery No. 9." General Hartranft provided this summary of the recapture of Fort Stedman by his Pennsylvania regiments (Federal left to right): The 208th stormed Batteries No. 11 and 12 and the lines to the fort; the 207th carried the west angle of Fort Stedman; the 205th and 211th the rear; the 200th the east angle; and the 209th carried Battery No. 10 and the remaining line to the right.[115]

After the war, during his successful campaign for the governorship of Pennsylvania, Hartranft would take the lion's share of credit for the recapture of Fort Stedman. Conversely, Captain Carter of the 3rd Maryland insisted Hartranft's two brigades and the other troops on the plain behind Stedman merely occupied a fort that had already been recaptured by the resurgent troops of the first division. (General Willcox agreed and supported his position by pointing to the nearly 1,000 prisoners and seven battle flags taken by his men.) Moreover, Carter claimed that as he passed through the Federal works alone, he convinced a Confederate regimental commander to surrender his entire unit in front of Fort Stedman. This display of bravado nearly cost Carter his life—first when he prematurely demanded the enemy surrender before any Federal troops had come into view, and again, when he brandished the surrendered Confederate flag and drew fire from Federal soldiers who mistook him for a "Johnnie Reb."[116]

Although Robinson's men of the 3rd Maryland and 100th Pennsylvania came away with only one battle flag, they claimed the capture of a large number of prisoners. Clarke wrote that upon regaining the Federal line, "the rear rank of Robinson's troops was promptly faced about from Battery No. 10 to Battery No. 12. We had charged past the right flank of the enemy and were in the rear of his right wing." The Federals were immediately confronted by a Confederate line of battle bearing down on them. When their calls for surrender went unheeded, the Northern soldiers braced for the attack. But as the graycoats drew near, "their guns began to be cast upon the ground, the line turned to the left, and the order, 'Strip off

114 *OR* 46, pt. 1, 332.

115 *OR* 46, pt. 1, 345; Hartranft, "The Recapture of Fort Stedman," 589.

116 Scott, *Forgotten Valor*, 619, 623-625.

your belts,' was complied with, and about 800 enlisted men and over 40 officers were prisoners of war."[117]

Other Union defenders manning the works above Stedman also told tales of wholesale captures. Captain John C. Boughton, commanding the 2nd Michigan in Battery No. 9, sought to cut off "Johnnies" escaping through "a ravine that runs laterally from the right of Stedman to the Appomattox." Boughton claimed his men "charged line with them to the foot of Spring Hill, and cut off the retreat and captured something over 300 prisoners. . . . Twenty minutes before 7 o'clock we re-occupied the picket-line."[118]

Major Theodore Miller, Tidball's inspector of artillery, had been passing word of the Confederate attack to Union batteries when he was intercepted by Confederates in the early morning darkness. To escape the bombardment of dueling cannons, Major Miller and his captors took cover in a bombproof near Fort Stedman. Given the fading morale of the Confederate soldiers, "and seeing our troops charging triumphantly into the fort, I started with my guards in a keen run toward our lines, calling on all the rebels around and near me to fall in and follow me, and I am happy to report that I succeeded in bringing about 250 or 300 of the enemy in this manner into our lines."[119]

Lieutenant Val H. Stone had been directing the fire from Battery No. 9 for almost three hours when, "At 8 a.m. some few of the enemy surrendered and came into the fort. One of the rebel officers informed me if I would cease firing that there were 200 or 300 who were under my fire (I was firing canister then) would come in. I did so, and some 300 came in." Stone was told by the same Confederate officer that if he had waited ten minutes to commence firing when the Confederate line had first approached before dawn, the Carolinians of Ransom's brigade would have taken both Battery No. 9 and Fort McGilvery.[120]

---

117 Anderson, *The Fifty-Seventh Regiment Massachusetts Volunteers*, 282.

118 *OR* 46, pt. 1, 327.

119 *OR* 46, pt. 1, 358-360.

120 *OR* 46, pt. 1, 190.

Part XI

Retreat Through A "Consuming Fire"

Weeks before Lee's attack, Union General McLaughlen had developed his own plan for a pre-dawn rush against the Confederate works opposite Fort Haskell. However, this and a similar proposal by Second Division commander Robert B. Potter had been tabled because of the risk inherent in storming heavily fortified positions. In addition, the massing of a large force would be required to execute a breach, thus raising the potential for great loss if the attack failed. In July 1864, Federal troops had successfully stormed the entrenchments flanking the Crater only to be decimated when the assault stalled. The Federals took heavy casualties when they sought refuge in the abyss created by the blast and when they retreated through the field of fire back to their own lines. As a result, General Grant decided that a frontal attack should be undertaken only when it became evident that Lee was attempting to vacate the Richmond-Petersburg defenses.[121]

Lee also knew of the risks involved, having avoided a major offensive strike on Union fortifications—unless attacked by Grant first—since as far back as the mid-May fighting around Spotsylvania Court House. According to General Walker, Lee agreed to the assault on Fort Stedman only because "desperate diseases require desperate remedies." Now, with the sun well up, the attack stalled, and the Union opposition organized and deadly, Lee's worst fears were realized. As Colonel Theodore Lyman of Meade's staff observed, "It was just the Mine turned the other way; they got in there and could not get out." The retreating Southerners found themselves exposed to an enfilading fire of artillery and musketry spewing from the deadly arc formed by the Federal infantry and batteries.[122]

The narrow corridor between the lines became little more than a killing field. "Every foot of the retreat was swept by a tremendous tempest of shot, shell, grape, canister—every missile that the engines of war cast from their iron lips," recorded regimental historians V. E. Turner and H. C. Wall of the 23rd North Carolina. "The artillery ploughed and tore up the ground so ceaselessly that in all but color the flying earth looked like a wind driven snowstorm." Many of the beleaguered

---

121 OR 46, pt. 1, 805-806.

122 Badeau, *Military History of U. S. Grant: From April 1861 to April 1865*, 3 vols., vol. 3, 449; Walker, "Gordon's Assault on Fort Stedman," 29-30; Theodore Lyman, *Meade's Headquarters 1863-1865: Letters of Colonel Theodore Lyman from the Wilderness to Appomattox* (Boston, 1922), 323.

Southerners elected to end their war by surrendering at Fort Stedman rather than risk maiming or death by going back the way they had come. The majority, however, bravely refused to give up even though they knew, as Confederate General Walker discovered, that the journey back "was a thousand times more hazardous than the advance because it was now in the full blaze of daylight." Walker joined his troops and fled at the double-quick across the "storm swept space" while the federal bullets "screeched and screamed like fiends. . . . At first I made progress at a tolerably lively gait, but I wore heavy cavalry boots, the ground was thawing under the warm rays of the sun, and great cakes of mud stuck to my boots; my speed slackened into a slow trot, then into a slow walk." To Walker, it felt as though it took him an hour to trudge back to his works and tumble, exhausted, over the parapet and into the arms of his surprised men.[123]

Many of those who survived the nightmarish journey back to their lines witnessed signal acts of bravery. When his leg was shattered, color bearer James Clark of the 56th North Carolina was seen handing off his flag. "Then," a comrade recorded, "seizing between his teeth the folds of his blanket, spread beneath him, he crawled over the ground until safely back in one of our rifle pits."[124]

One of the most poignant stories about this phase of the battle concerned Captain Joseph P. Carson of the Doles-Cooke brigade of Georgians. Carson was preparing his sharpshooters for battle the evening before the attack when his 18-year-old brother Bob appeared in camp. A courier for Gen. Philip Cook, Bob feared that his brother would be killed and demanded to accompany Joseph into battle for the purpose of retrieving his body and carrying it home to Georgia. Try as he might, Joseph could not dissuade his brother, even though "I reminded him that both of our brothers had been killed, and that our old father at home would look to him to lean on in his old age." Joseph then lent Bob his overcoat to shield him against the frigid night.

Both brothers joined the rush on Fort Stedman in the pre-dawn darkness. Joseph watched as Bob struggled to dislodge the tethered logs and spikes blocking their path into the fort. After the tide of battle turned against the Confederates and Joseph and his men began falling back, a comrade told the captain that his brother may have been killed in front of the fort. When he arrived at the spot, Joseph found his overcoat covering Bob's lifeless form. He had been shot through the heart. The surviving sibling and one of his men hoisted Bob's large frame onto their shoulders.

123 Turner and Wall, "Twenty-Third Regiment," 264; Walker, "Gordon's Assault on Fort Stedman," 28-29.

124 Graham, "Fifty-Sixth Regiment," 392.

"We started with it across the open space under a heavy fire. Neither my companion nor myself was struck," recalled Joseph, "but the body was shot through four times."[125]

General Gordon had escaped by sending his horse off with an orderly and trotting through the ravine that ran from Stedman northward toward the Appomattox River. As the last of the stragglers returned, Gordon made a quick assessment of his battered corps. To his dismay, even though he had sent three messengers, a Confederate regiment was still holding its advanced position in the Union works. Gordon told his staff that another runner must carry a withdrawal order to call back the isolated unit. Every orderly volunteered, wrote Gordon, but "Thomas G. Jones of Alabama insisted that as he was the youngest and had no special responsibilities, it should fall to his lot to incur the danger. . . . A portion of the trip was through a literal furnace of fire, but he passed through it, going and coming, without a scratch."[126]

At 8:32 a.m., General Parke telegraphed General Hunt at Meade's headquarters: "We have reoccupied Stedman and the whole line, capturing many prisoners. All is quiet now. Please send word to corps commanders to halt their troops. . . ."[127]

Part XII

Flag Of Truce

The smoke of battle had hardly settled on the scarred ground before Fort Stedman when several Confederate officers bearing a flag of truce appeared in front of the Southern lines. The delegation included Major Henry Kyd Douglas, Gordon's assistant adjutant general, who was "directed to open communications with the enemy at once, that the wounded between the lines might be cared for." His small delegation stood there for almost thirty minutes before Federal officers

---

125 Thomas, *Doles-Cook Brigade*, 42.

126 "Mr. Edward Crapsey's Letter," *Philadelphia Inquirer*, March 28, 1865, 1; Henry A. Chambers, *Diary of Captain Henry A. Chambers*, T. H. Pearce, ed. (Wilmington, 1983), 253; Gordon, *Reminiscences*, 412.

127 *OR* 46, pt. 3, 150.

ventured out to parley.[128] Major John D. Bertolette of General Hartranft's staff received the flag and read the handwritten message presented to him by Douglas: it was a formal request from General Gordon to retrieve the Confederate wounded and dead.[129]

While such a request was to be expected, IX Corps commander General Parke did not respond immediately. Grant had warned his general officers that Lee might attack to cover a withdrawal from Petersburg, and he had urged them to take advantage of this contingency. With communications fully restored, army headquarters had telegraphed Parke at 8:20 a.m. to "take the offensive, if practicable." Parke responded, "As far as I can learn the enemy's artillery is still in position, and I hardly think it practicable to attack their line with my available force."[130]

With Wheaton's division of the VI Corps having come up on Parke's left, and with two more Federal divisions from the V Corps on the march toward Fort Stedman, General Meade continued pressing for a counterattack. General Hunt telegraphed Parke again at 9:20 a.m.: "Is your decision definitive that you cannot attack? Troops are halted, moving to support you. The two divisions of Fifth Corps will be ordered to move on until halted by your orders." Parke replied, "I think it too late to attack now. The enemy's lines are unchanged. They made an attack with the determination of carrying our line, but failed. . . . Their lines are evidently now fully manned and prepared for us." It was at this time, when Parke was still communicating with two of General Warren's divisions of the V Corps (Crawford's and Ayres's), that Douglas's delegation appeared. It was not until noon that Parke informed Meade's headquarters that, "Major General Gordon has requested a flag of truce for the removal of the wounded and dead between the lines. I have acceded to his request, and authorized General Hartranft to make the necessary arrangements."[131]

An hour later Meade's staff was still mulling the possibility of mounting an attack between the Crater and Fort Stedman. "The commanding general," read the message handed to Parke, "directs that you make all preliminary arrangements prior to receiving orders for attacking with your corps at points proposed by Generals Potter and McLaughlen." However, because General Grant had already issued

---

128 "Mr. Theodore C. Wilson's Dispatch: Scene Presented by the Battle Field," *New York Herald*, March 28, 1865, 1. Henry Kyd Douglas, *I Rode with Stonewall, 329*.

129 *OR* 46, pt. 3, 123.

130 *OR* 46, pt. 3, 146, 150.

131 *OR* 46, pt. 3, 152, 153.

orders that his spring campaign was to begin on March 29, and with President Lincoln now visiting the front, the order for a Federal counterattack in front of Fort Stedman never came. Instead, the truce was approved for the hours of 2:00 p.m. to 4:00 p.m.[132]

Soon after Douglas's party appeared on the field that morning, combatants on both sides recognized the white flag and ceased firing. Thousands of men mounted the parapets, "occupying all positions available to sight-seeing" to take advantage of this rare opportunity to survey the battle scene with a minimal risk of being shot. A reporter from the *New York Herald* observed that "hundreds from both sides ran out to succor the wounded and behold the killed." As he stepped onto the slope to the right of the fort, the reporter saw "large numbers of rebels, writhing in pain and covered with clotted blood." The ground in front of the fort "was strewn with arms and plentifully covered with cartridge boxes and other accoutrements. In every ditch lay numbers of the enemy's dead and wounded." There were many more wounded and dead Confederates behind Union lines.[133]

Confederate Brig. Gens. William Gaston Lewis, Matthew Ransom, William R. Cox and others joined the conference. Douglas recalled that when General Hartranft finally appeared on the scene, the program for removing the wounded and the dead was quickly negotiated. During the course of their meeting Douglas and Hartranft discovered they had attended the same college. According to Douglas, that conversation sparked their lifelong friendship.

In the meantime, Douglas continued, "Men ran over the field from each side and gathered up their comrades, taking time, when they could, to exchange pipes, tobacco, penknives, hardtack, and anything that was tradable." According to the *New York Herald,* "many of the rebel privates left their line, and walked out to communicate with our men, and not perhaps very strange to relate, some fifty or more forgot to go back." When they realized what was going on, Confederate officers, among them General James Walker, rode out and put an end to the commiserating, hurrying the men back to their former positions.[134]

The battlefield was virtually clear of soldiers when Douglas presented the Union party with his "ghastly" receipt: "Received of Major [John D.] Bertolette 120 dead and 15 wounded in the engagement of the 25th March 1865." The

---

132 *OR* 46, pt. 3, 46, 153, 159.

133 "Mr. Theodore Wilson's Dispatch," 1.

134 Douglas, *I Rode with Stonewall,* 329; "Mr. Charles H. Hannam's Dispatch: Rebel Flag of Truce," *New York Herald,* March 28, 1865, 1.

Confederates would honor their part of the bargain—delivering Federal wounded and a list of 600 prisoners taken—during another truce the next morning.[135]

Part XIII

The Assessment

Among the latecomers to the scene of the fight were two of Robert E. Lee's sons, Major General William H. F. "Rooney" Lee and Captain Robert E. Lee Jr., who rode ahead of cavalry coming from 40 miles away. Captain Lee saw the dispiriting results of the morning's action in his father's face: "My brother and I had ridden ahead of the division to report its presence, when we met the General riding Traveller, almost alone, back from that part of the lines opposite the fort. Since then I have often recalled the sadness of his face, the careworn expression."[136]

The numbers compiled in General Meade's headquarters added up to the first significant Union victory of the siege since the battle of Poplar Spring Church (Peebles Farm) six months earlier. General Parke's summary of battle reports provided this listing of Federal losses sustained during the assault on Fort Stedman: 70 killed, 424 wounded, and 523 missing, for a total of 1,017. While the statistics, especially on the Confederate side, are the subject of dispute, they still pointed to a substantial Union victory. The Federal estimate of the prisoners taken—1,949 men and officers—became the generally accepted total.[137]

The prospect of seeing Confederate prisoners was one of the factors that motivated President Lincoln to make a personal visit to the front that day. Lincoln journeyed to City Point the day before to escape the prattle of Washington. The telegraph wire between Fort Stedman and City Point had been cut before dawn, and the fight was over before news indicating the gravity of the action reached Generals Grant and Meade. (Lincoln's first dispatch to Secretary of War Edwin M.

---

135 Douglas, *I Rode with Stonewall*, 329; OR 46, pt. 3, 158, 204.

136 Robert E. Lee, Captain, *Recollections and Letters of General Robert E. Lee* (Garden City, 1924), 147.

137 OR 46, pt. 1, 185, 316.

Stanton that morning spoke only of "a little rumpus up the line, ending about where it began.")[138]

When more details became available after the restoration of the telegraph, Lincoln sought to entrain for a previously scheduled review on the Western front, with a stop at Meade's Station for a look at Fort Stedman along the way. General Tidball claimed that when the President viewed the battlefield from the crest above Meade's Station, he got caught up in the moment: "The President, meeting General Hartranft, and supposing him to have done it all, dubbed him then and there a major general." The president completed his assessment of the prisoners taken upon his arrival at Patrick Station, near Poplar Spring Church on the Western front. When Meade offered him a report from General Parke on the action, Lincoln was reported to have pointed at the captives brought there, saying, "Ah, there is the best dispatch you can show me from General Parke."[139]

Estimates of other casualties on the Southern side—killed and wounded—were and remain incomplete because of the breakdown of the Confederate reporting system during the last days of the war. Southern participants challenged early Union estimates as unduly excessive, due in part to the perception of many observers that relatively low numbers of Southern troops were actively engaged on the battlefield. Opposing generals at the center of the action estimated that only 10,000 to 12,000 Confederates participated in the attack, rather than the 18,000 allegedly promised. After the war, Captain Frederick Phisterer compiled detailed statistics for Scribner's *Campaigns of the Civil War*. Phisterer concluded that total Southern losses in all categories at Stedman were 2,681—about seven percent of Lee's remaining effective troops.[140]

General Lee downplayed the scope and significance of his losses in his initial, terse report to Southern president Jefferson Davis, perhaps because he knew his communiqué would soon be published in the Richmond newspapers and then reprinted across the country. Lee's description of the action stated,

---

138 Porter, "Campaigning with Grant," 597.

139 James Sanford Barnes, "With Lincoln from Washington to Richmond in 1865," *The Magazine of History with Notes and Queries*, no. 161, vol. 41, no. 1, 41 (This is a reprint of an article that appeared in *Appleton's Magazine* in 1907); Scott, *Forgotten Valor*, 636; Lyman, *Meade's Headquarters*, 325.

140 Walker, "Gordon's Assault on Fort Stedman," 24; Hartranft, "The Recapture of Fort Stedman," 584. Confederate General Walker estimated 10,000 Confederates, while Union General Hartranft believed the number to be 10,000 to 12,000; Hodgkins, *Battle of Fort Stedman*, 45-46. Phisterer's total represents 8.34 percent of the estimate of 32,000 troops available to Lee below the Appomattox as developed by J. C. Babcock for General Meade. Babcock's dispatch to Meade dated March 25, 1865. See *OR* 46, pt. 3, 116.

At daylight this morning, Gen. Gordon assaulted and carried the enemy's works at Hare's Hill, capturing nine pieces of artillery and eight mortars and between five and six hundred prisoners, among them one Brigadier General and a number of officers at lower grades. The lines were swept for a distance of 400 to 500 yards to the right and left and two efforts made to recover the captured works were handsomely repulsed; but it was found that the inclosed works in the rear, commanding the enemy's main line, could only be taken at a great sacrifice, and the troops were withdrawn to their original position.

It being impracticable to bring off the captured guns, owing to the nature of the ground, they were disabled and left.

Our loss reported is not heavy. . . .[141]

General Gordon also filed what might best be called a skeletal (though overly optimistic) report, conceding only that, "The loss to my command in killed, wounded and prisoners probably exceeded that of the enemy."[142]

Many participants and observers, including Confederate military men, questioned Lee's judgment in launching the attack at all. Many thought it was nothing more than a "forlorn hope" and said and wrote as much. To General Grant's aide and chronicler, Adam Badeau, "It seemed almost as if the great defender was becoming dazed by misfortune, and finding himself shut in by lines of soldiers that he could not break, was madly dashing against the walls that he had no hope of penetrating."[143]

Union Major General Andrew A. Humphreys, in writing his history of the Virginia campaign, stated that Lee's plan of attack was fatally flawed in that the "three forts" required for inflicting a break in the Union line were non-existent. Humphreys argued that Lee should have instead sought to widen the breach, focusing his resources on Battery No. 9 and Fort Haskell. Brigadier General Henry L. Abbott, the IX Corps engineering chief, concurred in the importance of the

---

141 General Robert E. Lee's report of operations from February 5-8 and March 25, 1865 are found in OR 46, pt. 1, 382-383.

142 Major General John Brown Gordon's report, dated April 11, 1865, can be found in Janet Hewett, ed., OR *Supplement,* vol. 46, no. 95, 794-795.

143 Badeau, *Military History of U. S. Grant,* 449-450.

flanking forts: "If the inclosed works on right and left had not fixed a limit beyond which the enemy could not extend, I think a great disaster might have occurred."[144]

However, other experts saw the merit of Gordon's plan and Lee's agreement to launch it. Having anticipated just such an attack, General Grant allowed that, "The plan was very well conceived and the execution of it well done indeed, up to the point of carrying a portion of our line."[145] Artillery officer John Tidball disagreed with Humphreys's view that the "three forts," deemed of such importance by Gordon, were non-existent. After the war he stated in a letter to former Union general Orlando Willcox that Fort Friend, Battery No. 4, and Fort Avery were "no doubt" the "chief objective points" named by General Gordon and others. Fort Avery, Tidball argued . . .

> was in rear of that part of our line held by Potter's Division and in the same line with Fort Friend and Battery No. 4. Like these it was a regularly constructed enclosed work, mounting at that time, four 4-1/2 siege rifles, which commanded with their fire that part of our line from Fort Haskell to Fort Rice. Battery No. 4 was armed with three 30 pdr. Parrotts, commanding all that part of the line from the Appomattox to Battery No. 9. Fort Friend, being near your headquarters, was a strong little work.

> These were important works, judiciously located and armed as a provision against any break that the enemy might make in our line—such as did occur at Stedman. . . .

According to Tidball, Humphreys's error was later repeated in the writings of Phil Sheridan and others.[146]

Captain B. F. Dixon of the 49th North Carolina expressed the frustration of many Southerners by lamenting the fact that Ransom's brigade was not supported when it swept northward toward Battery No. 9: "I have always been able to find some sort of excuse for failures, but in this instance I stand to-day as I did on that day, and unhesitatingly say, 'Somebody blundered.'"[147]

The failure of Confederate supports remained an issue for decades. Humphreys quotes from a postwar statement by Gordon to the effect that the

---

144 Humphreys, *The Virginia Campaign of '64 and '65*, 317; OR 46, pt. 1, 172.

145 Grant, *Personal Memoirs of Ulysses S. Grant*, 408.

146 Scott, *Forgotten Valor*, 628.

147 B. F. Dixon, "Additional Sketch: Forty-Ninth Regiment," Clark, *North Carolina Regiments*, vol. 3, 158. H. A. London, Editor, "Battle of Fort Stedman," *The Chatham Record*, Wednesday, March 27, 1912.

reinforcements [Pickett's division] from James Longstreet's Corps "were delayed by the breaking down of trains, or by some other cause, and did not arrive at the appointed hour, which caused so great a delay that we did not get into the fort and upon the enemy's flank at as early an hour as was expected, and daylight found us with the plan only half executed."[148] Telegraphic records show that Lee alerted Gordon on the day before that the arrival of Pickett's division was questionable and that substitute troops were available. However, of all the additional brigades called to supplement Gordon's Second Corps troops, only Ransom's appeared on the field on time. Although the other five brigades had arrived after midnight on March 24, Wallace's came up late from its position on the left of Ransom, and the remaining four were not called up to attack Fort Stedman. Still, Gordon stuck to his story (quoted here by a Union veteran in 1904) and refused to shoulder any of the blame:

> Why did we fail? I'll tell you why. God did not intend that we should succeed. . . . He caused the axle of the last tender of the last section of the train that was bringing troops from Richmond to break, thus delaying the entire body of troops from reaching us. Had they arrived I believe that we should have captured City Point that morning. . . . God was in command."[149]

For General Willcox, the dramatic repulse of the assault provided vindication of his maligned Union division for its performance at the Crater: "[T]he result was, so far as I was concerned, more glorious in this case than it was disastrous in that, because besides those killed and wounded, my division captured 953 officers & men & 8 flags—which was more than my loss at the Crater in killed, wounded and missing." The *New York Times* concluded that the battle also vindicated General Parke and the troops of the IX Corps, opining that they "have in this affair paid the rebels back for their defeat at the explosion of the Petersburg mine, and henceforth will be held in as high esteem by them as any other in our army."[150]

The repulse at Fort Stedman elated General Meade, who exclaimed, "Wish they would try it every day." Late on the day of the failed attack Meade issued General Orders No. 13, which expressed hearty congratulations to the army on "the success of the operations of yesterday." Various units who took part in the action on March 25, 1865, were cited for their "firm bearing" and "conspicuous

148 Humphreys, *The Virginia Campaign of '64 and '65*, 320.

149 Trudeau, *The Last Citadel*, 354.

150 Scott, *Forgotten Valor*, 619; *New York Times*, March 28, 1865, 1.

gallantry." However, Meade assigned blame for the initial Confederate breakthrough to "the reprehensible want of vigilance of the Third Brigade, First Division, Ninth Corps." The censure appalled General Parke, who vigorously protested in favor of General McLaughlen and his men and pled with Meade to strike the statement from the record. Meade eventually acceded to his request, but not before copies of General Orders No. 13 had been printed and widely circulated. Meade's staff scrambled to quash the original version, but it was still read on parade before units of the Army of the Potomac, and it appeared in some East Coast newspapers.[151]

General Meade concluded General Orders No. 13 with an admonition for his troops to benefit from their experiences of that day:

> Two lessons can be learned from these operations: One that no fortified line, however strong, will protect an army from any intrepid and audacious enemy, unless vigilantly guarded; the other, that no disaster or misfortune is irreparable where energy and bravery are displayed in the determination to recover what is lost and to promptly assume the offensive.[152]

As suggested by the last line of Meade's order, the work of the day did not end with the recapture of Fort Stedman. Grant had anticipated that Lee might attempt a pre-emptive strike and withdraw from Petersburg before the Federals could "recover from their consternation." Grant's generals also knew that for Lee to mass his forces opposite Fort Stedman, he must have drawn off large numbers of troops from other points along the armed corridor. The failed Confederate assault was an invitation for a Federal counterattack elsewhere.[153]

When he received news of the assault on Fort Stedman, Grant telegraphed Major General John Gibbon, now commanding the XXIV Corps of the Army of the James: "The enemy have attacked on General Parke's front and broken through his line. This may be a signal for leaving. Be ready to take advantage of it."[154] Meade, as noted earlier, pressed Parke to counterattack with his IX Corps, but Parke continued to urge caution, stating that the formidable Confederate defenses in his front remained intact and fully manned. Still, the violent eruption at Fort Stedman

---

151 Nevins, ed., *The Personal Journals of Colonel Charles S. Wainwright*, 504; OR 46, pt. 3, 174, 222.

152 *OR* 46, pt. 3, 174.

153 Humphreys, *The Virginia Campaign or '64 and '65*, 320-321.

154 *OR* 46, pt. 3, 162.

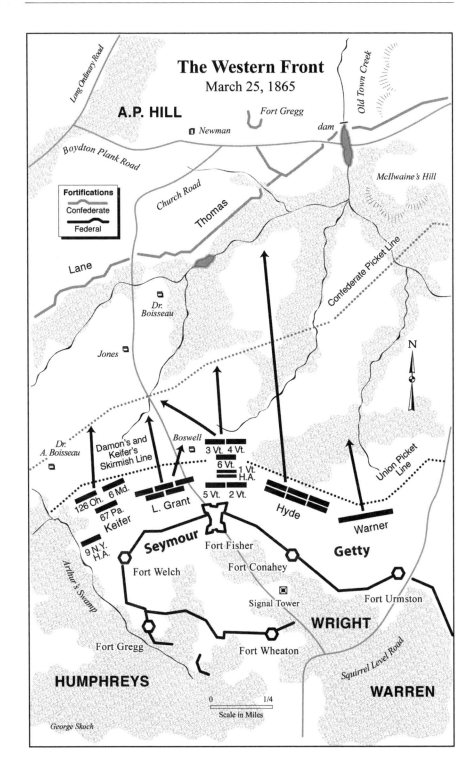

The Western Front
March 25, 1865

A.P. HILL

Fort Gregg

Newman

dam

Old Town Creek

McIlwaine's Hill

Boydton Plank Road

Long Ordinary Road

Fortifications
Confederate
Federal

Church Road

Thomas

Lane

Dr. Boisseau

Jones

Confederate Picket Line

N

Dr. A. Boisseau

Damon's and Keifer's Skirmish Line

Boswell

3 Vt. 4 Vt.

6 Vt.
1 Vt. H.A.

5 Vt. 2 Vt.

Hyde

Union Picket Line

Warner

126 Oh. 6 Md.

67 Pa.

L. Grant

Keifer

9 N.Y. H.A.

Getty

Seymour

Fort Fisher

Fort Conahey

Fort Welch

Signal Tower

Fort Urmston

WRIGHT

Arthur's Swamp

Fort Gregg

Fort Wheaton

Squirrel Level Road

HUMPHREYS

0   1/4
Scale in Miles

WARREN

George Skoch

sent aftershocks rumbling down the entire fault line formed by the opposing armies on the Western front.

Part XIV

Union Counter-Attacks on the Western Front

While General Parke was contemplating a flag of truce offered by the defeated Confederates in front of Fort Stedman, his fellow corps commanders on the other side of Petersburg—Humphreys and Wright—were already going on the offensive. Grant had warned his generals that Lee might attempt a pre-emptive strike as prelude to withdrawal west. Knowing that Lee must draw off troops from other portions of his line to mount such an assault, the Federals immediately began probing his defenses along the entire four-mile arc between Hatcher's Run to the west and Rohoic Creek (aka Old Town Creek) to the east.[155]

On the Western Front, Arthur's Swamp bisected the lines on a northwest to southeast course, passing just below Fort Fisher, the centerpiece of the Union line here. Below the swamp, Humphreys' II Corps faced west toward Henry Heth's Confederate division, while above the marshy ground Horatio Wright's VI Corps lined up opposite Cadmus Wilcox's division to the north, which was screened by the recent inundation of Rohoic Creek.

Anchoring the Federal left, Humphreys telegraphed Parke at 7:25 a.m., "I ordered out a reconnaissance some time ago. Shall I drive in the enemy's pickets all along my line, and, if I find his works slimly held attack him?" At this early hour, Parke still spoke for the Army of the Potomac: "The enemy hold Fort Stedman and are pressing us. [Yet] If their lines are weakened in your front I think it well to take advantage of it." Humphreys assigned Major General Nelson Miles, commanding his First Division, with the task.[156]

At 9:00 a.m., the 25-year-old Miles "threw out" two reconnoitering parties to "feel the enemy." Colonel George W. Scott of the First Brigade led skirmishers comprised of 200 men from the 61st New York Volunteers and 100 men from the 53rd Pennsylvania Volunteers. On Miles's right, the Pennsylvanians quickly drove

---

155 Porter, "Campaigning with Grant," 596.

156 OR 46, pt. 3, 121. This "Fort Fisher" below Petersburg should not be confused with the mammoth fort of the same name guarding the approach to Wilmington, North Carolina.

in skirmishers of McComb's Tennesse Brigade below Arthur's Swamp, and, to the left the New Yorkers met stiff resistance before seizing the Confederate picket line near Watkin's House. Before noon, Brigadier General Henry J. Madill, the division officer of the day, led the skirmishers forward again. The Federals occupied the length of the enemy's picket line across Miles's front; Scott brought up his entire brigade, and the Irish brigade of Col. Robert Nugent also moved "impetuously" forward.[157]

At noon, VI Corps commander General Wright mounted a similar attack to the left of Fort Fisher. Lieutenant Colonel George B. Damon advanced with 230 skirmishers of the 10th Vermont and 160 more from the 14th New Jersey. Lieutenant Colonel Binkley led supporting troops of the 110th and 122nd Ohio regiments. However, despite the best efforts of Colonel Damon, the mile-long line was driven back in disarray under "volleys of heavy musketry" from the Confederate rifle pits. Wright attacked again at 3:00 p.m. with a more robust force, with General Joseph Kiefer leading his brigade. The skirmish line was augmented on the left by the 10th Vermont and on the right by the 110th and 122nd Ohio regiments, supported by a column comprised of the 67th Pennsylvania, 6th Maryland, 9th New York Heavy Artillery, and 126th Ohio regiments.[158]

This time, with the visiting President Lincoln watching the action from nearby Fort Wadsworth, Wright's men quickly overran the picket pits to the left of Church Road. The men of Sam McGowan's brigade of South Carolinians, holding the Confederate center above Arthur's Swamp, saw the attack coming. Sharpshooter Berry Benson wrote:

> Our men, kneeling in the pits, take good aim and we can see how busy they are. It is but a minute before the enemy's line falters, appears about to break and flee. But look. The color bearer runs forward alone with his flag. With a shout that rings again, the blue line follows in a swift charge through our deadliest fire. They reach the works, and turning right and left, they sweep the line in both directions for a long distance, taking possession of half a mile of rifle pits.[159]

---

157 Williams, "Gen. Grant's Army, The Victory of Saturday . . . From Our Special Correspondent," *New York Times*, March 29, 1865, 1.

158 *OR* 46, pt. 1, 307.

159 Susan Benson Williams, *Berry Benson's Civil War Book: Memoirs of a Confederate Scout and Sharpshooter*, (Athens: 1992), p 177.

Wright's supporting troops pushed beyond the attacking force's front line, with Brigadier General Louis Grant's Vermonters charging past the Jones house.[160] Edwin Hyde's brigade of Getty's division veered to the right of the house, advancing in "mad career" before arriving at an impassable marsh beyond the Confederate rifle pits. General Lee challenged the Georgia regiments of Cadmus Wilcox's division, just back from the Stedman front, to regain the lost ground. Brigadier General James Lane, commanding the division due to Wilcox's illness, chose the 45th and 49th Georgia for the assignment. Colonel Simmons of the 49th Georgia led the charge downhill to strike the Federals like "a thousand bricks," pushing the bluecoats back to the Confederate picket line, from which point he engaged the enemy for the rest of the afternoon.[161]

To relieve pressure on his II Corps, General Humphreys launched a diversion on his left across Hatcher's Run. From General Hayes' division, held in reserve, Brigadier General William Smyth ordered out a contingent of 500 men from his brigade under Lieutenant Colonel S. A. Moore of the 4th Connecticut Heavy Artillery (reorganized from the 14th Connecticut Volunteers). Smyth's troops of the 12th New Jersey and the 69th and 106th Pennsylvania Volunteers drove the 60th Alabama from Crow's Ford to advance within sight of Boydton Plank Road. Smyth brought up his entire brigade in support, but Humphreys refused to spare any more troops for this sortie, and Smyth waited in his exposed position west of the Crow house.

Though vastly outnumbered, the Confederates pushed back hard against Humphreys above Hatcher's Run. Late in the afternoon, Cooke's brigade of North Carolinians returned from the scene of the Crater battlefield to join the defense with Young Moody's brigade (formerly Archibald Gracie's of Alabama, Bushrod Johnson's division, Richard Anderson's Corps). Attacking in the wake of Smyth's diversion, Cooke's sharpshooters drove Brigadier General McAllister's brigade back to an intermediate position in the contested corridor. At dusk, however, Moody's counterattack with the 41st, 43rd, and 59th Alabama regiments met with disaster. Apparently unaware that Federals still occupied the line vacated by the 5th New Hampshire above Watkins house, Moody's troops were decimated when they

---

160 OR 46, pt. 1, 304.

161 Thomas Hyde, *Following the Greek Cross, or Memories of the Sixth Army Corps* (New York, 1894), 243-244; John Hardeman, Company F, 45th Georgia Regiment, "In the Trenches Near Petersburg, VA, March 28, 1865." Army Heritage Education Center Collections, Carlisle, PA, and is quoted in William B. Styple, *Writing and Fighting from the Army of Northern Virginia, A Collection of Confederate Correspondence* (Kearny, 2003), 312-313.

charged "as if on drill" into the well-entrenched 124th New York commanded by Col. Charles Weygant.

At Skinner's Farm, Joe Davis's Mississippi brigade and MacRae's sharpshooters from North Carolina charged Colonel Nugent's Second "Irish" Brigade of Miles's division about 2:30 p.m., and when that failed, again at 4:10 p.m. Later, McComb's Tennessee brigade returned from The Crater to add weight to perhaps the heaviest fighting on the Western front. One reporter claimed that "the musketry firing was not surpassed by the battles of the Wilderness and Spotsylvania Court House." The Irish Brigade stood up to the work, but not without the support of Col. Augustus Funk's brigade, William Mintzer's brigade, and detachments from Griffin's division of the V Corps.[162]

It was not until 11:50 p.m. that night before General Humphreys confirmed his II Corps held the entrenched former Confederate picket line from the C. Smith house (just below Arthur's Swamp) southward to the Armstrong house near Hatcher's Run. From that point to Hatcher's Run, Humphreys had taken and held an intermediate line between the opposing rifle pits. By this time Smyth's brigade had been withdrawn from its unsupported position beyond Hatcher's Run.[163] In addition to any killed and wounded, Humphreys also claimed the capture of 365 Rebel prisoners.

Above Arthur's Swamp, the men of George Thomas' Confederate brigade, supported by artillery from the Norfolk Blues and sharpshooters from McGowan's brigade contested the fighting across the Jones farm for about two hours. Then, at 6:00 p.m., they watched as the Federals formed a mile-long line of battle in front of Fort Fisher. "The hill was blue as far as we could see, both to the right and left," wrote a Rebel captain in a letter home. "Our two regiments, numbering in all about 400 guns, fought them until they were within 50 yards of our front or works, they had nearly surrounded us, they having 5000, we 400! Our ammunition was about this time completely expended, and Colonel Simmons gave us orders to fall back. We had a hill of 250 yards to run up," he continued, "the enemy firing into us both right and left. We knew if we escaped it would be a miracle."[164]

---

162 J. L. Rhodes, "The Fight at Hatcher's Run: Mr. J. L. Rhodes' Letter," *Philadelphia Inquirer*, March 28, 1865, 1; *OR* 46 pt. 1, 210.

163 *OR* 46, pt. 3, 128.

164 Hardeman, Company F, 45th Georgia Regiment, "In the Trenches Near Petersburg, VA, March 28, 1865." According to Capt. Washington C. Irvine, the 14th and 35th Georgia regiments "moved in to help prevent" the capture of troops of the surrounded 45th and 49th regiments. John Fox, *Red Clay to Richmond, Trail of the 35th Georgia Infantry Regiment, C. S. A.* (Winchester, 2005), 296-297.

The long Union line of battle that overwhelmed the Confederate defenders comprised the brigades of Hyde, Warner, Hamblin, and Edwards, plus Damon's skirmishers. It rolled all the way across the broad corridor to the Southern works before falling back toward the overrun picket line. The action climaxed when Oliver Edward's troops of Wheaton's Union division fought off a double skirmish line from Alfred Scale's brigade to wrest control of McIlwaine's Hill overlooking the Boydton Plank Road.[165]

General Wright filed his battle reports the next day. He concluded that his VI Corps had moved his line forward an average of one-half a mile, and that this improved position had been hardened overnight.[166] Wright claimed that his corps netted 547 prisoners, raising Lee's losses for the day to about 4,000.

The importance of the Union successes of March 25, 1865, would be reflected in General Grant's subsequent report on the completion of the Richmond Campaign. In it, Grant concluded that Wright's proximity to the enemy set the stage for his breakthrough following the decisive battle at Five Forks farther west one week later. "The result of the offensive effort of the enemy the week before, when he [Lee] assaulted Fort Stedman, particularly favored this," explained Grant. "The enemy's entrenched picket-line captured by us at that time threw the lines occupied by the belligerents so close together at some points that it was but a moment's run from one to the other."[167]

*   *   *

The next day, March 26, General Lee sent a dispatch to President Davis reviewing the military situation and his rationale for the sortie on Fort Stedman. "I fear now it will be impossible to prevent a junction between Grant and Sherman," Lee concluded, "nor do I deem it prudent that this army should maintain its position until the latter shall approach too near."[168]

---

165 Elisha Hunt Rhodes, *The Second Rhode Island Volunteers at the Siege of Petersburg, Virginia,* (Providence, 1911), 28-29.

166 *OR* 46, pt. 3, 181-182.

167 *OR* 46, pt 1, 53.

168 Freeman, *Lee's Dispatches,* 341.

Editor's Conclusion

Planning for the daring attack included the participation of Gordon's II Corps, Pickett's division, two brigades from Cadmus Wilcox's division, two brigades from Bushrod Johnson's division and W. H. F. Lee's cavalry division. Most of the Confederates did not arrive in time for the attack, and the Confederates were driven back with heavy losses. The attack had no effect upon Union operations, and Lee lost thousands of veterans he could ill afford.

By weakening Wilcox's front (Lee's right) in preparation for the Fort Stedman effort, Lee gave the Federals of the II and VI corps the opportunity to seize parts of the picket line and capture hundreds of prisoners. The new Union position was now dangerously close to Confederate lines. It was from this front that the VI corps would advance on the morning of April 2 to break through Wilcox's lines and force the evacuation of Petersburg and Richmond.

Federal losses during the Fort Stedman operation were actually much higher than many sources, usually relate, and in fact totaled 2,087; Lee's Confederates however, lost about double that at 4,000.[169]

---

169 Horn, *The Petersburg Campaign*, 33.

Chapter 5

Prelude to the Five Forks Campaign

Battle of Lewis Farm (Quaker Road)

March 29-30, 1865

Editor's Introduction

Lieutenant General U.S. Grant's goal for this, his seventh offensive, was to force the Confederates out of their lines to defeat them in the open, and sever the South Side Railroad, one of the last two major logistical lifeline feeding Richmond and Petersburg. He planned a huge wheeling movement to outflank and turn the Confederate right flank to accomplish it. The Army of the Potomac's II Corps, under Maj. Gen. A. A. Humphreys, would cross Hatcher's Run on the Vaughan Road and Maj. Gen. Gouverneur Warren would form his V Corps on Humphreys's left at the junction of the Vaughan and Quaker roads. On the far left, Maj. Gen. Phil Sheridan, with Brig. Gen. Ranald Mackenzie's Army of the James cavalry, the Army of the Potomac's cavalry under Maj. Gen. George Crook (commanding what had been David McM. David Gregg's cavalry division), and the cavalry from the Army of the Shenandoah, would ride to Dinwiddie Court House.

On the night of March 25, Maj. Gen. Edward O. C. Ord pulled three divisions of the Army of the James out of the Bermuda Hundred and Richmond lines and arrived at Petersburg about 5:00 p.m. on the 28th. His departure was so secretive that Confederate Lt. Gen. James Longstreet did not realize the Federals had left his front. Sheridan, meanwhile, crossed to the south side of the James River March 27. Mackenzie's cavalry left the

Richmond lines on the night of the 28th, arrived in position the next evening and formed in rear of II Corps. Grant gave Mackenzie's troopers the job of protecting Warren's V Corps wagon train.

On the evening of March 28, the Union troops were arranged as follows: Three divisions of the XXIV Corps and XXV Corps held the trenches outside Richmond, while another division of the XXV Corps manned the Bermuda Hundred lines; Maj. Gen. John G. Parke's IX Corps held the ground from the Appomattox River on the right to Fort Davis, with Maj. Gen. Horatio Wright's VI Corps watching the front extending from Fort Davis to Arthur's Swamp; on Wright's left, Humphreys with II Corps held the line from Arthur Swamp to Hatcher's Run, where the Vaughan Road crossed it; Warren's V Corps was behind Humphreys, and Sheridan's cavalry was at Hancock Station on the military railroad; Ord's Army of the James infantry took the place of II Corps, with its line extending all the way to Hatcher's Run.

Grant's intent was to have the Army of the Potomac, except IX Corps, available for the campaign. The result was that Maj. Gen. George G. Meade, the commander of the Army of the Potomac, had some 60,000 men ready to go, Ord brought 17,000 infantry and 1,500 cavalry under Mackenzie, and Sheridan had 12,000 cavalry from the Army of the Shenandoah and the army of the Potomac. The disposable force available for the capture of Petersburg was 70,000.

Grant's orders to Sheridan for this offensive were issued on March 24:

> You may go out the nearest roads in rear of the Fifth Corps, pass by its left, and passing near to or through Dinwiddie, reach the right and rear of the enemy as soon as you can. It is not the intention to attack the enemy in his intrenched positions, but to force him out if possible. Should he come out and attack us or get himself where he can be attacked, move in with your entire force in your own way and with the full reliance that the army will engage or follow . . . as circumstances will dictate. I shall be on the field and will probably be able to communicate with you. Should I not do so, and you find the enemy keeps within his main intrenched line, you may cut loose and push for the Danville road. If you find it practicable, I would like you to cross the South Side railroad between Petersburg and Burkesville and destroy it to some extent.[1]

---

1   *OR* 46, pt. 3, 234.

Note that Grant's first priority was to force the Confederates out of their lines so Sheridan could defeat them. The destruction of the railroad was a secondary objective to be accomplished only if the first was not possible. Also note that Grant promised to come to Sheridan's aid: "Should he come out and attack us, or get himself where he can be attacked, move in with your entire force in your own way, and with the full reliance that the army will engage or follow, as circumstances will dictate." Once having destroyed the railroad, Sheridan could either return to Grant's army group or ride south and join Maj. Gen. William T. Sherman, who was advancing north through North Carolina toward Virginia.

Three days later on March 27, Meade dictated Grant's orders for the campaign to the Army of the Potomac. In essence, the plan called for the cavalry and the II Corps and V Corps to cross to the west side of Hatcher's Run. The infantry would push the Confederates into their lines and keep them from sending troops west to oppose the sweeping cavalry. Meanwhile, XXIV Corps and XXV Corps troops from the Army of the James—which had slipped away undetected from Longstreet's front outside Richmond north of the James River—would hold the ground vacated by the II Corps.

It is impossible to explain what trick of mental gymnastics enabled Grant to issue orders that said one thing to Sheridan ("Should he come out and attack us, or get himself where he can be attacked, move in with your entire force in your own way, and with the full reliance that the army will engage or follow, as circumstances will dictate") and something very different to Meade that essentially immobilized the Army of the Potomac in front of Lee's trenches (with the possible exception of Wright's VI Corps)? How could Meade assist Sheridan with his "entire force" if it was pinned down in front of the Confederate lines?

This offensive was the same basic plan that had failed time and again during Grant's previous offensives. In each case, instead of sending a mobile column strong enough to achieve his goal, Grant immobilized all but a fraction of his infantry by advancing them as close to the Confederate lines as possible. This strategy had two goals. First, Grant hoped that if the Confederates weakened their line to oppose the turning movement, he would be close enough to attack and break through. Second, he hoped that by pressing against the Confederate lines, he might fulfill the opposite goal of keeping the Confederates pinned down in their trenches while a relatively small command, a corps, for example, tried to turn the enemy flank to get to the South Side Railroad. In each previous effort, while the Federal flanking force floundered through woods, swamps, and along difficult road and paths, or waited in trenches for the Rebels oppositie them to strip their lines so they could assault, the Confederates did in fact strip their lines, assemble a strike force, and attack the flanking force. And so every previous effort failed. The Virginia Campaign of 1864-65 is replete with examples of Grant attempting to achieve too many goals with too little force, and failing to achieve any of them.

The first battle of what should be viewed as the Five Forks Campaign took place on March 29 at the Lewis Farm, when Warren and his V Corps attempted to approach the Confederate entrenchments as Grant had ordered. Warren was attacked there by Lt. Gen. Richard H. Anderson, but repulsed him. The second battle of the campaign took place two days later on March 31 when Warren attempted to advance on the White Oak Road. Under Gen. Robert E. Lee's watchful eye, Anderson attacked and routed two of Warren's three divisions, but the Federals eventually repulsed the attack and stood their ground.

Sheridan, meanwhile, moved to Dinwiddie Court House and was also expected to advance to the White Oak Road. Warren was continually instructed to extend his left flank and be ready to cooperate with Sheridan when he moved up to the road. Meade's orders on the 29th to both Warren and Humphreys concerning movements set for the 30th included the following: "The object of this movement is to force the enemy into his line of works and develop the same, and if he is found out of his line to give battle." Meade later acknowledged that Warren had accomplished this object in the fighting along the Quaker Road. By the end of the day on the 29th, however, Grant had still not informed Meade of the changes he was making in his operational plans. Sheridan told Grant that he would move up to the White Oak Road on the morning of the 30th to a position east of Five Forks. When Warren was informed of this move, he ordered a division under Romeyn Ayres to move toward the White Oak Road supported by another division under Samuel Crawford with the intention of cooperating with Wesley Merritt's cavalry of Sheridan's command. As it turned out, Merritt did not move as Sheridan indicated he would, but rode instead farther west. Although Sheridan reported him to be in possession of Five Forks that afternoon, this was not the case.

In making his plans for this offensive, Grant seems to have not taken into account what General Lee might do. Did it occur to Grant that Lee might do the same thing he himself had done with Ord's infantry divisions—pull men from the lines farther north? What would prevent Lee from shifting a division of infantry from north of the Appomattox River or from outside Richmond?

Part I

General U.S. Grant Prepares for Action

Following the battle of Bentonville, General Sherman's "Army Group" moved to Goldsboro, North Carolina. Here, Sherman's troops rendezvoused with the forces commanded by Maj. Gen. John M. Schofield. After arranging to have his troops take a well-merited rest, Sherman proceeded to General Grant's headquarters at City Point, Virginia.

At meetings on March 27 and 28, also attended by President Abraham Lincoln and Admiral David D. Porter in the wardroom aboard *River Queen*, Sherman explained the plan of operations which he had previously broached to Grant in a letter. Sherman stated that in case it became necessary to bring his "Army Group" to the Petersburg front to encompass the defeat of the Confederates, he would be ready to march by April 10. If he were required to make this movement, Sherman proposed first to threaten an attack on Raleigh, North Carolina. After executing this feint, Sherman's "Army Group" would veer to the right, striking the Roanoke River near Weldon, North Carolina, 60 miles south of Petersburg. At Weldon, Sherman's troops would be in an excellent position to move to Burke's Station, the junction of the South Side and the Richmond and Danville railroads. The occupation of Burke's Station would enable Sherman's "Army Group" to intercept General Robert E. Lee's Confederate army in the event that it should be compelled to fall back on either Danville or Lynchburg. If, in the meantime, Lee's hard-fighting Confederates continued to hold Grant at bay, Sherman would join the Union armies operating against Petersburg and Richmond.

Grant authorized Sherman to carry out his master plan. This was conditioned on the stipulation that Sherman received no further instructions. Grant, in turn, explained to Sherman the plan of operations that he had matured. The lieutenant general commanding stated he hoped his plan would lead to an early evacuation of the Petersburg lines by Lee's army. The meeting then adjourned, and Sherman returned to North Carolina.[2]

By the afternoon of March 28, Grant had completed his dispositions. The various units of his mobile striking force had moved into their advance staging areas and the troops were eager to take the offensive. At a staff meeting in Grant's

2   Andrew A. Humphreys, *The Virginia Campaign of '65,* 322.

City Point headquarters, a series of orders were drafted. Grant hoped these would set into motion a chain reaction which would force General Lee's army to abandon the fortifications guarding the approaches to Petersburg. Once the Confederates were driven out of the Petersburg defenses, the Union generals believed that their superior numbers and mobility would ensure the destruction of Lee's veteran army.

In accordance with the plan of operations outlined by Grant, the commander of the Army of the Potomac, General George G. Meade, prepared a set of instructions to guide his corps commanders. Maj. Gen. Andrew A. Humphreys was to hold the troops of his II Corps in their camps until 9:00 a.m. on the following day, "unless previously notified" that the Army of the James was in position. On moving out of the investment lines, Humphreys was to take position with "his right resting on or near Hatcher's Run and his left extending to the Quaker Road." Combat patrols would then be advanced. If the Confederates were discovered outside their works, Humphreys was to attack and drive them into their fortifications. The II Corps' train was to be parked near the Cummings house.[3]

Major General Gouverneur K. Warren's V Corps was alerted to be ready to march at an hour designated by Meade. Warren was admonished not to proceed beyond the junction of the Vaughan and Quaker Roads until Humphreys' troops had reached their initial battle station. After he had received information that Humphreys was in position, Warren was to advance along the Boydton Plank Road. The V Corps was to take position on Humphreys' left with his left flank refused. Warren, like Humphreys, was to throw forward a strong force of skirmishers. These would be charged with the task of driving in the Confederate outposts.

The two other corps (the VI and IX) which constituted the Army of the Potomac were to remain where they were. At the moment, these two corps were holding the investment lines east and south of Petersburg. In case the Rebels should pull troops out of the Petersburg defenses to meet the Union turning movement, the VI and IX Corps were to attack.

General Grant himself signed the order detailing the cavalry's role in the projected offensive. Maj. Gen. Philip H. Sheridan's troopers were to be on the move at the earliest possible hour on the 29th. The cavalry's line of march was not to be "confined to any particular road or roads." Grant, however, suggested that Sheridan march "by the nearest roads" passing to the rear of the staging area occupied by the V Corps. To outflank the Confederates, Sheridan, after having passed beyond the left flank of the V Corps, was to strike for Dinwiddie Court

---

3   OR 46, pt. 3, 224.

House. Grant observed that it was not his intention to attack the Rebels in their entrenchments, but to force them to abandon their powerful fortifications to avoid being encircled. In case the Southerners should leave the protection of their works and attack the cavalry column, Sheridan was to hurl his entire force against them. Grant promised Sheridan that the remainder of "the army will engage or follow the enemy as circumstances will dictate."

If the Confederates refused to take the field, Sheridan was authorized to cut loose from his base and strike for the Richmond and Danville Railroad. Furthermore, if it should prove feasible, Sheridan was to wreak havoc on the South Side Railroad at some point between Petersburg and Burke's Station. After having wrecked the two railroads, Sheridan was given two alternatives: he could either rejoin Grant's "Army Group" using a route to the south of his line of advance, or he could join General Sherman's forces in North Carolina.[4]

After reading his instructions, Sheridan walked out of Grant's cabin. The general followed, desiring to have a private conversation with the cavalry leader. A glance convinced Grant that Sheridan seemed to be "somewhat disappointed at the idea, possibly, of having to cut loose again from the Army of the Potomac, and place himself between the two armies (Lee's and Johnston's) of the enemy." Speaking up, Grant said, "General, this portion of your instructions I have put in merely as a blind." Grant then informed Sheridan that he expected the movement that was about to begin to result in the Federals' passing around Lee's right flank. This would force the Confederates to evacuate Petersburg and Richmond and lead to an early end of the long bloody conflict. Continuing, Grant remarked that "the nation had already become restless and discouraged at the prolongation of the war, and many believed that it would never terminate except by compromise." Grant informed Sheridan that the reason he had included the passages pertaining to the cavalry joining Sherman was that unless his plan proved successful it would be interpreted as a disastrous defeat.[5]

Under cover of darkness on the 27th, a portion of General Ord's Army of the James had been withdrawn from its camps on the north side of the James River. As the success of Ord's movement depended in great measure upon its secrecy, the general took a number of precautions. Several days before the projected operation, Ord quietly withdrew from the front lines most of the troops detailed to accompany his expeditionary force. After making a demonstration against the

---

4   *Ibid.*, 231, 234. Grant wished Sheridan to strike the Richmond and Danville Railroad near Burke's Station.

5   Ulysses S. Grant, *The Personal Memoirs of Ulysses S. Grant*, 2 vols. (New York, 1917), vol. 2, 300-301. All references to this source are to volume 2 unless otherwise indicated.

Confederate earthworks in the Darbytown road sector, Ord concentrated, in camps calculated to be concealed from the eyes of the Rebel scouts, the units slated to march to the Southside. The troops that were to be left behind were kept constantly on the move. Camps were shifted. Combat patrols sent out at frequent intervals to harass the Confederate outposts. To deaden the sound of the marching columns, the pontoon bridges across which the troops were scheduled to pass were covered with moist straw and compost.

When the XXIV Corps moved out, Maj. Gen. John Gibbon took two of his three divisions with him. Brig. Gen. Charles Devens' division was left behind to hold the line of works. Brig. Gen. William Birney's division of the XXV Corps also accompanied Ord when he moved to the Southside. Crossing the James River at Deep Bottom, the troops of the XXIV Corps—Brig. Gen. John W. Turner's division in the lead—marched to Broadway Landing on the Appomattox River. To avoid congestion, Birney's black division crossed the James River at Varina. Birney's troops rendezvoused with Gibbon's column at Broadway Landing.[6]

By 7:40 a.m. on the 28th, the last of Ord's infantry had crossed the Appomattox River. Turner's division, which had the lead, pushed on toward the Petersburg lines without resting. Both Gibbon's other division commanded by Brig. Gen. Robert S. Foster and Birney's division were badly jaded by the night march. Ord, therefore, permitted these two units to halt until noon. Recent heavy rains had turned the roads into ribbons of mud. Consequently, the Army of the James' trains were "much delayed." It was a number of hours before the last of the heavily loaded wagons rolled across the pontoon bridge.[7]

After the troops caught their second wind, the march was renewed. Before the afternoon was over, Foster's troops overtook Turner's division. At dusk, Gibbon's troops went into camp near Fort Siebert; and Birney's people bivouacked near Humphreys' divisions. The ground occupied by the Army of the James was immediately in the rear of the II Corps' staging area. General Gibbon was pleased with the way his troops had conducted the 36-mile march. He reported that his soldiers had performed "one of the most remarkable marches on record with very few stragglers."[8]

Ord's Cavalry, led by hard-riding Brig. Gen. Ranald S. Mackenzie, departed from its encampments on the north side of the James River on the evening of the

---

6   OR 46, pt. 1, 1160, 1173, 1179, 1236, 1238.

7   *Ibid.*, OR 46, pt. 3, 236.

8   *Ibid.*, OR 46, pt. 1, 1160, 1173, 1236, 1238.

26th. Crossing the James at Varina and the Appomattox at Point of Rocks, the cavalrymen reached Humphrey's Station at daybreak.[9]

The departure of the three divisions of infantry and one of cavalry division cut the Union strength north of the James River into two divisions. With this greatly reduced force, Maj. Gen. Godfrey Weitzel was expected to pin Lt. Gen. James Longstreet's Corps in position, while the Army of the Potomac and Sheridan's cavalry turned the Confederate right. In an effort to deceive the Southerners, the regimental bands were left behind and they played as usual. On the night of the 27th and for several nights afterwards, men detailed by Weitzel kept the fires going in the camps of the troops who had accompanied Ord

Before leaving for the Southside, General Ord, feeling certain that Grant's attempt to turn the Confederates out of their Petersburg defenses would be crowned with success, left written instructions for Weitzel's guidance in case Richmond was evacuated. Weitzel was informed as to the route he was to follow to avoid Rebel torpedoes (land mines) when he marched his men into Richmond.[10]

When General Meade received reports indicating that Ord's troops would reach the area behind the II Corps by dusk on the 28th, he re-adjusted his time table. Humphreys was alerted to have his troops on the road by 6:00 a.m. Upon receipt of this news, Humphreys drafted orders which would govern the II Corps' movements on the 29th. In accordance with Meade's directive, Humphreys announced that his troops would be ready to move at the designated hour and Vaughan Road would serve as the corps' line of advance.

Brigadier General William Hays' division would take the lead. After crossing Hatcher's Run, Hays was to deploy his troops north of the Vaughan Road. Hays' right flank was to be close enough to the stream to be covered by artillery posted at the point where the Vaughan Road crossed the river. Hays' division would also cover Dabney's Mill Road.[11]

Major General Gershom Mott's division followed Hays. After crossing Hatcher's Run, Mott's troops were to form north of the Vaughan Road. The left flank of the division was to be extended in the direction of the Gravelly Run Friends' Meetinghouse. Major General Nelson A. Miles' division would march behind Mott's. Once Miles' division had reached the right bank of Hatcher's Run,

9 *Ibid.*, 1244. When General Mackenzie's division left its camp near the New Market Road, it mustered 54 officers and 1,629 enlisted men.

10 *Ibid.*, 1160, 1227. In addition to Devens' division, Weitzel's command included Maj. Gen. August V. Kautz's division of the XXV Corps.

11 *Ibid.*, OR 46 pt. 3, 224-226.

the general was to post his troops on Mott's left. Miles' battle line was to extend from the vicinity of the Gravelly Run Friends' Meetinghouse across the Quaker Road.[12]

Each division commander was to cover his flank with a strong skirmish line. After the divisions had completed their deployment, the skirmishers were to advance and drive the Confederate outposts back inside their works.

Humphreys informed his subordinates that he expected troops from General Gibbon's XXIV Corps to relieve their outposts about 5:00 a.m. If Gibbon's troops failed to show up, Hays' people were not to delay their march. Miles and Mott, however, would each leave a brigade behind to hold the lines until Gibbon's soldiers put in an appearance.[13]

The commissary, ordnance, and quartermaster departments spent a busy day supplying the men of the II Corps. Each soldier was issued four days' rations of hardtack, coffee, and sugar. Salt meat to last one day was rationed to each individual. Enough cattle to last the Corps for three days were cut out from the army's herd. These would be driven with the division herds. In addition, sufficient hardtack, coffee, sugar, and salt to subsist the Corps for another eight days was loaded into the division supply wagons. Beef on the hoof calculated to last for ten days was allotted to the Corps herd. Forage for eight days was to be carried along on the expedition.

Instead of the usual 40 rounds of ammunition, each soldier would carry 50 on his person. Furthermore, enough ammunition to supply every soldier with another 20 rounds was loaded into the division wagons.

Since the army expected to move light and fast, the amount of artillery to be taken along was limited. One four-gun battery of 12-pounder Napoleons and one four-gun battery of 3-inch rifled artillery were to be allotted to each division. The three batteries that were to be left behind were to report to the IX Corps' chief of artillery, Brig. Gen. John C. Tidball.[14]

Meanwhile, General Warren had drafted instructions to govern the movements of his corps. Initially, Warren worked out his plans in accordance with a directive issued by Meade on the 27th. This memorandum, for some unexplained reason, was not delivered to Warren until the following afternoon. Maj. Gen.

---

12 *Ibid.*, 226.

13 *Ibid.*, 226-227. If it became necessary to leave the two brigades behind when the Corps took the field, the one from Mott's division was to be posted near the Tucker house battery and Batteries C and D. The brigade from Miles' division was to be stationed near Battery 4. *Ibid.*, 227.

14 *Ibid.*, 225-226.

Romeyn B. Ayres' division was scheduled to take the lead when the V Corps took the field. Two batteries and the Corps' pontoon train would follow close on the heels of Ayres' infantry. After breaking camp at 5:00 a.m., Ayres' troops were to cross Arthur's Swamp. Gaining the stage road, the division was to seize the crossing of Rowanty Creek near the Perkins farm. As soon as a bridgehead could be established, the pioneers were to lay a "double bridge." After the two batteries had crossed the pontoon bridge, Ayres' division would proceed to the junction of the Vaughan and Monk's Neck roads.

Major General Charles Griffin's division was to march behind Ayres' batteries. The remaining batteries and the wagons with the entrenching tools were to follow Griffin's soldiers. Maj. Gen. Samuel W. Crawford's division would come next. The Corps' trains would bring up the rear.

After entering the Vaughan Road, the Corps would proceed as rapidly as possible by way of J. Kidd's to Dinwiddie Court House. If the enemy was encountered, he was to be attacked. To expedite the march, officers were admonished to see that the men remained in the ranks and did not straggle. Warren warned "any man may be justifiably shot who . . . falls out without permission from the division commander."

As in the case of Humphreys' Corps, Warren's was stripped down so that it could travel light and fast. In this respect, Warren announced that as a battle was "expected the command must be as little encumbered as possible and prepared for action so that nothing will have to be sent to the rear when the fighting begins."[15] Only five four-gun batteries (three smoothbores and two rifled) would accompany the corps. The corps' four other attached batteries would be left behind.[16]

To keep the Confederates in the dark for as long as possible, Warren ordered the musicians to be left behind. After sounding reveille at the usual hour, the musicians would rejoin their units.[17]

---

15 *OR* 46, pt. 1, 797-798. The only vehicles authorized to accompany the corps across Rowanty Creek were one medical wagon and one army wagon loaded with hospital supplies to each brigade; and one army wagon with forage for each division. The ambulance train was to consist of one-half the vehicles assigned to the corps. In addition to the ammunition each soldier carried, another 20 rounds per man, was to be transported in the ordnance wagons. One sutler's wagon was authorized to accompany each brigade. Forage to last for one day was to be carried either in the spring wagons or on the horses. The remainder of the V Corps' wagons were to be parked near the Perkins house, and supplies brought forward as needed. *Ibid.*, 798.

16 *OR* 46, pt. 3, 230.

17 *Ibid.*, *OR* 46 pt. 1, 798.

Shortly after Warren had issued these orders, he received an important message from Meade's headquarters. Opening the dispatch, Warren discovered that Meade had changed his plans. The V Corps was not to go beyond the junction of the Vaughan and Quaker Roads until General Humphreys was in position. Upon being informed that Humphreys was ready, Warren would resume his advance. Turning into the Boydton Plank Road, Warren would take position with his right anchored on Humphreys' left.

Several hours later the thoroughly confused Warren received a third message from Meade's headquarters. Scanning the dispatch, Warren learned that Humphreys was uncertain of his corps' ability to reach the Quaker Road. Accordingly, Humphreys had been directed "to place his right within supporting distance of General Ord . . . ." Humphreys would then deploy his corps, letting his formation determine where his left flank would rest. In view of these circumstances, Meade thought it would be best if Warren's corps moved up the Quaker Road instead of the Boydton Plank Road.

This placed Warren in a quandary. He had one message directing him to advance up the Quaker Road and another up the Boydton Plank Road. Worse, Warren did not know that Humphreys' starting time had been changed. Warren calculated that if Humphreys marched at 9:00 a.m., the V Corps would reach the junction of the Vaughan and Quaker Roads long before the II Corps could get into position. Warren, therefore, determined to take up a strong position west of Rowanty Creek. Here he would wait while Humphreys completed his dispositions. As a result of his previous visit to the area in February at the time of the battle of Hatcher's Run, Warren was familiar with the terrain. He knew that there was a commanding ridge on the Hargrove farm. This was one-half mile east of the Boydton Plank Road. To be prepared to meet either eventuality, Warren determined to occupy this ridge with a strong detachment. He would hold the junction of the Vaughan and Quaker Roads with the remainder of his Corps.[18]

General Sheridan likewise spent the afternoon of the 28th reviewing his plans. General Crook's division was to be in the saddle at 5:00 a.m. Riding along the Jerusalem Plank Road, Crook's troopers were to march by way of Gary's Church and Ream's Station. A detachment of pioneers with three pontoon boats would accompany Crook's column. The cavalry planned to cross Rowanty Creek at Malone's Bridge. If necessary, the pioneers would throw a bridge across the stream. After crossing the creek, the Federals would strike for Dinwiddie Court House. Sheridan's two other divisions, Brig. Gens. George A. Custer's and Thomas C.

18 *Ibid.*, 798-799.

Devin's, were to hit the road as soon as Crook's cavalrymen had cleared the area. Custer and Devin would report to Maj. Gen. Wesley Merritt.

All the cavalry's wagons were to be assembled on the Jerusalem Plank Road. They would be organized into a convoy and escorted by a brigade to be detailed by General Merritt. The ambulances, however, were slated to accompany their respective divisions.

During the advance to Malone's Bridge, strong scouting parties would be thrown out to reconnoiter all the roads on the left of the column's line of march. After crossing Rowanty Creek, patrols would be pushed out as far as Stony Creek.[19]

The intelligence flowing into General Lee's headquarters on the 27th indicated that the Union was starting to stir restlessly. Lee felt that within a few days Grant would inaugurate an offensive designed to force the Confederates to abandon their Petersburg defenses. When the Federals moved out, Lee believed they would direct their movements toward the upper reaches of Hatcher's Run. This meandering stream covered the right flank of Lee's army. (Rising about 15 miles west of Petersburg, Hatcher's Run was not a part of the watershed of the Appomattox River. Instead the stream ran roughly parallel to the Appomattox for about seven miles and then it veered to the southeast to become one of the effluents of the Nottoway.) Between Hatcher's Run and the Appomattox lay the tracks of the vital South Side Railroad, one of Lee's two essential links with the fragment of the Cis-Mississippi Confederacy not yet occupied by the Yankees.[20]

General Lee realized that the South Side Railroad would undoubtedly be Grant's prime objective, if the Federals planned to drive the Confederates from Petersburg without having to storm the powerful fortifications. To reach the railroad, Lee correctly deduced that Grant would probably cross Hatcher's Run at a point some distance from the Rebel lines. To accomplish this, the Union army would have to march westward until it reached a point beyond the Confederates' right flank, and then strike for the railroad. Examining his maps, Lee observed that the roads which the Union army would use in gaining his right passed through a wooded area which was cut up by numerous small but troublesome streams. Because of the recent rains, these watercourses could be expected to be running bank full.

After consulting all his available sources of information, Lee decided that the Union army would probably cross Rowanty Creek at Monk's Neck Bridge. (Rowanty Creek was formed by the confluence of Hatcher's and Gravelly runs.)

19 *Ibid.*, OR 46, pt. 3, 234.

20 Douglas S. Freeman, *R. E. Lee : A Biography*, 4 vols. (New York, 1935), vol. 4, 22.

Having crossed Rowanty Creek, Lee believed the Federal column would strike for the South Side Railroad by way of Dinwiddie Court House and Five Forks. The marching distance was 15 miles or a 1 ½ days as the roads then were. If Lee endeavored to meet this thrust by merely lengthening his front, he would be compelled to extend his lines from the Claiborne Road to a point several miles west of Five Forks. This would be a prolongation of four miles, a distance the Confederates could not hope to protect adequately. Lee had already stretched his thin line almost to the breaking point. On the twenty-seven and one-half miles held by his infantry, Lee could count an average of only 1,140 men per mile.[21]

Helping to hold the lines on the north side of the James were two divisions of James Longstreet's Corps. At this time, these once formidable divisions had been reduced to about 6,400 effectives. It would take the advance elements of the two units a minimum of 12 hours to reach the Petersburg area in the event of a crisis.[22] Brigadier General Martin W. Gary's understrength mounted brigade was attached to Longstreet's Corps. Maj. Gen. Fitzhugh Lee's cavalry division was stationed on the Nine Mile Road guarding the crossing of the Chickahominy. This division mustered about 1,800 officers and men, but it was a two days' march from the point of danger.[23] The only other troops north of the James were the heavy artillery units, the Virginia Reserves, and the Local Defense Troops. This hodgepodge of troops which were assigned to the Department of Richmond totaled about 4,250, commanded by Lt. Gen. Richard S. Ewell.[24] Altogether at this time, Lee could muster north of the James about 10,000 infantry, 1,800 cavalry, and 750 heavy artillerists. To do this, however, he would have to call out all the Virginia Reserves and Local Defense Troops. Without using his second line troops, Lee could deploy about 7,500 infantry. Exclusive of Fitz Lee's cavalry, only Longstreet's two divisions could be used to reinforce the Confederate right.[25]

The Howlett Line between the James and Appomattox rivers was held by Maj. Gen. William Mahone's infantry division, almost 4,000 strong. In addition, the big guns along Mahone's line were manned by several heavy artillery companies and detachments from the Confederate navy. Mahone's front was nearly five miles long. The troops charged with the defense could not be reduced, because if the

---

21 *Ibid*, 22-24.

22 *Ibid.*, 24; OR 46, pt. 1, 388. The two divisions from Longstreet's Corps stationed north of the James River were commanded by Maj. Gens. Charles W. Field and Joseph B. Kershaw.

23 Freeman, *R. E. Lee*, vol. 4, 24.

24 *OR* 46, pt. 3, 1331.

25 Freeman, *R. E. Lee*, vol. 4, 24.

Federals secured a breakthrough at this point they would cut Lee's army in two and sever communications between Richmond and Petersburg.[26]

Major General John B. Gordon's Corps, supported by a heavy artillery concentration, occupied the sector from the Appomattox River east of Petersburg to the point where Lieutenant's Run passed through the Confederate lines. Gordon's front was slightly longer than four miles. After deducting his losses suffered in his March 25 dawn attack on Fort Stedman, Gordon was able to deploy about 5,500 soldiers. If the works had not been so formidable and all the ranges plotted, this would have been a hopelessly inadequate force for the task involved.[27]

Two divisions of Lieutenant General Ambrose P. Hill's Corps held the earthworks on Gordon's right. Hill's front extended from Lieutenant's Run to the fortifications covering the Boydton Plank Road at Burgess Mill. This was a distance of more than eight miles, and it was held by approximately 9,200 officers and men.[28]

To the right of Hill's Corps, guarding the White Oak and Claiborne roads, was Lt. Gen. Richard H. Anderson's small Corps. At this time, Anderson's troops consisted of Maj. Gen. Bushrod R. Johnson's division and Col. Hilary P. Jones' artillery. Johnson's division mustered about 4,800 officers and men.[29]

There was no cavalry on the army's right flank. The nearest mounted force was Maj. Gen. William H. F. "Rooney" Lee's division which was stationed at Stony Creek Station, 40 miles away by road. There were about 2,400 troops in Rooney Lee's command. On the 28th, while the Federals were preparing to take the field, Rooney Lee's division was reinforced by Maj. Gen. Thomas L. Rosser's division, approximately 1,200 sabers. Rosser's battered division had been serving in the Shenandoah Valley.

The only command which General Lee could count on as a reserve was Maj. Gen. George E. Pickett's division. On March 14, Pickett's troops had been transferred to the north side of the James to forestall a threatened sweep by Sheridan's cavalry. When the attack failed to materialize, Pickett's troops remained north of the river. At the time of the assault on Fort Stedman, Pickett's division was ordered to return to the Southside. Only one brigade, Brig. Gen. George H. Steuart's, was able to reach Petersburg on March 25 before the attack was suspended. Even so, Steuart's troops were not committed. Following the failure of

---

26 *Ibid.*; OR 46, pt. 1, 389.

27 Freeman, *R. E. Lee*, vol. 4, 25.

28 *Ibid.* Maj. Gens. Cadmus M. Wilcox and Henry Heth led the two divisions from A. P. Hill's Corps charged with the defense of this sector.

29 Freeman, *R. E. Lee*, vol. 4, 25.

the attack on Fort Stedman, Steuart's soldiers were permitted to camp near the city. Two of Pickett's brigades: Brig. Gens. Montgomery D. Corse's and William H. Terry's were halted before they reached Petersburg and bivouacked on Swift Creek. Pickett's other brigade, Brig. Gen. Eppa Hunton's, had remained north of the James. All told, the strength of Pickett's scattered command was approximately 5,000. Since the battle of Gettysburg, Pickett's troops had remained in the background. They had, in general, been assigned to quiet sectors on the front. The division had the highest rate of desertions in the Army of Northern Virginia, which was good evidence of low morale.[30]

It is instructive to learn just how thinly stretched Lee's army was at this time, and why his reserve was so small. The density of the Confederate infantry and the character of the various zones, as of March 27, 1865, were approximately as listed in the Table 1 on the next page.

To make matters worse, Lee received an urgent dispatch from General Longstreet. "Old Pete" informed Lee that General Gary's scouts had spotted Sheridan's cavalry on the previous morning near Malvern Hill. At the time they were sighted, the Union cavalry was moving up the right bank of the James. By 3:00 p.m., the last of the Federal column had passed from view. (Gary's scouts were correct. Devin's and Custer's cavalry division had crossed the James River at Deep Bottom on the 26th.) In addition, reports had reached Longstreet's command post indicating that Sheridan's troopers had left White House in great haste. Many saddles and bridles, a large quantity of ammunition, and many sacks of oats had been left behind. Prior to its departure from White House, it was stated that the Union cavalry had received 2,000 fresh horses from the remount service. The Confederate scouts were also told by the inhabitants that the troopers of Maj. Gen. August V. Kautz's cavalry division had bragged that they had been alerted and expected to go to North Carolina.[31]

In response to this news, Lee decided to concentrate most of his cavalry on the right flank of his army. A telegram was sent to General Longstreet, directing him to send Fitz Lee's division to the Southside. Longstreet was not too impressed with General Lee's plan to counter the Union thrust with cavalry. Old Pete thought that, instead of stripping all cavalry from his flank, it would be wiser if Lee constituted a special task force to deal with Sheridan's hard-driving troopers. Longstreet believed

---

30 *Ibid.*

31 *OR* 46, pt. 3, 1357-1358; *Ibid.*, *OR* 46, pt. 1, 1101. General Kautz had commanded the cavalry division attached to the Army of the James until March 20, 1865. On that date, Kautz was detached and placed in charge of an infantry division in the XXV Corps. General Mackenzie commanded of the cavalry division formerly led by Kautz.

TABLE 1	
Zone and Command as of March 27, 1865 and Length of the Line Held	Infantry per Mile of Defended Lines
North of the James	
Fitz Lee's cavalry on the Nine Mile Road	1,800
Longstreet, with Field's and Kershaw's divisions (chiefly in field works), five miles	1,360
Ewell, with Virginia Reserves, Local Defense Troops and heavy artillery (in heavy earthworks), two and one-half miles	740
Howlett Line	
Mahone's division (heavy works with naval and Heavy ordnance support), nearly five miles	740
From the Appomattox to Lieutenant's Run	
Gordon's Corps (heavy works, enemy very close), four miles	1,350
From Lieutenant's Run to Burgess Mill	
Wilcox's division of Hill's Corps (some heavy works chiefly field works, about four and one-half miles	1,100
Heth's division of Hill's Corps (works of the same type as Wilcox's, though not as strong, except at Burgess Mill), three and one-half miles	1,200
Average density of this line	1,150
Beyond Burgess Mill	
Anderson's Corps (light field works on extreme right), three miles	1,600
Average density (31,400 men on twenty-seven and one-half miles of line defended by infantry)	1,140
Pickett's division, a quasi-reserve	5,000
Cavalry at Stony Creek	2,400
Ordered to Stony Creek, Rosser's division	1,200

that this task force ought to be composed of "an efficient cavalry force with Pickett's division and two or three batteries." This command, Longstreet reasoned, could watch Sheridan and keep him off the two vital railroads. If the Union cavalry joined Sherman in North Carolina, this specially constituted task force would reinforce General Joseph E. Johnston's Confederate army. Longstreet concluded "I believe that our cavalry, supported by the infantry, will be more effective against the enemy's raiders than our cavalry alone. I believe that such a force in proper hands will be able to frustrate the objective of the enemy, as nearly all his horses must be somewhat exhausted."[32] Lee saw the logic in Longstreet's arguments. The decision having been made, Longstreet drafted orders for Fitz Lee to move his division at daybreak on the 28th to the Southside where he would report to General Lee. Since there was very little forage in the Petersburg area, Fitz Lee would take all the provender that he could collect with him when he marched. Lee's dismounted troopers were to be left behind to man the works on either side of the Nine Mile Road.[33]

At the same time, General Lee had alerted Rooney Lee to hold his division ready to move to the point of danger. General Lee planned to mass all his mounted troops, except Gary's brigade, on his extreme right.[34]

In a desperate effort to further increase his cavalry force, General Lee sent an urgent telegram to Lt. Gen. Jubal A. Early, the commander of the Department of Western Virginia and East Tennessee. Besides informing Early that Sheridan's cavalry was "probably on Grant's left," Lee inquired into the possibility of the departmental commander's dispatching one of Maj. Gen. Lunsford L. Lomax's brigades to Petersburg.[35] Early replied immediately to Lee's communication. He reported that his department was in danger and it would be impossible to send any troops to Petersburg. [36]

The news reaching Lee's headquarters from the scouts on the 28th was more foreboding than on the previous day. First, there was the report brought in by an 18-year-old girl whose parents lived inside the Union lines. At the risk of her life, she passed through the Union picket lines and informed the Confederate outposts that strong contingents from the Army of the James had crossed the James and Appomattox rivers. Lee immediately relayed this intelligence to General Longstreet. Old Pete then sent observers to check on the report. The first scouts who returned to the Confederate line reported that the only Union force that had

32 *Ibid., OR* 46, pt. 3, 1357.

33 *Ibid.*, 1358. There were 385 men and 5 officers in Fitz Lee's division that were without mounts and had to be left behind.

34 Freeman, *R. E. Lee*, vol. 4, 26-27.

35 *OR* 46, pt. 3, 1358. At this time, Gen. R. E. Lee ordered the 1st Maryland Cavalry, stationed at Gordonsville, to join Fitz Lee's division.

36 *Ibid.*, 1362.

crossed the river on the night of the 28th was a supply train. Later, several of Gary's scouts came in and confirmed the news that Sheridan's cavalry had moved to the Southside. In addition, they correctly reported that Mackenzie's division was still north of the James. Longstreet's scouts were unable to discover whether any of Ord's infantry and artillery had crossed the river. So far, the measures that Ord had taken to conceal the movement of his troops were working to perfection.[37]

Lee, however, could not afford to take chances. In spite of Longstreet's failure to penetrate the cordon with which Ord had veiled his movements, Lee alerted his subordinate to be prepared to release all the troops he could spare. As the next step in his campaign to protect his right flank, Lee executed the plan which Longstreet had broached on the preceding day. He would organize a special task force composed of cavalry, infantry, and artillery to deal with the threat posed by Sheridan's cavalry. Lee realized that he might have to augment this force if the cavalry were supported by infantry. But if he did, Lee hoped to do so without being compelled to draw troops from the Confederate Petersburg and Richmond lines in such numbers as to make a Union breakthrough inevitable. Lee's plan of operation was, in short, a compromise between the detachment of a major force and a long extension of his already attenuated defensive line.[38]

Lee, therefore, asked Longstreet to designate Pickett's division as the one to cooperate with the cavalry. In acknowledging Lee's communication, Longstreet stated that he did not think he could spare Pickett. But, he continued, the danger would be much greater if Sheridan were permitted to destroy the two railroads that served as the supply lines for the Army of Northern Virginia or to rendezvous with Sherman's army in North Carolina. Longstreet felt that the Confederates' only recourse was to "put a force in the field that can contend against" the Federals' mobile striking force. Curiously enough, there is no record of any preliminary discussion between Lee and Longstreet as to who should command the task force charged with stopping Sheridan's thrust.[39]

Once the decision to constitute a special task force had been made, instructions were drafted alerting Pickett's scattered brigades to be ready to move to the right. Lee could not bring himself to order Pickett to start moving his

---

37 *Ibid.*, 1359-1360; Freeman, *R. E. Lee*, vol. 4, 27.

38 *Ibid.*

39 *OR* 46, pt. 3, 1360.

brigades on the 28th. The general was still apprehensive lest the activities of Sheridan's cavalry were a feint designed to cover an attack north of the James.[40]

During the day, Lee replied to Early's message regarding the impossibility of sending one of Lomax's brigades to Petersburg. Besides expressing regret that the "paucity" of troops prevented Early from dispatching reinforcements, Lee ordered Early to send Lt. Col. William McLaughlin's Artillery Battalion to the Petersburg front.[41]

Part II

The Advance Begins: The V Corps Wins the Battle of the Lewis Farm

Long before daybreak on the 29th, reveille sounded in the camps of Sheridan's cavalry corps. As soon as the troopers had eaten breakfast, the officers mustered and inspected their units. After the regimental commanders had satisfied themselves that each man had drawn the prescribed 5 days' rations, the 30 pounds of forage and 40 rounds of ammunition, the buglers sounded "Boots and Saddles." The cavalrymen then swung into their saddles. It was daybreak when Sheridan's powerful mounted force, 9,000 strong, departed from the Hancock's Station staging area. Crook's division, with which Sheridan traveled, took the lead as the troopers rode southward along the Jerusalem Plank Road.[42]

The cavalry column marched by way of Gary's Church and Ream's Station. At Webb's Farm, the Union vanguard turned into the Malone's Bridge Road. Nothing exciting occurred to mar the march until Brig. Gen. J. Irvin Gregg's brigade, which was spearheading Sheridan's advance, reached Malone's Bridge. Much to his disgust, Sheridan discovered that the Confederates had burned the bridge. While Gregg's troopers waited for the pioneers to throw a pontoon bridge across the stream, they were fired on by a small Confederate detachment posted on the west

40 Freeman, *R. E. Lee*, vol. 4, 27.

41 *OR* 46, pt. 3, 1362.

42 *OR* 46, pt. 1, 1101, 1116.

bank. Dismounting, the troops blazed away with their Spencer carbines. The Rebels scattered, and the pioneers quickly bridged Rowanty Creek.[43]

Gregg's troopers then clattered across the swaying structure. Pressing forward, the troopers veered to the right and drove the butternuts across Stony Creek. Several prisoners were captured. When questioned, the Southerners told Sheridan that they belonged to Rooney Lee's division which was camped on the Weldon Railroad near Stony Creek Station. Information gleaned from the prisoners convinced Sheridan that the Confederate cavalry would not attack his powerful column. Examining his maps, Sheridan observed that if he pushed on to Dinwiddie Court House, Rooney Lee's command would be forced "to make a wide detour" if it were to rejoin the Army of Northern Virginia. Consequently, Sheridan decided to push on.[44]

Once the column had turned off the Jerusalem Plank Road, progress of the corps' wagon trains was slowed by "the almost impassable dirt roads" of this section of Virginia. The thousands of horses' hoofs and hundreds of wagon wheels turned the roads into ribbons of mud. Not wishing to be delayed by his trains, Sheridan decided to march without them. Custer's division was detached and remained at Malone's Bridge to assist and protect the trains from Rooney Lee's cavalry.[45]

Having provided for the security of his trains, Sheridan headed for Dinwiddie Court House. Gregg's brigade continued to lead Sheridan's advance. Several times during the march, Gregg's troopers clashed with small, roving-mounted Confederate patrols. These were easily brushed aside by the Union vanguard. Muddy roads, however, proved to be a bigger obstacle. It was 5:00 p.m. before the column reached Dinwiddie Court House. Even then, Batteries C and F of the 4th U.S. Light Artillery were bogged down. The artillerists were unable to accomplish the day's objective. After occupying Dinwiddie Court House, Sheridan posted the troopers of Devin's and Crook's divisions so that they covered the Vaughan, Flat Foot, Boydton Plank, and Adams roads. As soon as the officers reported that their men were in position, Sheridan permitted their units to camp.[46]

---

43 *Ibid.*, 1101, 1141.

44 *Ibid.*, 1101, 1116, 1141; *OR* 46, pt. 3, 267. Dinwiddie Court House consisted of a court house, a hotel, and a few farm houses. Davies' brigade camped on the Boydton Plank Road; the 1st New Jersey cavalry was posted on the Flat Foot Road. *OR* 46, pt. 1, 1143, 1148.

45 *Ibid.*, 1101, 1116, 1129.

46 *Ibid.*, 1101, 1116, 1141; *OR* 46, pt. 3, 267.

Custer's combative cavalrymen discovered that they had been given a most unpleasant assignment when they were detached and detailed to guard the trains. It was late afternoon before the last of the wagons crossed Rowanty Creek. To their dismay, Custer's troopers quickly discovered that the road west of the creek was worse, if possible, than it had been on the opposite side. The passage of Devin's and Crook's divisions had turned the road into a sticky slime. In a futile effort to expedite the march, Custer organized fatigue parties. These groups were put to work assisting the pioneers in corduroying the road. Progress, however, continued to be agonizingly slow. When darkness descended, the head of the train was seven miles from Dinwiddie Court House. Because the road was too narrow to permit a night march, the wagons were parked. After picketing the area, Custer permitted his exasperated troopers to bed down for the night.[47]

As a result of the excitement engendered by the projected offensive and the necessity for making last minute preparations, there was very little sleep in the camps of the V Corps on the night of the 28th. Long before daybreak, the soldiers had been fed and the units formed. As anticipated, Ayres' division was on the road by 3:00 a.m. As soon as the road was cleared, the other units of V Corps moved out in accordance with the march schedule established by Warren.[48] By 4:45 a.m., Ayres' vanguard reached the place where Monk's Neck Bridge had formerly stood. The few Confederates manning the outpost on the far side of Rowanty Creek fired several scattered shots at Ayres' scouts before taking to their heels. Obtaining a precarious footing on the ruins of the bridge and fallen trees, Ayres' infantry scrambled across the stream. After the bridgehead was established, a company of the 50th New York Engineers speedily laid a canvas pontoon bridge. After the bridge was declared passable for horses, Warren crossed with his escort. Hailing Ayres, Warren ordered the division commander to reassemble his troops and resume the advance. The troops on the left bank would cover the bridgehead.[49]

For the first mile beyond Rowanty Creek, the progress of Warren's column was slowed by the necessity to remove obstructions from the road. The Confederates had felled trees to impede the Union advance. Unlike Sheridan, Warren had little trouble with "General Mud." Warren reported that, except in the boggy areas, the roads were dry.[50]

47 *Ibid.*, pt. 1, 1116, 1129, 1134; *OR* 46, pt. 3, 267.

48 *Ibid.*, *OR* 46, pt. 1, 779, 870.

49 *Ibid.*, 799; *OR* 46, pt. 3, 253, 258.

50 *Ibid.*, *OR* 46, pt. 1, 799.

By 8:15 a.m., the head of the V Corps reached the junction of the Monk's Neck and Vaughan roads. Except for the few shots exchanged at the bridge and the felled timber, the Federals had failed to see any signs of Confederate activity. From an old black man who had been hiding in the woods near Crawford Church, Warren learned that there were no Rebel troops at Dinwiddie Court House as late as the previous day. Warren drafted a message containing this data and handed it to Capt. Gordon Winslow. The staff officer, accompanied by a ten-man escort, galloped up Vaughan Road to deliver copies of this dispatch to Generals Meade and Humphreys.[51]

While waiting to hear from army headquarters and after Winslow departed, Warren deployed his command. Ayres' division proceeded to the intersection of the Quaker and Vaughan roads and halted. Two of Ayres' brigades took positions at the intersection; the other was formed into line of battle and sent a short distance up Quaker Road. After Ayres' troops had moved off the road, Griffin's division occupied the commanding ground separating the headwaters of Great and Little Cattail runs. Griffin's troops were posted on the Chappell, Scott, and Hargrave farms. Two of Crawford's brigades covered the county road leading to R. Boisseaau's farm on the Boydton Plank Road. Crawford's other brigade—Brig. Gen. Richard Coulter's—guarded the corps' train. The trains were parked at the junction of the Monk's Neck and Vaughan roads.[52]

The country into which the V Corps had marched and where the subsequent operations were to be conducted:

> was of the forest kind common to Virginia, being well watered by swampy streams.
> The surface was level and the soil clayey and sandy, and, where these mixed together,
> like quicksand. The soil after the frosts of winter first leave it is very light and soft, and
> hoofs and wheels find but little support.[53]

Upon questioning the inhabitants, Warren learned that Brig. Gen. Rufus Barrington's North Carolina cavalry brigade had passed down Quaker Road the previous day. The farmers stated that the Confederate troopers had remarked that they were en route to Stony Creek.[54]

---

51 *Ibid.*, *OR* 46, pt. 3, 254.

52 *Ibid.*, *OR* 46, pt. 1, 799, 896; *OR* 46, pt. 3, 243, 259.

53 Survivors' Association', *History of the Corn Exchange Regiment*, 562.

54 *OR* 46, pt. 3, 254.

At 10:20 a.m., Maj. William Jay of Meade's staff galloped up to Warren's command post, and handed Warren a dispatch from General Meade. Opening the message, Warren found that he was to move his Corps up Quaker Road to the Gravelly Crossing. Furthermore, Meade thought that if Warren sent out patrols on his right, he would contact Humphreys' left near J. Slaughter's house.[55]

Replying to Meade's communication, Warren gave a brief resume of the position of his corps. He informed his superior that his skirmishers on Quaker Road had probably already penetrated as far as Gravelly Run. If they hadn't, Warren assured Meade, he would see that they did. Warren also passed on the information he had picked up concerning Barringer's activities.[56]

Warren continued to mark time while his patrols tried to establish a liaison with Humphreys' corps. When the fiery Meade received Warren's message, he simmered. It was evident that Warren had misinterpreted his orders. Instead of advancing in force up the Quaker Road, Warren had sent a force of skirmishers to the Gravelly Run crossing. Meade, calling to his chief of staff, Maj. Gen. Alexander S. Webb, told him to send a second message to Warren. After expressing his approval of the dispositions Warren had made to cover his left flank and rear, the general observed that "this must not prevent you moving your Corps up the Quaker Road across Gravelly Run . . . ." After he had crossed the stream, Warren was to form his corps facing north and anchor his right on Humphreys' left. Only after this maneuver had been completed would Warren provide for the security of his left flank. If possible, Warren was to hold the Boydton Plank Road.[57]

This message which General Webb signed at 11:20 a.m. was entrusted to Capt. Campbell D. Emery. A glance at the piece of paper convinced Warren that he had misunderstood Meade's intentions. Hailing a staff officer, Warren sent him racing to tell General Griffin to move his division up the Quaker Road. General Crawford was alerted to hold his command ready to support Griffin's advance. When he had taken care of this urgent business, Warren informed army headquarters of the measures he had undertaken to implement Meade's instructions.

Shortly thereafter, General Meade and his staff rode up to Warren's command post. After conferring briefly, the two generals accompanied Griffin's vanguard as it trudged up the Quaker Road.[58]

---

55 *Ibid.*; *OR* 46, pt. 1, 799.

56 *Ibid.*; *OR* 46, pt. 3, 254.

57 *Ibid.*, *OR* 46, pt. 1, 799; *OR* 46, pt. 3, 255.

58 *Ibid.*, *OR* 46, pt. 1, 800. Warren's command post was located at the intersection of the Quaker and Vaughan roads.

Unlike Sheridan's and Warren's corps, Humphreys' did not get started at the designated hour. It was 6:30 a.m.—one-half hour after the scheduled time—before Humphreys' advance division, Hays', moved out of the Petersburg investment line.[59] Turning into the Vaughan Road, the troops passed through the picket line and crossed Hatcher's Run without difficulty.

Even before all of the troops had reached the right bank, Hays sent a strong combat patrol composed of the 7th West Virginia, the 7th Michigan, and the 4th Ohio to reconnoiter the area into which the II Corps was moving. The bluecoats advanced about one and one-half miles without discovering any Confederates. They then retraced their steps and reported their findings to General Hays.[60]

When the patrol returned, Hays halted his division one-half mile west of Hatcher's Run.[61] In accordance with Humphreys' instructions, Hays deployed his troops about one-half mile north of the road. Two brigades—Brig. Gens. Thomas A. Smyth's and Col. James P. McIver's—were formed into line of battle. McIver's right flank rested near the run. The opposite side of the stream was held by the troops of General Gibbon's XXIV Corps. Hays' other brigade—Col. William A. Olmsted's—was held in reserve.[62]

Mott's division followed Hays' across Hatcher's Run. About one mile west of the run, Mott deployed his division north of the Vaughan Road. Two of Mott's brigades—Brig. Gens. Byron R. Pierce's and Robert McAllister's—were formed into line of battle; the other, Brig. Gen. Regis de Trobriand's, was held in reserve. The right flank of Pierce's brigade rested on the left flank of Hays' division. As soon as his troops were in position, General Mott put them to work throwing up a line of earthworks.[63]

Close on the heels of Mott's troops, Miles' soldiers marched out of their camp near the Squirrel Level Road. By 8:30 a.m., the last of Miles' division had crossed Hatcher's Run. Passing beyond the area where Mott was marshaling his soldiers, Miles stopped his command. Miles then formed his division north of the Vaughan Road; its right rested on Mott's unit and its left on Gravelly Run.[64] Since Miles had four brigades, he deployed three of them into line of battle—Brig. Gen. John

59 *Ibid.*, OR 46, pt. 3, 249.

60 *Ibid.*, OR 46, pt. 1, 766.

61 *Ibid.*, 675, 757, 791.

62 *Ibid.*, 757, 766.

63 *Ibid.*, 776, 781, 785.

64 *Ibid.*, 709-710.

Ramsey's on the left, Brig. Gen. Henry J. Medill in the center, and Col. George W. Scott's on the right. Col. Robert Nugent's brigade was held in reserve.[65] After the troops had taken their positions, breastworks were constructed.[66]

Except for Battery B, 1st Rhode Island Light Artillery, all the artillery units attached to the II Corps were parked once they had crossed Hatcher's Run. The Rhode Islanders, however, unlimbered their four 12-pounder Napoleons on the north side of the Vaughan Road about one-half mile west of the watercourse. Once they had emplaced their guns, the cannoneers trained them on Dabney's Mill.[67]

While the infantry was forming, Humphreys sent out several mounted patrols. By 9:00 a.m., one of them had succeeded in opening communications by way of the Vaughan Road with Warren's Corps. A second group moved up the valley of Gravelly Run to the Quaker Road. Encountering a few Confederate vedettes, the Yankees drove them up the Quaker Road. Beyond the "old saw-mill," the bluecoats were fired on by an infantry outpost. Because the Confederates were protected by breastworks, the Unionists returned and reported their findings to Humphreys.

When the division commanders completed their dispositions, they covered their fronts with a strong line of skirmishers.[68] Patrols were sent out to reconnoiter. The scouts returned with information that they had pinpointed the outlying Confederate defenses in this sector. They stated that the Confederate outposts were sheltered behind a line of breastworks covering the approaches to Dabney's Mill. This was about three-fourths of a mile in front of the ground held by the II Corps.[69] Humphreys, however, had to postpone his attack on these Confederate fortifications while Warren was getting into position.

Early on the 29th, Gibbon's Army of the James corps marched out of its camp behind Fort Siebert. In accordance with Grant's orders, Gibbon's troops moved into the entrenchments formerly held by the II Corps.[70] General Foster's division occupied the fortifications from Fort Sampson on the right to Hatcher's Run on the

65 *Ibid.*, 714, 724, 733, 744. Miles' division, unlike the others in the II Corps and V Corps, contained four brigades instead of three.

66 *Ibid.*, 733.

67 *Ibid.*, 791. The two batteries assigned to Mott's division were parked on the Vaughan Road near the Brown's house.

68 *Ibid.*, 676, 710, 714, 733, 766, 776. Among the regiments deployed as skirmishers by Miles' brigadiers were the 26th Michigan, the 126th New York, and the 140th Pennsylvania. Mott's battle line was screened by the 20th Indiana, the 17th Maine, and the 93rd New York. Hays' brigadiers threw forward the 7th Michigan, the 4th Ohio, and the 7th West Virginia.

69 *Ibid.*, 710, 776.

70 *Ibid.*, 1173.

left.[71] Turner's division was held in reserve and camped east of Hatcher's Run near the Vaughan Road.[72] During the early afternoon, two of Turner's regiments were sent across Hatcher's Run. These two units were posted in support of the four guns of Battery B, 1st New Jersey Light Artillery.[73]

Later in the day in accordance with General Ord's instructions, Gibbon saw that all his troops were supplied with four days' rations which were to be carried in their haversacks. Rations to last an additional eight days were stored in the corps' wagons. To the soldiers, this was a certain indication that a period of active campaigning was in the offing.[74]

General Birney's black division, which had accompanied Gibbon's corps to the Southside, remained at Humphreys' Station throughout the day.[75]

News that the Yankees had crossed Rowanty Creek reached General Lee's headquarters before noon. When the scouts brought in this information, they stated that infantry and cavalry had crossed the stream at Monk's Neck Bridge and were massing toward Dinwiddie Court House.[76] Lee, as he informed Longstreet, was unable to deduce from these fragmentary reports the immediate Union objective.[77] The situation, however, was so critical that Lee would have to take some action. Brig. Gen. Samuel McGowan's brigade of Wilcox's division was pulled out of the defense lines on the east side of Hatcher's Run. Following the withdrawal of McGowan's troops, Wilcox's three other brigades had to spread out to cover the vacated rifle pits. McGowan's brigade was sent to the sector west of Burgess Mill held by Anderson's corps.

With this business taken care of, Lee directed Pickett to transfer Corse's and Terry's brigades from the Swift Creek staging area to Petersburg. At Petersburg, Pickett was joined by Steuart's brigade. The three brigades then entrained on the cars of the South Side Railroad, which the railroad authorities had previously spotted in the Petersburg yards. The troops were then sent to Sutherland's Station, ten miles west of Petersburg, where they detrained. Many hours were required to

71 *Ibid.*, 1179.

72 *Ibid.*, 1214.

73 *Ibid.*, OR 46, pt. 3, 270.

74 *Ibid.*

75 *Ibid.*, OR 46, pt. 1, 1332, 1334-1336.

76 *Ibid.*, OR 46, pt. 3, 1362.

77 Freeman, *R. E. Lee*, vol. 4, 28.

make this shift. It was late on the night of the 29th before the last of Pickett's three brigades had been shuttled to Sutherland's Station.

While General Lee was drafting the orders for the movement of Pickett's and McGowan's soldiers, Fitz Lee rode up to his headquarters. The cavalryman informed his uncle that his division, which had left Nine Mile Road the day before, was in Petersburg. General Lee told his nephew that Sheridan was striking for Dinwiddie Court House. Lee stated that he thought the Union cavalry would concentrate at Five Forks before breaking up the South Side Railroad. Fitz Lee was to go to Sutherland's Station where he would be joined by Rooney Lee's and Rosser's cavalry and Pickett's infantry. Fitz Lee was then to attack Sheridan. General Lee was confident that the only way the raid could be stopped was to wrest the initiative from the Yankees. To ensure cooperation between the three cavalry divisions—which had not been under a unified command since Lieutenant General Wade Hampton's departure form the Virginia theater of operations—Lee told Fitz Lee to take charge of the cavalry corps. No written instructions, however, were given Fitz Lee on this matter. Fitz Lee was to give a strict interpretation of these verbal orders long after the entire complexion of affairs changed.[78]

Taking leave of his uncle, Fitz Lee rejoined his division. At an order from the general, the troopers again moved out. To reach the Sutherland's Station rendezvous area, Lee's cavalrymen took Cox Road as they rode out of Petersburg. Reaching Sutherland's Station, Fitz Lee's division camped, pending the arrival of Rooney Lee's and Rosser's troopers.[79]

As the next item on his agenda, General Lee issued instructions for Rooney Lee's and Rosser's division to report to Fitz Lee. Since Sheridan's column had cut direct communications between Petersburg and Stony Creek, these two divisions would have to detour to the west of Dinwiddie Court House if they were to carry out their assignment. Consequently, Rooney Lee's and Rosser's grey clads were unable to join Fitz Lee until the evening of the 30th.[80]

After arranging for the protection of the South Side Railroad, General Lee realized that steps would have to be taken to guard the Richmond and Danville Railroad. The latter railroad was almost as vulnerable to a Union raid as the former. Accordingly, Lee decided to use Pickett's other brigade, Hunton's, which was stationed north of the James, to fend off any raids the Federals might be planning on the Richmond and Danville Railroad. Eppa Hunton's brigade was to be

---

78 *Ibid.*, 28-29.

79 *OR* 46, pt. 1, 1298-1299.

80 *Ibid.*, 1299; Freeman, *R. E. Lee*, vol. 4, 28.

Lieutenant General
Richard H. Anderson
*Fredericksburg and Spotsylvania
National Military Park*

withdrawn from the rifle pits
flanking the Williamsburg Road. To
avoid the allurements of the
Richmond streets, Hunton's grey
clads were to cross the James River
by way of the pontoon bridge
located below the city and camp
near Manchester. From Manchester, Hunton's troops could be
shifted by rail to either Petersburg
or Burke's Station, as the situation
demanded. It was late afternoon before Gary's troopers relieved Hunton's infantry.
By then, however, the situation had changed drastically.[81]

Lee would have preferred to withdraw additional units from north of the James
to confront the Union threat to his right. But before doing this, he decided to get
Longstreet's reactions. When Lee informed Longstreet of the latest developments
on the Southside, he stated that Old Pete might have to come to Petersburg with
Field's division. In the meantime, Lee wanted Longstreet to ascertain what Union
troops were stationed north of the James.[82] Longstreet replied, "The usual force is
in our front, so far as we can learn. Our scouts are in from the enemy's line this
morning, and report affairs as usual." (Evidently, General Weitzel was carrying out
his mission. More than 60 hours had passed since Ord had led three of his infantry
divisions to the Southside, and still Longstreet was in the dark regarding this
movement.) Longstreet observed that if Fields' men were moved, the VMI Cadets
Local Defense Troops must be called out to take their places in the lines.[83]

81 *OR* 46, pt. 3, 1364.

82 Freeman, *R. E. Lee*, vol. 4, 29.

83 *OR* 46, pt. 3, 1363.

Meanwhile, General Anderson, whose Corps was directly threatened by the Union advance, began to institute measures which he hoped would enable his command to cope with the situation. General Johnson was authorized to recall his outposts as soon as he was satisfied that the Federals were moving in force up the Quaker Road. To cover the pickets' retreat, Johnson was directed to post one of his brigades in advance of the earthworks.[84]

About noon, Johnson learned from his scouts that a strong Union force (Warren's Corps) was coming up the Quaker Road. Johnson immediately forwarded this information to Anderson. The corps commander replied, directing Johnson to take his division, attack the bluecoats, and drive them back to the Vaughan Road. Just as Johnson's butternuts were starting to form, several excited cavalrymen galloped up. They informed Johnson that the foe was "retiring beyond Gravelly Run." Consequently, Johnson did not anticipate meeting the foe until after his troops reached the stream. When his division moved out of the works, Johnson had Brig. Gen. Henry A. Wise form his Virginia brigade into line of battle. One of Wise's regiments, the 34th Virginia, was detached and sent to support the cavalry patrols operating on the Boydton Plank Road. Brig. Gens. William E. Wallace's, Young M. Moody's, and Matthew W. Ransom's brigades marched by the flank in the rear of Wise's battle line. Wise's Virginians passed beyond the forks of the Boydton Plank and Quaker roads before they encountered any Federals. As the grey clads entered the skirt of the woods north of the junction, they were fired upon by Warren's skirmishers.[85]

Advancing up the Quaker Road, Warren's vanguard soon reached Gravelly Run. To their disgust, the Federals found that the Confederates had broken down the bridge. Undaunted, General Griffin shouted for Brig. Gen. Joshua L. Chamberlain to deploy his brigade into line of battle. Chamberlain's troops were to cross the run and occupy the rifle pits which were visible on the far side. Plunging into the water, Chamberlain's eager troops experienced considerable difficulty in wading across the waist-deep stream. Upon gaining the left bank, Chamberlain deployed and threw forward a battalion of the 198th Pennsylvanians as skirmishers. The remainder of the 198th Pennsylvania and the 185th New York were formed into line of battle on either side of the road. After these dispositions had been completed, Chamberlain's troops advanced and drove the Confederate outposts out of the earthworks guarding the crossing. Chamberlain's troops continued to push ahead until they reached Lewis' farm. Observing that the foe (part of

84 *Ibid.*, 1365.

85 *Ibid.*, OR 46, pt. 1, 1286-1287.

Major General Bushrod R. Johnson
Library of Congress

Johnson's division) was posted in strength on the opposite side of the clearing, Chamberlain halted the pursuit. No farther advance would be undertaken, pending the arrival of the remainder of Griffin's division.[86]

As soon as Chamberlain's troops had established a bridge-head, Warren directed Griffin's pioneers to construct a bridge. Within a short time, a usable structure was thrown across the stream. When this bridge was completed, the remainder of Griffin's division crossed the run. Warren and Meade now parted. The corps commander accompanied Griffin's division and the army commander returned to his command post. Later in the afternoon, the 50th New York Engineers, to help facilitate the crossing of the artillery, laid a pontoon bridge at this point. The banks were very steep and the artillery could not cross the pontoon bridge until proper approaches had been made. It therefore took the batteries considerable time to affect a passage of Gravelly Run.[87]

Having reached the right bank of Gravelly Run, the remainder of Griffin's division tramped up the Quaker Road. The road was choked with felled timber. To secure the advance of the artillery, the pioneers were put to work clearing away the obstructions. Even so, Griffin's troops forged ahead of the II Corps. Humphreys' troops, who were advancing on the right of Warren's Corps, were having a difficult

---

86 *Ibid.*, 800, 845, 847. The 198th Pennsylvania was formed on the right of the Quaker Road and the 185th New York on the left.

87 *Ibid.*, 800; *OR* 46, pt. 3, 255; Capt. Charles H. Porter, "Operations of the Fifth Corps on the Left, March 29, to Nightfall March 31, 1865, Gravelly Run," *Papers of The Military Historical Society of Massachusetts*, Vol. 6 (Boston, 1907), 215.

time working their way through the wooded countryside between the Quaker Road and Hatcher's Run.[88]

Upon overtaking Chamberlain's brigade at the Lewis farm, Griffin ordered his subordinate to resume the advance. Griffin also had Col. Edgar M. Gregory deploy his brigade on Chamberlain's left.[89] At this time, the firing on the skirmish line had practically died out. Consequently, Chamberlain reformed his battle line at the Lewis house. After reinforcing his battalion of skirmishers with a company from the 185th New York, Chamberlain moved his men forward. The brigade swept ahead. Chamberlain's skirmishers gained the woods on the far side of the clearing before the fire of the Confederates became severe. The general hoped that his battle line would likewise reach the timber before the grey clads sprang into action. This was not to be. Before the bluecoated battle line gained the woods, Wise's Virginians started to blaze away with a vengeance. Chamberlain's troops recoiled for an instant. Urged on by their officers, the Yankees recovered their poise and forged ahead. Attacking fiercely, Chamberlain's troops forced part of Wise's brigade to fall back into the open ground south of the junction of the Boydton Plank and Quaker roads.[90]

General Anderson rode up as Wise's troops were falling back. The corps commander directed Johnson to have Wallace's brigade support the part of Wise's brigade that still contested the Union advance. At a word from Wallace, his grim South Carolinians moved into the woods on the right of Wise's Virginians.[91]

After forcing Wise's grey clads to fall back about a mile, Chamberlain halted his brigade. Even though they had encountered only a few pockets of resistance, Gregory's Yankees were unable to keep pace with Chamberlain's troops. While Chamberlain was regrouping his brigade and waiting for Gregory to come up, Wise's and Wallace's soldiers launched a powerful counterattack. Soon, Chamberlain's troops were "completely enveloped in a withering fire." Taken by surprise, the Northerners were thrown on the defensive. At the end of one-half hour's combat, Chamberlain's left began to give ground. Redoubling the fury of their onslaught, the Rebels turned Chamberlain's left flank. Falling back, the Federals took position in a clearing. Here, the line occupied by the left flank of the

---

88 *OR* 46, pt. 1, 800.

89 *Ibid.*, 800, 853.

90 *Ibid.*, 847, 1287.

91 *Ibid.*, 1287.

brigade was parallel with the Quaker Road. Chamberlain's battle line, instead of being straight, was L-shaped.[92]

The Confederates quickly moved against Chamberlain's reorganized main line of resistance. So terrible was the Southerner's onslaught that Chamberlain despaired of holding his new position for longer than ten minutes. In desperation, the general sent a request to Col. Gregory (whose brigade had now arrived) to attack the Rebels on the right flank when they renewed their assault on his battered command. In the meantime, General Griffin had galloped up. Griffin assured Chamberlain that if he would hold on for five more minutes, the artillery would be up. Shouting this encouraging news to his men, Chamberlain succeeded in rallying them.

Two batteries had followed Griffin's division up the Quaker Road. While the infantry was able to march up the timber-strewn road with comparatively little difficulty, the artillery was stopped cold. Finally, however, the pioneers cut a path and Battery B, 4th U.S. Light Artillery thundered up the road. Reaching the Lewis clearing at a critical moment, the cannoneers unlimbered their four pieces. A section was emplaced on each side of the Lewis house. Going into action immediately, the artillerists hammered away at the oncoming Confederates. The two 12-pounder Napoleons on the west side of the house raked Wise's hard-charging Virginians with canister.[93]

When General Johnson observed that Wise's troops had closed to within canister range of the Union guns, he shouted for General Moody's Alabamians to move to the attack. The Alabamians formed on Wise's left and charge the guns. At a word from Moody, the cheering Alabamians started forward on the double.[94]

Supported by the fire of Battery B's four smoothbores, Chamberlain's left flank companies recovered the initiative. Counterattacking, they re-entered the woods. Feeling for an opening, the Confederates, following the arrival of Moody's Alabamians, started to exert tremendous pressure on Chamberlain's right and center. By this time, many of the Federals had fired up all the rounds in their cartridge-boxes. In addition, the cartridge-boxes of friend and foe were rifled. Many of the troops, refusing to trust the bayonet, began to slink to the rear. To stave off disaster, Chamberlain sent a second plea to Gregory for help. At the same time, General Griffin, sensing that his subordinate was in grave trouble, rushed

---

92 *Ibid.*, 847-848, 1287.

93 *Ibid.*, 848, 899, 1287. So close were the artillerists to the Confederate infantry that battery commander Lt. John Mitchell and four of his men were cut down.

94 *Ibid.*, 1287.

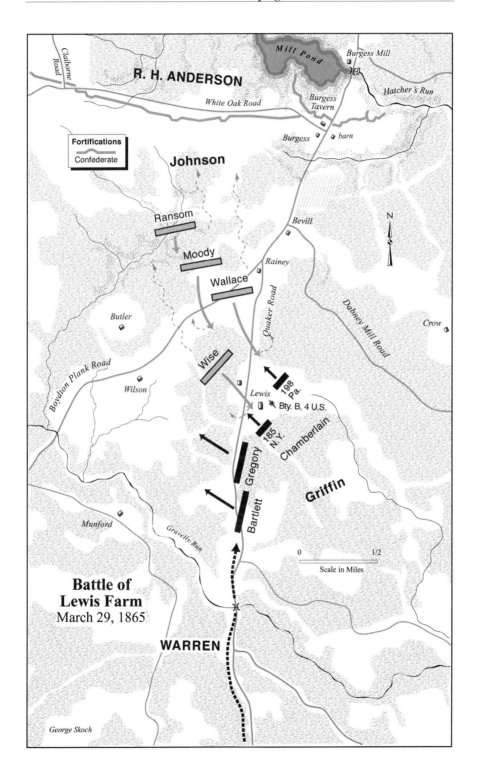

**Battle of
Lewis Farm**
March 29, 1865

George Skoch

three of Brig. Gen. Joseph J. Bartlett's regiments—the 1st and 15th Michigan and the 155th Pennsylvania—to Chamberlain's assistance. In response to Chamberlain's plea, Gregory sent the 188th New York. These fresh troops arrived none too soon. As they came up on the double, Chamberlain's battered brigade fell back on the Lewis house to protect the artillery.[95]

It seemed that Chamberlain was omnipresent. The general circulated along the battle line, urging his men to hold on for a few more minutes. The general became a target. Chamberlain's faithful charger "Charlemagne" was shot from under him, and the general's arm was disabled when his steed fell. A minie ball struck him in the chest, glanced over his chest, and left a painful wound and "a disreputable-looking coat." Chamberlain, however, refused to relinquish his command.[96]

Passing through Chamberlain's retreating brigade, the fresh regiments moved to the attack. On the right, Bartlett's three regiments led by Col. Alfred L. Pearson, who had grasped the colors of the 155th Pennsylvania, dashed straight toward the Confederate battle line.[97] As the 188th New York emerged from the woods into the Lewis clearing, Lt. Col. Isaac Doolittle saw that Bartlett's battle line was sweeping forward on the right. Deploying on the double, the New Yorkers joined in the charge. Taking cover behind piles of sawdust which served them as breastworks, the Southerners blazed away at the oncoming Yankees.

By this time, the southerners had had enough. When Anderson was informed that the Yankees had thrown in fresh troops and stopped his advance, he ordered Johnson to recall his soldiers. Covered by a strong rear guard, Moody's, Wallace's, and Wise's troops pulled out of the woods north of the Lewis farm. Falling back, the Southerners established a roadblock on the Boydton Plank Road. Johnson posted his troops on the edge of the woods north and east of the Bevill house.[98]

While Chamberlain's brigade was fighting for its life, General Warren observed that a country lane cut across the Quaker Road a little south of the Lewis house. The general felt that if he sent a detachment up this road, it might be able to gain the Boydton Plank Road and turn the Confederates right flank. Calling for Capt. Napoleon J. Horrell, Warren directed him to take the escort company and reconnoiter the lane.[99]

95 *Ibid.*, 848.

96 Survivors' Association, *History of the Corn Regiment*, 563.

97 *OR* 46, pt. 1, 848.

98 *Ibid.*, 858, 1287.

99 *Ibid.*, 800. Company C, 4th Pennsylvania Cavalry served as Warren's escort.

Before Horrell's troopers had gone far, they were fired upon by the outposts of the 34th Virginia. This regiment had been given the task of guarding the Boydton Plank Road. As soon as Warren learned that his escort company was in contact with the Rebels, he ordered General Crawford to take his division and support the cavalry. Before taking up the advance, Crawford had Brig. Gen. Henry Baxter deploy his brigade into line of battle. The right flank of Baxter's brigade rested on Griffin's left. Col. John A. Kellogg's brigade was massed in the rear of Baxter's unit. Once these dispositions were completed, Crawford sent his troops forward. Passing through the escort company's skirmishers, Crawford's battle line easily drove in the Confederate pickets covering the approaches to the Boydton Plank Road. By this time, Griffin's troops had broken the back of Johnson's attack. When Col. John T. Goode of the 34th Virginia learned that Johnson was falling back, he decided to do the same. Skillfully breaking contact with the bluecoats, the Virginians rejoined their comrades. Following the Confederates retreat, Crawford's troops reached the Boydton Plank Road.[100]

Two of Ayres' brigades crossed Gravelly Run close on the heels of Crawford's troops. Since the emergency had passed, these two units were held in reserve near the Spain house. For the time being, Ayres' other brigade, which was escorting the Corps' train, remained south of the run.[101]

About 4:00 p.m., General Humphreys received a message from army headquarters informing him that the V Corps, on his left, was advancing up the Quaker Road. Humphreys was directed to advance his Corps and connect his left with Warren's right.[102]

Earlier in the afternoon, several of Humphreys' subordinates had sent strong combat patrols to feel the Confederate defense in their sectors. On the right, one of General Hays' brigade commanders, Col. William A. Olmstead, had made a forced reconnaissance. Three of Colonel Olmsted's regiments—the 19th Maine, and the 59th and 152nd New York—were brought up from the reserve. Spearheaded by the 19th Maine, this combat patrol reached and occupied Dabney's Mill. Like Hays, Mott also sent three regiments to explore no man's land. After advancing about three-quarters of a mile, two of Mott's units—the 17th Maine and the 93rd New York—came upon a line of breastworks held by a few pickets. Brig. Gen. Byron R.

---

100 *Ibid.*, 884, 892. Two of Kellogg's regiments—the 6th and 7th Wisconsin—were formed into line of battle behind Baxter's troops. Kellogg's other regiment, the 91st New York, was massed on the left of the brigade, ready to be deployed either on the left flank of the battle line or in rear of the first line, as circumstances dictated.

101 *OR* 46, pt. 3, 255, 257.

102 *Ibid.*, *OR* 46, pt. 1, 676.

Pierce, who was in charge of the patrol, deployed part of the 93rd New York as skirmishers. Springing forward, the New Yorkers put the Confederates to flight and occupied the rifle pits west of Dabney's Mill.[103] The other regiment sent out by General Mott, the 20th Indiana, failed to spot any signs of Confederate activity.[104]

Accordingly, when Humphreys received his instructions to advance, he was reasonably certain that his men would not encounter much opposition. After the staff officers had relayed the word to Humphreys' subordinates, the II Corps battle line moved forward. Miles' left flank brigade, Ramsey's, established contact with Warren's right. As a result of the dense woods and tangled underbrush, this connection was repeatedly broken. Ramsey halted his brigade while communications were re-established.[105]

Suddenly, the roar of battle was heard from the direction of the Quaker road. Shortly thereafter, Humphreys received a message from army headquarters stating that General Griffin had been attacked by two Confederate divisions. Humphreys was directed to support Griffin's right with Miles' division.[106] After relaying the necessary instructions to Miles, Humphreys rode to the point of danger. By the time he reached Griffin's command post, the Confederates had fallen back. Here he was handed a message from Meade's headquarters, dated 5:40 p.m. Humphreys learned that Warren was scheduled to make another attack at 6:00 p.m. If Miles could be spared, Humphreys was to support Warren's advance. Furthermore, if Humphreys believed he could score any additional gains, he was to send his entire corps forward. Following the receipt of these instructions, Humphreys issued orders for his division commanders to continue the advance.[107]

Two of Griffin's brigades, Bartlett's and Gregory's, pressed forward hard on the heels of Johnson's rear guard. Warren, as usual, was at the front with the skirmishers. Union skirmishers gained the junction of the Boydton Plank and Quaker roads. Soon, before they reached the junction, Johnson's troops, in accordance with Anderson's directive, retired into the fortifications covering the White Oak road. Outposts were left by the Confederates to contest the Federals' drive.

---

103 *Ibid.*, 758, 785.

104 *Ibid.*, 781. The 20th Indiana had moved out to the left of Mott's division.

105 *Ibid.*, 676, 710.

106 *OR* 46, pt. 3, 250.

107 *OR* 46, pt. 1, 676.

Advancing beyond the junction, the Federals approached J. Stroud's farm. Confederate sharpshooters posted in the Stroud house picked off several bluecoats. A combat patrol from the 118th Pennsylvania, led by Captain George W. Moore and Lieutenant William T. Godwin, sprinted toward the house. Unable to stop the onrushing Yankees, the Southerners abandoned the building. Occupying the house, the bluecoats rushed to the windows and blazed away at the rapidly disappearing grayclads. A section of artillery posted behind an earthwork covering the White Oak road returned the Yankees' fire. The battery commander standing on top of the works directing the cannoneers paid no attention to the Yankees. The first shell from the Rebel field pieces passed over the house, the second struck it, and the third exploded in the chimney, wounding two men. Brick and plaster "flew about thick, enveloping the new occupants of the structure in dust and rubbish." The house was hurriedly evacuated.[108]

If Griffin's men were to attack the Confederate battery, they would have to cross a large open field. To make matters more difficult for Griffin's troops, the thick woods which flanked the Quaker road had prevented Crawford's and Miles' soldiers from keeping pace with them. Darkness blanketed the area before Crawford's and Miles' bluecoats drew abreast of Griffin's. In the light of these difficulties, Warren decided against an attack on the Confederate earthworks guarding the approaches to the White Oak road.[109]

Thus closed the battle of Lewis' Farm. The Confederates reported that they lost about 250 men in this engagement. General Warren listed his casualties as: 53 killed, 306 wounded and 22 missing. If the report of General Chamberlain is to be believed, the Confederates understated their losses. Chamberlain boasted that his brigade, on the 30th, buried 130 Rebels who had fallen in the battle. In addition, Warren reported the capture of about 100 Rebels.[110]

108 Survivors' Association, *History of the Corn Exchange Regiment*, 563-563.

109 *OR* 46, pt. 3, 245; *OR* 46, pt. 1, 801-802, 853, 862, 1287.

110 *OR* 46, pt. 1, 803, 849, 1287.

Part III

Grant Modifies His Master Plan

The favorable way in which events were developing on the 29th led Grant to change his plan of operations. He decided to have Sheridan, for the time being, forego his projected raid on the Confederate railroads. In a letter informing the cavalry leader of the day's happenings, Grant wrote: "I now feel like ending the matter (the investment of Petersburg) if it is possible to do so before going back." After telling Sheridan to forget about the raid, Grant ordered the cavalryman "to push round the enemy if you can and get onto his right rear." The cavalry would make this movement, Grant observed, in concert with the infantry. Grant cautioned Sheridan that the activities of the Confederate cavalry might cause him to modify his action. Sheridan was to put his new set of instructions into operation in the morning.[111]

At the same time, Grant addressed a message to Meade informing him that "Sheridan has received orders to push for the enemy's right rear in the morning, unless the position of . . . the Confederate cavalry makes a different course necessary." Grant also outlined for his subordinate the moves which he wanted the II and V Corps to undertake on the 30th. If Warren's advance up the Boydton Plank Road should compel the Confederates to fall back behind Hatcher's Run during the night, the II and V Corps were "to wheel to the right so as to cover all the crossing of the run." If the Rebels did not retire across the run, the Federals were to "push up close to his and feel out to . . . their left and endeavor to force him to this course."[112]

In the meantime, Meade had already drafted a set of instructions to guide his corps commanders. Warren was directed to have his V Corps resume the advance at 6:00 a.m. The right flank of the V Corps was to extend across the Quaker Road; its left was to be pushed into the countryside west of the road.[113]

Humphreys' II Corps was to move forward at the same time. The II Corps' right flank division of Hays' was to advance along the road leading from Dabney's Mill to J. Crow's farm. Miles' division on Humphreys' left would continue to

111 *Ibid.*, OR 46, pt. 3, 266.

112 *Ibid.*, 243.

113 *Ibid.*, OR 46, pt. 1, 803.

maintain contact with Warren's right, and if necessary, render support to the V Corps. Each of Humphreys' three divisions was expected to hold one brigade in reserve. Humphreys' and Warren's troops were to force the Rebels to fall back into their fortifications. If, however, the Confederates came out of their works, the Yankees were "to give battle."[114]

After evaluating Warren's after action reports from the afternoon of the 29th, the Union brass were reasonably certain that in the Burgess Mill sector, Griffin's division had forced the Confederates to retire into the earthworks. This intelligence, taken in conjunction with Grant's orders, caused Meade to modify his previous instructions to Warren. As soon as Warren had ascertained that Meade's interpretation of the tactical situation was correct, he was to extend his line to the left. Combat patrols would then be thrown out in an effort to pinpoint the Confederate positions west of the Boydton Plank Road. This dispatch reached Warren's command post an hour before midnight.[115]

At the same time, Grant issued orders for General Ord to have one of his divisions cross Hatcher's Run at 5:00 a.m. on the 30th. The soldiers from the Army of the James were to support Humphreys' Corps.[116]

The staff officer entrusted with Grant's message regarding the change in plans reached Dinwiddie Court House on the night of the 29th. Ushered into General Sheridan's headquarters, the aide handed the cavalry leader Grant's letter. Without a moment's hesitation, Sheridan made his plans to cope with the changed situation. Sheridan proposed to send General Merritt with Devin's division to gain possession of Five Forks. Crook's division would be held in reserve; Custer's would continue to protect the trains.[117]

It rained very hard throughout the night. When Devin mustered his division on the morning of the 30th, the rain was still falling. Before taking leave of Sheridan, Merritt received last minute instructions. Merritt was told that Devin's division was to advance via Adams Road to J. Boisseau's farm. If no opposition was encountered, the Federals were to turn into Crump Road and try to gain White Oak Road. Merritt then rejoined his command. When Merritt gave the word, the column moved out.[118]

---

114 *Ibid.*, OR 46, pt. 3, 251.

115 *Ibid.*, OR 46, pt. 1, 803.

116 *Ibid.*, OR 46, pt. 3, 269.

117 *Ibid.*

118 *Ibid.*, OR 46, pt. 1, 1116, 1122.

Except for several brief stops to remove a few felled trees from the road, the march was routine. Two miles north of Dinwiddie Court House, Merritt halted the division. In accordance with Merritt's instructions, Devin posted Col. Charles L. Fitzhugh's brigade at the intersection of Brooks and Adams roads. One of Fitzhugh's regiments advanced along Brooks Road and established a roadblock on the Boydton Plank Road. The rain-drenched column then continued to J. Boisseau's farm. Devin massed one of his two remaining brigades, Col. Peter Stagg's, at the junction of the Dinwiddie and Crump Roads. The general would use Brig. Gen. Alfred Gibb's brigade for reconnaissance. Altogether, Gibbs sent out three combat patrols. Two of Gibb's regiments—the 5th and 6th U.S. Cavalry—were sent up Dinwiddie Road with instructions "to feel and find the enemy." Maj. R. Murray Morris of the 6th Cavalry was in charge of this patrol. The 6th Massachusetts—Col. Casper Crowninshield commanding—moved across to reconnoiter Boydton Plank Road. Col. Charles L. Leiper's 6th Pennsylvania Cavalry advanced up Crump Road. The Pennsylvanians were to see if they could block White Oak Road. In addition, Leiper was to maintain contact with Harris' and Crowninshield's patrols.[119]

Within a short time the three Union patrols had established contact with Confederate outposts. These were the first butternuts that the cavalrymen had seen since leaving Dinwiddie Court House. Attacking, the bluecoats drove the Rebel vedettes back on their supports.[120]

Although no fresh reports from the endangered right reached Lee's headquarters on the morning of the 30th, the general became convinced that he would have to send additional reinforcements if he were to take the initiative against Sheridan. Any withdrawal from the Petersburg defense line was dangerous. But unless Lee was willing to have his right turned, there was no other alternative. Grimly, Lee issued instructions for General Gordon's Corps to assume responsibility for the defense of a two-mile section of the earthworks on the west side of Lieutenant Run. These trenches were held by Maj. Gen. Cadmus M. Wilcox's division. Once Gordon's troops had relieved Wilcox's, Lee would reinforce his endangered right. Gordon planned to use Maj. Gen. Bryan Grimes' division to relieve Wilcox's left flank units.

---

119 *Ibid.*, OR 46, 1116, 1122, 1128.

120 *Ibid.*

Having taken care of this business, Lee rode out to Sutherland's Station learned that Fitz Lee's division was en route to Five Forks. The general was disturbed to learn that Rooney Lee's and Rosser's troopers had not arrived from Stony Creek.[121]

Under the cover of darkness, Pickett's three infantry brigades had marched form Sutherland's Station to Burgess Mill. It was a cold, rainy night. The road was a ribbon of mud; the angry little streams athwart the division's path were almost past fording. On the morning of the 30th, Anderson, Pickett, Heth, and several other ranking officers were summoned to a conference with General Lee at Sutherland's Station.

At this meeting, the Rebel brass discussed various ways of dealing with Sheridan, but only two seemed promising. Heth expressed the view that, from his extended front, he might strike the advancing bluecoats a heavy blow. Pickett, however, seemed to have a better opportunity. He was told that he was to use his three brigades, and two of Johnson's (Ransom's and Wallace's) in the projected attack. As the initial step in Lee's battle plan, Pickett's command was to march west on Five Forks, where his infantrymen would rendezvous with Fitz Lee's cavalry. From Five Forks, with the cavalry in support, Pickett was to march toward Dinwiddie Court House and assail the Yankees. Six of Pegram's guns were slated to go with Pickett. If the Confederates could drive Sheridan from Dinwiddie Court House, they would frustrate the Federal drive to cut General Lee's vital supply lines. By these orders, Lee had carried out the suggestion originally advanced by Longstreet. A mobile task force had been concentrated and given the mission of guarding the army's right flank. This force, when assembled, would consist of about 6,400 infantry and 4,200 cavalry. Having completed his business at Sutherland's Station, Lee returned to Petersburg.[122]

Transfer of Johnson's two brigades to augment Pickett's task force had dangerously reduced the infantry strength of Anderson's small corps. Unless units were brought from other sectors to take their places on the lines, Anderson would have to spread his remaining men very thin. The position held by Anderson's Corps was important in itself, and it also constituted the sector from which troops could be drawn quickest in case additional reinforcements had to be sent to Pickett. Accordingly, Lee moved to shift additional troops into this area. Brig. Gen. William MacRae's brigade of Heth's Division was transferred from the east to the west bank of Hatcher's Run. MacRae's troops were stationed east of Burgess Mill. One of

121 Freeman, *R. E. Lee*, vol. 4, 30-31.

122 *Ibid.*, 31; Douglas S. Freeman, *Lee's Lieutenants: A Study in Command*, 3 vols. (New York, 1944), vol. 3, 657-658.

TABLE 2	
Zone and Command	Infantry per Mile of Defended Lines
North of the James	
Cavalry on the left flank, approximately 500	
Longstreet, with Field's and Kershaw's divisions (no change)	1,360
Ewell, with Virginia Reserves, Local Defense Troops and Siege Artillery (no change)	1,320
Howlett Line	
Mahone (no change)	740
From the Appomattox to Lieutenant's Run	
Gordon's, with two divisions, by the extension of line two miles to the Right, density reduced on fronts of four miles from 1,350	870
From Lieutenant's Run to Burgess Mill	
Major General Bryan Grimes' division of Gordon's Corps, two-mile front	870
Wilcox's division less McGowan's and Hyman's brigades but with line shortened to about two and one-fourth miles	1,100
Heth's division, strengthened by Hyman's brigade, line approximately three and three-quarters miles in length	7,787
Average density of this zone	1,370
Beyond Burgess Mill	
Anderson, with Johnson's division, less Ransom's and Wallace's brigades, but with Hunton's brigade of Pickett's division and McGowan's brigade of Wilcox's division added, three mile front	1,200
Mobile task force operating beyond the fortified lines at Five Forks	6,400 infantry 4,200 cavalry
Moving	
Pickett, to join Anderson	5,000 infantry
Cavalry, on the right flank	4,200 cavalry

Wilcox's brigades—Col. Joseph H. Hyman's—was transferred from the Lieutenant's Run area to the rifle pits south of Burgess Mill. Following the arrival on the west side of Hatcher's Run, McGowan's brigade was temporarily attached to Anderson's Corps. Hunton's brigade, which arrived from Richmond on the morning of the 30th, was assigned to hold the works near the junction of the Claiborne and White Oak Roads. Hunton would receive his orders from General Johnson. The trenches vacated by this shift to the right were occupied by Grimes' troops.[123]

The changes effected by Lee left the dispositions of the Confederate troops on the right on the 30th are as shown in Table 2 on the previous page.

During his advance from Sutherland's Station to Five Forks, Fitz Lee did not see the foe and continued to move down Dinwiddie Road. Before proceeding very far, the Southerners' vanguard established contact with Morris' combat patrol.[124]

Meantime, Pickett's column had also started for Five Forks along White Oak Road. The distance to be covered was little more than four miles. The road led through a flat, drab country of pine woods and small, open fields. Several roads, including Crump Road along which the 6th Pennsylvania was operating, approached White Oak Road from the south. Because Pickett's column was passing across their front, the Union troopers made the most of their opportunity. In addition, patrols sent by General Ayres established contact with Pickett's soldiers. Colonel Pegram's adjutant, Capt. V. Gordon McCabe, wrote in his diary:

> Our flank being exposed to the enemy, they harassed us with small bodies of cavalry without intermission. General Pickett, instead of pushing on, stopped, formed a regiment in line-of-battle, and awaited some attack. Much valuable time was lost in this way. A line of skirmishers marching on our flank would have been ample protection.[125]

Pickett thought the march "necessarily slow" because of the constant skirmishing. "In front," he reported, "we had to drive the enemy out of the way nearly the whole distance."[126]

---

123 Freeman, *R. E. Lee*, vol. 4, 32; *OR* 46, pt. 1, 1287. MacRae's sharpshooters, however, remained on the east side of the run.

124 *Ibid.*, 31; *OR* 46, pt. 1, 1299.

125 Armistead C. Gordon, *Memories and Memorials of William Gordon McCabe*, vol. 1 (Richmond, VA: Old Dominion Press, Inc., 1925), 163

126 Freeman, *Lee's Lieutenants*, vol. 3, 658-659.

Major Morris' combat patrol penetrated to within three-quarters of a mile of Five Forks without difficulty. The few Confederate scouts encountered were easily brushed aside. Suddenly, however, the situation drastically changed and the attackers became the attacked, as Fitz Lee's hard-hitting division arrived on the scene. Seizing the initiative, the Confederates quickly surrounded Morris' regulars. Undaunted by this turn of events, the Union troopers dug their spurs into their horses and cut their way out of the trap. Nevertheless, the Federals lost 3 officers and 20 men. The Rebels likewise suffered several casualties. Among the Confederates wounded was Brig. Gen. William H. Payne. Returning to J. Boisseau's farm, Morris informed General Merritt that a strong force of Rebel cavalry had occupied Five Forks.[127]

The other two patrols sent out by Gibbs—Crowninshield's and Leiper's—crossed Gravelly Run. Advancing up Boydton Plank Road, Crowninshield's cavalrymen successfully connected with Warren's V Corps. Having accomplished their mission, Crowninshield's troopers rejoined the brigade. Leiper's troopers penetrated to within a sort distance of White Oak Road. Here they spotted a strong infantry column marching westward toward Five Forks. After sending back news of his discovery, Leiper and his men feigned attacks on the Confederates' left flank. These harassing tactics proved to be effective, because the Rebels would halt and form line of battle. After the infantry had deployed, the cavalry could fall back. The Confederates would then re-assemble and resume the march. This operation was repeated several times during the afternoon, and the Southerners lost valuable time. The Yankees identified Pickett's command from several prisoners they had captured. Once the Confederates had passed beyond the point where Crump Road deadended into White Oak Road, Leiper's command retraced its steps and rejoined Gibbs' brigade.[128]

When General Devin learned of Major Morris' setback, he sent the 1st U.S. Cavalry and two of Colonel Fitzhugh's regiments to recover the lost ground. Advancing up Dinwiddie Road, the Union troopers penetrated to within a short distance of Five Forks. By this time, Pickett's troops had reached Five Forks. Spotting a strong infantry battle line moving toward them, the cavalrymen fell back.[129]

General Crook's division remained at Dinwiddie Court House for most of the day. Gregg's brigade was stationed at the point where Boydton Plank Road crossed

---

127 OR 46, pt. 1, 1122, 1128, 1299.

128 *Ibid.*, Freeman, *Lee's Lieutenants*, vol. 3, 658-659.

129 OR 46, pt. 1, 1122.

Stony Creek. If Rooney Lee's and Rosser's divisions were to rendezvous with Fitz Lee's, they would have to make a detour south of Stony Creek and west of Chamberlain's Bed, a typical narrow and sluggish Virginian stream. It meandered from south of Five Forks in a southerly direction towards Dinwiddie Court House. Roads crossed it at its two fords: Danse's and Fitzgerald's.

During the morning, one of Henry E. Davies' Jr. regiments, the 10th New York, rode up Boydton Plank Road and opened communications with Warren's Corps. When Sheridan learned that the Confederates had occupied Five Forks in force, he directed General Crook to reinforce Merritt with one brigade. Accordingly, Crook ordered Davies' brigade to move out. Reaching J. Boisseau's farm, Davies reported to Merritt. Because the Confederates gave no signs of exploiting the success which they had scored at Morris' expense, Merritt decided not to commit Davies' troopers. Though not called on, Davies' men remained in the saddle ready to spring into action at a moment's notice.[130]

On the night of the 30th, Devin's division, reinforced by Davies' brigade, bivouacked on J. Boisseau's farm. For security purposes, a line of outposts was established by the Federal officers to cover the camps.

Throughout the long dreary day, Custer's troopers continued to escort the trains. The heavy rains made this task a nightmare. Even with corduroying, progress was disgustingly slow. Large details were constantly at work laying "corduroy" and lifting the wagons out of mud holes. At times, a horse or mule would be seen standing on what appeared to be solid ground. Suddenly, one of the beast's hoofs would sink out of sight. As the animal struggled to catch itself, all its feet would disappear into the slime. The beast would then have to be pulled out of the Virginia quicksand by a detachment of soldiers. At dark, the head of the train halted four long, hard miles east of Dinwiddie Court House.[131]

The intensive scouting and patrolling carried out by Merritt's command enabled Sheridan to get a good idea of the strength of the Confederate force to his front. Between 40 and 50 prisoners, including some from Pickett's division, were bagged by Union troopers. One of the captured infantrymen told Sheridan that the Rebel cavalry was being concentrated at Five Forks. The same individual informed Sheridan that Pickett's division had come from Burke's Station. Supplemental reports reaching Sheridan's command post from the front corrected this misinformation. The Union scouts reported that Pickett's division was deployed along White Oak Road, with its right anchored at Five Forks. Sheridan relayed this

130 *Ibid.*, 1112, 1141, 1144.

131 *Ibid.*, 1116, 1129, 1134; Grant, *Personal Memoirs*, vol. 2, 302-303.

intelligence to Grant, along with the news that Merritt's command was encamped at J. Boisseau's.[132]

It was almost sundown when the head of Pickett's column reached Five Forks. There, as anticipated, Pickett found Fitz Lee. The cavalryman told Pickett that his troopers were in contact with the Yankees on Dinwiddie Road. So far, Lee stated, his grey clads had more than held their own. Pickett had intended to press on toward Dinwiddie Court House. But after conferring with Fitz Lee, he decided that, because of the late hour, the weariness of the troops, and absence of Rooney Lee's and Rosser's cavalry divisions, he would wait until morning.

Two of Pickett's infantry brigades moved down Dinwiddie Road about three-quarters of a mile. These units would be responsible for protecting the task force from a surprise attack. Advancing, the infantry encountered dismounted Union cavalry armed with Spencer carbines. Undaunted, the butternuts pressed ahead and the Yankees fell back. After a brisk clash, the Confederates occupied the designated ground. The other Confederate units bivouacked in the woods at the forks. Mercifully, the rain ceased about dark. During the night, however, it began to fall heavily again. The infantry were prepared for this, after a fashion. Colonel Pegram and his staff had neither blankets nor food. They had hoped to return that night to Burgess Mill.[133]

Shortly after the Confederates bedded down for the night, Rooney Lee's and Rosser's divisions reached Five Forks. The muddy roads and booming creeks had made the march from Stony Creek Station a nightmare. Following the arrival of these units, Fitz Lee assumed command of the cavalry corps. Col. Thomas T. Munford took charge of Fitz Lee's division.[134]

General Grant had written Sheridan on the night of the 29th, "We will act altogether as one army here until it is seen what can be done with the enemy."[135] Despite Grant's intentions, the Union cavalry and infantry had acted independently of one another throughout the day. Humphreys and Warren were informed only that Sheridan was operating on their left. This was all. Warren had been repeatedly warned on the 29th that he must guard and protect his left, while at the same time his right would maintain contact with Humphreys' Corps. Yet, in his letter to

---

132 OR 46, pt. 3, 324.

133 Freeman, *R. E. Lee*, vol. 6, 31-32; Freeman, *Lee's Lieutenants*, vol. 3, 659.

134 OR 46, pt. 1, 1299.

135 *Ibid.*, OR 46, pt. 3, 266; William W. Swan, "The Five Forks Campaign," *Papers of the Military Society of Massachusetts* (Boston, 1907), vol. 4, 278.

Sheridan, Grant had observed that "Our line is now unbroken from the Appomattox to Dinwiddie."[136]

The only other reference to cooperation between the infantry and cavalry up to this time is found in one of Warren's numerous communications to Meade, sent at 9:50 a.m. on the 30th. A short time before, one of Sheridan's staff officers, Capt. George L. Gillespie, had passed by Warren's command post while bearing dispatches to General Grant. Gillespie told Warren that Merritt's command was massing at J. Boisseau's farm before sending out patrols to feel for White Oak Road. When Warren informed his superior of these developments, he also reported that Ayres' division would be sent on a forced reconnaissance to W. Dabney's. Upon reaching that point, Ayres's troops would be in a position to "cooperate with General Sheridan if he comes within reach."[137]

By this time, however, Grant had decided that the operations for the day should be confined to the infantry. Taking into account the heavy rain that had been falling since the previous evening, Grant addressed a message to Sheridan. The lieutenant general commanding observed:

> The heavy rain of to-day will make it impossible for us to do much until it dries up a little or we get roads around our rear repaired. You may therefore leave what cavalry you deem necessary to protect the left and hold such positions as you deem necessary for that purpose and send the remainder back to Humphreys' Station, where they can get hay and grain. Fifty wagons loaded with forage will be sent to you in the morning. Send an officer back to direct the wagons back to where you want them. Report to me the cavalry you will leave back and the positions you will occupy. Could not our cavalry go back by the way of Stony Creek . . . [Station] and destroy or capture the store of supplies there?[138]

Following the receipt of this letter, Sheridan left Dinwiddie Court House and hastened to Grant's headquarters. Reporting to Grant's Gravelly Run command post, Sheridan urged the general to reconsider his order recalling the cavalry. Although the rain continued to pour down, the persuasive Sheridan succeeded in prevailing upon Grant to change his mind. The cavalry would not be withdrawn from Dinwiddie Court House. Grant expressed his hope "that some good might result from the presence" of Sheridan's troopers near Five Forks. Evidently,

---

136 Swan, "The Five Forks Campaign," 278-279; OR 46, pt. 3, 266.

137 Swan, "The Five Forks Campaign," 279; OR 46, pt. 3, 266.

138 OR 46, pt.3, 325.

Sheridan was so carried away with his arguments that he told Grant that his troopers had reached White Oak Road, which was not true. When Sheridan returned to Dinwiddie Court House, he carried an order from Grant to hold the positions on White Oak Road, even if it prevented the "sending back of any of . . . his cavalry to Humphreys' Station to be fed." If Sheridan thought it necessary, the 50 wagon loads of forage ordered to his command would be increased.[139]

During his return trip to Dinwiddie Court House, Sheridan stopped at Warren's command post. Before continuing his journey, Sheridan told Warren that he had issued instructions for one of his divisions to advance to White Oak Road.[140]

It appears that General Meade and his corps commanders operated at a marked disadvantage. They had not been given an opportunity, as Sheridan had, to know what Grant's plans were. General Meade's position was especially embarrassing. The wings of his Army of the Potomac were separated by Ord's Army of the James, which was independent of Meade. Humphreys and Warren were under Meade's direct command, but the general could only give the two Corps commanders orders as he received them from Grant.[141]

The heavy rainfall had also rendered it extremely difficult to keep the supplies of war matériel moving to Humphreys' and Warren's corps. Warren decided to have the trains, which had accompanied his troops across the Rowanty, moved north of Gravelly Run. Large fatigue parties had to be turned out to help the teamsters. Even so, it was hard going, because the wagons "were nearly immovable in the mud." Finally, the soldiers had to resort to the time-consuming task of corduroying to get the heavily loaded vehicles to the front. During the day, the portion of the V Corps' train which had been parked at Perkins' farm crossed the Rowanty and moved to the intersection of Monk's Neck and Vaughan roads.[142]

Colonel Theodore Lyman, a Meade staffer and diarist, reported that the heavy rains had "reduced the roads, already poor, to a hopeless pudding." "Gravelly Run," the colonel stated "was swollen to treble its usual size; and Hatcher's Run swept away the bridges and required pontoons."[143]

---

139 *Ibid.*, OR 46, pt. 3, 324-325; Swan, "The Five Forks Campaign," 280; Horace Porter, "Five Forks and the Pursuit of Lee," in *Battles and Leaders of the Civil War*, vol. 4, 709-710.

140 Swan, "The Five Forks Campaign," 280.

141 *Ibid.*, 280-281.

142 OR 46, pt. 1, 803; OR 46, pt. 3, 298-299. The V Corps trains were guarded by the 11th and 14th U.S. Infantry.

143 Swan, "The Five Forks Campaign," 281.

The orders for the advance of the infantry, however, were not countermanded. Before retiring on the night of the 29th, Warren prepared the orders which he hoped would enable his corps to carry out the mission which Meade had assigned it. According to Meade's directive, the V Corps was to force the Rebels back into their fortifications. In addition, Warren was to reconnoiter to the left to develop the Confederates position in the area adjacent to the Claiborne Road. Warren, therefore, ordered his three division commanders to hold their units ready to resume the advance at 6:00 a.m. Warren also alerted them to be on the lookout for a Confederate counterstroke.[144]

On the morning of the 30th, while Warren's troops were preparing to move out, Grant informed Meade:

> As Warren and Humphreys advance, thus shortening their line, I think the former had better move by the left flank as far as he can stretch out with safety, and cover the White Oak Road if he can. This will enable Sheridan to reach the . . . South Side road by Ford's road, and may be, double the enemy up, so as to drive him out of his works south of Hatcher's Run.[145]

Chief of Staff Webb reported that Grant's letter reached the headquarters of the Army of the Potomac early on the 30th. This communication was not in complete accord with the one Grant had sent to Sheridan on the evening of the 29th. Stating that the cavalry and infantry would "act together as one army here until it is seen what can be done with the enemy." In so far as the operations of the cavalry were concerned, Grant's dispatch to Meade was "at a decided variance with the letter to Sheridan of the same morning telling him to leave only such force as he deemed necessary to hold the left and send the remainder back to Humphreys' Station.[146]

During the night, Warren had had time to reflect on the tactical situation. He did not think it would be advisable to pursue his advance up Boydton Plank Road until Humphreys' corps was able to get into position on his right. (It seems that while Miles' scouts had established contact with the V Corps, his battle line, however, had failed to draw abreast of Griffin's division before halting on the 29th.) Warren was also worried about his left. The corps commander did not believe he could extend this flank "with propriety" until he could obtain some idea of

144 *OR* 46, pt. 1, 803.

145 *Ibid.*, *OR* 46, pt. 3, 282.

146 Swan, "The Five Forks Campaign, 282; *OR* 46, pt. 3, 266, 325.

Sheridan's movements. If his left flank division (Crawford's) moved forward, its left flank would "be in the air." When Warren sent a message to headquarters at 5:50 a.m., reporting that his corps was ready to move, he called Chief of Staff Webb's attention to these difficulties. In conclusion, Warren remarked that he considered the position then occupied by his corps as the best available unless Meade proposed to assault the Rebel fortifications at Burgess Mill.[147]

It was 8:30 a.m. before Warren received an answer from army headquarters. Meade replied through his chief of staff. When Warren glanced at the message signed by Webb, he received scant satisfaction. Webb informed Warren that General Meade did not think he occupied as much of the front as the strength of his corps warranted. Meade wanted Warren to use two of his divisions—Ayres' and Crawford's—to reconnoiter the Confederate right. Webb was unable to give Warren much information regarding Sheridan's movements. All that Webb would do in this respect was to state that Sheridan had been "ordered to attack or turn the enemy's right." Warren, however, was to act independently of Sheridan. If the Rebels moved out of their breastworks and assaulted Warren's left, the V Corps was to counterattack. In this eventuality, Meade promised to support Warren "with all the available force to be procured.[148]

In the meantime, Warren and Humphreys had exchanged messages. At 6:00 a.m., Warren informed Humphreys that he proposed to postpone his advance until such time as Miles' division drew abreast of Griffin's. Warren expressed himself as hesitant about sending Griffin's troops, unsupported, across the broad open field to their front. Since Miles' soldiers had to pass through a heavily wooded area, Warren felt it would be some time before they drew abreast of his corps.[149]

Replying to Warren's communication, Humphreys reported that his corps was moving ahead slowly through a dense and almost impenetrable swamp. In accordance with Warren's wishes, Humphreys stated that he had reiterated his instructions for Miles to re-establish contact with the V Corps. Despite Humphreys' efforts, it was almost 7:30 a.m. before Miles' bluecoats moved into position on Warren's right flank.[150]

At 6:00 a.m., Warren directed Griffin to have Bartlett's skirmish line feel the Confederate front. Bartlett's bluecoats were to ascertain if the Southerners had

147 *Ibid.*, OR 46, pt. 3, 298.

148 *Ibid.*

149 *Ibid.*, OR 46, pt. 1, 803-804.

150 *Ibid.*, 804.

pulled back from the earthworks which they had occupied when darkness put a stop to hostilities.[151]

A dense fog blanketed the area, so Bartlett determined to delay his reconnaissance in hopes that the atmosphere would clear. It was fortunate for the Federals that he made this decision. At 6:30 a.m., when the fog lifted a little, Bartlett discovered that the right flank of his skirmish line was within 150 yards of a line of Rebel rifle pits. The soldiers manning the Union outposts decided to see if they could entice some of the Rebels to desert. Loaves of bread were thrust on bayonets and held aloft. The bluecoats then shouted, "Hey, Johnny! Come over and get some fresh bread and coffee." None of the Southerners took advantage of the offer.[152]

A slight demonstration on the part of the bluecoats drew heavy fire. Satisfied that the grey clads held the earthworks in force, the Union skirmishers, having accomplished their mission, fell back a short distance.[153]

Following receipt of the message signed by Chief of Staff Webb, Warren, despite grave misgivings, prepared to carry out the directive "to extend his line to the left as far as possible." Ayres' division was called up from the reserve and massed at Mrs. Butler's. Reconnaissance parties were sent to explore the countryside west of Boydton Plank Road. After these items were attended to, Warren sent a letter to Meade's headquarters acknowledging the communication. Warren wanted to know what would happen if he extended "his line to the left as far as possible, using both Crawford and Ayres," and the Rebels suddenly flanked him. If this transpired, Warren wondered what he would counterattack with.

It was 9:55 a.m. before Warren received a reply to this dispatch. Webb observed that Meade was "very anxious" to have Warren cover as much of the front as possible consistent with the safety of his corps. Meade's intention, Webb wrote, was to have Warren deploy Griffin and Crawford to the front, while he used Ayres to cover the corps' left flank. In addition, Meade wanted the 3rd Pennsylvania Cavalry which was guarding Warren's train to report to army headquarters at the intersection of Monk's Neck and Vaughan roads.

In the meantime, Warren had received a letter from General Webb containing information regarding the Confederate fortifications. The chief of staff reported that he had recently questioned several deserters and prisoners. From these people, Webb had learned that the Confederate fortifications covered White Oak Road.

---

151 *Ibid.*, OR 46, pt. 3, 307.

152 Survivors' Association, *History of the Corn Exchange Regiment*, 564.

153 OR 46, pt. 3, 308-309.

Acknowledging Webb's message, Warren replied that the intelligence gathered by his scouts corroborated the information Webb had obtained about the location of the Confederates' main line of resistance. Continuing, Warren wrote that two deserters had stated that the earthworks flanking Boydton Plank Road were strong "with two lines of obstructions in front." These men reported that a large number of blacks had spent the 29th strengthening these works. Still thinking in defensive terms, Warren reported that Crawford's troops were throwing up a line of breastworks near Boydton Plank Road. In case of a repulse, Warren observed, these rifle pits would make a good rallying point.

This dispatch was received by Meade at 9:35 a.m. Ten o'clock passed and still Warren's Corps did not budge. In the meantime, Captain Gillespie had passed through the V Corps' lines. From the captain, Warren secured information concerning the position of Sheridan's cavalry. This news was promptly relayed to Meade. It appears that this was the first definite information that Meade had received of Sheridan's activities.[154]

At 10:15 a.m., Warren sent another message to headquarters explaining his delays. Warren told his superiors of his plans. He would push out Ayres' division in column as he had Griffin's on the 29th. If Ayres met the foe, he was to give battle. Meade was informed that, if need be, Warren would support Ayres "with nearly the whole Corps and follow up any advantage gained." In the event that he was worsted, Warren wrote, he had "a good place to reform on." Warren admitted that he was "a little slow," but he believed that it was the only way he could keep his "troops working together and conduct operations with certainty." The corps commander expressed the opinion that the roads and fields were getting too soft for artillery, and believed that Sheridan's cavalry would have trouble operating advantageously.[155]

At 10:30 a.m., Warren directed Ayres to make a reconnaissance in the direction of White Oak Road. Ayres was to take his division and move in a northwesterly direction from Mrs. Butler's toward S. Dabney's. As the column felt its way ahead, Ayres was to see that his scouts maintained contact with the corps' skirmish line, which would remain stationary. If Ayres' troops encountered any Confederates within a mile of Boydton Plank Road, they were to attack and drive them back. Ayres was admonished not to advance his main force farther than one mile, unless

---

154 *Ibid.*, 299-300. Swan, "The Five Forks Campaign," 284. General Grant had indicated to Meade that Sheridan was moving up Ford's Church Road in an effort to reach the South Side Railroad. Furthermore, Grant had informed Meade that the cavalry was operating at too great a distance from the Army of the Potomac to effect any direct cooperation.

155 OR 46, pt. 3, 300-301.

it was to secure an obvious advantage. The division would take up a strong position with its flanks secured. Scouts were to be sent "to reconnoiter and develop the character of the county and the enemy's position." Ayres was informed that Sheridan's cavalry was massed at J. Boisseau's farm and was examining Crump Road. In the event that Ayres encountered a superior force and could hold on, Warren promised to reinforce him with Crawford's division. For communication purposes, a detachment of Warren's escort accompanied Ayres.[156]

Grant at this time had a different opinion of what Warren's plan of operation should be. Writing to Meade, Grant observed:

> My idea was that we should try to extend our left so as to cross the White Oak road, say at W. Dabney's, or as near up to the enemy as we can. This would seem to cover all the roads up to Ford's road, by which Sheridan might then move and get on to the South Side road, and possibly double up the enemy and drive him north of Hatcher's Run.[157]

The South Side Railroad, at the point where it was crossed by Ford's Road, remained Sheridan's objective.

For informational purposes, Webb forwarded Grant's dispatch to Warren. The chief of staff reported that Meade, after examining Grant's message, could see no reason for any change in the instructions which he had already sent to Warren. Webb reported that Meade had received "no information of General Sheridan's movements beyond the general statement that General S. is to turn to the enemy's right."[158]

Warren was perplexed by Grant's and Meade's messages. It seemed to Warren that Meade, on receiving Grant's communication, should have signified to him whether or not he was to extend the left flank of his corps across White Oak Road. If he were not to block White Oak Road, Warren would have liked to know just how far his left was to move out. Had Warren been in communication with Grant, he probably would have sought to obtain definite information on this subject.[159]

By 11:30 a.m., signal corps personnel succeeded in extending the field telegraph to Warren's command post. The transmission of messages between Meade's and Warren's headquarters was thus greatly expedited.

---

156 *Ibid.*, 309-310.

157 *Ibid.*, 283.

158 *Ibid.*, OR 46, pt. 1, 807.

159 *Ibid.*

In an effort to clarify the matter, at noon, Warren addressed another communication to General Webb. After acknowledging the receipt of the dispatch enclosing the one from Grant, Warren inquired about Meade's statement that there was "no reason to change his previous orders." Warren pointed out that Meade had "never said definitely how far he was expected to extend nor the object desired." "General Grant," Warren observed, "is definite on both points, and if I am to attempt . . . to block White Oak Road myself at all hazards I don't shrink from it." Warren thought that perhaps General Humphreys, if required, might occupy part of the front occupied by the V Corps. The corps commander knew from bitter experience that he should extend his "left toward the White Oak Road with strong force and precaution against an attack from the enemy." Warren informed Webb that he had seen Sheridan, and the cavalry leader had ordered a division to White Oak Road. This, Warren believed, would simplify his scheduled movement.[160]

General Warren was annoyed by the vagueness of his orders. According to the word he received from Meade's headquarters, he was to extend his left and keep it well guarded—that was all. Grant, however, wanted Warren to shift to the left and support Sheridan's cavalry in an attempt to turn the Confederates' right. Warren inferred more from Grant's dispatch than Meade's. This disposition by Warren to know the object and extent of a movement directed by his superior officer was a fault in his military character.

Meade was more patient than Warren. An examination of the correspondence which passed between Grant and Meade on the 30th indicates that the commander of the Army of the Potomac knew very little of the lieutenant general commander's master plan. Furthermore, it should be observed that at noon Warren had met Sheridan. The cavalryman, at this time, told Warren that one of his divisions was scheduled to move north to White Oak Road.[161]

Grant forwarded some information regarding Sheridan's activities to Meade. Grant reported that the cavalry sent out by Merritt had encountered the Confederates in considerable force. The blue-coated patrols, as they advanced up the Dinwiddie and Crump Roads, found White Oak Road covered by the Rebel troopers. Pushing ahead, the Union cavalrymen were reported to have seized Five Forks. (Copies of this message were also sent to Humphreys and Warren.)[162]

160   *Ibid.*, OR 46, pt. 3, 302.

161   Swan, "The Five Forks Campaign," 287.

162   *OR* 46, pt. 3, 283.

Yet, as late as 2:00 p.m., Grant refused to commit himself on the degree of cooperation that should exist between Meade's infantry and Sheridan's cavalry. At that hour, the general telegraphed the President who was at City Point:

I understood the number of dead left by the enemy yesterday for us to bury was much greater than our own dead. The captives were larger than reported also, amounting to about 160. This morning our troops have all been pushed forward, and now occupy a line from which you see marked on the map as the Crow house across the Boydton Plank road north of where the Quaker road intersects it. Sheridan's cavalry is pushing forward toward the White Oak road, and I think this afternoon or to-morrow may push on to the South Side Railroad.[163]

As if Warren were not having enough troubles with his left, the badgered general could not ignore his right. At 11:20 a.m., Warren received a dispatch from Humphreys. The II Corps commander informed Warren that, at the moment, his line of battle extended "in a straight line past the Crow house" to the V Corps' right. Humphreys stated that he had directed Mott's and Hays' skirmishers and those on the right of Miles' division to see if they could reach Hatcher's Run. Consequently, Humphreys wanted to know if Warren intended to move forward.[164]

In reply, Warren pointed out that, as the Confederates were reported to be strongly entrenched, he would be unable to advance up Boydton Plank Road. The regiments on his extreme right, Warren commented, had been refused for the want of a connection the previous evening. These organizations would be able to cooperate in Humphreys' advance, General Miles, Warren continued, had his permission to make any adjustments in this sector that he thought practicable.[165]

Throughout the morning, Warren had been so busy receiving dispatches and giving orders that he had been unable to leave his command post. After eating lunch, Warren decided to visit the front. Proceeding up Quaker Road, Warren reached J. Stroud's just as Bartlett's skirmishers started to move forward. Prior to Warren's arrival, Griffin had been told by his scouts that the Confederates were pulling back. In the face of Humphreys' advance, the Southerners had determined to abandon their line of outposts in the Burgess Mill sector. To take advantage of this situation, Griffin authorized Bartlett to advance his skirmish line.[166]

163 OR 46, pt 3, 280-281

164 *Ibid.*, 280-281, 292.

165 *Ibid.*, OR 46, pt. 1, 806.

166 *Ibid.*, 807, 846.

Following this Confederate pull back, a personal reconnaissance convinced Warren that Griffin's battle line could now cross the open field in safety. In addition, an advance would enable the V Corps to gain possession of the point where Dabney's Mill Road debouched into the Boydton Plank Road. This would be an important gain because it would facilitate communication between the II and V Corps. Warren accordingly directed Griffin to advance his battle line.

Griffin relayed this information to his brigade commanders. Bartlett's line of battle, closely supported by Gregory's brigade, moved up Boydton Plank Road. On the right, Miles' bluecoats likewise forged ahead. Within a few minutes, the Federals occupied the field fortifications recently held by Johnson's outposts. Having gained their objective, the Northerners halted and took cover. A Rebel battery mounted behind a parapet near the Burgess house hammered away at the advancing Yankees with shot and shell. Two Union artillery units—Battery B, 4th U.S. and Batteries D and G, 5th U.S.—emplaced at the junction of the Boydton Plank and Quaker roads returned the butternut cannoneers' fire. No opposition from the Rebel infantry was encountered by Griffin's troops.[167]

As soon as his men had gained the abandoned rifle pits, Warren rode forward. Training his field glasses on the Confederate main line of resistance, Warren found that the fortifications covering Burgess Mill "were well located and constructed, and defended by infantry and artillery." The timber had been slashed and where there were no trees, an "abatis had been laid." It was apparent to Warren that any advance by the Federals up the Boydton Plank Road would be fiercely contested.

There was no further action along Griffin's front until late in the afternoon. At 4:00 p.m., Colonel Hyman's North Carolina brigade moved out of the fortifications. Driving in the Union skirmishers, the Rebels launched a sharp attack on Bartlett's battle line. Assisted by the fire of the two regular batteries posted at the junction, the blue-coated infantry easily beat off this sortie. Several prisoners were captured by the Federals. One of them, a member of the 34th North Carolina, told the Yankees that Hyman's brigade had moved into the Burgess Mill sector during the morning. Following Hyman's arrival, Johnson's division shifted to the right.[168]

As darkness approached, Griffin recalled Gregory's brigade; Bartlett's troops were left to hold the captured rifle pits. Returning to the junction, Gregory's soldiers camped in the field around the Stroud house.[169] Griffin's other brigade,

---

167 *Ibid.*, 807, 808-828, 853, 862-863, 899.

168 *Ibid.*, 808-809, 863, 899.

169 *Ibid.*, 853, 863. For security purposes, the left flank of Bartlett's brigade was refused.

Chamberlain's, spent the day at Lewis' farm burying the dead and collecting the wounded from yesterday's engagement.[170]

Ayres's division moved out about noon to make its forced reconnaissance toward White Oak Road. The route selected for the division's advance was the road which led from Mrs. Butler's house on Boydton Plank Road by the Holliday house. This road entered White Oak Road near Halter Butler's residence, which was a short distance west of the Claiborne Road. Ayres' vanguard reached Holliday's without encountering any opposition. The advance brigade, Col. Frederick Winthrop's, crossed the branch of Gravelly Run that was to play so important a part in the battle of White Oak Road on the next day. Observing that his troops were having difficulty getting across the rain-swollen stream, Ayres ordered his two other brigades, Cols. Andrew W. Denison's and James Gwyn's, not to cross. Taking position on the right bank of the branch, these two units began to entrench.[171]

Winthrop's brigade penetrated to within 600 yards of White Oak Road before halting. Skirmishers were then pushed to within 400 yards of the road. Captain Horrell with the support company succeeded in getting astride the road for a few moments. From their advance position in a small clearing, the Federals observed the afternoon's activities on the White Oak Road. The Yankees watched as a strong force of Rebel infantry—Pickett's command— marched westward toward Five Forks. When Griffin's troops moved to occupy the advance rifle pits flanking Boydton Plank Road, the sound of battle came drifting in from the east. For a few minutes, the Confederate column paused before pressing on. During this time, Ayres dashed off a message to Warren reporting that Rebel infantry was moving toward Burgess Mill. Warren, in turn, relayed this news to Meade's headquarters.[172]

After a few minutes, the Southerners resumed the march. Shortly thereafter, Captain Horrell's troopers captured a Rebel officer. The Confederate told the Federals that he belonged to Pickett's division and was in charge of a wagon train. This intelligence was forwarded to Meade.[173]

Reconnoitering the area north of Holliday's farm, Ayres reported that there were no Confederate entrenchments to his front. As Ayres interpreted his front, he was correct when he made this statement. At this time, however, the general was gazing out on the portion of White Oak Road west of the Claiborne Road junction. Had Ayres faced north instead of northeast, he would have observed that there was

170 *Ibid.*, 849.

171 Porter, "Operations of the Fifth Corps," 218; *OR* 46, pt. 1, 809, 871.

172 Porter, "Operations of the Fifth Corps," 219; *OR* 46, pt. 1, 808.

173 Porter, "Operations of the Fifth Corps," 219; *OR* 46, pt. 1, 808.

a fortified line covering White Oak Road at its convergence with Claiborne Road, which veered sharply to the right and extended to Hatcher's Run.[174]

News that Ayres' patrols were feeling their way toward White Oak Road west of Halter Butler's house spurred the Confederates to take action. General Lee issued instructions for General Johnson to deploy one of his regiments outside the works. No attack was to be made on the Federals at this time. If, however, this Union unit proved to be the left flank of the Army of the Potomac it would be assaulted at a later date. In accordance with Johnson's orders, the 41st Alabama moved out of the works, crossed White Oak Road, and took position athwart the Union line of advance. Before darkness put a stop to activities in this sector, the Alabamians were in contact with Ayres' scouts.[175]

Ayres, having accomplished his mission, covered his front with a line of outposts and waited for further developments. On his right, Ayres' skirmishers were in contact with Griffin's pickets. About dusk, Warren visited Ayres' command post. After approving Ayres' dispositions, Warren rode back to his headquarters, which he reached after dark.[176]

Crawford's troops spent the day strengthening their main line of resistance which paralleled Boydton Plank Road. The divisions' left flank rested on Gravelly Run and its right near the Stroud farm. In addition to throwing up breastworks, the troops kept busy slashing timber. The gunners of Battery D, 1st New York Light Artillery emplaced their four 12-pounder Napoleons west of the Rainey house. Here they would be able to furnish support to Crawford's infantry in case of a sudden Confederate onslaught.[177]

Before the II Corps resumed its advance on the 30th, it was reinforced by a division from the Army of the James. In accordance with the order from Grant, Ord directed General Gibbon to have one of his divisions cross Hatcher's Run and support Humphreys' Corps. Before retiring on the night of the 29th, Gibbon issued instructions for General Turner to have his XXIV Corps division on the road by 5:00 a.m. After crossing to the west side of Hatcher's Run, Turner would report to General Humphreys.[178]

---

174 Porter, "Operations of the Fifth Corps," 219.

175 *OR* 46, pt. 1, 1287.

176 *Ibid.*, 809-810, 871.

177 *Ibid.*, 892, 899.

178 *Ibid.*, *OR* 46, pt. 3, 269-270.

Turner's division moved out at 5:00 a.m. After crossing Hatcher's Run, Turner's troops marched to Dabney's Mill. Within one hour after leaving his camp, Turner, despite the terrible weather, completed his dispositions. As directed by Humphreys, Turner posted his command on the right of Hays' division. To make room for soldiers from the XXIV Corps, Hays' troops closed to the left. Turner's left flank rested on Dabney's Mill and his right on Hatcher's Run near Armstrong's Mill. Brigadier General Thomas M. Harris' and Lt. Col. Andrew Potter's brigades were deployed into line of battle. Harris' was on the left and Potter's on the right. Col. William B. Curtis' brigade was held in reserve.[179]

The speed with which Turner had formed his division enabled Humphreys to start his attack as scheduled. At 6:00 a.m., the powerful Union battle line started forward. A large number of skirmishers screened Humphreys' advance.[180]

It took Hays' division about two and a half hours to reach the area around J. Crow's farm. Since the bluecoats expected to encounter heavy resistance, their advance had been cautious. At J. Crow's, the Yankees found plenty of evidence in the form of abandoned gear and supplies which indicated that the Rebels had hurriedly evacuated this area during the night. Having reached his goal, General Hays put his troops to work throwing up breastworks. Two brigades—McIvor's and Olmsted's—were stationed on the lines, while Smyth's were held in reserve.[181]

After the troops started to dig in, Hays told Colonel Olmsted to send a combat patrol and see if he could locate the Confederates main line of resistance. Within a short time, a three-regiment patrol—the 19th Maine, the 184th Pennsylvania, and the 36th Wisconsin—moved forward. The Maine regiment, deployed as skirmishers, was supported by the other two units. After advancing about three-fourths of a mile through a belt of slashed timbers, the bluecoats spotted a Confederate strong point. The soldiers observed that this redoubt (Fort Powell), which was situated on the south bank of Hatcher's Run, mounted two guns. A second earthwork, in which one gun was emplaced, was also spotted. Both forts were within supporting distance of one another. After sending back news of his discovery, Olmsted had the soldiers of the 19th Maine open fire. The Maine men had previously occupied positions within 300 yards of Fort Powell. Unable to depress their cannon enough to play on the Yankees, the grey clads had to rely on

---

179 *Ibid.*, 322; OR 46, pt. 1, 1214. In reaching Hatcher's Run, Turner's troops marched by way of Squirrel Level and Vaughan roads.

180 *Ibid.*, 676; OR 46, pt. 3, 288.

181 *Ibid.*, OR 46, pt. 1, 757, 759, 764, 766. McIvor's brigade was posted on the right and Olmsted's on the left.

small-arms when they returned the Yankee's fire. The Confederates and the men of the 19th Maine sniped away at one another until 4:00 p.m. At that hour, the 36th Wisconsin moved forward and relieved the Maine regiment.[182]

Turner's troops kept abreast of Hays' battle line as it pushed ahead. As the advance continued, Turner's division found itself squeezed out of line. The reason behind this development was the sharp meander to the southwest described by Hatcher's Run in the portion of channel between Burgess and Armstrong's mills. To avoid being completely crowded out of position, Turner's division was forced to cross Hatcher's Run a second time. When the division halted and entrenched, Harris' left flank rested on the stream. On the opposite side of Hatcher's Run was Hays' right flank unit, McIvor's brigade. Potter's brigade on Turner's right was in contact with Foster's division.[183]

On Hays' left, Mott's battle line worked its way through a dense belt of undergrowth. The few Confederate pickets encountered were brushed aside. Mott's troops drove across the road linking Dabney's Mill with the Boydton Plank Road. A swampy branch of Hatcher's Run was also negotiated. After an advance of about three-quarters of a mile, the division halted and entrenched. The right flank of Pierce's brigade was posted west of the Crow house. Pierce's troops were in contact with Hays' bluecoats. De Trobriand's brigade, as on the previous day, was held in reserve by Mott. While Pierce's and McAllister's soldiers were throwing up earthworks, de Trobriand was called upon to furnish large fatigue details. Some of these groups were put to work repairing Dabney's Mill Road. Others were given the task of corduroying roads and building bridges to facilitate the movement of the Corps' artillery to the front.[184]

Miles' division with three brigades—Ramsey's, Madill's, and Scott's—deployed into line of battle had a rough time working its way through the thick woods and dense underbrush. Each brigade commander covered his front with skirmishers. During the night, Ramsey's brigade on the left lost contact with the V Corps. It was 7:30 a.m. before Ramsey's unit re-established contact with Warren's soldiers on their left. At 9:00 a.m., Miles' troops reached Dabney's Mill Road and the division halted, while the brigade commanders reformed their units. Since Miles' battle line was now abreast of Warren's, it would be dangerous to proceed farther without a corresponding movement on the part of the V Corps. Warren, however, refused to budge. Artillery was brought forward. The four

182 *Ibid.,* 759, 762; OR 46, pt. 3, 290.

183 *Ibid.,* OR 46, pt. 1, 1214.

184 *Ibid.,* 776, 781, 785, 788.

12-pounder Napoleons of Battery K, 4th U.S. Light Artillery were unlimbered at the junction of the Boydton Plank and Quaker roads. The cannoneers of Battery M, 1st New Hampshire emplaced their four 3-inch rifles a short distance to the left of Battery E.[185]

General Miles employed his other brigade, Nugent's, on fatigue details. Large detachments were drafted from Nugent's command and put to work corduroying roads.[186]

During the morning, two Confederate deserters surrendered to Miles' scouts. When escorted to the general's command post, the Southerners stated that they belonged to Scales' North Carolina brigade. (At this time, Scales was sick, and Hyman was in charge of the unit.) The duo informed the Federal officers that their brigade had been pulled out of the Petersburg lines long before daybreak. After crossing Hatcher's Run, their organization had occupied the rifle pits covering Burgess Mill. News of this interesting development was promptly relayed to Meade's headquarters.[187]

Early in the afternoon, Humphreys received instructions from Meade to move his troops as close to the Confederates' main line of resistance as possible. When this had been accomplished, he was to entrench his command. Humphreys would then make an inspection and notify headquarters as to how many troops would be needed to hold the front from Boydton Plank Road to Hatcher's Run.

The extensive scouting and patrolling carried out by his soldiers throughout the morning allowed Humphreys to pinpoint most of the Confederate fortifications. Humphreys knew that Hays' and Mott's troops had driven almost as close to the foe's works as possible. If these two units attempted to renew the advance, it would probably precipitate a general engagement. Only on the left, in Miles' sector, was there a chance of inching closer to the Confederate works without much fighting. Humphreys, therefore, issued instructions for Miles to push forward and examine the fortifications which the grey clads had erected to cover the approaches to Burgess Mill.[188]

Following receipt of Humphreys' orders, Miles' division resumed the advance. Covered by a strong force of skirmishers, the line of battle moved relentlessly ahead through the thick undergrowth. Because Mott's division held its ground, Miles' command pivoted on its right flank brigade, Scott's. On the left, Ramsey's left flank

185 *Ibid.*, 676, 710, 791.

186 *Ibid.*, 710, 724.

187 *Ibid.*, OR 46, pt. 3, 289.

188 *Ibid.*, 290, 295.

guided on the Boydton Plank Road. Skirmishers of the 53rd Pennsylvania pushed ahead and forced the Confederate outposts to fall back. As soon as their pickets had retired, the Southern artillerists opened fire on the bluecoats. Both Ramsey's skirmishers and his battle line were shelled by the Confederate cannoneers. This bombardment, however, proved to be so ineffective that, for all practical purposes, it was useless.[189]

When they moved forward, the skirmishers covering the advance of Miles' center (Madill's) and right flank (Scott's) brigades clashed with the Confederate pickets. The 111th New York, which was screening Madill's units, drove the Rebel skirmishers across the road linking J. Crow's with Boydton Plank Road. At the same time, the regiment covering Scott's advance, the 5th New Hampshire, struck and drove in the Rebel outposts.[190]

When General Humphreys learned that Miles' division had crossed Crow Road and was in full view of the Rebel fortifications, he ordered the advance stopped. Miles was directed to entrench his position. Within a few minutes Miles had his troops at work throwing up fortifications.[191]

At the time that Hyman's North Carolina brigade drove in Griffin's outposts, the grey clads made a feeble thrust against the left flank of Miles' division. Ramsey's skirmishers, two companies of the 53rd Pennsylvania, easily beat off the attack. About this time, Colonel Scott decided to relieve his skirmishers. The 5th New Hampshire was recalled and the 26th Michigan and the 140th Pennsylvania moved forward. Taking position near the Confederate fortifications, the sharpshooters from these two regiments exchanged shots with the grey clad snipers until darkness put a stop to the day's hostilities in this sector.[192]

After Miles' troops had started to dig in along Crow Road, the cannoneers of Battery E, 4th U.S. Light Artillery and Battery M, 1st New Hampshire Light Artillery limbered up their pieces. Moving up Boydton Plank Road, the gunners placed their eight guns in battery near the Rainey house. Just before dark, Battery B, 1st New Jersey Light Artillery left the artillery park at Brown's house. Using a road

---

189 *Ibid.*, OR 46, pt. 1, 744.

190 *Ibid.*, 714, 734. The 111th New York had relieved the 126th New York on the skirmish line just before the advance began.

191 *Ibid.*, OR 46, pt. 3, 295.

192 *Ibid.*, OR 46, pt. 1, 714, 734, 744.

opened by fatigue parties, the gunners headed for the front. The New Jersey battery emplaced their four 12-pounder Napoleons near the Crow house.[193]

When Humphreys reported to Meade at 4:00 p.m., he announced that the right flank of the II Corps was anchored on Hatcher's Run, at a point 400 yards east of the J. Crow house. The corps' left flank, he stated, rested at the junction of Boydton Plank and Dabney's Mill roads. Scouting parties had located the Confederate defense line in this sector and found two large redoubts. These formidable earthworks were about 600 yards in front of, and opposite the II Corps flanks. A third strong point, which was farther from the Union lines was also observed between the two redoubts. From time to time, the butternuts had employed the cannon emplaced in these works against Humphreys' troops. Humphreys informed his superior that his line was "already tolerably entrenched" and could be held by Mott's and Hays' divisions. This would leave Miles' command available for any other assignments Meade might be contemplating.[194]

Throughout the remainder of the wet afternoon, the rain-drenched men of the II Corps were kept busy throwing up earthworks and corduroying roads. Altogether, 1,300 men were ordered to report to Capt. Charles W. Howell for labor on the roads. The work on Dabney's Mill Road, which was the corps lateral line of communications, was hindered by a shortage of tools. By dark the fatigue parties from Nugent's brigade had laid only a mile of corduroy. When informed of this, Humphreys issued instructions for Miles to put every man he could spare on this project in the morning. In an effort to cheer up the water-soaked troops' lagging spirits, Humphreys authorized his division commanders to send for whiskey. Humphreys cautioned, however, that he didn't know where they would obtain the fiery stimulant.[195]

After covering their fronts with a strong line of outposts, Humphreys' division commanders permitted their men to bivouac. Since the corps was camped near the foe, the sentries were directed to sound the alarm in case of any unusual firing on the picket line. Before retiring, the brigade commanders were instructed to have their troops under arms at 4:30 a.m. After being formed the soldiers were to remain at their battle stations until daylight.[196]

---

193 *Ibid.*, 791. The 10th Massachusetts Battery also moved from the artillery park. Proceeding to Dabney's Mill, the Massachusetts unit parked its guns in a field.

194 OR 46, pt. 3, 290-291.

195 *Ibid.*, 291, 296. Captain Howell of the Engineer Corps had been assigned to the II Corps on March 29 by the Chief Engineer of the Army of the Potomac, Col. James C. Duane.

196 *Ibid.*, 297.

On the morning of the 30th, General Mackenzie's cavalry division of the Army of the James was transferred from Hancock's Station to Humphreys' Station. Later in the day, the cavalrymen broke camp for a second time and marched to Monk's Neck Bridge. Here, Mackenzie's troopers were tasked with guarding the trains of the Army of the Potomac, which were parked in the fields east of Rowanty Creek.[197]

Throughout the late afternoon and evening, the frequent exchange of messages between corps, army, and group headquarters continued. At 4:00 p.m., Warren informed Meade that Ayres' vanguard was near W. Dabney's and had White Oak Road under observation. Warren now felt confident of his position. He reported that his troops had fortified a line extending from Griffin's right almost to Gravelly Run. If Humphreys could take over the front held by Griffin's and Crawford's divisions, Warren told Meade, he would take his "Corps and block the White Oak Road."[198]

Although Warren sent this dispatch at 4:00 p.m., it did not reach Meade until 7:30 p.m. Evidently, the military telegraph was not functioning properly. Before relaying Warren's message to Grant's headquarters, Meade added his comments. Meade expressed himself as satisfied that Warren's suggestion was "the best thing we can do under existing circumstances—that is, let Humphreys relieve Griffin, and let Warren move on to the White Oak Road and endeavor to turn enemy's right." As he understood the situation, Meade told Grant, Ayres was between the two Dabney farms, and liable to be isolated. If Ayres were reinforced by the remainder of the V Corps, Warren "ought to overcome any opposition the enemy can make, except from strong entrenchments," Meade wrote.

In the meantime, Grant had received a number of interesting reports from other sections of the front. These messages indicated that General Lee was stripping the inactive sectors of his front of troops to counter the Union threat to his right. If this were true, Grant knew that some parts of the Confederate defense line must be very thinly held. Accordingly, General Ord and the commanders of the VI and IX Corps were directed to ascertain the feasibility of carrying the fortifications in their sectors by assault. Both Generals Wright of the VI Corps and Parke's of the IX Corps reported that it was practicable to storm the Rebel defenses. Orders were issued, scheduling an attack on the Petersburg defenses for daybreak on the 31st.[199]

---

197   *Ibid., OR* 46, pt. 1, 1244.

198   *Ibid., OR* 46, pt. 3, 304.

199   *Ibid.,* 284-285; Humphreys, *The Virginia Campaign of '64 and '65,* 329.

Evidently, Grant was beginning to despair of accomplishing anything decisive in the Burgess Mill area. After having alerted Ord, Parke and Wright to be ready to storm the works, Grant dashed off a letter to Sheridan. In this message, Grant broached the idea of reinforcing Sheridan with a corps of infantry. Grant wrote, "If your situation in the morning is such as to justify the belief that you can turn the enemy's right with the assistance of a corps of infantry, entirely detached from the balance of the army, I will so detach the Fifth Corps, and place the whole under your command for the operation." Sheridan was asked to let the general know his thoughts on the matter. If they were in the affirmative, Grant promised to draft the necessary orders. Sheridan was also advised of Grant's plan to hurl Ord's, Parke's, and Wright's troops against the Petersburg defenses.[200]

Grant, however, now had change of heart. He decided to call off the scheduled assault. In notifying Meade of this, Grant stated that Parke and Wright were to "watch their fronts and go in if the enemy strips to attack our left." Grant also informed Meade that he had "pretty much made up his mind on the course to pursue, and will inform you in the morning what it is." In the meantime, Humphreys and Warren were to "secure their present position and await further orders."[201]

Meade's message endorsing Warren's plan to turn the Rebel right reached Grant's headquarters before the lieutenant general commanding sent the telegram directing that Humphreys and Warren "secure their present situation and await further orders." Consequently, Grant added a postscript. Humphreys was to relieve Griffin's division, which in turn was to move to the left. Warren was to "get himself strong to-night."

Grant's telegram was in Meade's hands at 8:35 p.m. Meade immediately wired Humphreys his instructions. The commander of the II Corps was to have Miles' division relieve Griffin's troops and the units from Crawford's division that were holding the fortifications covering Boydton Plank Road. One of Mott's brigades would support Miles' shift to the left. Shortly thereafter, a communication was sent to Warren informing him that Humphreys had been ordered to relieve Griffin's and the troops occupying "the return on the Boydton Plank Road." After Griffin's troops were pulled out of the lines, they were to be sent to Ayres' support. Warren was to hold his "Corps ready to attack and await further orders."[202]

---

200 *OR* 46, pt. 3, 325.

201 *Ibid.*, 285. Grant planned to use General Warren's V Corps to support Sheridan's thrust.

202 *Ibid.*, 285, 291, 305.

Next, Meade acquainted Grant with the steps he had taken to implement his superior's instructions. He informed Grant that he had not assigned Warren a specific mission. Meade had inferred from Grant's telegram that the lieutenant general commanding would do this.[203]

Replying to Meade, Grant wrote, "Your orders to Warren are right. I do not expect to advance him in the morning. I supposed, however, that was now up to the White Oak Road. If he is not I do not want him to move up without further orders."

As yet, Grant had refused to take Meade into his confidence. As demonstrated by his letter to Sheridan, Grant was already seriously thinking of sending the V Corps to Sheridan. The commanding general, however, maintained a discreet silence on this subject in his communications with Meade.[204]

About 9:45 a.m., Grant received an important message from Sheridan informing him of what had transpired on the extreme left during the afternoon. Sheridan reported that Pickett's division was deployed along White Oak Road—its right at Five Forks and its left extending toward Petersburg.[205]

This information convinced Grant that Warren would not have the cavalry support, which he had been led to expect, on his left flank. Sheridan's troopers would be fully occupied with Pickett's soldiers. Warren, therefore, would have to be advised of this development and alerted to watch his left flank closely. After adding these comments, Grant forwarded Sheridan's communication to Meade.[206]

A few minutes later, Grant sent a supplemental telegram to Meade's headquarters. Grant observed that with the Confederates on White Oak Road and the Federal cavalry at J. Boisseau's farm, it was not "improbable" that the Southerners would launch an attack in the morning on Warren's left. Grant, therefore, issued instructions for Sheridan to be prepared to push to Warren's assistance if he were attacked. Continuing, Grant wrote:

> Warren, I suppose, will put himself in the best possible position to defend himself, with the notice that he has already received; but in adding to this I think it will be well to notify him again of the position of Sheridan's cavalry, what he reports the enemy's position on the White Oak Road, and the orders he has received.

203 *Ibid.*, 285.

204 *Ibid*; Swan, "The Five Forks Campaign," 293.

205 OR 46, pt. 3, 324.

206 *Ibid.*

If the Rebels raised the initiative, Grant thought it would be a good idea for Meade to direct Humphreys to help Warren. Humphreys could do this either by sending reinforcements to Warren or by going over to the attack on his own front.

Before receiving Grant's second telegram, Meade forwarded a copy of Sheridan's message to Warren. In addition, the general observed that, in view of the intelligence obtained by Sheridan, it would be necessary to alert Ayres. Meade also wanted Ayres reinforced "without delay, as the enemy may attack him at daylight." The commander of the Army of the Potomac presumed that Warren would use Crawford's division to support Ayres.

Meade, when he sent this message to Warren, failed to include Grant's endorsement to Sheridan's original letter. Grant had commented, "Warren will not, from this dispatch, have the cavalry support on his left flank that I expected. This information had better be sent to him, with instructions to watch closely on his left flank." This omission on Meade's part would have important repercussions.[207] Nor, so far as Warren was concerned, did Meade take notice of Grant's supplementary order that Warren be informed "again of the position of Sheridan's cavalry, what he reports the enemy's position on the White Oak Road, and the orders he has received."[208]

Only one more message was sent to Warren from Meade's headquarters on the 30th. At 10:35 p.m., Chief of Staff Webb informed Warren that Griffin's division would be relieved as soon as possible. General Humphreys was to contact Warren as soon as Miles' division had started for Boydton Plank Road.[209]

Replying to Grant's supplemental message, Meade reported that he had sent a copy of Sheridan's dispatch to Warren. Meade stated that Warren had been alerted "to put Ayres on his guard, as he might be attacked at daylight." Crawford was to move immediately to Ayres' assistance; Griffin was to take position within supporting distance as soon as relieved. By daylight, Meade reasoned, Warren "should have his whole Corps in hand ready for the defensive or offensive, and ought to be secure in either contingency, particularly as he can always fall back on Humphreys." Meade, however, could not bring himself to believe that the Rebels would be able to assemble a force large enough to do the powerful V Corps any harm. In closing, Meade observed that Warren had been given "no orders to advance, but simply to strengthen and secure his position." The V Corps would not be ordered to take the initiative unless Grant gave the word.

207 *Ibid.*, 286, 306, 324; Swan, "The Five Forks Campaign," 294-295.

208 *OR* 46, pt. 3, 286.

209 *Ibid.*, 306.

At 11:00 p.m., following the receipt of Meade's order to reinforce Ayres, Warren drafted a set of instructions to govern his corps' movements in the morning. At daybreak, Ayres was to reinforce his advance brigade (Winthrop's) with his entire division and Crawford was to hold his command ready to support Ayres. As soon as it relieved by Humphreys' Corps, Griffin's division was to move down Boydton Plank Road and join Ayres.[210]

In the meantime, Humphreys had been informed of the decision to use part of his corps to occupy the position currently held by Griffin's division. At 8:50 p.m., General Webb telegraphed Humphreys that he was to have Miles' division relieve Griffin's bluecoats. One of Mott's brigades would be used to support Miles. Humphreys would see that this order was executed as soon as possible.

Humphreys quickly drafted and distributed a set of instructions to his division commanders calculated to implement this directive. Hays was to call up his reserve brigade (Smyth's). All of Hays' troops were to be placed on the front line. The left flank of the division would then be extended to the left and part of the breastworks held by Mott's division occupied. Hays' soldiers would also be responsible for holding the picket line currently held by Mott's men. Once Hays' troops had relieved his right flank units, Mott was to shift his division to the left. Miles' division would be relieved. Two of Mott's brigades were to occupy the trenches from Hays' left to Boydton Plank Road. Miles' troops, in their turn, would relieve Griffin's division and hold "the return on the Boydton Plank Road." One of Mott's brigades was to support Miles' left flank. The three division commanders were alerted to be ready to carry out their scheduled movements at daybreak.[211]

Next, Humphreys addressed a message to Warren stating that he had been directed to relieve Griffin with Miles' division. The commander of the II Corps wanted Warren to give him a description of the position occupied by Griffin's troops. Since Warren had retired, the general's adjutant sent Humphreys a sketch and a description of the works held by Griffin's command.[212]

Editor's Conclusion

When the Confederates failed to continue the attack at the Lewis Farm and instead withdrew to their former White Oak Road Line, General Grant expanded General Sheridan's raid into a major offensive mission. As we

210   *Ibid.*, 286, 306.

211   *Ibid.*, 291, 294.

212   *Ibid.*, 293.

shall see in the next chapter, the Lewis Farm (Quaker Road) fighting, coupled with the bad weather, put the pieces in motion for the marching, riding, skirmishing, and fighting that occurred on March 30 and the battles of Dinwiddie Court House and White Oak Road the following day.

Chapter 6

The Five Forks Campaign

The Battles of Dinwiddie Court House and White Oak Road

March 30-31, 1865

Part IV

The Battle of Dinwiddie Court House

The courier bearing Grant's letter inquiring about placing the V Corps under Sheridan's control reached the cavalryman's headquarters early on the morning of the 31st. Replying to Grant's communication, Sheridan confidently stated that if the rain stopped and the ground dried, he believed he would either turn the Confederate right or score a breakthrough. He could do this if he were reinforced by an infantry corps. Sheridan, however, wanted the VI Corps and not Warren's V Corps. He observed that he "would not like the Fifth Corps to make such an attempt."

Next, Sheridan jotted off a few lines concerning the situation in the Dinwiddie Court House area. His scouts had just returned from the front with important news. They told Sheridan that the Rebels were busy throwing up breastworks at Five Forks. From the sound of the chopping, the scouts believed the fortifications extended at least a mile west of the vital crossroads. In addition, noises made by the

Major General Philip H. Sheridan
Library of Congress

trains on the South Side Railroad were distinctly audible to the Federals. All the trains seemed to be westbound.[1]

A number of hours elapsed before Sheridan's message reached Grant's command post. When Grant drafted his reply, he informed the cavalry leader that it would be impossible to give him the VI Corps. At the moment, the VI Corps was in the center of the Union line between the Appomattox and Hatcher's Run. "Besides," Grant continued, "Wright thinks he can go through the line where he is, and it is advisable to have troops and a commander there who feel so to cooperate with you when you get around." Grant was willing, however, to give Sheridan the II Corps instead of the V Corps. If this were agreeable with Sheridan, orders would have to be issued in the very near future to ensure that Humphreys' troops would be in position and ready for action by the morning of April 1. Before Sheridan could answer this dispatch, the situation had changed drastically.[2]

At 9:00 a.m. on the 31st, General Merritt reinforced his picket line. At the same time, Merritt directed Devin to send out several strong combat patrols. These groups were to undertake a forced reconnaissance of the Confederate positions covering White Oak Road. In accordance with Merritt's instructions, "old war horse" Devin sent Colonel Stagg's Michigan brigade up Crump Road; Colonel

1   OR 46, pt. 3, 380.

2   *Ibid.*

Major General Wesley Merritt
Library of Congress

Fitzhugh's brigade was dismounted and advanced up Dinwiddie Road. Devin's third brigade, Gibbs', was massed at J. Boisseau's. Gibbs' unit could be used to support Stagg's and Fitzhugh's troopers in case they were unable to handle the Confederates that they encountered.[3]

Davies' brigade of Crook's division which had been ordered to the front on the previous afternoon was also posted at J. Boisseau's. Patrols from Davies' brigade were given the task of watching the countryside west of Chamberlain's Bed. Crook's two other brigades—Cols. J. Irvin Gregg's and Charles Smith's—were based at Dinwiddie Court House. Detachments from these two commands picketed Boydton Plank and Flat Foot roads. The crossings of Stony Creek were also kept under close surveillance by Crook's troopers. Sheridan's third division, Custer's, guarded the wagon train which was still bogged down somewhere west of Malone's Bridge.[4]

Fitzhugh's and Stagg's troopers had not advanced very far up Dinwiddie and Crump roads before they came upon the Confederate outposts. Discovering that the Rebels held White Oak Road in force, Stagg's men fell back. After relaying this information to Devin, Stagg established a roadblock on Crump Road. The ground where Stagg formed his brigade was a short distance north of Gravelly Run.[5]

---

3   *Ibid.*, OR 46, pt. 1, 1116, 1122, 1128.

4   *Ibid.*, 1129-1130, 1141, 1144, 1154, 1156.

5   *Ibid.*, 1122; Swan, "The Five Forks Campaign," 303; *Atlas to Accompany the Official Records of the Union and Confederate Armies*, United States War Department. It was published in Washington, D.C. by the Government Printing Office in 1891-95. Plate LXXIV, No. 2.

As soon as his men had crossed a branch of Chamberlain's Bed about one mile southeast of Five Forks, Fitzhugh halted his brigade. He proceeded to deploy his dismounted troopers on either side of the road. Once his men had taken up a strong defensive position, Fitzhugh advanced two of his regiments—the 6th New York and the 1st U.S. (The 1st U.S., an organic part of Gibbs' command, had been temporarily assigned to Fitzhugh's brigade.) These two units penetrated to within a short distance of Five Forks before being checked. During the advance, the bluecoats captured several prisoners. On being questioned, the captives told the Yankees that Five Forks was "occupied by Pickett's division of infantry and at least a division of cavalry." This disturbing news was immediately forwarded to headquarters. In response to Sheridan's instructions, Devin directed Fitzhugh to hold his ground and open communications with Davies' brigade which was operating on his left. A glance at his maps showed Devin that Fitzhugh occupied "the apex of a triangle, the left of which was held by Davies' brigade and the right by Stagg's."[6]

In the meantime, one of Davies' patrols had obtained some interesting information regarding Confederate movements. A company of the 1st New Jersey Cavalry led by Capt. Samuel Craig crossed Chamberlain's Bed. Passing through the Confederate vedettes, Craig's troops swooped down upon and captured a Rebel outpost manned by infantry. The foot soldiers told the Yankees that Johnson's infantry and Rooney Lee's cavalry divisions were moving down the opposite side of Chamberlain's Bed toward Dinwiddie Court House. If this information was true, and the Southerners were allowed to continue their march unimpeded, they would turn Sheridan's left flank.[7]

Undoubtedly, this report caused Sheridan a few unpleasant moments, because it indicated that the Confederates had poured additional troops into the area. Since Sheridan had anticipated the arrival of Rooney Lee's troopers, the information that they were operating west of Chamberlain's Bed probably did not bother him very much. Sheridan, however, was troubled by the news that Johnson's troops had reinforced Pickett. The cavalryman had not calculated on this turn of events. Sheridan did not know, of course, that only two of Johnson's brigades were serving with Pickett. Now, to make matters worse, the foe had apparently seized the initiative. Instead of attacking, the aggressive Sheridan would have to use all his skill to check the Confederate effort to outflank his corps.

6   *Ibid.*

7   *Ibid.*, pt. 1, 1144, 1148.

Major General George Crook
Library of Congress

To counter this Rebel thrust, Sheridan decided to commit Crook's division. The extensive reconnaissance carried out by the Federals had revealed that there were two roads that crossed Chamberlain's Bed and gave ready access to their left flank. A short distance above the upper crossing, Chamberlain's Bed branched. The west fork, know as Bear Swamp, was crossed by Scott Road which connected Five Forks and Little Five Forks. Because it was presumed that the Confederates were advancing along Scott Road, the Federals, if they were to hold Dinwiddie Court House, would have to cover the two lower crossings: Danse's and Fitzgerald's. Davies' brigade which was already at the front was rushed westward from J. Boisseau's. Reaching the Lewis farm, Davies formed his brigade in the field east of Danse's Ford. The 3rd Battalion, 1st New Jersey Cavalry led by Maj. Walter W. Robbins was sent across Chamberlain's Bed. Robbins' troops were to see if they could locate the Rebel column reportedly advancing along Scott Road. Davies manned a line of outposts covering the approaches to the ford with Maj. James H. Hart's battalion of the 1st New Jersey.[8]

Colonel Charles Smith's brigade was rushed from Dinwiddie Court House to the point where Ford Station Road crossed Chamberlain's Bed at Fitzgerald's Ford. This was about one mile south of Danse's Ford which was guarded by Davies' troopers. After he had deployed his command, Smith sent a detachment of the 2nd New York Mounted Rifles across the stream. To ensure that Smith would have a

8 *Ibid.*, 1141, 1144, 1148; Humphreys, *The Virginia Campaign of '64 and '65*, 334.

timely warning of the approach of the Confederates, the New Yorkers established a picket line several hundred yards west of the ford.

One of Crook's three brigades—Gregg's—was held in reserve. Taking their station at the junction of Adams and Brooks roads, midway between the two fords, Gregg's troopers were ready to assist Davies and Smith in case they were needed.[9]

After having made these dispositions, Sheridan was confident that he could cope with the situation. Sheridan's main line of resistance now faced west instead of north. Fitzhugh's brigade held the right on Dinwiddie Road; Smith's the left at Fitzgerald's Ford; and Davies' the center at Danse's. Stagg's brigade, on Crump Road, guarded Fitzhugh's rear; while Gregg's and Gibbs' units constituted a strategic reserve. So certain of his position was the cavalry leader that he decided not to order up Custer's division at this time.[10]

The news that Rooney Lee's and Rosser's divisions had reached Five Forks early in the morning persuaded Pickett to press on toward Dinwiddie Court House, and he quickly formulated a well-thought plan of operations.

A short distance southeast of Five Forks, Munford's cavalry division took up its battle station astride Dinwiddie Road. Strong detachments from Munford's division were posted on Crump and Gravelly Run Church roads. Munford's mission was to hold White Oak Road and pin the Federal cavalry in position while the remainder of Pickett's task force turned Sheridan's left.

Spearheaded by Rooney Lee's and Rosser's cavalry, Pickett's infantry marched southward from Five Forks about 9:00 a.m. Scott Road served as the Confederate line of advance. The Southerners crossed Bear Swamp near the E. P. Scott farm. Chamberlain's Bed protected the exposed left flank of the greyclads column as it pushed ahead. In spite of the weather and hunger, the cavalry was in excellent spirits. The infantry, too, were alert and full of fight. At Little Five Forks, the Rebels turned into Ford Station Road. Pickett planned to re-cross Chamberlain's Bed at Fitzgerald's Ford and assail Sheridan's left flank. As soon as Munford heard the sound of Pickett's guns, he was to launch a frontal attack on the bluecoats.[11]

After crossing Chamberlain's Bed, Robbins' patrol found that the road leading to Danse's Ford was unprotected. Before proceeding, Robbins detached Companies K, L, and M and had them establish a roadblock. Accompanied by Company H, Robbins rode down the right bank of the stream as far as Fitzgerald's

9   *Ibid.*, 1141, 1156.

10   *Ibid.*, 1129-1130; Swan, "The Five Forks Campaign," 303.

11   Freeman, *Lee's Lieutenants*, vol. 3, 660; Humphreys, *The Virginia Campaign of '64 and '65*, 334; *OR* 46, pt. 1, 1299.

Ford, and conferred briefly with Colonel Smith. The general told the major that his scouts had not yet seen any Confederates. Robbins then retraced his steps, picked up his troopers holding the roadblock, and re-crossed the stream. The troopers were dismounted and their horses sent to the rear. Next, Robbins put his men to work building breastworks of fence rails. Hardly had Robbins' troopers completed the barricade before they heard the crackling of gunfire from the direction of Fitzgerald's Ford, and took cover. They then anxiously waited for the butternuts to appear.

The rest of Davies' brigade, with the exception of Hart's battalion, was posted in a field east of Danse's Ford. After Robbins' troopers had slowed the Confederate advance, Davies planned to counterattack and hurl the foe back into Chamberlain's Bed.[12]

About 11:00 a.m., Fitz Lee's vanguard—Barringer's North Carolina cavalry brigade from Rooney Lee's division—established contact with the picket line held by a detachment of the 2nd New York Mounted Rifles as it felt its way toward Fitzgerald's Ford. Fighting a skillful delaying action, the New Yorkers retired across the stream. Colonel Smith learned that his outposts were engaged, so he prepared to defend the ford. When the cavalrymen of the 2nd New York re-crossed the watercourse, they were dismounted. The 6th Ohio also dismounted and moved into position alongside the New Yorkers. Taking cover, the Unionists opened fire on the Confederate cavalrymen when they appeared on the opposite bank. Unable to breast the fire of the repeating carbines, the grey clads recoiled.

To exploit this temporary success, Col. Smith sent a battalion of the 1st Maine across the creek. The Maine men reached the right bank without difficulty. But as soon as the battalion deployed and started to advance, it ran into trouble. Encountering a powerful Confederate battle line composed of both mounted and dismounted troopers, the bluecoats were hurled back in confusion. The panic-stricken men either sought refuge among the "led horses" or plunged into the neck-deep stream.

As they approached Chamberlain's Bed, scouts from Barringer's brigade realized that the Federal cavalry had crossed it and were advancing to attack them. General Rooney Lee ordered Barringer to dismount his command and meet the Union advance. Colonel William H. Cheek's 1st North Carolina Cavalry was in front supported by Colonel James L. Gaines' 2nd North Carolina and Major James H. McNeill's 5th North Carolina. The 3rd North Carolina Cavalry and Beale's Virginia Cavalry Brigade stood in reserve and McGregor's Horse Battery was put

---

12 *Ibid.*, 1148.

into position. The fight between the Maine men and the three North Carolina regiments was severe. Among the Confederate casualties was Colonel Gaines who lost his right arm.

After reaching the creek, Barringer's brigade formed a line of battle. The 5th North Carolina Cavalry took position opposite Fitzgerald's Ford backed by the 2nd. Colonel Cheek's 1st North Carolina Cavalry formed 150 yards north of the ford. A gap of one hundred yards separated the right flank of the 1st and the left of the 5th. Barringer's plan was for the 5th to cross at the ford in columns of four and deploy to the right of and below the ford. The 2nd was to follow behind and once on the east bank to deploy in line of battle to the left and above the ford. After they reached the east bank the 2nd would form on the 5th's left. Meanwhile, the 1st would cross downstream. They would thus form a long continuous line, make their charge, drive back the Federals and pursue them. McNeill's 5th North Carolina Cavalry entered the creek as planned, every man holding his cartridge box high above the water with his left hand and his rifle with his right. The Federals opened a heavy fire on the dense mass. Nevertheless the regiment reached the east bank and deployed in line of battle on the right of the road, waiting for the 2nd North Carolina to cross.

Barringer sent a courier to McNeill to learn his situation. McNeill was advancing slowly, waiting for the supporting regiment to form on his left. He realized that the fire was so furious that it was better to advance than to stand. Colonel McNeill coolly said: "Please tell General Barringer that I am all right and advancing slowly for the Nineteenth [2nd] to form on my left that we may charge and carry those works. Ask him, please, to hasten the Nineteenth over."[13]

To distract Union fire from the 5th and 2nd regiments, Rooney Lee ordered the 13th Virginia Cavalry from Beale's brigade to charge across the ford mounted, just when the 2nd North Carolina was stepping forward to cross. Only the first squadron of the Virginians galloped into the creek, however, as the second squadron refused to follow and blocked the road so that the rest of the regiment could not advance. The 2nd closed in behind the first squadron of Virginians. Meanwhile, north of Fitzgerald's Ford, Colonel Cheek's 1st North Carolina Cavalry crossed the creek and, despite opposition from the 2nd New York Rifles, gained the east bank.

The battalion from the 1st Maine retreated before the charging cavalry, but Smith brought up the rest of the regiment which was stationed a mile to the rear behind a slight rise. Reunited, the regiment lay down in double rank formation on

13 Walter Clark, ed., *North Carolina Regiments*, 640-641.

top of the hill overlooking the ford. The 6th Ohio cavalry was formed in the woods on the left of the 1st Maine. As the first squadron of the 13th Virginia rode past, the 6th Ohio fired into it. When the Virginians neared the top of the hill, the Maine boys rose up and opened fire on them. As the Confederates recoiled, the 6th Ohio fired into their flank again and the 1st Maine followed them down the hill pouring volleys into them, causing them to break and retreat.

Trying to halt the fleeing Virginians, Barringer's brigade color-bearer waved his battle flag in his hand while Barringer's aides rushed at them on the enemy's side of the stream and tried to rally them, especially to keep them from riding headlong into the 2nd North Carolina Cavalry. But the horsemen crashed into the poor North Carolinians, pushing them down into the deep water at the lower side of the ford. At the ford, General Barringer mounted on his horse, observed the disaster that befell his brigade. He sent a courier to form the 5th along the top of the bluff. The men came up from the water and were supplied with ammunition as quickly as possible. Under the fire of the Tar Heels, the Union cavalry went back to their works on the ridge.[14]

The 1st North Carolina pursued the New Yorkers into the pines when bullets began falling in their right and rear. Cheek galloped to the right of his line and found the enemy moving up the creek in his rear. He withdrew his regiment as rapidly as possible and reformed in his original line on the west side of the creek.[15]

Sometime after 11:00 a.m., Pickett and his infantry reached Fitzgerald's Ford just after Rooney Lee's attack ended. Pickett rejected his plan to cross at Fitzgerald's, settling on Danse's Ford located one mile to the north, where there was supposed to be a bridge. He now formulated a new plan. Fitz Lee, with Rooney Lee's cavalry division and Ransom's two infantry brigades, was to cross Chamberlain's Bed at Fitzgerald's Ford. The three infantry brigades of Pickett's division and Rosser's cavalry division were to force their way across at Danse's Ford. Pickett's contingent reached Danse's Ford about 2:30 p.m.

Sheridan, as was to be expected, was elated by Smith's success. At 2:30 p.m., he dashed off a message to Grant informing him: "W. H. F. Lee attacked Smith's brigade, of Crook's division, on Chamberlain's Creek, and got cleaned out. I will now attack him and push First Cavalry Division (Devin's) against their infantry line." Sheridan also reported that Maj. Gen. Robert F. Hoke's division and three of Pickett's brigades were at Five Forks on the night of the 30th. (The cavalry commander was badly mistaken when he reported that Hoke's division was at Five

14 *OR* 46, pt. 3, 471.

15 *Ibid.*, 473.

Forks. Hoke's division was in North Carolina.) General Devin's division, Sheridan stated, was in contact with the line of outposts covering the Rebel infantry's Five Forks encampments. (Sheridan was wrong again. At this very minute, Pickett's infantry was preparing to force its way across Chamberlain's Bed at Danse's Ford. It was Munford's dismounted troopers that Devin's patrols had spotted near Five Forks.)

Despite the disastrous outcome of the efforts in the morning, Rooney Lee prepared to make another attack on the Chamberlain's Bed fords. The afternoon plan was for the 2nd North Carolina Cavalry, Colonel Gaines commanding, supported by the 5th North Carolina, to attack at the ford and for the 1st North Carolina to cross at the same place as it had in the morning. Although Sheridan's men had strengthened their positions by throwing up rifle-pits in the edge of the pines, Lee and Barringer were determined to renew the attack. For the second time and at nearly the same places the Confederates formed line of battle, from the experience of the morning every man knowing the danger that lay ahead.[16]

The 2nd North Carolina Cavalry met the same fate at the ford as did the 5th in the morning, and for half an hour the 1st North Carolina Cavalry, being the only Confederates on that side, were subjected to the concentrated fire of the entire line of the Union cavalry. To break the uneven contest, Rooney Lee ordered Beale's brigade to attack across the creek and come into the fighting on the left of the North Carolinians. Thus encouraged, both Confederate brigades rushed over Smith's rifle-pits, broke his line, and drove his men pell-mell through the pines, out into an open field. A few moments after this General Rooney Lee, at the head of a mounted squadron from the 5th, came up the road from the ford at a gallop. He charged across the open field and into the woods beyond, but the Union forces had already withdrawn.

Colonel Cheeks described the fighting in a letter to his wife the next day:

My Dear Alice:—We had a terrible fight yesterday. I lost eighty in my regiment. Colonel Cowles severely wounded; Maj. [Marcus] McLeod slightly; Captain Dewey killed; Captain Coleman killed. Thirteen other officers wounded, several of whom will die. John and Al were not hurt. Nearly all the brim of my hat shot off. My horse (the one I lately bought) shot twice, and killed.

My regiment fought more gallantly than I ever saw it before. We waded a creek waist-deep and seventy-five yards wide under heavy fire and drove the enemy from an [e]intrenched position. Will give you full particulars when I have more time. General

16 *Ibid.*, OR 46, pt. 3, 339; Clark, *North Carolina Regiments*, vol. 3, 640-641.

Lee complimented us in the highest terms. The Thirteenth Virginia was on my left, and after the fight gave me three most enthusiastic cheers. 'Boots and saddles' has sounded. Goodbye.

Rooney Lee is reported to have told a friend, "There was nothing done at Gettysburg more gallant than this charge of the 1st North Carolina Cavalry at Chamberlain's Run."

When General Crook learned that the Confederates had stormed across Chamberlain's Bed at Fitzgerald's Ford, he prepared to rush reinforcements to Smith's assistance. Because no Rebels had appeared at Danse's Ford, Crook ordered General Davies to support Smith. Davies would leave Robbins' battalion to hold the ford. Since the road was impassable for mounted troops, Davies' cavalrymen left their horses behind when they marched. As soon as his command had started for Fitzgerald's Ford, Davies rode ahead. The general wanted to find out how tidings were going with Smith's command. By the time Davies reached Fitzgerald's Ford, Smith's troopers had crushed the Confederate bridgehead. Davies, seeing that his command's services were not needed, wheeled his horse about. When the general encountered the head of his mud-spattered column, he ordered the troops to countermarch. An air of urgency was added to the situation when heavy firing broke out in the direction of Danse's Ford. This noise could mean only one thing—the Confederates had attacked Robbins' battalion. The troops, at a word from the general, moved off on the double.[17]

Shortly after Davies' brigade had started for Fitzgerald's Ford, Robbins' scouts reported that a strong force of Rebel infantry was approaching Danse's Ford. Moments later, the Confederate vanguard (Corse's brigade) attacked and drove in Robbins' pickets. General Corse then formed his brigade and moved to carry the crossing. While the Southerners had the advantage of numbers, this was partially nullified by the strong defensive position held by the bluecoats. Besides being protected by breastworks, the Yankees were deployed on lower ground. Corse's butternuts had to pass across the skyline to get at the Federals. Consequently, Robbins' troopers threw back the initial Rebel onslaught. Undaunted, Corse prepared to turn the Yankees' flanks. While a strong detachment of Corse's Virginians feigned another frontal attack, strong combat patrols infiltrated the woods to the right and left of the road. One of these groups succeeded in fording the stream above the crossing. Pressing forward, the patrol encountered the line of outposts manned by Hart's New Jersey battalion. Hart's troopers were easily

---

17 OR 46, pt. 1, 1144; Clark, *North Carolina Regiments*, vol. 3, 471-473.

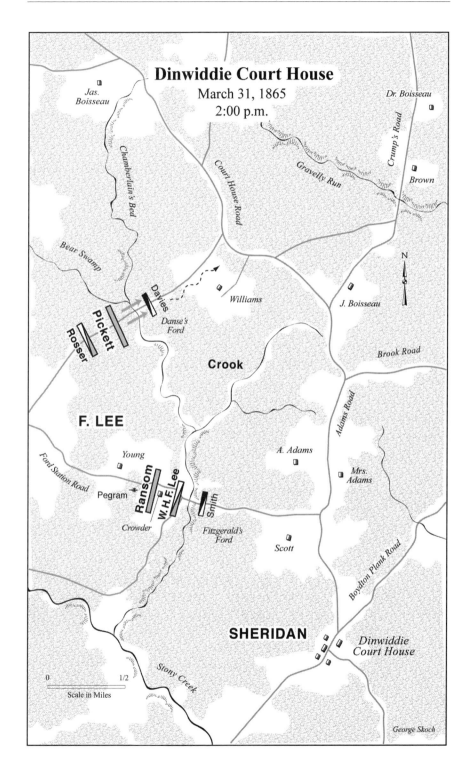

Dinwiddie Court House
March 31, 1865
2:00 p.m.

Jas. Boisseau

Dr. Boisseau

Crump's Road

Chamberlain's Bed

Court House Road

Gravelly Run

Brown

Bear Swamp

Davies

Williams

J. Boisseau

N

Pickett

Danse's Ford

Rosser

Crook

Brook Road

F. LEE

Adams Road

Young

A. Adams

Ford Station Road

Ransom

W. H. F. Lee

Mrs. Adams

Pegram

Smith

Crowder

Fitzgerald's Ford

Scott

Boydton Plank Road

SHERIDAN

Dinwiddie Court House

0   1/2

Stony Creek

Scale in Miles

George Skoch

brushed aside by the rugged Rebel infantry. Simultaneously, Corse's soldiers renewed their attack on Robbins' battalion. Robbins' troopers grimly held their ground until the grey clads had closed to within 15 yards. With his flank turned and his men unable to check this powerful frontal assault, Major Robbins abandoned all hopes of holding the ford. He shouted for his men to fall back. As the cavalrymen started to pull back, all thought of discipline vanished. It was every man for himself as the battalion came pouring back out of the bottom.[18]

Davies' brigade came up just as the Confederate infantry started to flood across the ford. The troopers, not used to marching, were badly jaded. In an effort to contain the bridgehead, Davies threw his command into the fray. The 10th New York was formed into line of battle astride the road. Major Robbins now succeeded in rallying a portion of his command. The reformed battalion took position on the New Yorker's left. Corse's Virginians attacked the roadblock immediately. After delivering two or three volleys, the New York regiment fled. Major Robbins' battered battalion was left to cover the New Yorkers' "shameful retreat." Pressing on, the Confederates came close to capturing the brigade's "led horses." At the last minute, the horse soldiers succeeded in saving their mounts.[19]

Davies' brigade had failed to check the Confederate advance. As soon as Corse's troops had established a bridgehead, Pickett sent the other four infantry brigades that were available wading across Chamberlain's Bed. To save his brigade from being cut to pieces, Davies gave orders to fall back to Adams Road. The general hoped to reorganize his battered command at that point. Colonel Hugh R. Janeway was directed to cover the retreat with the 1st and 2nd Battalions of his 1st New Jersey Cavalry. Janeway hurriedly deployed his two battalions across Danse's Ford road. Davies' troopers, after passing through Janeway's command, headed for the previously designated rendezvous. One of Colonel Stagg's Michigan regiments, which had been rushed to Janeway's support by General Devin, now put in an appearance. The Michiganders moved into position alongside the New Jersey unit.[20]

There was scant activity along Devin's picket line until 2:00 p.m. The Confederates precipitated what little action there was along Dinwiddie Road. To cover the right of Pickett's flanking column, Munford sent out several patrols. These groups carried out their assignment so successfully that the Federals kept

---

18 *Ibid.*, 1148-1149; Humphreys, *The Virginia Campaign of '64 and '65*, 334. Major Hart was killed in the fighting.

19 *OR* 46, pt. 1, 1148-1149.

20 *Ibid.*, 1122, 1144, 1149.

Brigadier General Thomas C. Devin
Library of Congress

their attention on White Oak Road. Devin's scouts failed to pick up any intelligence of Pickett's march down the west side of Chamberlain's Bed. When Devin learned that Five Forks was held by Pickett's division reinforced by at least a division of cavalry, he ordered Fitzhugh's troopers to fall back. Re-crossing Chamberlain's Bed, Fitzhugh's brigade retired about one-half mile. The brigade took up a new position covering the junction of Dinwiddie and Gravelly Run Church roads.[21]

About 2:30 p.m., Devin's troopers were surprised when the sound of heavy firing came rolling in from the southwest. Shortly thereafter, Devin received an urgent request from Colonel Janeway for help. Devin ordered Colonel Stagg to send one of his Michigan regiments to Janeway's assistance. (Stagg's brigade, except for the detachment manning the roadblock on Crump Road, had returned to J. Boisseau's farm.) In an effort to discover what was happening at Danse's Ford, Devin accompanied the Michiganders as they rode toward the sound of battle. Devin, arriving in the neighborhood of the crossing, found Davies' troopers "retiring precipitately." The general waved the Michigan regiment into position alongside Janeway's troopers. Next, he sought to rally Davies' frightened men. Finding that this was impossible, Devin called for his adjutant, Maj. Amasa E. Dana. Devin told the staff officer to hasten to Colonel Fitzhugh's command post and order Fitzhugh to move his brigade by the left flank and take position on the

---

21 *Ibid.*, 1122; *Atlas to Accompany the Official Records*, Plate LXXIV, No. 2.

road leading to Danse's Ford. One regiment would be left behind to hold Dinwiddie Road.[22]

As soon as Dana contacted Fitzhugh, the brigade commander hastened to carry out Devin's instructions. The 6th New York was detached to hold the roadblock, and the trumpeters were ordered to sound "Boots and Saddles." Fitzhugh's column moved off in a fast trot. Leaving Dinwiddie Road, Fitzhugh's brigade turned into the road leading to Danse's Ford. Some confusion ensued when stragglers from Davies' brigade broke through Fitzhugh's ranks. Finally, Fitzhugh's troopers caught up with Janeway's hard-pressed command. In accordance with Devin's orders, Fitzhugh dismounted and deployed his brigade. The troopers took position on either side of the road near the Williams house. Janeway's hard-pressed rear guard passed through Fitzhugh's ranks. Colonel Janeway then disbanded his group. The Michigan regiment reported back to Colonel Stagg; Janeway's troopers rejoined Davies' brigade, which was being reorganized near J. Boisseau's farm. Pressing forward hard on the heels of Janeway's rear guard, Corse's butternuts struck the fresh Union battle line. A bitter contest ensued. Fitzhugh's bluecoats were able to hold their own. Corse's heretofore irresistible sweep had been checked.[23]

The Yankees' jubilation, however, was short-lived as Munford now committed his division. Advancing down Dinwiddie Road, Munford's scouts established contact with the 6th New York. Before attacking, the colonel directed brigade commander Col. William A. Morgan to dismount several of his regiments. When the officers had formed their men into line of battle, Munford sent Morgan's brigade forward. The Confederate assault wave rolled over the New York regiment. Part of one of Colonel Stagg's Michigan regiments was rushed to the New Yorkers' assistance. Between them, the two Union units momentarily checked Munford's drive. Quickly regrouping, the Confederates again drove ahead, however, and the Union line collapsed.[24]

In an effort to enhance the pressure he could generate on Corse's front and get this stalled attack rolling, Pickett committed Terry's brigade. This increment to their strength enabled the Rebels to extend their right flank. To make matters worse for the Yankees, Devin learned that the 6th New York was in full retreat. Next, a powerful line of Southern infantry emerged from the woods to the general's front.

---

22 *OR* 46, pt. 1, 1122-1123; Swan, "The Five Forks Campaign," 303.

23 *OR* 46, pt. 1, 1123, 1144, 1149.

24 *Ibid.*, 1123, 1299. Colonel Morgan was in temporary command of the brigade formerly led by Munford.

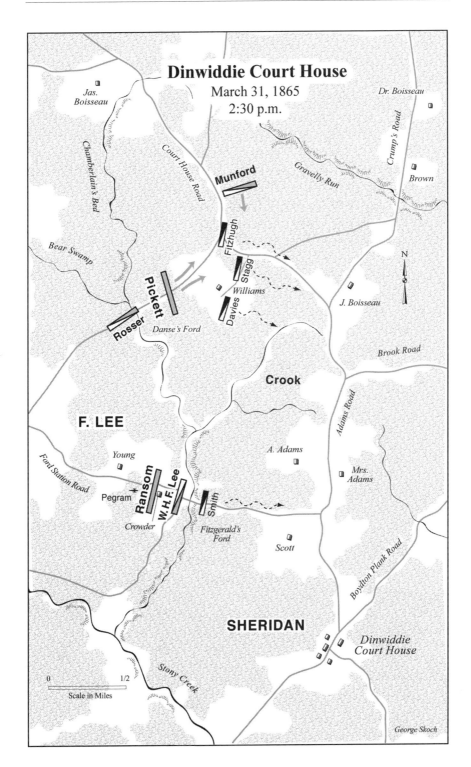

Dinwiddie Court House
March 31, 1865
2:30 p.m.

Jas. Boisseau

Dr. Boisseau

Crump's Road

Brown

Court House Road

Chamberlain's Bed

Munford

Gravelly Run

Bear Swamp

Fitzhugh

Stagg

Williams

Pickett

Davies

J. Boisseau

N

Rosser

Danse's Ford

Brook Road

Crook

Adams Road

F. LEE

Young

A. Adams

Mrs. Adams

Ford Station Road

Ransom

W.H.F. Lee

Pegram

Smith

Crowder

Fitzgerald's Ford

Scott

Boydton Plank Road

SHERIDAN

Dinwiddie Court House

0   1/2

Scale in Miles

Stony Creek

George Skoch

Devin realized that, if he left Fitzhugh's brigade where it was, it would be annihilated. He issued instructions for Fitzhugh to retire. At the same time, Devin called up Stagg's brigade.[25]

Covered by a strong rear guard, Fitzhugh's brigade retired a short distance. Stagg's Michiganders filed into position on Fitzhugh's left. Pushing rapidly ahead, Munford's butternuts quickly established contact with Fitzhugh's right flank units on Dinwiddie Road. The Federals beat off Munford's initial thrust. A second attack by the grey clads, however, was successful, and Fitzhugh's troopers fell back. Devin's defensive line had been rendered untenable. To cope with Munford, Fitzhugh redeployed his entire brigade athwart Dinwiddie Road. Stagg's Michiganders were left to deal with Pickett's infantry.[26]

Fitzhugh's and Stagg's brigades were unable to check the Confederate advance. Munford's troopers forced Fitzhugh's bluecoats back. At the same time, Pickett's infantry hammered away at Stagg's Michiganders. The two Union brigades fell back on J. Boisseau's farm, where General Davies was reforming his command. General Merritt sought to defend this strategic point. Devin's two brigades were deployed on the right; Davies placed his troopers on the left. Patrols were sent down Adams Road. These groups expected to open communications with the Federal troopers covering the Dinwiddie Court House.[27]

After driving back Stagg's brigade, Pickett moved to take possession of Adams Road. A combat team was sent through the woods. Reaching the vital road, the Confederates set up a roadblock. By this adroit move, Pickett succeeded in isolating the Union forces at Dinwiddie Court House from their comrades at J. Boisseau's farm.

The patrols sent out by Merritt were unable to get through Pickett's roadblock. To extricate his men from this dangerous situation, Merritt ordered Devin to take the two brigades—Fitzhugh's and Stagg's—and move across to Boydton Plank Road. In case the foe continued his push toward Dinwiddie Court House, Devin was to strike him in the flank and rear. Once he had mustered his command, Devin proceeded to carry out the first part of Merritt's instructions. Because Munford's Rebel division was hovering in the area, Devin screened his march with a strong rear guard. Though the Confederates adopted a threatening attitude, they did not attack. When his command reached A. Dabney's farm, Devin formed it into line of battle covering Plank Road. The "led horses" were brought up, and Devin prepared

---

25 *Ibid.*, 1123; Humphreys, *The Virginia Campaign of '64 and '65*, 335.

26 *OR* 46, pt. 1, 1123.

27 *Ibid.*, 1117, 1123, 1144.

to advance along Brooks Road and establish contact with Gibbs' brigade. At this time, Gibbs' brigade was covering the junction of Adams and Brooks Roads.[28]

Davies' brigade crossed the Boydton Plank Road shortly after Devin's troopers. Confederate patrols from Munford's division, both mounted and dismounted, harassed Davies' column. When Davies reached Plank Road, he assumed command of Devin's troops as ranking officer. One of Stagg's regiments, the 6th Michigan, was sent to check the Confederate pursuit. The Michiganders easily drove back the grey clad patrols that had been worrying Davies' men. Next, Davies issued orders suspending Devin's projected movement down Brooks Road. Instead, Devin was told to march to Dinwiddie Court House by way of Plank Road. It was starting to get dark when Fitzhugh's and Stagg's brigades reached Dinwiddie Court House. In accordance with Merritt's instructions, Devin moved his two brigades to Crump's farm, where they camped. Davies' unit also marched to Dinwiddie Court House. Here, the brigade was rejoined by the men with the "led horses." The troopers had not seen their horses since they had been sent to the rear early in the afternoon. Davies' brigade camped for the night on Great Cattail Run near the Kidd farm.[29]

When the foe had first appeared at Fitzgerald's Ford, Gregg's Pennsylvania brigade had been rushed to that point. Gregg posted his men in support of Smith's command. Smith's troopers, however, handled the situation without calling upon Gregg for help. Around 2:00 p.m., the sound of heavy firing drifted in from the north. Shortly thereafter, Gregg learned that the Confederate infantry had stormed across Chamberlain's Bed at Danse's Ford. Reports reached Gregg's command stating that Davies' brigade had been unable to check the grey clads' onslaught. Expecting to receive orders to march to his comrades' relief, Gregg alerted his regimental commanders to hold their men ready to move on a moment's notice.

Despite the bad news from the front, Sheridan refused to throw in his reserves until Pickett had committed himself. The cavalry leader was uncertain of the Confederates' intentions. Dinwiddie Court House might be their objective, or they might wheel to the left and drive up Boydton Plank Road in an effort to roll up the V Corps. Sheridan bided his time until Pickett's vanguard drove across Adams Road. This success enabled the Southerners to isolate three of Sheridan's brigades—Davies', Fitzhugh's, and Stagg's. Sheridan, hoping to convert this Confederate success into a disaster, ordered Merritt to march these three units across to Boydton Plank Road. If the grey clads pursued, Sheridan planned to strike

---

28 *Ibid.*, 1117, 1123; *Atlas to Accompany the Official Orders*, Plate LXXIV, No. 2.

29 OR 46, pt. 1, 1117, 1123, 1144.

them in the flank and rear. Next, Sheridan planned to organize his attacking forces. Gregg's brigade was to move across country and "attack the enemy in the flank and rear." Devin's third brigade, Gibbs', was to take position at the junction of Adams and Brooks roads. Gibbs' troopers were to delay Pickett's infantrymen in case they should strike for Dinwiddie Court House. A staff officer was sent to contact General Custer. The aide was to direct Custer to hasten to Dinwiddie Court House with two of his brigades. Custer's other brigade would be left to guard the train.[30]

Following the receipt of Sheridan's orders, Gregg's eager troopers, guided by a staff officer, rode off in the direction of the firing. After riding about a mile, Gregg halted his command. The 4th, 8th, and 16th Pennsylvania were dismounted and deployed into line of battle. There were no grey clads in sight. The Pennsylvanians, covered by a strong force of skirmishers, then worked their way cautiously forward, guided by the sound of heavy firing. Within a few minutes, the blue clads sighted Pickett's oncoming battle line. A fierce engagement ensued.[31]

A short time before Fitzhugh's and Stagg's troopers had been driven back on J. Boisseau's farm, Gibbs' brigade had taken position at the junction of Adams and Brooks roads. The four guns manned by the cannoneers of Batteries C and F, 4th U.S. Light Artillery were emplaced on the hill north of Dinwiddie Court House. When Gregg's Pennsylvanians moved forward, they established contact with Gibbs' left flank companies. Gibbs planned to get in touch with the remainder of Devin's division after it had retired to Boydton Plank Road, but he was unable to do so.

As soon as most of his infantry had reached the junction of Dinwiddie and Crump roads, Pickett formed his brigades into line of battle. Covered by a strong force of skirmishers, the Rebel infantry advanced on Dinwiddie Court House. Pickett's battle line guided its movements on Adams Road. Munford's troopers covered the infantry's left flank. Within a few minutes, Pickett's soldiers were in contact with Gregg's and Gibbs' hard-fighting troopers. On the Union left, Gregg's Pennsylvanians did not wait for the Confederates to charge. Pressing ahead, the bluecoats hurled the Confederate skirmishers back. In this thrust, a number of prisoners were captured by the Unionists, and sent to the rear. The Yankees held their own for almost two hours. Finally, however, Pickett's soldiers succeeded in dislodging Gibbs' brigade. The untimely retreat of Gibbs' command rendered

30 *Ibid.*, 1102, 1128, 1130, 1154.

31 *Ibid.*, 1154.

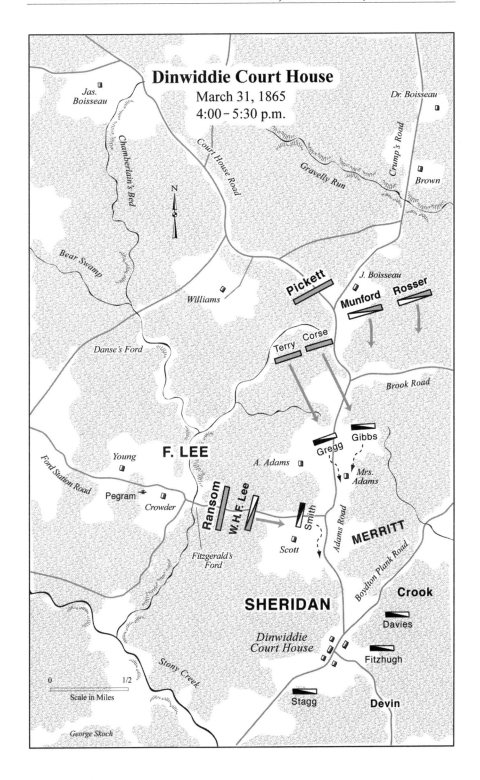

Dinwiddie Court House
March 31, 1865
4:00 – 5:30 p.m.

N

Jas. Boisseau

Dr. Boisseau

Chamberlain's Bed

Court House Road

Gravelly Run

Crump's Road

Brown

Bear Swamp

Pickett

J. Boisseau

Munford   **Rosser**

Williams

Danse's Ford

Terry   Corse

Brook Road

Gibbs

F. LEE

Young

A. Adams

Gregg

Mrs. Adams

Ford Station Road

Pegram

Crowder

Ransom   **W.H.F. Lee**

Smith

Adams Road

MERRITT

Fitzgerald's Ford

Scott

SHERIDAN

Boydton Plank Road

Crook

Davies

Dinwiddie Court House

Fitzhugh

Stony Creek

0   1/2
Scale in Miles

Stagg   **Devin**

George Skoch

Major General George C. Custer
Library of Congress

Gregg's position untenable. Covered by a strong rear guard, the Federals fell back.[32]

The combative Custer was overjoyed when a staff officer galloped up and told him to march to Dinwiddie Court House with two of his brigades. In accordance with Sheridan's instructions, Col. William Wells' brigade was detached and left to guard the wagons. Accompanied by Cols. Alexander C. M. Pennington's and Henry Capehart's brigades, Custer rode forward "at the trot." Upon reaching Dinwiddie Court House, the head of the column halted while Custer reported to Sheridan. The cavalry leader directed Custer to place his "command in position to support and relieve" Crook's division, which was being forced back by the Confederates. Rejoining his command, Custer directed Pennington to reinforce Smith's brigade at Fitzgerald's Ford. Capehart's troopers were to take position on the left of Adams Road. Just as Pennington was marshalling his command preparatory to carrying out Custer's instructions, one of Sheridan's staff officers galloped up. The aide told Pennington to deploy his brigade on Capehart's right.

By 5:30 p.m., Custer's command had taken position about one-half mile north of Dinwiddie Court House. Pennington's brigade was posted a short distance in front of and to the right of Capehart's. One artillery unit (Battery A, 2nd U.S. Light Artillery) reported to Custer. The "Boy General" had the artillerists unlimber their

32 *Ibid.*, 1128, 1154.

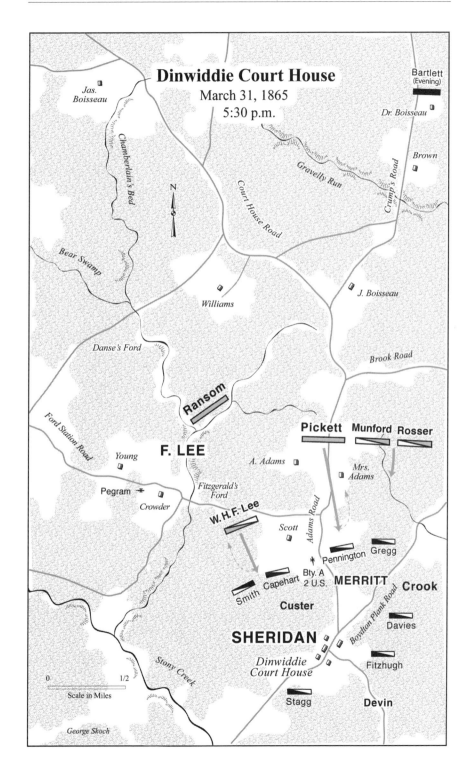

Dinwiddie Court House
March 31, 1865
5:30 p.m.

Jas. Boisseau

Bartlett (Evening)

Dr. Boisseau

Brown

Chamberlain's Bed

Gravelly Run

Crump's Road

Court House Road

N

Bear Swamp

Williams

J. Boisseau

Danse's Ford

Brook Road

Ransom

Pickett   Munford   Rosser

Ford Station Road

Young

F. LEE

A. Adams

Mrs. Adams

Pegram

Fitzgerald's Ford

Adams Road

Crowder

W.H.F. Lee

Scott

Pennington   Gregg

Smith   Capehart   Bty. A 2 U.S.

MERRITT   Crook

Custer

Boydton Plank Road

Davies

SHERIDAN

Dinwiddie Court House

Fitzhugh

0   1/2
Scale in Miles

Stony Creek

Stagg

Devin

George Skoch

four 3-inch rifles in the field on the left of Adams Road. His dispositions completed, Custer confidently waited for the Confederates to appear.[33]

Smith's troopers held Fitz Lee's command at bay until 5:30 p.m. Immediately after the Confederate horse artillery started to shell his command, Smith's scouts reported that Pickett's infantry was closing in on his brigade. (The retreat of Gregg's and Gibbs' commands had uncovered Smith's rear.)[34] If Smith's bluecoats remained where they were, they would be crushed between Pickett's advancing infantry and Fitz Lee's cavalry. Consequently, Smith ordered his men to fall back. Before they reached Dinwiddie Court House, Smith's people spotted Custer's battle line. Halting his command, Smith reformed his brigade on the left of Capehart's unit.[35]

As soon as Smith's brigade pulled back from Fitzgerald's Ford, Rooney Lee's and Rosser's cavalry divisions forded Chamberlain's Bed. Once the troopers had gained the left bank, Fitz Lee massed them on the right of Pickett's battle line. The Confederate infantry, after forcing Gregg's and Gibbs' units to give way, had resumed its push toward Dinwiddie Court House. Before they had advanced far, the Southerners encountered a fresh Union formation—Custer's division. It was getting late and darkness was not far off. Now that Fitz Lee was up, Pickett determined to make one final effort to smash Sheridan's Corps. The infantry would attack down Adams Road, while Fitz Lee turned the Union left. Munford's cavalry would cover the countryside between the Adams and Boydton Plank roads.[36]

Gregg's and Gibbs' battered commands had passed through Custer's line a few minutes before the Confederates emerged from the woods. Gregg's brigade was posted on the right of Pennington's brigade; Gibbs' was sent to the rear and rejoined Devin's division at Crump's farm. When the Confederates attacked, Pickett's infantry first assailed Pennington's troopers. (This Union command had taken position in advance of Custer's main line of resistance.) Pennington's brigade gave way. Falling back, Pennington reformed his command on the crest of a ridge on the right of Adams Road. This retreat enabled Pennington to re-establish contact with Capehart on his left. The grey clads failed to follow up on their

---

33 *Ibid.*, 1130, 1134. Only two of Pennington's regiments—the 2nd Ohio and the 3rd New Jersey—were formed into line of battle on the right of Adams Road. At this time, the 2nd Connecticut had not reached Dinwiddie Court House, and the 2nd New York was guarding the bridge that carried Boydton Plank Road across Stony Creek.

34 *OR* 46, pt. 1, 1157.

35 *Ibid.*, 1157.

36 *Ibid.*, 1130, 1134, 1157, 1299.

success. Pennington's troopers were given time in which to throw up fence rail barricades. When they did attack, the Confederates were thrown back by the troopers holding Custer's reorganized defensive line. A second attempt by Pickett's infantry to storm the Union position was also repulsed. Custer's troops then counterattacked and forced the Confederate skirmishers to recoil on their line of battle.[37]

In the meantime, Fitz Lee's cavalry had assailed the Union left. Smith's bluecoats, despite heavy losses, held their "ground under the hottest fire of which the enemy was capable," losing heavily all the while, till nearly dark." Smith now learned that his men had shot up all their ammunition. Consequently, he permitted them to fall back. Reforming on Adams Road, Smith's troopers "intimidated the advance of the enemy by presenting a good front, without a cartridge."[38]

It was now getting very dark; therefore, Pickctt ordered the attack suspended. When the fighting ceased, the two contending battle lines lay very close to each other. Pickett's infantry was massed astride Adams Road, with Fitz Lee's cavalry on the right and Munford's on the left. The Confederate picket lines extended from G. U. Brooks' on the left to Fitzgerald's Ford on the right. Two brigades of Custer's division held Sheridan's front on the night of the 31st. In anticipation of a dawn attack, Custer's men slept on their arms.[39]

After the fighting had ceased, Gregg's and Smith's troopers secured their "led horses." The two units then marched to Great Cattail Run, where they rendezvoused with Davies' brigade. Once he had regrouped his division, Crook permitted his men to camp. Following Custer's departure for the front, the wagon train was parked near the junction of Vaughan and Monk's Neck roads.[40]

While the Southerners had failed to score a sweeping success in the battle of Dinwiddie Court House, they had wrested the initiative from the aggressive Sheridan. If progress had been slow, it was because the Federal cavalry (most of them armed with seven-shot repeating carbines) had fought hard. The spirit of Pickett's hard-bitten fighters seemed as stout as ever. No reports were made by the Confederate leaders of the losses suffered by their commands in the battle of Dinwiddie Court House. In addition to the battle casualties, Pickett had lost the services of one of his brigadiers. During the day, General Terry had received a

---

37 *Ibid.*, 1130, 1134-1135.

38 *Ibid.*, 1157.

39 *Ibid.*, 1130; Humphreys, *The Virginia Campaign of '64 and '65*, 336.

40 OR 46, pt. 1, 1142, 1155, 1157; *Atlas to Accompany the Official Records*, Plate LXXIV, No. 2.

disabling injury. The ranking officer in the brigade, Col. Robert M. Mayo, assumed command of Terry's brigade.[41]

Having lost the initiative, Sheridan was forced to fight a delaying action. Each time the Confederates overcame a pocket of resistance, they were confronted by another. Nevertheless, by nightfall, Sheridan's Corps had been pushed back nearly to Dinwiddie Court House. Union losses during the day had totaled about 450.[42]

Late in the afternoon of the 31st, Grant sent a member of his staff, Brig. Gen. Horace Porter, to see Sheridan. Porter reached the junction of Adams and Brooks roads just as Gregg's and Gibbs' brigades were falling back. At this time, Porter recalled, one of Sheridan's bands, while under a heavy fire, was "playing 'Nellie Bly' as cheerily as if it were furnishing music for a country picnic."

Porter encountered Sheridan just before he reached Dinwiddie Court House. After Porter had reported on how the Army of the Potomac was faring, Sheridan remarked, "he had had one of the liveliest days in his experience, fighting infantry and cavalry with cavalry only." Sheridan told Porter "that he was concentrating his command on the high ground just north of Dinwiddie, and would hold that position at all hazards." Continuing, Sheridan declared, "that with the Corps of infantry he expected to be put under his command he could take the initiative the next morning and cut off the whole of the force Lee had detached." Sheridan, referring to Pickett's force, commented: "This force is in more danger than I am—if I am cut off from the Army of the Potomac, it is cut off from Lee's army, and not a man in it should ever be allowed to get back to Lee. We at last have drawn the enemy's infantry out of its fortifications, and this is our chance to attack it."

Sheridan begged Porter to hasten to Grant's headquarters and again urge the lieutenant general commanding to send him the VI Corps, "because it had been under him in the battles in the Valley of Virginia, and knew his way of fighting." Porter repeated the information which had been forwarded to Sheridan the previous evening regarding the VI Corps—namely, that Wright's Corps was on the right of the Army of the Potomac, and the only infantry force which could promptly join Sheridan was Warren's V Corps. With this business taken care of, Porter returned to Grant's headquarters. The staff officer reached Dabney's Mill at 7:00 p.m. and gave Grant a full report of Sheridan's operations.[43]

Evidently, Sheridan was not quite as confident of his position as he had led Porter to believe he was. When the cavalry leader composed a letter to Grant

---

41 Freeman, *Lee's Lieutenants*, vol. 3, 660; OR 46, pt. 1, 1268.

42 *OR* 46, pt. 3, 381.

43 Porter, "Five Forks and the Pursuit of Lee," 710-711.

describing the day's fighting, he wrote, "This force (Pickett's) is too strong for us. I will hold on to Dinwiddie Court-House until I am compelled to leave."[44]

Part V

The Battle of White Oak Road

It stopped raining on the afternoon of the 30th, but by 3:00 a.m. the next morning it started again. The streams continued to rise, and the roads were getting worse. Except where corduroyed, they were practically impassable. When Grant awoke and found that the rain had recommenced, he determined to do nothing until the precipitation ceased. The general's first order of the day was to Meade, sent at 7:40 a.m., announced, "Owing to the heavy rain this morning the troops will remain substantially as they are now, but the Fifth Corps should today draw three days' more rations."[45]

When he acknowledged Grant's telegram (at 7:45), Meade inquired if there were any objections to the II Corps also drawing three days' rations. The empty supply wagons would then be returned to the military railroad to be refilled.[46] Grant saw no objections. The II Corps was authorized to draw its rations.

Humphreys' and Warren's Corps had started taking up the positions which they had been ordered to assume the previous evening, about two hours before Grant issued his directive suspending all activities for the time being.

At daybreak, Ayres started massing his division near the S. Dabney house. First, the general issued orders calling up Denison's and Gwyn's brigades. These two organizations had spent the night camped on the left bank of the rain swollen branch of Gravelly Run, near Mrs. Butler's. After fording the three-foot deep stream, the two brigades marched to S. Dabney's, where they rendezvoused with Winthrop's command. In an effort to increase his striking force, Ayres sent an urgent dispatch to Warren. Ayres wanted the soldiers from his division who were manning the line of outposts relieved by men from some other unit. Ayres

---

44 *OR* 46, pt. 3, 301.

45 *OR* 46, pt. 3, 334; Freeman, *R. E. Lee*, vol. 4, 34. On the evening of March 30, Grant moved his headquarters to Dabney's Mill. Meade's headquarters at this time were on the Vaughan Road, in the triangle formed by the road, Generally Run, and a small tributary of the Run.

46 *OR* 46, pt. 3, 335.

Major General Gouverneur K. Warren
Library of Congress

informed his superior that he would
have already replaced the pickets
from his own command, but he did
not feel it would be wise to reduce
his strength at this time.[47]

A staff officer delivered this
message to General Warren at 6:10
a.m. Warren saw the logic behind Ayres' request. He dashed off a hurried reply,
informing Ayres "that the matter of relieving the pickets will be attended to at
once."[48]

For some unexplained reason, forty-five minutes elapsed before Warren
moved to secure a relief for Ayres' outposts. At 7 o'clock, Warren ordered General
Crawford to recall his pickets covering the Boydton Plank Road. Crawford would
then concentrate his division at the Holliday house. When his troops had reached
Holliday's, Crawford was to see that soldiers from his division relieved Ayres' on
the picket line. Crawford's men were to picket the front from Humphreys' left to a
point north of Holliday's. In case of a Confederate attack on Ayres' division,
Crawford was to move to his comrade's assistance. The pioneers from two of
Crawford's brigades were to be detached and left to throw a bridge across the rain
swollen branch of Gravelly Run that barred the passage of the corps' artillery.
Crawford would establish his command post at Holliday's house.[49]

Warren would have liked to visit Ayres' division and superintend the
operations at the front. In fact, he intended to leave for the point of danger "as soon
as the giving and receiving instructions necessary for the operations of the day
would permit." On the 31st, as on the 30th, the influx of dispatches received, and

47 *Ibid.*, 335, 368; pt. 1, 868.

48 *Ibid.*, pt. 3, 368.

49 *Ibid.*, 370; pt. 1, 812.

the orders that they made necessary, kept Warren at his headquarters and accessible to the telegraph until almost 9:00 a.m.[50]

The II Corps, as scheduled, had moved to take over the rifle pits held by Griffin's division. Since the Federals were on guard against a Confederate counterattack, they moved cautiously. Long before daybreak, General Hays issued instructions calling up General Smyth's brigade from the reserve. Moving to the front Smyth's troops halted in the rear of the trenches occupied by Pierce's brigade, the unit holding the right flank of Mott's main line of resistance. At dawn, Smyth's bluecoats relieved Pierce's soldiers. By this maneuver, Hays had succeeded in deploying his three brigades in the rifle pits—McIvor's on the right, Olmsted's in the center, and Smyth's on the left. The right flank of Hays' division was anchored on Hatcher's Run; its left flank joined Mott's right at the Taylor house. Hays had no reserve.[51]

As soon as Smyth's men had relieved Pierce, Mott's division shifted to the left. Mott's troops filed into the earthworks occupied by Miles' division. Two of Mott's brigades, McAllister's and Pierce's, were stationed in the breastworks. McAllister's left rested on the Boydton Plank Road, while Pierce's right was in contact with Hays' left at the Taylor house. De Trobriand's brigade was massed near the Rainey house, ready to move to Miles' assistance in case of an emergency.[52]

Upon being relieved by Mott's troops, Miles' division shifted across the Boydton Plank Road. Ramsey's and Madill's brigades relieved Griffin's troops in the fortifications. Nugent's and Scott's brigade were held in reserve. Throughout the morning, Miles gave his two reserve units various assignments. Nugent's soldiers were organized into fatigue parties and put to work slashing timber. The 5th New Hampshire of Scott's brigade was used to man Miles' picket line. When the New Hampshire regiment moved into no man's land, it was accompanied by two companies of the 64th New York.[53]

The II Corps batteries were not moved at this time. Three of the batteries were on the line and three were parked in reserve.[54]

50 *Ibid.*, pt. 1, 812.

51 *Ibid.*, 759, 766; pt. 3, 346.

52 *Ibid.*, pt. 1, 766.

53 *Ibid.*, 710, 714, 719, 724. Ramsey's brigade occupied the trenches on the left; Madill's those on the right.

54 *Ibid.*, 791. The four guns of Battery K, 4th U.S. Light Artillery and the four 3-inch rifles of Battery M, 1st New Hampshire Light Artillery were emplaced near the Rainey house; the four

By daylight, the II Corps had completed its shift to the left. When General Meade (at 7:30 a.m.) called for a report of the disposition of the II Corps, Humphreys replied:

> The position of my troops this morning is: Hays extending from right, near Crow House, to Taylor house; Mott from Taylor house to Boydton Plank Road. Miles has relieved Griffin in his position. . . . I find that Miles is strong enough in Griffin's position to admit of my putting de Trobriand's brigade in a little more central position from which it can move in a few minutes to the left.[55]

After being relieved by Miles, Griffin received instructions from Warren to move his division from the Boydton Plank Road to Mrs. Butler's. Griffin would mass his division at that point. Evidently, Griffin did not move promptly. When Humphreys reported to Meade (at 7:40 a.m.), he wrote: "Miles has relieved Griffin in his position, but Griffin has remained some hours."[56]

Warren, like Humphreys, was requested by General Meade (at 7:30 a.m.) to locate his units. The commander of the V Corps, however, hedged in his reply. Instead of telling where his divisions were, he indicated where he intended to post them. Warren, therefore, reported that Griffin's division would be concentrated at Mrs. Butler's, Ayres' near S. Dabney's, and Crawford's in between. In addition, Warren informed Meade of the existence of the road linking Mrs. Butler's on the Boydton Plank Road with W. Dabney's on the White Oak Road. At this time, Warren warned, this road is "not practicable" for wheeled vehicles. To make matters worse, the road crossed "a very difficult branch of Gravelly Run." Warren reported that he had all the pioneers he could spare working on a bridge. Even so, it would "take a long time to make" a practicable crossing for the wagons.

This telegram reached Meade's headquarters at 8:06 a.m. Meade immediately forwarded a copy of this message to Grant. In a covering dispatch, Meade commented that additional tools would be sent to the V Corps as soon as they could be moved to the front. Meade wanted to insure that the connecting road was rendered "passable for artillery and wagons at the earliest moment."[57]

12-pounder Napoleons manned by Battery B, 1st Rhode Island Light Artillery, were unlimbered near the Crow house.

55 OR 46, pt. 3, 346.

56 *Ibid.*, 346, 361.

57 *Ibid.*, 335, 346, 361.

A little before 8:30, the rattle of musketry from the direction of Humphreys' front became audible to the officers at Meade's headquarters. Messages were immediately sent to Humphreys and Warren. Humphreys was directed to ascertain and report the cause of the firing. Besides informing the commander of the V Corps of the skirmishers, Meade directed Warren to stand ready, if called upon, to rush his reserve to Humphreys' support. Meade, in compliance with Grant's directive, took this opportunity to inform his Corps commanders, "There will be no movement of troops today."

Making an investigation, Humphreys discovered that General Miles had sent a 60-man combat patrol from the 64th New York. Miles had done this in accordance with an order which Humphreys had issued to his subordinates. The division commanders were directed to reconnoiter the Confederate fortifications, try to capture prisoners, and ascertain the strength and identify of the units opposed to the II Corps. This information, Humphreys felt, would be invaluable in case an attack was ordered.

In carrying out this mission, Miles' combat patrol had clashed with Rebel pickets. After a few shots had been exchanged, the Southerners fled, leaving 16 prisoners in the Yankees' hands. The Confederates then sent a small detachment to drive back Miles' patrol, but it failed. Accompanied by their prisoners, the Yankees returned to their lines. Upon being questioned, the grey clads stated that they belonged to McGowan's South Carolina brigade. Furthermore, they identified Scales' brigade (under the temporary command of Col. Joseph Hyman) as the unit holding the lines on their left.[58]

Replying to Meade's communication, Warren explained that there was "a good deal of musketry firing going on in our lines by the men firing off their guns to put in fresh loads." Warren thought that, unless he completely lost contact with Humphreys, the force (Miles' division, reinforced by de Trobriand's brigade) which had relieved "Griffin is much more than under any circumstances could be needed there." If the Confederates, however, should break Humphreys' line or threaten to do so, Warren promised not to wait for orders to assist his brother officer.[59]

Meade had also informed Grant of the firing on the left of the II Corps' front. After stating that he had directed Warren to support Humphreys if necessary, Meade thought it would be a good idea if Grant alerted Ord. Meade reported that he had issued instructions for the II and V Corps to be supplied with rations. The

---

58 *Ibid.*, 346-347, 361. Lieutenant Colonel Welcome A. Crafts of the 5th New Hampshire was in charge of Miles' combat patrol.

59 *Ibid.*, 361.

general, however, expressed concern lest the condition of the roads render it impossible to re-victual Humphreys' and Warren's commands.

Following the receipt of Meade's dispatch, Grant telegraphed Ord to hold his troops ready to support Humphreys in case the II Corps was attacked.[60]

At 8:50 Warren received a message from Humphreys sent at 7:40. Humphreys wanted to know where Warren proposed to rest his right flank. At the moment, Humphreys reported, there was "a vacant space" on Miles' left.[61]

In answering Humphreys' dispatch, Warren stated that he was unable to "take up any regular line of battle on account of the woods and swamp." Instead, he had concentrated each of his divisions in a specified point so they could meet an attack from any direction with the line refused." Warren did not believe that the Confederates would be able to turn the II Corps left without Humphreys being forewarned, even if the V Corps moved away. As the troops were now deployed, Warren informed Humphreys, he could move Griffin and his supporting artillery into position on Miles' left in short order. A copy of the message to Meade locating the areas where Warren had posted his divisions, and a sketch map of the countryside west of the Plank Road, were also forwarded to Humphreys.[62]

At this time, Warren was not anticipating making any forward movements. Five minutes before he dictated the message to Humphreys, Warren received another telegram from Meade's headquarters. Meade again pointed out to his subordinate that "Owing to the weather no change will today be made in the present position of the troops." To take advantage of this hiatus, three day's rations and forage would be brought up and issued to the command. The empty wagons were to be sent to the rear to be refilled. Warren was admonished to "use every exertion to make practicable the roads to the rear. . . ."

During the night, Warren had received a copy of Sheridan's message to Grant reporting that Pickett's division was deployed along the White Oak Road, its right at Five Forks, and its left extending toward Petersburg. At 8:15 a.m. Warren relayed this communication to General Ayres. In his covering memorandum, Warren commented that he inferred from Sheridan's correspondence that Merritt's "small force" had been dislodged from the White Oak Road. Consequently, Warren warned Ayres that he would have to be on the lookout for a Confederate attack on his "left flank from the west as well as from the north." Ayres was also informed

60 *Ibid.*, 335, 374.

61 *OR* 46, pt. 1, 813.

62 *Ibid.*

that Crawford had been directed to mass his division at Holliday's, while Griffin's division was being concentrated at Mrs. Butler's.[63]

Although the Union brass did not know it, the left flank of Ayres' picket line extended about three-quarters of a mile beyond the point where the Rebel fortifications veered sharply north at the junction of the Claiborne and White Oak Roads. Ayres' presence in this sector was a result of the message which Warren had sent Meade at 4:00 p.m. on the 30th. At that time, Warren had written that he could take his "Corps and block the White Oak Road."[64] Meade had forwarded a copy of Warren's dispatch to Grant. The lieutenant general commanding had replied at 8:30 p.m., "It will just suit what I intended to propose—to let Humphreys' relieve Griffin's division and let that move farther to the left. Warren should get himself strong tonight."[65]

Later in the evening, Grant sent two telegrams to Meade. In both of these, Grant pointed out that Warren was not to attack without orders signed by him. Since it was feared that the Rebels were about to seize the initiative, Warren was to strengthen his position. Grant was correct in his estimate of the situation. Not only were the Confederates about to launch a powerful assault on the left flank of Warren's Corps, but Pickett's task force was preparing to move against Sheridan's cavalry.[66]

On the morning of the 31st, General Lee visited the sector held by Anderson's Corps. The general rode along the White Oak Road inspecting the fortifications as far to the west as the Claiborne road. Upon reaching "the return," Lee learned from General Johnson that Union troops (Ayres' division) which were in front of the works at this point were deployed with their "left flank in the air." To take advantage of this carelessness, and to preclude the possibility of the Federals' interposing between Pickett's task force and Anderson's fortified position, Lee determined to attack and roll up the exposed Union flank.

This would be a desperate gamble, because there were only four brigades available with which to undertake this task. To make matters worse, these four units came from three different divisions. Moody's and Wise's brigades belonged to Johnson's division, Hunton's to Pickett's, and McGowan's to Wilcox's. Accordingly, they would not be accustomed to working as a team. Johnson was placed in charge of the projected attack, under the general supervision of Anderson.

63 OR 46, pt. 3, 369.

64 Ibid., 304; Swan, "The Five Forks Campaign," 315.

65 OR 46, pt. 3, 285; Swan, "The Five Forks Campaign," 315.

66 OR 46, pt. 3, 285-286; Swan, "The Five Forks Campaign," 315-316.

The corps commander, however, seems to have taken little or no part in the subsequent engagement.[67]

Upon being given tactical control of the situation, Johnson quickly made his dispositions. McGowan's brigade, which was posted west of Burgess Mill, was pulled out of the rifle pits. When he formed his troops on the White Oak Road, McGowan moved to join Johnson at the junction of the Claiborne and White Oak Roads. Hyman's brigade extended to the left, and occupied the trenches vacated by McGowan's South Carolinians.

An air of urgency was added to the situation when Johnson spotted two Union battle lines (Winthrop's and Gwyn's) moving into the field west of Halter Butler's house. Johnson ordered Hunton's troops to leave the protection of the earthworks and take position in the woods north of the White Oak Road. The Alabama brigade was formed on Hunton's right. Since General Moody was ill, Col. Martin L. Stansel (the ranking regimental commander) was in charge of the Alabama brigade. At the same time, Johnson notified Anderson and Heth that he would attack as soon as he could form his line of battle. McGowan's grey clads now came hurrying up the White Oak Road. Johnson shouted for McGowan to deploy his men on Stansel's right. Within a few minutes, the three battle-hardened Rebel brigades had taken position in the woods north of the White Oak Road. Wise's brigade was on the ground but not in line.

Johnson was encouraged when he saw that the Union left flank was still dangling "in the air." Furthermore, the woods west of Halter Butler's field would screen the Confederates' approach march. Johnson, therefore, issued instructions for McGowan to take his brigade and assail the exposed Union flank. McGowan was to drive the Federals across the front of Johnson's other brigades. Hunton's and Stansel's troops would then move to the attack. Following the receipt of Johnson's orders, McGowan's South Carolinians crossed the road. Before McGowan's troops got into position, the Yankees suddenly resumed their advance.[68]

In the meantime, one of Ayres' staff officers had reached Warren's command post. The aide informed Warren that the Confederates still held a line of outposts south of the White Oak Road. (On the morning of the 31st, the 41st Alabama had continued to man the line of outposts which General Johnson had established covering the approaches to the White Oak Road.) Warren decided that, if his position were to be rendered secure from attack by the Five Forks Rebels, it would

67 Freeman, *R. E. Lee*, vol. 4, 33-34.

68 *OR* 46, pt. 1, 1287-1288.

be necessary to do something about the Rebel pickets. In addition, the general was afraid that the suspension of hostilities ordered by Grant would give the foe an excellent opportunity to reconnoiter the V Corps' position. Finally, Warren believed that his troops would be unable to obtain much rest during this hiatus in action operations unless there were "a greater distance" between his picket line and line of battle. As the situation then was, Warren felt that his men would have insufficient time to get under arms in case a strong force of butternuts "showed itself at the advance posts." To prevent any relaxation of vigilance until after his position had been made secure, Warren did not announce that orders had been received suspending all movements.

At 9:40 a.m. Warren telegraphed Meade that he had directed Ayres to drive in the Confederate outposts. In addition, Ayres was to see if he could ascertain the strength of the Rebel force holding the White Oak Road. A copy of this dispatch was forwarded to Ayres.[69]

General Meade approved of Warren's forced reconnaissance. At 10:30 Chief of Staff Webb informed Warren: "Your dispatch giving Ayres' position is received. General Meade directs that should you determine by your reconnaissance that you may get possession of and hold the White Oak Road you are to do so notwithstanding the orders to suspend operations today".[70]

Ayres' division, however, had moved forward and a desperate contest had been precipitated before Webb's communication reached Warren.

General Ayres spent a busy morning marshalling his division at S. Dabney's. As soon as all his units were up, Ayres proceeded to form his men in accordance with Warren's instructions. The troops were deployed east of S. Dabney's place in Halter Butler's field. This field was bounded on the north by the White Oak Road.[71]

Ayres had Winthrop form his brigade into line of battle north of the Holliday dwelling. The 140th New York was thrown out as skirmishers and covered Winthrop's battle line.[72] Gwyn's brigade was deployed into line of battle and took position en echelon on Winthrop's right.[73] These two brigades faced the White Oak Road, which was about one-fourth of a mile to their front. To protect his left flank, Ayres placed Colonel Denison's brigade in a wooded ravine west of the field. Two

69 *Ibid.*, 813; pt. 3, 362; Survivors' Association, *History of the Corn Exchange Regiment*, 368.

70 *OR* 46, pt. 3, 362.

71 *Ibid.*, pt. 1, 868; Porter, "Operations of the Fifth Corps," 224.

72 *OR* 46, pt. 1, 868, 873. From right to left, Winthrop's battle line was formed as follows: the 146th New York, 5th New York, and 15th New York Heavy Artillery.

73 *Ibid.*, 875.

Major General Romeyn B. Ayres
Library of Congress

of Denison's regiments, the 4th and 7th Maryland, patrolled the woods on the left of the brigade.[74]

It was a little after 7:00 a.m., when Crawford's division moved out of the breastworks covering Boydton Plank Road. The muddy road and the rain-swollen branch slowed down the pace of Crawford's march. Inspite of these difficulties, Crawford succeeded in massing his troops at Holliday's by 10:00 a.m.[75]

Meanwhile General Griffin concentrated his division at Mrs. Butler's. Protected as he was by the booming branch, Griffin held an impregnable position. Therefore, when Griffin's division had taken its position astride the wood road, arms were stacked, knapsacks unslung, and the men prepared breakfast. It now ceased raining and the sun, bright and warm, broke through the clouds. Blankets were spread out to dry, and the soldiers felt the "buoyancy always so distinctively dominant during the short rifts in seasons of continual contacts."[76]

Warren's artillerists would not be able to move their pieces to the front until the pioneers had completed the bridge. The eight guns manned by the gunners of Battery D and Battery E, 1st New York Light Artillery, therefore, were emplaced to cover the spot where the Boydton Plank Road crossed Gravelly Run. In addition, these two units would protect Griffin's left flank. Following the departure of Griffin's troops, Battery B, 4th U.S. and Batteries D and G, 5th U.S. Light Artillery

---

74 *Ibid.*, 874; Porter, "Operations of the Fifth Corps," 224

75 *OR* 46, pt. 1, 883, 892, 896.

76 Survivors' Association, *History of the Corn Exchange Regiment*, 568.

had remained in position at the junction of the Boydton Plank and Dabney Mill roads. They would furnish fire support to Miles' division of the II Corps.[77]

Shortly after Ayres had completed his dispositions, one of Warren's staff officers (Major Emmor B. Cope) galloped up to his command post. The aide-de-camp told Ayres that he was "to take the White Oak Road and entrench a brigade up on it." Ayres was also authorized to call upon Crawford for one brigade to support his attack. When Crawford received Ayres' request, he issued marching orders to Col. Richard Coulter's brigade. When Coulter reported to Ayres, he was directed to form his brigade in the rear of Winthrop's command. While Coulter's troops were filing into position, Winthrop's moved to the attack.

As soon as Coulter's brigade had advanced to reinforce Ayres, Crawford hastened to form his two other brigades. Brigadier General Henry Baxter's and Col. John A. Kellogg's brigades were massed in columns of regiments in a thick woods south of Halter Butler's field. Kellogg's organization was on the right and Baxter's on the left.[78]

In obedience to Warren's orders, Ayres at 10:30 a.m. sent Winthrop's brigade forward. Gwyn's troops supported Winthrop's advance on the right. Covered by the skirmishers from the 140th New York, Winthrop's grim battle line swept ahead. As they advanced across the field, the Federals were greeted by small-arms fire. At first, this was scattered, but as the Yankees drove closer to the White Oak Road, it increase in intensity. Lieutenant Colonel William W. Swan recalled:

> I sat on my horse between the two lines of reserves, watching Winthrop go forward steadily in painful silence. Not an enemy was to be seen, not a musket was fired, until the advancing troops were half across the field, when suddenly along the edge of the wood at the other end there appeared a long blue line of smoke. . .

The bluecoats were unable to see their tormentors who were concealed in the woods north of the road. Winthrop's soldiers, however, drove to within "ten to fifteen yards" of the road.[79]

At the time that Winthrop's brigade moved to the attack, McGowan's troops had not been able to get into position on Ayres' left. Consequently, when he saw the bluecoats coming across the field toward the White Oak Road, Johnson ordered his

77 OR 46, pt. 1, 899.

78 Ibid., 883, 868, 892, 896.

79 Ibid., 873; Porter, "Operations of the Fifth Corps," 225; Swan, "The Five Forks Campaign," 319.

"command to advance and meet the enemy's attack." Before Johnson's message could be relayed to his brigade commanders, a lieutenant in Hunton's brigade who had been watching Winthrop's advance sprung to his feet, waved his sword, and shouted "Forward!" Hunton's eager Virginians, answering the lieutenant's call, rushed from their places of concealment. Stansel's Alabamians moved to the attack on Hunton's right. McGowan had not completed his dispositions when Johnson's attack order reached his command post. His line was not formed, but his South Carolinians, on hearing the shouts of Hunton's troops, could not be restrained. Surging forward, McGowan's brigade assailed Ayres left flank.[80]

Hunton's Virginians and Stansel's Alabamians, in a short desperate contest, bested Winthrop's New Yorkers. To escape annihilation, Winthrop bellowed instructions for his soldiers to face about. Covered by a rear guard, the brigade fell back on the position occupied before the advance.[81]

When Colonel Gwyn saw the Confederates come pouring across the road, he led his brigade forward on the double. Before Gwyn's troops could intervene, Winthrop's command was in full retreat. Gwyn's battle line halted and blazed away at the oncoming Rebels. This served to check momentarily the Confederate drive. Encouraged by Gwyn's stand, Winthrop rallied his command. The Confederate onslaught was slowed. Reacting to this situation with his customary vigor, Johnson hurled Hunton's Virginians against Gwyn's line of battle. Stansel's Alabamians pressed against Winthrop's flank. The Alabamians' volleys struck Winthrop's brigade in the flank, and Winthrop's troops resumed the retreat. Colonel Swan recalled that:

> Winthrop's brigade then returned slowly to the branch of Gravelly Run. There was no order, however. Each man was looking out for himself and all were making for the entrenched line. . . . The men did not run. The stream was much swollen and at places too deep for the infantry to ford. I remember that I rode with Winthrop in rear of the retreating troops. My horse was killed, shot through the neck, from side to side, just as we entered the wood.[82]

Hunton's troops found the going more difficult. The Virginians centered their attack on the left flank and front of Gwyn's battle line. Following Winthrop's

---

80 Freeman, *R. E. Lee*, vol. 4, 34; *OR* 46, pt. 1, 1287-1288; Porter, "Operations of the Fifth Corps," 227.

81 *OR* 46, pt. 1, 871, 875.

82 *Ibid.*, 871, 875; Swan, "The Five Forks Campaign," 321.

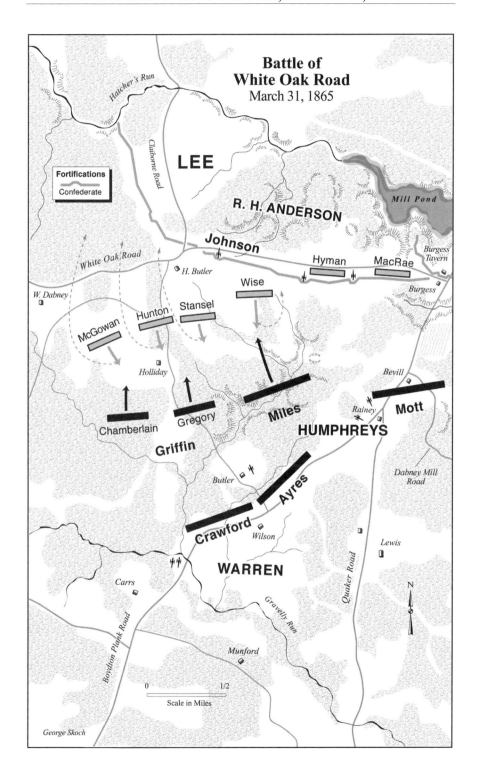

Battle of
White Oak Road
March 31, 1865

withdrawal, Gwyn's position became untenable. Hunton's troops turned Gwyn's flank. The regiment on the left, the 210th Pennsylvania, broke and fled. Gwyn's brigade fell back upon Crawford's division.[83]

In the meantime, McGowan's South Carolinians moved against Denison's brigade. Denison's Marylanders checked McGowan's initial thrust.

Coulter's brigade, which had been sent to reinforce Ayres' division, had not completed its deployment at the time that Winthrop suffered his repulse. Observing that Gwyn's troops were already moving to Winthrop's assistance, Coulter advanced to help Denison. McGowan by this time had renewed his attack on Denison's Maryland brigade. Infiltrating the woods to the left of the ravine held by Denison's battle line, the South Carolinians compelled the 4th and 7th Maryland to fall back. This success enabled McGowan's soldiers to enfilade the left flank of Denison's line, and the Marylanders were forced to evacuate the ravine. When they retreated, Denison's bluecoats fell back on Coulter's command. So shaken was the Maryland brigade by this setback that Denison was unable to reform his unit until after it had crossed the rain-swollen branch. Among the casualties in this fighting was Colonel Denison, who was wounded. He, however, refused to leave the field.[84]

After Denison's troops had passed beyond their field of fire, Coulter's battle line commenced to blaze away at McGowan's oncoming grey clads. Coulter's men, however, had been badly unnerved by the sight of Denison's frightened soldiers pounding for the rear. The officers of Coulter's left flank units found, much to their consternation, that McGowan's battle line overlapped theirs. Subjected to a deadly enfilade fire, the left flank companies eroded away, file by file. Three of Coulter's regimental commanders were cut down—wounded. The brigade then fell back in confusion. Before reaching the run, Coulter succeeded in rallying the hard-core elements of his command for several brief stands. Each time, however, the advancing Confederates smashed these pockets of resistance.[85]

It had been General Ayres' intention to reform his division in the edge of the woods on the south side of Halter Butler's field. When the Rebels overwhelmed Denison's and Coulter's brigades on the left, the general's plan was doomed. He then sought to rally his troops behind a ravine near the Holliday cabin, but he failed. Ayres' shattered division then retreated in confusion across the run.

---

83 *OR* 46, pt. 1, 875.

84 *Ibid.*, 869, 874; Porter, "Operations of the Fifth Corps," 227.

85 *OR* 46, pt. 1, 896; Porter, "Operations of the Fifth Corps," 227. The wounded officers were: Major Dennis R. Dailey of the 147th New York, Lieutenant Colonel Horatio N. Warren, of the 142nd Pennsylvania, and Major Henry H. Fish of the 54th New York.

In their initial surge, the Southerners had scored a sweeping success. Johnson's three brigades (Hunton's, McGowan's, and Stansel's) had routed Ayres' formidable reinforced division. Four Union brigades, mustering more than 5,000 officers and men, were in wild retreat. Having cleared the Yankees out of Halter Butler's field, Johnson's troops advanced into the woods that bounded the field on the south.

General Lee had been anxiously watching the progress of Johnson's attack. Lee feared that Hunton's brigade on the left of Johnson's battle line would lose contact with the troops holding the fortifications. Consequently, Lee ordered Wise's brigade which was held in reserve to advance and take position on Hunton's left. Wise proceeded to carry out Lee's instructions with his customary alacrity.[86]

When General Crawford learned that General Ayres, instead of being the attacker, had become the attacked, he ordered Baxter's and Kellogg's brigades deployed in the woods north of Holliday's cabin. Baxter formed his brigade on the right, Kellogg on the left.

Four of Baxter's regiments deployed into line of battle, while the 39th Massachusetts was thrown forward as skirmishers. Observing that the Rebels were advancing in great strength, Baxter reinforced the 39th Massachusetts with the 11th Pennsylvania. Both of these regiments were composed of hardened veterans. As soon as the retreating elements of Ayres' division had moved out of range, the skirmishers opened fire upon the Confederates. The butternuts were in full view as they charged across Halter Butler's field. Although but few in numbers when compared with the assaulting column, the two regiments caused Hunton to hesitate. After a brisk fire fight, the Confederates pushed ahead. The 39th Massachusetts and the 11th Pennsylvania were brushed aside. In this engagement, Lt. Col. Henry M. Tremlett of the 39th Massachusetts was mortally wounded. The colonel was carried from the field on a tent fly by several of his devoted men. Falling back, the bluecoats expected to rendezvous with the remainder of the brigade. But upon reaching Holliday's, they were unable to find any sign of their friends. Disgusted at being left to their fate, the two regiments "fell back without much order to the branch which they had crossed four hours before."[87]

Baxter encountered much difficulty in forming his battle line. Hundreds of Ayres' frightened soldiers rushed through the ranks of the brigade. By the time Baxter had completed his deployment, the skirmishers of the 39th Massachusetts and the 11th Pennsylvania were in contact with Hunton's Virginians. At first,

---

86 OR 46, pt. 1, 1288; Freeman, R. E. Lee, vol. 4, 34.

87 Porter, "Operation of the Fifth Corps," 227-228; Alfred S. Roe, The Thirty-Ninth Regiment Massachusetts Volunteers: 1862-1865 (Worcester, 1914), 281.

Brigadier General Samuel W. Crawford
Library of Congress

Baxter's right flank rested in the air. Gwyn's brigade now came flooding back from the front, and officers succeeded in rallying some of the braver souls on Baxter's right.

When the graycoats attacked Baxter's line of battle, they concentrated their efforts on his left. Within a few minutes, Stansel's Alabamians forced Baxter's left flank regiment to give way. Having gained an opening, the Southerners rolled up Baxter's brigade. Soon only the right flank regiment, the 107th Pennsylvania, was left on the field. Seeing the havoc that the Rebels were raising with Baxter's brigade, Gwyn's men had also disappeared. The Southerners now prepared to knock out the Pennsylvania regiment. Colonel Thomas F. McCoy, realizing that if he permitted his command to remain where it was, it would be surrounded, ordered his men to retreat. The Pennsylvanians reached the branch "with little loss."[88]

Colonel Kellogg had not completed his dispositions when Ayres' reinforced division fell to pieces. To check the rout, General Crawford directed Kellogg to deploy the elite 6th and 7th Wisconsin (once members of the "Iron Brigade") to arrest the retreat of Ayres' troops. The two Wisconsin regiments, however, found this impossible. Ayres' panic-stricken troops broke through Kellogg's ranks and threw the two Wisconsin regiments "into confusion." As soon as the fugitives had passed, Kellogg had the 6th and 7th Wisconsin close ranks. When his battle line was

88 *OR* 46, pt. 1, 892.

formed, Kellogg shouted for his troops to open fire on the advancing Confederates.

Kellogg now called up his third regiment, the 91st New York. The New Yorkers formed on the left of the 6th Wisconsin. Taking cover behind a slight rise, they raked the Rebel battle line with well-directed volleys. This caused a number of the grey clads to veer off to the left. At the same time, the 6th and 7th Wisconsin held fire in the face of the Rebel onslaught. The retreat of Baxter's brigade, however, had exposed Kellogg's right flank.

McGowan, observing that he was unable to smash Kellogg's brigade with frontal attacks, determined to bypass this island of resistance. Sweeping to the left, McGowan's troops passed around Kellogg's right flank. To cope with this dangerous situation, Kellogg had the 7th Wisconsin wheel to the right. Kellogg merely postponed the inevitable by this move. The Confederates had now succeeded in turning Kellogg's flanks. Worse, Rebel patrols had started to infiltrate the area in the rear of the brigade. Kellogg, confronted by this emergency, ordered his men to fall back behind the branch. The officer sent to relay this message to Col. Jonathan Tarbell of the 91st New York was wounded. Therefore, when Kellogg's brigade retreated the New Yorkers were left behind. Since the grey clads had already bypassed their position, Kellogg's soldiers had to conduct a fighting withdrawal. Several times, the Federals were compelled to cut their way through Confederate roadblocks. Crossing the run, the 6th and 7th Wisconsin took position near the bridge which the pioneers had recently completed.[89]

A number of minutes elapsed before Colonel Tarbell realized that his regiment was terribly alone. Rather than surrender, the colonel decided to fight his way out of the trap. The regiment fell back to the Holliday cabin. Here, the colonel succeeded in forming part of his command on the colors. He then determined to make one final attempt to slow the Rebel advance. This last-ditch stand by the regiment failed. Overpowered by the Confederates, the New Yorkers retreated across the branch. After crossing the run, Colonel Tarbell reformed his regiment, and posted it in support of Battery H, 1st New York Light Artillery.

Colonel Kellogg, in his "After Action Report," proudly claimed that his "command were the last organized troops to leave the field." This statement by the Union brigade commander is a clear indication of the scope of the Confederates success at this stage of the battle. The outnumbered Confederates had simply carried everything before them. Johnson's three brigades had swept the area between the White Oak Road and the run clean of organized Union troops. (It

89 *Ibid.*, 884, 886-887.

Major General Charles Griffin
Library of Congress

appears that Wise's Virginia brigade, when it was finally committed, did not engage the V Corps.) Two powerful Federal divisions (Ayres' and Crawford's) had been mauled. Warren's forced reconnaissance had ended in disaster.

It was about 10:30 o'clock when General Warren left for the front. The general intended to take charge of Ayres' forced reconnaissance. By the time Warren reached the run, Ayres' division was in full retreat. Crossing the stream, he hastened toward the point of attack. Before the general reached Crawford's command post, that officer's division was also falling back. In an effort to rally the soldiers, Warren seized the colors of a Pennsylvania regiment. Warren galloped up and down the lines, brandishing the banner, but the soldiers refused to stand and fight. It was evident that the men could not be induced to stop their retreat until they had placed the branch between themselves and Johnson's terrible men. The general, therefore, re-crossed the stream. Still flaunting the colors to encourage the disheartened troops, Warren, ably assisted by his more resolute subordinates, succeeded in curbing the panic. Regiments which had held together were deployed on the right of Griffin's division. The remainder of Ayres' and Crawford's regiments were rallied behind Griffin's main line of resistance. Here, the routed units were re-formed and the rolls called.[90]

90 *Ibid.*, 814, 887; Porter, "Operations of the Fifth Corps," 228; Roe, *The Thirty-Ninth Massachusetts*, 282.

It was about 11:00 a.m. when the sound of "heavy musketry" from the direction of White Oak Road became distinctly audible at General Griffin's headquarters at Mrs. Butler's. Without a moment's hesitation, Griffin had the "long roll" beaten. The command, "Fall in! Fall in!" rang out simultaneously with the crashing volleys. This order was obeyed with alacrity. Rifles were quickly taken from the stands and the regiments fell in on their colors. Griffin then put his division in motion toward the point of danger. When Griffin's troops reached the rise overlooking the branch, they witnessed a melancholy sight. They saw hundreds of their comrades falling back toward the stream as fast as their legs would carry them. As the wave of fleeing soldiers floundered through the waist-deep water, General Griffin's voice could be heard, "For God's sake, let them through, or they will break our line." In his "After Action Report," Griffin stated that his troops were "met by the Third Division [under Crawford] running to the rear in a most demoralized and disorganized condition, soon after followed by the Second Division [Ayres']." In accordance with Warren's instructions, Griffin quickly formed his division into line of battle along the left bank of the stream.[91]

News that the Confederates were sweeping everything before them caused the V Corps' chief of artillery, Brig. Gen. Charles S. Wainwright, to shift several of his batteries. The two artillery units (Battery D and Battery E, 1st New York Light Artillery) that had been guarding the Boydton Plank Road crossing of Gravelly Run limbered up their pieces. When they turned off the Plank Road at Mrs. Butler's, the gunners found the going exceedingly difficult. They literally had to lift their guns through the Virginia mud. Reaching Griffin's main line of resistance, the artillerists placed their guns in battery. Major Charles E. Mink saw that the four 12-pounder Napoleons of Battery H were unlimbered on a commanding knoll in a small field. The gunners trained their pieces on the woods beyond the run. They had an excellent field of fire. Captain Deloss M. Johnson of Battery D was unable to find such a favorable location for his four Napoleons. He emplaced them in a wooded area. Johnson's guns, accordingly, played but small part in the subsequent fighting.[92]

Griffin had barely completed his deployment before the Confederate skirmishers emerged from the woods on the opposite side of the branch. In general, the Rebel advance had followed the Union retreat along the wood road. The bluecoats watched as the Southerners descended a hill and crossed the swale that

91 OR 46, pt. 1, 814, 846; Survivors' Association, *History of the Corn Exchange Regiment*, 569. Griffin was mistaken on one point: Ayres' shattered division reached the run ahead of Crawford's. Chamberlain's brigade was deployed on the left of Griffin's line.

92 OR 46, pt. 1, 899.

separated the rise which they had just left from the one occupied by Griffin's division. It seemed evident to the Yankees that the Rebels intended to force their way across the run. Actually, the Southerners merely planned to make a forced reconnaissance. Mink's four Napoleons opened the engagement. The gunners raked the advancing Confederates with shell and canister. Moments later, Griffin's infantry started to blaze away. After a brisk engagement, the grey clads fell back about 400 yards.[93]

For the next several hours, Union and Confederate sharpshooters sniped at one another. Many of the bluecoats' skirmishers expended up to 80 rounds. Learning that the sharpshooters had about exhausted their ammunition, Lt. Col. Henry O'Neill of the 118th Pennsylvania called for a volunteer to carry cartridges to the line. It was a perilous undertaking. Sergeant George W. Stotensburg responded. He ran along the front from man to man, dropping a fresh supply of ammunition in the rear of each sharpshooter. The daring sergeant was shot at a number of times, but discharged his mission successfully and rejoined his regiment unharmed.[94]

As soon as Warren learned of the desperate state of affairs at the front, he sent a staff officer to contact General Humphreys. The commander of the II Corps was requested to make a diversion in favor of the V Corps. When he sought to obtain additional details of the extent of the setback suffered by the V Corps, Humphreys' staffers were unable to contact Warren. One of them did see Griffin, however. Griffin assured the aide that his division would be able to hold its line on the branch. Humphreys accordingly issued instructions for "General Miles to throw forward two of his brigades and attack the enemy."[95]

In the meantime, a large number of fugitives from the V Corps' debacle had descended on Miles' left flank brigade, Ramsey's. To cope with this situation, Ramsey established a straggler line manned by the 66th New York and the 116th Pennsylvania. These regiments took position behind Ramsey's main line. When the frightened soldiers entered Miles' lines, they were stopped and turned back.

It was about 12:30 when Miles received the orders from Humphreys to move to the relief of the V Corps with two of his brigades. Colonels Madill and Ramsey were alerted by Miles to be ready to take up the advance. Nugent's brigade would support Madill's and Ramsey's attack. Scott's brigade was called up from the reserve and relieved Madill's and Ramsey's commands in the rifle pits.

---

93 *Ibid.*, 815; Porter, "Operations of the Fifth Corps," 228.

94 Survivors' Association, *History of the Corn Exchange Regiment*, 569-570. Colonel William Sergeant of the 210th Pennsylvania was mortally wounded by a Confederate sharpshooter.

95 *OR* 46, pt. 1, 677, 815; pt. 3, 348.

When Miles gave the word, Ramsey's and Madill's battle lines moved out of the works. Swinging to the left, the two brigades advanced into the woods west of the Boydton Plank Road. Miles' troops reached the run a short distance beyond the right flank of the V Corps. Ramsey's brigade, which was on the left, waded the stream; Madill's lagged behind. Near the crest of a ridge several hundred yards beyond the branch, Ramsey's troops ran afoul of Wise's Virginians. A sharp engagement ensued. At this time, three of Ramsey's regiments (the 64th New York and the 145th and 183rd Pennsylvania) were on detached service. The brigade was, therefore, considerably understrength. Even so, the bluecoats, for several minutes, gave a good amount of themselves. Suddenly, however, without warning, the 148th Pennsylvania gave way "unceremoniously and in confusion." The retreat of the 148th left Ramsey's right flank regiment, the 53rd Pennsylvania, isolated. To escape destruction, the 53rd Pennsylvania likewise retired and re-crossed the run. Ramsey, realizing that it would be foolish to continue the conflict with just two regiments (the 66th New York and the 116th Pennsylvania), passed the word to fall back.

When he reached the left bank of the branch, Ramsey, in spite of the harassing fire of Wise's sharpshooters, quickly reformed his brigade. Subsequently, Ramsey bitterly castigated the conduct of Madill's command. He reported, "Had the Third Brigade [Madill] advanced with me, after crossing the run, instead of remaining idle spectators, the result of the assault would have been different and my brigade spared the mortification of a repulse."[96]

As soon as he had redeployed his troops into line of battle, Ramsey again led them across the run. Ramsey's bluecoats slowly closed on Wise's battle line which was formed along the crest of the ridge. In the meantime, Madill's brigade had forded the stream. While Ramsey's troops pinned Wise's grey clads in position, Miles proposed to turn the Confederates left flank with Madill's brigade. Madill's bluecoats, after crossing the branch, detoured to the right. The scouts soon reported that the brigade's battle line had passed beyond Wise's left flank. The colonel now wheeled his brigade to the left. Pressing eagerly forward, Madill's troops struck Wise's command on its exposed flank. So sudden and swift was this blow that Wise's Virginians were driven back in confusion. Over 100 prisoners and one stand of colors were left behind by the Southerners.[97]

All this time, Ramsey's soldiers exerted heavy pressure on Wise's front. When Wise's brigade collapsed in face of Madill's flank attack, Ramsey's soldiers dashed

---

96 *Ibid.*, 710, 714, 745, 750-751. The 145th and 183d Pennsylvania had been detailed to corduroy the Dabney Mill road; the 64th New York was on outpost duty.

97 *Ibid.*, 710, 734, 736, 738, 740. Captain Albert F. Peterson of the 64th New York and about 50 of his men rejoined the brigade in time to participate in the second advance across the run.

forward and secured the crest of the ridge. Miles decided to capitalize on his success. The mopping up operation would be left to Nugent's brigade; Madill's and Ramsey's troops would be entrusted with the pursuit.[98]

When Miles' troops attacked Wise's brigade, Hunton's soldiers shifted to the left to assist their comrades. This forced Stansel's Alabamians to extend to both the right and left to cover the V Corps line to their front. Convinced that his men would not be able to fight their way across the run, Johnson ordered them to hold the ground gained.

General Lee, accompanied by General McGowan, also reconnoitered the small watercourse behind which Warren's two shattered divisions had found sanctuary. After examining the terrain, Lee approved Johnson's decision to hold it. Returning to the White Oak Road, Lee tried to find some artillery and, if possible, some cavalry to send to Johnson's assistance.

It soon became evident to Johnson that his men were approaching exhaustion, and if they were to hold on, they would have to be reinforced. But there were no fresh troops available. General Anderson, upon being advised of the situation, ordered Johnson to withdraw his command. The troops were to be pulled back and occupy the line of breastworks south of the White Oak Road which Ayres' troops had thrown up the previous evening. The collapse of Wise's brigade had added an air of urgency to the situation. Screened by a rear guard, the Rebels abandoned their gains and fell back. In the course of this retrogressive moment, Hunton's and Stansel's brigades changed positions. By 3 o'clock, Johnson announced that McGowan's, Hunton's and Stansel's units had moved into their designated rifle pits. Stansel's Alabamians on the left held the angle, which formed the connection between "the return" and the field fortifications south of the White Oak Road. Wise's brigade, however, had been so roughly handled by Miles' Yankees that it was withdrawn inside the fortifications east of "the return."[99]

About the time that Madill's and Ramsey's troops marched out of the works, General Miles had trained his field glasses on the Confederate rifle pits west of the Plank Road. What the general saw convinced him that these trenches were unoccupied. Miles, therefore, ordered the 5th New Hampshire of Scott's brigade to charge this position. At this time, the New Hampshire regiment was manning the Union picket line in this sector. In moving to carry out Miles' instructions, the regiment became confused. Instead of attacking to their front, the soldiers from

---

98 *Ibid.*, 710, 734, 745. Before the day's fighting was over, Madill's brigade had captured 124 prisoners, and Ramsey's 160.

99 *Ibid.*, 1288; Freeman, *R. E. Lee*, vol. 4, 34. When Johnson's troops took position covering the White Oak Road, McGowan was on the right, Hunton in the center, and Stansel on the left.

New Hampshire obliqued sharply to the left. Shortly thereafter, they overran the right flank of Madill's brigade. Before a semblance of order could be restored, the Confederates had thrown troops into the heretofore deserted rifle pits and a splendid opportunity to penetrate the defenses in this sector had been lost.[100]

Upon witnessing the rout of Wise's brigade, Miles became convinced that he could carry the Confederates fortifications if he were reinforced by another brigade. Miles accordingly relayed this information to Humphreys. The corps commander authorized Miles to go ahead. To implement his decision, Humphreys ordered de Trobriand's brigade to support Miles' right. At the same time, the general notified Mott that he might have to rush a second brigade to Miles' assistance.[101]

De Trobriand's brigade had spent much of the morning massed in support of Miles' division near the Rainey house. At 9:30 o'clock, Ord had telegraphed Grant that the Confederates were marshalling troops east of Hatcher's Run.[102] A copy of Ord's message was in Humphreys' hands by 10:15. When Meade forwarded Ord's dispatch to Humphreys, he sent a covering communication. Meade left it up to the judgment of his corps commander whether to relieve the Army of the James by attacking, or send his reserve to Ord's assistance.[103]

Humphreys decided to rush his reserve (de Trobriand's brigade) to Ord's support. Consequently, de Trobriand's command was shifted to the right and stationed near the Crow house. When the Confederates attacked, they moved against Warren and not Ord. De Trobriand's presence on the right of the II Corps became superfluous. To obtain troops to support Miles' offensive, Humphreys again issued marching orders to de Trobriand. The disgusted troops retraced their steps. Returning to the Rainey house, de Trobriand's soldiers relieved Scott's in the rifle pits west of the Boydton Plank Road.[104]

Following the arrival of de Trobriand's bluecoats, Scott's men moved forward. The brigade soon overtook Miles' division. At this time, the division was cautiously working its way through the woods fronting the Confederate earthworks which covered the approaches to the White Oak Road. Miles had Colonel Scott deploy his brigade en echelon on the right of Madill's unit. Scott's mission was to protect the division's right flank. As the advance progressed, Scott's brigade and Madill's

---

100 OR 46, pt. 1, 710, 714, 719.

101 *Ibid.*, pt. 3, 348.

102 *Ibid.*, 374.

103 *Ibid.*, 347.

104 *Ibid.*, pt. 1, 781.

diverged. Miles halted his battle line. To plug this gap, Miles called up Nugent's brigade from the reserve. The sweep was then renewed. As the Federals forged ahead, they drove in the grey clads skirmishers. In this fighting, the 111th New York of Madill's brigade cut off and captured over 100 men and the colors of the 41st Alabama.

At 3:30, Miles' troops reached the edge of the abatis that protected the approaches to the Confederate fortifications. The left flank of Ramsey's brigade rested near Halter Butler's field. A glance at the formidable works and the "almost impassable slashing" convinced Miles that it would be "impossible to take them with the force available."[105]

Because his right flank unit (Scott's brigade) had lost contact with Mott's division, Miles decided he had better close to the right. The entire division then moved by the right flank. After forming a connection with de Trobriand's brigade of Mott's command, Miles put his troops to work throwing up earthworks. Several of Miles' units became scrambled in the confusion caused by the shift. When this situation was ironed out, Miles found that his brigades were deployed from left to right: Scott's, Ramsey's, Madill's, and Nugent's.[106]

When Miles' division marched off to the west in pursuit of Wise's Virginians, General Mott sought to maintain contact with his brother officer's command by extending his left flank. To do this, Mott was compelled to pull out part of de Trobriand's brigade from the earthworks. Leaving two of his eight regiments to guard the artillery, de Trobriand moved out. De Trobriand's brigade accomplished its mission by bridging the gap that had opened between Miles on the left and McAllister on the right. While de Trobriand's soldiers took position, they were subjected to a brisk shelling by Confederate artillery. The brigade then dug in.[107]

In the meantime, General Humphreys decided to have Mott make a forced reconnaissance of the Confederate fortifications east of the Plank Road. This movement, the general believed, would pin the Rebels down and keep them from detaching troops to oppose Miles' advance. Mott then alerted McAllister and Pierce "to assault the enemy's works on their respective fronts."

Pierce's attacking force on the right consisted of the 5th Michigan and the 1st Massachusetts Heavy Artillery. An unhappy combination of circumstances rendered Pierce's task difficult. To Pierce's right, there was a bend in Hatcher's

---

105 *Ibid.,* 710-711, 714, 740. As soon as Scott's unit overtook the division, the 5th New Hampshire rejoined the brigade.

106 *Ibid.,* 711, 714.

107 *Ibid.,* 776, 781.

Run. This meander restricted the movements of Pierce's battle line as it advanced to the attack. Worse, the Rebel batteries emplaced in front of the Crow house and near Burgess Mill (to the right and left of Pierce's front) caught the advancing Yankees in a deadly crossfire. Nevertheless, the general grimly formed his men. At 2:30 o'clock, he moved the two regiments forward. The bluecoats drove ahead on the double. Not until they reached the felled timber fronting the Rebel's works did the soldiers falter. Unable to work their way through the abatis, Pierce's men recoiled.[108]

McAllister planned to have a strong team feel the Confederates works covering Burgess Mill. The combat patrol from McAllister's brigade was composed of the 11th Massachusetts, the 120th New York, and a battalion of the 8th New Jersey. This force would be supported by the 11th New Jersey. At a word from McAllister, the combat patrol dashed forward. Working their way through the abatis, the bluecoats reached the crest of a ridge overlooking the Confederates main line of resistance. Several outposts were overrun by the Yankees and 15 pickets captured during the advance. Soon after this initial success, the Union drive ground to a stop. In addition to the musketry of the Rebel infantry, the Yankees came under an enfilade fire from the Confederate batteries. To save themselves, the bluecoats lay down. After his men had spent a very uncomfortable hour hugging the ground, McAllister received orders from Mott to recall them. The soldiers were drawn off, one by one, under a severe fire from Southern sharpshooters. This attack had cost McAllister's command a number of casualties.[109]

Hays' division also launched a limited attack on the Confederate defense line on the afternoon of the 31st. In the morning, General Smyth with the 108th New York had made a bold reconnaissance of his front. Smyth returned with information that the Rebels still held Fort Powell. Hays then ordered Smyth to capture this strong point. The attacking force consisted of the 1st Delaware, the 7th Michigan, the 4th Ohio, and the 7th West Virginia. After deploying his command into line of battle, Smyth moved against Fort Powell. Everything went according to plan until the Federals reached the broad belt of slashed timber fronting the strong point. The felled timber was so thick that the battle line was unable to get through. Smyth, therefore, sent his skirmishers into the abatis, and they succeeded in driving in the Rebel outposts. Taking position near the redoubt, the Northerners sniped away at the cannoneers manning the two guns emplaced in the work. Evidently, this

---

108 *Ibid.*, 776, 781, 785. In this attack, Pierce's combat team suffered 16 casualties: two dead and 14 wounded.

109 *Ibid.*, 788.

proved to be very disconcerting to the gunners, because they soon deserted their pieces and ceased firing. Since his battle line had been unable to penetrate the belt of slashed timber, Smyth was not able to capitalize on this situation. At dusk, Smyth recalled his sharpshooters and returned to the rifle pits.[110]

These thrusts on the part of Hays' and Mott's troops, in conjunction with the pressure Ord's Army of the James was exerting on the Rebel position east of Hatcher's Run, accomplished their purpose. When McAllisters' and Pierce's troops moved against the rifle pits held by Brig. Gen. John R. Cooke's brigade east of the Plank Road, General Heth asked General Wilcox for help. Wilcox, however, was unable to send his brother officer any assistance. At this time, Brig. Gen. James H. Lane's brigade, which was holding the fortifications on either side of Hatcher's Run, was under heavy pressure from Hays' and Ord's commands.[111]

The II Corps' batteries remained in the position they occupied at dark on the 30th until noon of the 31st. As the Rebel attack on Warren's Corps gathered steam, Battery B, 1st New Jersey Light Artillery and the 11th Battery, New York Light Artillery were ordered up by the corps' chief of artillery, Lieutenant Colonel John G. Hazard. Captain A. Judson Clark had his New Jersey artillerists emplace their four Napoleons in front of the Rainey house; the New Yorkers relieved one of the V Corps' batteries on the knoll to the east of the house. Opening fire with their four 3-inch rifles, the New Yorkers silenced a troublesome Rebel battery located in the peach orchard west of Burgess Mill. At the same time, Battery E, 4th U.S. and Battery M, 1st New Hampshire (which had been in position at the Rainey house since the previous afternoon) concentrated their attention on the large redoubt near the Boydton Plank Road. These two batteries were able to gain fire superiority over the Confederate guns mounted in the redoubt.

Under the cover of darkness, Clark's cannoneers limbered up their pieces and moved to the left. Utilizing a road recently opened by the pioneers, the battery reached the rifle pits held by Miles' division. The gunners then proceeded to emplace their pieces at strategic places along Miles' main line of resistance. What he had seen during the afternoon convinced Colonel Hazard that a smoothbore battery could be more effectively employed if mounted on the knoll occupied by the 11th New York. He, therefore, ordered Battery K, 4th U.S. Light Artillery to change places with the 11th New York. By 11 o'clock, this shift had been affected. At 1:00 p.m. Colonel Hazard called up the 10th Massachusetts Battery. The

---

110 *Ibid.*, 766. A line of outposts were stationed in the edge of the woods fronting Fort Powell by General Smyth.

111 Humphreys, *The Virginia Campaign of '65*, 333.

Massachusetts gunners, on reaching the front, emplaced their four 3-inch rifles on the right of Battery B, 1st Rhode Island Light Artillery at the Crow house.[112]

At dusk, Mott shifted McAllister's and Pierce's brigades to the west side of the Boydton Plank Road. Before moving to the left, the brigade commanders detached a number of troops. These men were left behind to hold the rifle pits when their units moved to the left.[113]

By 1:00 p.m. General Warren was satisfied that his corps could contain the Confederate attack. Griffin's division, supported by the fire of Mink's battery, had forced Johnson's' vanguard to fall back. At the same time, Ayres and Crawford had reformed their divisions. Warren now dashed off a message to Meade's headquarters telling of the morning's disaster. He told of his plans to recover the initiative. Already, he wrote, his skirmishers on the left had crossed the run. One of Griffin's brigades, supported by the reorganized portion of Ayres' and Crawford's division, was preparing to counterattack. When the advance started, it would pivot on the corps right flank. Warren calculated that his men would be ready by 1:45, unless the Rebels beat him to the punch.[114]

Warren, in announcing the time that his counterthrust was to begin, had underestimated the difficulties involved. It took longer than anticipated for Ayres and Crawford to complete their dispositions. In addition, the troops experienced considerable difficulty in crossing the rain-swollen branch. It was 2:30 before Warren gave the order to advance.[115]

Warren's failure to attack on time caused Meade to have serious misgivings. At 2:50 p.m., Chief of Staff Webb forwarded to Warren a copy of a message which Humphreys had sent to army headquarters. Humphreys reported that Miles' troops had taken prisoners from Pickett's Division. This intelligence led Humphreys to assume (incorrectly) that Pickett's division was opposite Miles' center. Humphreys had concluded that if Warren's wheeled to the right it would "take Pickett on his right flank." In his covering dispatch, Webb observed: "Since Miles is already well forward from your right flank the general commanding [Meade] considers that that

---

112 *OR* 46, pt. 1, 791. Battery B, 1st New Jersey remained on Miles' front a very short time. At midnight, the gunners limbered up their pieces and returned to the Boydton Plank Road. The pieces were then parked.

113 *Ibid.*, 785, 788.

114 *Ibid.*, pt. 3, 362.

115 *Ibid.*, pt. 1, 815.

must be secure. Miles is ordered to take the enemy's works supported by his own Corps. You will see the necessity of moving as soon as possible."[116]

Because this communication from Meade's headquarters reached Warren after he had started his advance, he ignored it for the time being. Subsequently, Warren pointed out: "The information about Pickett's division was erroneous, and was worse than useless to me. According to subsequent information his division was at that time some three or four miles away driving General Sheridan. Nor did Miles assault the enemy's breast-works as the dispatch led me to infer he would."[117]

When Warren set about organizing his counterattack, he and General Griffin rode to the left to confer with General Chamberlain. The two officers asked Chamberlain if, suffering as he was from the wounds incurred on the 29th, he felt able to spearhead the projected attack. Warren's and Griffin's language in this "exigency" was very strong. Chamberlain, though in considerable pain, was ready for the hazardous assignment. Griffin then gave Chamberlain his instructions. He was to regain the ground lost by Ayres' and Crawford's troops.[118]

At a command from Chamberlain, his troops forded the waist-deep run. As soon as all his men had gained the right bank, Chamberlain formed his brigade into double line of battle.[119] Gregory's brigade followed Chamberlain's across the branch. Like Chamberlain, Gregory deployed his command into two lines of battle—the 188th and 189th New York in front, the 187th New York in the rear. Gregory's unit moved into position on Chamberlain's right.[120] Bartlett, after crossing the stream, massed his brigade on Chamberlain's left rear. Ayres' division supported Griffin's troops on the left en echelon by brigades. Griffin's skirmishers commanded by Colonel Pearson covered Ayres' front; Crawford's division watched Griffin's right flank. The wood road served as the axis of Chamberlain's advance. The remainder of Warren's Corps guided their movements on Chamberlain's brigade.[121]

Brushing aside the few skirmishers encountered, Chamberlain's bluecoats reached Holliday's cabin with ease. When Chamberlain's troops emerged from the

---

116 *Ibid.*, pt. 3, 362-363.

117 *Ibid.*, pt. 1, 815.

118 William H. Powell, *The Fifth Corps* (New York, 1896), 783; Survivors' Association', *The Corn Exchange Regiment*, 570.

119 OR 46, pt. 1, 849. The 198th Pennsylvania was in front, and the 185th New York was in support.

120 *Ibid.*, 853.

121 Porter, "Operations of the Fifth Corps," 229-230; Powell, *The Fifth Corps*, 783.

woods into the southern edge of Halter Butler's field, they were greeted by a heavy fire. Chamberlain observed that there was a strong force of Confederates (Hunton's Virginians) ensconced in the rifle pits, which Ayres' troops had thrown up in the field prior to their retreat. Hunton's grey clads had "turned" these trenches. Additional Confederate soldiers could be distinguished in the edge of the woods which bounded the field on the north.

Chamberlain halted his brigade and rearranged his lines, which had been broken to some extent by the march through the ragged terrain and thick woods between the branch and Holliday's. Warren now rode up and directed Chamberlain to entrench. By this time, Chamberlain's advance line (the 198th Pennsylvania) had "gained a slight crest in the open field." Here, the Pennsylvanians were subjected to a galling fire by the Virginians holding the rifle pits. At the same time, sharpshooters posted in the woods which flanked Halter Butler's field on the east commenced to snipe away at the Yankees. It appeared to Chamberlain "that the enemy's position might be carried with no greater loss than it would cost us merely to hold our ground." When Chamberlain told Griffin of his observations, he received permission to push ahead.[122]

After he had readjusted his lines, Chamberlain led his cheering troops to the attack. As the Yankees surged across the field, the Rebel troops posted in the woods to the right poured several volleys into the flank of Chamberlain's battle line. In addition, Confederate artillery emplaced in "the return" had growled into action. The 198th Pennsylvania wavered. Chamberlain called for assistance; Gregory's brigade responded handsomely. Gregory's command, advancing by battalion en echelon to the left, dashed into the woods. The Rebel sharpshooters gave way in face of Gregory's sudden onslaught. Chamberlain's blue clads, their right flank secured, charged the works on the run. This time the determined Yankees were not to be denied. Chamberlain's troops reached the rifle pits and drove Hunton's Virginians from them in confusion. One regiment, the 56th Virginia, was cut off and much of it was captured. Pressing on, Chamberlain's and Gregory's soldiers stormed across the White Oak Road.[123]

Hunton subsequently recalled, "The 198th Pennsylvania wavered under the fire very decidedly, and a portion of it broke and ran. The balance of the line

---

122 OR 46, pt. 1, 849; Porter, "Operations of the Fifth Corps," 230.

123 OR 46, pt. 1, 849, 863; Porter, "Operations of the Fifth Corps," 230; Powell, *The Fifth Corps*, 784. Chamberlain's brigade lost "not more than 75" men in this attack. Along with the colors of the 56th Virginia, the Federals captured 135 Confederates.

reformed under my fire, advanced, and drove us back. I thought it was one of the most gallant things I had ever seen."[124]

Following the smashing Union attack, Hunton's brigade (without the 56th Virginia) retired into the fortifications. McGowan's grey clads had been isolated by Chamberlain's and Gregory's breakthrough to the White Oak Road. To rejoin their comrades, the South Carolinians had to detour to the north a considerable distance to bypass the Federal roadblock.[125]

When General Hunton returned from the fray, his scabbard had been bent almost double by a missile and he had three bullet holes through his clothes. General Lee greeted the doughty fighter briskly, "I wish you would sew those places up; I don't like to see them."

"General Lee," said Hunton, "allow me to go back home and see my wife and I will have them sewed up."

The answer amused Lee. "The idea," he replied, "of talking about going to see wives; it is perfectly ridiculous, sir."[126]

Chamberlain's and Gregory's soldiers had crossed the White Oak Road a short distance west of "the return." Warren was understandably elated by the success scored by Griffin's troops. The general thought that his men might be able to carry the fortifications guarding the junction of the Claiborne and White Oak Roads. If they could storm "the return" it would render the Confederate position south of Hatcher's Run untenable. Warren, therefore, ordered the advance suspended while he made a personal reconnaissance.

In the meantime, to secure his gains, Griffin had Chamberlain's and Gregory's soldiers throw up entrenchments. Ayres' division, which had not fired a round during the advance, was halted just short of the White Oak Road. Taking position near the W. Dabney house, Ayres' troops were faced west toward Five Forks. Like Ayres', Crawford's soldiers had not been engaged since leaving the branch. His division was posted northwest of the Holliday cabin. Its mission was to watch the gap between Griffin's right and Miles' left.[127]

Accompanied by a strong force of scouts, Warren rode forward. As the general's party approached the works, they "drew a very severe fire from the line, particularly of artillery." Nevertheless, Warren made a thorough examination of "the return." What he saw convinced the general "that the foe's defenses were as

---

124 Swan, "The Five Forks Campaign," 321-322.

125 *OR* 46, pt. 1, 1288; Humphreys, *The Virginia Campaign of '65*, 334.

126 Freeman, *R. E. Lee*, vol. 4, 35.

127 Porter, "Operations of the Fifth Corps," 230-231; *OR* 46, pt. 1, 816.

complete and as well located as any he had ever been opposed to." After concluding "that it would be useless to sacrifice the men in an assault," Warren retraced his steps.[128]

When Griffin's troops crossed the White Oak Road at 3:40, Warren dashed off a message to Meade's headquarters, telling of his gains. In addition, Warren reported that the Rebel fortifications veered sharply to the right. Warren had also seen General Miles, who announced that his division was "close up" to the Confederate works.[129]

It was about 5:00 p.m. before Warren received a reply to his message. Upon opening the dispatch, which was signed by Chief of Staff Webb, Warren found that he was to secure his position and protect, as well as possible, his left flank. Humphreys, Webb observed, had been directed to extend to the left and connect with Warren's right. Webb reported that Sheridan's cavalry was believed to be advancing. (At this time, Sheridan's troopers, in the face of Pickett's slashing attack, were falling back on Dinwiddie Court House.) Warren was authorized, if he wished, "to push a small force down the White Oak Road and try to communicate with Sheridan. . . ."[130]

Warren had already taken the precautions outlined in Webb's memorandum. Two of Griffin's brigades (Chamberlain's and Gregory's) were dug in along the White Oak Road. Gregory's right flank was in contact with Miles' left flank unit—Scott's brigade. The corps' left flank was guarded by Ayres' division. Crawford's division, reinforced by Bartlett's brigade, constituted the corps reserve. Wainwright's artillerists, however, had been unable to take their guns across the run. Consequently, the V Corps did not have any artillery support at the front.

The battle of White Oak Road, which had begun so disastrously for Warren's Corps, had ended in victory. Johnson's gallant Confederate command had seen its morning's gains wrested from it by the Union counterattack. Indeed, the Southerners were worse off than before, because they had lost control of the vital White Oak Road. They were now penned up in their works. The direct line of communications between Johnson's division and Pickett's task force had been severed. Worse was the effect of the battle on Confederate morale. The Southerners, after a brilliant start, had failed in their attempt to roll up the Union left. Furthermore, the Rebels had suffered losses which they could ill afford.

128 *OR* 46, pt. 1, 816; Powell, *The Fifth Corps*, 784.

129 *OR* 46, pt. 3, 363.

130 *Ibid.*, pt. 1, 677, 819, 1288.

All told, the Yankees reported that the battle of White Oak Road had cost them 177 killed, 1,134 wounded, and 594 missing. Of these casualties, the V Corps had suffered 1,407. General Johnson announced that his losses in the engagement totaled "about 800, including killed, wounded, and missing." In addition, Johnson claimed the capture of about 470 bluecoats.

TABLE 3							
Report of Casualties in the II Corps							
	Killed		**Wounded**		**Missing**		**Total**
Command	Officers	Men	Officers	Men	Officers	Men	
Miles' Division	5	40	12	233	1	41	423
Hays' Division	-	-	2	13	-	1	16
Mott's Division	-	6	1	58	2	42	109
Artillery Brigade	-	-	-	4	-	-	4
Total	**5**	**46**	**15**	**308**	**3**	**84**	**461**
Report of Casualties in the V Corps							
	Killed		**Wounded**		**Missing**		**Total**
Command	Officers	Men	Officers	Men	Officers	Men	
Cavalry Escort	-	-	-	1	-	-	1
Artillery	-	1	-	6	-	-	7
Griffin's Division	2	21	7	143	-	5	178
Ayres' Division	1	50	25	249	3	335	663
Crawford's Division	1	50	20	360	3	124	558
Total	**4**	**122**	**52**	**759**	**6**	**464**	**1,407**

Part VI

The V Corps Reports to Sheridan

When the fighting on the White Oak Road ceased, Warren's soldiers heard the roar of battle rolling up from the southwest. Warren, as well as his troops, was disheartened to observe that the distant rumble seemed to be receding. If this were true, it indicated that Sheridan had encountered a force which was giving him trouble. Instead of advancing, it seemed to the interested listeners that Sheridan was being steadily driven back by the Confederates.[131]

Warren accordingly determined to rush a force to the assistance of the cavalry. General Griffin was alerted to have Bartlett's brigade ready to move out. Bartlett was to march cross country and attack the Rebel force which was presumably driving Sheridan's cavalry on its naked left flank. Major Cope of Warren's staff was detailed to accompany Bartlett's column.

Preceded by Captain Horrell's escort company, Bartlett's brigade took up the march. The orders Bartlett had received from Warren were simple. He was to proceed toward the sound of the firing and attack the Rebels in the rear. After leaving the White Oak Road, Bartlett's troops advanced in a southwesterly direction. It was starting to get dark when the brigade passed through the picket line. The head of the column guided by the distant battle sounds. When the pickets shouted to the passing soldiers as to their intended destination, their inquiries were unanswered. Bartlett's people were as ignorant—except that the line of march trended toward the sound of battle—of their destination as were the men manning the line of outposts.

At first, the march led across a belt of open ground. When the vanguard reached a branch of Gravelly Run, the Federals left the fields and entered the timber. Locating a "wood road," Major Cope guided the column slowly forward. Before the soldiers had proceeded far into the timber, the firing died down. After advancing about one mile and crossing several arms of Gravelly Run, the head of the column debouched into an open field. On a hill in the soldiers' immediate front could be seen Dr. Boisseau's house.[132]

---

131 OR 46, pt. 1, 817.

132 *Ibid.*, 817, 821; Charles H. Porter, "The Fifth Corps at the Battle of Five Forks," *Papers of the Military Historical Society of Massachusetts*, VI, 239; Survivors' Association, *History of the Corn*

As Captain Horrell's troopers approached the doctor's outbuildings, they were fired on by Confederate pickets belonging to Munford's division. Quickly dismounting and deploying, Horrell's cavalrymen chased Rebel outposts from Dr. Boisseau's farm. Pressing eagerly ahead, Horrell's bluecoats drove the Southerners from the slope and across Gravelly Run. Since the Yankees did not attempt to cross the run, the Confederate troopers halted and took position covering the ford.[133]

It was already quite dark, and General Bartlett decided to take up a strong defensive position and wait for daylight. In the meantime, the general had learned from Major Cope that the Crump Road lay a short distance west of Dr. Boisseau's house. Bartlett therefore posted his brigade with its right flank anchored on the Crump Road; his front and left flank covered the road leading eastward from Dr. Boisseau's toward the Boydton Plank Road. Outposts were sent to relieve Horrell's troopers. Throughout the early part of the evening, the Federal and Confederate pickets sniped at each other from opposite sides of Gravelly Run.[134]

By the time that Bartlett had completed his dispositions, it was very dark. The Federals then turned their attention to the Confederate camp fires. Major Cope reported that these fires "seemed to stretch for miles on the south side of the run." In addition, the Yankees could hear the characteristic noises made by a large body of soldiers—wagons rumbling, men talking and shouting, and the thud of axes against trees. Most of the officers were in agreement that the exposed position occupied by Bartlett's brigade was "a perilous one and required considerable delicacy in handling." The night, however, cloaked the Union dispositions and helped add to the command's security.[135]

At 5:45, shortly before Bartlett's troops moved off, Warren received a message signed by Chief of Staff Webb. It had required 30 minutes to transmit this communication from Meade's headquarters to Warren's command post. Glancing at the dispatch, Warren discovered that he was to push a brigade down the White Oak Road. This force was expected to open communications with Sheridan and, if necessary, support the cavalry. Since the personnel at Meade's headquarters mistakenly thought that the firing was steadily drawing nearer, Webb felt that the

---

Exchange Regiment, 571-572. Bartlett's was the largest brigade in Griffin's division. At this time, Bartlett's brigade mustered nearly 2,500 officers and men. So far, in the Five Forks campaign, Bartlett's troops had not been seriously engaged. Three of Bartlett's regiments, however, were on detached duty at the time that the brigade was ordered to march to Sheridan's assistance.

133 Porter, "The Fifth Corps at the Battle of Five Forks," 239-240; *OR* 46, pt. 1, 821.

134 Porter, "The Fifth Corps at the Battle of Five Forks," 240.

135 *Ibid.*, *OR* 46, pt. 1, 821.

column which Warren was directed to send down the White Oak Road would not have far to go to establish contact with the cavalry.[136]

Warren, however, saw things different from the way the headquarters people did. He was convinced that the firing was not getting any closer. Instead, Warren correctly believed that the roar of battle was receding in the direction of Dinwiddie Court House. The general had talked with two of Sheridan's cavalrymen, a lieutenant and a sergeant, who had been cut off from their units by Pickett's attack. They told Warren that Sheridan's cavalry had been "attacked about noon by cavalry and infantry and rapidly driven back, two divisions (Crook's and Devin's) being engaged." Relaying this information to Meade, Warren reported that he had sent Bartlett's brigade to support the cavalry. Warren expressed his candid opinion that Bartlett's relief column would not arrive in time to be of assistance.[137]

A little after 6 o'clock, one of Merritt's staff officers reached Meade's headquarters. He told Meade that two of Pickett's brigades had advanced and secured a position between Sheridan's and Warren's commands. Furthermore, by this time, it had become apparent to the officers at army headquarters that the roar of battle was not getting any closer. They now came to the same conclusion as Warren—the firing was receding toward Dinwiddie Court House.

When Meade wrote Grant (at 6:35 p.m.), he told of these developments. Meade observed that if Sheridan were unable to overcome the Rebel force opposed to him, he would be obliged to contract the left flank of his Army of the Potomac. Meade warned Grant that if he were compelled to reduce his front, he "must do it tonight." Grant was also informed that Meade was ordering Warren to send a force down the Boydton Plank Road. This command would be charged with the mission of re-opening communications with Sheridan.

While Meade drafted Grant's message, Chief of Staff Webb sent fresh instructions to the commander of the V Corps. Warren was also informed that elements from Pickett's division had penetrated into the area between the V Corps and Sheridan's command. To cope with this situation, Warren was to send down the Boydton Plank Road the force previously ordered out the White Oak Road.[138]

When this message reached Warren, Bartlett's column had been gone for almost an hour. If he were to recall Bartlett's troops, it would require at least two hours for them to reach the Boydton Plank Road. By then, it would be too dark for Bartlett's troops to accomplish anything. He, however, thought of another solution

---

136 *Ibid.*, pt. 3, 363.

137 *Ibid.*, 364.

138 *Ibid.*, 338, 364.

to the problem. Because of the muddy condition of the "wood road" leading across to Holliday's, the artillery had been parked near the Boydton Plank Road. Three of Bartlett's regiments had been detailed to guard the artillery and the corps' wagons. Colonel Pearson was in charge of this force. Warren determined to send Pearson's command down the Boydton Plank Road.

Following receipt of his marching orders from Warren, Pearson started down the Plank Road. When the head of Pearson's column reached Gravelly Run, it was discovered that the stream was running bank full. The bridge had been broken down by retreating Confederates on the afternoon of the 29th. Since Warren had been required to operate without any cavalry to cover his left flank, he had made no effort to have the bridge rebuilt. Pearson was unable to proceed any farther until a new structure was built. After passing this information to Warren, Pearson let his men fall out and take it easy, while waiting for the pioneers to arrive and rebuild the bridge.[139]

After he had given Pearson his instructions, Warren sent another message to Meade's headquarters. He reported that it was too late to stop Bartlett; therefore, he had sent Pearson down the Plank Road. Warren promised to keep headquarters informed of Bartlett's progress.[140]

After directing his division commanders to secure the ground gained by entrenching their positions, Warren returned to his headquarters. (At this time, Warren's headquarters were at Mrs. Wilson's.) The general wanted to be near the telegraph, so he could keep in touch with General Meade throughout the night. By 8:00 p.m., Warren and his staff had reached Mrs. Wilson's.[141]

---

139 *Ibid.*, 817, 818, 820. The Plank Road was the direct route over which Sheridan communicated with Grant. It seems almost incredible that news that the bridge across Gravelly Run was out had not reached Grant's GHQ. Undoubtedly it had. On March 29, 30, and the early part of the 31st, staff officers and couriers were continually crossing the run and it was fordable. It had started to rain on the 30th and continued until the next afternoon. Streams that were easily passed on the 29th and 30th became difficult to cross on the 31st. Porter, "Fifth Corps at the Battle of Five Forks," 243-244.

140 *OR* 46, pt. 3, 364. By this time, Warren had thoroughly reconnoitered the Confederate defenses covering the White Oak Road. He informed headquarters, "We can see the enemy's breast-works for two miles east along the White Oak Road. If they are well manned they cannot be carried. I'm within 200 yards of where they turn off north from the White Oak Road."

141 *Ibid.*, pt. 1, 818. It was about four and one-half miles from Mrs. Wilson's to Meade's GHQ. Grant's headquarters were at Dabney's Mill, four miles from Warren's. About five and one-half miles separated Warren's and Sheridan's command posts. Grant's, Meade's, and Warren's former headquarters on the Quaker Road were connected by telegraph. The only contact between Sheridan's headquarters at Dinwiddie Court House and the other command posts was by courier.

In the meantime, Meade had received a reply to his 6:15 telegram to Grant. Besides sending Meade a copy of Sheridan's 2:30 p.m. message, Grant informed the commander of the Army of the Potomac that Colonel Porter had just returned from Dinwiddie Court House. Porter had told Grant that Devin's division "had been driven back in considerable confusion south of J. Boisseau's house." At the time that Porter had left Sheridan, Crook's division was moving to the front. Sheridan had told Porter that he expected Crook to turn the Rebel's flank. Grant stated that he hoped to get Sheridan's cavalry "onto the White Oak Road west of W. Dabney house." Up to this time, Grant wrote, Sheridan had failed to carry out his assignment. Furthermore, the way things were developing, there was no assurance that the cavalry leader would succeed. In this case, it would be necessary for Warren to watch his left. Grant believed that if Sheridan could hold on to Dinwiddie Court House, it would discourage any ideas the Confederates have of sweeping around Warren's left flank. Even so, Grant warned, Warren "cannot be too much on his guard."

In addition, Grant wanted Meade to have the Confederate prisoners captured in the battle of White Oak Road, closely questioned. He wanted to see if Lee had received any reinforcements from North Carolina. Sheridan had incorrectly identified Hoke's division as one of the units opposing him. This was the reason behind this request.[142]

Meade answered Grant at 7:10 p.m. He announced that he had learned nothing concerning the reported transfer of Confederate units from North Carolina to the Petersburg theater of operations. Meade added, however, that this certainly would not be an impossible move on the Rebel's part. Continuing, Meade reported that Capt. Michael V. Sheridan (General Sheridan's adjutant and brother) had just reached his headquarters. The captain told Meade that the Confederates were in possession of the Brooks road. If, as this news indicated, the Rebels had concentrated a large force of infantry to General Sheridan's front, Meade observed, the Plank Road was open to their advance. The captain had warned Meade that the Southerners would probably resume their attack on the cavalry corps in the morning. If they did, Meade was of the opinion that General Sheridan would either have to rejoin the army or to be reinforced. Meade did not believe it possible to detach any units from the Army of the Potomac to send to Sheridan. To justify his position, Meade pointed out that not only was his left flank resting in the air but that his line was dangerously extended.

142 *Ibid.*, pt. 3, 338-339.

After waiting 30 minutes and receiving no reply to his communication, Meade sent Grant another telegram. He again announced that Captain Sheridan was at his headquarters. The captain, Meade wrote, had said that General Sheridan had fallen back on Dinwiddie Court House, after having been "repulsed" by the Confederate infantry. In event that he was compelled to evacuate Dinwiddie Court House, Sheridan had told the captain that he would retire via the Vaughan Road.[143]

By 5 o'clock, another one of Sheridan's staff officers, Colonel John Kellogg, had galloped up to Meade's headquarters. Kellogg told Meade that Sheridan would be unable to hold Dinwiddie Court House in the face of a renewed Confederate onslaught. When he relayed this information to Grant, Meade broached the subject of transferring one of Gibbon's divisions to the right bank of Gravelly Run. Meade also thought that it would be a good idea to have Turner's division of the XXIV Corps march to Sheridan's assistance. Meade had predicated this suggestion on the assumption that Grant would deny him permission to contract his lines.

It was 11:45 p.m. before Grant replied to Meade's communications. When he did, Grant—who was becoming alarmed by the situation—ordered Meade to recall Warren's Corps. When Warren had massed his troops on the Boydton Plank Road, he was to send one division to Sheridan's relief. This column was to "start at once and go down the Boydton road."[144]

Following Warren's return to his headquarters at Mrs. Wilson's, he and Meade had been in frequent communication. At 8 o'clock, Meade warned Warren that Sheridan had been forced back on Dinwiddie Court House by a strong Rebel task force. The retreat of Sheridan's cavalry, Meade continued, had exposed the rear of the II and V Corps to attack and would "require great vigilance" on Warren's part. If Warren had sent a column down the Boydton Plank Road (as Meade had previously ordered), it was not to go beyond Gravelly Run.[145]

Because Pearson's troops had been unable to cross Gravelly Run, Warren had already taken the step which Meade urged. When Warren replied to Meade's communication (at 8:20 p.m.), he conveyed this information to army headquarters. In addition, Warren announced that Bartlett had penetrated "nearly down to the crossing of Gravelly Run." Warren said that he was confident that if Sheridan held on at Dinwiddie Court House, the foe would be unable to hold their gains and be compelled to fall back to Five Forks. Expressing strong opposition to a night

---

143 *Ibid.*, 339, 340.

144 *Ibid.*; Swan, "The Five Forks Campaign," 337.

145 *OR* 46, pt. 3, 364.

march, Warren observed, "I shall leave a good many men who have lost their way." Warren also inquired, "Does General Sheridan still hold Dinwiddie Court House?"

At 8:35 p.m., Warren received a telegram signed by Chief of Staff Webb marked "confidential." Scanning the message, Warren learned that headquarters was of the opinion that the Army of the Potomac would have to contract its lines. Warren would be required to hold, if possible, the Boydton Plank Road, resting his left flank on Gravelly Run. Hatcher's Run would be covered by Humphreys' II Corps and Ord's Army of the James. Warren was alerted to hold his men ready to carry out this order on "short notice."[146]

By this hour, Meade knew that Bartlett's brigade had taken position at Dr. Boisseau's. Nevertheless, Webb gave no intimation as to whether Bartlett was to hold his ground. The staff, in its anxiety for the safety of Humphreys' and Warren's Corps, had forgotten about this important information. Furthermore, Grant, as yet, did not now that Bartlett's brigade occupied a position on the left flank of Pickett's.[147]

Warren hated to see the army take the step outlined in Webb's memorandum. He was afraid that a retreat to the Boydton Plank Road would prove to be a heavy blow to the morale of his soldiers. Furthermore, the general felt that Pickett's force would be unable to hold its position in front of Dinwiddie Court House, because his corps threatened its left flank.[148]

Consequently, Warren, when he answered Webb's communication, argued that the Army of the Potomac should try to hold its gains. He pointed out that the fortifications which his troops had thrown up covering the Plank Road were "very strong." One division, if supported by artillery, could hold this line, Warren argued. The only way the Confederates could carry this position, Warren stated, would be by a strong column operating south of Gravelly Run. The general believed that if Meade followed the course of action which he proceeded to outline, the Confederates would find plenty to keep them busy. Warren would have Humphreys, reinforced by the V Corps' artillery, hold the Plank Road. The V Corps would be freed to cross Gravelly Run and assail the Rebels from one side, while Sheridan attacked from the other. Should the Southerners seek to reinforce Pickett, Bartlett's roadblock would force them to detour to the west. In summing up his

---

146 *Ibid.*, 364-365.

147 Swan, "The Five Forks Campaign," 338.

148 *OR* 46, pt. 1, 818.

argument, Warren announced, "Unless Sheridan has been too badly handled, I think we have a chance for an open field fight that should be made use of."[149]

Following receipt of Grant's 8:45 p.m. telegram directing him to send a division of the V Corps to Sheridan's assistance, Meade had Chief of Staff Webb prepare an order implementing this decision. Warren was instructed to pull back inside the earthworks covering the Boydton Plank Road. Griffin's division was to be sent to Dinwiddie Court House. Upon reaching the Court House, Griffin would report to Sheridan. General Humphreys' II Corps was to occupy the fortifications northeast of Mrs. Butler's house.[150]

Webb's message which had been sent at 9 o'clock was in Warren's hands 17 minutes later. Warren was distressed to learn that the ground which had cost so much blood was to be abandoned. Nevertheless, he proceeded to draft a set of instructions calculated to implement Grant's decision. General Ayres, who was nearest the Plank Road, was to withdraw his division and mass it near the Boydton Plank Road; Crawford was to follow Ayres and concentrate his troops behind the entrenchments southeast of Mrs. Butler's; Griffin was to recall Bartlett's brigade from its position at Dr. Boisseau's. When Bartlett had rejoined the division, Griffin was to return to the Boydton Plank Road. Griffin's soldiers would then move to Dinwiddie Court House, where the general would report to Sheridan. In executing this movement, the division commanders were admonished to take care and see that none of their pickets or any portions of their units were left behind. They were to put their organizations into motion immediately upon the receipt of this order, which Warren handed to his staff officers for distribution at 9:35 p.m.[151]

At this hour, all of Warren's command (with the exception of Bartlett's brigade, Pearson's three regiments, and the corps artillery), was based along the White Oak Road. Chamberlain's brigade of Griffin's division was on the north side of the road. Crawford's division was near the road on Griffin's right, and Ayres' in a similar position on his left. Accordingly, considerable time would be wasted while the staff officers were contacting the three division commanders. In addition, Griffin would have to recall Bartlett. At best, Bartlett could not be expected to withdraw his pickets and get back to the Boydton Plank Road before 1 or 2 'clock in the morning.[152]

---

149 *Ibid.*, pt. 3, 365.

150 *Ibid.*, 365-366. Meade informed Grant that he had ordered Warren to carry out the plan of operations advanced by the lieutenant general commanding.

151 OR 46, pt. 1, 820.

152 Swan, "The Five Forks Campaign," 341.

Evidently, Webb decided that his 9 o'clock dispatch to Warren needed clarification. At 9:20 p.m. he handed the telegrapher at army headquarters another message. Warren was to see that the division slated to join Sheridan started at once. In addition, Warren was given freedom "to act within the Boydton Plank Road" as he saw fit. Webb again informed Warren that Humphreys' II Corps would "hold to the road and the return."[153]

Warren replied to the chief of staff's communication at 10:00 p.m. He pointed out that there would be a considerable lapse of time before Bartlett's brigade would rejoin Griffin's division. Since Ayres' and Crawford's divisions were not engaged, Warren had determined to withdraw them first. Even so, Warren did not feel that the march of Griffin's division would be retarded, because, before the troops could cross Gravelly Run, the bridge would have to be rebuilt. The officer (Capt. William H. H. Benyaurd) whom Warren had sent to examine the crossing had pronounced it unfordable by infantry. Furthermore, Captain Benyaurd had stated a 40-feet span could be required to complete the bridge. The general informed Webb that he would exert himself to see that the bridge was passable by the time Griffin's division reached it.[154]

Warren's Corps was without pontoons. The pontoon train which had started with the corps on the 29th had been used to bridge Rowanty Creek and the Quaker Road crossing of Gravelly Run. To construct a span at the Boydton Plank Road crossing of Gravelly Run, Warren put his pioneers to work razing a house. This building would supply materials for the construction of the urgently needed bridge. Captain Benyaurd was put in charge of the project.[155]

In the meantime, Meade had been doing some deep thinking. Examining his maps, Meade came to the conclusion that Bartlett would be unable to rejoin Griffin in time for the division "to move with any promptitude" down the Plank Road. To facilitate Griffin's march to the point of danger, Meade issued instructions for Warren to attach another brigade to his division in place of Bartlett's. When Webb communicated this order to Warren, he reported that Sheridan had been attacked by four infantry brigades—three from Pickett's division, one from Gordon's Corps.[156]

When Warren noted that Webb's message had been sent at 9:40 p.m., he realized that army headquarters had not yet received his dispatch regarding the

---

153 OR 46, pt. 3, 366.

154 Ibid.

155 Ibid., pt. 1, 820.

156 Ibid., pt. 3, 366.

condition of the bridge. He trusted that, when Meade was apprised of this, he would agree that Bartlett would be able to rejoin Griffin before the bridge was passable. Consequently, Warren decided not to make any change in his marching orders for the time being. He would wait until Meade had received his telegram concerning the state of affairs at the crossing.[157]

Warren's 8:40 p.m. message suggesting that he be permitted to cross Gravelly Run with his entire corps and attack the Rebels' rear, while Sheridan assailed them in front, made quite an impression on Meade. At 9:45 p.m., Meade inquired of Grant, "Would it not be well for Warren to go down with his whole Corps and smash up the force in front of Sheridan?" Meade agreed with Warren that the II Corps could hold the line of the Plank Road. Unlike Warren, Meade did not think the Plank Road was the best line for the V Corps to operate along. Instead, he would have Warren move his entire corps up to the position held by Bartlett's brigade. From Dr. Boisseau's, Warren's troops would advance and take the Rebel force threatening Sheridan in the rear. "Or," Meade continued, "he could send one division to support Sheridan at Dinwiddie and move on the enemy's rear with the other two." Meade neglected to inform Grant that the battle plan had originated with Warren.[158]

This was the first news Grant had received that one of Warren's brigades was at Dr. Boisseau's on the Crump Road. Meade had been in possession of this information for at least an hour. Furthermore, Meade made no mention of the fact that he had already directed Warren to recall Bartlett's brigade. Grant seems to have held the opinion that at least part of Warren's Corps had already returned to the Plank Road.[159]

Replying to Meade's communication at 10:15 Grant tersely observed, "Let Warren move in the way you propose and urge him not to stop for anything. Let Griffin go on as he was first directed."[160] In a second telegram, Grant requested that Meade keep Sheridan posted on the dispositions being undertaken for his relief. Furthermore, Meade was to inform Sheridan that he was "to take general direction of the forces sent to him until the emergency for which they are sent is over."[161]

---

157 *Ibid.*, pt. 1, 821.

158 OR 46, pt. 3, 341.

159 Swan, "The Five Forks Campaign." 343-344.

160 OR 46, pt. 3, 342.

161 *Ibid.*

Shortly thereafter, Grant handed a dispatch to one of his staff for delivery to General Sheridan. Grant notified the cavalry leader that the V Corps had been ordered to his support. Two divisions were scheduled to march by way of J. Boisseau's; a third would move down the Boydton Plank Road. In addition, Grant announced that General Mackenzie's cavalry division of the Army of the James had been directed to join Sheridan. Mackenzie's troopers were to advance via the Vaughan Road. Grant, without having any justification for it, informed Sheridan that the V Corps should reach him "by 12 tonight." Sheridan, Grant wrote, would "assume command of the whole force sent to operate with him and use it to the best of his ability to destroy the force which his command has fought so gallantly today."[162]

As soon as Grant had approved his proposed plan of operations, Meade sent another message to Warren. The leader of the V Corps was informed that he was to send Griffin's division down the Plank Road. Ayres' and Crawford's commands were to join Bartlett's brigade at Dr. Boisseau's. They would then attack the rear of the Confederate force which was confronting Sheridan's cavalry. According to the latest intelligence reaching GHQ, Sheridan's troopers were reportedly posted a short distance north of Dinwiddie Court House. In case the Rebels bested the V Corps, Warren's line of retreat would be by way of the Brooks and Boydton Plank Roads. Meade urged Warren to move rapidly, so that he would reach the junction of the Brooks and Boydton Plank Roads ahead of the Confederates. Meade believed, however, that the foe would fall back toward Five Forks, in the face of Warren's advance. Warren was admonished to move light and fast. Any gear that would prevent the corps from moving cross country was to be left behind. Warren was to notify Meade as soon as his troops started to move.[163]

Meade's telegram was handed to Warren at 10:48 p.m. Upon reading it, Warren was distressed to learn that Meade still did not know about the bridge. Furthermore, Meade seemed to be unaware that a strong force of Confederates confronted Bartlett's brigade and held the right bank of Gravelly Run south of Dr. Boisseau's. Warren, had also received news from one of his staffers, Maj. William T. Gentry, that a Confederate force (Roberts' North Carolina brigade) held the junction of the Crump and White Oak Roads. The major, in attempting to communicate with Bartlett, had accidentally blundered into this roadblock. The major had escaped, but his orderly had been captured.

---

162 *Ibid.*, 381.

163 *Ibid.*, 367.

Warren knew that it had been one and one-half hours since he had issued instructions recalling his corps. The general assumed that, at this very minute, the troops were moving back along the "wood road" toward the Plank Road. If his orders were being obeyed, Ayres' division would be in the lead. If he followed Meade's orders to the letter, Griffin's division would have to be pushed to the head of the column, while Ayres' retraced its steps. To keep from wasting valuable time while the two divisions changed places, Warren determined to send Ayres' division instead of Griffin's to Sheridan's support.[164]

Answering Meade's message, Warren pointed out that on the receipt of Chief of Staff Webb's 9 o'clock dispatch, he had issued instructions for his divisions to retire from the White Oak Road. Ayres' division was to move first, to be followed in turn by Crawford's and Griffin's. Warren warned Meade that if he altered the march order during the night, it would produce wholesale confusion which would render all his "operations nugatory." To escape from this impasse, Warren informed Meade that, on his own initiative, he had decided to send Ayres's division to Sheridan. At the same time, he would take Crawford's and Griffin's divisions and move against the Rebel's flank and rear. Warren, however, cautioned army headquarters that, with the Confederates holding Gravelly Run below Dr. Boisseau's, he would not "accomplish the apparent objects" of Meade's directive. As a result of a break in the telegraph line, this message was delayed in transmission.[165]

After he had handed the signal officer the dispatch addressed to Meade, Warren (at 11:00 p.m.) drafted an order implementing this decision. Instead of halting his command near the Boydton Plank Road, Ayres would proceed down the Plank Road to Dinwiddie Court House and report to Sheridan. Crawford and Griffin, upon receipt of this order, were to halt and mass their divisions. The staff officers entrusted with the delivery of these orders would report to Warren the positions currently occupied by Crawford's and Griffin's commands.[166]

A number of problems, however, had arisen to plague the V Corps. Not the least of which was the shortage of staff officers. (On the evening of the 31st, there were only six staff officers at Warren's headquarters.) When Warren had moved to comply with Meade's 9:00 p.m. order, he had been forced to detail one officer to

---

164 *Ibid.*, pt. 1, 821-822.

165 *Ibid.*, pt. 3, 367, 417. Throughout the night, there had been a continual delay in the passage of orders between Meade's and Warren's headquarters. Colonel Swan attributed the lag to the fact that the telegraph line ended at Warren's former command post on the Quaker Road. Swan, "The Five Forks Campaign," 345.

166 OR 46, pt. 1, 822.

contact each of the three division commands. In addition, Warren had to send a member of his staff, Major Gentry, to get in touch with General Bartlett. In trying to reach Bartlett's command post, Major Gentry had blundered into the Confederate roadblock. When Gentry returned to report what had happened, Warren called for Major Cope, who had just returned from Dr. Boisseau's. Cope, who knew the way, was detailed to carry the message to Bartlett. Furthermore, Warren had sent an officer to order up the pioneers, and guide them to the Plank Road crossing of Gravelly Run. At the same time, another aide (Captain Benyaurd) was sent to check on the condition of the crossing.[167]

In the White Oak Road sector, the opposing lines were very close. If intelligence of the movement was to be kept from reaching the ears of the Confederates, the Union officers would have to forego the use of drums, bugles, and loud commands in arousing their units. Every order had to be relayed by word of mouth from each commander to his subordinates. As was to be expected, considerable time was lost while these orders were filtering down from the generals to the non-commissioned officers. To awaken the men, the sergeants and corporals had to shake them.[168]

To make matters worse, the night was "intensely dark and stormy." At the time that the staff officers reached Crawford's and Griffin's headquarters with Warren's 11 o'clock order, they discovered that the two divisions had not moved. By 1:00 a.m., the aides had returned to Warren's command post with this information.[169]

In the meantime, Meade's headquarters had been in frequent contact with General Humphreys' II Corps. When the decision to reposition the V Corps was made, Chief of Staff Webb telegraphed Humphreys. At 9:10 p.m., Humphreys was directed to have his men reoccupy the position held during the morning. The II Corps was to anchor its left flank on Mrs. Butler's and hold "the return."[170] Fifteen minutes later, Webb repeated this message. In addition, the chief of staff informed Humphreys, "General Warren is to be left free to act and is to send a division to General Sheridan at once."

In the wake of Meade's 10:15 p.m. communication altering Warren's orders, Webb sent another wire to Humphreys. The leader of the II Corps was informed

---

167 *Ibid.*, The staff officers present included: Col. Henry C. Bankhead, Majs. William T. Gentry and Emmor B. Cope, Capts. William H. H. Benyaurd, James W. Wadsworth, and Gordon Winslow.

168 *Ibid.*

169 *Ibid.*, 822-823.

170 *Ibid.*, pt. 3, 351.

that Warren was to move down the Crump Road and attack the Rebel force opposing Sheridan in the rear with two divisions. Warren's third division was to join Sheridan by way of the Boydton Plank Road. In view of these developments, Humphreys was to remain on the defensive and strengthen his position.

Replying to Webb's telegram, Humphreys announced that, according to the schedule he had worked out, his corps would fall back just before daybreak. His troops would reoccupy the rifle pits held on the morning of the 31st.[171]

Humphreys also dispatched a message to Warren. Besides informing Warren of the orders he had received from army headquarters, Humphreys wanted to know at what time the V Corps would march. Humphreys proposed to synchronize his movements with Warren's.[172]

Humphreys' communication reached Warren's headquarters at 12:30 a.m. Acknowledging the message, Warren pointed out that, at first, Meade had directed him to withdraw immediately the V Corps from the White Oak Road sector. Subsequently, he had been advised to attack the Rebels with two divisions of his V Corps, while sending a third down the Plank Road to reinforce Sheridan. Colonel Wainwright, with the corps artillery, was to remain on the Plank Road. Warren also expressed his belief that the position occupied by Bartlett's brigade would compel the Confederate force confronting Sheridan to withdraw before morning.[173]

Because the telegraph was not functioning properly, it was 11:45 p.m. before Meade's headquarters learned that the Gravelly Run bridge had been destroyed and it would take considerable time to rebuild. Meade accordingly dashed off a message to Warren. He inquired about the possibility of using an alternate route to send the division to Sheridan's support. Meade wanted to know if any time could be saved by sending the reinforcements by way of the Quaker Road. After pointing out to Warren that time was of the essence, Meade wrote, "Sheridan cannot maintain himself at Dinwiddie without reinforcements, and yours are the only ones that can be sent." Warren was urged to, "Use every exertion to get the troops to Sheridan as soon as possible." In case it became necessary, Warren was to use both the Boydton Plank and Quaker Roads to rush assistance to Sheridan. After signing the dispatch, Meade added a paragraph, "If Sheridan is not reinforced in time and compelled to fall back he will retire up the Vaughan Road."[174]

---

171 *Ibid.*, 351, 352.

172 *Ibid.*, pt. 1, 823.

173 *Ibid.*

174 *Ibid.*, pt. 3, 367.

At the same time, Meade telegraphed Grant. Meade informed his superior of the contents of the message which he had sent to Warren. Meade had apparently accepted Warren's thesis that the Confederates would fall back during the night. He informed Grant, "I think it is possible the enemy may retire from Sheridan's front tonight fearing an attack from the rear."[175]

It took Meade's 11:45 p.m. communication one hour and a quarter to reach Warren's headquarters. When he read the dispatch, Warren was shocked to discover that the Union brass was displaying "so much solicitude for General Sheridan's position and the necessity of reinforcing him directly." Warren felt that Sheridan's plight must be desperate if Meade were willing for the V Corps to forego its scheduled attack on the Confederate rear to march to Sheridan's assistance. Examining his maps, Warren discovered that, if his troops moved to Dinwiddie Court House by way of the Quaker Road, as suggested by Meade, it would require a march of over ten miles. Since the night was far advanced, Warren calculated that, if his troops marched via the route outlined by Meade, it would be impossible for them to reach Dinwiddie Court House before 8:00 a.m. By that time, the soldiers of the V Corps would be too late to be of any use to Sheridan in holding Dinwiddie Court House.

In the event that the Confederates occupied Dinwiddie Court House, Warren knew that a Union attack down the Boydton Plank Road would take them in the rear. A movement down the Plank Road would enable the entire V Corps to march as a unit. If one division were sent around by the Quaker Road (as Meade proposed), it would separate Warren's Corps into three groups. A hard night march, on top of the previous day's fighting, would sap the vigor of his soldiers, Warren believed. Accordingly, they could not be expected to go into action with much enthusiasm.[176]

In view of these considerations, Warren determined to disregard Meade's suggestions. Warren would hold Crawford's and Griffin's division where they were until such time as he learned that General Ayres' troops and established contact with Sheridan's cavalry. This time, Warren theorized, would not be wasted, because Crawford's and Griffin's badly jaded soldiers would get some needed rest.[177]

Having arrived at this decision, Warren (at 1:00 a.m.) informed Meade that he believed the pioneers would complete the bridge across Gravelly Run before his infantry could reach the Quaker Road. If, however, he was wrong, Warren

---

175 *Ibid.*, 342-343.

176 *Ibid.*, pt. 1, 823-824; Powell, *The Fifth Army Corps*, 794.

177 OR 46, pt. 1, 824.

promised to have Ayres' division follow the route proposed by Meade. Warren also informed Meade that he had heard from Captain Benyaurd, that it would not take the pioneers more than one hour to complete the structure.[178]

It was about 10:00 p.m. when General Ayres received Warren's 9:35 p.m. order directing him to fall back to the Boydton Plank Road. To reach the road, Ayres' division beat its way through about two miles of difficult country and cross a branch of Gravelly Run. By the time that Ayres reached Mrs. Butler's, he received the order directing him to march his command down the Boydton Plank Road. Leaving his soldiers to draw rations from the supply train which they met, Ayres hastened to Warren's headquarters. Here, Ayres was informed by Warren that Sheridan had been hard-pressed and needed assistance badly. It was impressed on Ayres that he must exert himself to get his division to Dinwiddie Court House. The general then rejoined his command.[179]

At 2:05 a.m., Warren received a message from Captain Benyaurd announcing that the bridge was open for traffic. Warren relayed this news to Meade and Ayres.[180]

As soon as General Ayres learned that Benyaurd's detachment had finished the bridge across Gravelly Run, he put his command into motion. Gwyn's brigade took the lead as the division moved down the Plank Road. According to Ayres, there had been little delay at the bridge. The Plank Road was good enough, but the fatigue of the night march, in conjunction with yesterday's battle, had pushed the men to the limit of their endurance. As customary, the men marched for 50 minutes and then were allowed to rest for ten minutes. During these stops, many of the soldiers fell asleep. To get the column moving again, "the officers had to use violence" to get the men on their feet. By 4 o'clock, the head of Ayres' column had penetrated to within one mile of Dinwiddie Court House. Ayres now encountered one of Sheridan's staff officers. This officer left Dinwiddie Court House at 3:20 and carried a dispatch from Sheridan to Warren.[181]

Ayres was told by the staffer that his column had arrived sooner than expected. In fact, Ayres' division had come a mile too far. The aide announced that Ayres should have turned into the Brooks road. If he had, the staffer remarked, the

---

178 *Ibid.*

179 Swan, "The Five Forks Campaign," 363-364. During the halt, cattle were butchered and the beef distributed.

180 *Ibid.*, 364; *OR* 46, pt. 1, 824.

181 Swan, "The Five Forks Campaign," 364; *OR* 46, pt. 1, 869, 876. Bowerman's brigade brought up the rear of Ayres' column.

division could have taken the Confederates from the rear. Ayres accordingly reversed his line of march. Returning to the Brooks road, the head of the division turned into it just as dawn started to break. The staffer did not remain with Ayres to show him the way, but galloped off to deliver Sheridan's message to Warren.

Shortly after the division started down the Brooks road, General Ayres sighted a Rebel picket sitting on a rail fence. Spotting the approaching column, the Confederate leaped off the fence, mounted his horse and rode off. Ayres halted his column and threw out a strong skirmish line. The skirmishers were directed to feel their way toward Dinwiddie Court House. Ayres believed that if there were any Confederates holed up in the area between Brooks road and the Court House, they would be trapped between his soldiers and Sheridan's cavalry.

When the skirmishers had moved off, the column resumed its advance along Brooks road. Colonel Swan recalled, "The march along the Brooks road was quite joyous. A clear day was breaking, and the cavalry bugles away to the left and then nearer were playing lively airs that told that the enemy had flown." Near the junction of the Adams and Brooks roads, Ayres encountered General Sheridan. When Ayres reported to Sheridan, he was directed to mass his division in the fields west of the junction and let his men prepare coffee. Taking position in the designated fields, Ayres' division rested on its arms until 2:00 p.m.[182]

The staff officer bearing Sheridan's message reached Warren's headquarters at 4:50 a.m. Upon reading the dispatch, Warren learned that Custer's division, which was deployed astride the Adams road, was guarding the approaches to Dinwiddie Court House. Sheridan reported that the Confederate main line of resistance covered the road linking the Adams road with Fitzgerald's Ford. Because Sheridan had received erroneous information indicating that Warren had one division at J. Boisseau's, he mistakenly believed that the V Corps was in the rear and almost on the flank of the Rebel battle line. Accordingly, Sheridan proposed to hold his position at Dinwiddie Court House. If the Rebels moved against Custer, Sheridan wanted Warren to hurl the division based at J. Boisseau's against the Southerners' left flank and rear. Even if the Confederates did not attack, Sheridan wanted the V Corps to go over to the offensive. The cavalry, Sheridan promised, would co-operate and try to seize the road linking Adams' plantation with Fitzgerald's Ford. If the cavalry were able to carry out its assignment, Sheridan believed that Warren would bag Pickett's entire command. The aggressive Sheridan had written,

---

182 *Ibid.*, 364-365; *OR* 46, pt. 1, 869, 871, 874, 876. The 8th Maryland was one of the regiments which Ayres deployed and threw forward as skirmishers.

"Do not fear my leaving here [Dinwiddie Court House]. If the enemy remains, I shall fight at daylight."[183]

Warren was distressed to learn that Sheridan had a mistaken impression of the tactical situation. There were no elements of the V Corps at J. Boisseau's. The closest that any of the units of the V Corps had been to J. Boisseau's was Dr. Boisseau's. It was a mile and one-fourth from the doctor's to J. Boisseau's. Moreover, during the night, Bartlett's brigade had been recalled from Dr. Boisseau's. Warren knew it would be impossible for him to carry out the plan of operations advanced by Sheridan.[184]

Following the receipt of Sheridan's message, Warren left his headquarters and returned to the White Oak Road. With dawn approaching, Warren wanted to give his personal supervision to the movements of Crawford's and Griffin's divisions.[185]

It was midnight when Bartlett's brigade evacuated its position at Dr. Boisseau's. The dark night, in conjunction with the narrow "wood road" made marching conditions difficult. Almost three hours elapsed before the last of Bartlett's troops rejoined Griffin's division near the White Oak Road. Bartlett's soldiers were allowed only a short rest. About 5:00 a.m., Griffin received his marching orders. One of Warren's staffers rode up to Griffin's command post, and told the general "to move up the First Division with all possible dispatch, via the J. Boisseau house, and report to General Sheridan." Griffin immediately alerted his brigade commanders to hold their units ready to move.[186]

The Confederates were known to be occupying in force the fortifications covering the junction of the Claiborne and White Oak Roads, so the V Corps officers thought it necessary to exercise extreme caution in executing the shift to the left. To screen his division's withdrawal from the rifle pits covering the White Oak Road, Griffin directed Colonel Gregory to have his pickets remain in position. After the division moved out, the pickets would be recalled and fall in behind Bartlett's brigade.[187]

Chamberlain's brigade took the lead when Griffin's division took up the march. At this hour, General Warren did not know that Pickett's task force was falling back on Five Forks. So far as Warren's information went, he expected to

---

183 *OR* 46, pt. 3, 419-420.

184 *Ibid.*, pt. 1, 824.

185 *Ibid.*, Swan, "The Five Forks Campaign," 371.

186 *OR* 46, pt. 1, 846, 863.

187 *Ibid.*, 854; Swan, "The Five Forks Campaign," 371.

meet the Rebels near J. Boisseau's. They had been there, he knew, as late as midnight. Sheridan, in his 3:00 a.m. dispatch from Dinwiddie Court House, had informed Warren that the Confederates were still there, and that the V Corps' advance would take them on their flank and rear. Not knowing when he might encounter the foe, Griffin had Chamberlain's brigade advance in line of battle. Under the impression that he would probably strike the Confederates before he reached J. Boisseau's, Chamberlain moved with great care. Gregory's and Bartlett's brigades swung along in column by battalions behind Chamberlain's. Griffin's line of march led westward across the fields south of the White Oak Road. When Chamberlain's soldiers reached the Crump Road, they wheeled to the left, the Crump Road now served as Griffin's line of advance.[188]

Since there was a possibly of a Confederate counterstroke, Warren had to be careful when it came to withdrawing Crawford's division. To cover his retrogressive movement, Crawford formed his division for battle. Coulter's brigade took position on the left; Baxter's brigade held the center; while Kellogg's troops watched the right. Baxter's troops were the last to retire. The 39th Massachusetts, deployed as skirmishers, covered Baxter's withdrawal. Warren accompanied Baxter's command until he became convinced that the Rebels had no notion of following the V Corps. Besides watching the enemy, the 39th Massachusetts checked straggling.

Both Coulter's and Baxter's brigades marched in line of battle. Kellogg, who held the post of danger, had his command move in column by regiments. In event of a Confederate attack, Kellogg could quickly deploy his soldiers to the right and rear. After detaching a skirmishers to keep the Rebels occupied, Crawford's division marched off toward the west.

As soon as the division was well on its way, the officers in charge of the skirmishers reassembled their men. They then hastened to rejoin their units. The Confederates, however, made no effort to follow the V Corps.[189]

General Warren's escort, after the departure of the corps, retired along the "wood road" toward the Plank Road. The cavalry had the task of turning back any men or supply wagons that had not received information regarding the V Corps' withdrawal from the White Oak Road.

Warren remained with Crawford until after the head of the division had turned into the Crump Road. Convinced by this time that he had been successful in his

188 Swan, "The Five Forks Campaign," 371; OR 46, pt. 1, 846, 849; Porter, "Fifth Corps at the Battle of Five Forks," 246.

189 OR 46, pt. 1, 879-880, 885, 889, 896; Porter, "Fifth Corps at the Battle of Five Forks," 246-247.

efforts to disengage his corps, Warren left Crawford. Accompanied by his staff, Warren rode forward and joined Griffin. It was a little after 9:00 a.m. when Warren reached Griffin's command post.[190]

At J. Boisseau's, Griffin's vanguard encountered Devin's cavalry division advancing up the Adams road. It was about 7:00 a.m. when Griffin's troops established contact with Sheridan's cavalry. Griffin stopped his division and reported to General Sheridan as directed. Sheridan ordered Griffin to halt his troops, mass them, and await further orders. Bodies of the men and horses killed in yesterday's fighting were scattered about the area. A soldier in the 118th Pennsylvania recalled that, as the column came to a halt: General Sheridan and his staff emerged from a neighboring wood. His appearance had not become familiar to the soldiers of the 5th Corps, nor had they yet become impressed with that personal magnetism which roused all fighting men with whom he came in contact.[191]

When Sheridan rode up, he asked Chamberlain where Warren was. To this inquiry, Chamberlain replied that he thought Warren was at the rear of the column.

"That's just where I should expect him to be!" said Sheridan. (Warren's reason for being at the rear while disengaging his troops has already been discussed.) The imputation cast on Warren's valor by this remark to one of Warren's subordinates could not be deemed productive of good discipline, even if there had been a shadow of truth in it. The officers and men of the V Corps, however, knew differently. "Warren was never the one to be in the rear when there was a fight going on. When anyone wanted to find him during a battle, they had to go to the front line to do it."[192]

Griffin, in accordance with Sheridan's instructions, massed his division across the Adams road, one-half mile south of J. Boisseau's. When Warren joined Griffin, he learned that Ayres' division was concentrated about three-quarters of a mile below Griffin's, near J. M. Brook's. Crawford's soldiers reached J. Boisseau's shortly after Warren. The division halted, and Crawford allowed his men to prepare breakfast and rest.[193]

While Warren was conversing with Griffin and waiting for instructions from Sheridan, a staff officer rode up. The aide handed Warren a message signed by

---

190   *OR* 46, pt. 1, 825.

191   Swan, "The Five Forks Campaign," 371; Survivors' Association, *History of the Corn Regiment*, 575-576.

192   Powell, *The Fifth Army Corps*, 798.

193   *Ibid.*, Swan, "The Five Forks Campaign," 371.

Chief of Staff Webb. The dispatch informed Warren that, as soon as the V Corps rendezvoused with the cavalry, he was to report to Sheridan for orders. General Meade also wanted Warren to submit a progress report. It was a little before 9:30 a.m. when this communication was delivered to Warren.[194]

General Webb had signed this order at 6:00 a.m. At the same time, Meade had sent a telegram to Grant. Meade concluded his message with these words, "Warren will be at or near Dinwiddie soon with his whole Corps and will require further orders."[195]

In absence of evidence to the contrary, these dispatches indicate that Gouverneur Warren was responsible to Meade up until 6 o'clock on April 1. Up until then, Warren "had met the intentions and expectations of his commanding officer, and have even exceeded, or anticipated them." Two divisions of the V Corps reported to Sheridan by or before 7:00 a.m.—two and one-half hours before the receipt of Webb's 6 o'clock communication.[196]

Warren immediately moved to comply with Meade's request. He reported that the V Corps had crossed Gravelly Run and was massed at J. Boisseau's. Warren pointed out that, while he hadn't met Sheridan "personally," Griffin had spoken with the cavalry leader. Delighted by his success in disengaging his corps, Warren informed headquarters, "The enemy did not follow with a single man when we left the White Oak Road this morning." Warren also broached the subject of re-victualizing his command. He believed that his troops could draw rations by way of the Boydton Plank Road.[197]

Warren's failure to report directly to Sheridan might have been a contributing factor to his relief later in the day. Colonel Horace Porter, a key Grant staffer, was

---

194 Porter, "Fifth Corps at the Battle of Five Forks," 247; *OR* 46, pt. 1, 825-826.

195 *OR* 46, pt. 1, 385.

196 Powell, *The Fifth Army Corps*, 794.

197 *OR* 46, pt. 3, 418. Commenting on the Confederate failure to attack his corps as it was disengaging, Warren observed: "It was a matter of wonder at the time, and has been ever since, how the enemy permitted our thus withdrawing with out following us up to see the way we took, even if it had been with only a regiment. He would thus early have gained the knowledge that our infantry was moving toward his detached force, under General Pickett, which we beat so badly toward evening. General Lee could then have re-enforced his detached troops or timely warned them to withdraw. I kept my skirmish line halted a long while after my advance set out in the morning, so as to cover the movement as late as possible, and deployed my escort to fall back on the Boydton Plank Road and delude any pursuing forces, if possible, into the belief that we had all retired in that direction. It was a want of vigilance that was most rare on their part and betokened that apathy which results from a hopelessness as to the use of further resistance". *Ibid.*, pt. 1, 826.

"positive that this delay in reporting was very annoying to Sheridan." Several other commentators also subscribed to this view. In fact, after resting for several hours, it seems to have occurred to Warren that it might be a good idea to have an interview with Sheridan. About 11:00 a.m., when he finally contacted the cavalry leader, Warren pronounced his manner "friendly and cordial." At this time, Sheridan was dismounted. After the two officers had conversed for a few minutes, Sheridan called for his horse and rode off toward the front. Following Sheridan's departure, Warren rejoined his command.[198]

Except for a daring coup carried out by three members of the 16th Michigan, the rank and file of the V Corps spent a quiet morning. Not knowing that the V Corps had been withdrawn from the White Oak Road, the three Michiganders passed to the west of the II Corps' picket line. The soldiers planned to rejoin their regiment, which was assigned to Bartlett's brigade. Encountering a captain and 14 men of the 16th North Carolina Cavalry Battalion, the Yankees forced the Southerners to surrender. Accompanied by their prisoners, the bluecoats rejoined their regiment south of J. Boisseau's.[199]

Following receipt of Meade's directive ordering the II Corps to fall back and occupy the fortifications covering the Boydton Plank Road. Humphreys drafted an order calculated to implement his superior's decision. The retrogressive movement was to begin on the right by Hays' and Mott's divisions. These two units were scheduled to retire by 3:30 a.m. Hays' division on the extreme right would occupy a line extending from Armstrong's Mill to the Taylor house; Mott's command in the center was to hold the rifle pits between the Taylor and Rainey houses. General Miles' division on the left was to fall back into the trenches covering the Boydton Plank Road. Miles' left flank rested on Gravelly Run, while his right flank held "the return." This dispatch went out from Corps headquarters at 1:30 a.m.[200]

At the stipulated hour, Colonel Olmsted (whose brigade had been shifted to the left on the previous afternoon to occupy the rifle pits vacated by Pearson's troops) mustered his command. By 6 o'clock, Olmsted's had reported to General Hays. The division commander had Olmsted's soldiers reoccupy the trenches on the left of McIvor's brigade, which they had formerly held.[201]

---

198 *Ibid.*, 829; Porter, "Fifth Corps at the Battle of Five Forks," 247-248.

199 *OR* 46, pt. 3, 419. The three Michiganders were: W. M. Cronkite, A. McCrory, and William Stubel.

200 *Ibid.*, 411.

201 *OR* 46, pt. 1, 760, 762.

Throughout the morning and early afternoon, Hays' division took it easy. At this time, Hays had two brigades—McIvor's and Olmsted's—in the trenches, and one in reserve, Smyth's. About 2:00 p.m., Hays issued instructions for McIvor and Olmsted to see if they could advance their lines closer to the Confederate main line of resistance. Covered by a strong skirmish line, the two brigades pressed forward. The Confederate outposts were easily driven in. All told, the Yankees advanced their line about 300 yards. On the right, McIvor's brigade was in contact with the XXIV Corps on the east side of Hatcher's Run. To secure their gains, McIvor's and Olmsted's troops threw up a new line of earthworks. Smyth's brigade moved and occupied the trenches recently vacated by Olmsted's troops. The ground gained by Hays' bluecoats on the afternoon of the 1st would be used by the division as its jumping off point when it moved against Fort Powell. The attack on that stronghold was scheduled for 4:00 a.m. on the 2nd.[202]

Mott's division returned without any incident worthy of note to the position which it had held on the previous morning. Upon reoccupying the breastworks between the Rainey and Taylor houses, Mott placed McAllister's and Pearce's troops in the rifle pits; de Trobriand's brigade was posted in reserve.[203]

Miles started pulling his troops from the ground which they had seized near the White Oak Road at 3:30 a.m. The Confederates made no effort to harass Miles' infantrymen as they retired. Accordingly, the withdrawal went off as scheduled. When he reached the Boydton Plank Road, Miles placed Scott's brigade on the left. Scott, who would protect the II Corps' left flank, rested his left on Gravelly Run. Colonel Ramsey's brigade held the rifle pits on the right of Scott's command. The brigade commanded by Colonel Madill held "the return" on the right of Ramsey's bluecoats. Madill's right flank was in contact with McAllister's left at the Rainey house. Miles' other brigade, Nugent's, was in reserve. During the day, Nugent's command was called upon to furnish large fatigue details for work on the fortifications.[204]

Not wishing to entirely waste the day, Miles saw that his men were supplied with rations and ammunition. In addition, the brigade commanders were directed to inspect their units to insure that their men's arms and accoutrements were in order.[205]

202 *Ibid.*, 757, 760, 762, 764, 766; pt. 3, 411.

203 *Ibid.*, pt. 1, 777, 781, 785, 789. Pearce's brigade was stationed on the right and McAllister's on the left.

204 *Ibid.*, 711, 714, 724, 734, 744.

205 *Ibid.*, 745.

With the exception of one battery, the II Corps' artillery was not engaged on the 1st. Shortly after daybreak, the cannoneers of Battery B, 1st Rhode Island positioned at the Crow house, opened fire on Fort Powell. The Rebels replied. After a short duel, the artillery fell silent. During the late afternoon, Battery B, 1st New Jersey was again placed in battery near the Rainey house. Since an uneasy quiet had settled over Humphreys' sector, the V Corps' artillery, which was temporarily attached to the II Corps, remained parked throughout the day.[206]

By the evening of the 31st, the last of the trains belonging to the Army of the Potomac had crossed Rowanty Creek. As soon as the last wagon had reached the west bank of the creek, General Mackenzie relayed this information to General Meade. At the same time, Mackenzie requested a fresh assignment.[207]

When Grant learned that Mackenzie's division was looking for work, he ordered Ord to send the unit to Dinwiddie Court House.[208] Upon the receipt of Grant's telegram, Ord issued instructions for Mackenzie "to get off as soon in the morning as possible." Grant was not satisfied with this move on Ord's part. A terse message went out under Grant's signature, "I want Mackenzie to go tonight. It may be too late in the morning." Grant then informed Meade of his plans to rush Mackenzie to Sheridan's assistance.[209]

It was too late, however, to change Mackenzie's orders. Accordingly, Mackenzie's division did not get under way until early on the morning of the 1st. It was about 3:30 o'clock when Mackenzie's troopers broke camp and crossed Rowanty Creek. Marching by way of the Monk's Neck and Vaughan Roads, the hard-riding troopers headed for Dinwiddie Court House.[210]

Editor's Conclusion

The Confederate cavalry and infantry attack on March 31 collapsed and tightly pressed the Union lines and, temporarily, at least, brought General Sheridan's major offensive move west and north to a halt. The Rebels, however, as we shall see in the third and final Five Forks Campaign chapter that follows, were unable to take advantage of their tactical success

---

206 *Ibid.*, 791-792, 899.

207 *Ibid.*, pt. 3, 382.

208 *Ibid.*, 378.

209 *Ibid.*, 341, 378.

210 *Ibid.*, pt. 1, 1244.

because of heavy columns of Union infantry approaching their left flank from the east. This new threat forced General George Pickett to pull back before daybreak and strengthen the absolutely vital road junction known as Five Forks. It was imperative for the Confederates to maintain their grip on the logistics hub, which General Lee ordered Pickett to hold at all hazards.

Chapter 7

The Five Forks Campaign
The Battle of Five Forks

April 1, 1865

Part VII

The Battle

A little before 10:00 p.m. on March 31, General Pickett received an important piece of news from Colonel Munford. The cavalry officer's scouts had captured two soldiers from Warren's familiar V Corps. These infantrymen belonged to Bartlett's brigade, which had pushed southwestward from the White Oak Road and occupied high ground at Dr. Boisseau's. The position held by this Federal unit was north of Gravelly Run and on the left and rear of Pickett's task force. It is uncertain whether Pickett knew the exact location of Bartlett's command. Nevertheless, the general decided that it would be unwise for his troops to try to hold the ground gained in the day's fighting.

According to Fitz Lee, Pickett believed that Bartlett's brigade spearheaded an advance of the entire V Corps. Pickett had already determined that Sheridan's cavalry held Dinwiddie Court House in force. Now, to make matters worse, he knew that the Union leaders were rushing infantry to Sheridan's assistance. Confronted by this situation, Pickett felt that he should not expose his force needlessly. It was better, he concluded, to take position where he could discharge his principal duty to afford protection to the right flank of the Army of Northern Virginia and the approaches to the South Side Railroad.[1]

Consequently, orders were issued for Pickett's force to pull back. The withdrawal was slated to start at 4:00 a.m., and would follow the line of the previous day's advance. By the hour fixed for the return march, it was apparent to Pickett and his officers that their left was being threatened by another Union column (Ayres' division) pushing down the Boydton Plank Road. As a result of the usual delays associated with breaking camp, it was daybreak (about 5:00 a.m.) before the last of Pickett's five infantry brigades (Corse's) began to slog northward through the mud. Colonel Munford's troopers covered the rear of Pickett's retreating column. At the same time, Rooney Lee's and Rosser's divisions re-crossed Chamberlain's Bed, and returned to Five Forks by way of Little Five Forks.[2]

Sheridan's vanguard (Custer's division) nipped at the heels of the retreating column. Even though the Federals failed to attack, they remained in sight or close enough to know what was transpiring. Sheridan, however, neither tried to force a fight nor cut off the Rebel guns and trains which had started for Five Forks at 2:00 a.m.[3]

The artillery had an uneventful march through the spring mud and by sunrise was parked on the ground it had occupied before yesterday's engagement. Hungry gunners, finding no rations, had to rob their horses of some of the animal's corn. Parched over the fire, the corn constituted the artillerists' breakfasts. Pickett probably fared no better. Even so, he brought back all his wounded, and his rear guard (Munford's division) watched Sheridan's movements closely. The Federals, Pickett concluded, at the moment did not aim to turn his right flank. Instead, they appeared to want to push a force between his task force and Anderson's Corps on his left. Subsequently, Pickett recalled "that he sent Lee a telegram to this affect and asked that a diversion be made to prevent his isolation."

When the infantry reached Five Forks during the forenoon, Pickett sent his wagons across Hatcher's Run. He would also have deployed his task force on the north bank of the stream, Pickett recalled, had he not received a telegram from Lee urging him to, "Hold Five Forks at all hazards. Protect road to Ford's Depot and

---

1   Freeman, *Lee's Lieutenants*, vol. 3, 660; OR 46, pt. 1, 1299; Humphreys, *The Virginia Campaign of '65*, 342.

2   Freeman, *Lee's Lieutenants*, vol. 3, 661; OR 46, pt. 1, 1264; Humphreys, *The Virginia Campaign of '65*, 342.

3   Freeman, *Lee's Lieutenants*, vol. 3, 661.

Major General George E. Pickett
Library of Congress

prevent Union forces from striking the South Side Railroad. Regret exceedingly your forced withdrawal, and your inability to hold the advantage you had gained."

This message was, in a sense, justification for the course Pickett pursued: Lee recognized that the withdrawal had been forced. At the same time, the telegram from GHQ forbade a farther retreat, for compelling reasons. If Five Forks were abandoned and the Federals able to reach the South Side Railroad and cut the wagon roads leading to the west along the south bank of the Appomattox, all would be lost. Again, if Pickett's force gave up Five Forks, the numerically superior Unionists would pass to the westward along the White Oak Road, circle the headwaters of Hatcher's Run, and turn the Confederate right flank. The position at Five Forks was weak, in itself; but, strategically, it was the most important on that sector of the front. It simply had to be defended.[4]

Pickett stopped at Five Forks. He later wrote that he assumed Lee had received his earlier telegram about his withdrawal. Accordingly, Pickett believed that Lee, in addition to making a diversion in his favor, would send him reinforcements. Operating on these assumptions, one historian argued that Pickett "may not have been vigilant or careful in deploying his troops to meet possible attack that day."[5]

4   *Ibid.*, 661-662; Humphreys, *The Virginia Campaign of '65*, 343.

5   Freeman, *Lee's Lieutenants*, vol. 3, 662. It is possible, but it does not seem probable, that Lee's telegraphic orders for Pickett to hold Five Forks covered an acknowledgement of Pickett's request for reinforcements and a diversion. A report from Pickett evidently had reached army headquarters on the morning of the 1st. Indications are, however, that it covered only the events of the previous night. In his report to Secretary of War Breckinridge on the evening of

The general posted Rooney Lee's cavalry division on the right, along the west boundary of Gillian's field. On his left, Pickett placed a regiment of Munford's mounted division—the 8th Virginia Cavalry. This unit was to maintain contact with Brig. Gen. William P. Roberts' under strength brigade. Roberts' command picketed the area between Pickett's left and the Confederate fortifications covering the junction of the Claiborne and White Oak Roads. Roberts' troopers were stout fighters but, like most of the Confederate organizations, the brigade had an acute shortage of experienced field officers. A stronger brigade should have been given this critical assignment.[6]

The Confederate main line of resistance covering Five Forks was held by the five infantry brigades of Pickett's task force. General Ransom's North Carolina brigade of Johnson's division was posted on the left. To afford protection to his left flank which was resting in the air, Ransom refused it. General Wallace's South Carolina brigade joined Ransom on the right. Next, and extending as far west as Five Forks, was Steuart's brigade. To Steuart's right was Mayo's command. Beyond Mayo, on the right flank, was Corse's brigade. Corse's, Mayo's and Steuart's brigade hailed from Virginia. Two of these three units (Mayo's and Steuart's) had been with Pickett at Gettysburg.[7]

Except for the refused left line, Pickett's main line of resistance paralleled the White Oak Road. The frontage held was about one mile and three-quarters in length. To strengthen their position, the Confederate officers had their men dig in. Pegram's six guns were placed along the line wherever the cannoneers could find fields of fire in the wooded countryside. Three of Pegram's pieces were unlimbered on Corse's right; the remainder were placed in battery at Five Forks. The eight guns manned by the cannoneers of Maj. William M. McGregor's Battalion were sent to bolster the right flank of the line.[8]

The remaining units of Munford's division were stationed along the Ford's Church Road, which led northward to the railroad. Rosser's division, which

---

the 1st Lee described Pickett's report of the night of March 31-April 1, but did not say anything to suggest that Pickett had appealed for assistance. See OR 46, pt. 1, 1263-1264. Absence of all evidence during the afternoon that Lee had any specific appeal from Pickett for help indicates that Pickett's memory of events was fuzzy when he wrote his report, or else that his telegram miscarried. It scarcely seems possible that so important message, if received at GHQ, would have been forgotten by Lee, by Colonel Walter Taylor, and by the others who wrote of the events of April 1. Freeman, *Lee's Lieutenants*, vol. 3, 662.

6   Freeman, *Lee's Lieutenants*, vol. 3, 662; Humphreys, *The Virginia Campaign of '65*, 344.

7   Freeman, *Lee's Lieutenants*, vol. 3, 663-664; Humphreys, *The Virginia Campaign of '65*, 344.

8   Humphreys, *The Virginia Campaign of '65*, 344.

constituted Pickett's strategic reserve, was posted north of Hatcher's Run to watch the trains. His division had been given this assignment, Rosser recalled, because the sore-backed, hard-ridden horses needed attention.[9]

Twenty-four years later, at Warren's court of inquiry, Fitz Lee explained why the Confederates had made their dispositions along the White Oak Road with less care than usual. Lee recalled:

> When we moved towards Five Forks, hearing nothing more of [Warren's] infantry's move which we had heard of the night before, I thought that the movements there, for the time being, were suspended, and we were not expecting any attack that afternoon, so far as I know. Our throwing up works and taking position were simply general matters of military precaution.[10]

Fitz Lee believed that his troopers and Pickett's infantry could handle any threat by Sheridan's cavalry. If the Union infantry left their lines to support Sheridan, then a corresponding force from Anderson's Corps would be rushed to Five Forks. Such was the reasoning of Fitz Lee as well as of Pickett.[11]

Either Fitz Lee and Pickett were ignorant of the details of the battle of White Oak Road, or they failed to realize its significance. Anderson's Corps was reduced by the losses suffered in the bitter fighting on the 31st, and two of its four brigades were already with Pickett. It was in no condition to render any further assistance to the forces on its right. Apparently, however, neither Fitz Lee nor Pickett realized this. Along with the rest of the Army of Northern Virginia, they cherished the general belief—a belief which helped to create a special esprit de corps—that Lee somehow could contrive to achieve the "impossible," even though, in this case, the line was stretched to the breaking point.[12]

The good showing made by his infantry in the battle of White Oak Road on the 31st had not deceived General Lee. He realized on the morning of the 1st that the situation was growing increasingly grave, even though his troops still grimly held the Petersburg lines. When he addressed a letter to President Jefferson Davis, Lee explained that when the Federals had extended their lines to Dinwiddie Court House, it had cut the Army of Northern Virginia off from the depot at Stony Creek.

9 *Ibid.*; Freeman, *Lee's Lieutenants*, vol. 3, 664.

10 Freeman, *Lee's Lieutenants*, vol. 3, 664.

11 *Ibid.*

12 *Ibid.*, 665.

The general reminded the President that the forage for the army's cavalry had formerly been delivered to that point.

Furthermore, it would now be more difficult to give up Petersburg, because Sheridan's rapid advance had deprived Lee of the use of the White Oak Road. From his position at Dinwiddie Court House, Sheridan could sweep around Lee's right flank and cut both the South Side and the Richmond and Danville Railroads. "This," in Lee's opinion, obliged the Confederates "to prepare for the necessity of evacuating their position on the James River at once, and also to consider the best means of accomplishing it, and our future course." There was no longer any hope, Lee left Davis to infer, that time remained for a slow removal of supplies from Richmond. He would like to have the President's view on the subject, Lee concluded. The general, however, felt that the situation was so dark that his continued presence at Petersburg was necessary. If either the President or Secretary of War Breckinridge came to Petersburg for a conference, Lee would be happy.[13]

Shortly after Lee had drafted this message, he received the message from Pickett telling of the forced withdrawal from the vicinity of Dinwiddie Court House. This was bad news. Looking at his map, Lee saw that it was only seven and one-half miles from Dinwiddie Court House to the South Side Railroad. If the railroad were to be saved, Pickett could not afford to give ground. Lee accordingly sent his, "Hold Five Forks at all hazards" communication to Pickett.

The one prospect of saving a dangerous situation continued to be the possibility that Grant might blunder and expose his "army group" to a Confederate counterattack. Lee accordingly proceeded to strengthen his position as far as practicable with artillery. He acted on the sound principle that this was the first essential to going over to the offensive in case Grant made a mistake.[14]

Brigadier General William N. Pendleton, Lee's Chief of Artillery, was ordered to transfer to the Petersburg lines a part of the reserve artillery. Seven guns belonging to Lt. Col. William T. Poague's battalion which been held in reserve near the Howlett Line were transferred to the Petersburg front. These guns were parked behind the sector held by Gordon's troops.[15]

At this time, Gordon's soldiers were very close to the breaking point, inasmuch as more than one-half of them had to be continuously on duty.[16]

---

13 Freeman, *R. E. Lee*, vol. 4, 35-36.

14 *Ibid.*, 36, 37.

15 *OR* 46, pt. 1, 1280.

16 Freeman, *R. E. Lee*, vol. 4, 37.

Beyond Gordon's right flank, A. P. Hill, who had returned that morning from an uncompleted sick leave, resumed leadership of a corps that was little more than a shadow of itself. All of Gordon's troops, plus that part of Hill's Corps east of Armstrong's Mill, now numbered only about 11,000 strong. They occupied—it could not be said they held—11 miles of front, from the Appomattox to Hatcher's Run.

Lee knew that this attenuation of his line was a desperate gamble with ruin, especially at a time when Pickett was retreating. To make matters worse, Confederate patrols captured troops belonging to the XXIV Corps. This was the first definite information that Lee had received that at least a part of the Army of the James had slipped away from Longstreet and crossed the James River. Lee was quick to act on this information. The general reasoned that, if the XXIV Corps had reinforced the Army of the Potomac in front of Petersburg, and no other units had taken its place, then Longstreet could go over to the attack and force Grant to transfer troops back to the northside. If, however, Longstreet did not feel he could successfully launch an assault, he could dispatch part of his corps to strengthen the Petersburg front. A telegram presenting these alternatives to Longstreet left Lee's headquarters on the morning of the 1st.

Having completed his morning's business at Army headquarters, Lee rode over to Anderson's command post. The general wanted to get a first-hand view of operations in that sector. Reaching the front, Lee learned that the Federals had "disappeared from the vicinity of the White Oak Road." Scouts sent out by General Johnson had returned with the information that the Yankees had moved to the west, in the direction of General Pickett's front. So far as the records show, Lee heard nothing more from Pickett.[17]

While waiting at Anderson's headquarters, Lee received a telegram from Longstreet. "Old Pete," replying to Lee's earlier communication, announced that Col. Robert Ould had told him that the Union troops remaining north of the James were black. At this very minute, Longstreet observed, his scouts were trying to verify this information. Since he believed the Union gunboats would frustrate any offensive activities which his corps might undertake. Longstreet thought it would be better if he used the troops that could be spared to reinforce the Southside.[18]

Answering Longstreet's telegram, Lee directed "Old Pete" to get ready to rush troops to Petersburg in case the scouts were able to confirm Colonel Ould's report.

---

17 *Ibid.*; pt. 1, 1288.

18 *Ibid.*, 1372. Colonel Ould was the Confederate agent in charge of the exchange of prisoners at City Point, Virginia.

Later in the day, Lee learned that General Roberts' brigade had captured several Union cavalrymen. Searching the prisoners, the Confederates found they had letters in their saddlebags which identified them as belonging to the 11th Pennsylvania Cavalry, a unit assigned to the division led by General Kautz. (At this time, the cavalry division formerly led by Kautz was commanded by Mackenzie.) Consequently, Lee fired off a wire to Longstreet asking him to ascertain what mounted units were on the northside. Longstreet sent Gary's brigade to investigate. "Old Pete's" theory was "that General Sheridan may have taken Kautz's cavalry, as they were fresh, and left a portion of his own in their place." (Longstreet was wrong in his contention. All of Sheridan's Corps had crossed the James on the night of March 26.)[19]

In addition to the smug overconfidence of Fitz Lee and Pickett, and their lack of understanding of the dread immediacy of the crisis, another factor entered the picture. It is probable that the third consideration, a very human one, led Fitz Lee and Pickett to assume that "general precaution" sufficed.

Before being recalled to Five Forks, General Rosser had spent a day on the Nottoway River. The shad were running in the stream. With a borrowed seine, the young general had a fine catch. Some of these he had placed in his headquarters ambulance and brought with him to Five Forks. As soon as Rosser was ordered to post his division north of Hatcher's Run, he arranged to have the fish cleaned and split. Next, the shad were placed on sticks in front of a brisk fire.[20]

Assured "that this would provide a meal delectable at any time and incredible in the hungry days of bone-gnarling war," Rosser invited Pickett and Fitz Lee to his shad-bake. Hungry and probably half wet, Pickett gratefully accepted. He promised to join his host at the designated place in one hour. Fitz Lee, with equal satisfaction, also accepted. Neither general lost any time in preparing to keep his appointment.[21]

It was after 2 o'clock when Fitz Lee swung into his saddle. But before the general started for the shad-bake, Colonel Munford galloped up on a foam-flecked horse and handed Lee a dispatch from Lt. Wythe B. Graham of the 8th Virginia Cavalry. (The lieutenant's unit had been tasked with maintaining contact between the left flank of Pickett's main line of resistance and Roberts' brigade.) According to Graham's story, Roberts' brigade had been attacked and overpowered by the Yankees (Mackenzie's division) east of Five Forks. Roberts' brigade had been shattered by this onslaught. Some of his North Carolinians had been driven back on

19 *Ibid.*, 1372, 1377; Freeman, *R. E. Lee*, vol. 4, 38.

20 Freeman, *Lee's Lieutenants*, vol. 3, 665-666.

21 *Ibid.*, 666.

Major General Fitzhugh Lee
Library of Congress

Anderson's lines guarding the junction of the Claiborne and White Oak Roads; the rest had fled westward and carried the tidings of the disaster to Graham's unit.

If this information were correct, then Sheridan had reached the White Oak Road and had severed the direct line of communication between Pickett's task force and Anderson's Corps. The "isolation" dreaded by Pickett was a reality. Reinforcements, if sent to him, would have to cut their way through a Union roadblock.

Fitz Lee was either "impatiently hungry or uncritically skeptical." He read the dispatch and remarked, "Well, Munford, I wish you would go over in person at once and see what this means, and, if necessary, order up your Division and let me hear from you." With that, the chief of cavalry rode off. Shortly thereafter, Munford saw Fitz Lee and Pickett riding up the Ford's Church Road together toward Hatcher's Run. At this time, Munford knew nothing of the two major generals' destination or of their reason for being together.

The unannounced departure of the two senior officers for a point approximately one and one-fourth miles from the front left Rooney Lee in charge of operations. Rooney Lee, however, was far out on the right and had received no word that his seniors had left the field. Furthermore, Rooney Lee probably had not been told of the clash on the left, in which the Union cavalry had routed Roberts' brigade. The senior among the cavalrymen facing the foe who had struck Roberts' North Carolinians was Munford. Since Fitz Lee had been acting as chief of cavalry, Munford had been in charge of the First Division. The infantry, in the absence of Pickett, had "Maryland" Steuart as their commander. Colonel Pegram was the ranking artillerist on the field.

None of these men (Rooney Lee, Munford, Steuart, or Pegram) knew that Pickett and Fitz Lee had ridden to the rear. The shad-bake was a social secret. Because the food was abundant, the affair was slow and deliberate, as every feast should be. If there was "something to drink," it probably was not shunned. Many of the Civil War officers did not hesitate to indulge even in the presence of the enemy. If the trio (Pickett, Fitz Lee, and Rosser) proceeded or followed their dinner with a little whiskey or brandy, there was no evidence, then or thereafter, that any of the three were inebriated.

The time slipped by "pleasantly," while the generals picked the bones from the broiled shad, two pickets dashed up. Reporting to the high ranking officers, they announced that the Yankees were advancing on all the roads that the task force was guarding. Rosser recalled:

> These reports were made to Pickett and to Lee and as the position at Five Forks was considered as well chosen and strong but little attention was given to the enemy's advance. I was suffering from my wound and as I was not immediately in command of the pickets I took no steps to reinforce them. Indeed the pickets were a part of . . . [Colonel] Munford's command and I, reporting direct to General Lee, and as he was present felt little or no concern about them.

Perhaps Rosser and his feasting comrades were the less concerned over the pickets' reports because there had not been any sound of action from the front; the Federals evidently were approaching but were not attacking. The officers at the front could be expected to cope with any small scale actions that might flare up.

Shortly after 4 o'clock, Pickett asked Rosser for a courier to take a message to Five Forks. Obligingly, Rosser offered two, one of whom, according to Rosser's rule, would ride ahead of but in sight of the second. Pickett drafted his dispatch and gave it to one of the couriers. They started down the Ford's Church Road. Doubtless, the conversation around Rosser's hospitable fire was resumed. Soon there came from the south of the run a burst of rifle fire. In plain view, on the other side of the stream, the generals saw the leading courier captured by the Federals. At the same moment, a blue coated battle line swept toward the Ford's Church Road.[22]

*   *   *

22 *Ibid.*, 666-669.

On the night of the 31st, General Sheridan's headquarters were at Dinwiddie Court House. When Sheridan received word that the V Corps would report to him, he was told that Warren's troops were in position near S. Dabney's. Looking at his maps, Sheridan saw that S. Dabney's was in the angle formed by the Boydton Plank and White Oak Roads. Sheridan was of the opinion that if Warren had moved according to Grant's expectations, "there would appear to have been but little chance for the escape" of Pickett's infantry which was deployed in front of Dinwiddie Court House. Accordingly, Sheridan at 3:00 a.m. dispatched his, "I am holding in front of Dinwiddie Court House" message to Warren.[23]

In anticipation of a resumption of the fighting on the 1st, Custer's troopers had slept on their arms. Custer's division was posted on the high ground about three-quarters of a mile north of Dinwiddie Court House. About the time that the first streaks of dawn appeared on the eastern horizon, Custer's scouts discovered that the Confederates, under the cover of darkness, had retired from the Federals' immediate front. Custer communicated this information to Sheridan.[24] Upon receipt of this important intelligence, the cavalry leader called for General Merritt. Sheridan directed Merritt to follow the retreating Rebels with Custer's and Devin's divisions.[25]

At this time, only two of Custer's brigades (Capehart's and Pennington's) were on the field. Wells' brigade was guarding the wagon train, which had parked for the night near the junction of the Vaughan and Monk's Neck roads. A staff officer thundered off with instructions for Wells to rejoin the division. Custer led his men up the Adams road. At the junction of the Adams and Brooks roads, Custer encountered Ayres' vanguard. So far, Custer's advance had been unopposed. In his "After Action Report," Sheridan attributed the rapid Confederate retreat in part to the advances of Ayres' division.[26]

Following the appearance of Ayres' column, Merritt determined to use Custer's division to turn the Confederate right. Since the countryside west of the Dinwiddie Road was unsuited for mounted operations, Merritt had Custer dismount and deploy his troopers into line of battle. Pennington's brigade was formed on the right and Capehart's on the left. When Custer gave the word, his

23 OR 46, pt. 1, 1130. For the details of Sheridan's 3:00 a.m. communication to Warren, see Part 6 of Chapter 6.

24 *Ibid.*, 1130.

25 *Ibid.*, 1104.

26 *Ibid.*, 1100, 1130. Sheridan also pointed out, "General Ayres was unable to get into the enemy's rear in time to attack as expected owing to the darkness and bad roads."

troops moved forward through the woods. The left flank of Capehart's brigade guided its movement at first on Chamberlain's Bed and later on Bear Swamp.[27]

Only a few Confederates (mostly stragglers) were encountered by Custer's cavalrymen as they swept ahead. On the extreme left of Custer's battle line, the men of Capehart's brigade encountered a Confederate patrol guarding the place where Scott road crossed Bear Swamp. After a brief stand, the grey clads beat a hasty retreat. The advance was then renewed and Custer's troops penetrated to within several hundred yards of the White Oak Road before again encountering any opposition. This time, however, the aggressive Custer decided not to attack. It was apparent to Custer and his men that any farther advance would be bitterly contested. Reconnoitering the Confederate position, Custer reported:

> The enemy had evidently resolved to oppose our farther advance with the greatest determination. Heavy lines of earth-works were discovered, extending for miles in either direction along our front. In advance of these were strong barricades of rails, logs, and other obstructions. Every point seemed to be strongly manned with infantry and artillery.[28]

To test the strength of the Confederate position, Custer ordered his brigade commanders to send out combat patrols. Pickett's grim infantry easily beat off the sharp sorties launched by these patrols. Rebuffed in his efforts to find a soft spot in Pickett's main line of resistance, Custer ordered his men to suspend the attack but to hold their ground gained.[29]

General Devin's troopers had ridden out of their Crump's Farm encampment at an early hour. The division followed Custer's troopers on the Adams road. When Merritt ordered Custer to move across country, he directed Devin to march up the Dinwiddie Court House Road and reoccupy his old position at J. Boisseau's. At J. Boisseau's, Devin encountered General Griffin's vanguard.

When the position at J. Boisseau's had been secured, Devin led his troopers on toward Five Forks. Devin's advance brigade, Colonel Stagg's, was fired on as it prepared to ford Chamberlain's Bed. Scouts were thrown out. They soon returned with information that Confederate infantry was watching the crossing and the position would not "be taken without a hard fight." Devin accordingly directed

---

27 *Ibid.*, 1117, 1130, 1135. Colonel Pennington deployed three regiments into line of battle, while holding a fourth (the 2nd Ohio) in reserve.

28 *Ibid.*, 1130, 1135. In reality, the line stretched for one and three-quarters miles.

29 *Ibid.*, 1118, 1130.

Colonel Fitzhugh to dismount his brigade. Fitzhugh's troopers were to wade the creek. When Fitzhugh gave the word, his blue clads stormed across the creek. Despite the galling fire of the Confederates, the dismounted troopers carved out a bridgehead. After the Rebels had started to give way, Stagg waved his mounted brigade to the attack. The 1st and 6th Michigan, reinforced by the 1st U.S. Cavalry of Gibb's brigade, crossed the stream on the left of Fitzhugh's command; the 5th Michigan protected the right flank of the bridgehead. In the meantime, General Gibbs deployed his brigade (without the 1st U.S.) to cover the right flank and rear of Devin's division.[30]

When the bridgehead had been secured, Devin determined to seize the wooded area between Chamberlain's Bed and the White Oak Road. When Devin gave the word, the division drove forward. Fitzhugh's dismounted battle line pressed up the Dinwiddie Road "at the charging step." Fitzhugh's troopers were flanked on the left and right by their mounted comrades. The 1st and 6th Michigan and the 1st U.S. Cavalry were on Fitzhugh's left, the 5th Michigan on his right. Driving in Pickett's outposts, Devin's cavalrymen closed on the Confederate main line of resistance.

As they approached Five Forks, the Yankees "developed a strong line of breast-works . . . filled with masses of infantry." Before being checked by the fire of Pickett's infantry, Devin's mounted contingents in some places closed to within 20 yards of the works. In several instances, men from Fitzhugh's dismounted brigade even crossed the breastworks. Before being beaten off, the troopers captured and dragged off several prisoners. Convinced that the Confederate position was too strong to carry, Devin's cavalrymen fell back into the woods south of the White Oak Road. Devin regrouped his division. Fitzhugh's brigade was posted on the left, and Stagg's on the right. At this time, Stagg also dismounted his command.

Following Fitzhugh's and Stagg's repulse, Devin ordered up Gibbs' brigade. Gibbs dismounted and deployed his unit on the right of the 5th Michigan. The right flank of Gibbs' brigade rested near the Barnes house. One of Gibbs' regiments, the 1st U.S. Cavalry, remained mounted.[31]

On Custer's right, Pennington's brigade was in contact with the 1st Michigan. Following Devin's repulse, Lt. Col. George R. Maxwell of the Michigan regiment informed Pennington that he had lost contact with the unit on his right. Maxwell told Pennington that he was gong to try to reestablish a connection with the remainder of Devin's division. As soon as Maxwell's Michiganders rode off toward

30 *Ibid.*, 1118, 1123.

31 *Ibid.*, 1123, 1124, 1128.

the east, Pennington, believing that it would be tempting disaster to hold his position with his right flank resting in the air, retired a short distance. Next, he shifted his brigade to the right. Near the Scott road, Pennington spotted Fitzhugh's brigade. Following his repulse, Fitzhugh had fallen back to regroup. Pennington halted and formed his command in a thick belt of woods, about 600 yards south of the Confederate breastworks. The Scott road separated Pennington's and Fitzhugh's commands. While waiting for further orders, the dismounted Union troopers threw up log breastworks.

It was about 11:00 a.m. when Sheridan's tardy wagon train reached Dinwiddie Court House. Colonel Wells permitted his men to rest until 1:00 p.m. At that hour, he had "boots and saddles" sounded and the troopers swung into their saddles. Proceeding to the front, Colonel Wells reported to General Custer near the left of Sheridan's battle line.[32]

One of Sheridan's three divisions, Crook's, saw little action on the 1st. At an early hour, Crook's division rode from their camp on Great Cattail Run to Dinwiddie Court House. Davies' and Smith's brigades were given the task of guarding the train, following Wells' departure. To carry out this assignment, Davies and Smith posted their cavalrymen in the fields north of the village. One of Davies' regiments was detached and sent to watch the bridge which carried the Boydton Plank Road across Stony Creek.[33]

Crook's other brigade, Gregg's, was given a more active assignment. Crossing Chamberlain's Bed at Fitzgerald's Ford, Gregg's troopers occupied Little Five Forks. The possession of this strategic crossroads enabled Gregg to control the roads leading to the left and rear of Custer's division. After having secured the crossroads Gregg threw out a number of patrols. One of these groups moved up the Gillian road and established contact with the 2nd West Virginia of Capehart's brigade. Another patrol visited Stony Creek. Only a few Confederates (less than twenty) were sighted by this unit. The 8th Pennsylvania made a forced reconnaissance down "the Dinwiddie Court House road" and scattered the few Rebels encountered. By his vigorous scouting and patrolling, Gregg made certain that there would be no surprise attack on Sheridan's left flank.[34]

During the morning, Sheridan learned that General Mackenzie's division had reached Dinwiddie Court House. Considering the fact that Mackenzie's men had been in the saddle since 3:30 a.m., Sheridan ordered him to rest his command.

32 *Ibid.*, 1135, 1139.

33 *Ibid.*, 1144, 1149, 1157; "Map of the Battle Field of Five Forks," Files, National Archives.

34 *OR* 46, pt. 3, 436-437.

Mackenzie accordingly halted his people in the fields north of the Adams house. After being warned to hold themselves ready to march at a moment's notice, the cavalrymen dismounted.[35]

*   *   *

A few minutes before noon, Lt. Col. Orville E. Babcock of Grant's staff reached Sheridan's headquarters. Babcock told Sheridan:

> General Grant directs me to say to you, that if in your judgment the Fifth Corps would do better under one of the division commanders, you are authorized to relieve General Warren, and order him to report to General Grant, at headquarters.

Sheridan replied that he hoped such a drastic step as that would not become necessary. The general then turned to a discussion of his plans.[36]

After Custer's and Devin's probing attacks had pinpointed Pickett's main line of resistance, Sheridan worked out his battle plan. Sheridan would have Custer make a feint toward Pickett's right. Simultaneously, the Confederate's left flank would be assailed by Warren's V Corps. Devin's division, bolstered by Pennington's brigade, was to make a frontal attack on the entrenchments as soon as the sound of firing indicated that the V Corps was engaged. If this onslaught proved successful, Pickett's task force would be cut off from the Army of Northern Virginia and driven westward.[37]

Early in the afternoon, General Sheridan sent a staff officer to order up the V Corps. Captain George L. Gillespie was also sent to the rear. Gillespie (an engineer and a Sheridan staffer) was directed to turn the head of Warren's column, when it came up, into Gravelly Run Church road. In addition, Gillespie was to "put the Corps in position on this road obliquely to and at a point but a short distance from the White Oak Road and about one mile from the Five Forks.[38]

---

35 *OR* 46, pt. 1, 1104, 1244.

36 Porter, "Five Forks and the Pursuit of Lee," 711-712.

37 Humphreys, *The Virginia Campaign of '65*, 344.

38 *OR* 46, pt. 1, 1104. Sheridan indicated in his "After Action Report" that Gillespie had reconnoitered the area. At Warren's Court of Inquiry, Gillespie testified: ". . . that he had made no reconnaissance of the enemy's works before the attack; that the cavalry had moved directly up the [Dinwiddie] road and gradually pressed the enemy behind his works; that he did not know that there was a return. Nor did he know its direction from the position where the Fifth Corps was [forward formed;] that he was instructed by General Sheridan to select ground

It was 1:00 p.m. when Gillespie reached J. Boisseau's where Warren had his command post. As soon as Warren learned that Sheridan wanted him to order up his infantry, he called for Col. Henry C. Bankhead. The general told the colonel to have the division commanders bring up their units at once. Warren, in an effort to facilitate the movement, specified to Bankhead that Crawford's division would move first, to be followed by Griffin's and then Ayres'.[39]

Galloping off, Bankhead personally gave Crawford and Griffin their marching orders. Since he had been directed to see that the head of the column started off on the correct road, Bankhead sent another officer (either Major Emmor B. Cope or Capt. James W. Wadsworth) to contact General Ayres. In Bankhead's opinion, the orders were obeyed promptly, and "the troops moved out as expeditiously as the nature of the road and the crowded state it was in (being blocked up with led cavalry horses) would admit."[40]

While Bankhead saw that the marching orders were transmitted to the division commanders, Warren went to see Sheridan. Warren wanted "to inform himself of the use to be made of his troops, so that no time would be lost on their arrival." Proceeding up the Dinwiddie Road, Warren visited Sheridan's command post. The cavalry leader tersely explained the tactical situation to Warren and what his plan of operations was. (At this time, Sheridan probably told Warren that the Confederate left flank was anchored near the junction of the Gravelly Run Church and White Oak Roads.) Having satisfied his curiosity, Warren rode back to the junction of the Gravelly Run Church and Dinwiddie Roads. Turning up the Gravelly Run Church road, Warren thoroughly examined the ground where Sheridan had directed him to marshal his corps. To prevent the Confederates from discovering the Union plans, Warren had his escort under Captain Horrell patrol the countryside as far north as the White Oak Road.[41]

Sheridan had told Warren that he wanted him to form his entire corps before sending it to the assault. He wanted to insure a single sledgehammer-like blow instead of a series of piecemeal thrusts. Furthermore, the cavalryman stated "that the formation was to be oblique to the road, with the right advanced, with two divisions in front, and the third in reserve behind the right division." The number

---

which would hold General Warren's Corps close under the right flank of Devin's command and beyond the observation of ht enemy, as he wanted to put Warren in as a turning column." Humphreys, *The Virginia Campaign of '65*, 347.

39 *OR* 46, pt. 1, 829, 831.

40 *Ibid.*, 831.

41 *Ibid.*, 829.

of assault waves and the frontage to be occupied by the corps was left up to Warren. A reconnaissance of the area convinced Warren that it would be best if his two assault divisions advanced in the "equivalent of three lines of battle." Both of the division commanders were to deploy two of their brigades in front, each brigade formed into double line of battle. Their third brigade would be centered behind the first two assault waves. Warren's third division would be posted in column of battalions in mass behind the right division.

General Crawford's division which took the lead when the Corps started for the front reached Gravelly Run Church first. While marching up the Dinwiddie Road, Crawford's vanguard cleared the road of led horses and wagons to enable the column to pass. As soon as he reached the church, Crawford proceeded to deploy his division in accordance with Warren's instructions. Baxter's brigade was formed on the right and Kellogg's on the left; Kellogg's left flank rested on the Gravelly Run Church road. Coulter's brigade was centered behind Baxter's and Kellogg's commands. Each brigade commander formed his unit into double line of battle.[42]

General Griffin's division arrived at Gravelly Run Church close on the heels of Crawford's command. As he rode up, Griffin was met by Warren. Pointing to the ground where he wished Griffin to form his division, Warren remarked that he wished the division commander "to be as expeditious as possible." Griffin would mass his division behind Crawford's. He had Bartlett and Chamberlain form their brigades in triple line of battle. Bartlett was on the left and Chamberlain on the right. Griffin's other brigade (Gregory's) was to report to Chamberlain. Chamberlain had Gregory form one of his regiments (the 188th New York) into line of battle on the right of Chamberlain's brigade. The 189th New York was deployed as skirmishers and took position in front of Chamberlain's command. Gregory's third regiment (the 187th New York) was given the mission of covering Griffin's right flank.[43]

---

42 *Ibid.*, 829, 831, 880, 885, 887, 889-890, 897. Kellogg's first line consisted of the 6th and 7th Wisconsin, the 91st New York formed his second line. Baxter had the 107th Pennsylvania, the 97th New York, and the 39th Massachusetts in his advance line; the 16th Maine and the 11th Pennsylvania formed his rear line. From right to left, Coulter's first line consisted of the 56th and 88th Pennsylvania Consolidated and the 94th New York. His second line had the 147th New York on the right, the 95th New York in the center, and the 181st and 142nd Pennsylvania Consolidated on the left.

43 *Ibid.*, 830, 832, 838, 850, 854, 860. Chamberlain's brigade was massed in three lines of battle. Bartlett likewise formed his brigade into three lines of two battalions each; one small regiment was deployed as skirmishers in front, and one regiment (the 155th Pennsylvania) was held in reserve.

Ayres' division, the smallest in Warren's Corps, reached the marshaling area last. Warren was waiting for Ayres when he rode up. Calling to the division commander, Warren requested him "to form his troops as expeditiously as possible, because General Sheridan desired to attack the enemy immediately." While Ayres was engaged in deploying his division on the west side of the Gravelly Run Church road, Warren again urged his subordinate to hurry.[44]

In forming his command, Ayres deployed Bowerman's Maryland brigade on the left and Gwyn's brigade on the right. Winthrop's brigade was centered behind the two advance brigades. All of Ayres' brigades formed into double line of battle. Skirmishers were advanced by Bowerman and Gwyn. The Gravelly Run Church road separated Gwyn's right from Crawford's left.[45]

General Crawford's division had been placed on the right of the Gravelly Run Church road. If "the return" in the Confederate line were located where Warren had been led to believe it was, Crawford's center would strike it and be the first to enter the works. In case Crawford was unable to carry the "return," Griffin would be there to sustain him and to take advantage of any success scored. General Ayres was to engage the Confederate troops holding the earthworks paralleling the White Oak Road and prevent reinforcements from being rushed to the unit (Ransom's brigade) holding "the return."[46]

When they moved to the attack, Warren directed his division commanders "to keep closed to the left and to preserve their direction in the woods, by keeping the sun, then shining brightly, in the same position over their left shoulders."[47]

The total length of the front occupied by the V Corps was about 1,000 yards. In the three days since crossing Rowanty Creek, Warren had seen the effective strength of his corps shrink from about 15,000 to 12,000 officers and men. In addition to the battle casualties and the men on detached service, many of soldiers had straggled.[48]

While the division commanders were placing their units, Warren prepared a sketch map depicting the presumed tactical situation. Copies of this document were distributed to the division commanders. According to Colonel James W. Forsyth,

---

44 *Ibid.*, 832.

45 *Ibid.*, 832, 869, 872, 874, 875. Gwyn's initial battle line was composed of: the 3rd and 4th Delaware, the 157th and 191st Pennsylvania. The 210th Pennsylvania constituted the second line. The 190th Pennsylvania was thrown forward as skirmishers.

46 Humphreys, *The Virginia Campaign of '65*, 346.

47 *OR* 46, pt. 1, 830.

48 *Ibid.*

Sheridan's chief of staff, the cavalry leader also saw a copy of Warren's diagram and instructions. The division commanders were told, as far as time would permit, to explain the map to their brigade commanders. Attached to the sketch was a brief outline of Sheridan's plan of attack. Warren informed his generals that the corps was to advance in a northwestwardly direction until it reached the White Oak Road. It would then wheel to the left and take a position at right angles to the road. As soon as the infantry was engaged, Custer's and Devin's cavalrymen were to charge. At this stage of the operations, Warren observed all the cavalry except Mackenzie's division was on the left of the V Corps. Mackenzie's troopers were reported to be advancing westward along the White Oak Road.[49]

Throughout the time that his corps was deploying, Warren "used all the exertions possible to hasten" his troops' arrival at the point of departure. To Warren, it seemed that everything was working smoothly and the soldiers "marched at once to their assigned positions without a halt."[50]

The ground on which the corps formed was rough and wooded, and cut up by numerous ravines. In addition, it was out of sight of the Confederate works, so that the direction of advance ordered depended solely upon the roadways and the supposed location of the Confederate fortifications along the White Oak Road. It was about 2:00 p.m. when General Griffin received instructions to move to the marshaling area. To reach Gravelly Run Church from the position occupied. Griffin's troops had to march about two and one-half miles along a narrow, woody road. Consequently, from the time (1:00 p.m.) that Sheridan issued his orders to bring up the V Corps, until Warren had completed his dispositions, slightly over three hours had elapsed. Most observers agreed that this was not an unreasonable length of time "when it is remembered that the length of the Corps was such, when stretched out on the road, that the leading file must have arrived on the new ground before the rear file quitted the old."[51]

During this time, Sheridan visited Warren and expressed his "apprehension that the cavalry which continued to fire on the enemy, would use up all their ammunition" before the V Corps was ready to advance. Replying, Warren told Sheridan that it would be 4:00 p.m. before he could complete his dispositions. Warren, however, remarked that he "was ready to move at once with whatever was at hand if Sheridan directed, and let the rest follow." Sheridan, wanting to strike one tremendous blow with his entire command, refused. Warren felt that Sheridan's

49 *Ibid.*, Swan, "The Five Forks Campaign," 376.

50 *OR* 46, pt. 1, 831.

51 Swan, "The Five Forks Campaign," 374-375; Powell, *The Fifth Army Corps*, 802.

"impatience was no greater apparently" than his own. The commander of the V Corps tried, however, to repress his impatience and prevent any outburst, which "would tend to impair confidence in the proposed operations" by the troops involved.[52]

Sheridan, however, saw things differently. Riding over to Gravelly Run Church, he reported that he found the V Corps "coming up very slowly." The cavalryman observed in his "After Action Report":

> I was exceedingly anxious to attack at once, for the sun was getting low, and we had to fight or go back. It was no place to entrench, and it would have been shameful to have gone back with no results to compensate for the loss of the brave men who had fallen during the day.[53]

To the impatient Sheridan, it appeared that Warren was not exerting himself to get his Corps up and into position. Sheridan felt that Warren gave "the impression that he wished the sun to go down before the dispositions for the attack could be completed."[54]

Warren, in his "After Action Report," hotly denied this implication on his military character. He wrote:

> Against General Sheridan's most ungenerous statement that I gave him the impression that I wanted the sun to go down, I simply place my denial, and trust that my whole conduct in life, and especially in this war, sustains me in it. The sun did not set until two hours and a half after the formation was completed.[55]

The trouble between the two generals was their conflicting personalities. Just because Warren, the introvert, didn't ride around "swearing and cursing at a fearful rate," he was dragging his feet, in Sheridan's opinion.[56]

While the V Corps was getting into position at Gravelly Run Church, Sheridan learned that Meade had pulled back the left flank of General Humphreys' II Corps. Instead of fronting the White Oak Road, Miles' division now held a line covering the Boydton Plank Road. This retirement on the part of the left flank division of the

---

52 *OR* 46, pt. 1, 831.

53 *Ibid.*, 1105.

54 *Ibid.*

55 *Ibid.*, 831.

56 Porter, "The Fifth Corps at the Battle of Five Forks," 250.

II Corps disturbed Sheridan. He was afraid that a strong Rebel column might march down the White Oak Road and strike Warren's Corps in the flank and rear. If the Confederates adopted this course of action, it would frustrate Sheridan's plans. To deal with this possibly dangerous situation, Sheridan ordered up Mackenzie's division.[57]

Following the receipt of the eagerly awaited instructions to move to the front, Mackenzie put his division into motion. Mackenzie's troopers proceeded up the Adams and Dinwiddie Roads to J. Boisseau's. Here, Mackenzie turned his column into the Crump Road. In accordance with Sheridan's orders, Mackenzie planned to establish a roadblock on the White Oak Road. If Mackenzie were able to carry out this task, he could afford a measure of protection to Warren's exposed flank.[58]

As Mackenzie's division rode up the Crump Road, Col. Samuel F. Spear's brigade took the lead. Spear used Maj. James E. McFarlan's battalion of the 11th Pennsylvania Cavalry to screen his advance. About one-half mile south of the White Oak Road, the Pennsylvanians encountered Confederate pickets. Driving in the outposts, the bluecoats "soon developed a considerable force" of Roberts' North Carolinians. The Confederates were posted in a line of rifle pits in the edge of a wood along the White Oak Road with an open field to their front. Preparatory to attacking, Major McFarlan deployed Companies G and H to the right and left of the Crump Road. The troopers of these two units remained on their horses. Next, McFarlan dismounted Companies B and F. These men were posted farther to the right and left in the woods. The rest of the regiment closed on the advance guard.[59]

As soon as the Pennsylvanians completed their dispositions, General Mackenzie ordered them to engage the Rebels. Observing that the rapid fire delivered by his cavalrymen (the 11th Pennsylvania was armed with Spencer carbines) kept the grey clads pinned own, Mackenzie placed himself at the head of Maj. Robert S. Monroe's battalion (Companies A, C, E and K). When Mackenzie gave the word, the Pennsylvanians charged in column of fours. At first, the Federals thundered through the field on the left of the road. Suddenly, the column cut across the road and struck the left flank of Roberts' position. Led by Mackenzie, the Pennsylvanians poured over the works and into the White Oak Road beyond. In the face of this onset, the North Carolinians fell back in confusion.[60]

---

57 *OR* 46, pt. 1, 1105.

58 *Ibid.*, 1105, 1244.

59 *Ibid.*, 1254.

60 *Ibid.*, 1254-1255.

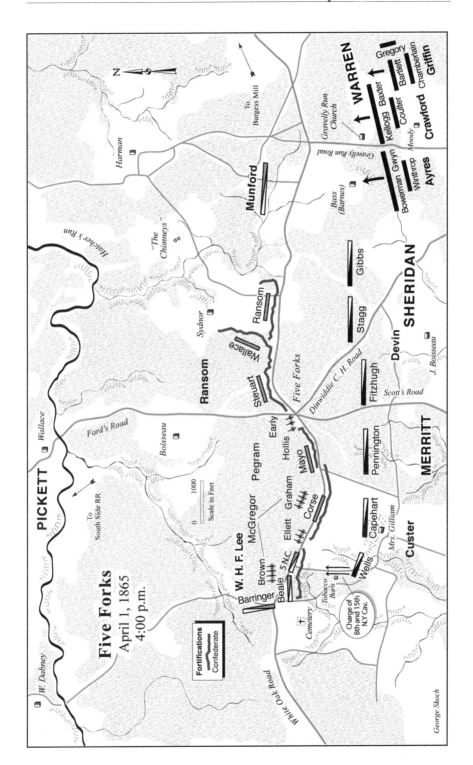

Five Forks
April 1, 1865
4:00 p.m.

Fortifications
Confederate

Scale in Feet
0   1000

N

George Skoch

Colonel Thomas T. Munford
USAHEC

The remainder of the 11th Pennsylvania supported the daring charge, and reached the Rebel line close on Mackenzie's heels. Following the Union breakthrough, the North Carolinians scattered. Some of the Rebels fell back to the west and joined Pickett's task force at Five Forks; the rest made their way eastward and joined General Anderson. After mopping up several pockets of resistance, Mackenzie mustered his command. Except for the loss of several valuable officers, the rout of Roberts' brigade had cost the Yankees a relatively small number of casualties.[61]

When he was informed of Mackenzie's smashing success, Sheridan issued a new set of instructions. After detaching a small force to watch the White Oak Road, Mackenzie was to join Sheridan. After detailing a battalion of the 5th Pennsylvania Cavalry to man the roadblock on the White Oak Road, Mackenzie started for Five Forks. The 1st Maryland took the lead as the division rode westward along the White Oak Road. Just as Mackenzie was getting ready to order the Marylanders to charge, the V Corps came pouring across the road. Mackenzie accordingly halted his command.[62]

The deployment of Warren's V Corps in the fields at the Gravelly Run Church had been bold and unconcealed. Munford, who was charged with guarding the left flank of the Confederate main line of resistance, watched these preparations. He

---

61 *Ibid.*, 1244, 1254-1255. Among the casualties were Capt. William Lancaster, killed, and Maj. Robert B. Monroe and Lt. Oscar S. Mathews, mortally wounded. In addition, Colonel Spear was wounded in the mopping up operations.

62 *Ibid.*, 1105, 1244.

sent courier after courier to tell either Pickett or Fitz Lee that the Yankees were getting ready to strike. Neither general could be found. Nobody seemed to know where the generals had gone; no instructions had been left regarding the forwarding of dispatches. Capt. Henry C. Lee of Fitz Lee's staff vainly rode the length of the line without learning any more than the baffled messengers.[63]

Each of the unit commanders, on his own responsibility, undertook to get ready to resist the impending onslaught. In this, they did not always co-operate with one another. Subsequently, Munford recalled:

> All this time Warren's swarming blue lines were plainly visible from the White Oak Road, forming into line and preparing to assault Pickett's left; Devin's partially dismounted cavalry was keeping up a sharp continuous fire along the whole of our infantry front, as if preparing to attack our right, and Custer's dismounted division was demonstrating. . . . And I was still without orders.

To prepare for the attack that he knew was certain to come, Munford dismounted and deployed his division on the left of Ransom's refused flank. A few "pens" built of rails from nearby fences were thrown up by Munford's troopers, and the inevitable attack dourly awaited.[64]

*   *   *

As soon as Ayres had completed his dispositions (which was about 4:15, or within 15 minutes of the hour designated by Warren), the order was given for the V Corps to attack. When the advance began, Generals Sheridan and Warren, and Colonel Porter rode at the head of Ayres' division. Pressing forward, the Union battle line marched through the belt of woods north of Gravelly Run Church. Entering the fields which surrounded the Barnes house, the skirmishers covering the advance of the V Corps flushed and drove in the Confederate outposts. Before he reached the woods on the far side of the field, a staff officer told Ayres "that there were indications of the enemy off to the left front." Growing apprehensive of an attack on his left, Ayres alerted Winthrop to be ready to bring up his brigade should the division be attacked. Shortly thereafter, Warren's troops burst across the White Oak Road. Here, the corps encountered General Mackenzie's cavalry

63 Freeman, *Lee's Lieutenants*, vol. 3, 670.

64 *Ibid.*, 670-671.

division. The troopers had arrived in this area a jump ahead of the infantry.[65] Reporting to Sheridan, Mackenzie was ordered to strike out toward Hatcher's Run. He would then turn west and get possession of the Ford's Church road. In addition, Mackenzie would cover the right flank of the V Corps.

Warren now realized that his corps had crossed the White Oak Road east of the left flank of the Confederate main line of resistance. To make it more perplexing, Crawford's troops (marching more quickly than Ayres), had crossed the road first. Already the two divisions had started to diverge. Warren thought it was probable that Pickett's defensive line was posted in the edge of the woods about 300 yards north of the road. He accordingly continued to lead his corps in a northwesterly direction.[66]

Almost immediately after Ayres' division crossed the White Oak Road and entered the field beyond, his troops received small-arms fire from the west. This fire originated with Ransom's North Carolina brigade, which was holding the refused flank of Pickett's defense line. The Federal officers now realized that the Confederate entrenchments did not extend as far east as they had assumed. Warren had been led to believe that the Rebel left was anchored near the junction of the Gravelly Run Church and White Oak Roads. Neither Capt. Gillespie nor Warren's escort had made any effort to ascertain the exact resting place of the Southerners' left. The Federal brass evidently felt that if they undertook any reconnaissance activity in this sector, it might put the Confederates on their guard and betray the plan of attack.[67]

Fortunately for Ayres' left flank unit (Bowerman's brigade), Ransom's grey clads were stationed in a thick belt of woods which, as Warren later recalled, made their fire, less than usually destructive," because the heavy vegetation disrupted their aim. Furthermore, the refused flank which faced the Federals was comparatively short—less than 150 yards. Understanding the tactical situation, Ayres immediately changed front to the left and faced "the return." In carrying out this maneuver, Bowerman's brigade faced and filed to the left. Ayres called up Winthrop's brigade from the reserve. Winthrop's troops moved into position on Bowerman's left on the double. His disposition completed, Ayres led his division to the attack. Ayres' battle line of "weather-beaten" veterans moved down the slope

65 OR 46, pt. 1, 832, 869; Humphreys, *The Virginia Campaign of '65*, 347; Porter, "Five Forks and the Pursuit of Lee," 713; Swan, "The Five Forks Campaign," 378; Porter, "Fifth Corps at the Battle of Five Forks," 250.

66 OR 46, pt. 1, 832, 869; Humphreys, *The Virginia Campaign of '65*, 347; Swan, "The Five Forks Campaign," 378.

67 *Ibid.*

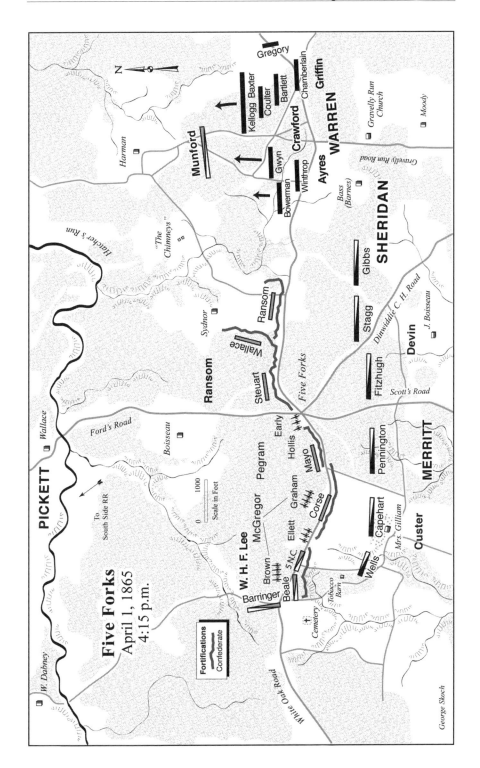

Five Forks
April 1, 1865
4:15 p.m.

George Skoch

toward the woods with a steady swing that boded no good for Pickett's task force, earthworks or no earthworks.[68]

Ayres' rapid change of front caused his right flank brigade, Gwyn's, to get well ahead of Crawford's division. Since Ayres' division was the pivot in the V Corps' wheel to the left, his troops had a shorter distance to move than the others. This was dangerous, because it exposed Gwyn's troops to possible flank attack. Gwyn's soldiers sensed this; there was some wavering in the ranks. Subsequently, Ayres confessed that he experienced anxiety when he learned that his right flank was resting in the air.[69]

Sheridan seemed to be omnipresent as Ayres's troops charged "the return." When Ransom's North Carolinians opened fire, Ayres' blue clads faltered for an instant. Observing this, Sheridan put the spurs to his horse and galloped along the battle line from left to right, shouting words of encouragement. Colonel Porter recalled that Sheridan called out, "Go at 'em with a will. Move on at a clean jump or you'll not catch one of them. They're all getting ready to run now, and if you don't get on them in five minutes, they'll every one get away from you! Now go for them."

Just then, one of the skirmishers was hit in the neck; blood spurted as if the jugular vein had been cut. "I'm killed!" the soldier cried, as he slumped to the ground. "You're not hurt a bit," Sheridan cried, "pick up your gun, man, and move right on to the front." Such was the electric effect of Sheridan's words that the wounded soldier snatched up his rifled-musket and rushed forward a dozen paces before he collapsed, never to rise again.[70]

At the time of Warren's assault, Sheridan was mounted on his favorite black horse, "Rienzi." This was the steed that had carried the general from Winchester to Cedar Creek. Colonel Porter remembered that, on April 1:

> The roads were muddy, the fields swampy, the undergrowth dense, and "Rienzi," as he plunged and curveted, dashed the foam from his mouth and the mud from his heels. Had the Winchester pike been in a similar condition, he would not have made his famous twenty miles without breaking his own neck and Sheridan's too.

68 OR 46, pt. 1, 869; Porter, "Five Forks and the Pursuit of Lee," 713; Powell, *The Fifth Army Corps*, 803.

69 OR 46, pt. 1, 832, 869.

70 Porter, "Five Forks and the Pursuit of Lee," 713.

Sheridan watched when Gwyn's troops started to recoil. Dashing into the midst of the broken lines, Sheridan called out, "Where is my battle flag?" As the color-sergeant rode up, Sheridan seized the crimson and white standard. Brandishing the colors, the general shouted words of encouragement to the infantrymen, and urged them to close their ranks. All this time, the minies were humming through the air, like a swarm of bees. One pierced the battle flag; another killed the color-sergeant, yet another wounded Capt. Andrew J. McGonnigle in the side, others cut down two or three of the staff-officers' horses.[71]

In his successful effort to rally Gwyn's soldiers, Sheridan dashed from one part of the line to another, "waving his flag, shaking his fist, encouraging, threatening, praying, swearing, the very incarnation of battle." Porter recalled, "It would be a sorry soldier who could help following such a leader."[72]

Ayres and his officers were also equal to the challenge. Recklessly exposing themselves, they quickly had the situation under control. Drawing his saber, Ayres led his shouting soldiers forward. His veterans, "who now behaved as if they had fallen back to get a 'good-ready'," eagerly followed the general. With fixed bayonets and a rousing cheer, the infantrymen dashed toward the breastworks protecting "the return." Since the entrenched section of Pickett's main line of resistance which faced east was only about 150 yards in length, Ayres' right flank, Gwyn's brigade, overlapped it

Even before the Yankees reached the works, a number of Ransom's North Carolinians lost their nerve and took to their heels. Realizing that it would be impossible to stop the flood of Federals, the gunners of McGregor's battery limbered up their four pieces. The artillerists, applying the whips to their horses, pulled out of the earthworks in the nick of time. Sweeping everything before them, Ayres' combat-ready infantry came storming over the works. The color-sergeant of the 190th Pennsylvania gained the distinction of planting the first stand of colors on the breastworks. All of Ransom's North Carolinians who declined to flee were killed or captured. Ayres' troops had seized "the return," the key to Pickett's position.[73]

Sheridan spurred "Reinzi" up to the angle. With a mighty leap, the horse carried his rider over the works, and landed in the middle of a line of Confederates

---

71 *Ibid.*; pt. 1, 869.

72 Porter, "Five Forks and the Pursuit of Lee," 713.

73 *Ibid.*; OR 46, pt. 1, 869-876. The return" was between 700 and 800 yards west of the junction of the Gravelly Run Church and White Oak Roads, instead of in the vicinity of the junction. Powell, *The Fifth Army Corps*, 804.

who had thrown down their arms and were cowering behind the earthworks. Several of the Rebels called out, "What do you want us-all to go to?" The general's "rage turned to humor, and he had a running talk with the 'Johnnies' as they filed past." "Go right over there," Sheridan said, gesturing toward the rear. Continuing, the general kept up a steady banter. "Get right along, now. Drop your guns; you'll never need them any more. You'll all be safe over there. Are there any more of you? We want every one of your fellows."[74]

In addition to seizing the key to the Confederate position, Ayres' troops had captured over 1,000 prisoners and a number of battle flags. The Yankees, however, had not emerged unscathed from the attack on "the return." Among the Union casualties were two of Ayres' three brigade commanders, Colonels Winthrop and Bowerman. The former was mortally and the latter severely wounded. Colonel James Grindley of the 146th New York took temporary charge of Winthrop's unit, while Col. David L. Stanton of the 1st Maryland assumed command of the Maryland brigade.[75]

Shortly after Sheridan entered the works, his orderly rode up and announced, "Colonel Forsyth of your staff is killed, sir." "It's no such a thing," cried Sheridan, "I don't believe a word of it. You'll find Forsyth's all right," he continued. Inside of the next ten minutes, Forsyth rode up. Sheridan then learned that it was colonel Winthrop who had fallen in the attack on "the return." The general did not appear surprised when he saw Forsyth. "There! I told you so," he exclaimed when Forsyth appeared.[76]

Instead of allowing Ayres to press ahead, Sheridan ordered him to halt and reform his division. While officers regrouped their units, patrols mopped up scattered pockets of resistance that had been isolated by the breakthrough. As soon as it became apparent that the Confederate line had given way, Ayres was directed to resume the advance. When the division again moved off, it swept the ground

---

74 Porter, "Five Forks and the Pursuit of Lee," 713.

75 *OR* 46, pt. 1, 569, 870-873. Colonel Grindley reported that his brigade captured four stand of colors. Four enlisted men (Cpl. August Kauss of the 15th New York Heavy Artillery, Sgt. Robert F. Shipley of the 140th New York, and Sgt. Thomas J. Murphy and Pvt. David Edwards of the 146th New York), were recommended for and received the Medal of Honor for capturing these flags. Colonel Stanton credited his command with capturing two stand of colors. Lieutenant Jacob Keogle of the 7th Maryland and Pvt. Joseph Stewart of the 1st Maryland received the Medal of Honor for this feat. Gwyn's brigade also captured two battle flags.

76 Porter, "Five Forks and the Pursuit of Lee," 713-714.

behind and on either side of the Rebel fortifications. Holding his men in hand, with Grindley's brigade in the lead, Ayres' division marched westward.[77]

When the Confederates in "the return" opened fire on Ayres' division, Warren observed that the fight at the angle would fall on Ayres, and not Crawford as planned. Warren sent a staffer to instruct Crawford "to oblique his division to the left and close up this interval." As soon as Warren pinpointed Ransom's left flank, he called for Major Cope. The major was told to contact Griffin. On doing so, Cope was to direct Griffin "to bring his division toward the White Oak Road, by the left flank, in order to be in better supporting distance" of Ayres' command.[78]

When Ayres changed direction to the left, Warren was not the only senior officer who knew Crawford and Griffin were "getting too far away." Ayres knew it. He sent a message for Griffin "to come up on his right." Griffin also knew it. His practiced ear told him that the battle had opened. Leaving his division for a moment, he rode at full speed to Ayres' command post and asked, "What is up?" "Nothing much," replied Ayres, "nothing new; the same old story. Crawford has gone off and left me to fight alone." Griffin, after promising to see if he could do something to help his comrade, hastened off after his division.

Sheridan also sent orders for Crawford and Griffin to come in on Ayres' right.[79]

In the meantime, Warren had established a temporary command post in the field east of "the return." Pending the return of his aides, Warren did not feel justified in shifting his position. Here, he could get information from all points at once, and utilize the many eyes of his staff and those of his commanders, instead of giving all his attention to a particular point to the neglect of others. In Warren's opinion, the time had not arrived for him to place himself at the head of an assaulting column. The dynamic Sheridan, however, had a different view. He felt that Warren should be leading and lending encouragement to his troops.[80]

After a few minutes had elapsed and he had heard nothing from the staff officers he had sent to get in touch with Crawford and Griffin, Warren became convinced that their divisions "must have passed on beyond" General Ayres' right. Leaving several members of his staff at his command post with instructions to contact him if anything important developed, Warren went to look for Crawford's and Griffin's divisions. As he approached the "Chimneys," the general was fired

---

77 *OR* 46, pt. 1, 870.

78 *Ibid.*, 832-833, 837; Humphreys, *The Virginia Campaign of '65*, 348.

79 Swan, "The Five Forks Campaign," 396.

80 *OR* 46, pt. 1, 833.

upon. He subsequently learned that these were the volleys which caused Gwyn's brigade to recoil.[81]

Notwithstanding Warren's diagram and orders to swing to the left on reaching the White Oak Road, Crawford's division had continued to barge ahead. The division passed several hundred yards beyond the road before it began to wheel to the left. After changing directions, Crawford's skirmishers encountered and drove in a few of Munford's pickets. The division's line of advance "led through bogs, tangled woods, and thickets of pine, interspersed with open spaces here and there, Crawford's left flank brigade (Kellogg's) lost contact with Ayres' division.[82]

General Warren, while en route to the "Chimneys," encountered Kellogg's brigade. Just as the general rode up, Kellogg's unit had pivoted to the left and taken position at right angles to its line of advance. Warren accordingly ordered Kellogg to hold this ground—it was in a clearing—until another brigade could come up and form on his right. The general then passed on into the woods in search of Crawford. Warren, however, was unable to locate his missing division commander. Nevertheless, the general sent one staff officer after another into the woods. They were to tell Crawford to wheel his other two brigades to the left and close upon Kellogg's brigade.

When Warren emerged from the wood, he discovered that Kellogg's brigade had disappeared. Sheridan, alarmed at this "wandering off," had sent several staff officers to recall Crawford. One of these, finding Kellogg standing idle, had ordered him forward.

Advancing rapidly, Kellogg's brigade swept through the Sydnor field. As Kellogg's battle line approached the Sydnor house, one of Munford's combat patrols stationed inside opened fire. The Confederates succeeded in momentarily checking Kellogg's advance. In a successful effort to get his stalled advance rolling, Kellogg ordered Colonel Tarbell of the 91st New York to bring up one of his battalions from the reserves. Tarbell came up on the double and deployed his New Yorkers on the left of Kellogg's battle line. Taking position, Tarbell's battalion engaged Munford's dismounted troopers at short range.[83]

As soon as Tarbell's New Yorkers dislodged the Rebels from the house, the advance was resumed. Kellogg's march to the west was rapid, because by the time

81 *Ibid.*

82 *Ibid*, 880; Powell, *The Fifth Army Corps*, 804.

83 *OR* 46, pt. 1, 885, 887; Swan, "The Five Forks Campaign," 397.

the rest of Crawford's division entered Sydnor's field, his unit had vanished into the woods on the far side.[84]

In the meantime, Major Cope had contacted Crawford. When the major found the general, he was east of the "Chimneys." In accordance with Cope's instructions, Crawford swung Baxter's brigade around to come in on Kellogg's right, Coulter following. Unable to find Kellogg's brigade, which had moved off, Crawford advanced toward the "Chimneys." On doing so, he called up Coulter's brigade and formed it on Baxter's left. Crawford's division then moved westward, driving in Munford's dismounted troopers. This opposition, however, caused the division to continue to bear to the northwest.[85]

Because the countryside was heavily wooded, troops moving rapidly through it could not be readily overtaken. After Crawford's and Griffin's divisions had wheeled to the left, their commands entered the open ground at the northern end of the R. Sydnor farm. This was about 800 yards north of "the return." It was here (at the "Chimneys") that Warren finally got in touch with General Griffin.[86]

Griffin's First Division had started off from the Gravelly Run Church behind Crawford's command. As the division swept toward the White Oak Road, it drifted toward the east. By the time Griffin's troops crossed the road, they had been uncovered. They now forged ahead of Crawford's division, which was at this time on their left. In accordance with the instructions he had received, Griffin wheeled his division to the left after it crossed the White Oak Road.[87]

Pushing ahead, Griffin's skirmishers easily drove in Munford's outposts. After his people had advanced a mile without encountering any fortifications, Griffin sensed that something had gone wrong. When the sound of heavy firing began to roll in from the left, Griffin halted his division in the wood northeast of Sydnor's field. By this time, Crawford's division had dropped out of line and veered off to the right. General Chamberlain, whose brigade was on the right of Griffin's battle line, recalled:

> Our instructions were to keep closed to the left on Bartlett's brigade, and also to wheel to the left in moving, the design being to strike the enemy in flank. We advanced through an open wood with nothing but light skirmishes in our front for some time.

84 Swan, "The Five Forks Campaign," 397.

85 *Ibid.*, 398.

86 Humphreys, *The Virginia Campaign of '65*, 349; OR 46, pt. 1, 833.

87 *Ibid.*, 838.

The constant change of direction to the left made the march on the right flank exceedingly rapid.

General Bartlett had also been troubled when he observed that the firing to his left was steadily increasing in tempo. Riding to the left, the general entered Sydnor's field. On the opposite side of the cleared area, Bartlett saw distinctly the Confederate left flank.[88]

In the meantime, General Griffin had made a personal reconnaissance. From Sydnor's field, the general watched the Rebel movement along the White Oak Road. About this time, Major Cope rode up. Hailing Griffin, the major told the general that Warren wanted him "to bring his division toward the White Oak Road, by the left flank." Griffin directed his three brigade commanders to face their men to the left. Before these instructions reached General Bartlett, however, all of his brigade, with the exception of three regiments (the 1st Michigan, the 20th Maine, and the 155th Pennsylvania), had drifted off to the right and joined Crawford's division.[89]

Placing himself at the head of Bartlett's three regiments, Griffin marched across Sydnor's field. When Chamberlain saw the division flag moving to the left, he followed with his command and the 188th New York of Gregory's brigade. Before Griffin proceeded far, he encountered Warren near the "Chimneys." Warred directed his subordinate to attack the Confederates holding the angle. The Corps commander then rode back to Ayres' position. By the time Warren reached the White Oak Road, Ayres' soldiers had stormed "the return."[90]

Since the capture of "the return" rendered Griffin's presence at that point superfluous, Warren decided to change the mission he had assigned the First Division. Major Cope was sent galloping off with instructions for Griffin to alter his line of march. Griffin was to push westward and attempt to get astride the Ford's Church road. By the time Cope reached Griffin, his division had nearly crossed Sydnor's field. Following the receipt of these fresh instructions, Griffin wheeled his division to the right. When the advance was renewed, the division's line of march was parallel to, and north of the White Oak Road.[91]

---

88 *Ibid.*, 838, 850, 861.

89 *Ibid.*, 837-838, 861.

90 *Ibid.*, 832, 837-838, 850. Chamberlain's brigade marched out of the woods by the left flank and, passing southeast of the "Chimneys," proceeded up the ravine in the direction of the firing. Swan, "The Five Forks Campaign," 398.

91 *Ibid.*, 837-838.

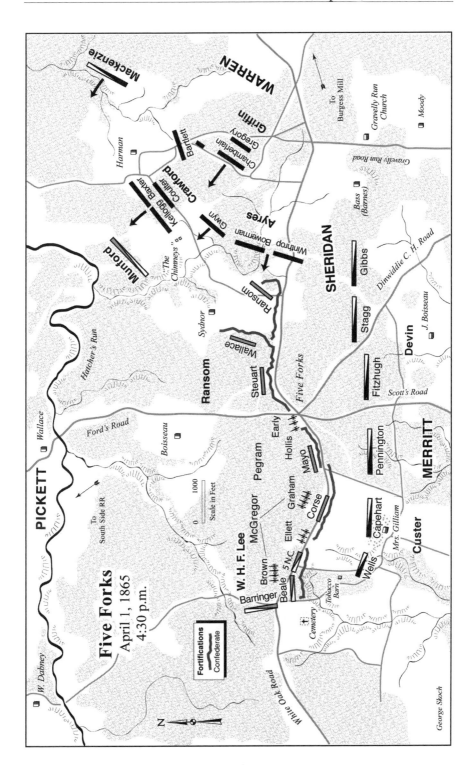

Five Forks
April 1, 1865
4:30 p.m.

After moving forward about three quarters of a mile, Griffin's troops encountered a strong force of Confederates, posted in the woods at the western edge of Sydnor's field. On being routed from "the return," the survivors of Ransom's brigade had fallen back toward Five Forks. The collapse of Ransom's North Carolinians had made Wallace's position untenable. Wallace's grey clads therefore hurriedly evacuated the rifle pits west of the angle. Wallace's retreat, in turn, had uncovered Steuart's position. In an effort to contain the Union breakthrough, the three brigadiers sought to establish a reorganized defense line in the timber on the west side of Sydnor's field. Besides protecting Five Forks, this position covered the vital Ford's Church road. Their new line was at right angles to the fortifications paralleling the White Oak Road. Light field works were hurriedly thrown up by the Confederates.[92]

In moving against the reorganized Confederate main line of resistance, Chamberlain's brigade (reinforced by the 188th New York) constituted the left wing and Bartlett's brigade the right wing of Griffin's battle line. Two of Gregory's regiments (the 187th and 189th New York) followed along behind. Advancing on the double, Griffin's soldiers "moved up rapidly under the crest of a hill." When Chamberlain gave the word, his eager troops charged the works, and tore a gaping hole in the Rebel line. The right wing of Chamberlain's command—the 185th New York and Maj. Edwin A. Glenn's battalion of the 198th Pennsylvania—poured through the hole and drove toward the White Oak Road. At the same time, the 188th New York and Capt. David L. Stanton's battalion of the 198th Pennsylvania maintained heavy pressure on the greyclads' front.[93]

Bartlett's three regiments hit the Confederate line a short distance to the right of Chamberlain's breakthrough. Encountering fierce resistance, Bartlett's right flank recoiled. One of Bartlett's regiments, the 155th Pennsylvania, was bested by the Confederates in a desperate hand-to-hand encounter in which the clubbed musket was freely used. To escape the galling fire poured into their ranks by the Rebels, a number of Bartlett's soldiers sought cover behind the rifle pits carried by Chamberlain's troops.

Union officers realized that if the frightened men were allowed to take cover in the earthworks, they would be helpless in case of a determined Confederate counterstroke. It took "the utmost personal effort of every general and staff officer

---

92 *Ibid.*, 839, 850; Humphreys, *The Virginia Campaign of '65*, 349.

93 OR 46, pt. 1, 850, 854, 856. At first, the 187th and 189th New York had been deployed as skirmishers. When Griffin advanced against the new Confederate line, the skirmishers were recalled. By the time that the officers in charge of the 187th and 189th New York mustered their troops, the rest of the division had moved off.

present" to rally Bartlett's troops. As soon as the men had been reformed, they deployed at right angles to the captured works. When Chamberlain learned of Bartlett's difficulties, he rushed the 185th and 188th New York to his comrade's assistance. Passing to the rear of the 1st Michigan and the 20th Maine, the New Yorkers advanced to the attack. Bartlett's troops, seeing that help was on the way, took heart and pressed ahead. The thick woods, in conjunction with the ebb and flow of the battle, caused Griffin's units to become badly scrambled. Nevertheless, this fresh Union push proved too much for Steuart's, Ransom's, and Wallace's battered brigades. Abandoning the fight, the Southerners fled the field, leaving about 1,500 prisoners and several battle flags in the hands of the victorious Unionists.[94]

Meantime, Bartlett and Chamberlain, assisted by several staff officers, rounded up a large number of stragglers (between 150 and 200) who were cowering in the edge of the woods. These men were reorganized and pushed back into the fray. While engaged in this disagreeable business, Chamberlain sighted Colonel Gwyn's headquarters flag in the open field in his rear. The general sent one of his staff officers, Lt. George C. Fisher, to ask Gwyn to come to his assistance. Gwyn cheerfully fell in with Chamberlain's suggestion. Leading his brigade forward, Gwyn arrived in time to contribute to the Confederate downfall.[95]

Griffin did not pause to let his men celebrate their success. Instead, he had his generals reform their brigades at right angles to the White Oak Road. Resuming the advance, Griffin's division drove westward, mopping up die-hard Confederates as it advanced. At Five Forks, Griffin's soldiers met Fitzhugh's and Pennington's dismounted troopers, who had just carried the Rebel fortifications at this point. On the right, Bartlett's troops gained the Ford's Church Road and captured a train of ambulances and wagons. Ayres' division reached Five Forks on the heels of Griffin's combat-ready bluecoats.[96]

Meanwhile, Crawford's battle line had advanced across the northern end of Sydnor's field and into the woods beyond. As they forged steadily ahead, Crawford's soldiers drove Munford's dismounted troopers before them. Reaching and crossing the Ford's Church road, Crawford's bluecoats captured seven ambulances and several wagons belonging to Wallace's brigade. These vehicles, along with a large number of prisoners, were sent to the rear. The prisoners were

94 *Ibid.*, 839, 850, 854, 861, 865, 868. The commander of the 20th Maine, Lt. Col. Walter G. Morrill, reported that his regiment captured the colors of the 9th Virginia.

95 *Ibid.*, 850.

96 *Ibid.*, 839, 868.

escorted to the rear so rapidly that Crawford's provost marshal was unable to keep an accurate tally. Kellogg, whose brigade had preceded the division, reported to Crawford.[97]

After Ayres' soldiers had captured "the return," Warren started off once more to see if he could locate Crawford. Tracing Crawford's line or march from Sydnor's field by the wounded coming to the rear, Warren finally located his missing division. When Warren found Crawford, he was on the east side of the Boisseau farm with his division in good order facing west. Without a moment's hesitation, Warren directed Crawford to wheel his division to the left and face it southward. The corps commander knew that with Crawford's division astride the Ford's Church road, he was in possession of one of the two avenues of escape open to Pickett's task force.[98]

As soon as Crawford had completed his dispositions, Warren ordered him to drive on Five Forks. The roar of the Rebel artillery was a clear indication to Warren that the Confederates still held the vital crossroads.[99]

Coulter's brigade was selected to spearhead the attack. Coulter deployed two of his regiments (the 121st and 142d Pennsylvania) on the left of the Ford's Church road, the rest of the brigade was formed on the right of the road. Crawford's two other brigades (Kellogg's and Baxter's) were massed en echelon on Coulter's right. When Warren gave the word, the division took up the advance. As it approached the woods which bounded the Boisseau farm on the south, the Union battle line was greeted by a scathing fire.[100]

Four of Bartlett's regiments (the 16th Michigan, the 1st Maine, and the 91st and 118th Pennsylvania), after becoming separate from their parent unit, had taken position on the right of Crawford's division. Two of the regiments (the 16th Maryland and the 91st Pennsylvania) had crossed and re-crossed Hatcher's Run during the course of the march to Boisseau's field. When Crawford wheeled his division to the left, these two units took position on the right of Baxter's brigade.[101] Three companies of the 1st Maine had also forded Hatcher's Run. Encountering one of Rosser's patrols, the Maine men charged and routed the Rebel horsemen. Re-crossing the stream, the three companies rejoined their comrades. Upon

97 *Ibid.*, 881; Humphreys, *The Virginia Campaign of '65*, 349-350.

98 *OR* 46, pt. 1, 835, 881, 897.

99 *Ibid.*, 835.

100 *Ibid.*, 835, 881, 897.

101 *Ibid.*, 866.

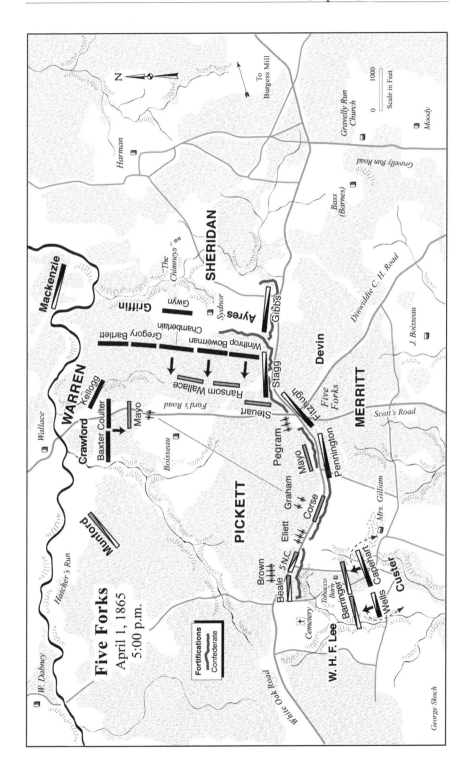

N

To Burgess Mill

0   1000
Scale in Feet

Gravelly Run Church

Moody

Harman

Gravelly Run Road

SHERIDAN

Bass (Barnes)

MacKenzie

The Chimneys

Griffin

Gwyn

Sydnor

Ayres

Gibbs

Dinwiddie C. H. Road

J. Boisseau

Gregory Bartlett

Chamberlain

Winthrop Bowerman

Stagg

Devin

Five Forks

WARREN

Kellogg

Ransom Wallace

MERRITT

Wallace

Baxter Coulter

Mayo

Ford's Road

Stuart

Fitzhugh

Scott's Road

Crawford

Boisseau

Pegram

Mayo

Pennington

Munford

Hatcher's Run

PICKETT

Graham

Corse

Mrs. Gilliam

Ellett

Brown

S.N.C.

Capehart

Beale

Tobacco Barn

Custer

W. Dabney

Five Forks
April 1, 1865
5:00 p.m.

Fortifications
Confederate

Cemetery

Barringer

Wells

W. H. F. Lee

White Oak Road

George Skoch

reaching the Ford's Church road, Warren gave the 1st Maine and the 118th Pennsylvania the task of watching the ford across Hatcher's Run.[102]

Following his sudden departure from the shad-bake, Pickett galloped back across Hatcher's Run. A short distance south of the stream, Pickett sighted a line of Munford's grim cavalrymen facing eastward. They were falling back in the face of Kellogg's lightning-like advance. At this very minute, the Union skirmishers were within 100 yards of the Ford's Church road. Directing the Confederates was Colonel Munford. He was recognized by Pickett, who inquired, "What troops are these?" Munford replied that "they were part of Fitz Lee Division." Taking a second glance at the bluecoats, Pickett implored, "Do hold them back until I can pass to Five Forks."

A young captain in the 3rd Virginia Cavalry, James Breckinridge, heard Pickett's appeal. Placing himself at the head of his command, Breckinridge charged the advancing Federals. This brief counterattack cost Breckinridge his life, but it probably saved Pickett's. The general threw himself forward on his horse, with his head on the side away from the foe, and successfully ran the gauntlet of several hundred yards of furious infantry fire.[103]

Fitz Lee likewise tried to rejoin his troopers by using the route pioneered by Pickett. He was too late. By the time Fitz Lee crossed Hatcher's Run, Kellogg's troops had reached the Ford's Church road. Fired upon, Fitz Lee turned back and attempted to lead Rosser's reserve division toward Five Forks by way of the Ford's Church road. The Confederate troopers, however, were unable to smash the Union roadblock and fell back. Next, Fitz Lee deployed Rosser's division astride the Ford's Church road, north of Hatcher's Run. Rosser was to keep the Federals from reaching the South Side Railroad.[104]

When he reached Five Forks, Pickett, in an effort to contain the Union breakthrough, sought to organize a new main line of resistance. Already, his subordinates, on their own initiative, had established and manned a line parallel to, and east of the Ford's Church road. (At this very moment, the troops holding this position (Ransom's, Steuart's, and Wallace's) were locked in a fierce contest with Griffin's Union division. Having just escaped from Crawford's troops, Picket knew that, unless he blocked the Ford's Church road, his new defense line would quickly be rendered untenable. He accordingly pulled Mayo's Virginia brigade out of the

---

102 *Ibid.*, 863, 867.

103 Freeman, *Lee's Lieutenants*, vol. 3, 669-670.

104 *Ibid.*, 670; pt. 1, 1299-1300; Robert H. Moore II, *Graham's Petersburg, Jackson's Kanawha and Lurty's Roanoke Horse Artillery* (Lynchburg, VA: H. E. Howard, 1966), 32.

entrenchment west of Five Forks. Reinforced by Graham's two guns, Mayo's Confederates moved into position on the double. The Virginians were also joined by stragglers from Ransom's and Wallace's units. Mayo's troops were deployed in the woods to the left and the right of the Ford's Church road. To reach the Confederate position, the Yankees had to cross Boisseau's field. Captain Graham had his gunners unlimber their two pieces near the road. Having completed their disposition, the Rebels grimly awaited Crawford's advance.[105]

As they pressed forward, Coulter's troops "suffered severely" from the fire of Mayo's infantry and Graham's battery. Undaunted, however, they swept steadily ahead. Crawford's other two brigades (Baxter's and Kellogg's) and two of Bartlett's regiments (the 16th Michigan and the 91st Pennsylvania) supported Coulter's drive down the Ford's Church road. Entering the woods at the south end of Boisseau's field, Coulter's troops smashed Mayo's brigade. A large number of Mayo's Virginians threw down their arms, and the remainder retreated in a southwesterly direction. (When Mayo's troops broke, the Confederates still held Five Forks.) Reaching Gilliam's field, Colonel Mayo succeeded in partially reforming the portions of his brigade that had survived the debacle. Pickett, observing the condition of the brigade, ordered Mayo to get across country to the South Side Railroad. Mayo's troops reached the railroad without further adventure "in great disorder."[106]

Besides taking a large number of Mayo's infantry, Coulter's troops captured Graham's two guns. A large number of ambulances also fell into the Federals' hands at this point.[107]

Following the rout of Mayo's brigade, Warren directed Crawford to oblique his division to the right. Warren wanted to place Crawford's troops astride the White Oak Road to the west of Five Forks. If he could do this, the last avenue of retreat open to Pickett's task force would be closed. In marching through the woods, Crawford's battle line was guided by the sound of the firing which was rolling in from the southwest. (At that point, Custer's and Rooney Lee's cavalry commands were locked in a grim struggle.) In advancing to the west, Crawford's left flank passed to the north of Five Forks. As soon as Crawford's troops had moved off, Warren started for Five Forks. Before reaching his destination, Warren

---

105 Humphreys, *The Virginia Campaign of '65*, 350; Moore, *Horse Artillery*, 32.

106 *Ibid.*; OR 46, pt. 1, 835, 881, 897; Swan, "The Five Forks Campaign," 402-403; Moore, *Horse Artillery*, 32.

107 OR 46, pt. 1, 835, 888, 897; Moore, *Horse Artillery*, 32.

encountered the 1st U.S. Cavalry riding up the Ford's Church road. The general directed the cavalrymen to file to the left and march to Crawford's support.[108]

When General Pickett saw that Mayo could not hold his position on the Ford's Church road, he called for General Corse. He directed Corse to change front to the left and deploy his troops along the west side of the Gilliam field. When formed, Corse's main line of resistance was at right angles to the White Oak Road. To attack Corse's Virginians, the Federals would have to cross an open field. Corse's task would be to hold this ground for as long as possible to cover the escape of Ransom's, Steuart's, and Wallace's brigades. At this time, the battered remnants of these three shattered commands were pouring westward through the woods in "complete disorder." To strengthen their position, Corse's troops threw up light field fortifications. Rooney Lee's cavalry division, which had held its own in the face of Custer's attacks, was positioned south and west of Corse's Rebels.[109]

General Mackenzie's cavalry division had advanced on the right of the V Corps. Riding rapidly, Mackenzie's troopers cut in behind the right and rear of Munford's picket line. The Confederate troopers gave way "without much resistance" in the face of Mackenzie's onslaught. On two occasions, however, the Rebel horsemen endeavored to make a stand. The first time, a squadron of the 1st Maryland led by Capt. Henry C. Erich charged and broke up the Confederate combat patrol. When another pocket of resistance slowed the Union advance, Mackenzie waved a battalion of the 5th Pennsylvania to the attack. As soon as these Southerners had been scattered, the march was resumed. During the course of their sweep, Mackenzie's troopers bagged a large number of prisoners, who were turned over to Warren's infantry. With the advent of darkness, Mackenzie halted his command and reported his position to Sheridan.[110]

It was after 9 o'clock before Mackenzie heard anything from Sheridan. At that time, he received instructions to have a detail relieve the infantry of the responsibility of guarding the ford where the Ford's Church road crossed Gravelly Run. It was about 10:00 p.m. before the troopers reached the ford and relieved the two companies of the 1st Maine that had been watching the crossing.[111]

---

108 *Ibid.*, 835; Porter, "Fifth Corps at the Battle of Five Forks," 253.

109 Humphreys, *The Virginia Campaign of '65*, 351; OR 46, pt. 1, 835.

110 OR 46, pt. 1, 1244-1245, 1251.

111 *Ibid.*, 864-865. At 7:00 p.m., Major Willis Spear with his two companies of the 1st Maine took position at the ford. When they approached the bank of Hatcher's Run, the Federals were fired on by a detail of Rosser's command posted on the far side. The Yankees returned their fire. After about an hour, General Mackenzie rode up and told Spear that his men were

After being driven across the Ford's Church road by Crawford's division, Munford remounted his people. Munford then proceeded to the Confederate right, where he reported to Pickett. Realizing that the battle was lost, Pickett ordered Munford to cross to the north side of Hatcher's Run and join Fitz Lee. Swinging to the west of Crawford's line of advance, Munford's troopers crossed Hatcher's Run at W. Dabney's. Darkness blanketed the area by the time Munford reported to Fitz Lee.[112]

When Sheridan issued orders for Warren to assault the Rebel left, he told Merritt "that the cavalry must cooperate." Preparatory to carrying out his assignment, Merritt ordered his division and brigade commanders to have their units charge the works as soon as Warren committed his infantry. Since Custer was on the extreme left of the Union line, Merritt sent a staff officer to brief him on the role his division was to play in the scheduled assault. Custer was to engage the Rebel force on his left, while maintaining contact with Devin's division on his right. Custer was to keep one brigade continually mounted, "to make the most of a pursuit when the enemy was dislodged from his works."[113]

As soon as the first crashing volley came rolling in from the east, Devin led his dismounted division against the Confederate fortifications covering the White Oak Road. Devin had previously dismounted all of his troopers except the 1st U.S. Cavalry. Captain Lord, the commander of the 1st U.S. Cavalry, had been alerted to keep his men in the saddle, so they would be ready to take up the chase in case of a breakthrough, General Merritt reported:

The cavalry, without a moment's hesitation, rushed into close quarters with the enemy . . . . The enemy's artillery in the works commenced firing rapidly, but owing to the woods obscuring the view where the cavalry line was operating, this fire was necessarily inaccurate and not very destructive. A hotter musketry fire than on this day has seldom been experienced during the war. Fortunately for us the enemy, firing from

---

shooting at their own comrades. Mackenzie then asked Captain Charles F. Sawyer to have his company cross the run. Sawyer refused, stating that he had seen the foe. Next, Mackenzie requested Captain William G. Howes to send a patrol across. In the meantime, the soldiers on the north bank had started answering the Maine men's "halloos" with the cry that they were the "Ninth New York Cavalry." Sawyer, however, refused to let Howes carry out Mackenzie's request. Two sergeants (unknown to Sawyer) volunteered to cross the run. On doing so, they were captured. This convinced Mackenzie that he had been mistaken, and he returned to his camp.

112 Humphreys, *The Virginia Campaign of '65*, 353; OR 46, pt. 1, 1300.

113 OR 46, pt. 1, 1118, 1130.

breast-works, aimed high, else the casualties in the command must have been very much greater.[114]

West of the road, Pennington's dismounted brigade of Custer's division also advanced to the attack. At the time the attack began, Pennington was absent. He was at Custer's command post, located near the Gilliam house. Custer called for Pennington to tell him to send for his "led horses." The general, contrary to Merritt's orders, planned to use Pennington's brigade to support his attack on the Rebel right. Before the staff officer could return with the "led horses," the sound of heavy volleys became audible. This indicated to the officers that Warren had engaged the foe. Within a few minutes, Pennington became convinced that firing had broken out in the sector held by his brigade. After assuring Pennington that he was mistaken, Custer rode off. Scarcely had Custer disappeared before one of Pennington's staffers galloped up and informed the colonel that Merritt had thrown his unit into the attack. Springing into his saddle, Pennington headed for the front.[115]

Meantime, Merritt's initial attack on Pickett's line had been checked when Pennington's brigade gave way. Just as Pennington rode up, he found his troopers retiring in confusion. Pennington, in his "After Action Report," attributed this setback to three factors:

> The failure of his brigade to maintain contact with Fitzhugh's unit on the right, Custer's removal of Capehart's brigade which had been posted on the left, and, finally, the fact that his men were nearly out of ammunition.[116]

The retreat of Pennington had exposed their left, so Devin's troopers were compelled to pull back. While Devin and his brigade commanders regrouped their commands, Pennington secured a fresh supply of ammunition from Devin's division. A team of volunteers led by Capt. Albert C. Houghton, under heavy fire, distributed the ammunition to the men on the battle line.[117]

As soon as the brigade commanders had reformed their units, the attack was resumed. For a second time, Pennington's right flank faltered. This time, however, Devin's troopers did not fall back. Instead, they continued to exert pressure on the

114 *Ibid.*

115 *Ibid.*, 1135.

116 *Ibid.*, 1118, 1124, 1135.

117 *Ibid.*, 1124, 1135-1136.

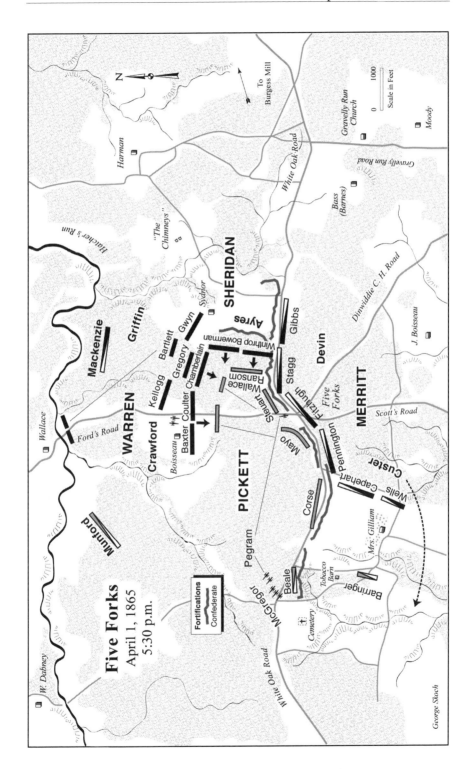

Five Forks
April 1, 1865
5:30 p.m.

Fortifications
Confederate

Scale in Feet
0   1000

N

To Burgess Mill

George Skoch

Major General W. F. H. (Rooney) Lee
Library of Congress

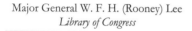

sector of the front held by Steuart's Virginians and Wallace's South Carolinians. Colonel Porter was an interested observer of Merritt's attack. He reported that:

> The natty cavalrymen with tight-fitting uniforms, short jackets, and small carbines swarmed through the pine thickets and dense undergrowth, looking as if they had been especially equipped for crawling through knot-holes. Those who had magazine guns created a racket in those pine woods that sounded as if a couple of army corps had opened fire.[118]

Following Ayres' breakthrough, the Confederates were compelled to withdraw a large number of Steuart's and Wallace's troops from the earthworks. These soldiers were used to man the new defensive line which the Rebel officers had established at right angles to the White Oak Road. Not until Mayo's brigade was pulling out of the trenches and sent to oppose Crawford's advance did Pennington's blue clad troops make any headway.[119]

After Colonel Pegram posted his guns, he lay down on the field and dropped off to sleep. The crash of Warren's opening volley awakened the colonel with a start. Swinging into his saddle, Pegram raced toward the point of danger. By the time that Pegram reached Five Forks, the Union cavalry had joined in the battle. Pegram took his battle station by the three guns emplaced west of the Ford's

118 *Ibid.*, 1124, 1136; Humphreys, *The Virginia Campaign of '65*, 350-351; Porter, "Five Forks and the Pursuit of Lee," 714.

119 *OR* 46, pt. 1, 1136; Humphreys, *The Virginia Campaign of '65*, 350-351.

Church road. These three pieces covered the strategic crossroads. Serving their guns with skill, the artillerists blasted away at the oncoming bluecoats. From the dismounted troopers repeating carbines came a continuous storm of bullets.

"Willie" Pegram admiringly watched the contest with the spirit that led General Heth to remark that the young colonel was "one of the few men who, I believe, was supremely happy when in battle." Without bothering to dismount, Pegram rode out between the guns. "Fire your canister low," he cautioned the gunners. Suddenly, Pegram pitched and fell from his horse. "Oh, Gordon," he cried to his adjutant, Gordon McCabe, "I'm mortally wounded; take me off the field."

Adjutant McCabe found this a difficult task, because the Unionists had seized positions near the guns. McCabe, however, finally succeeded in placing his dying friend on a stretcher. After seeing that the colonel was carried a short distance to the rear, McCabe returned momentarily to the battery. Retracing his steps, McCabe placed Pegram in an ambulance and had it started for Ford's Depot on the South Side Railroad.[120]

The detachment left behind by Mayo, Steuart, and Wallace (and their three supporting guns) found it difficult to hold the breastworks in the face of slashing attacks by Devin's and Pennington's troopers. Their position, however, became untenable when Griffin's infantry came rolling in from the east. Unable to stop the advance of the V Corps, the soldiers began to leave the rifle pits and drift to the rear. To capitalize on the situation, the dismounted cavalry charged the works. Spearheaded by Fitzhugh's brigade, the dismounted cavalrymen poured over the fortifications. Simultaneously, Devin committed the 1st U.S. Cavalry. Clearing the breastworks at a bound, the regulars thundered off after the fleeing Confederates. In the mopping up operations which ensued, the cavalry leaders reported that their men captured nearly 1,000 prisoners, two battle flags, and two guns. Two brigades, Fitzhugh's and Pennington's, claimed that they reached the guns first. General Merritt, in his "After Action Report," however, gave Fitzhugh's brigade credit for this success.[121]

Griffin's and Ayres' divisions reached Five Forks immediately after the cavalry carried the position. The large number of units which had converged on the strategic crossroads caused considerable confusion. As soon as Sheridan and his officers had restored a semblance of order, a pursuit was organized. Devin wheeled his division to the left, and rested his right on Griffin's division. Ayres' division was

---

120 Freeman, *Lee's Lieutenants*, vol. 3, 683.

121 *OR* 46, pt. 1, 1118, 1124, 1136; Swan, "The Five Forks Campaign," 403-405. Both of the captured pieces were 3-inch rifles. The Confederates abandoned these guns; they were not taken in a hand-to-hand encounter.

massed behind Griffin's. Upon the completion of these dispositions, the Union battle line rolled westward. The White Oak Road served as the axis of the Federal advance.[122]

Immediately before Warren's attack, Custer had massed Capehart's and Wells' brigades opposite the Rebel right. In accordance with Merritt's instructions, Custer had remounted these two units. When the sound of heavy firing in the east reached Custer's ears, he prepared to attack. To cover his advance and draw the fire of the grey clads' artillery, Custer directed the 15th New York of Wells' brigade to feign a frontal attack on Corse's main line of resistance. After the 8th New York had engaged the Rebel artillery, Custer would lead Capehart's and Wells' brigades forward and try to turn Corse's right flank. Corse's Virginia infantry brigade had been reinforced by one of Rooney Lee's brigades which had been dismounted.[123]

When Custer gave the word, the 15th New York threw down fences in front of the Confederate works. Next, the regiment, covered by a strong force of skirmishers, charged the battery. The determined New Yorkers, despite being exposed to a "terrible cross-fire" from the Southern infantry posted in rifle pits and behind barricades, charged up to the muzzles of the canister-belching guns. Repulsed, the New Yorkers fell back. A second attempt to reach the guns also ended in failure and the regiment retreated, leaving a number of dead and wounded scattered on the field.[124]

As soon as the 15th New York launched its frontal attack on Corse's brigade, Custer moved forward with Capehart's and Wells' commands. Before the Confederates could shift the position of their guns, Custer's troopers had swept around their right flank. Pushing eastward, Custer sought to seize a position in the rear of Corse's line. Before Custer secured his objective, Rooney Lee intercepted his column with a mounted charge by the 2nd and 3rd North Carolina Cavalry. Mounted men of the blue and the gray moved simultaneously to the attack. The fighting ebbed and flowed. Rooney Lee's troopers, however, held their position and Custer's lunge to turn the Rebel right was checked. Custer was unable to smash Rooney Lee's command and cut his way through and join the Union forces

---

122 OR 46, pt. 1, 839, 851, 1124.

123 *Ibid.*, 1130-1131, 1139; Humphreys, *The Virginia Campaign of '65*, 351; See Major General Wesley Merritt, "Testimony," Warren Court of Inquiry, in Janet B Hewett, OR *Supplement,* vol. 9, 850; Confederate Brig. Gen. Richard M. T. Beale, *Ibid.,* OR Supplement, 617; Paul B. Means, "Sixty-third Regiment," in *North Carolina Regiments,* vol. 3, 646-647; Richard H. Moore II, *The First and Second Stuart Horse Artillery,* 141.

124 OR 46, pt. 1, 1131, 1139. In his After Action Report, George Custer mistakenly credits the 8th New York with the attack on the battery.

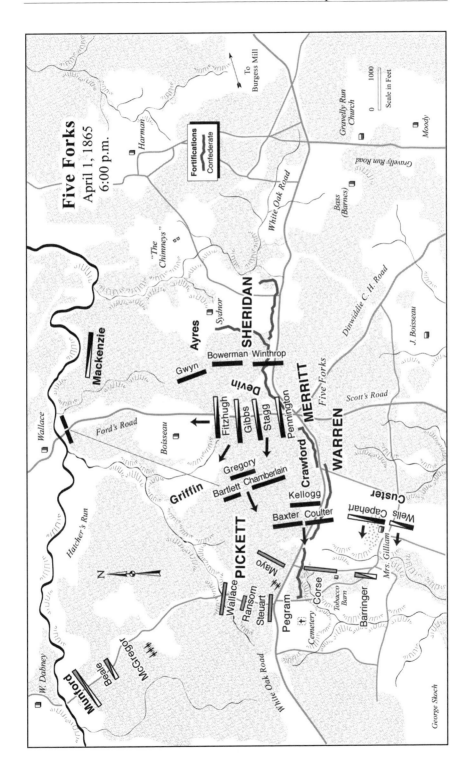

Five Forks
April 1, 1865
6:00 p.m.

Fortifications
Confederate

Scale in Feet
0   1000

George Skoch

approaching from the east. Under cover of Rooney Lee's attack McGregor's battery and Beale's cavalry brigade withdrew from the field and headed north through the woods or on the Ford road towards Hatcher's Run and safety. This must have been embarrassing and frustrating to the aggressive "Boy General," because the roar of battle was steadily drawing near, a certain indication that Warren was driving the Confederates before him.[125]

When Warren overtook Crawford's division, he found the troops in position in the edge of the woods on the east side of Gilliam's field. The right flank brigade, Kellogg's, of Crawford's division was massed in the timber north of the White Oak Road. At the same time, Custer's division was held at bay south and west of the field by Rooney Lee's troopers. Warren was distressed to observe that Crawford's soldiers were hesitant about moving against the breastworks held by Corse's Virginians on the opposite side of the field. It seems that the rapid advance through the woods had disorganized Crawford's formations. While there had been no order to halt, and many of the junior officers were urging their men to resume the advance, the soldiers, "not feeling the influence of their commanders," refused to budge.[126]

After allowing a few minutes for the officers to reform their units, Warren rode into the field, the corps flag in his hand. The general was accompanied by Captain Benyaurd and other staff members then present. As he rode along he called for those within hearing to follow him. Everywhere along the front, the color-bearers and officers sprang forward. With a mighty shout, Crawford's division drove to the attack. In spite of a scathing fire, the blue clads rolled over Corse's brigade. A large number of Confederates were made prisoners, and the remainder dispersed. Sergeant Hiram A. Delavie of the 11th Pennsylvania (Baxter's brigade) captured the colors of the 32nd Virginia. When within a few paces of the works, General Warren's horse was shot from under him. To shield the general, Lt. Col. Hollon Richardson of the 7th Wisconsin leaped between Warren and the foe. The colonel was cut down, badly wounded. One of the general's orderlies was killed.[127]

Following the defeat of Corse's brigade, Crawford's troops pushed westward along the White Oak Road, mopping up scattered pockets of resistance. The

---

125 *Ibid.*, 1131, 1139; Humphreys, *The Virginia Campaign of '65*, 351; Means, "Sixty-third Regiment," 646-647; Moore, *Stuart Horse Artillery*, 141-42.

126 Porter, "Fifth Corps at the Battle of Five Forks," 253; Humphreys, *The Virginia Campaign of '65*, 351-352; OR 46, pt. 1, 835, 881.

127 *Ibid.*

column proceeded about one-half mile. There were no more Confederates in sight and it had started to get dark so Warren halted the pursuit.[128]

When General Pickett ordered Corse into position on the west side of Gilliam's field, he directed Rooney Lee to be prepared to fall back toward the South Side Railroad. Using his mounted brigade to cover his dismounted unit, Rooney Lee fought a skillful delaying action. The retreat was slow and deliberate. After the collapse of Corse's brigade had exposed his left, Rooney Lee quickened the pace of his withdrawal. Even then, Custer was unable to cut off any appreciable number of Lee's troopers. Pressed by Custer's bluecoats, Rooney Lee's troopers passed up the W. Dabney road. After crossing Hatcher's Run, Rooney Lee's division marched to the Ford's Church road, where the general reported to Fitz Lee. Custer followed the Confederates for about six miles. Darkness, however, compelled Custer to give up the pursuit. Retracing their steps, Custer's troopers camped upon the battlefield. Here, Pennington's brigade rejoined the division.[129]

The shattered remnants of Corse's, Ransom's, Mayo's, Steuart's, and Wallace's brigades made their way through the woods and fields north of the White Oak Road. After wading Hatcher's Run, the survivors of the disaster gained the W. Dabney road. By the time the troops had reached the vicinity of the South Side Railroad, the officers had restored a semblance of order. After the units had been partially re-formed, Pickett moved his command toward Exeter mills at the mouth of Whipponock Creek. He planned to ford the Appomattox at that point and rejoin the Army of Northern Virginia.[130]

As soon as he halted Crawford's division, Warren called for Colonel Bankhead. The general told the staffer to find Sheridan and report what had happened. In addition, Bankhead was to ask for fresh instructions. When the colonel returned to Warren's command post, he told the general that orders had already been sent. Shortly thereafter, Colonel George A. Forsyth rode up and at 7:00 p.m. handed Warren the following message: "Major-General Warren, commanding Fifth Army Corps, is relieved of duty, and will report at once for orders to General Grant, commanding Armies of the United States."[131]

Warren's apparent lackadaisical attitude at the time that he was marshaling the V Corps at Gravelly Run Church had grated on Sheridan's nerves. Commenting on this, in his "After Action Report," Sheridan observed: "General Warren did not

128 Humphreys, *The Virginia Campaign of '65*, 352; OR 46, pt. 1, 835, 881.

129 Humphreys, *The Virginia Campaign of '65*, 352; OR 46, pt. 1, 1131.

130 Humphreys, *The Virginia Campaign of '65*, 355.

131 OR 46, pt. 1, 835-836; pt. 3, 420.

exert himself to get up his Corps as rapidly as he might have done, and his manner gave me the impression that he wished the sun to go down before dispositions for the attack could be completed."[132]

A little later, Sheridan exploded. The incident which triggered Warren's relief was the unsteadiness shown by Gwyn's brigade in the attack on "the return." Sheridan reported:

> During this attack I again became dissatisfied with General Warren. During the engagement portions of his line gave way when not exposed to a heavy fire, and simply from want of confidence on the part of the troops, which Warren did not exert himself to inspire.

Sheridan accordingly drafted an order relieving Warren of command of the V Corps. At the same time, Sheridan directed Griffin to take charge of the corps and push the Rebels down the White Oak Road. (General Bartlett would assume command of Griffin's division; Pearson was to take over Bartlett's brigade.) By this time, however, Sheridan and Griffin had reached Five Forks and the victory was complete.[133]

Little dreaming that his relief from the command of his corps had ever been thought of, Warren hastened to Sheridan's command post. His object was to try to persuade Sheridan to reconsider his action. The reply he received, "Reconsider? H——! I don't reconsider my determination."[134]

Writing of Warren's relief, Capt. Charles H. Porter observed:

> This, on the field of battle, after the most successful day's work that he had ever taken part in, was Warren deprived of the command of the Corps which he had commanded since March, 1864, and a position he had earned by the right of soldierly courage and brilliant operations on many fields. Beginning at Big Bethel, his name is associated with every field which the Army of the Potomac was engaged.[135]

Sergeant William A. Mentzer of the 39th Massachusetts told of seeing:

---

132 *Ibid.*, pt. 1, 1105.

133 *Ibid.*, 839, 1105; pt. 3, 420-421; Swan, "The Five Forks Campaign," 405.

134 Porter, "Fifth Corps at the Battle of Five Forks," 254; Powell, *The Fifth Army Corps*, 809.

135 Porter, "Fifth Corps at the Battle of Five Forks," 254.

Sheridan at Five Forks with his staff, riding along the rear of our lines, shouting, "See the Sons of B——s run! Give them H—l, boys!" After going a little way into the woods we came to the rear of the Rebel works, where I saw a lad behind the same firing at our folks. Jamming on my bayonet I jumped to the works and order him to come out; he looked up and had the impudence, with a smile on his face, to say, "I wish you would let me fire these five cartridges." I think I swore some and told him I'd put the bayonet right through him unless he came out at once, and he came. When going to the rear with my prisoner I saw General Warren riding the same way, but not till the next mooring did I know that our great and good leader had been relieved of his command.[136]

Editor's Conclusion

The question raised at the end of Introduction for Chapter 5 was this: What would prevent Lee from shifting a division of infantry from north of the Appomattox River or from outside Richmond? As we have now seen, this is precisely what happened. Lee ordered Maj. Gen. George Pickett's division to shift south of the Appomattox and he assembled the Army of Northern Virginia's cavalry under Maj. Gen. Fitzhugh Lee. This combined force nearly destroyed Sheridan's command at Dinwiddie Court House on March 31. Sheridan was so badly shaken by the near-disaster that Grant had to transfer Warren's V Corps from in front of the Confederate lines at Burgess Mill to Five Forks. It was this combined Federal forces that attacked Pickett at Five Forks on April 1. The Confederates lost the battle for many reasons, one of which was because Pickett and his second in command, Fitzhugh Lee, were absent during the battle.

Could Lee have won the battle at Five Forks? We will never know with certainty. What we do know, however, is that the Confederates failed to notice that three divisions of infantry and one division of cavalry had left Longstreet's front and moved opposite Petersburg. Lee's plans for such an event were to have Longstreet join him with Maj. Gen. Charles Field's division, which would have gone a long way toward defeating Warren and Sheridan. Lee also could have marched down the White Oak Road from Burgess Mill and struck the V Corps in flank during the Battle of Five Forks. The V corps had withdrawn from his front, but Lee seems not to have bothered to learn that Warren's corps had shifted and was attacking Pickett.

---

136 Roe, *The Thirty-Ninth Massachusetts*, 286.

The defeat at Five Forks and loss of the key road junction exposed and lost the South Side Railroad to the Confederates. Lee's last logistical lifeline had been cut, as had his best route of evacuation from Richmond and Petersburg. On the morning of April 2 Grant attacked and broke through the Confederate lines, General Lee advised President Jefferson Davis that he could no longer hold, and the evacuation began.

Chapter 8

The VI Corps Scores a Breakthrough

April 2, 1865

Editor's Introduction

Shortly after 8:00 p.m., as soon as he learned of Maj. Gen. Phil Sheridan's victory at Five Forks, Lt. Gen. U. S. Grant informed Maj. Gen. George Meade of Sheridan's success and added, "Humphreys must push now, or everything will leave his front and be concentrated against Sheridan. Inform Parke of this and tell him to be on the watch to go in."[1]

At this hour the assault columns of the various corps had not been formed for a 4:00 a.m. attack Grant wished to launch. Meade replied, "In pursuance to your instructions orders have been sent to Humphreys to assault at 4 a.m. tomorrow. . . . Do you mean he is to attack tonight? Orders were sent to both Wright and Parke to morrow at 4 a.m. . . . Your last

---

1 *OR* 46, pt. 3, 397.

dispatch says "Parke should be notified to watch. Do you mean his orders are to be changed?"[2]

Grant replied, "Generals Wright and Parke should both be directed to feel for a chance through the enemy's lines at once, and if they can get through should push on to-night. All our batteries might be opened at once, and if they can get through should push on to-night."[3]

Twenty-five minutes later Grant told Meade, "I believe with a bombardment beforehand the enemy will abandon his works. If not pursued Sheridan may find everything against him." Humphreys, added Grant, should press forward his skirmishers and attack if the Rebels were found leaving their trenches. If the enemy continued to hold their lines, he added, Humphreys should send Miles's division down the White Oak Road to reinforce Sheridan. Parke, Wright, and Ord, meanwhile, should open their artillery and push skirmishers forward and attack if the enemy gave way.[4]

Meade's corps commanders and Ord reported it was so dark that their men could not see well enough to move forward. In fact, the Confederates did not abandon their positions and turn on Sheridan. The Union guns opened about 10:00 p.m. and the bombardment of Lee's lines lasted until 2:00 a.m. The infantry assaults that followed began about 4:30 a.m., thirty minutes behind schedule.

The night of April 1 found Maj. Gen. George Pickett's defeated forces scattered and disorganized. After crossing Hatcher's Run, Gens. Rooney Lee and Tom Munford joined Fitzhugh Lee at Church's Crossing, near the Ford Road junction with the South Side Railroad. Fitz Lee informed his uncle, army commander Robert E. Lee, of the defeat at Five Forks, and General Lee then sent Lt. Gen. Richard H. Anderson's infantry to join Fitz Lee and help Pickett reassemble his command and hold the critical Southside Railroad. Leaving only a small force behind, Anderson abandoned his position at Burgess Mill at 6:30 p.m. and marched west while staying north of Hatcher's Run. Anderson joined Fitz Lee at 2:00 a.m. on the morning of April 2. The Army of Northern Virginia's intention was to defend the Southside Railroad at Sutherland's Station with Maj. Gen. Bushrod

2   Meade to Grant, 8:30 p.m.April 1, 1865 OR Vol. 46, pt 4, 397.

3   OR 46, pt. 3, p. 397.

4   *Ibid.*

Johnson's division, Brig. Gen. Eppa Hunton's brigade of Pickett's division, and the fugitives from Pickett's command.[5]

That same evening of April 1, two divisions of Warren's V Corps spent the night deployed across the White Oak Road near Gravelly Run Church. His third division camped near the Ford Road. Sheridan's cavalry camped on the Gilliam Farm near Five Forks while Mackenzie's cavalry from the Army of the James bivouacked near the Ford Road crossing of Hatcher's Run. Later that evening, Sheridan was joined by Miles's division of Humphreys's II Corps, directed there by General Grant to block any Confederate advance from Burgess Mill with the goal of hitting Sheridan's right flank on the White Oak Road. The II Corps's other two divisions faced Confederate defenses held by Lee's army.

Late that night after informing Sheridan he was sending him Miles' division, Grant also told the cavalry commander of his plans to attack Lee's lines at Petersburg at 4:00 a.m. He ended his message by adding, "From your isolated position I can give you no specific directions but leave you to act according to circumstances. I would like you however to get something done to the South Side road even if they do not tear up a mile of it." Sheridan replied to Grant at 12:30 a.m. that he intended to sweep the White Oak Road and all north of it down to Petersburg.[6]

5   *OR* 46, pt. 1, pp. 1124, 1288-1289.

6   *OR* 46, pt. 3, p. 434, 454.

Part I

Wright Prepares to Strike

S hortly after 4:00 p.m. on April 1, 1865, the telegraph operator in Maj. Gen. Horatio Wright's VI Corps headquarters jotted down a message which came over the wire from General Meade's headquarters: General Wright was to assault the works to his front at 4:00 a.m. Should this attack prove successful, Wright was to be prepared to "follow it up with all the force under . . . [his] command, except the garrisons of the enclosed works and supports to the batteries" which he had in the lines. After carrying the Rebel defenses, Wright's troops were to push for the Boydton Plank Road and endeavor to establish contact with the assaulting columns to their right and left. It would be left up to Wright, since he was familiar with the area, to determine where the blow would fall. Wright was advised that the units to his right and left—the IX Corps and the Army of the James—were to launch simultaneous attacks.[7]

Having been alerted some 48 hours before that a major push was impending, General Wright and his staff were already working out a plan of attack. Wright was careful in selecting the point to be assailed. Besides making a personal reconnaissance of the VI Corps front, Wright interviewed dozens of officers who were familiar with the Rebel fortifications opposite Forts Fisher and Welch. At this point, the Union earthworks jutted to within 5,000 feet of the Petersburg perimeter.

On March 25, Wright had undertaken a limited offensive in the Fort Fisher sector to support the Union counterattack on Fort Stedman. Soldiers of the VI Corps had advanced, captured, and held an entrenched picket line approximately halfway between Forts Fisher and Welch and the Petersburg defenses. After they were refaced, these rifle pits would allow Union storming parties to execute a covered approach to within 2,500 feet of the Confederate trenches.[8]

The ground between the lines in the Fort Fisher area had been cleared of trees and offered "few natural obstructions, "except for the marshes which "intersected the Rebs' front. The sector to be assailed was near the VI Corps left flank. Northeast of the Fort Fisher salient, the area fronting the Confederate works was inundated, while beyond the flooded area was the formidable belt of fortifications

---

7   OR 46, pt. 3, 422.

8   OR 46, pt. 1, 903; Humphreys, *The Virginia Campaign of '64 and '65*, 321.

centering on the lead-works." In Wright's opinion, an attack in those sectors was out of the question.

When the Federal generals studied the works in front of Fort Fisher through their glasses, they saw that they consisted of an "extraordinary strong line of rifle pits, with deep ditches and higher relief." To reach the Southerners main line of resistance, Wright and his staff calculated their men would have to feel their way through one or two lines of abatis. A number of redoubts in which artillery was emplaced were pinpointed along this line at strategic spots. Wright recalled that the Confederate officers might look upon the works as impregnable. Subsequent to the assault, Wright noted, "but for the successes of the 25th ultimo, in which the corps carried the entrenched picket-line of the enemy . . . the attack of the 2nd . . . could not have been successful."[9]

Having selected the area where his attack would be delivered, Wright addressed a circular outlining his battle plan to his division commanders. The assault would be made at 4:00 a.m. on the Confederate defenses between the Jones house and the corps' left flank. Brig. Gen. Frank Wheaton's division was to take the right; Brig. Gen. George W. Getty's division the center; and Brig. Gen. Truman Seymour's division the left. In forming, Getty's troops would be in advance, and Wheaton's and Seymour's en echelon. The division commanders were to mass their units by brigades with regimental fronts. Understrength regiments would be consolidated so as not to extend the column too much. Division commanders were to form their units as near the picket line as practicable, and advance when the signal gun at Fort Fisher was discharged. When they organized their columns of attack, Wright recommended that Wheaton form his division "left in front," and Seymour "right in front, so as to deploy to the right and left, if the need arose."

The picket line would be advanced at the same time. If feasible, the skirmishers were to enter the Rebel works. Where checked by the fire of the Confederates, the pickets were to take cover, blaze away, and endeavor to pin down the grey clads posted in the trenches.

Troops occupying the fortifications from Fort Howard to Fort Urmston were to be cut to the minimum, as would the garrisons charged with the defense of Forts Gregg, Sampson, and Cummings. The force holding the rifle pits linking these works was to be reduced by nine-tenths, while the trenches connecting Forts Urmston and Gregg were to be abandoned.

Five four-gun batteries: Battery E, 5th U.S. Light Artillery; the 1st and 3rd Batteries, New York Light Artillery; and Batteries G and H, 1st Rhode Island Light

9 OR 46, pt. 1, 903.

Artillery were to accompany the attacking force. Of these units, a battery would be assigned to each division. The other two would be held in reserve. The three other batteries of the corps were to remain in the works to the right of Fort Fisher and to the left of Fort Gregg. Commanders of these units were to look to corps Chief of Artillery Capt. Andrew Cowan for instructions.[10]

Pioneers would accompany the vanguard of each assaulting column; their task was to cut a path through the abatis and any other obstructions encountered. Sharpshooters were to be deployed where they would do the most good.

Troops left to occupy the investment line would be alerted to hold themselves ready to repulse Confederate counterattacks, or to rejoin their units in case the desired breakthrough was achieved.

Units slated to participate in the onslaught were to be put into motion for the marshalling area "tonight," so that they could "complete" their formation before 4:00 a.m. Wright cautioned his subordinates that "perfect silence" was mandatory until the moment the signal gun was discharged.

Should the VI Corps succeed in breaching the Rebel line and gaining the Boydton Plank Road, its subsequent movements would be made in conformity with orders from General Meade.[11]

The sweeping victory scored by Sheridan's command at Five Forks late on the afternoon of April 1st, caused General Grant to pressure Meade to start offensive operations east of Hatcher's Run at an earlier hour than scheduled.

At 8:40 p.m., Grant notified Meade that the VI and IX Corps should "be directed to feel for a chance to get through the enemy's lines at once." If they found an opening, they were to "push on tonight." "All our batteries," Grant observed, "might be opened at once without waiting" for the assault columns to get into position. Meade was to inform his corps commanders of the rout of the Five Forks Confederates.[12]

At 9:00 p.m., General Meade notified the commanders of his II, VI, and IX Corps that General Sheridan's cavalry and the V Corps had driven the Confederates from Five Forks, "capturing several batteries, over 4,000 prisoners, and numerous trains." To keep the Rebels from rushing reinforcements to restore

---

10 *OR* 46, pt. 3, 423-424. The Jones house had burned in the fighting on March 25. Battery E, 5th U.S. Artillery was armed with four 12-pounder Napoleons; the 1st New York with four 3-inch rifles; the 3rd New York with four 12-pounder Napoleons; Battery G, 1st Rhode Island with four 3-inch rifles; and Battery H, 1st Rhode Island with four 12-pounder Napoleons. *OR* 46, pt. 1, 660.

11 *OR* 46, pt. 3, 424.

12 *Ibid.*, 397.

Major General Horatio G. Wright
Library of Congress

the situation in the Five Forks sector, Meade wanted the three corps commanders to feel the Southerners' lines to their front. If the opportunity presented itself, they were to "push on tonight." The II, VI, and IX Corps artillery was to start hammering the Rebs' works, without waiting for the assaulting columns to form.

Wright moved to see that his superior's instructions were carried out. Orders were issued for the artillery to open and the skirmish line to advance. Staff officers were sent to direct Wheaton and Getty to have their divisions move out and be ready to attack. Seymour's division was alerted to be ready to support this thrust.[13]

It was almost 10:00 p.m. when Captain Cowan received instructions from General Wright "to open fire on the enemy's lines with all the batteries." Cowan relayed this news to his subordinates. A "moderate" bombardment was commenced and continued for about three hours. The Federal cannoneers pointed their pieces at the area where it was known that the Rebels were in the habit of posting their pickets.[14]

Meanwhile, at 9:05 p.m., Grant telegraphed Meade that in view of the Confederate disaster at Five Forks, he felt that a bombardment might compel the grey clads to abandon their Petersburg fortifications. If they were not pressed, Grant feared that General Lee might concentrate an overwhelming force against Sheridan. Maj. Gen. John G. Parke and Horatio Wright were to put their artillery into action and push forward their pickets and sharpshooters. If Lee had started to

13 *Ibid.*, 407.

14 OR 46, pt. 1, 1009-1012.

pull his butternuts out of the Petersburg defenses, the VI and IX Corps were to "push directly after him."[15]

Thirty minutes later, Meade notified Wright and Parke that he was forced to modify his 9:00 p.m. order. As Grant had directed, they were to bombard the Rebel lines and make a forced reconnaissance of the works to their front. If it were discovered that the Confederates were withdrawing troops to counterattack Sheridan, they were to go after them.

At 10:05 p.m., Wright acknowledged the receipt of Meade's 9:00 and 9:35 p.m. dispatches, and informed headquarters of the steps he had taken to carry out Meade's 9:00 p.m. directive.

Prior to the receipt of Wright's latest dispatch, Meade's Chief of Staff, Brig. Gen. Alexander S. Webb, addressed a note to Wright, "Assault as you please," the chief of staff wrote, "but feel with your skirmishers and batteries . . . while you are preparing your columns."[16] Webb handed the message to Capt. William S. Worth, who placed it in Wright's hands a little before 11:00 p.m.

Before acknowledging the communication, Wright issued a circular addressed to his division commanders and Chief of Artillery Cowan. They were again informed that the assaulting columns would be formed as directed and held ready to advance at 4:00 p.m. The battery which had been sent out in front of the lines to shell the Confederates, in accordance with Grant's orders, was to be recalled before the troops formed. At the same time, the pickets would cease firing.[17]

Wright was taken aback as he studied Webb's paper. He felt that Webb was chiding him for not being ready to attack sooner. Replying, Wright assured Webb that everything would be ready, and the VI Corps would "go in solid." Wright was confident that when they went in, his troops would make "the fur fly." Since his division commanders were familiar with Meade's battle plan, Wright assured Webb, there would "be no hesitation from want of knowledge of what is expected." If his troops did half as well as he expected, they would crack the Rebs line 15 minutes after he had said go, Wright added.

After reading Wright's telegram, Meade sought to calm his corps commander's ruffled feelings. Meade informed Wright that he was "quite sick, and trusted to General Webb to attend to matters." He accordingly wished to apologize for the tenor of Webb's 10:15 p.m. dispatch, which had been composed when

15 OR 46, pt. 3, 397-398.

16 *Ibid.*, 422.

17 *Ibid.*, 425.

headquarters was under the impression that Wright didn't intend to attack until 4:00 a.m., as previously ordered.[18]

A copy of Meade's 9:00 p.m. message to his corps commanders took 50 minutes to reach General Grant's Dabney's Mill headquarters. When he looked at it, Grant was disgusted to see that Meade had misinterpreted his instructions. Grant had never intended for Wright and Parke to attack "without forming assault lines." They were to have their batteries open fire and "feel out with skirmishers and sharpshooters if the enemy is leaving, and attack in their own way."[19]

At 11:45 p.m., Wright reported to Meade that the VI Corp's artillery had gone into action and that there was firing on the picket line. The division commanders were busy forming their "assault columns" and would attack at 4:00 a.m. It would be impossible, Wright notified Meade, for his generals to get the troops massed in time to step up the timetable. Unless he received orders to the contrary, Wright would send his troops forward as scheduled.[20]

General Meade relayed Wright's "will make fur fly" dispatch to Grant's headquarters. On doing so, Meade pointed out that Wright's preparations were made "in accordance with his original order." These plans, Meade noted, he had approved and if given the go ahead, he would order the VI Corps to carry them out.

Grant liked the way Wright talked. Replying to Meade's communication, Grant instructed Meade to let Wright proceed as originally planned.[21]

Because Meade had retired for the night, at 12:25 a.m., Chief of Staff Webb notified Wright that General Grant was responsible for the orders for the VI Corps to assault "as soon as possible." The orders from the Army of the Potomac headquarters had been drafted in spirit. Webb urged Wright to attack as early as he could "with any hope of success."

Sixty-five minutes later, Webb notified Wright and Parke that the storming columns were to move forward at 4:00 a.m. All orders conflicting with this time were suspended.[22]

* * *

18 *Ibid.*, 423.

19 *Ibid.*, 399.

20 *Ibid.*, 423.

21 *Ibid.*, 399.

22 *Ibid.*, 477.

Upon the receipt of the orders from Meade directing that the artillery be put into action and forced reconnaissance undertaken of the Rebel works, Wright transmitted copies to his division commanders and Chief of Artillery Cowan. In a covering memorandum, he urged the officers to closely examine the ground over which their assaulting columns were to march. When they did, they were cautioned to be careful not to attract the grey clads' attention. Since it could be fatal for the Union plans if intelligence of the preparations reached the foe, Wright cautioned his division commanders to make certain that "only reliable men" were detailed for outpost duty. If any soldiers of questionable loyalty were on the picket lines they were to be relieved.[23]

Wright's three division commanders issued confidential instructions to the leaders of their brigades on steps that would be taken to guarantee the success of the projected assault. General Wheaton announced that his division (the First) would be massed near Fort Fisher inside the works with Joseph H. Hamblin's 2nd Brigade bringing up the rear. The brigades were to be *en-echelon*. Each brigade commander to cover his front with a skirmish line, which was to "extend a sufficient distance to the right of each brigade front to more than cover and protect its flank."

No less than 35 axes to be carried by the advance line of each brigade, with which to assist the pioneers in hewing a way through the abatis.

In the advance, the brigades were to preserve a sufficient interval to prevent the front line of one from mingling with the rear rank of another. The lines in each brigade were to be kept well apart, not less than 50 paces, and one line should not crowd another. The interval between lines could be increased to conform to the character of the ground. It would probably be necessary for Col. Oliver Edwards' unit to march more rapidly than Penrose's and Hamblin's. Should the troops of General Getty's division gain ground to the right or left in advance, Colonel Edwards would have to conform to their movements.

After storming the trenches to his front, Col. Edwards was to hold them and make such disposition with his right flank as would assist in Penrose's troops in entering the rifle pits to his right. Penrose's bluecoats were to assist Hamblin's soldiers in the same fashion. If any of the brigades, upon approaching the Confederate works, found the ditch in their front impassable, its commander was to halt his front line, have it engage the foe, and move his other lines to the right or left and probe for a soft spot.

---

23 *Ibid.*, 425. Wright had cause for worry on this score. Earlier in the day, four men of Wheaton's division (one from the 4th New Jersey and three from the 40th New Jersey) had deserted to the foe. *Ibid.*, 426.

No lights were to be permitted or matches struck after the division had debouched from the main works. Noise would be curtailed. Orders were to be given in a "low tone." General Wheaton recommended that the troops constituting the second and third assault waves not be allowed to cap their pieces. The division sharpshooters were to report to Colonel Edwards.[24]

Getty and Seymour issued similar instructions to their brigade commanders.

*   *   *

It was a little before midnight when General Getty's troops marched from the division camps. The soldiers moved in light marching order, leavinag their canteens and knapsacks behind. A detachment from the 61st Pennsylvania remained behind to garrison Fort Urmston; the 62nd New York held Forts Tracy and Keene.[25]

*   *   *

A soldier in the Vermont Brigade reported:

The night of April 1st was dark, damp, chilly and gloomy. All was quiet along the line of the corps, although preparations were quietly going on. Tents were struck, personal effects which had accumulated, were assorted, the greater part of which were cast aside. Ammunition was served, knapsacks packed and left on the ground to be taken in charge by the Quartermaster. Haversacks were filled, muskets loaded, but uncapped, bayonets fixed. The special orders were read to each company, after which the commander reported that all was in readiness.[26]

*   *   *

According to regimental historian Penrose G. Mark of the 93rd Pennsylvania: The ranking officers of the regiment: Captains B. Frank Hean and P. G. Mark, along with the other regimental commanders were called to Col. James M. Warner's headquarters. After Warner read Wright's orders to the assembled officers, he

24 Ibid., 427.

25 OR 46, pt. 1, 953-954.   •

26 Charles H. Anson, "Assault on the Lines of Petersburg, April 2, 1865," in War Papers Read Before the Commandery of the State of Wisconsin, Military Order of the Loyal Legion of the United States (Milwaukee, 1891), Vol. 1, 89.

Brigadier General George W. Getty
Library of Congress

dismissed them. It was after 10:00 p.m. when Hean and Mark returned to their camp. Instructions for the troops to get ready were issued. Within a few minutes, the soldiers were busy making the usual preparations for going into battle: short letters were written and messages given to non-combatants to be sent home "in case of accidents." Useless clothing and playing cards were dispensed with, and as little as possible packed in the knapsacks. Some more careful than others, wrote their names, company, and regiment on pieces of paper and pinned them on their blouses, so as to be identified if killed. Cartridge boxes and canteens were filled and muskets carefully examined; rations were packed in haversacks; and the inevitable wooden pipe and tobacco bag were carefully placed where they could be as easily reached as cartridges.

Finally at midnight the word came to Captain Hean "to form on the regimental parade ground without noise; to join the brigade (Warner's) and move out between the enemy's line and ours in front of Fisher." While the regiment was forming at midnight, knapsacks were collected and placed under guard at the fort. In the dark and damp of the early morning, the smoke from the artillery hung like "huge clouds near the ground deepened the obscurity and made our movements somewhat slow."[27]

---

27 Penrose G. Mark, *Red: White: and Blue Badge, Pennsylvania Volunteers, a History of the 93rd Regiment* (Harrisburg, 1911), 321.

*   *   *

Getty's column passed the breastworks and abatis to the right and left of Fort Welch through openings cut for that purpose. After hiking about one-half mile, the division halted in rear of the captured rifle pits. Here, Getty massed his brigades in columns by regiments. From the area where Getty marshaled his brigades, a slight ravine ran toward the Rebel line, 650 yards away. The ravine and the ground on either side to Getty's front had been covered with pines. These trees had been cut for fuel during the winter; the stumps and brush remaining, with water standing in the lower spots. At the point where the ravine passed through the Confederate works, there was a gap about 50 feet across. To cover this opening, the Rebs had placed several cannons in redoubts on the rising ground on either side of the ravine.[28]

*   *   *

Brigadier General Lewis A. Grant's Vermont brigade rested its left on the ravine; the other units in the advance would guide on the men from the Green Mountain State.[29] By 1:00 a.m., Grant had completed his dispositions, and the troops were told to lie down while the other units were forming.[30] Col. Thomas W. Hyde's 3rd Brigade was posted on Grant's right,[31] while Colonel Warner's brigade was on the extreme right. As Warner's men filed into position, they were fired on by Confederate pickets and several men were cut down.[32] Even so, "not a word was heard, men standing shoulder to shoulder were silent, as men by their side were hit. This inability to return the fire of the Rebs was 'misery intensified to the men.'"[33]

28 Anson, "Assault on the Lines of Petersburg, April 2, 1865," 89; *OR* 46, pt. 1, 953-954.

29 *OR* 46, pt. 1, 953-954.

30 *Ibid.*, 968. From front to rear, Grant massed his regiments: the 5th, 2nd, 6th, 4th, and 3rd Vermont Infantry regiments, and two battalions of the 1st Vermont Heavy Artillery.

31 *Ibid.*, 975; Frederick D. Bidwell, *History of the Forty-Ninth New York Volunteers* (Albany, 1916), 85-86. Hyde's column of attack was formed in four lines. The first line consisted of the 49th and 77th New York, the second of the 1st Maine, the third of the 61st Pennsylvania, and the fourth of the 43rd and 122nd New York.

32 *OR* 46, pt. 1, 962-963. Warner's brigade was formed into column of regiments on the right of Hyde's brigade: the 102nd Pennsylvania constituted the first line, the 139th Pennsylvania the second, the 93rd Pennsylvania the third and fourth lines, and the 98th Pennsylvania the fifth.

33 Mark, *Red: White: and Blue Badge*, 321-322.

*   *   *

Getty told his brigade commanders that when the advance began, they were "to force their way through all opposition and obstructions into the enemy's works." After carrying the Confederates' position, the troops were to be halted, reformed, and held ready to cope with any emergency.[34]

*   *   *

For nearly four hours Getty's soldiers were called to lie on their arms on "the cold, damp ground, awaiting the time when the booming gun from Fort Fisher should signal them to charge, drive home that mighty wedge of humanity, strike to the very heart of the Confederacy and to the life blood of treason and rebellion."[35]

*   *   *

General Wheaton's division moved out of its camps near the Weldon Railroad at 10:30 p.m. One of the soldiers recalled that at that hour "the moon was shining brightly, and the night was calm and beautiful, only disturbed by occasional discharges of artillery and the plunging and bursting of shells." Penrose's column, after marching about one and one-half miles, halted briefly near Globe Tavern. About midnight, "the moon went down," and the artillery roared into action. This cannonade, one of the soldiers described, as "surpassing all we had before witnessed."[36]

*   *   *

The troops were halted in rear of Fort Fisher to allow Getty to complete his dispositions. As soon as Getty's division was out of the way, Wheaton led the way through the works. The 3rd Brigade, Colonel Edwards commanding, was massed in column of assault in three lines, 22 paces to the right and rear of Getty's left flank brigade. Seventy-five volunteers from the 37th Massachusetts armed with Spencer Repeating Rifles were deployed as skirmishers to cover the brigade front. Besides

34 *OR* 46, pt. 1, 954.

35 Anson, "Assault on the Lines of Petersburg, April 2, 1865," 89.

36 Alanson A. Haines, *History of the Fifteenth Regiment New Jersey Volunteers* (New York, 1883), 301.

the 20 axmen from the pioneers, Edwards saw that a number of men in his front were issued axes to assist the pioneers in cutting a path through the obstructions. While forming, Edwards' bluecoats were harassed by the fire of the Confederate pickets.[37]

*   *   *

Colonel Penrose deployed the New Jersey Brigade in four lines, 30 paces behind to the right of Edwards' unit;[38] Colonel Hamblin's troops took position in double line of battle, 30 paces to the right and rear of Penrose's. A detachment of sharpshooters from the 49th Pennsylvania armed with Spencers was deployed as skirmishers on Hamblin's right. Looking to their left and rear, Hamblin's soldiers saw Fort Fisher silhouetted against the skyline.[39]

*   *   *

Clinton Beckwith of the 121st New York noted in his diary that his regiment had "scarcely gotten into position when we were ordered to lie down." About this time the pickets began shooting, as Beckwith supposed to cover the noise of our forming, and we were treated to the sensation of lying upon a field for a long time exposed to the fire of the enemy's skirmishers without any shelter. Every once in a while some one would get hit with a ball, and we could hear his cry of anguish as the lead tore through. Finally our men, by stopping their fire and crying, "April Fool, Johnnies," restored quiet, and for a long time we lay perfectly quiet, waiting for the time to come when we could move forward. There was some firing away to our right but not more than usual.[40]

*   *   *

37 *OR* 46, pt. 1, 910, 941, 945. Edwards deployed his brigade from right to left: first line, the 37th Massachusetts and the 5th Wisconsin; second line, the 119th and 49th Pennsylvania and the 2nd Rhode Island; third line, the 82nd Pennsylvania.

38 *Ibid.*, 910, 927-928. Penrose's brigade was massed in column of regiments from front to rear: the 40th, 4th, 10th, and 15th New Jersey Infantry regiments.

39 *Ibid.*, 910, 931, 940. Colonel Hamblin's first line had the 65th New York on the right and the 2nd Connecticut Heavy Artillery on the left; his second line consisted of the 95th Pennsylvania and the 121st New York, the New Yorkers on the left.

40 Isaac O. Best, *History of the 121st New York Infantry* (Chicago, 1921), 209-210.

Brigadier General Truman Seymour
Library of Congress

It was after midnight before General Seymour's two-brigade division marched through the works. As the head of the column approached the area where the division was to deploy, the soldiers came under fire. "By some mischance or misapprehension," the Union outposts posted in this area commenced shooting at the Confederate pickets. The grey clads retaliated and the Feds got the worst of this exchange, as the Southerners' missiles swept through the "dense masses" behind the pickets. A number of men were killed or wounded. Union officers feared that their massed units would open fire. If this happened, it would "seriously interfere with, if not break up, the plan of attack."

*   *   *

The shooting spread to the right and along Getty's front, where a number of officers were cut down. In Colonel Hyde's brigade, the losses were especially serious—two regimental commanders were mortally wounded and carried to the rear. General Grant was struck in the head and compelled to turn over command of the Vermont brigade to his senior regimental commander—Lt. Col. Amasa S. Tracy of the 2nd Vermont. In the end, however, the officers got control of the situation and everything quieted down. Generals Wright and Seymour were impressed with the way their men behaved, for they stood the fire "without returning a shot or uttering a word to indicate their presence to the enemy."

*   *   *

Colonel J. Warren Keifer's brigade was massed into column of assault in rear of the rifle pits captured on March 25. Keifer's right flank rested on "an almost impassable swamp and ravine." On the opposite side of the ravine was the Vermont brigade. As if the sniping of the grey clad sharpshooters wasn't bad enough, the "deep darkness and the deep swamps" plagued Keifer's bluecoats.[41]

*   *   *

Colonel William S. Truex's brigade of Seymour's division reached the ground it was to occupy at 12:30 a.m. To his front, Truex made out through the gloom of the Union outposts, while to his rear he could see the outline of Fort Welch. Truex formed his brigade in three lines of battle to the left and rear of Keifer. Although his scouts warned him that he was within 150 yards of the Rebs' picket line, Truex succeeded in completing his dispositions without attracting the grey clads' attention. After his soldiers had been on the ground about one half-hour, Confederate pickets on the left began banging away. Shooting soon spread to Truex's front and continued for about 60 minutes. At first, this musket fire caused confusion, but when it slackened the men calmed down. Though this firing was extremely galling, Truex's troops didn't reply. This was especially hard on the 87th Pennsylvania, which was made up largely of recruits.[42]

*   *   *

Chief of Artillery Cowan, in compliance with Wright's instructions, had ordered Battery E, 1st New York to report to General Seymour; the 3rd New York Battery to General Getty; and Battery H, 1st Rhode Island to General Wheaton. The 1st New York Battery and Battery G, 1st Rhode Island would be held in

41 OR 46, pt. 1, 903, 978, 992. Before moving out, Keifer's brigade, with the exception of the 138th Pennsylvania, occupied the works from Fort Fisher to Fort Gregg. The 138th Pennsylvania garrisoned Fort Dushane. Keifer formed his command into three lines of battle. From right to left Keifer's first line consisted of: the 110th and the 126th Ohio, and the 6th Maryland; his second line of the 9th New York Heavy Artillery; his third and rear line of the 122nd and the 138th Ohio, and the 67th Pennsylvania.

42 *Ibid.*, 978, 981-982; Helena A. Howell, *Chronicles of the One Hundred Fifty-First Regiment New York State Volunteer Infantry 1862-1865* (Albion, 1911), 98-99. Truex's first line had the 10th Vermont on the right and the 106th New York on the left; the second line was composed of the 14th New Jersey on the right and the 151st New York on the left; the 87th Pennsylvania constituted the third line.

reserve. At 2:00 a.m., the five batteries which were to accompany the assaulting columns were relieved from duty in the works and parked near Fort Fisher.

*   *   *

Captain George W. Adams of Battery G, 1st Rhode Island called for volunteers from the batteries that were to remain in the works. Twenty men were selected by the captain. With this detachment, Adams was to accompany the storming parties and take charge of turning the Confederate field pieces. Adams, before moving out, saw that his volunteers were equipped with rammers, lanyards, and friction primers.[43]

*   *   *

On the night of April 1, the works to be assaulted by the VI Corps were defended by troops from Maj. Gens. Cadmus M. Wilcox's and Henry Heth's divisions. During the past five days, a number of Wilcox's and Heth's units had been shifted west of Hatcher's Run to counter the Union thrust toward Five Forks.

*   *   *

Daybreak on March 27 had found Wilcox's and Heth's commands, about 9,200 strong, charged with the defense of eight miles of front, extending from Lieutenant Run on the east to Burgess Mill to the southwest. Wilcox's four brigades on the left held about four and one-half miles of front.[44]

*   *   *

On March 29, General Robert E. Lee issued orders for General Wilcox to have one of his brigades, Brig. Gen. Samuel McGowan's, report to General Heth. Accompanied by McGowan's South Carolinians and three of Brig. Gen. William MacRae's regiments (the 44th, 47th, and 52nd North Carolina), Heth was to cross

---

43 *OR* 46, pt. 1, 902, 910.

44 Freeman, *R. E. Lee*, vol. 4, 30.

Hatcher's Run and operate against the Union columns which were threatening to turn the Army of Northern Virginia's right.[45]

*   *   *

Brigadier General James H. Lane's brigade was given the task of holding the rifle pits from which McGowan's soldiers were withdrawn. Upon relieving McGowan, Lane posted his regiments: the 28th, 37th, 18th, and 33rd North Carolina from right to left. The right flank of the 28th North Carolina was anchored near the brown house in front of General MacRae's winter quarters, while the left of the 33rd rested on the branch near Mrs. Banks'.[46]

*   *   *

The withdrawal of McGowan's brigade reduced the density of the troops holding Wilcox's sector from 1,000 to 888 men per mile. General Lane, on inspecting his front, found that the interval between men varied from six to ten paces.[47] On Lane's right, Col. W. J. Martin of the 11th North Carolina, who had remained behind when MacRae had moved to the southwest, reported that the men in the trenches from his regiment and the 26th North Carolina were "5 or 6 feet apart."[48]

*   *   *

On March 30, General Lee called on General Wilcox for another brigade—Col. Joseph H. Hyman's. Troops from Maj. Gen. Bryan Grimes' division of the II Corps moved into the rifle pits formerly held by Hyman's grey clads. As soon as Hyman and his North Carolinians reported to General Heth, they marched westward and took position across the Boydton Plank Road, west of Hatcher's Run and just south of Burgess Mill. General MacRae, at the same time, crossed to the west of Hatcher's Run with the 44th, 47th, and 52nd North Carolina. The transfer of Hyman's brigade reduced the front held by Wilcox's division to about two and

45 Caldwell, *The History of a Brigade of South Carolinians*, 207; Martin, "History of the 11th North Carolina Regiment," 56.

46 *OR* 46, pt. 1, 1285.

47 *Ibid.*, Freeman, *R. E. Lee*, vol. 4, 30.

48 Martin, "History of the 11th North Carolina Regiment," 54.

one-quarter miles, while the sector for which Heth was responsible remained the same—three and three-quarter miles.[49]

*   *   *

The six miles of earthworks between Indian Town Creek and Burgess Mill, at dark on April 1, were defended by six brigades. Brig. Gen. Edward L. Thomas' Georgia brigade was on the left. The Georgians' left flank was anchored on Indian Town Creek. Lane's North Carolinians defended the sector from the branch near Mrs. Banks' to the brown house in front of MacRae's winter quarters. Two of MacRae's regiments, the 11th and 26th North Carolina, occupied the rifle pits on Lane's right. From left to right, Col. Andrew M. Nelson's Mississippi brigade and Brig. Gen. William McComb's Maryland and Tennessee brigade, and the 44th, 47th, and 52nd North Carolina of MacRae's brigade held the fortifications to Burgess Mill. (MacRae and his three regiments had been shifted during the day back to the east side of Hatcher's Run.) Thomas and Lane reported to Wilcox, while MacRae, Nelson, and McComb looked to Heth for instructions.[50]

Part II

Wright's Troops Overrun the Confederate Earthworks

The assaulting columns of the VI Corps were in position before 4:00 a.m., but it was unusually dark for that hour. Wright realized only too well that it would be impossible to launch a coordinated attack until day had started to break. He therefore took upon himself the responsibility of postponing the onslaught. Within 40 minutes, it was light enough for the soldiers "to see to step, though nothing was discernible beyond a few yards." Wright now gave the word; the crew manning the Fort Fisher signal gun fired a blank round.[51]

So far as anyone could recall, the general, field, and staff officers of Getty's division went into the fight on foot. Charles H. Anson reported, "The Vermont Brigade had been selected to lead the charge, every man understood such to be the

49 Freeman, *R. E. Lee*, vol. 4, 32-33.

50 *Ibid.*, 43.

51 *OR* 46, pt. 1, 902.

case; but few orders were given, and those in a whisper; guns were loaded, but uncapped, bayonets fixed."[52]

A heavy bombardment had broken out along the IX Corps' front, so not all of Getty's brigade commanders heard the report of the Fort Fisher signal gun. A staff officer soon hailed Colonel Tracy of the Vermont brigade and told him that the signal gun had been discharged and that his unit was the guiding brigade: the troops on the left and right were waiting for the Vermonters to advance. At a word from their officers, the men rose to their feet, leaped over the rifle pits, and took up the advance. The lines, which were massed, advanced successively, each moving forward as the preceding wave gained 100 yards. For several moments, Getty recalled, "nothing was heard but the tramp and rustle of the advancing columns." As the Rebels' picket line defended by McGowan's sharpshooters was gained, the silence was shattered by a "scattering volley." The troops responded with a ringing cheer and pushed ahead in the face of a galling small-arms fire, which was now spilling from the earthworks to their front. Rebel artillery on the division's left and right roared and caused the lines of the Vermont brigade to waver. Colonel Tracy reported that this was the day's most critical moment.[53]

A soldier recalled:

No word was spoken, as they (the Vermonters) came upon and passed over the entrenched picket line. No sound broke the stillness until the enemy's pickets, conscious of some power advancing upon them like a mighty ocean wave, with unbroken crest, delivered their fire and ran to cover in disorder. Then went up a shout from 2,500 loyal hearts, taken up and repeated by the oncoming host. The charge was on! The leading brigade pressed forward on the line designated, unconsciously angling slightly to the left and into the ravine not a man flinching, though many considered it a "forlorn hope." Consternation seized the Confederates within their entrenchments; rushing to their guns, a terrible fire of shot, shell and canister, was soon pouring into the advancing columns, especially from the forts located to the right and left of the ravine.[54]

Day was breaking and the Confederates, if the advance slowed, would discover what was transpiring. The hesitation, however, was only momentary; the Green Mountain boys pushed forward with a determination that knew no such word as

52 Anson, "Assault on the Lines of Petersburg, April 2, 1865," 88.

53 OR 46, pt. 1, 954, 962, 968.

54 Anson, "Assault on the Lines of Petersburg, April 2, 1865," 91-92.

fail. Case-shot and canister came whistling out of the gloom. Fortunately for Getty's division, most of these projectiles passed overhead. Though considerable confusion was engendered by the character of the ground and the dim light, resolute men rushed ahead to assist the pioneers in hewing an opening through the abatis. Officers and men vied with each other in the race for the works. Passing through these gaps, the Federals crossed the ditch and swarmed over the works defended by the right flank companies of the 37th North Carolina.[55]

The Vermont brigade on the left brushed away the double line of abatis "like cobwebs and the men swarmed over the works with yells and cheers that struck terror to the rebels flying in all directions." In crossing the ground in front of the abatis, casualties in the Vermont brigade were "numerous." While passing through the abatis, "all formations were broken, each man seemed determined to be in the lead, and, not unlike other instances many claimed to have been the first to grapple with a Johnny in a hand-to-hand conflict. It has been conceded, however, that the 'Yellow Flag' was the first over the works."[56]

Men of the Vermont brigade claimed for one of their number, Capt. Charles G. Gould of the 5th Vermont the honor of being first man in the VI Corps to mount the Rebel breastworks. Scaling the parapet, Gould found a muzzle of a rifle musket jammed against his chest. The weapon misfired. As the captain leaped down into the redoubt, a North Carolinian slashed him in the face with a bayonet. After sabering the Reb, Gould pulled the bayonet from his wound. Moments later, the intrepid captain was struck on the head with a saber, while another Johnny bayoneted him in the back. Gould sought to escape. Placing his hands on the interior slope of the parapet, Gould sought in vain to vault over the works. But with his strength ebbing, the captain slumped. A sergeant in the 5th Vermont rushed to Gould's assistance. Dropping his rifle-musket, the burly sergeant grasped his captain and tried to help him over the parapet. A Confederate saw what was happening, and caught the captain from behind. At this, the sergeant snatched up

---

55 *OR* 46, pt. 1, 954, 962, 968, 1285.

56 *Ibid.*, 969, 974; Anson, "Assault on the Lines of Petersburg, April 2, 1865," 89, 92. Among the officers killed or wounded in front of the abatis were: Lt. George C. French of the 1st Vermont Heavy Artillery who was killed as he gallantly cheered his men on, while Lt. G. C. Hawkins of the 3rd Vermont was wounded. Captain E. G. Ballow was struck by a shell fragment and compelled to retire from the field. The 1st Vermont Heavy Artillery carried "a yellow flag, distinctive in beauty; printed upon its silken folds were the memorable words 'Freedom and Unity.'"

his rifle-musket, dealt the Reb a deadly blow, and lifted Gould over the works. Both men rolled into the ditch, where they were safe from the deadly minies.[57]

Soldiers from the Vermont brigade entered a redoubt to the right of the ravine and captured four guns. Urged on by Lt. Col. Ronald A. Kennedy, men of the 5th Vermont swung to the left, crossed the hollow, and stormed a small work defended by the 28th North Carolina mounting two guns. Color-Bearer Jackson Sargent was the first to scale the parapet and plant the "State Colors of Vermont"; he was followed by Cpl. Nelson E. Carle with the national colors. Seymour's division coming up, the 5th Vermont bore toward the right and rejoined the brigade. After passing to the left of the white house and reaching the wooded crest beyond, Colonel Tracy called a brief halt to allow his officers to reform their units.[58]

Colonel Hyde's initial assault wave halted at the edge of the swamp fronting the Rebels' abatis. As soon as the soldiers of the 49th and 77th New York had re-adjusted their lines, they stormed through the openings in the abatis cut by the pioneers and over the works. They were followed over the parapet by the three other lines. Some confusion occurred because of the darkness, "but the colors of the different regiments and those directly about them, guided by the fire of the enemy, went straight on to their destination."[59]

After entering the defenses, Lt. Col. Stephen C. Fletcher of the 1st Maine called for Capt. Augustus Merrill. Fletcher told Merrill to take a few skirmishers and see if he could ascertain the enemy's position and strength in our front. "Accompanied by 20 men, the captain advanced through the woods and came upon a hastily abandoned Rebel camp—McGowan's winter quarters. Here, the bluecoats captured a lieutenant and three men belonging to Hill's Corps. Questioning the grey clads, Merrill learned that the Southerners "would make but slight resistance this side of Hatcher's Run." Meanwhile, other units from Hyde's brigade forged ahead. Colonel Hyde succeeded in reforming about 200 men into line of battle at a point near the South Side Railroad, a mile beyond the breakthrough.[60]

Colonel Warner's troops to the right of Hyde's column closed to within a few paces of the Rebel pickets (McGowan's sharpshooters) before they were

---

57 Anson, "Assault on the Lines of Petersburg, April 2, 1865," 92-93.

58 *OR* 46, pt. 1, 969, 974.

59 *Ibid.*, 976. When the advance began and the first line moved forward, Colonel Hyde reported, "After they had advanced 100 yards the second advanced, the third in like manner, and the fourth after the third had gone 250 yards in advance, the first line got nearly up to the picket-pits of the enemy before their movement was discovered; swept them easily, followed by the second and third."

60 *Ibid.*, 976-977.

discovered. The space between the outposts and the rifle pits was uneven and swampy. Furthermore, it was still quite dark, and the Confederate artillery had opened. These factors combined to throw Warner's assaulting columns into "great confusion." The first line, the 102nd Pennsylvania, wavered. Major James McGregor of the 139th Pennsylvania, whose unit was following, feared that his soldiers would become intermixed with those from other units. He shouted for the color-sergeants to push ahead. When the 139th Pennsylvania arrived in front of the abatis, McGregor found that it wasn't as formidable as he had feared. It was quickly passed. The troops followed their color-bearers over the works, behind which were discovered many of Lane's North Carolinians "who appeared only too glad of the opportunity" of being taken prisoner. Soldiers of the 93rd and 102nd Pennsylvania crossed the works at the same time. A brief halt was called while prisoners were collected and sent to the rear. Without much organization, Warner's brigade pushed on toward the South Side Railroad. Finally, Warner and his officers "with great difficulty" halted and reformed their commands about a mile from the breached defenses.[61]

Cannoneers of the 3rd New York Battery entered the works, close behind Getty's infantry. In accordance with instructions from Capt. William A. Harn, the New Yorkers unlimbered their four Napoleons and opened fire on several Rebel guns emplaced in a work to the right of the breakthrough. After a few minutes of hot action, the Federal gunners silenced the Rebel pieces.[62]

General Wheaton's division advanced to the right of Getty's column of assault. Each wave in Wheaton's phalanx guided left, "each brigade taking up the movement toward the enemy's lines as soon as the troops on its left had gained the prescribed distance of 100 paces between lines." Wheaton's bluecoats encountered "a sharp musketry and artillery fire," from which their losses were comparatively small, considering the distance that they had to pass over and the abatis that had to be hewed away.

During the advance through the gloom, the commands became "more or less disordered." The lines in many cases merged. Wheaton had seen that extra axes, besides those carried by the pioneers, had been issued to the men of the first wave. Apparently, the abatis in the sector against which Wheaton directed his division was more formidable than in the area assailed by Getty. Wheaton reported that his men "were astonished to find these obstructions such serious obstacles and so difficult

61 *Ibid.*, 963-966; Mark, *Red: White: and Blue Badge*, 322.

62 *OR* 46, pt. 1, 1010, 1013.

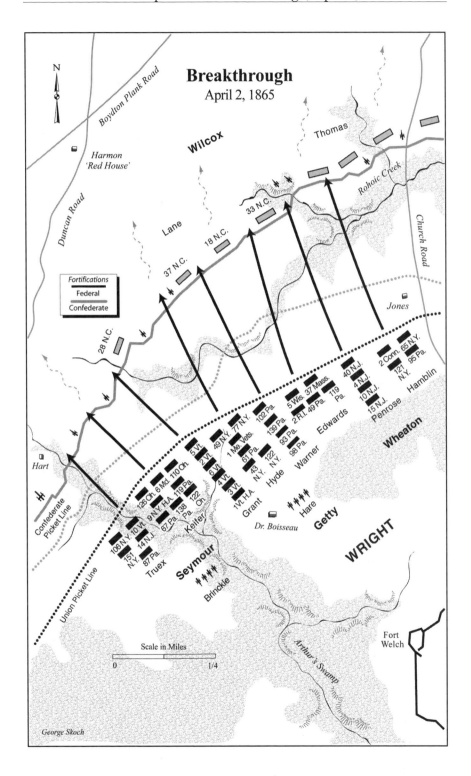

Breakthrough

April 2, 1865

George Skoch

to remove." While the pioneers were cutting openings, they were subjected to "a severe canister and musketry fire."[63]

Colonel Edwards' troops cheered wildly as they beat their way through two lines of abatis, crossed the ditch, and mounted the Rebel works. Soldiers from the 37th Massachusetts and the 5th Wisconsin were first to plant their colors on a large redoubt. Rebel artillerists standing by their pieces sent several charges of canister crashing into the onrushing bluecoats. After a bitter hand-to-hand struggle, the Yanks found themselves in possession of the work, where they listed the capture of three guns, about 40 prisoners, and a battle flag.[64]

The 2nd Rhode Island which was following the 5th Wisconsin lost contact in the gloom. Diverging to the right, the regiment crossed two lines of abatis. The Rhode Islanders found themselves in front of a Confederate emplacement mounting one gun. Sweeping over the parapet, the soldiers from Rhode Island drove the grey clads from their defenses and through an encampment. First Lt. Frank S. Holliday, placing himself at the head of a small party, stormed a two-gun Confederate battery. After capturing the pieces, the Yanks turned them on the fleeing Southerners.[65]

When they crossed the works, several of Edwards' officers saw that the butternuts still held the earthworks to their right from which they hammered Penrose's and Hamblin's onrushing brigades with small-arms fire, canister, and shell. Major William C. Gray of the 119th Pennsylvania wheeled his regiment to the right. Advancing along the line of works, Gray's bluecoats captured three redans with seven guns and a large number of prisoners.[66]

Colonel Edwards, accompanied by a number of soldiers, pushed for the railroad. The 37th Massachusetts in its advance passed through a camp and turned to the demolition teams. Several wagons and a number of tents filled with clothing, officers' baggage, and quartermaster's stores were put to the torch.

Sergeant James Young of Company D, 5th Wisconsin and a score of men first reached the South Side Railroad. As they approached the tracks, a locomotive and a string of cars rumbled by. The soldiers blazed away but were unable to stop the

---

63 *Ibid.*, 910.

64 *Ibid.*, 941, 945, 952. Captain John C. Robinson of the 37th Massachusetts was one of the first to reach the abatis, where he was wounded. Corporal Richard Welch of Company E, 37th Massachusetts knocked down the rebel color-bearer, took the flag, and shot one of the gunners as he was discharging his piece.

65 *Ibid.*, 951.

66 *Ibid.*, 950.

train. A man from the signal corps on horseback had accompanied Young's detachment. He rode up to a pole, rose in his saddle, climbed the pole, cut the wire, and after descending attached the wire to a battery, which he had fastened securely to his saddle. For the next several minutes, he sat his horse coolly receiving the Reb dispatches.

After crossing the Boydton Plank Road, Lt. Col. Elisha Rhodes of the 2nd Rhode Island called a halt. He formed his men into line of battle and awaited further orders.[67]

It was so dark that Penrose's New Jersey brigade could "see only a few paces in advance. "The skirmishers supposed to screen Penrose's advance failed to do so, and the 40th New Jersey spearheading the column encountered a scathing fire from Rebel outposts. The 40th New Jersey which today was getting its first taste of combat faltered. Coming up from behind, the 4th New Jersey commingled with the 40th. Urged on by Colonel Penrose, the two regiments overran the Confederate pickets, capturing a number of grey clads. Here, a portion of the 4th New Jersey halted and reformed.

Penrose's brigade now diverged to the left. As it did, the 10th and 15th New Jersey closed up on the first line. Part of the New Jersey brigade entered a section of the Rebel defenses already carried by Edward's bluecoats. Spotting two abandoned 3-inch rifles, a detachment led by Capt. Charles R. Paul of Penrose's staff took possession. A guard was placed on the guns, and they were loaded within a few minutes. Two companies of the 37th Massachusetts dashed up and claimed the field pieces. When Penrose's men protested, the soldiers from Massachusetts pushed them away.[68]

On the right of the New Jersey brigade, soldiers recoiled before "the terrible fire" of the Confederates. Spencer-armed riflemen of the 37th Massachusetts blazed away at the Rebs, pinning them down, so that "a handful of men under protection of their volleys, found a standing place under the angle of a parapet where they could not be reached by artillery or struck by riflemen unless exposed themselves." After each volley, a few more men crossed the glacis and joined their comrades in the defiladed area in the angle of the works. Soon there were enough Federals to storm the redoubt.

When the bluecoats surged over the parapet, the defenders showed the greatest obstinacy. "Some refusing to surrender were shot. One, William Cheatham, said he would never surrender; when a man of the 15th (New Jersey)

---

67 *Ibid.*, 946, 951, 953; Mark, *Red: White: and Blue Badge*, 322.

68 OR 46, pt. 1, 927-929; Haines, *History of the Fifteenth Regiment New Jersey*, 301.

before the words were hardly spoken, drove a bayonet through his body. Major (J. Augustus) Fay of the 40th (New Jersey) led a storming party, which was joined by men from all our regiments. He (Fay) was uninjured, but had a number of bullet holes in his clothing. The color-bearer in the fort would not give up his flag, and the major had to draw his pistol and wound him before he would drop them."[69]

Meanwhile, Lt. Col. Baldwin Hufty's battalion of the 4th New Jersey had joined the 119th Pennsylvania in mopping up the rifle pits to the right of the breakthrough.[70]

After reforming his brigade, Colonel Penrose had his officers check the rolls. At the same time, the troops turned about 200 disarmed Confederates over to the people from the provost-marshal's department.[71]

It seemed to the soldiers of Colonel Hamblin's brigade that the signal gun would never be discharged. Anson Ryder, who lay beside diarist Beckwith, remarked, "I would rather charge than lie here in this suspense and misery." As the first grey of dawn began to show, the gun "belched." The soldiers of the brigade scrambled to their feet, closed ranks, and plunged forward into the darkness.[72]

Colonel Hamblin's column of assault "advanced en echelon of twenty paces to rear and right" of Penrose's brigade. A number of circumstances (the semi-darkness, a ground fog, and the nature of the terrain), caused the brigade's lines to be thrown into "some confusion" by the time they reached the Confederate defenses. The 65th New York gained the honor of being the first regiment in the brigade to plant its colors on the parapet. Before reaching the Confederate rifle pits, the 121st New York divided. Most of the men along with the colors entered the works farther to the right than intended, capturing two guns. One of these pieces was immediately turned on the Rebels, loaded, and fired by Sgt. Redford Dustin of Company F.[73]

One of the men of the 121st New York wrote:

the Rebel works were marked by jets of flame from their rifles as they fired upon us. Another instant and we were up to their abatis, and we got into a tangle looking for a place to get through. Finally some fellow to our left sang out, "Here's a road," and a lot of us made for it, and followed it on a run to the Rebel works at that point a fort.

69 Haines, *History of the Fifteenth Regiment New Jersey*, 301-302.

70 *OR* 46, pt. 1, 929.

71 *Ibid.*, 927.

72 Best, *History of the 121st New York Infantry*, 210.

73 *OR* 46, pt. 1, 931, 935, 936.

Climbing up the sides, it being now light enough to see a few paces ahead, I went in through the embrasure of the guns, one of which had been firing on us. The Johnnies had run back among the huts and were firing back at us. We ran down toward them and they ran back into the field. Quite a number hid in the huts, and our fellows hunted them out.[74]

Colonel Hamblin now lost control of his unit. Colonel James Hubbard of the 2nd Connecticut Heavy Artillery with one force drove for the railroad, another detachment swung to the right,[75] while a third party led by Maj. J. W. Cronkite of the 121st New York struck for the Boydton Plank Road, and "fired into the running Rebs, and . . . into some wagons which were passing." The bluecoats used their bayonets to twist off the telegraph wire. Within a few minutes, the Confederates counterattacked and compelled Cronkite's detachment to abandon its toehold on the Boydton Plank Road.

The troops advancing to the right joined the 119th Pennsylvania and Hufty's battalion in sweeping the Rebs out of their works to the right of the breakthrough. As they drove ahead, the colors of the 65th New York in the van, the Federals captured a redoubt armed with three guns. Spencer-armed soldiers from the 49th Pennsylvania screened the right flank of the column, as it drove through rapidly crumbling Confederate defenses toward Fort Gregg. In doing so, the sharpshooters bagged a number of Confederate pickets. As soon as the column was halted by the fire of Confederate guns emplaced in Fort Gregg, Capt. James T. Steuart wheeled his sharpshooters to the left. This movement brought them face to face with a redan mounting three guns. Steuart called for his men to charge. Sweeping across the ditch, the bluecoats entered the stronghold, capturing 3 guns, 3 officers, and 25 enlisted men.[76]

Lt. Col. Charles A. Milliken was in charge of the Union picket line to the right of the point of attack. Milliken's pickets kept pace with Wheaton's division to their left. Overrunning the Rebel outposts, the Federals captured and disarmed between 400 and 500 Johnnies. Milliken's men claimed that they entered the redoubt near the Jones house ahead of Wheaton's division. Swinging his skirmishers to the right, Milliken assisted Wheaton's troops in enlarging the breakthrough.[77]

74 Best, *History of the 121st New York Infantry*, 210-211.

75 OR 46, pt. 1, 931-932. The party swinging to the right consisted of detachments from the 65th and 121st New York, the 2nd Connecticut Heavy Artillery, and the 95th Pennsylvania.

76 *Ibid.*, 935-936, 940; Best, *History of the 121st New York Infantry*, 211.

77 OR 46, pt. 1, 962.

A section of Battery H, 1st Rhode Island Light Artillery accompanied Wheaton's assaulting columns. Almost as soon as the troops had carried the works, the cannoneers, amid a cracking of whips and shouts, drove up and put their pieces into action. Throwing their pieces into battery, they opened fire on a section of Rebel artillery which was enfilading Wheaton's troops from the right. The Federal cannoneers quickly gained the upper hand; the Rebel guns withdrew. At this, Battery H ceased firing, limbered up their pieces, and moved to the left.[78]

As General Wheaton recalled, his troops "were perfectly wild with delight at their success in this grand assault." Considerable difficulty was encountered by the officers in reforming the brigades.[79]

General Seymour's division had advanced to the left of Getty's. As soon as the signal gun was discharged, Colonel Keifer's column of assault drove forward. Scattered clumps of underbrush and several "marshy ditches" were encountered and caused confusion. Keifer's first wave (the 110th and 126th Ohio, and the 6th Maryland) rolled over the Confederate picket line, capturing a number of grey clads.

"Without halting or discharging a piece," the column surged toward the Rebels' main line of resistance. Men began to drop as they came under a heavy fire. Seconds seemed like hours, as the pioneers cut a route for the troops through the double line of abatis. Crossing the ditch, the Yanks scaled the earthworks, to the left of a salient angle. Six officers and about 20 enlisted men from the 6th Maryland claimed the honor of planting the first stand of colors on the works in the sector assailed by Seymour's division. Several minutes elapsed before these soldiers were joined by other men of the regiment. During this time, a fierce hand-to-hand struggle took place, as soldiers of the 11th and 26th North Carolina vainly sought to seal the breach.[80]

The 126th Ohio crossed the ditch a short distance to the right of the 6th Maryland. Entering the Rebel rifle pits, the Ohioans captured a number of prisoners. To the Buckeye's right and left were redoubts in which diehard Confederates continued to hold out. From these works, the Southerners blazed away at the Federals with small-arms and artillery. Col. Benjamin F. Smith quickly reformed his regiment. Swinging to the left, the 126th Ohio advanced against one of the redoubts.[81]

---

78 *Ibid.*, 1010, 1014.

79 *Ibid.*, 910.

80 *Ibid.*, 992-993, 1000. In this fight, Maj. C. K. Prentiss, Capt. Thomas Coker, and Lt. Thomas Duff and Thomas H. Goldsborough were severely wounded.

81 *Ibid.*, 1005.

To the right of the area penetrated by the 126th Ohio, the 110th Ohio broke through. Troops from that regiment captured four pieces of artillery, 400 prisoners, and two battle flags.[82]

The 9th New York Heavy Artillery, on approaching the abatis obliqued to the left, and broke through the Rebels' line to the left of the point penetrated by the 6th Maryland. Storming a redoubt, the New Yorkers captured four guns. These pieces were manned and turned on the retreating butternuts with effect. As soon as he could reform his regiment, Lt. Col. James W. Snyder wheeled it to the left and swept down the rifle pits. Encountering a deep swamp, the Yanks waded it and carried a second redoubt mounting two guns.[83]

Within a few minutes, Keifer's brigade had captured 10 pieces of artillery, a large number of prisoners, three battle flags, and Maj. Gen. Henry Heth's headquarters flag.

Colonel Keifer's third line (the 122nd Ohio, the 67th and 138th Pennsylvania) followed the other units through the abatis and into the works. A number of the regimental commanders had difficulties regrouping their units, after they had entered the fortifications. While several units swung to the left to roll back the Confederate line, others drove for the South Side Railroad. Two of these regiments, the 122nd Ohio and the 138th Pennsylvania, followed the rapidly retreating Confederates for several miles in a northwesterly direction. The Boydton Plank Road was crossed and a short distance beyond, a camp was overrun and prisoners taken.

Soldiers from the 138th Pennsylvania reached the South Side Railroad, cut the telegraph wires, and ripped up two rails. As they were returning to their regiment, Cpl. John W. Mauk and Pvt. Daniel Wolford lost their way and encountered two mounted Confederate officers. The Rebs drew their pistols and called on the Yanks to surrender. One of the officers shouted that other Confederates were coming. Undaunted, Mauk and Wolford fired—the corporal unhorsed one of the officers,

---

82 *Ibid.*, 1003. Lieutenant Colonel Otho H. Binkley in his after-action report cited a number of his men, "The flags were captured by Private Isaac Jones, Company H, and Sergt. Francis M. McMillen, Company C. . . . Capt. George P. Boyer made himself conspicuous by his activity and bravery. Adjt. William H. Harry, Lieuts. John T. Sherer, A. A. Hubbard, D. S. French, and Amos Shaul deserve great credit for the manner in which they conducted themselves during the engagement. First Sergt. John W. Hays, commanding Company A, and Sergt. Richard Pearson, commanding Company G, are entitled to mention for their good conduct during the assault, in which the latter was severely wounded. Sergt. Thomas Goe, Company D, in charge of three men, caused 130 rebels to surrender to him; among those were 3 captains and 4 lieutenants. Corpl. Keeran McKenny, Company C, was the first to reach and capture a four-gun battery, overpowered two rebels who refused to surrender to him." *Ibid.*, 1003-1004.

83 *Ibid.*, 1002.

while the private missed. Fearful that other Johnnies would show up, Mauk and Wolford fled and rejoined their unit. Subsequently, it was learned that the officer Mauk had killed was one of Lee's corps commanders—the redoubtable Ambrose P. Hill.[84]

Colonel Truex led his cheering troops forward at the double-quick. A "terrible fire of musketry and artillery" was encountered before the first line had advanced more than a few steps. Since it was quite dark, many of the units became scrambled. Within a few moments, the blue-coated tide had engulfed the Confederate picket line. In passing the abatis, the lines were "considerable broken." Part of the 10th Vermont on the right became separated and wasn't seen again by Lt. Col. George B. Damon for several hours. The colonel with the rest of his regiment crossed the ditch and scaled the parapet, which at that point was from 12 to 15 feet high. The 10th Vermont won the distinction of being the first unit in Truex's brigade to plant its colors inside the works; it was closely followed by the 106th New York and the 14th New Jersey. Soldiers of the 14th New Jersey entered the Confederate rifle pits defended by Martin's North Carolinians near an unpainted barn.

Within a few moments, Truex's troops rounded up about 300 Confederates who had grounded their arms. The prisoners were sent to the rear without guards; infantrymen were detailed to take charge of the five guns emplaced along the works carried by the brigade.

As soon as the officers of the 10th Vermont and the 106th New York could reform their units, Colonel Truex had them wheel their regiments to the left. Moving off on the double, the Federals charged down the line, rolling back the foe as they advanced. The Yanks overran a redoubt and captured 150 Rebs and two wagons. After pausing briefly to regroup, the battle line rolled on. A second redoubt was attacked. The Confederates evacuated the work and retired into a third redoubt. The 14th New Jersey, which had been called up to support the 10th Vermont and the 106th New York, was the first unit to enter the strongpoint which mounted two guns. Here, Truex's command was reinforced by the 6th Maryland and the 7th New York Heavy Artillery of Keifer's brigade.[85]

Grey clad battle lines now emerged from the woods to the right and from the open ground in front of the captured redoubt. The Unionists held their ground for about 20 minutes in the face of this slashing counterthrust. Over-powered, the Yanks retired across the swamp and into the next redoubt. Major William Wood

---

84 *Ibid.*, 993, 1008; Oscela Lewis, *History of the One Hundred and Thirty-Eighth Regiment, Pennsylvania Volunteer Infantry* (Norristown, 1866), 153-155.

85 OR 46, pt. 1, 982, 986-987, 990-991; Howell, *Chronicles of the One Hundred Fifty-First Regiment New York*, 98-99.

and a detachment of the 7th New York Heavy Artillery took charge of the four guns mounted in the fort. The New Yorkers turned these pieces on the oncoming Confederates. By this time, grey clad artillerists had manned the two guns in the recaptured redoubt. With these pieces, they engaged Wood's cannoneers in a lively duel. Within a few minutes, the New Yorkers succeeded in dismounting one of the Rebel guns.[86]

The redoubt was reoccupied without a struggle. Without pausing, the Federals advanced on the next redoubt, which was also given up almost without a struggle by the grey clads. Inspecting the work, the Northerners found that they had captured four guns, caissons, and several teams. About one-half mile beyond, Seymour's troops met the XXIV Corps. A halt was called to allow Seymour to communicate with General Wright.[87]

One of the division hospitals, Wheaton's, had been set up by Surgeon Redford Sharp near Fort Fisher, within the Union defense line. By daylight, the first of the walking wounded began to trickle back from the front, followed by the litter cases. From then until 4:00 p.m., the surgeons worked feverishly in "dressing wounds, extracting bullets and amputating limbs. There were the usual sad and terrible scenes of suffering and death." Thirteen of the wounded expired after receiving treatment. All told, 300 cases were handled during the day by Dr. Sharp and his team. Among these were a number of Confederates, "who shared the attention bestowed by the surgeons and expressed their gratitude for kindness shown." As fast as possible, ambulances took the wounded to the general hospital at City Point.[88]

Editor's Conclusion

By late morning on April 2, Grant had driven the Confederates from the line jutting southeast from Battery No. 45 and had sealed Petersburg off by deploying troops from the Army of the Potomac and the Army of the James close to the Dimmock Line. Now, he set about trying to block other possible Confederate escape routes. Grant issued new orders to Sheridan:

---

86 OR 46, pt. 1, 979, 982, 986, 991, 1000, 1002.

87 *Ibid.*, 979, 982-983, 991, 993.

88 Haines, *History of the Fifteenth Regiment New Jersey*, 302-303.

Lieutenant Colonel Commissary of Subsistence, and Acting Aide-de-Camp
RICHIE HOUSE, April 2, 1865-12.30 p.m.

Major-General SHERIDAN:

I would like you to get the Fifth Corps and all the cavalry, except Mackenzie, across the Appomattox as soon as you can. You may cross where you please. The position and movements of the enemy will dictate your movements after you cross. All we want is to capture or beat the enemy. There is a pontoon train with the army. If you want it send an officer to conduct it where it will be required.

U. S. GRANT[89]

In reply to Grant's message to block the Chesterfield county roads, Sheridan told Grant that all the Confederates had left Petersburg earlier that afternoon, and therefore there was no point in crossing to Chesterfield county: "From what has transpired here I think, beyond a doubt, that the enemy's troops, wagons, and, in fact, everything that is left of them, have moved off and are moving toward Burkeville Junction. With these impressions and your instructions I am in some doubt as to the result of my moving north of the Appomattox. I think everything has left Petersburg, or is leaving it." He ended by informing Grant that his cavalry was fighting the fugitives beyond the Namozine Road.

Sheridan's obstinacy allowed some 40,000 Confederates to escape the Richmond and Petersburg front via Chesterfield county roads, for its ultimate surrender a week later at Appomattox Court House.

89 *OR* 46, pt. 3, 488-489.

The Retreat to Appomattox

April 2–9, 1865

by Chris Calkins[1]

By 8:00 p.m. on April 2, 1865, the dejected troops of General Lee's Army of Northern Virginia began crossing the Appomattox River from Petersburg over four bridges. As the wagons following rumbled across, the various elements moved into Chesterfield County and Lee's evacuation plans were implemented. Under generals James Longstreet (First-Third Corps, combined with A. P. Hill's Corps after his death on April 2) and John B. Gordon (Second Corps), the troops leaving the Petersburg lines would follow routes along the River, Hickory, and Woodpecker roads, and eventually reach Amelia Court House on the Richmond & Danville Railroad. Units of the Confederate army under Maj. Gen. William Mahone would leave their positions along the Howlett Line, while others evacuate the defenses surrounding Richmond from the east and southeast. Lee hoped to rendezvous his troops at Amelia—thirty miles to the west—where he had expected supplies to be waiting for his men and animals. After issuing the rations to the army, he planned to follow the rail line 104 miles to Danville and hopefully link up with the Army of Tennessee under Gen. Joseph E. Johnston in North Carolina.

---

1 Ed Bearss did not include anything beyond the breakthrough on April 1. In order to complete the narrative of the Petersburg story, Chris Calkins, author of *Battles of Appomattox Station and Appomattox Court House, April 8-9, 1865* (with Edwin C. Bearss) and *Battle of Five Forks* (The Virginia Civil War Battles and Leaders Series) agreed to work with Ed to research and write this short chapter. He based his research on the *Official Records* and other sources.

Approximately 58,000 Confederate forces left the Richmond-Petersburg front and were pursued by 76,113 soldiers in the Federal army.

Lieutenant General Richard S. Ewell led troops out of Richmond and was followed by Naval and Marine forces from Drewry's Bluff. South of the Appomattox River, and moving through Dinwiddie County, were remnants from the fighting along White Oak Road and the Five Forks area under generals Fitzhugh Lee and Richard Anderson who now commanded the forces of generals George Pickett and Bushrod Johnson. This element of Lee's army would be pursued by the Federal forces of General Sheridan's cavalry and General Meade's Army of the Potomac. General Grant, along with Major General E. O. C. Ord's Army of the James, would march parallel to the South Side Railroad as they headed toward Burke's Station to cut off Lee's advance in that direction.

On April 3, the Union Army occupied both Richmond and Petersburg, and continued to pursue and fight the retreating force at Namozine Church in Amelia County. This would become a running fight between both Northern and Southern cavalry forces with the V, II, and VI Corps of the Army of the Potomac right behind. The IX Corps followed the Army of the James and worked diligently to realign the gauge of the South Side Railroad to accommodate the rolling stock of Grant's Military Railroad. Ord's forces were composed of the XXIV Corps, along with units of the XXV Corps comprised of United States Colored Troops.

As the Confederate army continued its trek toward Amelia Court House on April 4, additional rear guard action took place at Deep Creek, Tabernacle Church, and Beaverpond Creek. While Lee's forces trudged into the county seat village, staffers were sent down to the rail station to look for the expected rations which did not materialize. As more troops of the Army of Northern Virginia piled into Amelia Court House, Lee made the fateful decision to appeal to the local citizens for any surplus food rations they may have had, thus expending precious time in waiting around the county seat. Up to this point, he had had a one-day's lead on Grant's army but now would lose it. In his after action report of the campaign, Lee noted, "This delay was fatal and could not be retrieved."

Realizing that Lee was concentrating his force at Amelia, fast riding Union cavalry and accompanying infantry swung around to the southwest of town and headed west for Jetersville, the next station on the Richmond & Danville Railroad. Located south of Amelia Court House and across Lee's line of march, Federal troops began entrenching themselves to thwart any advance made by the Confederates. After receiving this distressful news, Lee decided to make a night march around the dug-in Union army at Jetersville, and head for Farmville where he was informed that 80,000 rations would be waiting for him. Before marching that evening, the general learned that a wagon train intended for his son's soldiers—those of Gen. George Washington Custis Lee—had been pounced upon

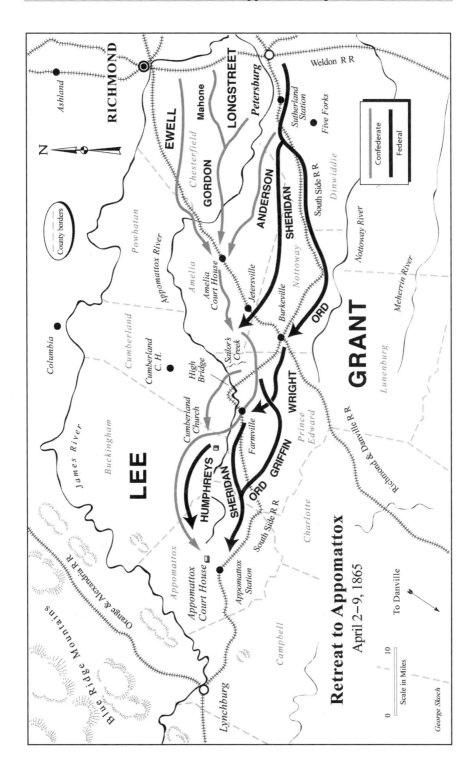

Retreat to Appomattox
April 2–9, 1865

George Skoch

by Federal cavalry and was destroyed near Painesville. Both forces would clash at nearby Amelia Springs until nightfall.

On the morning of April 6th, word reached Humphreys' II Corps that the tail end of Lee's column was moving past the Amelia Springs resort north of Jetersville and along a ridge running parallel to Flat Creek. Federal skirmishers were dispatched in pursuit and now the II Corps was in motion. They would eventually be following the Confederate column which was strung out as follows: Longstreet, Anderson, Ewell, the main wagon train, and Gordon acting as rear guard. Continual fighting would take place in a running gun battle. Every so often Gordon's men would make a stand similar to that of the hamlet of Deatonsville. Eventually the armies would come to the crossing of Little Sailor's Creek where a final rear guard action would take place that evening.

Farther to the south, at Burke's Station, Ord's Army of the James moved along the South Side Railroad. Determining that Lee's column was heading toward Farmville, and that the nearby High Bridge might be used to cross the Appomattox River, the general dispatched two infantry regiments: the 54th Pennsylvania and the 123rd Ohio, along with three companies of the 4th Massachusetts Cavalry to destroy it. Approaching the 126-foot-high and 2,400-foot long railroad structure from the south, the "bridge burners" were soon pounced upon by members of Fitzhugh Lee's cavalry. In desperate hand-to-hand fighting, the horse soldiers lost heavily in rank on both sides. The Federal losses were Colonel Theodore Read (killed) and Col. Francis Washburn (mortally wounded). The Southern forces lost Brigadier General James Dearing (mortally wounded and the last Confederate general to die in the war) along with majors John Knott and James Thomson, and Col. Reuben Boston (all killed). The High Bridge was saved from destruction for the time being.

Back at Sailor's Creek, Sheridan's three cavalry divisions led by generals George Custer, Thomas Devin, and George Crook, took turns attacking Lee's wagon train along his line of march. Carrying out hit-and-run tactics at the major crossroads, the Union cavalry was able to cause a gap in the Confederate column and cut off those elements under Anderson and Ewell along Little Sailor's Creek. To alleviate some of the pressure behind Ewell, the main wagon train and Gordon would turn onto another roadway that crossed Sailor's Creek at Double Bridges two miles farther north. It was now near 5:00 p.m. and the battles of Sailor's Creek were about to begin.

Sailor's Creek would become three separate engagements, all fought simultaneously and spread out about one to two miles apart. Ewell's Corps would be assaulted by Horatio Wright's VI Corps at the Hillsman farm and along Little Sailor's Creek. Anderson, with Pickett and Johnson, would make their stand a mile farther beyond at Marshall's Crossroads. They would be attacked by Union cavalry commanded by Gen. Wesley Merritt. At the confluence of Big and Little Sailor's Creek, Gordon protected the wagons and faced off against Humphreys at Lockett's farm. Nightfall would bring an end to the fighting at the creek with a terrific loss for Lee's Army of Northern Virginia.

The toll was 7,700 Southerners who were either killed, wounded, or captured. The general officers taken prisoner were: Richard Ewell, Custis Lee, Seth Barton, Joseph Kershaw, James Simms, Dudley Dubose, Eppa Hunton, and Montgomery Corse. Federal estimates for casualties amounted to 1,180 men of which 170 were killed. The day closed with Ord's men skirmishing with Longstreet at Rice's Depot on the South Side Railroad.

With the Federal army now on his heels, Lee decided to make another night march as his men moved toward and into nearby Farmville. Some would cross the Appomattox on the High Bridge, while others on the wagon bridge below. Gordon's Corps would then follow the railroad into Farmville, while another contingent, led by Mahone, marched directly to Cumberland Court House via the Jamestown Road. South of the river others would follow the direct road into Farmville while skirmishing at the Sandy and Bush river crossings. Lead elements of Longstreet's Corps reached Farmville where they found the waiting rations at the train station. Distribution began among the hungry Confederate soldiers but soon Federal cavalry advanced upon Farmville and the trains were closed up and sent westward to Pamplin's Depot. Lee then ordered his troops to cross the Appomattox River into Cumberland County with instructions to burn all bridges behind them including High Bridge and the lower wagon bridge, four miles down river.

Three miles north of the town of Farmville, the Army of Northern Virginia began entrenching near Cumberland Church to protect their wagon train as it continued its westward movement. Constructing trenches in a "fish hook" fashion, Mahone's division held the left flank position while Gordon and Longstreet's men filled in the rest of the defensive line.

The threat against this line soon came in the form of Humphreys' II Corps. Earlier that morning, the Federals reached High Bridge as the Confederates began burning a few of the western spans. Extinguishing the fire on the lower wagon bridge over the Appomattox River, the Northern soldiers made a passage and then headed the five miles to Cumberland Church. Finding the Confederates entrenched there, preparations were made to assault the position held by Mahone. Unable to turn the flank, nightfall brought an end to the fighting as Lee's men began their third night march in a row. Their destination was Appomattox Station—thirty-eight miles away—where more supply trains awaited them. That night, General Grant, now in Farmville and from his headquarters in the local Prince Edward Hotel sent his first dispatch to Lee concerning the possibility of surrender. Upon receiving and reading the message the Confederate commander handed it to Longstreet, who remarked "Not yet." At the same time, President Lincoln, at City Point, received a message from Grant who informed him that Sheridan sent correspondence that "If the thing is pressed I think that Lee will surrender." Lincoln responded "Let the thing be pressed."

By following the various routes to Appomattox Station via Appomattox Court House, Lee's men had a march of some eight miles farther than had they stayed south of the river and paralleled the South Side Railroad. This left that route open to the Union army of only thirty miles to the station. To pressure the Confederate line of march, both the II and VI Corps followed behind Lee's troops while the rest of the Federal army stayed south of the river on the shorter road. Their line of march was Sheridan's cavalry, Ord's Army of the James, and the rear being brought up by Griffin's V Corps.

On April 8th, both armies tramped along in their race to Appomattox Station and the supply trains waiting for them there. In the lead, Custer's troopers received information about the location of these trains and set off to capture them before Lee's troops could get there. Leading the Confederate line of march this day was the surplus wagon and artillery train under Brig. Gen. R. Lindsay Walker. After passing through Appomattox Court House his men went into camp about a mile from the station.

As the armies moved along this day pretty much unmolested, a series of messages were passed between Grant and Lee. In one concerning the possibility of surrender, Grant received a message from Lee asking what terms would be offered. This provoked a series of correspondence between the two until a face-to-face meeting was decided upon the next day.

Custer's cavalry reached the four supply trains at Appomattox Station first that evening and captured them without a major incident. Seeing Walker's artillery going into position, the Union troopers made a series of attacks on their camp, eventually scattering the Confederates and capturing 25 cannon. This engagement now placed elements of the Federal army across the route Lee had intended too follow in his march toward Danville.

Lee, now setting up his headquarters near Appomattox Court House, heard the fighting three miles away at the station and realized that the Federal army was now in his front. Earlier that day, with his army down to two corps, he switched the line of march so that Gordon now led the army with Longstreet holding the rear. Fitzhugh Lee's cavalry would support Gordon's Corps.

Instructing Gordon to prepare for a breakthrough attempt early on April 9, preparations were made for a morning attack. Assembling his men at the edge of the village and supported on his right flank by cavalry, at dawn the Confederate battle line moved forward and encountered elements of Crook's cavalry. These were easily pushed back but then, along a far ridge, Union infantry were seen forming in battle line. These proved to be soldiers of Ord's Army of the James. As they began making their forward movement, Gordon's men realized that their escape route was sealed off so they began to fall back toward the village. Soon another threat faced them as Griffin's V Corps arrived on the scene and began to move upon Gordon's left flank. Word was sent to Lee of the impending situation and soon white flags of truce began appearing along Gordon's battle line. The fighting ground to a halt as it did likewise in the Confederate rear now being pressed by the Union II and VI Corps. Grant, by employing a giant pincers movement, had forced Lee's army into submission made possible by the situation provided at Farmville. The two generals now set about to meet and discuss the terms of surrender.

The surrender proceedings took place on April 9 at the village home of Wilmer McLean. By 3:30 p.m., the Army of Northern Virginia was no longer a fighting force to be contended with. The war in Virginia was finally over and the Appomattox Campaign was successfully completed by Grant's army.

Afterword

The Petersburg Campaign offers interesting lessons. On the strategic level, the Overland Campaign battles leading up to the opening of the siege demonstrate that the battles of annihilation President Lincoln and Generals Halleck and Grant sought to inflict upon Lee proved more destructive to the Army of the Potomac than to the rebel army. From May 5 to June 12, Grant instructed General Meade to make the Army of Northern Virginia his primary focus; he sought to cripple it instead of forcing it to fall back upon Richmond. By the time the Union troops arrived opposite Petersburg, their army was badly damaged and too weak to seize a nearly undefended city. For eight months Meade's men suffered in the Petersburg trenches, boiling in summer and shivering in the winter. It was only the arrival of the previously detached VI Corps and Phil Sheridan's cavalry from the Shenandoah Valley that enabled Grant defeat Lee at Five Forks, cut the final railroad, and seize Petersburg and Richmond.

One tactical innovation the Confederates adopted during this period (and which is routinely overlooked) was the further development of their sharpshooter battalions. Most of these units had been formed in 1863. Each brigade had a battalion of 200 men (operating in teams of three) who exploited gaps in Union lines of battle. Their effective firing helped turn back or rout nearly every offensive Grant mounted against Petersburg. As the quality of

Union soldiers deteriorated, one Southern battalion became more than a match for any single Union regiment—and often a match for an entire Union brigade.

Similarly, the Federals experimented with skirmishers armed with Spencer repeating rifles. In the VI Corps breakthrough on April 2, 1865, for example, skirmishers armed with Spencers helped suppress Rebel fire from the trenches while storming columns broke through the lines.

Despite the paucity of books and published articles on the Petersburg Campaign, its effect on Civil War was significant and decisive. Within a week of the fall of Petersburg and Richmond, Lee's exhausted army was trapped and surrendered at Appomattox Court House (April 9). Slightly more than two weeks after Lee's men put down their arms, Joseph E. Johnston surrendered his army in North Carolina (April 26). Richard Taylor surrendered on May 4. This effectively ended the fighting east of the Mississippi River. Three weeks later Lt. Gen. E. Kirby Smith, in command of the Trans-Mississippi Department, followed suit. It is now clear that once Lee's Army of Northern Virginia died, Southerners everywhere lost hope and gave up.

Bibliography

Manuscripts

Library of Congress, Washington, D.C.
    Cadmus Marcellus Wilcox, Papers, 1846-1887
National Archives, Washington, D.C.
    Horace Rugg Court Martial Transcript, Record Group
    Map of the Battlefield of Five Forks
Pennsylvania Historical Society Collection
    Joseph Carter, "History of the Third Brigade, First Division, Ninth Corps"
Virginia Historical Society, Richmond, VA
    Cadmus M. Wilcox, Petersburg Campaign Report, Lee Headquarters   Collection
    R. H. Anderson, Narrative of Services Oct '64—April '65, Lee Headquarters   Collection
University of North Carolina, Chapel Hill, NC
    H. A. London Papers
    Samuel Walkup Diary
    William Gaston Lewis, Personal Papers
Virginia State Library, Richmond, VA
    John F. Sale Diary

Newspapers

New York Herald, March 28, 1865.
New York Times, March 28, 1865, March 29, 1865.
Our Living and Our Dead, May 13, 1874.
Philadelphia Inquirer, March 28, 1865.
Raleigh Daily Confederate, February 23, 1865.
Richmond Times Dispatch, March 28, 1865.
The Chatham Record, March 27, 1912.
Washington Daily Times, March 26, 1865.

Official Publications

United States Dept. of the Army. *The Medal of Honor of the United States Army*, Washington, D.C.: U.S. Government Printing Office, 1948.

United States War Department. *The War of the Rebellion: A Compilation of the Official Records of the Union and Confederate Armies*. 128 vols. Washington, D.C.: U.S. Government Printing Office, 1880-1901.

United States War Department. *Atlas to Accompany the Official Records of the Union and Confederate Armies*. Washington, D.C.: U.S. Government Printing Office, 1891-1895.

Published

Ammen, S. Z. *Maryland Troops in the Confederate Army from Original Sources: Material Gathered in 1879 from the Men Who Led and Fought*. Thomas Clemens Collection, American Military History Education Center (Carlisle, PA).

Anderson, John. *The Fifty-Seventh Regiment of Massachusetts Volunteers in the War of the Rebellion Army of the Potomac*. Boston: E. B. Stillings & Co., 1896.

Andrus, Michael J. *The Brooke, Fauquier, Loudoun, and Alexandria Artillery*. Lynchburg: H.E. Howard, 1990.

Anson, Charles H. "Assault on the Lines of Petersburg, April 2, 1865." In *War Papers Read Before the Commandery of the State of Wisconsin, Military Order of the Loyal Legion of the United States*, Vol. 1. Milwaukee: Burdick, Armitage & Allen, 1891.

Badeau, Adam. *Military History of U. S. Grant*. 3 vols. New York: D. Appleton and Company: 1868-1881.

Barnes, James Sanford. "With Lincoln from Washington to Richmond in 1865." In *Magazine of History with Notes and Queries*, vol. 41, no. 161 (1931).

Barrier, J. D. "Breaking Grant's Line." In *Confederate Veteran*, Vol. 33 (1925).

Bartlett, Napier. *Military Record of Louisiana, Including Biographical and Historical Papers Relating to the Military Organizations of the State*. Baton Rouge: Louisiana State University Press, 1992.

Barton, Randolph. "The Battle of Hatcher's Run." In *Confederate Veteran*, Vol. 17 (1909).

Beale, R. L. T. *History of the Ninth Virginia Cavalry in the War Between the States*. Richmond: B. F. Johnson Publishing Company, 1899.

Best, Issac O. *History of the 121st New York Infantry*. Chicago: W. S. Conkey Co., 1921.

Bidwell, Frederick David. *History of the Forty-Ninth Volunteers*. Albany: J. B. Lyon Co., 1916.

Billings, John D. *The History of the Tenth Massachusetts Battery of Light Artillery in the War of the Rebellion, 1862-1865*. Boston: The Arakelyan Press, 1909.

Bradwell, I.G. "Holding the Line at Petersburg." In *Confederate Veteran*, Vol. 28 (1920).

——————. "Gordon's Brigade after the Valley Campaign." In *Confederate Veteran*, Vol. 18 (1910).

Brooks, U. R. *Butler and His Cavalry in the War of Secession 1861-1865*. Columbia: The State Company, 1909.

Caldwell, J. F. J. *The History of a Brigade of South Carolinians, Known First as "Gregg's," and Subsequently as "McGowan's Brigade."* Philadelphia: King and Baird, 1866.

Calkins, Chris. National Park Service Lecture. June 1, 2004.

Chambers, Henry A. *Diary of Captain Henry A. Chambers*. T. H. Pearce, ed. Wilmington: Broadfoot Publishing Co., 1983.

Clark, Walter, ed. *Histories of the Several Regiments and Battalions from North Carolina in the Great War 1861-'65*. 5 vols. Wilmington: Broadfoot Publishing Co., 1996.

Committee of the Regiment. *History of the Thirty-Fifth Regiment Massachusetts Volunteers, 1862-1865*. Boston: Mills, Knight, & Company, 1884.

—————. *History of the Thirty-Sixth Massachusetts Volunteers, 1862-1865*. Boston: Press of Rockwell and Churchill, 1884.

Cooke, Charles M. "Fifty-Fifth Regiment." In Walter Clark, ed., *Histories of the Several Regiments and Battalions from North Carolina in the Great War 1861-'65*, Vol. 3. Wilmington: Broadfoot Publishing Co., 1996.

Cooke, John Esten. *Wearing of the Gray: Being Personal Portraits, Scenes and Adventures of the War*. Bloomington: Indiana University Press, 1959.

Cowper, Pulaski, compiler, and Gallagher, Gary W., ed., *Extracts of Letters of Major-General Bryan Grimes, to his Wife: Written While in Active Service in the Army of Northern Virginia, Together with Some Personal Recollections of the War*. Wilmington: Broadfoot Publishing Co., 1986.

Cox, William R. "The Anderson-Ramseur-Cox Brigade." In Walter Clark, ed., *Histories of the Several Regiments and Battalions from North Carolina in the Great War 1861-'65*, Vol. 4. Wilmington: Broadfoot Publishing Co., 1996.

Davis, Jefferson. *The Rise and Fall of the Confederate Government*, 2 vols. New York: D. Appleton and Co., 1881.

Dixon, B. F. "Additional Sketch: Forty-Ninth Regiment." In Walter Clark, ed., *Histories of the Several Regiments and Battalions from North Carolina in the Great War 1861-'65*, Vol. 3. Wilmington: Broadfoot Publishing Co., 1996.

Douglas, Henry Kyd. *I Rode With Stonewall: Being Chiefly the War Experiences of the Youngest Member of Jackson's Staff from the John Brown Raid to the Hanging of Mrs. Surratt*. Chapel Hill: The University of North Carolina Press, 1940.

Dunlop, W. S. *Lee's Sharpshooters; or, The Forefront of Battle*. Little Rock: Tunnah & Pittard, 1899.

Fox, John. *Red Clay to Richmond, Trail of the 35th Georgia Infantry Regiment, CSA*. Winchester: Angle Valley Press, 2005.

Freeman, Douglas Southall, ed., *Lee's Dispatches: Unpublished Letters of General Robert E. Lee to Jefferson Davis and the War Department of the Confederate States of America, 1862-65*. New York: G.P. Putnam's Sons, 1915.

—————. *Lee's Lieutenants, A Study in Command*, 3 vols. New York: Charles Scribner's & Sons, 1942-1944.

—————. *R. E. Lee: A Biography*, 4 vols. New York: Charles Scribner's & Sons, 1934-1935.

Gerrish, Theodore. *Army Life: A Private's Reminiscences of the Civil War*. Portland: Hoyt, Fogg & Donham, 1882.

Goolsby, J. C. "Crenshaw Battery, Pegram's Battalion, Confederate States Artillery: Graphic Account of the Effective Career of this Gallant Organization." In *Southern Historical Society Papers*, Vol. 28 (1900).

Gordon, Armistead C. *Memories and Memorials of William Gordon McCabe*. Vol. 1. Richmond: Old Dominion Press, Inc., 1925.

Gordon, John B. *Remininiscenes of the Civil War.* Baton Rouge: Louisiana State Univeristy, 1993.

Graham, Robert D. "Fifty-Sixth Regiment." In Walter Clark, ed., *Histories of the Several Regiments and Battalions from North Carolina in the Great War 1861-'65,* Vol. 3. Wilmington: Broadfoot Publishing Co., 1996.

Grant, Ulysses S. *Personal Memoirs of U. S. Grant.* 2 vols. New York: The Century Company, 1917.

Haines, Alanson A. *History of the Fifteenth Regiment New Jersey Volunteers.* New York: Jenkins & Thomas Printers, 1883.

Hale, Laura Virginia and Phillips, Stanley S. *History of the Forty-Ninth Virginia Regiment: "Extra Billy Smith's Boys."* Lanham: S.S. Phillips and Associates, 1981.

Hartranft, John. "The Recapture of Fort Stedman." In *Battles and Leaders of the Civil War,* edited by Robert Underwood Johnson and Clarence Clough Buel, Vol. 4. New York: The Century Co., 1887.

Hewett, Janet B., Trudeau, Noah Andre, and Suderow, Bryce A. *Supplement to the Official Records of the Union and Confederate Armies.* 100 vols., Wilmington: Broadfoot Publishing Co., 1994.

Hodgkins, William H. *The Battle of Fort Stedman (Petersburg, Virginia), March 25, 1865.* Boston: Privately Printed, 1889.

Hopkins, William P. *The Seventh Regiment Rhode Island Volunteers in the Civil War, 1862-1865.* Providence: Snow and Farnham, 1903.

Howell, Helena A., compiler. *Chronicles of the One Hundred Fifty-First Regiment New York State Volunteer Infantry 1862-1865.* Albion: A.M. Eddy, 1911.

Humphreys, Andrew A. *The Virginia Campaign of '64 and '65.* New York: Charles Scribner's Sons, 1883.

Hyde, Thomas. *Following the Greek Cross, or Memories of the Sixth Army Corps.* New York: Houghton, Mifflin and Company, 1894.

Jones, Hamilton C. "Fifty-Seventh Regiment." In Walter Clark, ed., *Histories of the Several Regiments and Battalions from North Carolina in the Great War 1861-'65,* Vol. 3. Wilmington: Broadfoot Publishing Co., 1996.

Kiefer, Joseph Warren. *Slavery and Four Years of War: A Political History of Slavery in the United States.* 2 vols. New York: G.P. Putnam's Sons, 1900.

Kilmer, George L. "Assault and Repulse at Fort Stedman." In *Century Magazine* (Vol. 34, September, 1887).

Lane, James H. "History of Lane's North Carolina Brigade." In *Southern Historical Society Papers,* Vol. 9 (1881).

—————. "Twenty-eighth North Carolina Infantry." In *Southern Historical Society Papers,* Vol. 24 (1896).

Lee, Robert E. *Recollections and Letters of General Robert E. Lee.* Garden City: Doubleday, Page & Co., 1924.

Lewis, Osceola. *History of the One hundred and Thirty-Eighth Regiment, Pennsylvania Volunteer Infantry.* Norristown: Wills, Iredell, & Jenkins, 1866.

Longstreet, James. *From Manassas to Appomattox: Memoirs of the Civil War in America.* Philadelphia: J.B. Lippincott, 1896.

Lyman, Theodore. *Meade's Headquarters 1863-1865: Letters of Colonel Theodore Lyman from the Wilderness to Appomattox.* Boston: The Atlantic Monthly Press, 1922.

Mark, Penrose G. *Red: White: and Blue Badge, Pennsylvania Volunteers, a History of the 93rd Regiment, known as the "Lebanon Infantry" and "One of the 300 Fighting Regiments" from September 12th, 1861 to June 27th, 1865*. Harrisburg: The Augbinbaugh Press, 1911.

Martin, W. J. "History of the 11th North Carolina Regiment." In *Southern Historical Society Papers*, Vol. 23 (1895).

Means, Paul B. "Sixty-third Regiment." In Walter Clark, ed., *Histories of the Several Regiments and Battalions from North Carolina in the Great War 1861-'65*, Vol. 3. Wilmington: Broadfoot Publishing Co., 1996.

Moore II, Robert H. *Graham's Petersburg, Jackson's Kanawha and Lurty's Roanoke Horse Artillery*. Lynchburg: H. E. Howard, 1996.

————. *The First and Second Stuart Horse Artillery*. Lynchburg: H. E. Howard, 1985.

Nash, Eugene A. *A History of the Forty-Fourth Regiment New York Volunteer Infantry in the Civil War, 1861-1865*. Chicago: Donnelly, 1911.

Nevins, Allan, ed. *A Diary of Battle: The Personal Journals of Colonel Charles S. Wainwright, 1861-1865*. New York: Harcourt, Brace, & World, 1962.

Osborne, E. A. "Fourth Regiment." In Walter Clark, ed., *Histories of the Several Regiments and Battalions from North Carolina in the Great War 1861-'65*, Vol. 1. Wilmington: Broadfoot Publishing Co., 1996.

Osbourne, Hampden. "The Struggle for Fort Mahone." In *Confederate Veteran*, Vol. 25 (1917).

Porter, Charles H. "Operations of the Fifth Corps on the Left, March 29, to Nightfall March 31, 1865; Gravelly Run." In *Papers of the Military Historical Society of Massachusetts*, vol. 6. Boston: Military Historical Society of Massachusetts, 1907.

————. "The Fifth Corps at the Battle of Five Forks." In *Papers of the Military Historical Society of Massachusetts*, vol. 6. Boston: Military Historical Society of Massachusetts, 1907.

Porter, Horace. *Campaigning with Grant*. New York: The Century Company, 1897.

————. "Five Forks and the Pursuit of Lee." In *Battles and Leaders of the Civil War*, edited by Robert Underwood Johnson and Clarence Clough Buel, Vol. 4. New York: The Century Co., 1887.

Powell, William H. *The Fifth Army Corps (Army of the Potomac), A Record of Operations During the Civil War in the United States of America, 1861-1865*. New York: G. P. Putnam's Sons, 1896.

Rhodes, Elisha Hunt. *The Second Rhode Island Volunteers at the Siege of Petersburg, Virginia*. Providence: Rhode Island Soldiers and Sailors Historical Society, 1911.

Roe, Alfred S. *The Thirty-Ninth Regiment Massachusetts Volunteers: 1862-1865*. Worcester: Regimental Veteran Association, 1914.

Roulhac, Thomas R. "Forty-Ninth Regiment." In Walter Clark, ed., *Histories of the Several Regiments and Battalions from North Carolina in the Great War 1861-'65*, Vol. 3. Wilmington: Broadfoot Publishing Co., 1996.

Rowland, Dunbar. *The Official and Statistical Register of the State of Mississippi, 1908*. Nashville: Press of the Brandon Printing Company, 1908.

Scott, Robert Garth. *Forgotten Valor: The Memoirs, Journals, & Civil War Letters of Orlando B. Willcox*. Kent: Kent State University Press, 1999.

Sorrel, G. Moxley. *Recollections of a Confederate Staff Officer*. Jackson, TN: McCowat-Mercer Press, 1958.

Stedman, Charles. "The Forty-Fourth North Carolina Infantry." In *Southern Historical Society Papers*, Vol. 25 (1897).

Stephens, Robert Grier, ed., *Intrepid Warrior, Clement Anselm Evans: Confederate General from Georgia; Life, Letters, and Diaries of the War Years*. Dayton: Morningside Bookshop, 1992.

Stevens, Robert J. *Captain Bill: The Records and Writings Of Captain William Henry Edwards (and Others) Company A, 17th Regiment South Carolina Volunteers, Confederate States of America: a History and Genealogy of Chester County, S.C.* Richburg: Chester District Historical Society, 1985.

Stone, DeWitt Boyd, Jr., ed. *Wandering to Glory: Confederate Veterans Remember Evans' Brigade*. Columbia: University of South Carolina Press, 2002.

Sturgis, Thomas, by companion, "Prisoners of War." In *Personal Recollections of the War of the Rebellion: Addresses Delivered Before the Commandery of the State of New York, Military Order of the Loyal Legion of the United States*. Fourth Series, edited by A. Noel Blakeman. New York: G.P. Putnam's Sons, 1912.

Styple, William B. *Writing and Fighting from the Army of Northern Virginia, A Collection of Confederate Correspondence*. Kearny: Belle Grove Publishing, 2003.

Survivors' Association, *History of the Corn Exchange Regiment 118th Pennsylvania Volunteers, From their First Engagement at Antietam to Appomattox*. Philadelphia: J. L. Smith, 1888.

——————. *History of the 121st Regiment Pennsylvania Volunteers*. Philadelphia: Press of Burk & McFetridge Co., 1893.

Swan, William W. "The Five Forks Campaign." In *Papers of the Military Historical Society of Massachusetts*, Vol. 6. Boston: Military Historical Society of Massachusetts, 1907.

Thomas, Henry W. *History of Doles-Cook Brigade: Army of Northern Virginia, 1861-1865*. Atlanta: Franklin Printing and Publishing, 1903.

Tidball, Eugene C. *"No Disgrace to My Country": The Life of John C. Tidball*. Kent: Kent State University Press, 2002.

Trudeau, Noah Andre. *The Last Citadel: Petersburg, Virginia, June 1864—April 1865*. Baton Rouge: Louisiana State University Press, 1993.

Turner, V.E. and Wall, H.C. "Twenty-Third Regiment." In Walter Clark, ed., *Histories of the Several Regiments and Battalions from North Carolina in the Great War 1861-'65*, Vol. 2. Wilmington: Broadfoot Publishing Co., 1996.

Walker, Francis A. *History of the Second Army Corps in the Army of the Potomac*. New York: Charles Scribner's Sons, 1886.

——————. "The Expedition to the Boydton Plank Road, October, 1864." In *Papers of the Military Historical Society of Massachusetts*, Vol. 5. Boston: Military Historical Society of Massachusetts, (1906).

Walker, James A. "Gordon's Assault on Fort Stedman, March 25, 1865: A Brilliant Achievement." In *Southern Historical Society Papers*, Vol. 31 (1903).

Wall, H. C. "The Twenty-Third North Carolina Infantry." In *Southern Historical Society Papers*, Vol. 25 (1897).

Wells, Edward L. *Hampton and His Cavalry in '64*. Richmond: B. F. Johnson Publishing Company, 1899.

Williams, Susan Benson. *Berry Benson's Civil War Book: Memoirs of a Confederate Scout and Sharpshooter*. Athens: University of Georgia, 1992.

Williamson, J. Pinkney, *History of the Crater and Ten Months Siege of Petersburg*. n.p., n.d.

Woodbury, Augustus. *Major General Ambrose E. Burnside and the Ninth Army Corps*. Providence: S.S. Rider & Brother, 1867.

Index

John Matthew IV

About Edwin C. Bearss

Edwin Bearss is a world-renowned military historian, author, and tour guide known for his work on the American Civil War and World War II. Ed, a former WWII Marine severely wounded in the Pacific Theater, served as Chief Historian of the National Park Service from 1981 to 1994.

Ed is the author of dozens of articles and many books, including *The Campaign for Vicksburg* (3 vols.), *Receding Tide: Vicksburg and Gettysburg—The Campaigns That Changed the Civil War* (with J. Parker Hills), *Fields of Honor: Pivotal Battles of the Civil War*, and many more. Ed discovered and helped raise the Union warship *USS Cairo*, which is on display at Vicksburg National Military Park. His book on the subject is entitled *Hardluck Ironclad: The Sinking and Salvage of the Cairo*.

About Bryce A. Suderow

Bryce Suderow is a Civil War writer and researcher living in Washington, D.C. He received his bachelor's at Knox College and earned a master's in American history at Sonoma State University. His master's thesis, *Thunder in Arcadia Valley*, was published in 1985 (University of Missouri). Bryce has also published many articles in a number of Civil War periodicals and is recognized as one of the finest archival researchers working today. With Bryce's help, the current book on Petersburg might never have been published.